Migrations and Mobilities

Published in cooperation with the Castle Fund, established by
Mr. John K. Castle. The Castle Fund is housed in Yale University's
Program in Ethics, Politics, and Economics in honor of
Mr. Castle's ancestor, the Reverend James Pierpont,
one of Yale's original founders.

Migrations and Mobilities

Citizenship, Borders, and Gender

EDITED BY

Seyla Benhabib and Judith Resnik

NEW YORK UNIVERSITY PRESS

NEW YORK AND LONDON

NEW YORK UNIVERSITY PRESS
New York and London
www.nyupress.org

Library of Congress Cataloging-in-Publication Data

Migrations and mobilities : citizenship, borders, and gender /
edited by Seyla Benhabib and Judith Resnik.
p. cm.
Includes bibliographical references and index.
ISBN-13: 978-0-8147-7599-8 (cl : alk. paper)
ISBN-10: 0-8147-7599-3 (cl : alk. paper)
ISBN-13: 978-0-8147-7600-1 (pb : alk. paper)
ISBN-10: 0-8147-7600-0 (pb : alk. paper)
1. Citizenship. 2. Citizenship—Social aspects. 3. Emigration and
immigration—Social aspects. 4. Aliens. 5. Women alien labor. 6. Women
refugees. I. Benhabib, Seyla. II. Resnik, Judith.
K3324.M54   2009
323.6—dc22   2008044241

New York University Press books are printed on acid-free paper, and their
binding materials are chosen for strength and durability. We strive to use
environmentally responsible suppliers and materials to the greatest extent
possible in publishing our books.

Manufactured in the United States of America
c   10 9 8 7 6 5 4 3 2 1
p   10 9 8 7 6 5 4 3 2 1

To our children, Laura Ilana Colomba Schaefer and Jonathan Jeffrey Curtis-Resnik, and to the children of others, as they move around the globe.

Seyla Benhabib
Judith Resnik

Contents

Introduction: Citizenship and Migration Theory Engendered

Seyla Benhabib and Judith Resnik

Nations, Citizens, and Others

The permeability of national borders can be seen not only by the ease with which words and images move through an internet unfettered by geographical constraints but also by the movement of people across national borders and of transnational legal and moral precepts shaping discourses around the globe.[1] In 1910, some thirty-three million of the 1.7 billion in the world's population lived in countries as migrants.[2] By 2000, estimates were that about 175 million of six billion people were at some distance from their countries of origin.[3] During the last three decades of the twentieth century alone, seventy-five million people moved across borders to settle elsewhere.[4] Yet, even with this volume of movement, less than 4 percent of the world's population undertakes migrations.

Thus our interest is simultaneously in those who move and those who stay put. Whether migrant or landlocked, *where* a person is—literally and physically—has profound effects on that person's life. One's place on the planet frames the availability of food, of basic goods and broader economic opportunities, of personal security and health care, of social connections with other members of one's family as well as of the possibility for ties to larger communities, and of legal recognition as a property owner, a worker, a recipient of social services, health care, and education, a family member, a voter, an office holder, a lawful resident, and a citizen.

The relevance of mobility, combined with the relevance of place, makes questions of immigration and citizenship both pressing and contested in countries around the world. A simplistic presumption is that citizens

1

residing in a given nation-state are in a reciprocal relationship with that country, recognized as members entitled to rights, protection, material support, and political loyalty. Noncitizens—lumped together into an undifferentiated whole—sit outside that circle of rights and obligations.

But the variety of migration patterns and of legal regimes governing access to residence, citizenship, and to the social and economic resources of the state undermines these propositions. While some people never move, others could be conceptualized as "commuters" going back and forth regularly between countries and building up or attenuating ties to more than one place. In contrast, some noncitizens enter for a brief period of time to supplement the income of their families, to whom they are eager to return. Yet others reside outside their families' countries of origin for decades and are part of other vibrant communities making lasting marks on their host countries. Still others are involuntary migrants tossed out and seeking safety from states that would do them harm. Their numbers are poignantly large; as of 2006, some twenty-five million people were refugees, asylum seekers, or displaced persons.

Given the breadth of the potential questions raised by these trends, clarification of both our terminology and our central interests is in order. Migrations are related to globalization, involving the increased movement around the world of goods, services, information, and capital of all kinds, as well as of legal, political, and moral norms.[5] Migrations are about people in transit, both as *immigrants* and as *emigrants*. Someone migrates *from* some place to another, rendering every migrant an *emigrant* from one country or locality and an *immigrant* in another.

While local and regional migrations (often shifting from rural to urban settings) within state-territories raise important questions related to economic and social identities, this volume is concerned with the effects of movements *across* state boundaries on the relationship of persons and rights. Given the nature of the current nation-state system and of the dual commitments of the international order to territorially demarcated states and to a human rights regime, cross-border movements are legal and political as well as socioeconomic and cultural matters.

Central to the discussion is the concept of *citizenship*, which is a legal, an economic, and a cultural event, denoting official recognition of a special relationship between a person and a country. Entailed in this political contract are obligations of protection and guarantees against deportation, expatriation, and denationalization.[6] Historically, citizenship has been transmitted or acquired through different methods, of which four—*jus soli, jus sanguinis,* a mix thereof, and naturalization—are common around the world. *Jus soli,* or "birthright citizenship," means that a person born on the given state's territory has the right to citizenship without further inquiry. *Jus sanguinis* disregards territorial claims and bases the inheritance of citizenship rights on the citizenship status of one or both parents. A third form mixes these two ideas by requiring that a person be born in a given state and that either or both of the parents are also citizens or long-term legal residents of that state.[7] The fourth method, naturalization, is the acquisition of citizenship by migrant foreigners. Almost all of the world's nations permit naturalization, but the criteria for doing so vary widely and can impose hurdles, including years of residency, marriage to a national, demonstration of knowledge about language and history, and renunciation of an affiliation to another country.[8] The patterns and the rules of migrations and citizenship come with histories and contexts, sometimes of voluntary association and more often of imperialism and colonialism, forceful acquisition of territories of indigenous peoples, and the consequences of trade practices, including human trafficking and slavery.

The facts raise the question of how to frame discussions: Ought one start with nation-states as givens? Or should one begin with a focus on persons living in particular areas? In many instances, one could argue that rather than people crossing borders, the border "crossed" them by ignoring that they were already members of preexisting polities—some of which are called "first nations" or "indigenous" and others of which were configured through prior boundary settlements. In terms of those people in transit, moving from one locale to another, we note that many are ex-, neo-, and postcolonials of the nations in which they reside or to which they seek admission, raising normative questions about whether shared histories, interactions, memories, and experiences impose obligations or constraints.

As the image of a border crossing a person suggests, the boundaries of nation-states are not static but drawn or redrawn in the face of conflict. Today's realignments include disaggregations, such as those of new states from what had been Yugoslavia, as well as new aggregations, sometimes in federalist states as well as through the invention of new forms such as the European Union (EU), offering opportunities for the layering of citizenship that insist on the coherence of ties to subparts as well as to the whole.

Some would argue that a stronger dynamic is at work here and that we are watching the end of the nation-state, as global economic, environmental, and political forces make that form of government insufficient or obsolete.⁹ But while the meaning of state sovereignty may be under revision, nation-states remain a critical form of organization. Even porous borders continue to define networks of obligations and constitute real barriers, rendering some persons aliens or intruders. Further, when countries join together to promulgate legal commitments to universal norms that transcend sovereign boundaries and that constrain sovereign prerogatives, they do so through conventions reliant on national authority for implementation. These treaties can be conceptualized either as internally contradictory or as changing the import of territorial sovereignty.

With or without these transnational conventions, sovereign states do not function as equals. The power of national sovereignty varies radically depending upon resources and political organization, such that neither countries nor their residents are all in the mobility market in the same way. As Saskia Sassen has pointed out, migrations occur under structured configurations of "pull" and "push" factors. Some migratory patterns become established through the economic interdependencies of sending and receiving countries over periods of time.¹⁰ Moreover, competition exists for skilled migrants.¹¹ Yet some people, fully rooted in a place where they have great opportunities or to which they feel deep affiliation, are delighted to stay put. Others may be open to moving, but only to certain locales under specified conditions. Some people are so in need of work that they have little possibility of shopping opportunity sets,¹² and others—refugees—are involuntarily displaced.

A host of reform proposals—raising or lowering barriers as well as arguing for new categories—have been proffered, accompanied by a robust political debate and literature addressing the various meanings of citizenship and sovereignty.¹³ All too often, gender is missing from these conversations,¹⁴ and the migrant—if imagined as a person at all—is presumed to be a man traveling alone in search of work. The burden of this volume is to alter this imaginary so as to bring squarely into focus the fact that citizens, migrants, refugees, and members of host communities are not disembodied individuals (or, by default, men) but are adults or children traveling with or leaving family members. Moreover, the mobility of some has consequences for or corresponds to the immobility of others. All of these persons are engendered in their relationships with others, with the wage workforce, and with the polities from which they came and those that they seek to enter.¹⁵

Gender as a Category in Transnational Legal Regimes

Our intervention in this volume is to bring gender equality claims into the discussion of the four other major principles regularly invoked in this area—the free movement of persons; the need for protection of refugees; the jurisdictional authority of sovereign states over their borders; and the obligation to respect family ties, including through family reunification. Our argument is that the laws, policies, moralities, and theories of citizenship, as well as of sovereignty, jurisdiction, family life, and migration, must grapple with the way histories of discrimination and subordination based on gender affect the conceptualization and implementation of opportunities, rights, and burdens, as well as the nation-state's powers. When one inflects citizenship, sovereignty, and migration theories with gender analysis, new questions emerge both about feminist conceptions of women and men and about political theories of the state. In short, once gender is in sight, "each eye sees a different picture."[16]

The chapters of this book are shaped by this thesis, as they also illuminate disagreements about the normative desirability of the categories of "citizen" and "state" and their implications for women and men in different parts of the globe. Because many of the essays are also framed in reference to transnational laws on nationality, migration, asylum, and equality that form the backdrop for contemporary debates, a brief review of some of the relevant legal provisions, their allocation of authority, and the mechanisms by which they are implemented is in order. Our focus is on five such laws: the 1948 Universal Declaration of Human Rights (UDHR),[17] followed in 1951 by the Convention on Refugees (the 1951 Refugee Convention),[18] the 1966 International Covenant on Civil and Political Rights (ICCPR)[19] and related Comments on Family Reunification, the International Covenant on Economic, Social, and Cultural Rights (ICESCR) of the same year,[20] and the Convention on the Elimination of All Forms of Discrimination against Women (CEDAW), which entered into force in 1981.[21]

In 1948, shortly after World War II and the formation of the United Nations, its member states promulgated the Universal Declaration of Human Rights, which addresses all of our themes—equality, sovereignty, mobility, citizenship, and families. The declaration's preamble states that the "peoples" of the United Nations' Charter affirmed their faith in "the dignity and worth of the human person and in the equal rights of men and women."[22] All persons, "without distinction of any kind, such as race, colour, sex, language, religion, political or other opinion, national or social origin, property, birth or other status," are entitled to dignified treatment regardless of "the political, jurisdictional or international status of the country or territory to which a person belongs."[23] Furthermore, both women and men "of full age" are to enjoy "equal rights as to marriage" and to "found families"—"the natural and fundamental group unit" of society—and are entitled to protection by the state.[24]

Moving from questions of equality and family life within a nation-state to the issue of mobility, Article 13 of the UDHR recognizes a freedom of movement across boundaries. While stating a right to *emigrate* from a country, the UDHR does not specify the conditions under which one could exercise a parallel right to *immigrate*, to enter a country.[25] Similarly, while proclaiming in Article 15 that everyone has "the right to a nationality"[26] and, moreover, that "[n]o one shall be arbitrarily deprived of his nationality nor denied the right to change his nationality,"[27] the UDHR does not outline the qualifications that trigger that right nor the criteria that would render a deprivation arbitrary.

These provisions need to be read against a background premise of the United Nations Charter itself, which is built upon deference to the national order. "Nothing contained in the present Charter shall authorize the United Nations to intervene in matters which are essentially within the domestic jurisdiction of any state or shall require the members to submit such matters to settlement under the present Charter."[28] Of course, the question is what issues were "essentially within the domestic jurisdiction of a state." The history of the clause's drafting suggests that it was shaped in response to concerns in the United States that the United Nations's commitment to human dignity and nondiscrimination could be used (as indeed people tried to do) by opponents of racial segregation.[29]

The 1948 UDHR also recognizes the needs of refugees. Article 14 anchors a right of asylum that was detailed soon thereafter in the 1951 Convention on Refugees. Under that convention, a person seeking asylum has to show persecution based on one of five categories—race, nationality, religion, political opinion, or membership in a particular social group.[30] Not on that list was gender. While the 1948 UDHR was innovative in banning discrimination predicated on "sex," attention to women's equality did not pervade the UN approach to many issues. In the 1990s, the United Nations (as well as the European Union and the Commonwealth) became committed to what is called "gender mainstreaming," i.e., asking questions about the effects of all policies on women and men.[31]

Reflective of its era as well, the 1951 Convention on Refugees focused neither on the role gender played in shaping experiences of persecution nor on whether women should be understood as falling within the category of a "social group" or ought to be added as another category in the enumerated list. But, as Talia Inlender explores in her essay, that question is being pressed on many fronts now. Inlender argues that individuals seeking asylum ought to be able to make their claims to decision makers who understand the existence of what she terms "gender-specific" forms of persecution (such as forced pregnancy) as well as "gender-based" persecutions (which target women who violate a polity's conventions about women's roles).[32]

Inlender's analysis notes that, by 1991, the United Nations had taken up some aspects of the gender question for refugees. In its *Guidelines on the Protection of Refugee Women*, the United Nations advised receiving nations to consider how women who transgress gender norms could be put at risk and ought to be seen as proper candidates for asylum.[33] Inlender goes further than these guidelines by arguing that gender should both be included under the five categories already listed as the basis for asylum and also be added as an independent sixth basis to recognize the way women, qua women, are at risk of persecution. Other commentators, however, are leery of conceptualizing gender as a category akin to "race, nationality, religion, political opinion, or membership of a particular social group" because it entails essentializing women. Whichever position one espouses, engendering discussions of asylum seekers enables one to see that gender already is operating in the world of asylum adjudication. Actions that are oppositional to regimes can take diverse forms, from bearing arms to staffing safe zones for militants.[34] Moreover, the methods by which dissidents or out-group members are oppressed can also vary depending on whether the targeted groups are women or men, with the use of rape illustrating a tactic imposed particularly on women.[35]

Invocations of international law prompt questions of implementation. Because the UDHR is "only" a declaration of principles and does not detail mechanisms for enforcement, some argue that it does not function sufficiently *as* law, while others see it as a different kind *of* law that works through mechanism other than command and control.[36] As illustrated by Inlender's discussion, through its 1991 Guidelines on Refugee Women, the High Commissioner on Refugees[37] has sought to influence decision making in member states about how to evaluate claims of refugees and has had a profound impact in some jurisdictions.[38]

Another common method of implementation for UN provisions is the chartering of "expert bodies" or committees to elaborate the meaning of conventions. Such committees promulgate "general comments" and receive reports from member states, which are obliged to detail how they are compliant with or failing to live up to their commitments as parties to conventions. Further, in some jurisdictions (but not generally in the United States), international obligations can be a direct source of rights that are legally enforceable through litigation in national courts.[39]

Another of the United Nations' basic statements relevant to citizenship—the 1966 International Convention on Civil and Political Rights (ICCPR)—elaborates various of the UDHR's commitments to equality and mobility by putting those propositions into the structure of oversight through an expert body and public reporting. Focused on "political and civil rights" such as voting, marriage, and holding offices or owning property, the ICCPR states that "[a]ll persons are equal before the law and are entitled without any discrimination to the equal protection of the law."[40] The ICCPR requires states to "ensure to all individuals within its territory and subject to its jurisdiction the rights recognized in the present Covenant, without distinction of any kind, such as race, colour, sex, language, religion, political or other opinion, national or social origin, property, birth or other status."[41]

The ICCPR provides that both adults and children have "the right to acquire a nationality" but does not address what the predicates are for the exercise of that right.[42] In terms of mobility, the ICCPR reiterates that persons "lawfully within the territory of a State" shall have the freedom to stay, to leave, or to return from their "own country" (consistent with "national security, public order, public health or morals or the rights and freedoms of others").[43] The ICCPR recognizes as well the authority of states to expel aliens upon determinations by competent authorities of grounds to do so.[44]

Complementing the ICCPR is another convention of the same era— the International Covenant on Economic, Social, and Cultural Rights (ICESCR), which also entered into force in 1976. As its name suggests, its focal points are associative rights, including collective labor action, and its concerns include social security, education, and health. The ICESCR underscores the place of groups in a political order.

Another landmark in the recent history of transnational covenants and one that takes up directly questions of gender-based inequality is the Convention on the Elimination of All Forms of Discrimination against Women (CEDAW), which entered into force in 1981. As of 2007, more than 180 states (albeit not the United States) were parties.[45] The central precept of CEDAW is set forth in Article 3, which provides that

> States Parties shall take in all fields, in particular in the political, social, economic and cultural fields, all appropriate measures, including legislation, to ensure the full development and advancement of women, for the purpose of guaranteeing them the exercise and enjoyment of human rights and fundamental freedoms on a basis of equality with men.[46]

CEDAW also reaffirms rights to nationality, and moreover that women have rights equal to men "to acquire, change or retain their nationality" independent of their status as married or their husbands' citizenship status.[47] Further, women are to have "equal rights with men with respect to the nationality of their children."[48]

Given the traumas of dislocation of World War II and the deliberate destruction of families and communities, it is not surprising that family reunification itself is directly addressed by the United Nations as well as under the laws of many jurisdictions, including Europe and the United States. As part of its "General Comment" on Article 23 of the ICCPR, the UN Human Rights Committee explained that member states, working in "cooperation with other States," are required "to ensure the unity or re-unification of families, particularly when their members are separated for political, economic or similar reasons."[49] Furthermore, Article 10(1) of the UN Convention on the Rights of the Child (to which 193 states are parties, but again not the United States) also recognizes the need of children to cross borders for family reunification.[50]

In her contribution to this volume, Catherine Dauvergne helps us to understand through her analyses of the interaction between citizenship and immigration laws in Australia, Canada, and the United States[51] how family reunification has been a dominant category for admissions in all three countries, and how that route has been an important one for women to use to cross borders. More generally, Dauvergne argues that economic migration and humanitarian migration, which join family reunification to form the three major legal routes for admission, have created patterns reinforcing notions of women's dependence and men's independence.

As the European Union is committed to the free movement of persons and goods within its boundaries, it too has stipulated provisions for family unity. Moreover, forty-six nations subscribe to the 1950 European Convention on Human Rights and Fundamental Freedoms (ECHR), which insists on the right of "everyone" to "respect for his private and family life" and to "no interference" by public authorities with those rights except as is "necessary in a democratic society in the interests of national security, public safety or the economic well-being of the country."[52] A 2003 EU Council directive provides, for example, that persons lawfully living within the European Union but nationals of nonmember states are, subject to limitations, entitled to the host nation's granting admission to their children for the purpose of family reunification. That directive also recognizes that member states can condition family reunification on extant rules such as that requests on behalf of minor children be submitted before a child is a certain age.[53]

Four aspects of these major provisions, namely, the UDHR, the Convention on Refugees, the ICCPR, the ICESCR, and CEDAW—deserve special note. First, these transnational conventions undermine an absolutist theory of sovereignty that presumes that a sovereign nation has complete control over what occurs within its borders. By becoming states parties, nations cede authority (a form of sovereignty)—at least in theory—as they commit to complying with these precepts. Furthermore, in the human rights conventions, states parties agree to report on their efforts to comply.[54]

Second, these transnational conventions often operate in aspirational modes. Compliance with treaty obligations is uneven. Moreover, many conventions come with built-in escape hatches, in that states can condition their agreement through "reservations, understandings, or declarations" (RUDs) that limit their commitments. While some commentators are dismissive of these less-than-full obligations, RUDs may be vehicles by which transnational rights can be domesticated more slowly, enabling some forms of adaptation that open doors to considering perspectives different from one's own.[55] In Resnik's terms, "jurisdictional seepage" occurs through "law's migration" even as legal boundaries continue to do significant substantive work.[56]

Third, in addition to constraining sovereignty, these conventions also support sovereignty, in that all rely on the sovereign state to give meaning to their agreements and to decide how to comply with the rights defined. These are agreements among nation-states to be implemented by nation-states, predicated on the baseline of the UN Charter itself, which purports to carve out a domain of the "domestic" free from the "transnational."

Furthermore, even in those instances when conventions include the ability of individuals to bring direct complaints to member bodies about noncompliance,[57] remedies for noncompliance are limited. Enforcement is primarily at the national level.

Fourth, while one can find many commitments to the freedom to cross borders and to prohibitions on discrimination, one finds no shared affirmative commitments to the criteria for citizenship or for obtaining the status of lawful resident alien. The conditions under which nonnationals must be admitted to a state or to citizenship therein are not specified.[58]

That point brings us to the chapter by Catherine Dauvergne, who argues that "liberal discourses of equality and inclusion are left to citizenship law while immigration law performs the dirty work of inequity and exclusion." As she explains, a widely shared assumption is that sovereign nations "are morally justified in closing their borders, subject to exceptions of their choosing."[59] Dauvergne analyzes the implications of these propositions for women and men: "while women and men are approximately equally represented in the international population of refugees" and of asylum seekers, in the United States, Canada, and Australia, men are more likely to be admitted, perhaps because they undertake the dangers of the journey or perhaps because families selectively fund transit or perhaps (as Inlender's work suggests) because they are more able to obtain entry under these categories.

The silences and enforcement gaps in transnational conventions thus reflect the tensions between, on the one hand, an understanding of nation-states as defined by their ability to constitute their own internal rules of membership that reflect and generate shared identities supportive of democratic practices and, on the other hand, the universalist aspirations that all humanity has obligations to protect the dignity of and to provide for others.[60] Furthermore, the statements of equality of treatment as to gender and other criteria are often left with their content underspecified, in deference to the variety of practices, laws, economic arrangements, and religious and cultural commitments that shape relationships in ongoing polities. These gaps, generalities, and silences are part of what discussions of migration, mobility, and citizenship must take into account.[61] Further, the theme of growing barriers is also apparent in these chapters as a consequence of what Dauvergne describes as a "worldwide crack-down on illegal migration."[62] All the authors of this volume make plain that the burdens of these barriers are not borne evenly by persons or nations around the world.

Citizenship and Migration Embodied in Cross-National Families: Mothers, Fathers, Children, and the Nation-State

The story of one migrant—a Colombian mother named Joyce, a single parent who traveled to the Netherlands to visit her sister and explore life there while leaving her six-year-old daughter Emily in the care of other family members—illustrates the difficulties that families face. As Sarah van Walsum explains,[63] after the expiration of a tourist visa, Joyce remained in the Netherlands illegally until she obtained a residence permit based in part on her relationship with a Dutch man, with whom she subsequently became the parent of another child.

The Dutch authorities rejected Joyce's application for her daughter to join the family on the grounds that under Dutch law, Joyce had failed to demonstrate that during the period of separation, she had maintained an "effective family bond," which is to say that, despite the geographic separation, she had been effectively involved in the financial support and upbringing of the child. By the time Joyce lost her appeal, she was a Dutch citizen who had given up her Colombian nationality.

Thereafter, she turned to the European Court of Human Rights (ECtHR) because, as noted above, Article 8 of the ECHR prohibits unnecessary interference with family life. By then, other immigrants—including fathers—had tested the meaning of the "effective family bond" and the ECtHR had determined that the fact that a parent left a country of origin to travel abroad was not in itself sufficient to presume that a parent had made the decision to abandon a child who remained behind. Given litigation in both the domestic and European courts, Dutch immigration policies were rewritten to clarify that "effective family bonds" would be recognized for those children legally related to parents and that, unless children were living on their own, authorities would not assume a rupture from the sole fact of a parent's migration.[64]

Van Walsum makes clear that, when making evaluations about the provision of "effective care," officials had preconceived views about "good mothers" or "good fathers" that were predicated on cultural assumptions shaped by the customs in both host countries and countries of origin. Further, as she artfully illuminates, feminist efforts to obtain recognition in domestic law of the rights of those providing "substantive" care (in contrast to a focus on the status of a person as legally the parent) had influenced some decision makers to undervalue the legal status of migrants as parents and their needs to have other persons give care to their children when those parents traveled abroad. The challenge is to shape laws and practices that recognize a range of life choices and are respectful of the variations in family care patterns and of the "perspective of migrant mothers."

As van Walsum and others in this volume explicate, women's mobility is rarely a simple matter of the movement across state boundaries of a single, isolated individual. Women's mobility is a nodal point in a network of relationships that almost always involves dependent children, dependent elderly, the men with whom women are affiliated, and other family members or other women who—as Linda Bosniak and Aihwa Ong explore— are parts of networks in which women, both givers and recipients of care, are reliant on others.[65]

Van Walsum has provided one paradigm: a mother in one country becoming its national while her child is in another. Jacqueline Bhabha brings another issue into sharp focus: children as citizens themselves, with rights against deportation, caught up in complex webs in which their parents may be forced out of their children's countries. As we outlined above, citizenship rights often descend (by blood and place of birth) from parents who serve—in Bhabha's words—as "the anchor to which children are attached."[66] In theory, citizenship rights provide permanent access to living in a country. Furthermore, in theory, rights of family unity give noncitizen family members access to residency in countries where their relatives live. But as Bhabha demonstrates, asymmetries exist, and while parents may be able to bring their children to them, citizen-children are not always able to use their status to determine that of their parents.

Bhabha's rich analyses range from the United States to Canada to Ireland, France, and the responses of the European Court of Justice and the European Court of Human Rights. She details how issues that could be configured as "family law" can be dealt with through courts that regularly deal with family disputes or can be retitled as issues of "immigration" and then assigned for decision making to officials generally charged with policing national borders. In the United States, the treatment of citizen-children is particularly harsh in that, under current law, the United States Board of Immigration Appeals relies upon the criterion of "extreme hardship" to determine whether nondocumented migrant parents can be subject to deportation. Extreme hardship is not defined to include the disruption of child-parent relations; indeed, that is the baseline against which hardship is measured, because an applicant for a waiver of deportation must show that the harms are "substantially different from, and beyond, that which would normally be expected" when an alien leaves behind "close family members."[67]

Between the September 11 attacks on the United States and 2004, "over 4.7 million people were compelled to leave . . . for immigration reasons"; some three million citizen children have parents lacking "a regular immigration status."[68] Thus, many of those forced out are parents. As a consequence, the citizen-child's theoretical right to nondeportation is undermined, rendering it a "denuded status." When their parents are expelled, these children may well follow, but having lived all their lives in the United States, they can end up in countries where they know neither the language nor the customs.

In contrast, some decisions from the European Court of Justice as well as from the European Court of Human Rights have recognized a "child-centered approach" that takes seriously a nation's obligations to its children-citizens. The case of *Zhu and Chen v. Secretary of State for the Home Department* (discussed by Jacqueline Bhabha as well as Patrizia Nanz)[69] is exemplary. In this case, the parents, Chinese nationals with economic interests in a company in the United Kingdom, sought to avoid the Chinese policy penalizing parents for the birth of a second child. They arranged to have their daughter, Catherine Zhu, born in Belfast, Northern Ireland, and thereby for her to acquire birthright citizenship as well as mobility rights to reside elsewhere in the European Union. When the child was six months old, the mother and daughter moved to Great Britain and, relying on the child's birthright citizenship, applied for residence permits. Both the British and Irish governments objected that the choice of Belfast as a birth place was an abuse of EU law and that the child ought not to be considered a national entitled to protection under the relevant directive.[70]

That position lost in the European Court of Justice, which held that even a "very young minor who is a Community National" who fulfills the legal insurance and resource requirements enjoyed "a right to reside for an indeterminate period" within the European Union. The Court further concluded that, if the child met the legal residency and citizenship requirements, her primary caregiver also gained residency rights in order to give effect to the child's right. Of course, absent an understanding that the "primary caregiver" could be defined to include more than one person, that conception did not unite the entire family. Currently, in both the European Union and the United States, commentators are questioning the wisdom of birthright citizenship and using decisions that permit or deny

residency based on citizen-children's needs in arguments advocating limiting access to this form of entitlement to citizenship.[71]

Thus significant questions are raised about what justifications can support asymmetries between derivative rights borne from the citizenship
and residency rights of children as compared to those rights passed on
by those parents to their children; whether the unit of analysis for citizenship and residency rights should be individuals or families; which persons
should qualify for recognition as "family" members; what relevance the
physical places of those members has; and how gender analyses affect the
responses.[72] Even under a simplified model, focused only on the biological mother and father of a particular child, citizenship rights have varied
depending on whether a citizen parent is a mother or a father and where
a child is born.

Moreover, such patrilineal or matrilineal membership rules (and conflicts over them) can be found in many cultures and religions as well as in
nation-states.[73] Indeed, the contemporary human rights conventions that
insist on the irrelevance of the nationality of a spouse were formulated
in response to histories of discrimination based on an interaction among
gender, nationality, and marriage rules. During certain periods in the
United States, for example, citizen women who married men who were
not U.S. citizens could lose their U.S. citizenship.[74]

These gendered family-citizenship dramas have such power that they
are regularly the stuff of art, as Linda K. Kerber discusses through her
analyses of the case that inspired the Puccini opera, *Madama Butterfly*
(which was later revived in a Broadway musical as *Miss Saigon*). The basic
plot line is that a United States naval officer, stationed in the early part of
the twentieth century in Asia, seduces a young woman who then bears
his child. His promised return entails a broken promise, for he is accompanied by an American national wife, and the young Asian woman then
attempts suicide.

Kerber asks, What passport should that child have? "In the Meiji period, as in the West until roughly World War I, practices of documenting
individual identity were underdeveloped. . . . Was the child a Japanese
subject? . . . Not until 1985 was Nationality Law in Japan revised to permit Japanese women to transmit Japanese citizenship to their children."[75]
Under United States law at the time, the unmarried male citizen did not
transmit his citizenship status, but, had his child been born on United
States soil (including a navy ship, deemed United States territory), birthright citizenship would have been recognized.[76]

Such rules left thousands of children stateless, and this problem forms the analytic centerpiece of Kerber's commentary on the import of citizenship and the vulnerability of those who stand outside its parameters. As she recounts, gender continues not only to set the social and economic boundaries generating such configurations but also to do legal work. Under current United States law, citizen mothers and fathers who parent children abroad are not equally able to transmit citizenship. A federal statute provides that children born abroad of U.S. citizen mothers acquire citizenship at birth, while children of U.S. citizen fathers have to be acknowledged legally as their offspring before the child reaches the age of eighteen.[77]

A challenge to this statute on the grounds that it violated equal protection under the United States Constitution lost in the United States Supreme Court in a judgment rendered five to four. Deferring to Congress, the majority concluded that the statutory distinction was related to "important governmental objectives" forwarded by the presumptively rational distinction between mothers who, under the majority's view, were likely to have more contact with their children born abroad than would their fathers.[78] As a practical matter, as Kerber notes, more men are stationed abroad and can father more children than their female counterparts can produce; hence the rule operates to narrow the doors to citizenship for offspring born outside the United States. As Kerber powerfully demonstrates, the risks to those without recognized forms of citizenship cannot be overstated.[79]

Political, Economic, and Social Citizenship

Elucidating the role played by gender in migration and citizenship, van Walsum and Bhabha focus on international family movements, whereas Kerber's eye is trained on the way gender, intersecting with rules privileging place or parentage, leaves some without a state willing to call them members. Inlender's analysis of asylum, in turn, details distinctive means by which women engage in political action, rendering them outcasts as they try to alter a state's policies. In general what we see as core citizenship activities are predicated on traditions that train us to look to certain indices and ignore others. It is history at which Cynthia Patterson takes aim, as she shows how a narrow understanding of the classical conception of citizenship has all too deeply colored the Western conception and has wrongly generated as a model the privileges of free, adult, property-owning members of the Greek polis and of the Roman Empire as the paradigm of citizenship.[80]

Patterson argues that there are great discrepancies between theories of citizenship and the realities of its expression, which result "from making Aristotle stand for Athens on the one hand and Roman jurists for Rome on the other—and ignoring the historical context of both in which citizenship was an arena of on-going contestation with variable consequences (economic, social, religious, as well as political) for women and families and for aliens as well as the native born."[81] Because women did not vote or hold office in Athens or Rome, it has been assumed that they were excluded from citizenship. If, however, one looks beyond a formal understanding of the political as centered on the institutions of running and holding office, jury duty, and the military, and takes into account the many ways in which membership in the community is expressed, "the character of female and/or provincial citizenship becomes more interesting."[82]

As Patterson explains, around the year 451/o B.C.E., Pericles proposed to the Athenian Assembly that "anyone who was not born of two citizen parents should not have a share (*metechein*) in the polis." Patterson underscores that the Athenians did not vote on who was to be a "citizen" but rather on who could "share in the city." And this shareholding was expressed through the use of the term "*astos*" "to denote the parental citizen *couple* necessary for that 'shareholding.'" Yet it is the word "*polites*" that has usually carried the weight of discussions of citizenship in the ancient world.

Through meticulous documentation, Patterson reveals that women as *astoi* both had legal rights and protections (for example, against rape and adultery) and participated extensively in public religion, in the celebration of civic festivities, and in the care for the dead and funeral rituals. In Rome as well, which was never a democracy like Athens and which did not extend the *suffragium* (right to vote) to all male citizens, women of the republican elite held certain rights and privileges, placing them above lower-class male citizens. At that time, determining whether women were citizens then required a decision about what kind of participation counted as a mark of citizenship. If citizenship was understood more broadly as "sharing in the city" and if citizenship voice was seen as including public actions related to life and death and not just as a matter of whether women partook in certain political institutions, women were indeed citizens in the ancient world, with a status that was expressed and displayed through a variety of activities.[83]

We need thus to take Patterson's insight forward so as to focus on expressions of citizenship today that fall outside the parameters of conventional political citizenship. In the ancient world, propertylessness and la-
boring for others disqualified one from holding political citizenship. But,
as modern industrial democracies universalized the condition of wage
labor to all genders, races, and ethnicities, the complex interdependence
between work and citizenship emerged and, with it, the nomenclature
of "economic citizenship."[84] Until recently, however, the influence of the
ancient model on Western political thought made some form of property ownership of land the decisive criterion for citizenship. Jean-Jacques
Rousseau and Immanuel Kant, as well as Thomas Jefferson, were united in
their belief that landed property was necessary to assure nondomination
and to make a man "independent of the will of another."[85]

With the transition from an economy based on small commodity production, in which such forms of land ownership were meaningful, to an
industrial society of generalized commodity production, in which land
ceased to be the main source of wealth, the citizen became increasingly the
wage earner, dependent upon some form of salaried or wage-earning employment. T. H. Marshall, in his famous essay on "Citizenship and Social
Class," theorized that economic rights to form trade unions and to receive
unemployment compensation, retirement pensions, and health care benefits were the culmination of the rights of citizenship in democracies.[86]

In their contributions to this volume, Linda Bosniak and Aihwa Ong
address different aspects of this complex relationship between forms of
economic dependence and independence and one's status as a rights
holder. Bosniak proceeds from a broad observation that

> [t]o the extent that progressive social theorists, including feminist theorists,
> continue to press to redefine the *substance* of citizenship—to extend our
> conception to include more robust conceptions of "social citizenship" or
> "equal citizenship" or "democratic citizenship," and to incorporate new do-
> mains, like the workplace and the home, as sites of citizenship practice—we
> ought, I think, to be particularly sensitive to the questions of exclusion and
> subordination implicated in this discussion. Citizenship for whom? Citi-
> zenship where?[87]

As large numbers of women enter into the various sectors within the
labor force (for example, in the United States, about 75 percent of women
with children between six and seventeen work outside their homes), some

of the household labor that they once performed is undertaken by other women, who themselves often cross borders to take such jobs. "A good deal of the care work that was conventionally performed by wives and mothers (or female extended family members) is now performed by non-family members pursuant to commercial exchange or contract." This com-modification of domestic labor is both raced and classed and, increasingly, has a transnational dimension in which the migration of foreign women enables resident women to do different kinds of wage work. While both resident women and migrant women are economic agents, only resident women are now entitled to citizenship.

Bosniak resists the idea of citizenship as a "zero sum game" in which wealthier women gain their status at the "expense" of domestic workers. Rather than insist on a "universalist conception," Bosniak seeks to buf-fer against "citizenshiplessness" by arguing for the need to disaggregate aspects of citizenship so as to identify mechanisms of subordination and to provide specific protection for those without citizenship. Bosniak raises the concern that if the problems are seen only in all-or-nothing citizen-ship terms, then practical protections—such as protection of work hours and wages—might be forestalled because of the complexity of the larger political and legal challenges presented when transnational domestic workers seek protection.

Her intervention builds on some countries' traditions and institutions in which certain rights and obligations have long existed independent of political citizenship. In the United States, for example, aliens both pay taxes and serve in the military. Further, even if undocumented, aliens formally enjoy expressive and associational rights as well as procedural, contract, and property rights and access to public schools, which (while under assault) thus far attach to "personhood" and not only to citizen-ship. Yet, since 1996 in the United States, rights of access to health care and social welfare programs have also contracted.[88]

Aihwa Ong also focuses on foreign female workers as she pro-vides arresting accounts of the predicament of "foreign maids" in Asian metropoles, with "approximately 140,000 domestic workers . . . in Singa-pore, 200,000 in Malaysia, and 240,000 in Hong Kong."[89] An estimated ten million Asians, about half of whom are female, are "transient aliens," and some have been held as "sex slaves" or otherwise horridly abused; the "frequency and ferocity of abuses against foreign maids index a brew-ing human rights crisis over the emergence of neo-slavery in Southeast Asia."[90]

Ong analyzes "the interrelationships of labor markets, nationalisms and moral economies"[91] that generate this phenomenon. Some countries (such as the Philippines and Indonesia) are senders, with workers trained by various authorities (including NGOs) under a rubric which makes a connection "between free choice in seeking overseas employment [and] the young women's sense of moral indebtedness and sacrifice for their families."[92] As net remitters of earnings to their families and kin, these "maids" have become a highly prized "asset" for the economies of the countries involved. But a role that empowers them as workers at home does little to alter what may be called "domestic slavery" under conditions of economic globalization. As Ong details, employers often hold their domestic workers' passports and work papers. Foreign domestic helpers do not apply for citizenship, but instead may only hope for their contracts to be renewed. Of the countries studied, Hong Kong alone provided foreign maids with special work visas that protect minimum wages and days off. And the tenuous nature of such protections can be seen during times of economic crises; in 1997–98, close to nine hundred thousand migrant workers were expelled from Malaysia, Singapore, and Hong Kong.

What might be done? Ong is skeptical towards a language of human rights that includes a "logic of exception" that creates categories of persons outside the zone of citizenship and those within. She is also skeptical of the ability of transnational and local NGOs to intervene in light of the "competition for foreign jobs among labor-sending countries" and the complexity of having a young, female presence in the intimate domain of the household. While some NGOs have relied on the media to make plain the suffering of "racialized" women at work, these groups have pressed for the protection of the physical well-being of these women alone ("biowelfare"), rather than situating them as members of a global humanity. NGOs do not generally demand rights of citizenship for migrant workers, and not all workers want to lose or attenuate the citizenship that they have. Seeing NGOs as parties to and subject to national agendas and capitalist interests, Ong argues that NGOs are "not the actors of a 'postnational constellation,' in the Habermasian sense of an emerging global civil society."[93]

Valentine Moghadam, focused on another region of the world, provides a very different account than Ong of the effects of an international human rights regime, of transnational civil society, and of a global public sphere.[94] Moghadam, who considers case studies from the Republic of Iran and the Kingdom of Morocco through a comparative interest in countries like Egypt, Algeria, and Turkey, explores the way "local communities or national borders" are affected by globalized norms. She asks, "What of the migration and mobility of feminist ideas and their practitioners? How do local struggles intersect with global discourses on women's rights? What role is played by feminists in the diaspora, and what is the impact of the state?" By analyzing the formation of women's rights and feminist organizations both within specific countries and through transnational feminist networks, she argues that international conferences and treaties such as CEDAW have created tools that women tailor to their own contexts.[95]

Moghadam maps the "significant variations in women's legal status and social positions across the Muslim world."[96] Yet in general, "similar patterns of women's second-class citizenship"[97] can be identified in terms of family life and economic opportunity. Across national boundaries, citizenship is transmitted through fathers, and marriage laws give men rights that women do not have. In both Iran and Morocco, for example, the state, the family, and economic forms of dependency create what Moghadam calls the "patriarchal gender contract."[98]

Responding in the 1980s to efforts to strengthen application of gendered Muslim family law to women living in diverse national and cultural contexts, various women's networks came into being. For example, nine women (coming from Algeria, Sudan, Morocco, Pakistan, Bangladesh, Iran, Mauritius, and Tanzania) formed an action committee that resulted in Women Living Under Muslim Laws (WLUML), an organization that serves as a clearinghouse for information about struggles and strategies. WLUML includes women with differing approaches to religion; some are antireligious while others, such as Malaysia's Sisters in Islam, are observant. Thus, some work to abandon religious strictures while others challenge interpretations of religious laws and make arguments from within texts and traditions.

Moghadam identifies features of these efforts that distinguish the work of these groups from their counterparts in North America and Europe. For example, many Middle Eastern women's groups display "a tendency to work with men and to engage state agencies"[99] rather than adopt more radical feminist postures, as have some groups in other parts of the world who show more skepticism toward the possibility of state-based reforms.[100] Moghadam posits that groups such as WLUML serve to mediate the exchange between universalist equality claims and local conditions. By reviewing conflicts in Iran and in Morocco on family rights, Moghadam argues that WLUML, along with the Women Learning Project, had an impact by sparking an interaction between state-centric and transnational action. Thus, Moghadam concludes that "[t]he integration of North and South in the global circuits of capital and the construction of a transnational public sphere in opposition to the dark side of globalization has meant that feminism is not 'Western' but global."[101] She notes the following irony in global struggles: just as these struggles for women's equality require revisiting the discourse of universalistic human rights, the conditions of global migrations raise questions about whether to aspire to global citizenship, to particularized affiliations, or to combinations thereof. Further, Moghadam also suggests that the more culturally embedded a group is within a nation-state, the more effective could be its efforts to incorporate universalist norms.

Layering Citizenship, Federalist States, Multiculturalism, and Gender

Thus far, we have focused on women, men, and children moving across borders and either gaining status recognition or not. We turn now to two related ideas: groups of migrants affiliated with each other and living in somewhat distinct cultures within their host country, and federated or confederated governments in which citizens of preexisting states come together into one unit even as they insist on the continuing autonomy (sometimes termed "sovereignty") of the subdivisions. Obvious examples today are the United States, Canada, and the European Union, in which one is simultaneously a citizen of a state or province or nation and of the larger entity as well. Further, it is worth recalling that layered affiliations are not novel in that some colonials were both subject-citizens of an empire, such as Britain, while simultaneously being Australian or Canadian. Moreover, Commonwealth status can still be relevant to obtaining citizenship in the United Kingdom.

How should we understand citizenship, gender, and borders in these contexts? How do commitments to pluralism, multiculturalism, and universal rights play out? What roles ought to be accorded to the UN conventions, to national lawmaking, and to courts? Whose voices get heard and who speaks for or is understood as representing the interests of subgroups when conflicts emerge? Are jurisdictional allocations gender-coded (such as the assignment of "matters that are essentially within the domestic jurisdiction" to the nation-state by the UN Charter)? And what work does the division into domestic versus national jurisdiction do in inscribing gender distinctions? Intense debate surrounds issues of whether and when nation-states ought to encourage or to accede to multiple affiliations that constitute culturally differentiated forms of citizenship.

For example, from the perspective of the nation-state, one could identify advantages, such that a state may use communities of migrants as resources, providing networks, skills, and competencies to enhance a state's own standing in a global world. Alternatively, one can worry about the degree to which such communities deviate from national norms and retain allegiances to their home countries. Migrants' insistence on their subcultural connections are interwoven with their experiences in host countries, the degree of difference between host and home country, and the hospitality or the hostility of the host country.

In many respects, these are familiar issues in the political and legal theory of any federation, as it is often through conflicts over degrees of autonomy that one identifies which national normative commitments are so foundational as to trump subpolities' variations. Moreover, the problems of subgroup deviance are also familiar in the historical sense, in that migrants have long joined together in a new country to insist on their own delineations so as to adhere to distinctive customs rather than to be totally immersed in the culture in which they now live. Drawing on examples from earlier centuries of Chinese, Jewish, and Indian migrations, one could model these experiences as a diaspora, in which communities insist on their distinct identity and strong connections to another place that is their "home." Alternatively, given that globalized networks of transportation, communication, electronic media, and banking and financial services enable people living in one place to participate in and be connected to communities at a great distance, one could see these multiplying ties as representing people's experiences of having more than one "home country" and thus as pluralizing allegiances.

Our contribution here is to put gender at the forefront of these debates and to see how the tensions between migrant cultures and those of their host nations, interlaced with gender, are sites of contestation in this volume as exemplified by the lively philosophical divergence among David Jacobson, Audrey Macklin, and Angelia Means.[102] Jacobson's interest is in the "competing demands of immigrant communities, multicultural aspirations, and women's rights."[103] In his view, the evolution of international norms of justice, along with erosion in the sovereign ambit of the nation-state, have created a tendency in the courts to privilege individual "bodily self-possession" and free choice, including that of women, and this is leading the courts to uphold women's human rights to bodily integrity and freedom from patriarchal and communal fiat. This development is, in practice at least, geographically bounded and, in Western countries, socially and politically fraught vis-à-vis some immigrant communities.[104]

Jacobson's examples include practices that impose upon women's bodies, such as requiring female genital cutting, "marriage by capture," or the forcible return of a woman to her family's traditions. Jacobson then looks to law, and particularly to the courts, in which claims or defenses of such practices are stated in oppositional terms that put women's rights into conflict with "culture." Through the "judicialization of politics,"[105] argues Jacobson, courts and other branches of government use gender "as a means of excluding certain 'undesirable' cultural practices." In these struggles (including transnational violence as represented in 9/11), "the rights of women are a key leitmotif."[106]

Jacobson's questions have engaged many scholars, some of whom do not share his reading that "when women's rights clash with patriarchal culture, in the great preponderance of cases the rights of women trumps the claims of such cultures, legally and in public opinion."[107] For example, a 1996 analysis, "Individualizing Justice through Multiculturalism: The Liberal's Dilemma," by Doriane Lambelet Coleman, argued a different trend, at least in the United States, in which a "cultural defense" was used as mitigation of charges of criminal assaults such as rape, battery, and murder against the women involved.[108] (Jacobson might respond that the criminal charges vindicate his point, in that recognition of women's rights puts "culture" on the defensive.)

Data collection is one difficulty; reported judgments are a thin slice of what occurs in courts, where it is difficult to learn about all of the cases filed, defenses made, and charges dropped. More generally, beyond specific opinions in the small number of reported cases, identifying what to count as an instance of a government's privileging women's self-possession is not obvious. Beyond such empirical challenges are theoretical questions, because the juxtaposition of "culture" to "gender" is itself problematic, as is demonstrated in the debate raised by Susan Moller Okin's question: "Is Multiculturalism Bad for Women?"[109] Mapping the many world cultures (ancient and modern) that were patriarchal rather than emancipatory in their views of women and the defenses of "multicultural citizenship rights" by Will Kymlicka and others, Okin argued that the celebration of "different cultures" missed the harms to women.[110] Yet many feminist theorists rejected the positioning of women in opposition to culture, as they argued that it was not emancipatory to suggest that women had to make a choice between "your culture or your rights."[111] In the last few years, another question—wearing a headscarf—has come to embody (pun intended) these issues. In several countries, Muslim women and girls in professional and educational settings have been told that they may not wear head coverings. Litigation and legislation has resulted, along with a good deal of feminist commentary insisting that these women's agency has been undervalued.[112]

Furthermore, a women versus culture approach tends to exoticize both women and culture, as if "others" have these conflicts whereas practices in the United States or the West are not themselves predicated on deeply held cultural views of gender-coded social rôles and rules. The ever-present painful example is violence against women, which knows no national or cultural boundaries.[113] Yet, when states become active in pursuit of such harms, the concern is that prosecutions will be aimed at the marginal cultures, in some contexts resulting in the criminalization of the male members of economically or racially vulnerable minorities.

Such concerns shape the contributions of Audrey Macklin and Angelia Means, who seek to deconstruct the binarisms of gender versus cultural identity. Like Jacobson, Macklin puzzles about what law is supposed to do in the face of practices that could be oppressive to women in minority subcultures. Like Jacobson, she also considers female genital mutilation (FGM), which the Canadian Criminal Code explicitly made illegal in 1997. Macklin recounts that her initial concern was that "[s]ingling out FGM for special mention [. . .] seems to implant a marginalizing narrative into legal text."[114] But that insertion did not come from action by the dominant national culture alone, but from "encultured women" engaged in a campaign as they formed coalitions with mainstream feminist organizations to persuade the Canadian Parliament to take action that they believed would "unequivocally convey the message of its illegality to affected communities."[115] The criminal deterrent was thought to be a useful complement to education and consciousness raising.

Macklin's other case study involves the question of what could be styled "contracts versus rights." Many countries now promote "alternative dispute resolution" procedures to create state-enforced private settlements of conflicts in lieu of adjudication of rights.[116] Under the law of the Canadian Province of Ontario, women are rights holders when families dissolve and they can seek compensation for household labors that enabled their husbands to develop careers. Ontario also permits resolutions through negotiation, which results in "domestic contracts." In addition, when disputants use arbitration, these outcomes are enforceable in court. (In contrast, in Quebec, family law arbitrations are advisory rather than binding.)

In 2003, a then-new Islamic Institute for Civil Justice offered to arbitrate family and inheritance conflicts under Muslim law, prompting an inquiry about whether faith-based arbitration ought to be given legal force. Opposition came from the Canadian Council of Muslim Women, who worked with the transnational group, Women Living Under Muslim Laws (WLUML), also discussed by Moghadam. Reliant on networks "as Canadians, as women, as immigrants, and as Muslims," the opponents built constituencies both locally and globally, just as they argued on the basis of both national and transnational principles, including the UDHR's commitments to dignity and equality. Proponents of faith-based resolutions were similarly domestic and international—including organizations such as "the Christian Legal Fellowship, the Salvation Army, B'nai Brith, the Sunni Masjid El Noor, and the Ismaili Muslims." The denouement was Canadian legislation, which does not prohibit parties from turning to faith-based tribunals but gives such judgments no legally enforceable effect.

As Macklin explains, both cases rest on liberal principles concerned with the capacity of dependents to make volitional judgments. Specifically, political campaigns relied upon a shared appreciation that minors cannot knowingly consent to FGM and that immigrant women would be particularly vulnerable to their husbands. Moreover, the resistance to faith-based family dispute resolution was built on a general critique that family law ought not to be a regime permitting "parties to 'opt-out' of public norms and public scrutiny, leaving vulnerable women of all faiths and ethnicities with inadequate legal protection."[117] Yet, in Macklin's judgment, proponents of criminalizing FGM "underestimated the coercive power of the criminal justice system, while the anti-Islamic tribunal activists overestimated the equilibrating power of the civil justice system."[118] Moreover, commentators on both laws will probably underappreciate how politically important encultured women, often presumed to be voiceless, were. As Macklin details, those women played central roles, expressing "political citizenship in the public sphere of law reform" and doing so through transnational and transcultural claims of equality.[119] "Claiming their entitlement as legal citizens of Canada to participate in governance, they demanded equal citizenship as Canadian women. At the same time, they pointedly refused to renounce their cultural citizenship or to confine their gender critique to the specific cultural context."[120]

Such practices not only make the meaning of citizenship more complex by revealing the interaction of the language of universal rights and culturally embedded identities; they also expand the vocabulary of public claim making in democracies. It is with the transformation of democracies through such practices that Angelia Means is concerned. Means writes from the perspective of political philosophy, informed by a vision of "strong democracy," defined as relying on participatory politics instead of solely on individualistic rights-based perspectives to shape and change democratic processes. These strong democracies are evolving into a new type of political society: "a type of society that can leave behind the ideology of national identity; . . . that has undergone the requisite socio-economic modernization, is thoroughly adapted to cultural modernity (with its characteristic differentiation between law and ethical/cultural/religious worldviews) and has well-developed (and integrated) formal and informal public spheres."[121]

For Means, the challenge of integrating the claims of gender and culture into the public spheres of existing democracies, whether through legal, political, cultural, or social institutions, ought not to be conceived of in technical or strategic terms, focused on fixing a piece of legislation or tweaking a practice. Rather, the point is to push democracies towards another form of society, constantly reaching "for the inclusion of the other"[122] by bringing legal-doctrinal presence and emergent social groups into encounters and conversations, thus contributing to the reflexivity of the identity of the "democratic we." In such encounters the "others" as well as "we" are transformed through multiple democratic iterations. Even as she launches a strong defense to consider the "individual's equal right to cultural expression to be akin to the right of religious expression," and therefore deserving of protection, Means emphasizes how the conversation between law and minority cultures both challenges existing laws and changes the cultures themselves. For, "in the context of strong democracy, cultures (like religions) can be expected to evolve, to become complex, contrarian, and differentiated, and, ultimately, to make their peace with the idea of equal rights for all, including women's rights."

Unlike Jacobson, who is leery of a robust judicial role, Means has great ambitions for what courts can do. She urges constitutional courts to take an active role as meta-public spheres and to determine the boundaries of the cultural struggles of the present. Means wants courts to guarantee to all the right of equal freedom by protecting their freedom of speech and public access; by rejecting discrimination; and by reiterating private rights in the light of the multicultural, countercultural, and contrapunctual perspectives of new members. The role of the courts, in her account, is not to provide "a comprehensive conception of moral freedom that fills in the substantive content of personal liberty and moral autonomy, but rather, to pursue 'political freedom through law.'"

We turn from questions of cultures within nation-states to questions of cultures arising within federations or unions, entities whose self-definition includes two ideas: that subnational units have some degree of autonomy to generate distinctive norms; and that individuals can simulatnaeously be members or citizens of both the subunit and the larger one. Patrizia Nanz's interest is thinking about gender in the context of the emergence of European citizenship and the intra-European migration flows.[123] As she reminds us, before 1992, Europeans were "market citizens" but were "considered foreigners when traveling or living outside their country of origin." But in 1992 (under the Maastricht Treaty, which was agreed to in that year and became effective the following year), they gained the rights to move freely across borders and reside in any of the member states and to vote in and run for municipal and European Parliamentary elections where they resided. Citizenship in any of the EU member states provides EU citizenship.[124]

As educational and professional opportunities transcend nation-states, a new political space is emerging encompassing the twenty-seven nation-states of the European Union. But is that new union a demos? How can a meta-EU-citizen identity come into being? Nanz focuses on two mechanisms interacting and generating the "disassociation of nationality (belonging) from citizenship (legal status)" through which aliens and nationals become open to exchanges of intercultural citizenship practices. One is formal law, found in treaties and elaborated through directives and courts, and the second is the practices of the peoples of Europe, moving across national borders and embracing "dual national identities and multiple allegiances."[125]

As Nanz lays out, some of the legal predicates to the development of a European demos are entitlements to free movement of persons and families and the equal treatment of aliens and nationals. Nanz explains how the European Union's initial economic principles of the 1950s of equal pay for equal work developed into a more far-reaching insistence on equality and prohibitions against discrimination.

In the early 1960s, the European Court of Justice (the ECJ, sitting in Luxembourg) ruled that EU rights took "direct effect," operable directly at national levels and to be enforced by national courts.[126] (In contrast, for example, treaties ratified by the United States are not necessarily the source of rights for individuals in either national or state courts.) In 1998, the ECJ established the principle that nations cannot discriminate against nonnational EU citizens, and the concept of equality came to be understood to enable nonnationals to have family members join them in their countries of residence and thus developed into the understanding that rights to mobility were not predicated on one's own work status alone.

Nanz then takes up the question of entitlements to welfare through an analysis of the 1998 case of Martinez Sala[127] and concludes that this ruling is mixed from a feminist perspective. This judgment "widened the conferral of social advantages and family benefits beyond the bounds of economic activity" and therefore made EU citizenry the basis for some national welfarist policies.[128] But the ECJ reached the decision on the basis of the national court's holding that Ms. Martinez Sala was not a "worker" under the governing regulations, and hence did not recognize the ways in which a single parent without wage work contributes as another kind of "worker" to the economy.[129]

New legal questions emerge from circumstances in which a national of one country moves to another EU nation. Nanz also moves from legal principles to practices as she examines the attitudes of intra-EU migrants toward EU citizenship. Repeatedly, migrants "with high levels of national identity are more likely to identify with Europe" than those with lower levels of political identification, leading Nanz to reject "zero-sum conceptions of national versus European identity." Nanz sees these EU migration rights and the development of "situated postnational citizenship" as potentially of benefit to women, including non-EU nationals.

Vicki Jackson is also intrigued by the interaction among citizenship theory, federalism, and equality rights, as she looks worldwide to sort out their possible relationships. Jackson sees the advantages of a world in which national identities have meaning, in part to enable territorial connections that are based upon "rooted geography of living" rather than "based solely on ascriptive identity." Moreover, like Nanz, Jackson is insistent on layered relationships, in which one can be a citizen, in a meaningful sense, of more than one polity. Rather than denationalize citizenship, both Jackson and Nanz are eager to explore both expressive and legal mechanisms to pluralize citizenship and to accommodate experiences of persons as deeply related to more than one polity. Jackson is unwilling to assume that egalitarians ought to aspire to a world that is postnational and in which the meaning of citizenship is attenuated. Jackson sees nation-states as the engine for enforcement of rights and the places for participation to make or remake legal entitlements. "Undermining the civic affiliations embraced by national citizenship may have costs to maintaining the significance and viability of democratic governmental spaces."[130] Moreover, "equality of citizenship" has been used to "enhance women's access to public life, education, and economic advancement."[131]

Jackson also takes up the issue of whether federalist models of government might actually be better equipped than unitary systems for enabling women to gain equality.[132] By definition, federations offer more places for political participation and possibly some "closer to home." Some empirical data—from the United States and elsewhere—find a correlation between women's office holding and subunits, such that women are more likely to hold jobs in state legislatures and judiciaries than in the federal system. But given the many variables entailed (including whether an electoral system is proportional, how elections are financed, and the numbers of parties), causal claims should not be made. Federations could offer other advantages, including policy competition and training in sustaining a sense that policy disagreements are positive aspects of a country's identity. Yet the content of variation is key, for federations (infamously the United States) have tolerated discrimination. Further, unitary governments may make implementation of equality norms easier to monitor.

Citizenship, Human Rights, Jurisdictions, and Borders—Engendered

This volume aspires to reorient the lively debate concerning globalization, borders, migration, and citizenship by bringing together law, politics, and theories that highlight the way gender categories illuminate and enrich the analyses. All contributors struggle with the meaning of community and the hopes for equality in a world racked with dissension, violence, and subordination. We join the authors of this volume and, we hope, its readers, in aspiring to help shape intellectual and political iterative processes that refuse to ignore the injuries imposed in the name of the nation-state while acknowledging the ways in which these communities can shelter and enable their members. While we—the coeditors—are both committed to Benhabib's formulation of a "right to have rights,"[133] we have somewhat different views of the roles to be played by transnational precepts and nation-states. Resnik sees the generativity of "affiliation by law"[134] resting importantly at local and national levels in which one can either live safely and with respect or not, while Benhabib is more skeptical of this form of social ordering and pleads for robust interaction between cosmopolitan norms and local practices.

We raise these differences only in passing and deliberately in conclusion to this introduction as a way of inviting readers to join us in our efforts to understand the implications of these positions in the fast-changing world in which some of us move, some of us stay put, and all of us are marked by the interaction between those places and our genders, races, ages, ethnic affiliations, resources, and histories.

NOTES

1. Both of us have benefited from our many conversations with our editor, Deborah Gershenowitz, and with our colleagues and coteachers, Robert Post and Reva Siegel, as well as from the generous, generative, and thoughtful research and camaraderie of talented students, including Talia Inlender, Chavi Keeney Nana, Stella Burch, Angelica Bernal, Vasudha Talla, and Dane Lund. We are grateful for the generous support of Yale University's Castle Fund in subsidizing the publication of this book and the Migrations and Mobilities Conference held in New Haven, Connecticut in 2003 and cosponsored by Yale's Women Faculty Forum, its Law School, the Woodward Fund, the Yale Center for International and Area Studies, and the Crossing Borders Initiative. Our thanks to those entities, to the leadership of Linda Lorimer and Gus Ranis, to others of our colleagues at Yale and especially to Vilashini Cooppan, as well as to Rachel Thomas of the Women Faculty Forum, who joined us in its planning, and to the participants whose discussions inform our work. We each enjoy the pleasure of intellectual companionship and thus our thanks to Jim Sleeper and to Denny Curtis.

2. The population data come from the United Nations Population Division, "The World at Six Billion," ESA/P/WP.154, 1999. Migration data are from Hania Zlotnik, "Past Trends in International Migration and Their Implications for Future Prospects," in *International Migration into the 21st Century: Essays in Honor of Reginald Appleyard*, ed. M. A. B. Siddique (Boston, MA: Edward Elgar

Publishing, 2001), 227–61. See also the Migration Information Source, a source of data for population and migration information published by Migration Policy Institute, available at http://www.migrationinformation.org/datahub/comparative. cfm.

3. Zlotnik, "Past Trends in International Migration," supra note 2; Migration Information Source, http://www.migrationinformation.org/datahub/comparative. cfm.

4. United Nations Population Division, *International Migration Report 2002*, ST/ESA/SER.A/220, 2002, 20.

5. Economic models of migration see its welfarist potential to improve the standard of living through enabling workforces to expand in those countries whose economies are likewise increasing, so long as immigration policies can optimize through selection the skill sets needed in a particular place. See Jagdish Bhagwati, "Incentives and Disincentives: International Migration," *Review of World Economics* 120, no. 4 (1984): 678–701; World Bank, *Global Economic Prospects 2006: Economic Implications of Remittances and Migration* (Washington, DC: World Bank, 2006). Questions arise as soon as one disaggregates the benefits to ask about which countries or persons suffer gains and losses. See Joel P. Trachtman, "International Law of Economic Migration: Toward a Fourth Freedom," *available at* http://law.bepress.com/cgi/viewcontent. cgi?article=2483&context=alea (Draft, March 2008).

6. See Nottebohm Case (Liechtenstein v. Guatemala), 1955 I.C.J. 4, 23 (Judgment of April 6, 1955). There, the International Court of Justice defined citizenship as "a legal bond having as its basis a social fact of attachment, a genuine connection of existence, interest and sentiments, together with the existence of reciprocal rights and duties." What those rights and duties are varies from country to country, and moreover, both native-born and naturalized citizens may lose their status. Expatriation is a sanction used by some countries; naturalized citizens may also be at risk of denaturalization if citizenship was obtained by fraud. This distinction is discussed in Trop v. Dulles, 356 U.S. 86, 126 (1958) (Frankfurter, J., dissenting).

7. See generally Linda Bosniak, "Denationalizing Citizenship," in *Citizenship Today: Global Perspectives and Practices*, eds. T. Alexander Aleinikoff & Douglas Klusmeyer (Washington, DC; Carnegie Endowment for International Peace, 2001), 237–52; Peter Schuck and Rogers Smith, *Citizenship without Consent: Illegal Aliens in the American Polity* (New Haven, CT: Yale University Press, 1985). The prevalence of citizenship through one's parents or one's place of birth results in "97 out of every 100 people alive today" obtaining "political membership solely via circumstances beyond their control," a form of inheritance constituting a property right that Ayelet Shacher argues is unfair and imposes redistributional obligations on those who benefit from it. See Ayelet Shacher, "The Worth of Citizenship in an Unequal World," *Theoretical Inquiries in Law* 8 (2007): 367.

8. The possibility of being a citizen of more than one country is both available and becoming more prevalent. See Stanley A. Renshon, "Dual Citizens in America: An Issue of Vast Proportions and Board Significance," *Center for Immigration Studies Backgrounder* (July 2000), *available at* http://www.cis.org/articles/2000/back700.html; Peter J. Spiro, "Perfecting Political Diaspora," *New York University Law Review* 81 (2006): 207. See generally Graziella Bertocchi & Chiara Strozzi, "Citizenship Laws and International Migration in Historical Perspective," *CEPR No. 4737* (2004): 1–48; Yasemin Soysal, *Limits of Citizenship: Migrants and Postnational Membership in Europe* (Chicago, IL: University of Chicago Press, 1994); Patrick Weil and Randall Hansen, *Dual Nationality, Social Rights, and Federal Citizenship in the U.S. and Europe* (New York: Berghahn Books, 2002).

9. See Jean-Marie Guehenno, *The End of the Nation-State,* trans. Victoria Elliott (Minneapolis: University of Minnesota Press, 1995); David Jacobson, *Rights across Borders: Immigration and the Decline of Citizenship* (Baltimore, MD: Johns Hopkins University Press, 1996).

10. Saskia Sassen, *The Mobility of Labor and Capital: A Study in International Investment and Labor Flow* (Cambridge: Cambridge University Press, 1988).

11. Catherine Dauvergne, "Globalizing Fragmentation: New Pressures on Women Caught in the Immigration-Citizenship Law Dichotomy" (in this volume).

12. Linda Bosniak, "Citizenship, Noncitizenship, and the Transnationalization of Domestic Work" (in this volume); Aihwa Ong, "A Bio-Cartography: Maids, Neoslavery, and NGOs" (in this volume).

13. More generally, see Daniel Adler and Kim Rubenstein, "International Citizenship: The Future of Nationality in a Globalised World," *Indiana Journal of Global Legal Studies* 7 (2000): 519–48; Aleinikoff and Klusmeyer, *Citizenship Today: Global Perspectives and Practices,* supra note 7; Alexander Dobrowolsky, "(In)Security and Citizenship: Security, Immigration, and Shrinking Citizenship Regimes," *Theoretical Inquiries in Law* 8 (2007): 629; Peter Spiro, *Beyond Citizenship: American Identity after Globalization* (Oxford: Oxford University Press, 2008); Carol M. Swain, ed., *Debating Immigration* (Cambridge: Cambridge University Press, 2007).

14. The literature is building. See generally Karen Knop, ed., *Gender and Human Rights* (Oxford: Oxford University Press, 2004); and Sarah van Walsum and Thomas Spijkerboer, eds., *Women and Immigration Law* (New York: Routledge-Cavendish, 2007); Nancy Fraser, "Reframing Justice in a Globalizing World," *New Left Review* 36 (2005): 1; *Women Immigrants in the United States* (Washington, DC: Woodrow Wilson Center, Migration Policy Institute, 2002), *available at* http://www.wilsoncenter.org/topics/pubs/womenimm_rpt.pdf; Eveyln Nakano Gleen, *Unequal Freedom: How Race and Gender Shaped American Citizenship and Labor* (Cambridge, MA: Harvard University Press, 2002); Richa Nagar, Victoria Lawson, Linda McDowell, and Susan Hanson, "Locating Globalization:

Feminist (Re)Readings of the Subjects and Spaces of Globalization," *Economic Geography* 78 (2002): 257–84; Ayelet Shahar, "Against Birthright Privilege: Redefining Citizenship as Property," in *Identities, Affiliations, Allegiances*, eds. Seyla Benhabib, Ian Shapiro, and Danilo Petranovic (Cambridge: Cambridge University Press, 2007), 257–85.

15. For analysis of variations in receptivity to migrants, which is not uniform, see Alexander Aleinikoff, *Semblances of Sovereignty: The Constitution, the State, and American Citizenship* (Cambridge, MA: Harvard University Press, 2002); Benedict Anderson, *Imagined Communities: Reflections on the Origin and Spread of Nationalism* (London: Verso, 1983); Seyla Benhabib, *The Rights of Others: Aliens, Residents, and Citizens* (Cambridge: Cambridge University Press, 2004); Jacqueline Bhaba, "Border Rights and Rites: Generalisations, Stereotypes, and Gendered Migration," in *Women and Immigration Law*, eds. Sarah van Walsum and Thomas Spijkerboer (New York: Routledge-Cavendish, 2007), 16; Bonnie Honig, *Democracy and the Foreigner* (Princeton, NJ: Princeton University Press, 2001); Kim Rubenstein, "Advancing Citizenship: The Legal Armory and Its Limits," *Theoretical Inquiries in Law* 8 (2007): 508.

16. These are Joan Kelly Gadol's famous words. "The Social Relations of the Sexes: Methodological Implications of Women's History," *Signs* 1, no. 4 (1976): 811. See also Joan Scott, "Gender: A Useful Category of Historical Analysis," *American Historical Review* 91, no. 5 (1986): 1053–75.

17. Universal Declaration on Human Rights, G.A. res. 217A (III) (Dec. 10, 1948) [hereinafter, "UDHR"].

18. Convention relating to the Status of Refugees, G.A. res. 429 (V) (entered into force April 22, 1954) [hereinafter, "1951 Convention"].

19. International Covenant on Civil and Political Rights, G.A. res. 2200A (XXI), 21 U.N. GAOR Supp. (No. 16) at 52, U.N. Doc. A/6316 (1966), 999 U.N.T.S. 171 (entered into force Mar. 23, 1976) [hereinafter, "ICCPR"]. As of 2007, 152 countries were parties.

20. International Covenant on Economic, Social, and Cultural Rights, G.A. res. 2200A (XXI), 21 U.N. GAOR Supp (No. 16) at 49, U.N. Doc. A/6316 (1966), 993 U.N.T.S. 3 (entered into force Jan. 3, 1976) [hereinafter, "ICESCR"].

21. The Convention to Eliminate All Forms of Discrimination Against Women, United Nations, General Assembly Resolution 34/180, Dec. 18, 1979 (entered into force, Sept. 3, 1981), *available at* http://www.un.org/womenwatch/daw/cedaw/econvention.htm [hereinafter, "CEDAW"]. These provisions are, of course, augmented by many others. See Declaration on the Human Rights of Individuals Who Are Not Nationals of the Country in Which They Live, G.A. res. 40/144, annex, 40 U.N. GAOR Supp. (No. 53) at 252, U.N. Doc. A/40/53 (1985) (providing such "aliens" with rights to leave, liberty of movement within a country, as well as to have their spouses and minor children of legal aliens be admitted to join and stay with them, and to protect them from expulsion by requiring opportunities

for hearings and for decision-making not predicated on discrimination based on "race, colour, religion, culture, descent or national or ethnic origin"); Convention on the Reduction of Statelessness, 989 U.N.T.S. 175 (Dec. 13, 1975) (requiring that nations grant nationality rights, under certain conditions, to "persons born in its territory who would otherwise be stateless"); Migration for Employment (Revised) (ILO No. 97), 120 U.N.T.S. 70, (Jan. 22, 1952) (providing that members of the ILO make work policy and migration policies known and treat fairly "migrants for employment"); Declaration on Territorial Asylum, G.A. res. 2312 (XXII), 22 U.N. GAOR Supp. (No. 16) at 81, U.N. Doc. A/6716 (1967).

22. UDHR, supra note 17, Preamble, para. 5.

23. Ibid., art. 2.

24. Ibid., art. 16. The 1958 Convention on the Nationality of Married Women, 309 U.N.T.S. 65 (Aug. 11, 1958), also recognized that marriages or divorces between aliens and nationals ought not to "automatically affect the nationality of the wife." Ibid., art. 1. Further, a man who denounced his citizenship could not "prevent the retention of nationality by [his] wife." Ibid., art. 3. In addition, alien wives were to have "specially privileged naturalization procedures" through their husbands. Ibid., art. 3.

25. UDHR, supra note 17, art. 13.1 ("Everyone has the right to freedom of movement and residence within the borders of each state."); art. 13.2 ("Everyone has the right to leave any country, including his own, and to return to his country.").

26. UDHR, supra note 17, art. 14.1 ("Everyone has the right to seek and to enjoy in other countries asylum from persecution."); art. 14.2 ("This right may not be invoked in the case of prosecutions genuinely arising from non-political crimes or from acts contrary to the purposes and principles of the United Nations.").

27. Ibid., art. 15.1 ("Everyone has the right to a nationality."); art. 15.2 ("No one shall be arbitrarily deprived of his nationality nor denied the right to change his nationality.").

28. Charter of the United Nations, 59 Stat. 1031, T.S. 993, 3 Bevans 1153 (entered into force Oct. 24, 1945), art. 2, para. 7 [hereinafter, "UN Charter"].

29. Unsuccessful efforts to do so were undertaken in the 1940s by several organizations that petitioned the United Nations to deal with human rights violations in the United States. See, e.g., NAACP, *An Appeal to the World! A Statement on the Denial of Human Rights to Minorities in the Case of Citizens of Negro Descent in the United States and an Appeal to the United Nations for Redress* (1947). Further, in litigation in the United States, arguments were predicated on both the UDHR and the UN Charter, invoked for the proposition that racial segregation was illegal as a matter of international law. While a few courts agreed, the United States Supreme Court reread the parameters of the equal protection guarantees in the United States Constitution to base its prohibition on segregation

on national law. See Judith Resnik, "Law's Migration: American Exceptionalism, Silent Dialogues, and Federalism's Multiple Ports of Entry," *Yale Law Journal* 115 (2006): 1591–1614; see also Mark Mazower, "The Strange Triumph of Human Rights, 1933–1950," *The Historical Journal* 47 (2004): 279.

30. As provided in Article 1 of the 1951 Convention, such a person must be one who has a

> well-founded fear of being persecuted for reasons of race, religion, nationality or political opinion, is outside the country of his nationality and is unable or, owing to such fear or for reasons other than personal convenience, is unwilling to avail himself of the protection of that country; or who, not having a nationality and being outside the country of his former habitual residence, is unable or, owing to such fear or for reasons other than personal convenience, is unwilling to return to it. (1951 Convention, art. 1.A.2)

31. In the 1995 Fourth World Conference on Women, concerns were heard about the lack of a focus on women in the human rights discourse. Thereafter, commitments to considering the fact and import of gender in all arenas of policy were made. See Report of the Economic and Social Council for 1997, *Mainstreaming the Gender Perspective into All Policies and Programmes in the United Nations Systems*, U.N. GAOR, 52d Sess., Supp. No. 3 IVA, U.N. Doc. A/52/3 (1997). Claims of some success as well as critiques have followed. See Rachael Lorna Johnston, "Feminist Influences on the United Nations Human Rights Treaty Bodies," *Human Rights Quarterly* 28 (2006): 148–85; Hilary Charlesworth, "Not Waving but Drowning: Gender Mainstreaming and Human Rights in the United Nations," *Harvard Human Rights Journal* 18 (2005): 1.

32. Talia Inlender, "Status Quo or Sixth Ground? Adjudicating Gender Asylum Claims" (in this volume). When asylum is denied, the applicant may be returned to the country of origin, but under international law this "refoulement" is not to occur if threats remain, and instead that person is to be sent to a designated safe third country. See Canadian Council for Refugees, Canadian Council of Churches, Amnesty International, and John Doe v. Her Majesty the Queen, [2007] F.C. 1262 (Can.).

33. Inlender, "Status Quo or Sixth Ground?," 362. See also, Office of the High Commissioner for Refugees, *Guidelines for the Protection of Refugee Women*, U.N. Doc. ES/SCP/67 (July 21, 1991).

34. This point parallels the discussion of how in ancient times, women and men also expressed their political citizenship in different ways. See Cynthia Patterson, "Citizenship and Gender in the Ancient World: The Experience of Athens and Rome" (in this volume).

35. See Nora Markard, "Gendered Violence in 'New Wars': Challenges to the Refugee Convention," in van Walsum and Spijkerboer, *Women and Immigration Law*, supra note 14, 67–85.

36. That critique has been made more generally about many forms of international law. See Martti Koskenniemi, *The Gentle Civilizer of Nations: The Rise and Fall of International Law, 1870–1960* (Cambridge: Cambridge University Press, 2001). Yet, national jurists can conclude that, by ratifying treaties, domestic obligations change, and some courts within the United States, for example, have invoked the UDHR as well as the UN Charter as bases for their judgments. See Resnik, "Law's Migration," supra note 29.

37. Statute of the Office of the United Nations High Commissioner for Refugees, G.A. res. 428 (V), annex, 5 U.N. GAOR Supp. (No. 20) at 46, U.N. Doc. A/1775 (1950).

38. As Inlender notes, governments in some countries—including Canada, Australia, and the United States—have used those guidelines when promulgating administrative regulations, and further, some courts have relied on them when assessing whether immigration officials have erred in not recognizing asylum claims.

39. See also Canadian Refugee Council decision, Canadian Council of Churches, Amnesty International, and John Doe v. Her Majesty the Queen, [2007] F.C. 1262 (Can.). Medellín v. Texas, 128 S.Ct. 1346 (2008).

40. ICCPR, supra note 19, art. 26 (prohibiting discrimination on any ground such as "race, colour, sex, language, religion, political or other opinion, national or social origin, property, birth or other status").

41. ICCPR, supra note 19, art. 2.1 states, "Each State Party to the present Covenant undertakes to respect and to ensure to all individuals within its territory and subject to its jurisdiction the rights recognized in the present Covenant, without distinction of any kind, such as race, colour, sex, language, religion, political or other opinion, national or social origin, property, birth or other status."

42. ICCPR, supra note 19, art. 24.3.

43. ICCPR, supra note 19, art. 12.1.

44. ICCPR, supra note 19, art. 12.3 states, "[t]he above-mentioned rights shall not be subject to any restrictions except those which are provided by law, are necessary to protect national security, public order (*ordre public*), public health or morals or the rights and freedoms of others, and are consistent with the other rights recognized in the present Covenant."

45. CEDAW, supra note 21; see also Judith Resnik, "Categorical Federalism: Jurisdiction, Gender, and the Globe," *Yale Law Journal* 111 (2001): 619–47.

46. CEDAW, supra note 21, art. 3.

47. CEDAW, supra note 21, art. 9.

48. CEDAW, supra note 21, art. 10.

49. UN Human Rights Committee, ICCPR General Comment No. 19–Art. 23-A/45/40 Vol. I (1990).

50. The UN Convention on the Rights of the Child states at art. 10(1) that "States Parties shall further ensure that the submission of such a request [to enter

or leave a State Party for the purpose of family unification] shall entail no adverse consequences for the applicants and for the members of their family." G.A. res. 44/25, annex, 44 U.N. GAOR Supp. (No. 49) at 167, U.N. Doc. A/44/49 (1989) (entered into force Sept. 2, 1990) [hereinafter, "CRC"].

51. Dauvergne, "Globalizing Fragmentation" (in this volume).

52. Convention for the Protection of Human Rights and Fundamental Freedoms, 213 U.N.T.S. 222 (entered into force Sept. 3, 1953), as amended by Protocols Nos. 3, 5, 8, and 11, which entered into force on 21 September 1970, 20 December 1971, 1 January 1990, and 1 November 1998, respectively [hereinafter, "ECHR"], art. 8.

53. See Council Directive 2003/86/EC on the Right to Family Reunification, L 2512/12. This provision applies to "members of the nuclear family, that is to say the spouse and the minor children." Ibid., Preamble para. 9. A challenge to this provision for insufficiently respecting the fundamental right of family unification was rejected by the European Court of Justice. See Case C-540/03, *European Parliament v. Council*, 2006/C 109/02. The ECJ held that international instruments (the ICCPR and UN CRC) do not create individual rights to be allowed to enter the territory of a state nor to prevent member states a certain "margin of appreciation" as they evaluated applications for family reunification. See also Helene Lambert, "The European Court of Human Rights and the Rights of Refugees and Other Persons in Need of Protection to Family Reunion," *International Journal of Refugee Law* 11 (1999): 427.

54. See generally Hanna Beate Schöpp–Schilling, ed., *The Circle of Empowerment: Twenty-Five Years of the UN Committee on the Elimination of Discrimination against Women* (New York: Feminist Press, 2007); Hanna Beate Schöpp–Schilling, "Treaty Body Reform: The Case of the Committee on the Elimination of Discrimination against Women," *Human Rights Law Review* 7 (2007): 201–24.

55. See Valentine Moghadam, "Global Feminism, Citizenship, and the State: Negotiating Women's Rights in the Middle East and North Africa" (in this volume); see also Jennifer Nedelsky, "Communities of Judgment and Human Rights," *Theoretical Inquiries in Law* 1(2), Article 1 (2000), *available at* http://www.bepress.com/til/default/vol1/iss2/art1.

56. See Resnik, "Law's Migration," supra note 29, 1582–1611; Judith Resnik, "Gendered Borders and United States' Sovereignty," in van Walsum and Spijkerboer, *Women and Immigration Law*, supra note 14, 44–65.

57. See Optional Protocol to the Convention on the Elimination of Discrimination against Women, GA res. A/54/4 (entered into force December 22, 2000) [hereinafter, "CEDAW Optional Protocol"].

58. One recent provision—the Declaration on the Rights of Indigenous Peoples, U.N. Doc. A/RES/61/295 (Sept. 13, 2007)—does provide in art. 33.1 that "[i]ndigenous peoples have the collective right to determine their own citizenship in accordance with their customs and traditions" as well as the right to

"obtain citizenship of the States in which they live." As Linda Kerber discusses in this volume, some traditions, including those of nation-states, base citizenship on either patrilineal or matrilineal rules. Linda Kerber, "The Stateless as the Citizen's Other: A View from the United States" (in this volume).

59. As Dauvergne notes, Michael Walzer's work, *Spheres of Justice: A Defense of Pluralism and Equality* (New York: Basic Books, 1983), has been influential in shaping this position. For different views, see Joseph Carens, "Aliens and Citizens: The Case for Open Borders," *Review of Politics* 49 (1987): 251; David Abraham, "Doing Justice on Two Fronts: The Liberal Dilemma in Immigration," *University of Miami Legal Studies Research Paper No. 2007-19* (June 2007), *available at* http://ssrn.com/ abstract=1005448); Seyla Benhabib, "Twilight of Sovereignty or the Emergence of Cosmopolitan Norms? Rethinking Citizenship in Volatile Times," *Citizenship Studies* 11(1) (February 2007): 19–36.

60. See generally, Benhabib, *The Rights of Others*, supra note 15; Josh Cohen and Charles Sable, "Extra Rempublicam Nulla Justitia," *Philosophy & Public Affairs* 33 (2005): 147–75; Thomas Nagel, "The Problem of Global Justice," *Philosophy & Public Affairs* 33 (2005): 113–47; Martha Nussbaum, "Beyond the Social Contract: Capabilities and Global Justice," in *The Political Philosophy of Cosmopolitanism*, eds. Gillian Brock and Harry Brighouse (Cambridge: Cambridge University Press, 2005), 196–249; Amartya Sen, "Elements of a Theory of Human Rights," *Philosophy & Public Affairs* 32(4) (2004): 315–56; *Rationality and Freedom* (Cambridge, MA: Harvard University Press, 2002); *Development as Freedom*, (New York: Knopf, 1999).

61. Compare Benhabib, *The Rights of Others*, supra note 15; Judith Resnik, "Law as Affiliation: 'Foreign' Law, Democratic Federalism, and the Sovereigntism of the Nation-State," *International Journal of Constitutional Law* 6, no. 1 (2008): 33–66.

62. Dauvergne, "Globalizing Fragmentation," 333–356; Swain, *Debating Immigration*, supra note 13.

63. Sarah K. van Walsum, "Transnational Mothering, National Immigration Policy, and European Law: The Experience of the Netherlands" (in this volume).

64. Van Walsum, "Transnational Mothering," 231–233.

65. See Linda Bosniak, "Citizenship, Noncitizenship, and the Transnationalization of Domestic Work"; Aihwa Ong, "A Bio-Cartography: Maids, Neoslavery, and NGOs."

66. Jacqueline Bhabha, "The 'Mere Fortuity of Birth?' Children, Mothers, Borders, and the Meaning of Citizenship" (in this volume). Elsewhere, she addresses children as refugees. See Jaqueline Bhabha and Mary Crock, *Seeking Asylum Alone: Unaccompanied and Separated Children and Refugee Protection in Australia, the U.K. and the U.S.* (Sydney: Themis Press, 2007).

67. Bhabha, "'Mere Fortuity of Birth'?," 209 (citing Matter of Montreal, 23 I & N. Dec. 56, 59 [BIA, 2001]).

68. Bhabha, "'Mere Fortuity of Birth'?" See also Gerald L. Neuman, "Discretionary Deportation," *Georgetown Immigration Law Journal* 20 (2006): 611. The process by which decisions are made in general has been demonstrated through a detailed empirical study of asylum claims. Jaya Ramji-Nogales, Andrew I. Schoenholtz, and Philip G. Schrag, "Refugee Roulette: Disparities in Asylum Adjudication," *Stanford Law Review* 60 (2007): 295–412.

69. See Patrizia Nanz, "Mobility, Migrants, and Solidarity: Towards an Emerging European Citizenship Regime" (in this volume).

70. See Article 7 of Council Directive 2003/86/EC on the Right to Family Reunification, L 2512/12, which requires that the "sponsor" (as defined in Article 2(c), show the ability to financially support and provide health care and accommodation for uniting family members. In Case C-200/02, Zhu & Chen v. Sec'y of State for the Home Dep't, 3 C.M.L.R. 48 (2004) (ECJ), the UK and Irish courts argued that a minor child could not fulfill these requirements and thus could not the support the application of family reunification for a parent. See also, Bhabha, "'Mere Fortuity of Birth'?," 205.

71. Peter H. Schuck, *Citizens, Strangers, and In-Betweens: Essays on Immigration and Citizenship* (Boulder, CO: Westview Press, 1998).

72. Restrictive definitions in some countries may violate transnational covenants. See P. R. Ghandhi and E. Macnamee, "The Family in UK Law and the International Covenant on Civil and Political Rights 1966," *International Journal of Law and the Family* 5 (1991): 104.

73. One of the cases that is often discussed involves membership in the Santa Clara Pueblo, in New Mexico. See Judith Resnik, "Dependent Sovereigns: Indian Tribes, States, and the Federal Courts," *University of Chicago Law Review* 56 (1989): 671; Catharine A. MacKinnon, "Whose Culture? A Case Note on Martinez v. Santa Clara Pueblo," *Feminism Unmodified: Discourses on Life and Law* (Cambridge, MA: Harvard University Press, 1987), 63–69.

74. See Nancy F. Cott, "Marriage and Women's Citizenship in the United States, 1830–1934," *American Historical Review* 103 (1998): 1440.

75. Kerber, "The Stateless as the Citizen's Other," 78.

76. The Fourteenth Amendment to the U.S. Constitution, ratified in 1868, which guarantees that "all persons, born or naturalized in the United States, are citizens of the United States and of the state in which they reside."

77. See 8 U.S.C. § 1409.

78. See Nguyen v. INS, 533 U.S. 53 (2001). See also Vicki Jackson, "Citizenships, Federalisms, and Gender," 461.

79. See Kerber, "The Stateless as the Citizen's Other" (in this volume); see also Audrey Macklin, "Who Is the Citizen's Other: Considering the Heft of Citizenship," *Theoretical Inquiries in Law* 8 (2007): 333.

80. Patterson, "Citizenship and Gender in the Ancient World" (in this volume).

81. Ibid., 48.

82. Ibid., 49.

83. See Bonnie Honig, "Antigone's Anachronism? Homeric Mourning in Democratic Athens," Paper Presented at Yale Law Theory Workshop, Yale Law School, November 29, 2007. This paper was, in part, a response to Judith Butler, *Antigone's Claim: Kinship between Life and Death* (New York: Columbia University Press, 2000).

84. Alice Kessler-Harris, "In Pursuit of Economic Citizenship," *Social Politics: International Studies of Gender, State, and Society* 10, no. 2 (2003): 157–75.

85. See Jean-Jacques Rousseau, "Discours sur l'économie politique" (1755), in Jean-Jacques Rousseau, 3 *Oeuvres Complètes*, eds. Bernard Gagnebin & Marcel Raymond (Paris: Gallimard, 1964), 239, 263 ("[T]he right of property is the most sacred of all the rights of the citizens, and more important, in certain respects, than freedom itself."); Jean-Jacques Rousseau, *The Social Contract* [1762], Book 1, ch. 9, "Of Estate," trans. and introduced by Maurice Cranston (Middlesex: Penguin Books, 1978), 65–68; Immanuel Kant, "The Metaphysics of Morals, 1797," in *Kant: Political Writings*, ed. Hans Reiss (New York: Cambridge University Press, 1991), 139–40 (arguing that economic independence is a necessary empirical precondition to free citizenship and distinguishing between "active" citizens, who have a right to vote and exercise political influence, and "passive" citizens—including women, minors, and wage laborers who possess "the freedom and equality of all men as human beings" but lack political rights); "Letter from Thomas Jefferson to James Madison (Oct. 28, 1785)," reprinted in *The Papers of Thomas Jefferson VIII*, ed. Julian P. Boyd (Princeton, NJ: Princeton University Press, 1953), 682 (describing private property as a corollary to democracy because land ownership allowed men to achieve economic security and to develop self-reliance and observing that "small land holders are the most precious part of a state").

86. T. H. Marshall, *Citizenship and Social Class and Other Essays* (London: Cambridge University Press, 1950).

87. Bosniak, "Citizenship, Noncitizenship, and the Transnationalization of Domestic Work," 127. See also Laura Maria Agusin, "A Migrant World of Services," in van Walsum and Spijkerboer, *Women and Immigration Law*, supra note 14, 104–23.

88. See Plyler v. Doe, 457 U.S. 202 (1982); Shawn Fremstad and Laura Cox, *Covering New Americans: A Review of Federal and State Policies Related to Immigrants' Eligibility and Access to Publicly Funded Health Insurance* (Washington, DC: Kaiser Foundation, 2004). But rights of noncitizens have contracted in recent times; for further elucidations of the "disaggregation" of rights, see Benhabib, *The Rights of Others*, supra note 15; Soysal, *Limits of Citizenship*, supra note 8; Sassen, *The Mobility of Labor and Capital*, supra note 10.

89. Ong, "Maids, Neoslavery, and NGOs," 158.

90. Ibid.

91. Ibid., 160.

92. Ibid., 162.

93. Ibid., 178–179.

94. Ibid.; Moghadam, "Global Feminism, Citizenship, and the State" (in this volume).

95. Benhabib calls such processes of interaction between the local and the global "democratic iterations"; see Benhabib, *The Rights of Others*, supra note 15, 3; Seyla Behabib, *Another Cosmopolitanism: Sovereignty, Hospitality, and Democratic Iterations* (Oxford: Oxford University Press, 2006) (including replies to Benhabib's Berkeley Tanner Series lecture by Jeremy Waldron, Will Kymlicka, and Bonnie Honig); Resnik, "Law's Migration," supra note 29; Resnik, "Law as Affiliation," supra note 61.

96. Moghadam, "Global Feminism, Citizenship, and the State," 260.

97. Ibid.

98. Ibid., 258.

99. Ibid., 263.

100. Ibid.

101. Ibid., 271.

102. David Jacobson, "Multiculturalism, Gender, and Rights" (in this volume); Audrey Macklin, "Particularized Citizenship: Encultured Women and the Public Sphere" (in this volume); Angelia Means, "Intercultural Political Identity: Are We There Yet?" (in this volume).

103. Jacobson, "Multiculturalism, Gender, and Rights," 304.

104. Ibid., 305.

105. See Ran Hirschl, *Towards Juristocracy: The Origins and Consequences of the New Constitutionalism* (Cambridge, MA: Harvard University Press, 2004); Ran Hirschl, "The Judicialization of Mega-Politics and the Rise of Political Courts," *Annual Review of Political Science* 11 (2008): 93; Alex Stone Sweet, *Governing with Judges* (Oxford: Oxford University Press, 2000).

106. Jacobson, "Multiculturalism, Gender, and Rights," 325.

107. Ibid., 310.

108. Doriane Lambelet Coleman, "Individualizing Justice through Multiculturalism: The Liberal's Dilemma," *Columbia Law Review* 96(5) (1996): 1093–1167. Coleman in turn examined several specific cases in which "cultural practices" were argued as defenses to rape-as-courtship, marriage-by-capture, wife beating, and female genital mutilation. Ibid., 1105–12.

109. Susan Moller Okin, "Is Multiculturalism Bad for Women?" in *Is Multiculturalism Bad for Women?*, eds. Joshua Cohen, Matthew Howard, and Martha C. Nussbaum (Princeton, NJ: Princeton University Press, 1999).

110. Will Kymlicka, *Multicultural Citizenship Rights: A Liberal Theory of Minority Rights* (Oxford: Oxford University Press, 1996). For an account of these

debates, see Seyla Benhabib, *The Claims of Culture: Equality and Diversity in the Global Era* (Princeton, NJ: Princeton University Press, 2002).

111. Ayelet Shachar, *Multicultural Jurisdictions* (Cambridge: Cambridge University Press, 2001); Judith Resnik, "Dependent Sovereigns," supra note 73, 671.

112. Seyla Benhabib, *The Rights of Others*, supra note 15; Resnik, "Living Their Legal Commitments: Paideic Communities, Courts, and Robert Cover," *Yale Journal of Law and the Humanities* 17 (2005): 17; Joan Scott, *The Politics of the Veil* (Princeton, NJ: Princeton University Press, 2007); Nusrat Choudhury, "From the Stasi Commission to the European Court of Human Rights: l'affaire du foulard and the Challenge of Protecting the Rights of Muslim Girls," *Columbia Journal of Gender and Law* 16(1) (2007): 199–396.

113. See UNICEF, *Domestic Violence against Women and Girls* (United Nations Children's Fund Innocenti Research Ctr., Innocenti Digest No. 6, 2000), *available at* http:// www.unicef-icdc.org/publications/pdf/digest6e.pdf.

114. Macklin, "Particularized Citizenship," 280.

115. Ibid., 281.

116. See Judith Resnik, "Procedure as Contract," *Notre Dame Law Review* 80 (2005): 593.

117. Macklin, "Particularized Citizenship," 292.

118. Ibid., 293. For another critical analysis of these events, see Sherene H. Razack, "The 'Sharia Law Debate' in Ontario: The Modernity/Premodernity Distinction in Legal Efforts to Protect Women from Culture," *Feminist Legal Studies* 15 (2007): 3–32.

119. Macklin, "Particularized Citizenship," 298; see also *Bruker v. Marcovitz*, [2007] S.C.J. No. 54 (Can).

120. Macklin, "Particularized Citizenship," 279.

121. Means, "Intercultural Political Identity," 381.

122. See Jürgen Habermas, *The Inclusion of the Other: Studies in Political Theory* (Cambridge, MA: MIT Press, 1998).

123. Nanz, "Mobility, Migrants, and Solidarity."

124. A different approach to EU citizenship is proffered by Rainer Bauböck in his essay, "Why European Citizenship? Normative Approaches to Supra-National Union," *Theoretical Inquiries in Law* 8 (2007): 453. He proposes "equalization of most citizenship rights (including the franchise in local elections) for permanent residents of the Union independent of their nationality and developing common norms for the acquisition and loss of citizenship status in member states." Ibid., 488.

125. See also Dieter Grimm, "Integration by Constitution," *International Journal of Constitutional Law* 3 (2005): 193–208; Miguel Maduro, "Contrapunctual Law: Europe's Constitutional Pluralism in Action," in *Sovereignty in Transition*, ed. Neil Walker (Oxford: Oxford University Press, 2003).

126. See Case 26–62, Van Gend & Loss v. Netherlands Inland Revenue Administration, 1963 E.C.R. 1; see generally, Angela Ward, *Judicial Review and the Rights of Private Parties in EU Law* (Oxford: Oxford University Press, 2007).

127. Case C-85/96, Martinez Sala v. Freistaat Bayern [1998] E.C.R. 1-2691.

128. The ECJ has, thus far, remained committed to a broad application of the principles that social benefits should be afforded to those who live on the territory of a member state. See Case C-212/05, Gertraud Hartmann v. Freistaat Bayern (18 July 2007), citing *Martinez Sala* for the proposition that German child-raising allowance constitutes a social advantage within the meaning of Article 7(2) of Regulation No 1612/68 and upholding the right of the nonworking spouse of an EU national working in another member state to a social benefit in the form of child care. Ibid., para. 22; see also Case C-180/99, Khalil, Chaaban, Osseili v. Bundesanwalt fuer Arbeit/Nasser v Landeshauptstadt Stuttgart/Addou v Land Nordrhein-Westfalen (11 October 2001), citing *Martinez Sala* for a broad personal application of rights enumerated in Article 51 of the EC Treaty and upholding the right of the self-employed in another member state to social security benefits. Ibid., para. 33.

129. Nanz, "Mobility, Migrants, and Solidarity," 416–17 (citing the 2001 *Grzelczyk* and 2004 *Collins* judgments as landmarks in this respect).

130. Jackson, "Citizenships, Federalisms, and Gender," (in this volume).

131. Ibid., 449; see also Ratna Kapur, "The Citizen and the Migrant: Postcolonial Anxieties, Law, and the Politics of Exclusion/Inclusion," *Theoretical Inquiries in Law* 8 (2007): 537.

132. For the role that gender has played in giving meaning to distinctions between the work of "federal" and state governments in the United States, see Suzanne Mettler, *Dividing Citizens: Gender and Federalism in New Deal Public Policy* (Ithaca, NY: Cornell University Press, 1998); Judith Resnik, "'Naturally' without Gender: Women, Jurisdiction, and the Federal Courts," *New York University Law Review* 66 (1991): 1682–1772; Reva B. Siegel, "She, the People: The Nineteenth Amendment, Sex Equality, Federalism, and the Family," *Harvard Law Review* 115 (2002): 947–1046.

133. Benhabib, "Twilight of Sovereignty," supra note 59.

134. Resnik, "Law as Affiliation," supra note 61.

I

Situated Histories of Citizenship and Gender

1

||||||||||||||||||||||||||||||||||||||||||||||||||||

Citizenship and Gender in the Ancient World: The Experience of Athens and Rome

Cynthia Patterson

Introduction: Two Stories

In the mid-fourth century before the common era, a woman named Neaira, an ex-slave and former prostitute, stood trial in Athens on the charge of *xenia*, of being an alien posing as a citizen by acting the part of the wife of an Athenian. In raking the accused over the coals of Athenian civic values, the prosecutor, a certain Apollodorus, who was himself the son of an enfranchised ex-slave, implicated Neaira's entire household, children and Athenian "husband" alike, in a crime that he claimed had corrupted the moral integrity of the citizenship body.

The rhetorical climax of the speech was the charge that Neaira's daughter, by implication her mother's double, had participated in a sacred rite of the city reserved only for pure-born Athenians. In conclusion, Apollodorus urged the male jurors to imagine the rage of their female relatives if Neaira were allowed to "have the same share as they in public life and religion" and called upon them to vote "one in defense of his wife, another his daughter, another his mother, another the city and its laws and religion, so that those women are not seen to be held in equal esteem with this whore."[1] The speech for the defense does not survive and the verdict is unknown. Whatever the outcome, Apollodorus's attack details the remarkable career of a woman (by his own admission still notably beautiful when she appeared in court) who began life as a slave, managed to buy her own freedom, and lived a free life of some stability in Athens for thirty years prior to her trial.

Three hundred years later, in Rome in the midst of a civil war, the triumvirs (Octavian, Antony, and Lepidus) ordered the fourteen hundred richest Roman women to submit an inventory of their property and furnish whatever portion was requested thereof. The women so taxed first protested to the wives of the triumvirs and then "forced their way to the tribunal of the triumvirs in the Forum," where a certain Hortensia spoke publicly on their behalf, asking, "why should we pay taxes when we have no part in the honors (offices), the commands, the statecraft, for which you contend against each other with such harmful results?" Rebuking the men for the destructive civil war through which the women had lost "our fathers, our sons, our husbands, and our brothers," Hortensia insisted that Roman women would give willingly to the cause of war with the Gauls or Parthians but "for civil war may we never contribute, nor ever assist you against each other!" Angered or, perhaps, startled, the triumvirs tried to drive the women from the forum; but when the crowd protested on the women's behalf, the embattled rulers agreed to reconsider. The next day they issued a shortened list of female property owners along with a general requisition from "citizens and strangers, freedmen and priests, and men of all nationalities without a single exemption."[2] Hortensia won a place in history (if not her case) as one of those women, says an ancient writer, "whom neither the condition of their nature nor the cloak of modesty could keep silent in the Forum."[3]

Neither of these stories presents the usual and classical image of ancient citizenship that one encounters in modern discussions: for Athens (and Greece), Aristotle's political principle of men "ruling and being ruled"; and for Rome, the juridical articulation of public rights or duties from which women were excluded.[4] Rather, the emphasis is on family, property, and religion. This discrepancy between theories of citizenship and the realities of its expression results from making Aristotle stand for Athens on the one hand and Roman jurists for Rome on the other—and ignoring the historical context of both, in which citizenship was an arena of ongoing contestation with variable consequences (economic, social, religious, as well as political) for women and families and for aliens as well as the native born. The ancient experience with citizenship and citizenship rules in both the democratic polis of Athens and the imperial domain of Rome (neither one a state or nation in the modern sense) challenges a purely political or juridical notion of citizenship and in some respects anticipates contemporary discussions of citizenship as "membership" in diverse and not necessarily political or national contexts. In this chapter, I discuss the experience of citizenship in Athens and in Rome with emphasis on the meaning of citizenship for women and their families and the opportunities available for those without political privilege or status to participate in the larger community and, in some cases, to cross boundaries set by theory or law.

Since women did not vote or hold office in either ancient society (not a surprising exclusion given the connection of office holding with military service or command in both, especially Rome),[5] their citizenship is often denied or considered "second-class" or passive.[6] A similar argument portrays the citizenship of residents within the vast Roman Empire as for the most part inactive, since few could actually exercise political power, i.e., vote or hold office in Rome. If, however, we look at the ways in which citizenship in the ancient world was larger than politics, and at the multiple ways in which membership in the community was expressed and experienced, these conclusions become problematic and the character of female and/or provincial citizenship becomes more interesting. The ancient world, I submit, contributes more to the contemporary discussion of citizenship than simply political theory or juridical definition alone.

I. Athens

In the middle of the fifth century B.C.E., roughly a hundred years before the trial of Neaira, Athens was at the height of her power in the Aegean world; her navy was preeminent and her Aegean allies from the Persian wars a generation earlier were discovering that they were now subjects of an imperial rule.

At the same time, the Athenian *politeia* (constitution) itself was becoming more democratic, with the full assembly of (male) citizens and representative council of five hundred (male) citizens, chosen by lot for one-year terms, taking on major responsibility for domestic and imperial policy under the leadership of ten popularly elected generals. (Pericles was a general throughout his long political career.)

At this historical moment, in the year 451/0 B.C.E., Pericles proposed to the Athenian assembly that "anyone who was not born of two citizen parents should not have a share (*metechein*) in the polis." The demos approved the proposal. In reporting the decision, the author of the Aristotelian *Athenaion Politeia* (Constitution of the Athenians) offers only the brief explanation that the passing of the law was "on account of the large

The Aegean Sea and Greece. Map copyright 2007, Ancient World Mapping Center (www.unc.edu/awmc). Used by permission.

number of citizens (*politai*)," leaving historians to piece together a larger context.[7] Pericles' law perhaps replaced an earlier one requiring only that the male parent be a citizen for his child to be a citizen, for a number of prominent Athenians of earlier generations were offspring of an Athenian father and foreign mother. On the other hand, the law may have simply standardized customary practice. In any case, the key point is that the law drew a line around the political "family" of Athens, membership in which was now a privilege protected by law and only available to outsiders (including the subjects of Athens's empire) who were formally "adopted" by vote of the demos.[8]

The language of the law as reported by the *Athenaion Politeia* is significant. The Athenians did not vote on who was or was not to be a "citizen," but rather on who could "share in the city"; further, the law uses an interesting dual form of the word "*astos*" (city dweller) to denote the parental citizen *couple* necessary for that shareholding.[9] Both of these expressions have important implications for the character of Athenian citizenship in general and women's citizenship in particular, yet it is the word *"polites"* (as used in the *Athenaion Politeia*'s explanation of the law) that has generally carried the terminological weight of the discussion of Athenian and Greek citizenship. Why that is so has a lot to do with Aristotle.

Aristotle's Citizen

Any discussion of citizenship in Athens and in Greece, in general, has to confront the influence of Aristotle's *Politics*.[10] In Book 1, Aristotle articulates a teleological definition of the polis in which the polis is the natural "end" of a progression of human associations, beginning with the household organized for the sake of the necessities of life, extending through the village, and arriving at completion in the polis that exists for the sake of the "good life."[11] Then, at the opening of Book 3, Aristotle asks, "Who is the citizen (*polites*) and what is the meaning of the term?"[12] His answer, arrived at after the rejection of residence and possession of legal status as adequate criteria, is that citizens "in the strictest sense" (explicitly excluding children and the aged, exiles, and the disenfranchised) are those who share in the government of the state by sharing in the administration of justice and the deliberations of the political assembly.[13] The definition is essentially functional. A citizen is defined not by birth or by membership in any human association, but by what he does. The "he" in the previous sentence is not generic; for Aristotle, the essential mark of the *polites* is holding the "indeterminate offices" of assemblyman and juror,[14] positions that were held exclusively by adult men in all societies of which he had knowledge. The result of this definition, Aristotle acknowledges, is the awkward exclusion of some members of the community—boys and old men, and also resident aliens—necessary for the existence of the state. To these, Aristotle gives a "qualified" citizenship. About women he says nothing. The silence is striking but not surprising. The traditional interpretation simply takes this silence as exclusion or at least lack of interest, but recent critics suggest that Aristotle's vision of the state in its larger dimensions did in fact embrace women as essential participants.[15] Given his discussions elsewhere, about women's virtue, women's education, and (the dangers of) women's property owning, Aristotle's silence in Book 3 of the *Politics* may then be similar to the silence of American political writers of the early republic. Linda Kerber, for example, has suggested that this silence should not be taken "literally"—i.e., should not be understood to mean that "they were silent about that relationship [female citizenship] because they were not thinking about it."[16]

Whatever one concludes about Aristotle's views, they cannot be viewed as the summation of Athenian ideas on citizenship and the state.[17] As we saw in Pericles' law of 451/0 B.C.E., Athenians expressed community membership with language that could and did embrace what we can call female citizenship, and that fact opens up possibilities for a more than political understanding of what citizenship was and is. Before looking specifically at the consequences of citizen status for women in Athens—both those of Athenian birth and those, like Neaira, who lived as aliens (euphemistically "guests") within the polis—a few comments on the implications of this language may be useful.

The Astoi

"Anyone who is not born from two *astoi* shall not share in the polis."[18] "*Astos*" is a Greek term as old as Homer, denoting the "insider" as distinct from, and often in explicit contrast with, the *xenos,* or foreign "outsider." For example, in one of the term's earliest appearances, in the *Odyssey,* Odysseus is covered with mist so that neither "wife nor *astoi* nor friends will recognize him,"[19] and somewhat later Pindar writes of veneration offered the Olympic victor from both *astoi* and *xenoi.*[20] These passages (and others) suggest that "*astoi*" in the plural referred to the community as a whole, men and women, and no one would dispute that in the phrase "born from two *astoi,*" "*astoi*" means one man and one woman.

But are *astoi* really citizens? Some modern commentators (and in fact the standard Greek lexicon, Liddell/Scott) have suggested that the insider status denoted by "*astos*" (fem. "*aste*") included "civil rights only" with full political citizenship reserved for those called, as in Aristotle Book 3, "*politai.*" A contrasting suggestion is that in Athens "*astoi*" originally referred to the elite "nobility" who lived in or around the *astu,* the town center, as opposed to the *demos* (people) as a whole.

As I have argued elsewhere, these distinctions are faulty, the first because "*astoi*" is in fact used in contexts that are clearly political (e.g., Aeschylus's Athena chooses the "best of the *astoi*" for her new homicide court)[21] and the second because there is simply no example of such a contrast in any Athenian text. The difference between the terms is in fact more connotative than denotative, with "*astoi*" carrying the meaning of "one's own" in a communal sense (analogous to kin within the family) and *"politai"* conveying the more individual sense of the relationship of citizen to state. A good example is Apollodorus's charge against Neaira that she was "neither born an *aste* nor made a *politis.*"[22] An analogous situation exists with the proper adjectives *"Athenaios/a"* and *"Attikos/e"*—both descriptive terms for a native resident of Athens, a polis that included the 1,000-square-mile Attic peninsula. Women were more likely to be called *"Attikai"* than *"Athenaiai,"* just as they were more likely to be included in the *astoi* than the *politai*. However, their status as privileged insiders—and members of the polis *"Hoi Athenaioi"* ("the Athenians")—is quite clear and incontrovertible in two key areas: law and religion.[23]

Women and the Law

In the early sixth century B.C.E., the Athenian lawgiver Solon laid the foundation for Athenian citizenship. According to Athenian tradition and his own surviving poetry, Solon established the most basic privilege of Athenian citizenship, freedom of the person. With his abolition of debt slavery and freeing of Attic "mother Earth" from its bondage, no Athenian could be a slave within Attica (of course, outside Attica, the Athenian law had no authority). Slaves were now necessarily and by definition *xenoi*. According to the biographer and moralist Plutarch (writing some seven hundred years later but using Athenian sources), Solon made an exception in the case of an unmarried daughter who was found to have "been with" a man. She could be sold, having in effect given up her status with her action.[24] No example of the enforcement of the rule survives.

Although this rule overtly reveals the asymmetrical standards for sexual behavior in Athens (and antiquity in general), it suggests as well that Athenian women were *in general* protected from enslavement and also that women were considered responsible agents. The latter point is evident also in the Athenian law on *moichheia* (usually translated 'adultery,' the single quotation marks indicating that it is not quite the same thing).[25] In Athenian law, adultery was a crime committed by the man who entered the house and bed of another man; various accounts exist as to his punishment if found guilty, ranging from monetary payment to public humiliation, perhaps depending on the nature of the case or the will of the wronged husband. The adulterer's female partner (the language of the law is "the woman with whom adultery was committed") was also punished. Her husband was required to divorce her and she was banned from the sanctuaries of the city. These are substantial penalties—in essence, as will be seen in the next section, the loss of key features of her citizenship.

The woman found in 'adultery,' like the unmarried daughter found to have been "with" a man, had by her action disqualified herself from "having a share in the city." What is particularly striking, and indicative of the privileged citizen *body*, is that, initially, she is not physically punished, as was customary in other ancient societies. If, however, the woman so convicted (and once again there are no known cases) ignored these restrictions and appeared in a public sanctuary, the law (we are told) permitted anyone to inflict punishment on her short of death.[26]

The woman's citizen body was also protected in a more basic way by Athenian laws on assault (including sexual assault). Although an early Athenian law (quoted rhetorically by one ancient litigant) allowing a man to be killed with impunity who was found "upon" a woman of the household and saying nothing about the intentions of the female involved, suggests to some commentators that the Athenians did not distinguish adultery and rape, a more balanced appraisal confirms that like violence against a man or child, violence against women was a serious and distinct offense ("deserving the death penalty several times over," says a character in a fourth-century comedy).[27] The protection of the citizen body extended to both men and women. Some might respond by saying that, in the case of women, this protection is more properly understood as the protection of the honor of the male head of household, but a valid counterresponse is that for men and women in Athens, citizenship was bound up with family membership and citizen honor with family or household integrity. That much is clear in the story of the "family" of Neaira.

Women in Public Religion

Athenian law protected (at least in theory) male and female citizens, but a more active aspect of Athenian women's insider status was their involvement in public religion. When the Athenians established a new cult of Athena Nike (Athena as goddess of victory) in the mid-fifth century, they decided that her priestess would be chosen democratically (by lot) "from all the Athenians."[28] Two other prominent priestesses who appear in the historical record were the priestesses of Athena Polias ("of the city") and of Demeter, both chosen traditionally from elite Athenian families. Herodotus reported that it was the priestess of Athena Polias who publicly encouraged the Athenians to evacuate their city in the face of the Persian

Parthenon East Frieze (fifth century B.C.E.): Central scene (over the entrance to the temple). The priestess of Athena (central figure) receives footstools from two girls, and the priest receives the goddess's new robe from a temple boy (far right). Photograph: Alison Frantz EU 136. American School of Classical Studies. Used by permission.

invasion, by reporting that Athena's sacred snake had itself departed.[29] We hear also of a certain Theano, the priestess of Demeter, who refused to curse the traitor Alcibiades, saying that her role was to bless rather than to curse.[30]

The civic importance of women as participants in public religion, however, is most vividly and powerfully displayed in the Ionic frieze of the Parthenon. The frieze represents the Panathenaic ("all Athens") procession as part of the festival celebrating Athena's "birthday," including contingents of women who appear on the east side of the frieze and lead into the official ceremony over the temple's entrance, presided over by the priestess of Athena Polias and the city's magistrate in charge of religion (the *archon basileus*).

It is a solemn moment, showing women moving with dignity, high on the exterior walls of the most important religious building in the city.

The public personae of the priestesses of Athena Polias and Athena Nike may have been the inspiration for the title character and her "second-in-command" in Aristophanes' antiwar comedy *Lysistrata*, first produced in 411 B.C.E., in the latter years of the Peloponnesian War. In the

Parthenon East Frieze (fifth century B.C.E.): Procession of women.
Photograph: Alison Frantz EU 142. American School of Classical Studies.
Used by permission.

play, Lysistrata (whose name means "dissolver of armies") organizes and carries out a sex strike to bring the men of Greece to their knees and put an end to the war. She is supported by Myrrhine, a lesser figure but effective striker, who turns the acropolis into a bedroom in order to torment her husband (in the illogic of the comic plot, the latter is still at home in Athens).

At the time the play was produced the priestess of Athena Polias was a woman named Lysimache ("dissolver of battle"), in whose honor the Athenians later erected a bronze statue. The marble base for the statue and a very fragmentary inscription still remain, together with a Roman marble copy of a portrait head that has been identified as Lysimache. According to the much later Roman polymath Pliny, Lysimache held the office of priestess of Athena for sixty-four years, and the inscription seems also to record that fact.[31] Moreover, Myrrhine too had a real-life namesake in the first (democratically chosen) priestess of Athena Nike, for whom there survives an inscribed epitaph:

> This far-seen tomb is that of the daughter of Callimachos,
> Who was the first to tend the temple of Nike;
> Her name shared in her good fame, for by divine
> Fortune she was called Myrrhine. Truly
> She was the first who tended the statue of Athena Nike
> Chosen by lot out of everyone, Myrrhine, by good Fortune.[32]

In Aristophanes' comedy, which, like all Athenian drama, has some serious advice to give the assembled audience, a male magistrate rebukes the chorus of women for their "interference" in the business of men. The women respond with a vigorous claim to a stake in the business of the polis:

> Here we begin, all you citizens (astoi), to deliver
> advice that will benefit the city.[33]

They justify their public speech by recounting the public religious career (ending with the role of basket bearer as seen on the Parthenon frieze):

> As soon as I turned seven, I was an Arrephoros;
> then when I was ten I was a Grinder for the Foundress:
> and shedding my saffron robe I was a Bear at the Brauronia;
> And once, when I was a fair girl, I carried the Basket, wearing a
> necklace of dried figs.[34]

And the advice follows:

> Thus I owe it to the city to offer some good advice. And if I *was* born a woman, don't hold it against me if I manage to suggest something better than what we've got now. I have a stake (*metesti moi*) in our community: my contribution is men. You miserable geezers have no stake: you've squandered your paternal inheritance, won in the Persian Wars, and now pay no taxes in return.[35]

Earlier in the play, Lysistrata herself offered a famous image of the "fabric" of the community:

> Consider the City as fleece, recently shorn. The first step is Cleansing: Scrub it in a public bath, and remove all corruption, offal, and sheepdip. Next, to the couch for Scutching and Plucking: Cudgel the leeches and similar

vermin loose with a club, then pick the prickles and cockle burs out. As for
the clots—those lumps that clump and cluster in knots and snarls to snag
important posts—you comb these out, twist off their heads, and discard.
Next, to raise the city's nap, you card the citizens together in a single basket
of common weal and general welfare. Fold in our loyal resident aliens, all
foreigners of proven and tested friendship and any disenfranchised debtors.
Combine these closely with the rest. Lastly, cull the colonies settled by our
own people: these are nothing but flocks of wool from the city's fleece, scattered throughout the world. So gather home these far-flung flocks, amal-
gamate them with the others. Then, drawing this blend of stable fibers into
one fine staple, you spin a mighty bobbin of yarn—and weave, without bias
or seam, a cloak to clothe the City of Athens![36]

What is striking in this earthy recipe for civic harmony is the inclusion of
the larger community. Lyistrata herself, like her real-life model Lysimache,
is an Athenian citizen, an *aste*, but her sense of community extends further than the citizen elite. Perhaps women, restricted by their gender from
the exercise of full political participation, have as a consequence a greater
appreciation of the importance of "weaving" in the noncitizen part of
the community. The point will be relevant to Antigone's defense of burial
"rights" discussed later in this chapter.

"Having a Share": Family and Polis

"I have a share in the commonwealth," say the female chorus of the
Lysistrata.[37] The words take us back to the key language of the Periclean
law on polis membership: who is to "have a share in the polis"? This
phrase was in fact the most common way of expressing membership in
the Athenian polis and accentuates a number of important and interre-
lated aspects of that membership. First, citizenship is understood as active
participation—"having a share"—rather than simply legal status. Second,
citizenship brings concrete goods and rewards, including, for example, a
share in the public distribution of meat on Athena's birthday or in the
goods and glories of the Athenian empire. Third, citizenship is akin to
family membership. The same words express family inheritance ("I have a
share") as express political inheritance. Thus, rather than being antitheti-
cal to the family—an association or *koinonia* marked by clear differences
in role and responsibility according to age and sex—the polis was in a real
sense a "super-family" or "family of families."

The analogy gains additional force when we consider the bilateral character of Athenian inheritance law, in which females inherited after males in each generation to the degree of "children of cousins" and maternal relatives followed paternal relatives to the same degree. The man's prior claim, as well as the woman's lack of independent economic agency when she did become an heir, is unmistakable evidence of the subordinate and dependent position of women in Athens, but does not negate the significance of the woman's place as "share-holder" in both family and city. Only Athenians, male and female, could own a "piece of Attica" and inherit Athenian land.[38]

Care of the Dead: A Civic Responsibility

Athenians, male and female, constituted the privileged "insider" elite of their polis and received the concrete benefit of its success. "All good things from all over the world flow in to us," said Pericles.[39] The occasion on which Pericles spoke those proud words was a public funeral for the dead from the first year of the Peloponnesian War. Women participated in this ceremony and were on hand to hear the public oration (and perhaps to criticize it: Plutarch reports that the elderly Elpinice publicly rebuked Pericles for speaking in praise of a war against fellow Greeks although the other women "treated him like an Olympic victor").[40] The funeral for the war dead happened once a year, but the women's responsibility for the care of the dead was year-long. Athenian law (traditionally of Solon) regulated the performance of funeral rites drawing attention to the female role:

> They shall carry out the deceased on the day after they lay him out, before the sun rises. The men shall walk in front and the women behind. No woman less than sixty years of age shall be permitted to enter the chamber of the deceased, or to follow the deceased when he is carried to the tomb, except those who are within the degree of children of cousins.[41]

Most often, this law is cited as evidence of the restriction on female activity;[42] that may be accurate, but the law also reveals an important domain of female citizenship: the care of the dead. The legal language, "those within the degree of children of cousins," is the formal (and legal) definition of the family in classical Athens; these women, related to the deceased as sister, daughter, granddaughter, grandniece, or cousin, have a legal right *and* responsibility to perform his (or her) funeral rites.

A similar construction of responsibility for Athenian men, it can be noted, occurs in the Athenian homicide law, in which the responsibility for pursuit of the murderer (and ability to pardon) rests with those related to the deceased "to the degree of sons of cousins" and in inheritance law, where claim to an intestate estate extended to "children (male and female) of cousins." In this way we can see both men's and now women's familial status as the basis of their citizen status in the larger community, the "family of families" that was classical Athens.

Women played a major part in the funeral ritual, washing the corpse and performing lament. They also, and as significantly, had primary responsibility for tomb cult, the ritual commemoration of the dead at the tomb. The scene is a frequent one depicted on Athenian painted pottery.[43]

Athenian drama again takes us further. The most powerful (and provocative) presentation of women's role in burial occurs in Sophocles' *Antigone*. When Creon, the new king (or tyrant) of Thebes, declares that Antigone's brother, Polyneices, should go unburied because he died as an enemy of the city, bringing an Argive army against the city and his twin brother Eteocles, Antigone refuses to accept her uncle's decree and attempts to carry out the burial ritual. She is apprehended, and when challenged by Creon with the question "did you dare to disobey the law?" responds by asserting the existence of "unwritten laws" supported by the gods requiring the burial of the dead. Although Antigone's own concern is quite limited—only her brother's unburied corpse, she asserts, could have led her to this act of civic disobedience—the principle she articulates with her appeal (for the first time in Greek literature) to "unwritten laws" is broader: the dead must be buried.

In her final lament to the chorus, Antigone testifies to her commitment to her family *and* city responsibilities. "When you died," she says, addressing her dead parents and her brother Eteocles, "with my own hands I washed and dressed you all, and poured the lustral offerings on your graves."[44] The familial duty to bury her brother is in Antigone's mind also a public duty overriding the decree of the ruler. In this way, drawing on her familial duty, Antigone articulates a larger human principle, and creates a powerful challenge to a narrow view of citizenship as limited to the domain of the political. Or, we could say, Antigone's view of citizenship completes and makes whole Creon's narrow conception of civic duty. In the funeral speech for the war dead mentioned earlier, Pericles cites Athenian respect for the "unwritten laws" whose transgression carries public shame. Perhaps he had learned something about citizenship from *Antigone*.[45]

The Eleusinian Mysteries: A Different Model of Community

The humanistic notion of citizenship as entailing a responsibility for a community larger than politics and larger than citizens alone is also central to the Athenians' custodianship of the Eleusinian mysteries, one of antiquity's most open and broadly inclusive religious rites. According to myth and the elegant "Homeric Hymn to Demeter," Demeter came to Eleusis mourning the abduction of her daughter Persephone by Hades, the god of the underworld. The King of Eleusis built her a temple, yet still she refused to relent and to allow the earth to bloom until Zeus at last ordered a compromise in which Persephone would return to her mother for two-thirds of the year, so creating both the seasons and the agricultural year. Thus Eleusis, which in classical times was no longer an independent kingdom but one of the many *demes* (townships) making up the Athenian polis, was home to the worship of the goddess Demeter and her daughter Persephone and to sacred "mysteries," well kept throughout antiquity, that promised initiates happiness after death.[46]

The Athenian polis had authority over both the sanctuary and its rites, whose priests and officials were part of the larger Athenian civic administration. The only requirements for participation, however, were knowledge of the Greek language and absence of the pollution of homicide.[47] Within those two conditions, the rites were not merely panhellenic but ecumenical.

I will end this section with two examples, one from the story of Neaira and one from the career of Augustus (also known as Octavian), that will lead into the next section of the chapter. According to Apollodorus once again, Neaira was one of several "foundling" girls brought up to be slave prostitutes by a Corinthian woman and owner of a brothel; when in Corinth, the orator Lysias (a resident alien in Athens) visited the brothel and became very fond of one of Neaira's "sisters"—so much so, says Apollodorus, that he took her to be initiated into the Eleusinian mysteries with him.[48] How the young woman enjoyed the experience, he does not say. Her life was probably not much improved but, again, the mysteries' promise was for happiness *after* death.

Approximately three hundred years later, the Roman triumvir Octavian, after defeating Antony and Cleopatra at the battle of Actium in 31 B.C.E., took time out to visit Eleusis and take part in the mysteries. (He, like most Romans of his class, was fully fluent in Greek; whether he could claim to be free of the pollution of murder is more problematic.) Octavian (or Augustus, the name he took soon after his victory) participated again in the year 19—at a special extra celebration held specifically at his request.[49] Augustus no doubt used his imperial authority to dictate that second celebration, yet the fact that he wanted to be part of a ritual that was so broadly inclusive is remarkable. His personal response to the experience is not recorded, but there doesn't seem to be any reason to suppose that he was promised anything different or more than anyone else.

The Athenians responded to Augustus's interest in Eleusis by dedicating there a substantial monument to Augustus as "savior and benefactor" and to his wife Livia as well.[50] Athens at this time was a simple provincial town with a habit of taking the wrong side in Roman imperial politics. They had sided with Pompey against Julius Caesar and with Brutus and Cassius against Antony, but now perhaps they had things straight. The way in which Roman rule and Roman citizenship came to intersect and interact with Athenian traditions is an interesting story in its own right— and is the focus of the second half of this chapter.[51]

II. Rome and the Roman Empire

Sometime in the year 212 C.E., at the beginning of the century in which the Roman Empire faced major crises on all fronts, the emperor Caesar Marcus Aurelius Severus Antoninus Augustus (otherwise known as Caracalla) decreed that all free residents of the empire (with some exceptions) were thenceforth Roman citizens.

The significance and circumstances of this decree are the subject of ongoing discussion;[52] any interpretation requires some understanding of the origins of Roman citizenship in the Republican era (from 509 B.C.E.) and its development and extension as Rome became an empire (from the mid-third century B.C.E.).[53]

Roman citizenship, like Athenian citizenship, was rooted in family membership but had a distinctive Roman accent that is evident, for example, in Livy's retelling of the story of the political role played by the Sabine women who were the first Roman wives:

> The women besought their fathers on this side, on that their husbands,
> that fathers-in-law and sons-in-law should not stain themselves with impi-
> ous bloodshed, nor pollute with parricide the suppliants' children, grand-
> sons to one party and sons to the others. "If you regret," they continued,

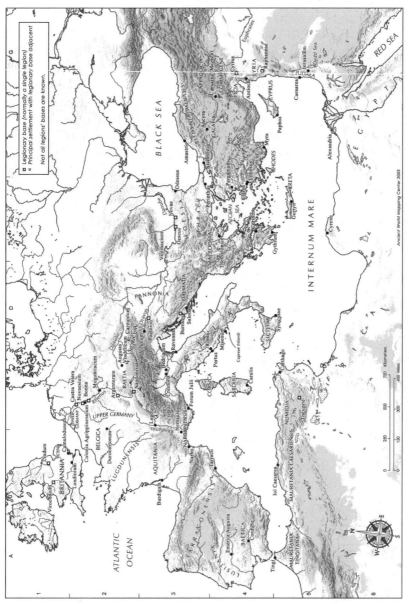

Roman Empire in 69 C.E. Map copyright 2007, Ancient World Mapping Center (www.unc.edu/awmc). Used by permission.

"the relationship that unites you, if you regret the marriage-tie, turn your anger against us. . . ." (1.13.4)[54]

Marriage, here between Sabine and Roman, and the kinship it produces stand at the beginning of the political order (after the act of violence that precipitated it). The right of marriage (*ius conubium*) was a privilege of Roman status, reserved for Roman citizens; for those on whom Rome bestowed a kind of partial citizenship and whom it classified as "*cives sine suffragium*" (citizens without the vote); or for those with "Latin rights." In addition, the related right of commerce (*ius commercium*)—of trade protected by access to the law—was a key right of both Roman and "Latin" citizenship. *Ius suffragium* (the right of voting) made the *ius civile* complete—for men only, that is.

Thus, citizen status was constructed as a juridical status providing access to the protection of Roman private law of person and property—and for men, access to political participation (and military service). As in Athens, there were implicit distinctions made according to gender, but the juridical distinction was between citizen and foreigner (*civis* and *peregrinus*), not between male and female. It is noteworthy that Latin status was expressly said to be "without the vote" while that disability was simply assumed (or traditional) for the Roman woman (*civis Romana*). Unlike Athens, however, Rome was never a democracy and the *suffragium* of all male citizens was not equal; rather, each citizen was classified according to age and property and his vote counted accordingly in block units, so as to significantly privilege the old and the wealthy.[55] Thus, Roman citizenship openly privileged the wealthy in a manner that might allow the elite wives or daughters, despite their lack of *suffragium*, to claim a status above the lower-class male citizen. The acknowledged hierarchical levels of citizen identity also provided a model for a citizenship that eventually came to embrace a much larger community than any Athenian could have imagined.

Roman citizen status (of all classes) came with a proper Roman name indicative of legitimate family membership (although again not all families were equal). For men, this Roman name consisted of a *praenomen, nomen* (family name proper) and often *cognomen* (distinguishing individual branch or special achievement)—thus Gaius Julius Caesar and Gnaeus Pompeius Magnus. For women, the simple feminine form of the family name was sufficient—e.g., Caesar's daughter was simply Julia—a reflection of the strong relation they retained with their paternal family. The support of Roman elite women for the political causes and careers of their male

Grave relief of Aurelius Hermia and his wife Aurelia Philematium (first
century B.C.E.). The couple are freed slaves of the same owner (Lucius Aurelius)
as indicated by their name and the abbreviation "L L." In the inscription, the
two each speak in the first person, revealing that the wife predeceased her
husband and asserting her claim to the traditional Roman female virtues of
chastity and fidelity. Photograph: British Museum (copyright The Trustee
of the British Museum). Used by permission.

relations is well known;[56] and, in general, Roman marriage—with the privileges it bestowed—became a particularly cherished Roman ideal.[57] One of
the most distinctive features of Roman citizenship, and in fact a result of
its connection with family membership, was the way in which any newly
freed slave became "in name" an adopted son or daughter of his or her
former owner and thereby a new Roman citizen. So the new citizens Aurelius and Aurelia (figure 1.5), both former slaves of a Roman of the *nomen*
Aurelius, openly displayed their new status in their joint funeral relief.

The openly "conjugal" stance (in image and text) is notable–this
new citizen husband and wife could be the parents of Roman sons and
daughters.

As the Roman "city-state" expanded through Italy and then the Mediterranean in the third through the first centuries B.C.E., definitions and
rules of citizenship became highly contested issues. Contrary to later

encomiastic tradition, Rome did not generously open her citizen rolls to outsiders; Roman citizenship remained a jealously guarded privilege until, in the early first century B.C.E., a bitterly fought war with the Italian allies convinced the Romans of the wisdom of bringing all free Italians into their commonwealth. In later years the privilege was furthered extended to favored provincials.

In a typically pragmatic manner, the Romans developed a two-tiered system of citizenship in which local customs and identity could continue under the larger umbrella of Roman law and, for the privileged, Roman citizenship. From this perspective, "*civitas Romana*" became a broadly inclusive notion, capable of embracing not only Italy and the western provinces but also people of widely different statuses and cultures—and certainly of both sexes. Again, the key is a family and a name. In a manner analogous to that of the freed slave, provincials entered the Roman civic body as adopted family members, whose new Roman name indicated their new Roman status (so those given citizenship under Caesar were all Julii, etc.). Roman status could be more or less useful and more or less utilized.

Perhaps the most celebrated case of a provincial citizen exercising his "citizen rights" is that of the apostle Paul, a Roman citizen who drew upon his right to "appeal to Caesar" and so traveled to Rome and to his death. Some years later we hear again of such insubordinate Roman citizens in a letter of the early second century C.E. from Pliny, governor of Bithynia-Pontus, to the emperor Trajan. Pliny asks his emperor for instructions on dealing with Christians and informs him of what he has done so far, including the torturing of "slave deaconesses" and the transferring of Roman citizens to Rome.[58] More typically, however, Roman citizens in the provinces tended to be supporters of the Roman order in elite positions within provincial cities and towns, as we will see in the case of Athens's own Roman citizen and civic philanthropist, Herodes Atticus.

Roman Athens

Roman citizenship in its imperial extension throughout the empire was useful in tying the provincial elite to the Roman governing elite; this can be seen particularly well in Roman Athens after the wars of the first century B.C.E. when the Athenian elite finally seems to have become reconciled to Roman imperial rule.[59] The Athenian response is most evident in the sphere of religion—a notable reminder again of the importance of public religion both for Athenian citizens and for the larger community.

By the time of Augustus (ruled 31 B.C.E.–14 C.E.) the annual rites of Demeter at Eleusis were an established "international" event. So it is no surprise that Augustus took the opportunity of visiting Eleusis and taking part in the mysteries after the battle of Actium in 31 B.C.E. and again in a special celebration held at his request in 19 B.C.E. As noted earlier, the Athenians responded to imperial interest in Eleusis by dedicating there a monument to August, "Savior and Benefactor," and to his wife, Livia, as well.[60] The hierophant (priest) of the mysteries at the time was most likely the same prominent Athenian, Zenon of Marathon, who served as priest of the new cult of Roma and Augustus on the acropolis in Athens; the cult was housed in a new, small but elegant, circular temple just northeast of the Parthenon. In this way, the Athenian elite can be seen as cooperating not only in the imperial participation in traditional Athenian religion but also in the worship of the Roman rulers (and their city) as divinities alongside the traditional Athenian gods.

The Roman entry into the civic religion of Athens is evident in the theater of Dionysos as well. Although Roman officials most likely attended the theater, Roman presence was marked most notably by the inclusion of "thrones" for the priests of Augustus and of Rome among the special front-row seats reserved for priests and priestesses of the Athenian polis. The men and women who filled these positions (and seats) seem to have been prominent Athenians already connected with civic religion (including Eleusis) who were proudly exhibiting a new role and new Roman identity.[61]

The Athenian family that devoted itself most zealously to Roman rule—and benefited from that zeal—was that of Herodes, or Tiberius Claudius Herodes Atticus. Herodes, a Roman citizen and friend of the Roman emperor Marcus Aurelius (ruled 160 C.E.–181 C.E.), came from a family that had cultivated relationships with Roman rulers since the early first century C.E., serving among other things as priests of Augustus and as "general" or "custodian" of the city. The remarkable thing, however, is that by this time (almost two centuries after Augustus's first visit to Eleusis), a new cosmopolitan image of Roman rule had emerged that drew equally on Greek (particularly Athenian) traditions and Roman traditions. Hadrian, the philhellenic peripatetic emperor, styled himself as a new Pericles and undertook to complete the temple of Zeus Olympios in Athens left unfinished since before the time of Pericles. Meanwhile, in Athens, Herodes devoted himself to refurbishing his native city with theaters and athletic facilities and to polishing his own image as a Greek philosopher, now a partner with the Roman ruling elite.

The most articulate spokesman, however, of the expanded community of the Roman Empire was Herodes' younger contemporary, the moralist and biographer Plutarch. Plutarch spent time in Athens at Plato's Academy and was a Roman citizen, but remained throughout his life (60 C.E.– 125 C.E.) a citizen of the small city of Chaeronea in Boeotia, so that, he explained "it would not become even smaller."[62] He was also a priest at the sanctuary of Apollo at Delphi, and wrote numerous essays on issues of religion, including such titles as "The Gods' Slowness to Punish," "Why Are the Delphic Oracles No Longer Given in Verse," and "On Isis and Osiris." Plutarch wrote his series of "Parallel Lives of Noble Greeks and Romans," matching each Greek figure with a comparable Roman one, in order to illustrate the consequences of moral character in public life and also to demonstrate the traditions on which a Greek and Roman partnership or common culture could be based.

The subjects of Plutarch's biographies are all men in public life, but his "Moral Essays" ("Moralia"), including such topics as "Advice on Marriage," "Sayings of Spartan Women," and "The Virtues of Women," display a remarkable interest in women's experience and, we might say, women's "citizenship" in the cosmopolitan world in which he lived. In "The Virtues of Women" (dedicated to Clea, the priestess of Apollo at Delphi, to whom he also dedicated "On Isis and Osiris"), Plutarch asserts that women deserve public recognition for their virtue as much as men and praises the Roman custom that allows public funeral orations for both men and women; he further claims that "the virtue of a man and woman is one and the same,"[63] although "fortitude, prudence, and justice" may show themselves in different ways in women than in men.

Variety is apparent also among men, he notes. With this introductory argument and with the comment that "many worthy things, both public and private, have been done by women," Plutarch relays twenty-seven stories, some mythical, some historical, from the larger Mediterranean world—Celts to Persians—in which women respond with intelligence, self-sacrifice, and public acts of courage in the face of tyranny or external threat. In the first and one of the more charming stories, we hear that after the Trojan ships were blown off course in their escape from Troy and landed at last in Italy, the Trojan women judged that it was time to settle down. So they burned the Trojan ships—and then, to preempt any angry response from their husbands, rushed to greet them with kisses and embraces, distracting the men long enough for the wisdom of their action to sink in. In another, the women of Amphissa (near Delphi) stood guard over sleeping female celebrants through the night to protect them from an occupying military force. Or, in another, the virtuous wife of a murderous tyrant in Cyrene bided her time, made her plans, and eventually brought about his overthrow (the tyrant's mother was burnt alive and he himself sewed up into a leather sack and tossed into the sea). Typically, the individual woman's heroism involves defense of her person or protest at sexual violation by tyrants (the traditional crime of the tyrant), so linking in a quite traditional way the public and private virtue of women (and vices of men).

Although Plutarch was clearly not challenging the traditional gender roles of his time (note that the Cyrenean Aretaphila, after throwing the tyrant in the sea, "spent the rest of her days quietly at her loom"),[64] and his female heroes have a certain rhetorical artificiality, nonetheless his stories bring women into the sphere of public virtue and imagine their active participation in their communities. By articulating these extraordinary female "public deeds," which often are both prompted by and expressed through familial relationships,[65] Plutarch challenged his contemporary audience to think about men and women as public as well as private partners in their communities, just as "Noble Greeks and Romans" are partners in the running of the empire. (He also hopes the stories will entertain.) As an elite Greek whose Roman citizenship was not exercised in political office holding or military command, Plutarch may have been in an ideal position to understand and articulate a sense of community broader than the political.

When a century later, in 212 C.E., the emperor Caracalla decreed that all free residents of the empire were Roman citizens, his aim may have in part been to increase the revenues from the inheritance tax paid only by citizens (male and female); but the decree was also most certainly a recognition of the extent to which the Roman Empire had become a complex but ecumenical community under the umbrella of Roman rule—the *civitas romana,* which later served as the model for Augustine's *civitas dei.*[66] By this time, the legal and political substance of Roman citizenship was quite minimal for most citizens, but the power of "Romanitas" and the imagined community of Roman citizens was profound. Rome was not in the end eternal, but it did last for a good long while—a stability due certainly in large part to its creative use of its own or others' traditions and constructions of citizenship, allowing or at least tolerating diverse sorts of community and at times the crossing of borders.

Conclusion

In the very different world of the twenty-first century, but nonetheless a world with some of the same problems of reconciling political rule and multiple local and/or religious identities, the experiences of Athens and Rome may still have something to offer. In antiquity, religion, with its cults, ceremonies, and rites, allowed and encouraged the participation of a broad spectrum of the population and the crossing of territorial, political, and social boundaries. Religion in the modern world has more often had the opposite effect. Nonetheless, for creativity, strength, and longevity, a community needs to be held together by more than political participation and to embrace diverse identities in some common shared experience without losing the distinctiveness of citizenship identity as active participation and privilege. Women, who have a long history of crossing borders and creating new families and communities, played an important part in the ancient polities of Athens and Rome. Important newfound rights of political participation in the modern world should not obscure the importance of the citizenship roles women have long held.

NOTES

1. Apollodoros, *Against Neaira* [Demosthenes] 59,111 and 114. Trans. Christopher Carey, *Trials from Classical Athens* (London: Routledge, 1997), 207.

2. Appian, *Civil Wars*, 4.32–4, qtd. in Mary Lefkowitz and Maureen Fant, *Women's Life in Greece and Rome* (Baltimore, MD: Johns Hopkins University Press, 1982), 207–8.

3. Valerius Maximus, *Memorable Deeds and Sayings*, 8.3, qtd. in Lefkowitz and Fant, *Women's Life*, supra note 2, 206.

4. J. G. A. Pocock presents this summary of "classical citizenship" (without footnotes or textual references). See J. G. A. Pocock, "The Ideal of Citizenship since Classical Times," in *The Citizenship Debates: A Reader*, ed. Gershon Shafir (Minneapolis: University of Minnesota Press, 1998). For a clear and nuanced discussion of citizenship from a contemporary standpoint, see Linda Bosniak, "Citizenship," in *Oxford Handbook of Legal Studies*, eds. Peter Kane and Mark Tushnet (Oxford: Oxford University Press, 2003), 183–201. My discussion of the multiple aspects of ancient citizenship is indebted to Bosniak's survey of the topic. The most explicit ancient expression of what is generally taken as the classical theory of political citizenship can be found in Ulpian: "Women are excluded from all

civil and public duties and so they cannot be judges, hold magistracies, bring legal claims for others, represent others in court. . . . " Ulpian, *Digest,* 50.17.2, qtd. in Thomas McGinn, *A Casebook on Roman Family Law* (Oxford: Oxford University Press, 2004), 457. The explanation offered by another jurist for this exclusion is simply "tradition." Ibid.

5. In Rome, the consuls and praetors were the chief executive and military officials, and the Roman voting assembly that elected them was essentially the army in assembly, the Comitia Centuriata; for details, see Claude Nicolet, *The World of the Citizen in Republican Rome,* trans. P. S. Falla (Berkeley: University of California Press, 1980), chap. 7. The Athenian democracy elected each year ten generals, who in the fifth century were the most important political officials as well; the situation changed in the fourth century with the increasing use of mercenary soldiers and the importance of finance for running the democracy. For details, see Mogens Hansen, *Athenian Democracy in the Age of Demosthenes* (Oxford: Oxford University Press, 1991).

6. "The Athenian democracy was a 'men's club' whose active members were restricted to men descended from parents who are both Athenian citizen." Elaine Fantham, Helene Peet Foley, Natalie Boymel Kampen, Sarah B. Pomeroy, and H. A. Shapiro, *Women in the Classical World: Image and Text* (Oxford: Oxford University Press, 1994), 74. Cf. Sue Blundell, *Women in Ancient Greece* (Cambridge, MA: Harvard University Press, 1995), 128 ("[F]or Athenian women 'citizenship' meant only that they had a share in the religious, legal, and economic order of the Athenian community."). Similarly, Robin Osborne denied Athenian women's citizenship on the ground that they (along with children and slaves) were excluded from the "honors" of the law courts. See Robin Osborne, "Religion, Imperial Politics, and the Offering of Freedom to Slaves," in *Law and Social Status in Classical Athens,* eds. Virginia Hunter and Jonathan Edmondson (Oxford: Oxford University Press, 2000), 80–81.

7. *Athenaieon Politeia* (Ath.Pol.) 26.4. The *Ath.Pol.* is a political history of Athens from the seventh through the fourth centuries B.C.E., concluding with a description of the author's contemporary fourth-century government. Although the work is collected among Aristotle's works and shows some similarities to Aristotle's political writing, there is reason to doubt the attribution, hence the designation "Aristotelian."

8. For discussion, see Cynthia Patterson, *Pericles' Citizenship Law of 451/0 B.C.* (New York: Arno Press, 1981) and, most recently, Cynthia Patterson, "Athenian Citizenship Law," in *Cambridge Companion to Greek Law,* eds. David Cohen and Michael Gagarin (Cambridge: Cambridge University Press, 2005), 267–89, with references. In general, for matters of Athenian law, see Stephen Todd, *The Shape of Athenian Law* (Oxford: Oxford University Press, 1993); for Greek law, see David Cohen and Michael Gagarin, eds., *Cambridge Companion to Greek Law* (Cambridge: Cambridge University Press, 2005).

9. *"Ex amphoin astoin."* The dual was an archaic grammatical form for "two" and was rarely used except in cases of a pair, for example, "eyes," "hands," or "parents").

10. Aristotle, "Politics," in *The Complete Works of Aristotle,* vol. 2, ed. Johnathan Barnes (Princeton, NJ: Princeton University Press, 1984).

11. Ibid., 1252b30.

12. Ibid., 1275a1. Book 2 is devoted to a critique of imagined (Platonic) and real *poleis* (Sparta, Crete, and Carthage).

13. Ibid., 1275a18–34.

14. Ibid., 1275a.

15. See Susan D. Collins, *Aristotle and the Rediscovery of Citizenship* (Cambridge: Cambridge University Press, 2006), chap. 5 with bibliography.

16. Linda Kerber, "The Paradox of Women's Citizenship in the Early Republic: The Case of Martin vs. Massachusetts, 1805," *American Historical Review* 97 (1992): 354. "Silence," she goes on to say, "is a social construction, related to an ability to verbalize and a control of access to the forums of public discussion." Ibid.

17. Aristotle himself (died 322 B.C.E.) was not a citizen of Athens but lived for a number of years in the city as a resident alien during the later part of the classical era and Athenian independence; his view of classical Athenian politics was from a distance, both temporally and personally. He seems to have privileged in his definition of citizenship those very political privileges that he never enjoyed. For the rights and responsibilities of resident aliens in Athens (male and female), see David Whitehead, *The Ideology of the Athenian Metic* (Cambridge: Cambridge University Press, 1976).

18. Law Attributable to Pericles, *Ath.Pol.* 26.4 (author translation).

19. Homer, *The Odyssey,* 13.192.

20. Pindar, *Olympian One,* 7.89–90.

21. Aeschylus, *Eumenides,* 437.

22. [Demosthenes], *Against Neaira,* 107.

23. See Cynthia Patterson, *"Hai Attikai:* The Other Athenians," *Helios* 13 (1986): 49–67.

24. Plutarch, *Solon,* 23 (author translation).

25. The Greek law on *moicheia* is a much debated topic. See Cynthia Patterson, *The Family in Greek History* (Cambridge, MA: Harvard University Press, 1998), chaps. 3 and 4, with bibliography.

26. [Demosthenes], *Against Neaira,* 86.

27. The complete quotation from Menander, *Dyskolos* 289–93 (trans. Norma Miller), in which the brother of a young woman accuses his sister's suitor of improper intentions, goes as follows: "Your idea is to seduce an innocent girl—a respectable man's daughter—or you're watching your chance to do something [i.e., rape] that deserves the death sentence, several times over." For discussion

of these issues and the laws involved, see Patterson, *The Family in Greek History*, supra note 25, 165–74.

28. I.G. (Inscriptiones Graecae) I 35. Translation can be found in *Ancient Greece: Social and Historical Documents from Archaic Times to the Death of Socrates* (2nd ed.), ed. Matthew Dillon and Lynda Garland (London: Routledge, 1994), 12.36; See Patterson, supra note 23, "Hai Attikai: The Other Athenians," 53.

29. Herodotus, 8.41.

30. Plutarch, *Alcibiades*, 22.3.

31. David Lewis, "Notes on Attic Inscriptions: Who Was Lysistrata?," *British School at Athens* 50 (1955): 1–6. Cf. Jeffrey Henderson, *Aristophanes' Lysistrata* (Oxford: Oxford University Press, 1987), xxxvi–xli, who accepts the Lysimache-Lysistrata identification but doubts that Aristophanes' Myrrhine is intended to recall the priestess of that name.

32. SEG 12.80 trans. in Dillon and Garland, *Ancient Greece: Social and Historical Documents*, supra note 28. See also Christoph Clairmont, "The Lekythos of Myrrhine," *Studies in Classical Art and Archaeology: A Tribute to Peter Heinrich von Blanckenhagen* (Locust Valley, NY: J.J. Augustin, 1979).

33. Although it is often said that women did not attend the theater in Athens, there is in fact no good reason to believe that they were officially excluded and—given that the theater was part of the public festival of Dionysos—good reason to think that many women would have been there. See Maurice Rehm, *The Play of Space* (Princeton, NJ: Princeton University Press, 2002), 50 with note.

34. *Lysistrata*, trans. Jeffrey Henderson (Loeb Classical Library, Cambridge, MA: Harvard University Press, 2000), 638–47. The women (using the singular first person as is common for the Greek chorus) offer here a sort of "*cursus honorum*" of their religious life. The "Foundress" is Artemis and the Brauronia is her festival at Brauron in eastern Attica. The "basket bearers" appear on the Parthenon frieze (above figure 1.1) representing the procession in honor of Athena. For discussion of female religious roles, see Mary Lefkowitz, "Women in the Panathenaic and Other Festivals," in *Worshipping Athena: Panathenaia and Parthenon*, ed. Jennifer Neils (Madison: University of Wisconsin Press, 1996); Joan Connely, *Portrait of a Princess: Women and Ritual in Ancient Greece* (Princeton, NJ: Princeton University Press, 2007). For general background on Greek religion, see Louise Zaimont and Pauline Schmitt Pantel, *Religion in the Ancient Greek City* (New York: Cambridge University Press, 1992).

35. Ibid., 648–54.

36. Douglass Parker, trans., *Aristophanes, Four Comedies* (Ann Arbor: University of Michigan Press, 1969), 44–45. Aristophanes is notoriously difficult to translate. I use two different translations because each one seems to capture best the meaning and tone of the particular passage cited.

37. These words of course were written by a man (Aristophanes) and performed by a chorus of men dressed as women. The extent to which that fact

undermines their significance is disputed. Froma Zeitlin, "Playing the Other: Theater, Theatricality, and the Feminine in Greek Drama," *Representations* 11 (1985): 63–94, takes the extreme view that Athenian drama is all about men, with nothing to say about real women's experience. Others, however, have more nuanced views. See especially Josine Blok, "Virtual Voices: Toward Choreography of Women's Speech in Classical Athens," in *Making Silence Speak: Women's Voices in Greek Literature and Society*, eds. Andre Lardinois and Laura McClure (Princeton, NJ: Princeton University Press, 2001).

38. On Athenian property and family law, see Todd, *The Shape of Athenian Law*, supra note 8; and Patterson, *The Family in Greek History*, supra note 25.

39. Pericles, in *Thucydides*, 2.38.

40. Plutarch, *Life of Pericles*, 28.

41. Demosthenes 43 ("Against Makartatos") 62 (trans. Murray).

42. See, e.g., Fantham, Foley, Kampen, Pomeroy, and Shapiro, *Women in the Classical World*, supra note 6, 76.

43. See espeically John Oakley, *Picturing Death in Classical Athens: the Evidence of the White Lekythos* (Cambridge: Cambridge University Press, 2004).

44. Sophocles, *Antigone*, 955–57.

45. For discussion of Antigone's argument and moral position see especially Helene Foley, *Female Acts in Greek Tragedy* (Princeton, NJ: Princeton University Press, 2001); see also the essays in *Antigone's Answer: Essays on Death and Burial, Family and State in Classical Athens*, ed. Cynthia Patterson, *Helios*, special issue, 335 (Lubbock: Texas Tech University Press, 2006).

46. Helene P. Foley, ed., *The Homeric Hymn to Demeter: Translation, Commentary, and Interpretive Essays* (Princeton, NJ: Princeton University Press, 1993). For the promise, see lines 480–82.

47. See ibid., 66.

48. [Demosthenes], *Against Neaira*, 59.21.

49. Kevin Clinton, "Eleusis and the Romans: Late Republic to Marcus Aurelius," in *The Romanization of Athens*, eds. Michael C. Hoff and Susan I. Rotroff (Oxford: Oxbow Books, 1997), 161–81.

50. Ibid.

51. I have omitted here, in the interest of brevity and the Athens/Rome contrast, the story of Athens's fall to Macedonian rule in the late fourth century. Democracy—and democratic citizenship—survived Philip and even Alexander, but not the rough rule of the "Successors." For Hellenistic Athens, see Peter Green, *Alexander to Actium* (Berkeley: University of California Press, 1990).

52. For a good discussion of the significance of this decree, see Peter Garnsey, "Roman Citizenship and Roman Law in the Late Empire," in *Approaching Late Antiquity: The Transformation from Early to Late Empire*, eds. Simon Swain and Mark Edwards (Oxford: Oxford University Press, 2004).

53. Rome had an empire before it had an "emperor" (the first of whom was Augustus 31 B.C.E.–14 C.E.).

54. Livy 1.13.4, quoted in Nicolet, *The World of the Citizen in Republican Rome*, supra note 5, 22.

55. Ibid.

56. See, e.g, Judith Hallet, *Fathers and Daughters in Roman Society* (Princeton, NJ: Princeton University Press, 1984).

57. On Roman marriage, see Susan Treggiari, *Roman Marriage: Iusti Coniuges from the Time of Cicero to the Time of Ulpian* (Oxford: Oxford University Press, 1991). On the Roman belief in marriage's centrality for their society, see Gordon Williams, "Some Aspects of Roman Marriage Ceremonies and Ideals," *Journal of Roman Studies* 48 (1958): 16–29.

58. Naphathi Lewis and Meyer Reinhold, *Roman Civilization: Selected Readings* (New York: Columbia University Press, 1990), 550–51. Early Christianity's challenge to Roman civic traditions is an important topic that I cannot consider here.

59. Before the early empire Athenians were not becoming Romans or vice versa. Christian Habicht, "Roman Citizens in Athens (228–31 B.C.)," in *The Romanization of Athens*, supra note 49, 9–17.

60. Ibid.

61. Daniel J. Geagan, "The Athenian Elite: Romanization, Resistance, and the Exercise of Power," in *The Romanization of Athens*, supra note 49, 24–25; Anthony J. S. Spawforth, "The Early Reception of the Imperial Cult in Athens: Problems and Ambiguities," in *The Romanization of Athens*, supra note 49, 188–191.

62. Plutarch, *Life of Demosthenes*, 2.

63. Plutarch, "The Virtues of Women," 242.

64. Ibid., 257.

65. For example, the Persian women rallied the defeated troops by meeting them outside the city, raising their skirts, and challenging them to have courage, saying "you can't take refuge here" (5). Interestingly (or disconcertingly) the same or a similar story is told by Plutarch of the Spartan women. Plutarch, "Sayings of Spartan Women," *Moralia*.

66. Garnsey, "Roman Citizenship and Roman Law," supra note 52, 150–55.

|||||||||||||||||||||||||||||||||||||||||||||||||||

2

The Stateless as the Citizen's Other:
A View from the United States

Linda K. Kerber

I begin by asking an anachronistic and playful but nevertheless deeply tragic question: What passport would the ill-fated child of Madame Butterfly and Captain Pinkerton carry? Normally, historians do not turn to an opera libretto for inspiration. Yet this story carries with it hints that help us map the landscape of statelessness in U.S. history, from the founding generation to the present.

It is a subterranean tale that haunts the imperial imagination. The roles have been dramatized over and over again—the man whom the American military has deployed in a strange landscape in a foreign part of the globe; the exotic woman whom he impregnates and abandons. Giacomo Puccini relied on American sources when he wrote the opera *Madame Butterfly*, which had its premiere at La Scala a century ago, in 1904. Puccini was inspired by a play of the same title, written by David Belasco, which he saw in London in 1900 in the Duke of York's Theatre. Belasco based his play on a novella by the Philadelphia writer John Luther Long, who, in his turn, was revising a fictionalized memoir by the French writer Pierre Loti.[1]

Whether in novella, play, or opera, the lover is Benjamin Franklin Pinkerton, a U.S. naval officer whose name signals the self-made, cynical American. He beds a trusting Japanese girl, tricking her into breaking with her family. She is pregnant when Pinkerton leaves with his fleet, promising to return. Slowly it dawns on Cho-Cho-San that this respectable military man cannot be counted on; nor will the laws of his nation enforce his promises to her.

In Long's story, Cho-Cho-San speaks in broken English; but as the reader adapts to the way she talks, she becomes a figure whom we respect

THE DEATH OF BUTTERFLY

Butterfly has blindfolded her son, whose name is Trouble, so that he cannot see her suicide. Puccini's stage directions specify that she give the child a doll and an American flag to distract him. The photo is probably of the famous American soprano Geraldine Farrar, in a production before 1913. From *The Victor Book of the Opera: Stories of One Hundred Operas with Five-Hundred Illustrations & Descriptions of One-Thousand Victor Opera Records* (Camden, NJ: Victor Talking Machine Co., 1913), 224.

and with whom we sympathize. Cho-Cho-San clings to the dream of Pinkerton's return—with the robins, as he has promised—and she resolves not to beg:

> He don' naever egspeg we got this nize bebby, account I don' tell him. I don' kin tell him. I don' know where he is. But—me? I don' tell if I know, account he rush right over here, an' desert his country, an' henceforth git in a large trouble—mebby with that President United States America, an' that large Goddess Liberty Independence![2]

A year later, the fleet returns, and she sees him on the deck of a ship in the harbor, arm in arm with a blonde woman; the woman introduces herself to the American consul as Mrs. Benjamin Pinkerton when Cho-Cho-San happens to be in the room. Devastated, Cho-Cho-San attempts suicide with her own father's sword, inscribed "To die with Honor / When one can no longer live with Honor."

Cho-Cho-San ("San" is an honorific; we're speaking of "Miss Cho-Cho") has been reinvented in our own time as Miss Saigon. Now the composers are French—Claude-Michel Schönberg and Alain Boublil—and the setting is the American war in Vietnam. Boublil has been explicit about how Pierre Loti's fiction resonated with what he learned while growing up in Tunisia: "Vietnam was a French colony and a French mistake before it became an American one." The authors were also inspired by a 1985 photograph of an airlift of "bui-doi"—the mixed-race children of American soldiers and Vietnamese women.

Schönberg and Boublil have transformed Pinkerton into Chris, an appealingly naive American soldier, authentically in love with Kim, a young woman from a respectable family who has been driven to work as a bar girl. When they are separated by the hurricane of war, Kim is brave and resilient, even prepared to kill to protect the child whom Chris does not know he has fathered. Some years later, when Chris finds out about the child, he is back in the United States and married. He is ravaged by guilt and the desire to be a true father to his child. His American wife can suggest no solution except to adopt the child themselves. Even in the context of decent people trying to do the right thing, the only way for Miss Saigon to make a respectable future for her child is to disappear. The music stops with her suicide. *Miss Saigon* has had its own stunning success; the London and New York productions ran for ten years each. Duplicate productions have been staged in dozens of other cities around the world.

So now to our anachronistic question: What passport would the child of Madame Butterfly and Captain Pinkerton carry? In the Meiji period in Japan, as in the West until roughly World War I, practices of documenting individual identity were underdeveloped, and the strict system of passport controls with which we have come to be familiar had yet to be invented. Long after Admiral Perry "opened" Japan to foreign intrusion in 1853, it remained rare for Japanese subjects to leave the island. Still, trying to answer the question is a useful exercise.

Was the child a Japanese subject? In the Meiji period, where the story is set, the concept of national civic identity was weak. What counted for legitimacy was inclusion in the father's family registry. Not until 1985 was Nationality Law in Japan revised to permit Japanese women to transmit Japanese citizenship to their children.[3] In Butterfly's time, an illegitimate birth was frequently disguised by the child being registered as the offspring of the woman's parents, born late in their lives; but in the story, Butterfly has broken from her family, so this registration is unlikely.[4]

Was the child an American citizen? If Butterfly had stowed away on Pinkerton's ship and given birth to their baby on American soil, the child would have been a citizen at birth, even if Butterfly had never married

Pinkerton. The Fourteenth Amendment of the U.S. Constitution, ratified in 1868, guarantees that "all persons, born or naturalized in the United States, are citizens of the United States and of the state in which they reside." If Pinkerton had married Butterfly, he would have transmitted his citizenship to their child wherever that child was born. But Butterfly does not stow away, nor does Pinkerton marry her, nor does he claim or legitimize the child, who therefore has no claim on the United States. In the United States, nonmarital children born overseas to American citizen fathers are not citizens until the father legitimizes them. Unrecognized by either nation, Butterfly's baby is effectively stateless.

A century stretches between our time and Pinkerton's. His story has been relived countless times, and the American answer to the passport question has not substantially changed. The practices that define which children born abroad are to be considered citizens from birth and which must be naturalized still take into account the status of the mother and the status of the father asymmetrically. Indeed, a case involving these issues came before the U.S. Supreme Court as recently as 2001, and in dealing with it, the Court found itself contemplating Americans' assumptions about belonging and protection, about birthright citizenship and its absence.

Tuan Ahn Nguyen was born in 1969. His father, Joseph Boulais, was an American army veteran who, after his discharge from service in Germany, went to Vietnam in 1963 as a civilian employee of a construction company. Boulais had a son with a Vietnamese woman. In a reversal of the Madame Butterfly trope, the Vietnamese mother abandoned her son at birth. In this true story, the father is the nurturer: Boulais remained in Vietnam, married another Vietnamese woman, and cared for his son. In the chaos of the collapse of the Saigon regime in 1975, Nguyen was brought to the United States along with other refugees and was reunited with his father and stepmother; from the age of six, he grew up in Houston in his father's home.

Various statutes provide that children born abroad whose parents are married to each other, at least one of whom is a citizen, are citizens at birth, so long as one parent has lived in the United States for five years, at least two of which were after age fourteen. But should the parents *not* be married to each other, and if only one is a U.S. citizen, then the sex of the citizen parent has major consequences. In a practice that reaches back to medieval England—when the older rule that the bastard was the child of no one was revised to make the bastard the child of the mother (continuing to free the father from any obligation to that child), extended when the American colonies reified the practice in the form of statutes that provided that children fathered by slave masters "followed the condition of the mother"—birthright citizenship for children born overseas to unmarried couples is transmitted effortlessly only through the mother. But the law requires that a child born overseas to an unmarried citizen father and a foreign woman is not a citizen unless the father acknowledges paternity legally and provides financial support until the child reaches the age of eighteen.

So Nguyen was not a citizen. Although Joseph Boulais provided financial support, he neglected to register the birth officially or to demonstrate a blood relationship with the child. So long as life moved along quietly, what did formal paperwork matter? But in the early 1990s, Nguyen was found guilty of two counts of sexual assault on a minor and was given an eight-year prison sentence. While he was serving his term, Congress, responding to a rising tide of anti-immigrant sentiment, tightened the rules for lawful permanent residents such as Nguyen. Conviction for an aggravated felony now meant deportation. And in 2001, a five-to-four U.S. Supreme Court majority denied Nguyen's father's claim that he should have been able to transmit birthright citizenship to his child on the same terms that an American citizen woman can.[5]

In reaching this decision, the Supreme Court wrestled with the meaning of gender equity, scrutinizing Section 1409 of the Immigration and Nationality Act of 1952 and its subsequent revisions (the statute that makes distinctions between the way men and women confer citizenship on nonmarital children born abroad). The members of the Court considered whether the statute met the high level of scrutiny that has been required since 1996. To meet that standard, those who defend discrimination on the basis of sex must show an "exceedingly persuasive justification" for that discrimination. It must serve "important governmental objectives," and the discriminatory means employed must be "substantially related" to the achievement of those objectives. Writing for the majority, Justice Anthony Kennedy defended the additional requirements placed on men to legitimize a nonmarital child on the grounds that these rules ensure that an authentic parent-child bond exists; that bond, in turn, could be counted on to transmit the values of citizenship (the important governmental objective). Boulais was not being burdened more severely than nonmarital fathers of children born within the United States who are required to exhibit their relationship to the child. Moreover, requiring men to legitimize their nonmarital children guarded against error or trickery: "Given the 9-month interval between conception and birth, it is not always certain," Justice Kennedy observed, "that a father will know that a child was conceived, nor is it always clear that even the mother will be sure of the father's identity. This fact takes on particular significance in the case of a child born overseas and out of wedlock." As for the birthright citizenship transmitted by the nonmarital birth mother, that, Kennedy thought, merely equalized her situation with that of the married mother or of the nonmarital mother who was in a position to return to the United States to bear her child.[6]

Lurking behind the reasoning of the majority opinion lay a fear that was not spoken in the opinion, but that was spelled out at length in the brief filed by the Department of Justice in support of making distinctions between mothers and fathers: "Congress minimized the burdens on unwed mothers who seek citizenship for their children . . . in order to advance its important interest in avoiding statelessness." In the United States, citizenship accompanies birth on American soil, whatever the citizenship or marital status of the parents. But in most nations, citizenship is traced through bloodline and only secondarily through place of birth. By the law of many nations, including nations in which the United States has had a substantial military presence, a child born out of wedlock inherits the citizenship of the mother.[7] There was, the Department of Justice argued, a real danger: "that the foreign-born children of unwed citizen mothers might become stateless if they were not eligible for United States citizenship, because the children would not be eligible for citizenship in the country of birth or in the country of the unwed father."[8]

Congress had recognized this danger in 1940 and again in 1952, framing the law to "insure that the child shall have a nationality at birth." In Germany, South Korea, and Japan (and to a lesser degree in Thailand), "the danger of statelessness in the event that the [nonmarital] father does not acknowledge the child remains a concern."[9] Men and women were differently situated in exposing their nonmarital child to the risk of statelessness: "The foreign-born child of an unwed American mother is at much greater risk of losing his or her 'status in organized society' than the foreign-born child of an unwed American father."[10] Congress left nonmarital children of U.S. citizen fathers exposed to the vagaries of the individual men's variable sense of personal responsibility and the rules of the countries in which they happened to be born.

"One concern in this context," Justice Kennedy observed, "has always been with young people, men for the most part, who are on duty with the

Armed Forces in foreign countries." Over one million military personnel were stationed in foreign countries in the year Nguyen was born.[11] In a dissenting opinion in one of the cases that formed a backdrop to *Nguyen*, Judge Andrew Kleinfeld of the Ninth Circuit Court of Appeals had emphasized that Congress understood full well what they were doing:

> This statute was passed during the Korean War. Members of Congress knew that American soldiers who went abroad to fight wars, and caused children to be conceived while they were abroad, were overwhelmingly male, because only males were drafted, so that the number of children born illegitimately of male citizens might be large enough to affect immigration policy, while the number of illegitimate children of female citizens would be negligible. They may also have sought to minimize the administrative burden on the Department of Defense for paternity and citizenship claims respectively by the women the soldiers left behind and their children. This may not be pretty, but it is a rational basis for the sex distinction. . . . Some noncustodial fathers of children born out of wedlock do not care to pay child support if it can be avoided.[12]

In other words, even those men representing the United States abroad have the Court's permission to father children out of wedlock and abandon them. "I expect very few of these are the children of female service personnel," Ruth Bader Ginsburg wryly observed to uncomfortable laughter in the courtroom during the oral argument in *Nguyen*. "There are these men out there who are being Johnny Appleseed."[13] In arriving at its judgment about gender equity, the Supreme Court responded to the fear of statelessness.

*   *   *

Statelessness is a subject that most historians of the United States have treated as belonging to other national histories—those of Jews, Gypsies, Palestinians. That U.S. history is taken to be innocent of engagement with the subject is yet another example of the habits of American exceptionalism. Since the *meanings* of statelessness have changed over time, the subject is one that should command the attention of historians as well as humanitarians.

In recent years, when some boundaries between states have become more plastic, "statelessness" has sometimes been given a positive valence. Statelessness can be made to sustain a cosmopolitan dream. The dreamers include many citizens of the member states of the European Union, whose passports carry them over the borders of twenty-five nations, and hundreds of thousands of people who hold more than one passport, often wealthy people with property on two continents. For these people, a destabilized citizenship is an enriched citizenship. Such people may speak cheerfully of multiplied citizenships, a comfortable cosmopolitanism, being a citizen of the world. If citizenship is about what might be called state*full*ness, then some people are rich in it.[14]

Somewhat less expansively, but with more stability, simple dual nationality is increasingly common. One result of the technological and economic changes we call globalization is that more and more people now live outside their natal countries—the UN's 2000 estimate was some 185 million, and the number is clearly growing. Sometimes parents share the same nationality; international marriages are also increasing in frequency. Increasing numbers of children hold citizenship of one country through descent and of another by *jus solis*—birth on the soil.[15]

The old tradition that required the renunciation of all other nationalities at the time of naturalization has substantially—but not completely—eroded. Canada dropped its renunciation requirement in 1947. The 1997 European Convention on Nationality accepts dual nationality, although some countries, including Germany, require adults who gained dual citizenship at birth to make a choice of nationality when they reach adulthood. In an effort to enable expatriates to protect themselves against increasingly harsh U.S. deportation laws and heightened discrimination, and responding to the hesitation, on sentimental and practical grounds, of expatriates to take oaths of naturalization, Mexico and some other Latin American countries changed their laws in the late 1990s to embrace dual citizenship (generally with provision to eliminate dual voting). And although the first item in the United States of America's oath of naturalization is the renunciation of allegiance to "any foreign prince, potentate, state or sovereignty of whom or of which I have heretofore been a subject or citizen," the Department of State puts virtually no energy into enforcing this provision. In 1967, the U.S. Supreme Court ruled that voluntary denationalization must be explicit—that even voting in a foreign election did not imply expatriation. In a powerful opinion, Justice Hugo Black wrote that the intention of Congress in the era of the Fourteenth Amendment had been "to put citizenship beyond the power of any governmental unit to destroy." Without a specific and voluntary renunciation, the Court held, "Congress has no power to divest a person of citizenship." Consular officials now abide by that rule; even the holding of dual nationality in the face of the naturalization oath is not construed by the Executive Branch as voluntary relinquishment.[16]

Yet even the enriched state is still defined by borders. Inside those borders are citizens and subjects, legal permanent residents, refugees, undocumented aliens. It has become essential to a state's identity that it be able to distinguish between those who belong—and are vulnerable to taxation and conscription—and those who do not. Citizens' identities are secured by passports, which they must have in order to leave the nation and in order to reenter it. International law limits the power of a nation to exclude or deport its own nationals; U.S. citizens have a virtually absolute right to enter the United States.[17] Legal permanent residents leave with nonbinding assurances that they can reenter; they are vulnerable if the rules or policies change while they are away. In times of danger—as during summer 2006 in Lebanon—the United States will seek to evacuate its citizens; but lawful permanent residents (green card holders) generally are not entitled to emergency and protective services provided by the U.S. government and must turn to the nearest diplomatic representative of the country of which they are nationals.[18] Undocumented aliens had better leave by the invisible modes by which they came. Most nations require a visa of foreigners who enter, and thus control admission at their borders. The ultimate "other" to the citizen is not the citizen of a different country, not the multiply passported, but rather those who lack passports of any sort; the stateless are defined by what they *lack*.

When Hannah Arendt—who herself was stateless for more than a decade—wrote memorably about statelessness a half-century ago, it was technically a legal term of art, describing "a person who is not considered as a national by any State by the operation of its law."[19] The stateless person may be a refugee, but not necessarily, for in times of peace a state may not have much interest in emphasizing vulnerability. A refugee may be a stateless person—but not necessarily. If a refugee has a state, it is a state to which he or she is unable or unwilling to turn for protection; a stateless refugee is presumed not to have access to state protection at all.[20] (The German constitution explicitly provides that people cannot be denationalized if that would expose them to statelessness.)[21] The 1948 Universal Declaration of Human Rights asserts that "[e]very person has a right to a nationality." The 1954 Convention Relating to the Status of Stateless Persons prohibits expulsion of stateless persons "save on grounds of national security or public order," but provides no oversight or enforcement

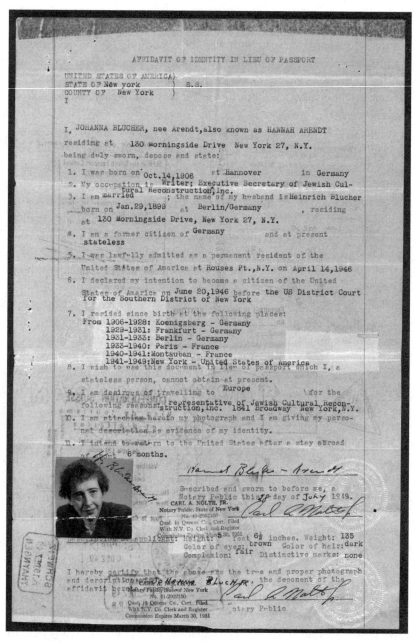

AFFIDAVIT OF IDENTITY IN LIEU OF PASSPORT

UNITED STATES OF AMERICA)
STATE OF New York   ) S.S.
COUNTY OF   New York   )
I

I, JOHANNA BLUCHER, nee Arendt, also known as HANNAH ARENDT

residing at   130 Morningside Drive New York 27, N.Y.

being duly sworn, depose and state:

1. I was born on Oct.14,1906   at Hannover   in Germany
2. My occupation is Writer; Executive Secretary of Jewish Cultural Reconstruction, Inc.
3. I am married   ; the name of my husband is Heinrich Blucher
   born on Jan.29,1899   at Berlin/Germany   , residing
   at 130 Morningside Drive, New York 27, N.Y.
4. I am a former citizen of Germany   and at present
   stateless
5. I was lawfully admitted as a permanent resident of the
   United States of America at Rouses Pt.,N.Y. on April 14,1946
6. I declared my intention to become a citizen of the United
   States of America on June 20,1946 before the US District Court
   for the Southern District of New York
7. I resided since birth at the following places:
   From 1906-1928: Koenigsberg - Germany
        1929-1931: Frankfurt - Germany
        1931-1933: Berlin - Germany
        1933-1940: Paris - France
        1940-1941: Montauban - France
        1941-1949: New York - United States of America
8. I wish to use this document in lieu of passport which I, a
   stateless person, cannot obtain at present.
9. I am desirous of travelling to Europe   for the
   following reasons: representative of Jewish Cultural Reconstruction, Inc. 1841 Broadway New York, N.Y.
10. I am attaching hereto my photograph and I am giving my perso-
    nal description as evidence of my identity.
11. I intend to return to the United States after a stay abroad
    of about 6 months.

                        Hannah Blücher – Arendt

                Subscribed and sworn to before me, a
                Notary Public this 7 day of July 1949.
                CARL A. NOLTE, JR.
                Notary Public, State of New York   Carl A. Nolte
                No. 41-2902150
                Qual. in Queens Co., Cert. Filed
                With N.Y. Co. Clerk and Register
                Commission Expires 5.30, 1951   feet 6½ inches. Weight: 135
                        Color of eyes: brown Color of hair: dark
                        Complexion: fair Distinctive marks: none

I hereby certify that the above are the true and proper photograph
and description of Johanna Blucher, the deponent of the
affidavit hereof. Notary Public, State of New York
                No. 41-2902150
                Qual. in Queens Co., Cert. Filed
                With N.Y. Co. Clerk and Register   Carl A. Nolte
                Commission Expires March 30, 1951   Notary Public

Hannah Arendt's "Affidavit of Identity in Lieu of a Passport, 1949." Note answers
to questions 4 and 8. Box 4, Hannah Arendt Papers, Manuscript Division,
Library of Congress, Washington, DC.

mechanism. Neither the United States nor Canada ratified the 1954 convention, apparently because both were concentrating on the overwhelming problem of refugees and displaced persons after the war and feared that the convention's recognition of de facto (as well as de jure) stateless persons might encourage them to seek "a new nationality for the sake of convenience."[22]

In our own historical moment, the contours of statelessness are somewhat different than they were in the immediate aftermath of World War II. It is true that statelessness is the formal description of lack. But statelessness is also a condition that changes over time, dynamically created and re-created by sovereignties in their own interests, defining the vulnerable in ways that affirm the invulnerable, and in the process revealing changing domestic values and changing power relations across international boundaries.

The nightmare of statelessness—of the man, woman, or child without a country—exists everywhere in our own time. As the meanings of work, racial identity, and gender identity have shifted over time under the stress of war, political struggles, global economic relations, and developing ideologies, vulnerability to statelessness has been reconfigured. The definition of statelessness itself has expanded.

In the United States now, perhaps the most chilling signal that reconceptualization is possible is the presence of a vigorous political attack on the Fourteenth Amendment's guarantee of birthright citizenship, an attack that destabilizes one of the strongest founding principles of American identity and makes highly likely the increase of statelessness. Although a parent receives no immigration benefits from having a U.S. citizen child until that child turns twenty-one, this attack has been soaked with the complaint that pregnant women enter the United States illegally in order that their children may claim citizenship by birthright, in effect tricking the generous provision of the Fourteenth Amendment.[23]

The United Nations High Commissioner for Refugees (UNHCR) now speaks of "effective nationality" and "ineffective nationality," and of de facto statelessness.[24] It has broadened the definition to include "the unprotected."[25] "Statelessness spells vulnerability," writes the immigration lawyer Stephen Legomsky. "In a world built on nationality, one simply cannot leave home without it. . . . Every individual needs one sovereign state to play the role of guardian angel."[26]

The pace of attention paid to the issue of statelessness can be traced in the lineage of fiction and nonfiction writings, where we can track with chilling accuracy the rise and fall of the threat of statelessness throughout the world. There is Edward Everett Hale's classic novella *The Man without a Country*, written during the Civil War and republished dozens of times since, especially during World War I and World War II, most recently shortly after 9/11.²⁷ There are films—*Casablanca* (1942), *I Was a Male War Bride* (1949), *Lady without a Passport* (1950), and most recently Steven Spielberg's *Terminal* (2004). The only monograph in the field was published seventy years ago: Catheryn Seckler-Hudson's 1934 *Statelessness: With Special Reference to the United States (A Study in Nationality and Conflict of Laws).*²⁸ In the aftermath of World War II, when the Atlantic world was swarming with displaced people, Hannah Arendt wrote what remains the most powerful set of reflections on statelessness—the stunning ninth chapter of *The Origins of Totalitarianism*, written between 1945 and 1951, when she herself was stateless.²⁹ Attention to statelessness receded again in the 1960s, reemerged modestly when attention was claimed by refugees from Vietnam and by the contested condition of Palestinians, and then exploded in our own time.³⁰

The UNHCR has recognized that distinctions between stateless people and refugees are somewhat less sharp than they once were. It now describes stateless people as one of several categories among the 20.8 million who represent a "population of concern."³¹ Refugees are the largest category, accounting for roughly 40 percent of the total. Other categories are asylum seekers and "internally displaced persons" who, once uprooted, fall through the cracks of current human rights law. Although international conventions have long provided protections against *refoulement*—the expulsion of persons who have the right to be recognized as refugees—its practice is increasing as asylum seekers are increasingly sent back to their nations of origin or to third countries, many of which will not provide them safety.³² Some 2.4 million people are conservatively estimated by the UNHCR to be stateless, living "in a Kafkaesque legal vacuum," their numbers uncertain, hard to document, "non-persons, legal ghosts."³³

These "persons of concern" introduce a new dimension into our understanding. Stateless persons have been commonly understood to be a population made vulnerable by movement; Philip Nolan, the "Man without a Country" in the nineteenth-century novella, is forced out of the state he calls home. But citizenship ties can be fractured in stasis as well as in movement; liminal people who have not moved physically can find that state boundaries have shifted, and the protections that citizenship was thought to provide can suddenly evaporate. A good example is the now stateless citizens of the former Soviet Union who have not obtained nationality in any of the new countries that succeeded the USSR.[34]

Imprisonment heightens vulnerability. In the normal course of events, the citizen can claim some measure of state protection when abroad. If arrested, a U.S. citizen who is charged with a crime while in another country can expect a personal visit and assistance from a U.S. consular officer. (The consul staff may not be able to resolve the problem, but they can be counted upon to make a good faith effort to try.) The stateless person has no consul to whom to turn.

Extreme economic vulnerability also can propel people into something that looks like statelessness; they dare not ask for asylum, and often have no one whom they can ask for it. In this situation, most notably, are the millions of desperate laborers, many of whom are women, who can escape the dire circumstances of their home countries only by accepting airfare from traffickers who transport them to labor situations close to slavery, in which they have no recourse against the exploitation and anger of their employers.[35] Indeed, the term "slavery" is once again in use as a descriptor of current conditions, and among the conservative estimates of the number of slaves in the world today is Kevin Bales's of twenty-seven million.[36] In February 2006, the UNHCR called on states "to cooperate in the establishment of identity and national status of victims of trafficking, many of whom, especially women and children, are rendered effectively stateless."[37]

Gender has, in fact, been a key factor in the history of statelessness. Only recently have gender-specific asylum claims such as rape, dowry-related violence, and coerced female circumcision been recognized, and that recognition has been sporadic. Among refugees, in settings in which gender and age demographics are provided by the United Nations High Commissioner for Refugees, adults divide evenly between men and women, but women are much more likely to be accompanied by children. Most significant, as Jacqueline Bhabha has recently emphasized, crude numbers do not describe the situation as women experience it: there is a substantial disparity in exposure to statelessness between men and women refugees and asylum seekers in different parts of the world, which emerges only when microclimates are examined. "In every single developing country of asylum neighboring the refugees' country of origin, women and children refugees substantially outnumber adult males [representing nearly 80 percent of the refugees]. . . . [I]n every developed state, male asylum seekers far outnumber females." Women historically have had less access than men have had to "the formal and informal structures that facilitate migration (state agencies, travel agents, smugglers, family funding)," and this lack of access, along with their "dependent family status, resource inadequacy, personal history and social positioning, which militate against a self-perception as an autonomous asylum seeker, [is] likely to be [a] powerful [impediment] to individual flight," Bhabha observes.[38]

In short, statelessness did not disappear with World War II, nor is the United States innocent of its terrors. How are we to understand its resilience—the continued reconstruction of an absence? Is it possible that the state *needs* its negation in order to know itself?

To historicize statelessness is to write a history of the practices of race, gender, labor, and ideology, a history of extreme otherness and extreme danger. It is time, I think, to examine the phenomenon in the long course of American history, and also as it now presents itself—in the context of new, turn-of-the-century wars, in the context of American fears of terrorism, and when, as likely as not, it is the woman who lacks the country.

*   *   *

The work of Hannah Arendt is a crucial starting point for any examination of statelessness. I begin where she—with her perfect pitch for irony— begins, in the era of state building that marks the opening of the modern era. She calls our attention to the paradoxes of the age of the democratic revolutions of the eighteenth century. Americans spoke of "inalienable rights," the French of "the rights of man," both "*inalienable* because they were supposed to be independent of all governments; but," writes Arendt, "it turned out that the moment human beings lacked their own government and had to fall back on their minimum rights, no authority was left to protect them and no institution was willing to guarantee them. . . . [What was] supposedly inalienable, proved to be unenforceable."[39]

The democratic transformations of the late eighteenth century paradoxically gathered an increasingly mobile population, one no longer tied to the soil, into populations fictively tied to a nation. As Robert Wiebe brilliantly discerned, systematized citizenship had great advantages for the state: it simplified taxation, and it provided an identifiable pool of male citizens vulnerable to military conscription. And in these redefinitions, it might be added, distinctions between those who belonged to a state and those who lacked one were invented, elaborated, and expanded.[40]

In the United States, where the foundations were weaker, nation-state building did not go as far as it did in France, which in 1792 began to construct a new civil order in which citizenship required a stabilized personal identity; criteria of residence, parentage, age, and status were regularized, even extending to reshaping naming practices, such as those of Jews, that were regarded as exotic.[41] Even in the more relaxed United States, however, state building and its centralization was key—that is the struggle, after all, between the Articles of Confederation and the federalist coup that made the Constitution. Were you inside the new polity? Outside? By 1856, Congress had asserted the exclusive right to issue passports.[42]

The process of constructing the nationally integrated state—the state that defined the rights of citizens and simultaneously defined who was to be excluded—stretched out across the long nineteenth century, from the confederation of colonies that made a revolution against Britain at the end of the eighteenth century to the state that was Britain's defender in 1917.

By the middle of the eighteenth century, the Swiss scholar Emmerich de Vattel's *Law of Nations* had made explicit a century of political development that had taken place since the state system established by the Treaty of Westphalia, which ended the Thirty Years' War in 1648. States were to be understood as moral entities, creating a moral international law of their own devising. In that context, Eliga Gould has brilliantly argued, those who are outside the state system can easily be understood as being outside the law; the stateless float in an immoral world. The Empire for Liberty protected its citizens against statelessness in part by strengthening distinctions among those of European descent inside the borders and placing Indians, slaves, and pirates outside the protective boundary, in a stateless realm of problematic morality and ethics.[43] Giorgio Agamben's long meditation on the indispensability of absences to the definition of the state is helpful here; the state requires the "state of exception" to define what it is not.[44] The new concept of citizenship required its opposite, its state of exception. Nation building has its ironies; the stateless becomes the citizen's other.

Nowhere is absence—and the dependence of the state on its own construction of the stateless—more sharply limned than in the contradictory centrality of slavery to the new republic. Slaves' presence was central to the economy of the new republic, yet their absence from its protections was central to the agreement—the three-fifths compromise—that made the federal Constitution possible. Slaves were the exception to "We the People," frozen in Agamben's state of exception; they were, as Christopher Tomlins brilliantly puts it, "the living dead of the United States

Constitution," violently, shockingly disfigured by the clause that counted slaves as three-fifths of a person for the purposes of representation.[45]

In 1773, as Massachusetts patriots were challenging the Tea Act, enslaved inhabitants petitioned the legislature: "We have no Property. We have no Wives. No Children. We have no City. No Country." Three years before Thomas Jefferson was to articulate a fundamental right to the "pursuit of happiness," they described themselves repeatedly as "unhappy," described their "greatest unhappiness," and signed themselves, wistfully, "FELIX."[46] Like Arendt's stateless people, slaves were deprived

> of a place in the world which makes opinions significant and actions effective . . . belonging to the community into which one is born is no longer a matter of course and not belonging no longer a matter of choice. . . . They are deprived, not of the right to freedom, but of the right to action; not of the right to think whatever they please, but of the right to opinion.[47]

On the eve of the Civil War, voting with the majority in *Dred Scott v. Sanford*—a decision that arguably helped to bring the war into being— Associate Justice Peter V. Daniel of Virginia stated what he took to be truth: that among Africans, "there never has been known or recognized by the inhabitants of other countries anything partaking of the character of nationality, or civil or political polity; that this race has been by all the nations of Europe regarded as subjects of capture or purchase; as subjects of commerce or traffic." His is a blunt definition of permanent statelessness.[48] The state of exception continued to define the boundaries of the nation, and it would take the explosion of civil war, and millions of deaths, to destabilize it.

Indians were also stateless against the Constitution, neither foreign nor domestic, existing in the interstices of the landscape and the law. Like the British before them, Americans chose definitions where it suited their interests. Sometimes the Indians were foreign, organized in force, led by chiefs, resembling a state. The new United States conducted treaties with Indians—some twelve between 1785 and 1819 with the Cherokee alone. "No one has ever supposed," Chief Justice John Marshall mused in 1830, "that the Indians could commit treason against the United States."[49]

But Americans could just as readily define Indians as savages, people who had no state formation to which recognition was due. In the Declaration of Independence, they figure only as "the merciless Indian Savages whose known rule of warfare, is an undistinguished destruction of all ages, sexes and conditions." Indians have no state; they are vaguely the "inhabitants of our frontiers." Thus no tribe was included as a party to the peace treaties among the United States, Britain, and France, even though the Indians of the Old Northwest had successfully defended their claim to lands north of the Ohio River. (What would it have meant to include the Indians directly in the peace settlement, already multinational, of 1783?) In 1847, Justice Roger Taney observed that "the native tribes . . . have never been acknowledged or treated as independent nations. . . . On the contrary, the whole continent was divided and parcelled out, and granted by the governments of Europe as if it had been vacant and unoccupied land."[50] By the late nineteenth century, even though treaties reserved vast expanses of land for Indians, maps in general circulation showed only the states of the United States, with no acknowledgment of Indian lands.

In 1830, in *Worcester v. Georgia*, Marshall admitted (his word) that the Cherokee, although not a foreign state, "yet, having the right of self government, they, in some sense, form a state . . . [but] they may not be admitted to possess the right of soil." They had, he thought, "a peculiar relation" to the United States.[51] It was indeed peculiar: forced into removal, their lands a state without soil, they truly constituted a "state of exception." For this exception, Marshall offered the convoluted concept of a "domestic dependent nation."[52] In that dependent nation, individuals had no reliable claims against the United States; locked into the landscape, they could not declare their autonomy. The authorization of removal, one Cherokee leader would try to persuade Congress, was a "scheme . . . to denationalize us."[53] And indeed it did. The Trail of Tears did not lead to vacant land; it led to lands already inhabited by other peoples, who had no reason to welcome the newcomers. The Fourteenth Amendment assigned citizenship to "all persons born or naturalized in the United States and subject to the jurisdiction thereof." In 1884, the Supreme Court ruled that an Indian born in the United States but within the geographic boundaries of tribal authority (already so undermined that it could offer little protection against the state) was not born "subject to the jurisdiction" of the United States and therefore was not a citizen at birth.[54] By 1903 it was established that Congress had plenary power to abrogate any Indian treaty. Native Americans lacked, in Arendt's words, "a place in the world which makes opinions significant and actions effective."

In a willful refusal to respect the relationship that Indians had with each other and with their lands, U.S. policymakers failed to acknowledge that while citizenship for Americans meant strengthening their civil and property rights, citizenship for Native Americans meant dispossession. Not until 1924 did all Indians get the right to vote; not until the New Deal was tribal authority grudgingly recognized within narrow limits.[55] Finally the stacked deck was reshuffled; the state mattered, and Indians' opinions mattered. Issues could be addressed, challenges could be seriously made. Indians did not always get their way, and still do not. But the challenges are carried on within the boundaries of the state. Sometime in the 1930s, it ceased to be reasonable to construe Indians as stateless.

The legal baggage carried from the colonial era into the republic included the concept of *coverture*, a set of rules and practices that linked married women to the state through their husbands, defining them as "covered" by their husbands' legal identity. The culture of coverture had no room for the concept that there might be limits to a husband's sexual access to his wife's body. It embedded the husband's control of the wife's body, property, and earnings in the heart of the marriage contract. Married women were thus extremely vulnerable under the law: as one judge in the Supreme Judicial Court of Massachusetts observed in 1805, "a married woman has no more political rights than an alien."[56] In this culture—and Americans were not peculiar; these practices persist in other nations into our own time—the common sense of the matter was that when a male citizen married a foreign woman, his citizenship stretched to embrace her. She did not even have to go through the process of naturalization. But when a woman citizen married a foreign man, she lost her citizenship, and, depending on the laws of the other country, statelessness loomed. Even President Ulysses S. Grant's daughter was denationalized when she married an Englishman in 1874, and it took a special act of Congress to reinstate her citizenship when she was widowed. "Are we aliens because we are women?" demanded abolitionist Angelina Grimke.[57]

No one definitively answered Grimke's question until 1907, when Congress passed a statute, and 1915, when the U.S. Supreme Court upheld it, that provided that the marriage of a woman citizen to a foreigner produced her denaturalization, even if she had been born in the United States. The Expatriation Act confirmed that hundreds of American-born women were no longer citizens. When World War I began, many hundreds of American-born women who had married men from countries with which the United States was at war were required to register as alien enemies.[58] Yet not all of their husbands' homelands embraced them as citizens. Once

American women seized the vote, one of the first things for which they used it was to press for the integrity of married women's citizenship.

At the turn of the twentieth century, in the aftermath of the Spanish-American War of 1898 (which stretched, in the Philippines, at least to 1902), the United States invented the ambiguous and unstable category of "noncitizen national" to describe a new status of people who lived under the U.S. flag without the full range of constitutional protections that flag normally carries. When the United States acquired the Philippines, Guam, Cuba, and Puerto Rico, Congress and the Supreme Court devised a series of related statutes, decisions, and conceptualizations that defined the status of these places in ways that simultaneously, as Christina Duffy Burnett eloquently puts it, took "control over territory while avoiding many of the responsibilities that sovereignty implies." Like other imperial powers—the British in India, Africa, and elsewhere; the Germans in Africa; the French in North Africa and Asia—the United States, through the Supreme Court, simultaneously asserted sovereignty while holding that these territories were "*neither* foreign *nor* part of the United States."[59] Despite the extension of numerous federal statutes to these territories, they could not look forward to developing into states. The U.S. Supreme Court drew a distinction between "incorporated territories," such as those that had been covered by the Northwest Ordinance of 1787, and "unincorporated territories," such as Guam and the Philippines. When Congress provided a Bill of Rights for the Republic of the Philippines after quashing an insurgency in 1902, it omitted the right to bear arms and the right to a jury trial. The Constitution did not follow the flag. At the borders, Congress exercised plenary power, largely excused from constitutional oversight by the courts.[60] In the aftermath of 1898, as the United States developed an empire, some geographical configurations—states—were defined by the United States as fully peopled by citizens; other geographical configurations were colonies, inhabited by subjects who were not, and could not be, citizens. The nation experimented with the creation of ambiguous spaces between the domestic and the foreign, between the national and the international, between sovereignty and subjugation. And in those spaces lay great potential for statelessness.

*   *   *

The mature modern state, John Torpey has written, can be said to have accomplished three defining seizures: the first, described by Marx, is the appropriation of the means of production from workers by capitalists; the second, described by Max Weber, is the appropriation of the means of violence from individuals by the state; and the third is the expropriation by the modern state of the legitimate means of movement across national boundaries. This last is a characteristic of state formation in the twentieth century, a century in which documentation of a relation to the state or its lack became a defining aspect of statelessness.[61]

In the early years of the twentieth century, before visas were required for entry into the United States, and when the United States understood itself to be in great need of new labor, most of the people who entered at Ellis Island lacked documents of any sort.[62] By contrast, the words "undocumented alien" now describe a condition of danger in relation to statelessness.

Throughout the century, grassroots movements for opening borders—to refugees, displaced persons, and the stateless after World War II; to a wider range of ethnicities in the remarkable immigration reforms of 1965—were in tension with skepticism and caution, embodied most obviously in the continued enforcement of the Chinese Exclusion Acts (not repealed until 1943), the Immigration Restriction statutes of the 1920s, the political restrictions of the McCarren-Walter Act of 1952, and the refusal of the United States to be party to a number of international conventions that included the stabilization of nationality, notably the 1954 Convention on Statelessness and the 1979 Convention on the Elimination of All Forms of Discrimination against Women, which the United States signed but has not ratified.

Statelessness continued to figure in American life in the twentieth century. The disruption of national boundaries devised by the Treaty of Versailles in the aftermath of World War I gave already well-established federal claims of plenary power at the borders considerably more frequent occasions on which to be deployed. The fascists' rise to power intensified the pressures. In this context, Fridtjof Nansen, the League of Nations's High Commissioner for Refugees, devised a passport that granted departure without the right of return and was widely used as an identification and travel document by the USSR and Eastern European countries. The Nansen Passport was a devil's bargain.[63] In its wake, Britain, France, and the United States hastened to stabilize and seal their borders against the millions of refugees and stateless whom the post-Versailles remapping of the European landscape created.[64] But what contemporaries called "nationality problems" entered anyway. It was the fault of the airplane, one political scientist dourly reflected in 1930, for exacerbating population movements and heightening the visibility of the vulnerable.[65]

The United States Immigration Act of 1924 reduced entry into the United States by some 85 percent of what it had been on the eve of World War I. Once the statute was backed by enforcement mechanisms, Mae Ngai writes, deportation "amounted to permanent banishment under threat of felony prosecution." The clash between the new statute and the explosive aftermath of the war meant that the difference between the immigrant and the refugee began to blur; even more blurred became the difference between the refugee and the stateless. Fleeing the Nazis, thousands of stateless Jews begged for sanctuary and were turned back at the U.S. borders.[66]

The forced displacements of the 1940s from World War II and the Cold War that followed it—in Europe, in India/Pakistan, in the Middle East—turned uncountable numbers of people into refugees (between seven and eleven million, it is estimated, for Europe alone). Most of these "displaced persons" were not technically stateless, since they were entitled to the passports of their home countries, but few could safely return there. Nearly a quarter-million Jewish displaced persons (DPs) were in zones occupied by the Allies in Germany, Austria, and Italy in early 1946. Those from Germany or Austria had been denationalized by the Nazis and were technically stateless; those from Poland, where a pogrom killed forty Jews in 1946, had good reason to refuse to return. The response of the United States ranged from hostile to guarded; it was understood to be a generous gesture when President Harry Truman reserved to DPs half the quotas already in place for immigrants from Europe and allowed NGOs (as well as individuals) to certify that they would not become a public charge. Even so, barely five thousand DPs, less than 10 percent of total European immigrants, entered the United States that year. Only in 1948, after intensive lobbying and much legislative struggle, did Congress authorize a capacious statute that authorized the admission of two hundred thousand over and above immigration quotas in two years (extended for another two years and another two hundred thousand visas in 1950). Even then, the State Department and Immigration and Naturalization Service dragged their collective feet, understanding themselves, as historian Roger Daniels puts it, to be "gatekeepers whose function was to 'protect' America from foreign contagion." Among those admitted, only about 15 percent were Jewish, many of whom were stateless.[67]

In the twentieth century, until well after World War II, it was common practice for married women to travel on their husbands' passports. The implications—that husband and wife would always be together, that she would not leave the country without him—are harmless only in times of peace and quiet. Suspicion of foreigners soaked the political atmosphere during World War I and in the years that followed; restrictive immigration legislation in the 1920s and its even more restrictive interpretation in the 1930s was supplemented by major decisions of the U.S. Supreme Court that made people of various nonwhite and non-African ethnicities ineligible for naturalization and enforced these rulings retroactively.

The Cable Act, passed in 1922 in the midst of a movement for immigration restriction, secured married women's nationality—up to a point. If an American woman married a foreign man who was himself eligible for citizenship, but went overseas with him to live, she lost her citizenship; if she wished to return (perhaps as a widow), she would need to naturalize (that is, she could not reclaim her original birthright citizenship), and she would first have to enter under the immigrant quota of her husband's nation. She could not pass her own American citizenship to her children.[68]

Despite the Cable Act's promise to stabilize the nationality of native-born women, should such a woman marry a man who was *ineligible* for citizenship (as were people from China; Japan was added in 1922, "Hindus" in 1923, and Filipinos in 1925), she was considered to have renounced her citizenship and could not easily reclaim it if the marriage ended in death or divorce.[69] When the Supreme Court declared in 1923 that Hindus could not be naturalized, Mary Das's naturalized husband lost his citizenship, and she was retroactively denied a passport even though she had been born in the United States. The only advice the State Department (still thinking in the old concepts that linked married women's identity with their husbands') had to offer was that she might consider divorcing her husband or remaining stateless while she searched for some other country to be naturalized in. She was, she wrote in an angry essay published in *The Nation*, "A Woman without a Country."[70]

Women from nations that expatriated them when they married an alien—countries that then included Britain and Canada, and still include some states that impose an automatic change in nationality status on women who marry foreigners[71]—could become temporarily stateless when they married American men after the passage of the Cable Act. "Women without a Country Are in Straits from the New American Nationality Law" was the headline of an article in the *New York Times* in 1922. And, writes Candice Bredbenner, "most resident immigrant women who married Americans after the passage of the Cable Act became stateless on debt due from her late allies, if America will forego her claims upon Britain of half that amount.

America's capacity to cancel is enormously greater. Her national income is expanding at the rate of £2,000,-000,000 a year, equal to half the total national income of Great Britain. She will pay off her internal war debt in twenty-five years. America has a great opportunity to be magnanimous; and magnanimity will be twice blessed—it will bless her and the world at large.

England, at great risk to herself, has reestablished the gold standard. It is important for America that this should be stabilized and that other countries should get back to it. The cancelation of the European debts to America would materially assist that end. It would save America from the otherwise inevitable inflation. If America insists upon the payment by Europe of £80,000,000 a year on account of these debts, there is bound to be such a disturbance of her economic life as will cost her far more than she receives from this source.

The best side of the American nation cannot feel comfortable in the thought that the tribute she is levying upon her late allies is keeping the workers in those countries for the next sixty years on short rations. It would be more in harmony with the altruistic sentiment which swept over the American continent ten years ago for her now to say that, out of her great abundance, she will make this further contribution to the restoration of the economic prosperity of the world.

A Woman Without a Country

By MARY K. DAS

I AM an American-born woman. My ancestors came from England to America in the year 1700. By the existing double standard of the American Government, I am not only rendered alien, but a stateless alien. My husband, a Hindu, was a naturalized American citizen when I married him. He had secured his certificate of naturalization from a United States District Court in 1914, having previously resided in the United States for eight years. The United States State Department three times gave him passports with which he traveled all over the world. He still holds his American naturalization certificate, but today he is told by the State Department that he was never an American citizen, because "the judges, who during the last quarter of a century or more naturalized Hindus to American citizenship, by due process of law, did not know the meaning of the United States naturalization laws, and so these judges from all parts of the United States acted illegally." This interpretation is based upon a recent decision rendered by a United States Supreme Court judge who is himself a naturalized citizen, who held that "high-caste Hindus are not white persons according to the commonly accepted meaning of the term, and thus are ineligible to American citizenship." Before we were married my husband went to several lawyers and asked if I stood the least chance of losing my citizenship in marrying him. These experts, one a former adviser to the State Department, told him that this could never happen, because the United States could not and would never apply a Supreme Court decision retroactively.

Last year when I asked the State Department for a passport to go to Europe my request was refused on the ground that I was "no longer an American citizen, having lost my American citizenship by [my] marriage with an alien ineligible to citizenship." This I disclaimed, and still disclaim, for at the time of my marriage and up to the present day my husband is in possession of his naturalization papers. But by fiat of the State Department my husband and I are stateless.

The amazing stand taken by the United States authorities is "that Hindus who are deprived of their American citizenship revert to their former British status." Is this stand due to total ignorance of the British law? The British law says that any British subject who renounces British nationality willingly, by naturalization into any other country, cannot revert to British citizenship automatically, in case the said subject wishes to do so; but must be naturalized according to British law, after living at least five years in some British territory. Now, it is apparent that without a passport an alien cannot enter British territory for the purpose of taking up residence; and there is no record of British authorities offering safe conduct to an Indian who has become an American citizen and then been deprived of American citizenship, to go to British territory, under promise of renaturalization in the course of time. Requests to the British Government to enter British territory, made by Indians who have lost their American citizenship, have either been refused or no notice has been taken of them. So when the American Government arbitrarily takes from us (American women and Hindus naturalized as American citizens) our American citizenship and protection, violating the scraps of paper given us in the form of naturalization certificates, it takes from us our safety and our standing in any community no matter where we may take refuge.

According to the Cable Act, an American woman marrying an alien ineligible to citizenship loses her American citizenship. An American man may marry a Japanese, Chinese, Hindu—any woman he pleases. To do so does not lose him his citizenship. But an American woman is penalized when she exercises this right granted the American man. She may marry a Negro from Africa and not lose her American citizenship, but if she marries a Hindu, Chinese, or Japanese, however high his reputation as a scholar, she loses her American citizenship. I feel that an American woman should not be penalized for marrying the person she loves. Marriage is not a matter of convenience; it has a spiritual bearing and none has the right to dictate the inner life of an individual.

The National Woman's Party has sought to remedy the situation by amending the Cable Act, but the House Immigration Committee refused to report out the bill. Some Representatives and Senators, members of the Immigration Committees of the two houses of Congress, hold that the ideal of Americanism should keep any American woman from marrying any foreigner, particularly an Asiatic. One Senator said that he would do all he could to defeat any amendment to the Cable Act which would give the right of American citizenship to any American woman marrying any foreigner. The American patriots who think that such provincialism is Americanism would do well to remember what Theodore Roosevelt said on an allied topic:

Our nation fronts on the Pacific, just as it fronts on the Atlantic. We hope to play a constantly growing part in the great ocean of the Orient. We wish, as we ought to wish, for a great commercial development in our dealings

In this essay, Mary K. Das emphasized her family's American lineage and her own fury: "An American man may marry a Japanese, Chinese, Hindu—any woman he pleases. To do so does not lose him his citizenship. . . . I feel that an American woman should not be penalized for marrying the person she loves. Marriage is not a matter of convenience; it has a spiritual bearing and none has the right to dictate the inner life of an individual" (The Nation, August 4, 1926, 105).

with Asia; and it is out of the question that we should permanently have such development unless we freely and gladly extend to other nations the same measure of justice and good treatment as we expect to receive in return. . . . I ask fair treatment for the Japanese, as I would ask fair treatment for Germans, Englishmen, Frenchmen, Russians, or Italians.

I am not pleading today for the right of Asiatics to become American citizens. But I hold that the attitude of the United States Government toward Hindus who were naturalized before the adverse Supreme Court decision is worse than the alleged attitude of Soviet Russia or the Mexican Government, against which the United States State Department so bitterly complains, in enacting retroactive laws depriving Americans of their vested rights. The State Department, declaring that Hindus who were naturalized by United States judges according to due process of law, to whom naturalization certificates were given upon the authority of the United States Government, are no longer American citizens, is violating a solemn contract. Has the American Government fallen to such a state of degradation that to it the civil rights of its citizens have less value than property rights?

In the Driftway

THE noon sun was hot on the Corne d'Or, but the Drifter had ordered the awning taken off his caique, and it was his own fault if he sweltered among the embroidered cushions. His boatman must be even hotter, bending over the flask-handled, fork-bladed oars, but he still beamed on the Drifter and talked Turkish to him. They passed the fleet of fishing boats, anchored close together with their masts crowded like pins on a cushion. From the right bank came the notes of a song that sounded suspiciously like "Jesus Wants Me for a Sunbeam"; in front of a large cross-topped building a column of girls was parading melodiously. The Drifter reflected that tolerance can be overdone. Yet the forest of minarets on the Stamboul side was still intact after generations of missionary songs. Perhaps tolerance is good strategy after all.

* * * * *

"LANGUAGE first originated in the use of gestures by primitive man; it is now used by children and idiots and in foreign countries, as in ordering a meal in Paris." The Drifter remembered his favorite definition, the effect of three months' study of psychology on the brain of a college student, as he sought to explain to his boatman that he would like to go ashore and eat lunch. He pointed to his mouth, he pointed to the shore, he talked English with a questioning inflection. He has a theory that any two humans, given time, can evolve a common language. Once he heard a fellow-American, abandoning words in despair, do complicated business with an Italian chauffeur by nothing but a series of eloquent grunts. This time too the boatman understood. He selected a little cafe with a balcony over the water and put the Drifter ashore.

* * * * *

COFFEE has the same name in all languages, and it is the national drink of Turkey. But the Drifter was hungry. In vain he asked for food in all the languages in which he is able to ask for food; in vain he appealed to the narghile-smokers industriously puffing at their tubes, while a yard or so away their fire burned and caldron bubbled. Better to interrupt a man at his pra his bath, his love-making than at his narghile. The D tested his theory thoroughly and gestured like a primitive man indeed. The more he pointed to his m the more coffee he was given. Nothing seemed fa from the Turkish mind at half past twelve o'clock food. But Constantinople is an international city an streets are full of amateur interpreters. Before lon proprietor led a boy to the Drifter's table. "Y a-t-il de manger?" asked the Drifter hopefully. The boy shoo head. "Etwas zu essen?" No better. It was the turn. "Russky?" he suggested. The Drifter pondere at last found three words: "Ya chochu yest—I want to The boy smiled and explained. The proprietor was prised but equal to the occasion. He led the Drifter, many a bow, to the kitchen of his house next door, a him select the materials for his own salad. If the D had insisted he might even have mixed it.

THE DRIF

Correspondence

Officially Pure

To THE EDITOR OF THE NATION:
    SIR: It will interest Nation readers to know th librarian of the Congressional Library is doing his or he for the cause of purity. Havelock Ellis's "Studies in th chology of Sex" cannot be taken out of the library. ' of that kind aren't circulated indiscriminately," the le the desk, age 25, told me.
    Washington, D. C., July 14   JOHN T. MOUT

Saving Germany for Chewing Gu

To THE EDITOR OF THE NATION:
    SIR: The latest development in the Americanizat Europe prompts me to make the following remarks: A "saved" Germany for democracy. Then you sent G Dawes and Mr. Young to save German industry from ruptcy and the German workingman from a fair wage. latest missionary is Mr. Wrigley. He is out to save G teeth and German digestion. And German newspapers, ćars, subways, back fences, and store windows are full well-known "Spearmint" signs. Verily, the American of Europe proceeds apace. With the help of a few more plans for other countries and a few more shiploads of c gum, you will soon have Europe safely in your vest poc
    Berlin, Germany, July 5   LIESBETH WEI

Oliver Cromwell on Prohibition

To THE EDITOR OF THE NATION:
    SIR: While we are having the truth about Puri and prohibition of alcoholic beverages, is it not to the p rake out these sentences from one of Oliver Cromwell's l
    Your pretended fear lest Error should step in, is the man who would keep all the wine out the country men should be drunk. It will be found an unjust unwise policy to deprive a man of his natural libe upon the supposition he may abuse it. When he d abuse it, judge.
The curious, and the dubious, will find this passage in th written by Cromwell to the Governor of Edinburgh c tember 12, 1650.
    Berkeley, California, July 14   B. H. LEH

their wedding days and remained so until they earned a naturalization certificate."[72] In the United States in the interwar years, "woman" was a category of instability and potential statelessness; most individual cases of statelessness involved women and arose from marriage.[73]

As fascists moved from harassing Jews to murdering them, naturalized women, many of them Jewish, desperately tried to bring husbands and fiancés into the United States during the 1930s. They organized themselves as the Citizen Wives Organization, established in an office by the Hebrew Immigrant Aid and Sheltering Society in New York. In the context of fascist expansion, the inability of American women, whether citizens by birth or by naturalization, to transmit their citizenship to their stateless children or husbands spelled danger. Even when the Naturalization Law was revised in 1930, its changes were not made retroactive; a citizenship that married women could take with them wherever they went was not fully achieved until the 1960s.[74]

The problematic national identity of married women, and their exposure to statelessness, was a key item on the League of Nations's human rights agenda. But the League's work was aborted by the onset of war. The American member of the League's Committee of Experts on the Legal Status of Women, Dorothy Kenyon, was deeply disappointed to lose the chance to pursue these questions, and after the war she worked hard, and successfully, to be appointed to its successor, the UN Commission on the Status of Women. Although red-baiting derailed Kenyon's UN career, she and her allies doggedly kept the issue alive. In 1957, the United Nations created a "Convention on the Nationality of Married Women," forbidding compulsory expatriation.[75] The issue was not solved. Signatories to the Convention on the Elimination of All Forms of Discrimination against Women (CEDAW), adopted in 1979, undertake to ensure that "neither marriage to an alien nor change of nationality by the husband during marriage" shall automatically change the nationality of the wife, force upon her the nationality of the husband, or render her stateless. But although the United States signed the treaty, Congress never ratified it. In any event, there is virtually no enforcement mechanism for any provision of CEDAW; in some nations today, women who marry foreign men lose their citizenship, exposing themselves and the children of their marriages to statelessness.[76]

Children—often subsumed in the category "women and children"—have had and continue to have their own specific vulnerabilities to statelessness.

In the United States, where "all persons born or naturalized in the United States and subject to the jurisdiction thereof, are citizens of the United States and of the State wherein they reside," children are citizens at birth. But the meanings of citizenship are different for children and adults, not least because children are spared or excused from the key rights and obligations of citizenship: to vote, to serve on a jury, to perform military service. The 1989 Convention on the Rights of the Child provides that every child (including children born to noncitizen parents in the territory of a state party to the convention) "shall be registered immediately after birth and shall have the right from birth to a name, [and] the right to acquire a nationality." It provides that "States Parties shall ensure the implementation of these rights . . . in particular where the child would otherwise be stateless." But the Convention, which the United States has signed but has not ratified, does not stipulate obligation to confer nationality, and there is no enforcement mechanism. Among the states that today grant nationality only through the father are Algeria, Bangladesh, Kuwait, and Saudi Arabia.[77]

A crudely drafted American statute of 1802 excluded foreign-born marital children of American fathers from citizenship. Had they the misfortune to be born in a nation in which citizenship followed blood rather than birth—a category that grew as the Code Napoleon spread—these children could find themselves without any citizenship at all. In 1855, it was American fathers (not mothers) who transmitted citizenship to their children, and that continued to be the case well into the 1930s.

When adults are deported or interned, their citizen children go with them. The most notorious example of this is the U.S. internment camps of World War II, where the birthright citizen children of Japanese-American parents (some of whom were themselves birthright citizens) were confined without recourse.[78] The Bracero Program of 1948–1964 involved several million Mexican men as temporary contract laborers; by the time it ended, many had built families in America. Their citizen children could not force a pause for reconsideration; they left with their parents. In the aftermath of 9/11, an uncounted number of citizen children have risked or actually faced the deportation of noncitizen parents.[79]

A Civil War statute provided that a deserter would lose his "rights of citizenship"; by the time it was embedded in the Nationality Act of 1940, the wording had been made so capacious that the deserter would simply lose his "citizenship." Over the course of World War II, some twenty-one thousand men were convicted of desertion from the army, and some seven thousand of them were separated from the service and rendered stateless. These figures do not include the navy and marines. The scope of the problem was not recognized until 1958, when a deserter applied for a passport. Deeply dismayed that the law conceded to "the military authorities complete discretion to decide who among convicted deserters shall continue to be Americans and who shall be stateless," Chief Justice Earl Warren wrote the ringing opinion in *Trop v. Dulles*:[80]

> Citizenship is not a license that expires upon misbehavior. . . . We believe . . . that use of denationalization as a punishment is barred by the Eighth Amendment [against cruel and unusual punishment]. . . . The punishment strips the citizen of his status in the national and international political community. . . . While any one country may accord him some rights . . . no country need do so because he is stateless. . . . In short, the expatriate has lost the right to have rights.[81]

Although he did not cite her, Warren had clearly read Arendt.

After the Illegal Immigration Reform and Immigrant Responsibility Act of 1996 required deportation for what immigration law referred to as aggravated felony convictions and defined as such felonies an expansive range of crimes, minor as well as serious, thousands of permanent legal residents were subject to deportation. If they were stateless, or came from nations with which the United States had no treaty of reciprocity (including Vietnam and, at the time, Cambodia), there was no obvious place to send them. In Seattle, Assistant Federal Public Defender Jay Stansell found an entire floor of the Federal Detention Center devoted to nearly two hundred prisoners who had prospect of neither freedom nor deportation. In the spring of 2001, a hundred such cases were brought together for appeal for habeas corpus proceedings and a limit to the indefinite detention to which they were subject. Among them was the stateless Kestutis Zadvydas, who had been born to Lithuanian parents in a refugee camp in Germany. He was not a citizen of Germany (which does not recognize *jus solis*) and not a citizen of Lithuania (or of Russia, which succeeded the former Soviet Union, of which Lithuania had been a part when he was born); nor had he ever been naturalized in the United States, although his family had moved there when he was eight years old. The crime for which he was convicted made him deportable after 1996, but no country would accept him. The 1954 Convention on Statelessness promises that all persons—it does not say all persons not convicted of crime—have a right to a nationality; but there is no practical provision for enforcing that promise.[82]

During the Supreme Court argument, while defending indefinite detention in response to a series of questions from Justice Ginsburg, Deputy Solicitor General Edwin Kneedler found himself saying, in an eerie reprise of Edward Everett Hale's Civil War novella *The Man without a Country*, that "one way to remove the alien [who has no country to go to] would be to put him on a boat." And when Stansell emphasized the vulnerability of one of the youthful prisoners—his inability to speak the language, his lack of contacts if he were to be sent back to Cambodia—Justice Antonin Scalia was skeptical: "It is up to you to find a country to get sent back to. The burden is not on us."[83]

But the Supreme Court ruled (although Scalia dissented) that although the attorney general "may" continue to detain aliens who present risks to the community, he does not have unlimited discretion.[84] "[O]nce an alien enters the country . . . the Due Process Clause applies to all 'persons' within the United States, including aliens, whether their presence here is lawful, unlawful, temporary or permanent." Stansell's clients were spared indefinite detention—a limbo not unlike statelessness—only until the administration found a place to which to deport them. Once a repatriation agreement was negotiated with Cambodia, some were deported to that country, where they knew no one, and whose languages they did not speak.[85]

Indefinite detention has long been the norm at the U.S. Naval Station at Guantánamo Bay, Cuba, which identifies itself as the United States's "oldest U.S. base outside the continental United States" and host to the "War on Terrorism Detainee Mission."[86] Guantánamo is now the prison for men captured in Afghanistan and elsewhere who are thought to have fought for al-Qaeda. In three separate decisions in 2004, justices of the U.S. Supreme Court expressed their suspicion of unlimited detention and simultaneously limited severely the ability of the detainees to test it. But these decisions were narrowly framed, and the general thrust of the Patriot Act of 2001, the proposals to strengthen it in 2003 (the most severe, which came to light only in a leaked draft, were never passed), and the Military Commissions Act of 2006, all make indefinite detention a familiar strategy. Some men have been held in indefinite detention for five years; some were in their teens when they were first imprisoned.[87] Indefinite detention may be our contemporary opposite of expulsion. Guantánamo, the island prison where the American flag flies, inhabited by men whose own nations cannot ensure them decent prisoner-of-war treatment, is today's floating prison of men without a country.

If citizenship is linked to work—as it is in Judith Shklar's understanding of citizenship as the "right to earn," T. H. Marshall's understanding of social citizenship as the right to basic material well-being, and Alice Kessler-Harris's understanding of economic citizenship—then what citizenship can be claimed by those trapped jobless in the underworld of the globalized marketplace?[88] It is estimated that 14,500 to 17,500 people are illegally trafficked in or through the United States each year against their will, despite the Thirteenth Amendment's strictures against involuntary servitude. The Victims of Trafficking and Violence Protection Act of 2000, and its steady reauthorization and expansion, most recently in 2005, recognizes something of the scope of the problem in the United States. As of 2008, thirty-three states had laws making trafficking a state felony offense.[89] Anthropologist Aihwa Ong has argued that in the last generation, "the norms of good citizenship in advanced liberal democracies have shifted from an emphasis on duties and obligations to the nation to a stress on becoming autonomous, responsible choice-making subjects who can serve the nation best by becoming 'entrepreneurs of the self.'"[90] Those who lack resources—and 70 percent of the world's poor are women—are almost bound to fail that entrepreneurial challenge.[91]

Labor trafficking is the third-largest international criminal enterprise, behind only drug and arms smuggling, producing billions of dollars in profit. (The United Nations Protocol to Prevent, Suppress, and Punish Trafficking in Persons, Especially Women and Children is the internationally agreed upon definition.)[92] Although this traffic involves both men and women, the largest categories by far are in the kinds of work in which women are most likely to be found: domestic service; marginally skilled labor in hotels, restaurants, and nursing homes; and sex work. So long as labor contracts are taken at face value, the realities of trafficking remain masked. Ambiguous borders cloud the margins between Ong's "mobile homo economicus" and the trafficked, between the trafficked and the refugee, between the refugee, the "essentially stateless," and the stateless.

Contemporary vulnerabilities to "essential statelessness" were recently made transparent by the largest successfully prosecuted human trafficking case in U.S. history, involving over two hundred Vietnamese and Chinese women and some men imported to work in near-slavery conditions at the Daewoosa garment factory in American Samoa. Opened in 1999, Daewoosa held contracts with several important American retailers of clothes, including JC Penney and Sears, which could import from Samoa at lower tariffs with products labeled "Made in American Samoa." In April 2002, the High Court of American Samoa awarded $3.5 million (approximately thirteen thousand dollars, or two years' salary, each—far less than minimum wage) to more than two hundred workers; in 2003, the U.S. Federal District Court in Hawaii sentenced Kil Soo Lee, the proprietor of the by then defunct factory, to forty years in prison for extortion, money laundering, and—in a rare invocation of the Thirteenth Amendment— "involuntary servitude." The workers who were imported into American Samoa were technically citizens of Vietnam and of China, but they had little hope of protection from either country. The government of Vietnam acknowledged its own general mandate to assist Vietnamese nationals residing overseas, but as in many countries where it is national policy to encourage labor migration, government ministries and offices have multiple responsibilities, and overseeing or protecting the interests of workers usually falls below expanding labor exports and serving the interests of labor exporters. No Vietnamese consul visited the Daewoosa factory.[93] In this context, and when home states decline to protect them effectively, the UNHCR's conclusion of February 2006 is especially apt: trafficked women and children are "essentially stateless."[94]

* * *

The dream of a cosmopolitan citizenship—and the nightmare of its absence in statelessness—in American history is a complicated one, whose presence we are only just beginning to acknowledge. In trying to understand the expansive meanings embedded in the status of statelessness, we come to consider not only questions of who can be a citizen and on what terms but also some of the instabilities of public/private distinctions, of the way the personal and the political merge, and of the way in which the state regularly relies on the microclimates of the workplace, the bedroom, and the birthing room to sustain national citizenship.

Behind the public story is a backstory of distrust: a distrust of the future complexities of sorting out the claims of thousands of people who might well conclude that they can claim citizenship retroactively, and a distrust of women as tricksters, accompanied by a belief that men should be able to pick and choose for which of their children they will be responsible. These issues have such resilience not only because they are stereotypes based on actual trends but also because these issues are rooted in concepts that reach back to the founding era, when the property regime of coverture ensured that married women's relation to the state was filtered through their husbands.

The categories that define who is vulnerable to statelessness have been refigured since the 1930s, when Catheryn Seckler-Hudson sought to provide it with a syntax. Statelessness is not a static conceptual matter; it now breaks along the fault lines of perceptions of state security, race and ethnicity, ideal workers, and gender. Indeed, the fault lines are not themselves always clear. Hannah Arendt has reminded us of the difficulty of distinguishing between stateless refugees and "normal" resident aliens. "Who," she asked, "will guarantee human rights to those who have lost their nationally guaranteed rights?" Statelessness is now created through the daily decisions of captors in prisons such as Abu Ghraib and Guantánamo, who decide who is entitled to the protections of international law and who is not. Today's transnational market in domestic labor is filled with people who are not technically refugees, but who are homeless in that they have left their home country, who are citizens of one country but undocumented aliens where they work. By far most of these people are women, many of whom, like Miss Saigon, slide all too easily into the international traffic in women and into the United Nations High Commissioner for Refugees' understanding of "ineffective nationality" and "de facto statelessness." In this volatile political context, statelessness is no longer so easily measured only by the presence or absence of a passport; it is a state of being, continually produced by new and increasingly extreme forms of restriction and by the creation of new categories of stateless human beings.

And so it may be that—from the days of the founding to our own time—the state has needed the stateless: needed them at some deep level, to construct what it is not; needed them for its own definition, to stabilize its own borders and boundaries. It is widely understood—thanks not least to Nansen and to Arendt—that statelessness haunted twentieth-century Europe. Statelessness has also haunted the United States throughout its history, from its oxymoronic founding as a republic of slavery to our own time. "Once they had left their homeland they remained homeless; once they had left their state they became stateless; once they had been deprived of their human rights they were rightless." Arendt's heartbreaking words conspicuously begin not with a crime but with an apparently neutral behavior: "once they had left." It is the leaving that makes the individual or community vulnerable, whether or not the leaving was itself voluntary. But if, for Arendt, twentieth-century statelessness was triggered by a single act, statelessness today, in particular in relation to the borders and borderlands of the United States, is most usefully understood not only as a status but as a practice, made and remade in daily decisions of presidents and judges, border guards and prison guards, managers and pimps. The stateless are the citizen's other. The stateless serve the state by embodying its absence, by providing frightening models of the vulnerability of those who lack sufficient awe of the state. The stateless serve the state by signaling who will not be entitled to its protection, and throwing fear into the rest of us.

And yet.

Is it possible to end not with the nightmare, but with the dream? Is it possible, still, to imagine a citizenship of the world?

Herman Melville imagined it—Melville, who had been a seaman on an immigrant ship, fleeing the Ireland of the Great Hunger. "Let us waive that agitated national topic," he wrote in *Redburn*,

> as to whether such multitudes of foreign poor should be landed on our American shores; let us waive it, with the one only thought, that if they can get here, they have God's right to come; though they bring all Ireland and her miseries with them. For the whole world is the patrimony of the whole world; there is no telling who does not own a stone in the Great Wall of China.[95]

Melville's dream has recently been invoked by Aristide R. Zolberg, professor of political science emeritus at the New School in New York, whose connection with the subject was forged when he himself was a child hidden from the Nazis. Zolberg calls on us to address the central asymmetry in international human rights law: if indeed "everyone has the right to leave any country, including his own," we need the concomitant principle: "Everyone has the right to enter any country." The world was made better in 1990, "when Hungary opened up its border to Austria, providing to masses of East German vacationers the possibility of driving their sputtering Trabants to freedom, and the processes unleashed by this turn of events amounted to a major turning point in world history." Zolberg muses, "the strict confinement of individuals to membership in the states under whose jurisdiction they happened to be born negates their being as members of a common species."[96]

Now, Zolberg is no fool, and he recognizes that "under present world conditions, in the absence of border controls, the world's affluent countries would be quickly overwhelmed by truly massive flows of international migrants in search of work, social benefits and safety. . . . The prospect imposes a major constraint on the application of the Melville principle." But at the very least, we can shift our starting point, searching for an ethical immigration policy that places the burden of proof on those who would restrict.

The end of the Cold War and the successes of the European Union have turned much critical attention toward inherited understandings of citizenship; whatever "globalization" is understood to be, it is having an impact on the way people understand their relationship to the jurisdictions in which, as Zolberg says, "they happened to be born." Identities shift and fracture; the relation of national identity to religious, gender, class, and ethnic identities blurs and re-forms. Millions of people right now are experiencing what it is like to be members of a nation and the European Union simultaneously. It may be possible to feel our way into a meaningful cosmopolitanism, in which a robust international law protects human rights in reliable ways, and reliance on the vagaries of the single nation-state is less essential. We are in the early days, but we can watch the dream expand in the European Union, which every day offers fresh examples of federalism in practice and of the framing of a robust and expansive international law of equity and human rights, practiced in courts of relatively recent invention: the International Court of Justice, the European Court of Human Rights, the International Criminal Court. As the European Union embraces new members, including Bulgaria and Romania, it may well be that we are living in the early years of a new and vibrant cosmopolitanism. We may not be able to assess this for fifty years; even a century is not long as these things go—we are in a time frame in which we repeatedly invoke the Treaty of Westphalia, after all. The United States itself has deep ambivalence toward these developments—being "often at the forefront of efforts to redress human rights abuses and to bring the world under the power of international law," as Harlan Cohen has observed, while at the same time being "equally careful to remain outside such legal schemes."[97] That the United States hesitates to play a leading role in this enterprise is to be regretted, but already we see a telling rhetorical shift, from talk of "civil rights"—rights that rely on the nation for maintenance—to "human rights," with the claim that the validity stretches

King Gustavus V of Sweden presents the Nobel Prize for
Literature to Pearl Buck, December 1938. Courtesy of Pearl S. Buck
International, www.pearl-s-buck.org.

throughout humanity. "The time may have come once again," writes
Ralph W. Mathisen, thinking of the expansive imperial citizenship of
Rome, "for a form of citizenship unburdened by the baggage of nation-
alism or political allegiances."[98]

While we are engaged in constructing an authentically capacious citizenship, we can be strengthened by the example of efforts by individuals
to forge such a citizenship out of their own desperation. So let me end as
I began, now with a third version of Madame Butterfly, this one by the
novelist Pearl Buck; this one written in 1952; this one stretching across the
globe, engaging the Atlantic as well as the Pacific; this one with a wistfully

optimistic ending (which is the more believable for its imperfection and the deep sadness at its core).

Josui is a modernized Cho-Cho-San, who navigates between the United States and Japan in the context of the postwar occupation in Pearl Buck's mesmerizing novel *The Hidden Flower*.[99] Married by Japanese rite in Japan, despite her skeptical family, Josui actually goes to the United States to marry her American soldier under American law, but discovers that he is from Virginia, where interracial marriage is illegal, as it would be until 1967. His wealthy family pressures him—threatening the loss of his inheritance—should he move with Josui to New York, and he capitulates to them, abandoning her (as Pinkerton and Chris, in their different ways, abandoned their commitments to their Asian lovers). The scion of the First Families of Virginia is humiliated in the readers' eyes as spineless, unreliable, and without ethics. While Josui is pregnant with the child of her faithless American "husband," she is wooed by her Japanese former suitor—himself a fine young man, eager to enter the modern world, who has remained loyal and loving during her absence. But he cannot find the strength to bear the shame that in his society would accompany not only marrying a divorced woman but also raising the biracial child of her first husband. He will marry her, but not if she brings the child back to Japan. And so Josui returns to America, to Los Angeles, as far away from Virginia as she can get. She gives birth to her son in a charity clinic. In a marvelous twist of fate, she is saved from giving him up for anonymous adoption by the intervention of a refugee Jewish woman physician, who has lost all that made her life worthwhile in the Holocaust, but whose heart is stirred by Josui's infant. The doctor adopts the infant, who is key to her new life; Josui can return to Japan a respectable woman to make a new life of her own. The exemplars of the ethics of a cosmopolitan world are these two women—the Butterfly who finds a way to ensure her child's future without having to kill herself; the survivor of the Holocaust who stretches her hands across the Pacific, across boundaries of language, race, and nation. Together they will make a world in which state boundaries are less important than ethics and love.

NOTES

This article was originally published in the *American Historical Review*, February 2007. In its original version, it was offered as the Harald Vyvyan Harmsworth Memorial Lecture at Oxford University in 2006 and as the Presidential Address to the American Historical Association in 2007. These notes have been updated to 2008.

I have many people to thank for their good counsel as this project developed over an extended period of time. My debts in the United Kingdom include invigorating conversations with Simon Newman, Jane Caplan, Desmond King, Matthew Nicholls, Peter Thompson, Nicholas Bamforth, Tony Badger, Matthew Gibney, Guy Goodwin-Gill, and Brad Blitz. I am grateful to the Citizenship Study Group at the Radcliffe Institute for Advanced Study in 2003 and to my colleagues at the University of Iowa Department of History and College of Law. Over the years, I have depended on the wise counsel of many scholars: Thomas Bender, Jacqueline Bhabha, G. Daniel Cohen, Nancy Falgout, Paula Fass, Michael Grossberg, Charles Hawley, Elizabeth Hillman, Frederick Hoxie, Stephen Legomsky, Gerda Lerner, Barbara Schwartz, Mark Sidel, Avi Soifer, Christopher Tomlins, Barbara Welke, and Marilyn Young, all of whom must be absolved from responsibility for any misinterpretations of mine. My greatest debt is to Mary Dudziak, who understood this project when it was just a gleam in my eye, and has offered wise counsel from the beginning.

1. Kaori O'Connor, "Introduction," in Pierre Loti, *Madam Chrysanthemum* (1901; repr. London: Kegan Paul International, 1985), viii, 335.

2. John Luther Long, *Madame Butterfly*, chap. 10, originally published in *Century Illustrated Magazine*, January 1898; reprinted in Maureen Honey and Jean Lee Cole, eds., *"Madame Butterfly" and "A Japanese Nightingale": Two Orientalist Texts* (New Brunswick, NJ: Rutgers University Press, 2002).

3. Vera Mackie, "Feminist Critiques of Modern Japanese Politics," in Bonnie Smith, ed., *Global Feminism since 1945* (London: Routledge, 2000), 182–83, 190. See also Chikako Kashiwazaki, "Citizenship in Japan: Legal Practice and Contemporary Development," in T. Alexander Aleinikoff and Douglas Klusmeyer, eds., *From Migrants to Citizens: Membership in a Changing World* (Washington, DC: Carnegie Endowment for International Peace, 2000), 434–71.

4. On this point I am grateful for the good counsel of Patricia Steinhoff and Robert Straton of the University of Hawaii. Straton, "Patriarchy in Meiji Japan" (Ph.D. diss., History, University of Hawaii, 2006).

5. Tuan Ahn Nguyen v. INS, 533 U.S. 53 (2001). I have written about this case in "Top Court Took a Step Backward on Gender Bias," *Boston Globe*, June 23, 2001, and "Toward a History of Statelessness in America," *American Quarterly* 57 (September 2005): 727–49. See also Kristin Collins, "When Fathers' Rights Are Mothers' Duties: The Failure of Equal Protection in *Miller v. Albright*," *Yale Law Journal* 109 (2000): 101–42.

6. Nguyen, supra note 5, 53, 60, 65–66, and Tuan Ahn Nguyen v. INS, Brief for Respondent, December 13, 2000, 10. This is a development that many feminists had supported, in an effort to strengthen the rights of unmarried birth mothers within the United States. See Lehr v. Robertson, 463 U.S. 248 (1983).

7. Nguyen, Brief for Respondent, supra note 6, 34. On the transmission of citizenship, good places to start are Sarah A. Adams, "The Basic Right of Citizenship: A Comparative Study," Center for Immigration Studies, Washington, DC, Summer 1994, http:// www.cis.org/articles/1993/back793.html (accessed January 11, 2007). An important survey with very helpful charts is Patrick Weil, "Access to Citizenship: A Comparison of Twenty-Five Nationality Laws," in T. Alexander Aleinikoff and Douglas Klusmeyer, eds., Citizenship Today: Global Perspectives and Practices (Washington, DC: Carnegie Endowment for International Peace, 2001), 17–35.

8. Nguyen, Brief for Respondent, supra note 6, 8.

9. Ibid., 19, 36.

10. Ibid., 42.

11. Nguyen, supra note 5, 65.

12. United States v. Ahumada-Aguilar, 189 F.3d.1121 (9th Cir. 1999).

13. Oral Argument in Nguyen, supra note 5. It should be emphasized that the minority was unpersuaded. In dissent, Sandra Day O'Connor stressed the principle—well established, she argued, in a long train of decisions stretching back to the 1970s—that "sex based statutes deny individuals opportunity." The dissenters did not agree that the statute ensured "that children who are born abroad out of wedlock have, during their minority, attained a sufficiently recognized or formal relationship to their United States citizen parent—and thus to the United States—to justify the conferral of citizenship upon them," since biological mothers could also be neglectful of their relations with their children. Nguyen, supra note 5, 79. That administrative convenience may not be used as justification for discrimination on the basis of sex had been established in Reed v. Reed, 404 U.S. 71 (1971), the first decision in which the Court found discrimination on the basis of sex to be a denial of equal protection of the laws. Ruth Bader Ginsburg, then thirty-eight years old, and ACLU director Mel Wulf wrote the brief for Sally Reed, who challenged the Idaho rule that when separated parents competed to serve as administrator of their dead son's estate, the father must be preferred.

14. Arjun Appadurai, "Patriotism and Its Futures," Public Cultures 5, no. 3 (1993): 423–24; Aihwa Ong, Flexible Citizenship: The Cultural Logics of Transnationality (Durham, NC: Duke University Press, 1999); Linda Bosniak, "Denationalizing Citizenship," in Aleinikoff and Klusmeyer, Citizenship Today, supra note 7, 237–52. A contradictory trend has been the effort of some wealthy individuals to relinquish their citizenship, and of the manipulations of corporate nationality to avoid paying taxes. A place to begin to consider this is G. Warren Whitaker and B. Dane Dudley, "Departing Is Such Sweet Sorrow: Giving Up U.S. Citizenship

or Residence," *Probate and Property* 19 (September/October 2005): 10–12. I am grateful to Stanford Ross for this point.

15. Among the many discussions of this subject are David A. Martin and Kay Hailbronner, eds., *Rights and Duties of Dual Nationals: Evolution and Prospects* (The Hague: Kluwer Law International, 2003), especially Martin, "Introduction: The Trend toward Dual Nationality," 3–18; and Aleinikoff and Klusmeyer, *From Migrants to Citizens*, supra note 3, especially Miriam Feldblum, "Managing Membership: New Trends in Citizenship and Nationality Policy," 475–49.

16. Afroyim v. Rusk, 387 U.S. 253 (1967); Martin, "Introduction," supra note 15, 6.

17. Stephen Legomsky, "Why Citizenship?" *Virginia Journal of International Law* 35 (1994–1995): 289. See International Covenant on Civil and Political Rights, Article 12.4, adopted by the United Nations 1966, entered into force 1976; adopted by the United States and entered into force 1992.

18. Consular officials are guided in this matter by the *Foreign Affairs Manual*, vol. 7, 012—Eligibility: Section c. The manual does provide, however, that "[w]hen an L[egal] P[ermanent] R[esident] applicant has exceptionally close and strong ties to the United States, and overriding humanitarian and compassionate grounds exist, [the consular official may] request guidance from CA/OCS/ACS about the propriety of providing the service, with the understanding that the host government may not, and is not obligated to, honor a request from the U.S. Government on behalf of such an individual." I am grateful to Charles Hawley, vice consul, U.S. Consulate General, Ho Chi Minh City, Vietnam, for this reference.

19. The 1954 Convention Relating to the Status of Stateless Persons entered into force June 6, 1960, but as of September 2006, only sixty states had signed and ratified it. The United States is not among them. The text is conveniently found on the UNHCR website: http://www.unhcr.org/protect/PROTECTION/3bbb0abc7.pdf (accessed January 11, 2007).

20. Andrew Brouwer for UNHCR, "Statelessness in Canadian Context: A Discussion Paper," July 2003, 23, http://www.unhcr.org/ protect/PROTECTION/40629ffc7.pdf (accessed January 11, 2007).

21. Basic Law, Section I, Basic Rights; Article 16: (1) "German citizenship may not be taken away. Citizenship may be lost only pursuant to a law, and against the will of the concerned person only if they do not become stateless as a result." Gisbert H. Flanz, ed., *Constitutions of the Countries of the World* (Dobbs Ferry, NY: Oceana Publications, 2003), n.p.

22. Universal Declaration of Human Rights, 1948, Article 15; Convention Relating to Stateless Persons, Article 32; UNHCR, "Statelessness in Canadian Context," supra note 20, 8.

23. On the inability of noncitizen parents to benefit from the citizenship of their child, see 8 U.S.C. section 1151(b)(2)(A)(I). An argument for reinterpreting

the Fourteenth Amendment was made by Peter H. Schuck and Rogers M. Smith in *Citizenship without Consent: Illegal Aliens in American Polity* (New Haven, CT: Yale University Press, 1985). More recently it was made in the Brief of Amicus Curiae Eagle Forum Education and Legal Defense Fund in Support of Respondents in *Yaser Esam Hamdi et al. v. Rumsfeld*, 542 U.S. 507 (2004). An effort to undermine birthright citizenship by statute was defeated in the immigration reform bill of December 2005. For an international overview, see Andrew Grossman, "Birthright Citizenship as Nationality of Convenience," Proceedings of the Third Conference on Nationality, Council of Europe, October 2004, http:// uniset.ca/naty/maternity/ (accessed January 11, 2007). In 1993, Representative Elton Gallegy of California sponsored a constitutional amendment that would have changed the language of the Fourteenth Amendment to read, "All persons born in the United States . . . of mothers who are citizens or legal residents of the United States . . . are citizens of the United States." See "The Birthright Citizenship Amendment: A Threat to Equality," *Harvard Law Review* 107 (1994): 1026–43. For a defense against the constitutional attack, see Walter Dellinger, "Statement before the Subcommittees on Immigration and Claims and on the Constitution of the House Committee on the Judiciary," December 13, 1995, http://www.usdoj.gov/ olc/deny.tes.31.htm (accessed January 11, 2007).

24. International conventions on statelessness were established in 1954 (Convention Relating to the Status of Stateless Persons) and 1961 (Convention on the Reduction of Statelessness). They can conveniently be found at http://www.ohchr. org/english/law/stateless .htm and http://www.ohchr.org/english/law/statelessness.htm (both accessed January 11, 2007). The UNHCR web page, http://www. unhcr.org/ protect/3b8265c7a.html (accessed January 11, 2007), framed as an answer to the question "Who is stateless?," is very helpful. It has this current definition: "A stateless person is someone who is not recognized by any country as a citizen. Several million people globally are effectively trapped in this legal limbo, enjoying only minimal access to national or international legal protection or to such basic rights as health and education." The UNHCR site also has convenient links to texts of conventions, case law, and UN reports. Among the most useful are UNHCR, "2005 Global Refugee Trends: Statistical Overview of Populations of Refugees, Asylum-Seekers, Internally Displaced Persons, Stateless Persons, and Other Persons of Concern to UNHCR," Geneva, June 9, 2006, http://www. unhcr.org/cgi-bin/texis/vtx/events/opendoc. pdf?tbl=STATISTICS&id=4486ceb12 (accessed January 11, 2007). A very good resource is UNHCR, "Statelessness in Canadian Context," supra note 20.

25. Carol Batchelor, "Stateless Persons: Some Gaps in International Protection," *International Journal of Refugee Law* 7, no. 2 (1995): 232–59.

26. Legomsky, "Why Citizenship?," supra note 17, 299–300.

27. Edward Everett Hale, *The Man without a Country* (Boston: Little, Brown, 1865), first appeared in the *Atlantic Monthly* in 1863. It was reprinted steadily

throughout the nineteenth century; several editions were timed to coincide with the Spanish-American War. For Hale's own reflections on the origins of the story, see E. E. Hale, "The Man without a Country," *Outlook* 59 (May 5, 1898): 116. There was another flurry of printings the year after Hale died in 1909. Prompted by World War I, Harvard Classics published its edition in 1917. On the edge of World War II, with the world filled with stateless people who had not denounced their country but who were desperate for sanctuary, the circulation was energized again by cheap copies distributed to schoolchildren. (That may be the form in which I first read it.) It was most recently reprinted by the Naval Institute Press in 2002.

28. Catheryn Seckler-Hudson, *Statelessness: With Special Reference to the United States (A Study in Nationality and Conflict of Laws)* (Washington, DC: Digest Press, 1934), published under the auspices of the Department of International Law and Relations of the American University Graduate School, with a preface by Ellery C. Stowell, who described statelessness as "an inexcusable anomaly" and an "intolerable condition."

29. Hannah Arendt, *The Origins of Totalitarianism* (New York: Harcourt, Brace, 1951).

30. For a judicious assessment, see Lex Takkenberg, *The Status of Palestinian Refugees in International Law* (Oxford: Clarendon Press, 1998), especially chap. 5: "Laws Relating to Stateless Persons." "Palestinians who were displaced as a result of the 1948 war are at the same time both refugees and stateless persons," Takkenberg observes. Their situation is made more unusual because they were not displaced from a state; the citizenship they once held in the British mandate was erased in 1948.

> Gradually, the legal and political impairment of being stateless, not belonging to a state, not having a national passport, became more significant. . . . Although the host states have generally provided permanent residency status to those refugees who took direct refuge . . . during and in the aftermath of the 1948 war . . . with the exception of Jordan, citizenship has generally not been available, not even for second or third generation refugees. (347–50)

Takkenberg concludes that "the entity 'Palestine' currently does not fully satisfy the international legal criteria of statehood. . . . Palestinians who have not acquired the nationality of a third state therefore continue to be stateless for the purpose of international law" (181). In *The Iron Cage: The Story of the Palestinian Struggle for Statehood* (Boston: Beacon Press, 2006), his judicious history of the impact of the absence of nationality, Rashid Khalidi observes that without a Palestinian state to maintain a central archive of documents, the historical record is greatly and permanently impoverished (xxxv). The UNHCR has been cautious about how it describes Palestinians, generally treating them as stateless but making rhetorical room for those who do not agree; thus the wording of the

UNHCR Global Appeal 2005 Middle East Regional Overview: "although Palestinians may not be considered as stateless since a Palestinian state has technically existed since the approval of UN General Assembly Resolution 181 (1947), some three million have been unable to return to their homes and their legal status has constantly been disputed by the Israeli government." UNHCR, *UNHCR Global Appeal 2005 Middle East Regional Overview*, December 2004, http://www.unhcr. org/pubs/pub4412b28d5c.pdf, 189. For a careful analysis of the ambivalent citizenship offered—and denied—to Palestinian Arabs resident in Israel between 1948 and 1952, see Shira Nomi Robinson, "Occupied Citizens in a Liberal State: Palestinians under Military Rule and the Colonial Formation of Israeli Society, 1948–1966" (Ph.D. diss., Modern Middle East History, Stanford University, 2005), chaps. 1 and 2.

31. A good place to begin is the UNHCR home page, especially "2005 Global Refugee Trends," http://www.unhcr.org/statistics/ STATISTICS/4486ceb12.pdf (accessed January 11, 2007).

32. For the definition of *"refoulement,"* see http://portal.unesco. org/shs/en/ ev.php-URL_ID=4145&URL_DO=DO_TOPIC&URL_SECTION=201.html (accessed January 11, 2007). The definition is included in the UN Convention Relating to the Status of Refugees of 1954, Article 33(1): "No Contracting State shall expel or return ('refouler') a refugee in any manner whatsoever to the frontiers of territories where his life or freedom would be threatened on account of his race, religion, nationality, membership of a particular social group or political opinion." But not all countries are parties to the UN Convention. See the important essay by Stephen H. Legomsky, "Secondary Refugee Movements and the Return of Asylum Seekers to Third Countries: The Meaning of Effective Protection," *International Journal of Refugee Law* 15 (2003): 567–677.

33. UNHCR, "The World's Stateless People: Questions and Answers," September 1, 2006, http://www.unhcr.org/basics/BASICS/452611862.pdf (accessed January 11, 2007). For the estimate of nearly 2.4 million stateless, see UNHCR, "Refugees by Numbers 2006 Edition," http://www.unhcr.org/cgi-bin/texis/vtx/basics/ opendoc. htm?tbl=BASICS&id=3b028097c#Stateless (accessed January 11, 2007). This report includes the observation that

> [t]he Universal Declaration of Human Rights underlines that "Everyone has the right to a nationality." Unfortunately, circumstances have conspired to deny many of that right, often leaving them in a Kafkaesque legal vacuum. . . . As a result of a concerted effort to improve the data provided by states, the number of stateless people identified as being of concern to UNHCR rose sharply from 1,455,900 in 2005 to 2,381,900 at the beginning of 2006. Although precise numbers are still difficult to estimate, UNHCR believes the actual total of people without a country to call their own may be at least 11 million.

34. See UNHCR, "Statelessness in Canadian Context," supra note 20, 16.

35. For a recent example, see Amy Waldman, "Sri Lankan Maids Pay Dearly for Perilous Jobs Overseas," *New York Times*, May 8, 2005, A1, detailing "exploitation so extreme that it sometimes approaches 'slaverylike' conditions, according to a recent Human Rights Watch report on foreign workers in Saudi Arabia."

36. Kevin Bales, *Disposable People: New Slavery in the Global Economy* (Berkeley: University of California Press, 2004), 9; stunning photographs are included in Andrew Cockburn, "21st Century Slaves," *National Geographic* 204 (September 2003): 2–25.

37. UNHCR, "Statelessness: Prevention and Reduction of Statelessness and Protection of Stateless Persons," February 14, 2006, http://www.unhcr.org/excom/EXCOM/43f1f6682.pdf (accessed January 11, 2007).

38. Jacqueline Bhabha, "Demography and Rights: Women, Children, and Access to Asylum," *International Journal of Refugee Law* 16 (2004): 232, 235; see also Bhabha, "'More Than Their Share of Sorrow': International Migration Law and the Rights of Children," *Saint Louis University Public Law Review* 22 (2003): 253 n. 1.

39. Arendt, *The Origins of Totalitarianism*, supra note 29, 291–93.

40. Robert Wiebe, "Framing U.S. History: Democracy, Nationalism, and Socialism," in Thomas Bender, ed., *Rethinking American History in a Global Age* (Berkeley: University of California Press, 2002), 239. For a similar perspective based on European examples, see John Torpey, *The Invention of the Passport: Surveillance, Citizenship, and the State* (Cambridge: Cambridge University Press, 2000), chap. 1.

41. For the process in France, see Gérard Noiriel, "The Identification of the Citizen: The Birth of Republican Civil Status in France," in Jane Caplan and John Torpey, eds., *Documenting Individual Identity: The Development of State Practices in the Modern World* (Princeton, NJ: Princeton University Press, 2001), 29–47.

42. James H. Kettner, *The Development of American Citizenship, 1608–1870* (Chapel Hill, NC: University of North Carolina Press, 1978), chap. 7; Torpey, *The Invention of the Passport*, supra note 40, 95.

43. Eliga H. Gould, "Zones of Law, Zones of Violence: The Legal Geography of the British Atlantic, circa 1772," *William and Mary Quarterly* 60 (2003): 471–510; and Gould, "States, Statelessness, and the Law of Nations in the British Atlantic, circa 1756" (unpublished paper, American Society of Legal History, 2005).

44. I am grateful to Christopher Tomlins for prompting my thinking on these matters. Giorgio Agamben, *Homo Sacer: Sovereign Power and Bare Life*, trans. Daniel Heller-Roazen (Stanford, CA: Stanford University Press, 1998), 18.

45. See Christopher Tomlins, "The Threepenny Constitution (and the Question of Justice)," *Alabama Law Review* 58.5 (2007: 979–1007).

46. "Petition of the Africans, Living in Boston, 1773," in James Oliver Horton and Lois E. Horton, *Slavery and the Making of America* (New York: Oxford University Press, 2005), 51. In a 1792 debate in the French Assembly, a deputy would

say, "slaves have no civil status. Only the free man has a city, a fatherland; only he is born, lives and dies a citizen." Quoted in Noiriel, "The Identification of the Citizen," supra note 41, 29.

47. Arendt, *The Origins of Totalitarianism*, supra note 29, 296.

48. Dred Scott v. Sanford, 60 U.S. 393 (1856). See also Mark Janis, "Dred Scott and International Law," *Columbia Journal of Transnational Law* 43 (2005): 763.

49. Worcester v. Georgia, 31 U.S. 515 (1832).

50. U.S. v. Rogers, 45 U.S. 567 (1846).

51. Worcester v. Georgia, supra note 49.

52. Cherokee Nation v. the State of Georgia 30 U.S. 1 (1831).

53. John Ross in 1840, quoted in William McLoughlin, *After the Trail of Tears: The Cherokees' Struggle for Sovereignty, 1839–1880* (Chapel Hill: University of North Carolina Press, 1993), 28. I am grateful to Frederick Hoxie for this reference, and for an extended conversation that helped me develop these ideas.

54. Elk v. Wilkins, 112 U.S. 94 (1884).

55. The best overview of these matters is to be found in R. David Edmunds, Frederick E. Hoxie, and Neal Salisbury, *The People: A History of Native America* (Boston: Houghton Mifflin, 2007).

56. Martin v. Commonwealth, 1 Mass. 347 (1805). I have discussed this case at some length in *No Constitutional Right to Be Ladies: Women and the Obligations of Citizenship* (New York: Hill and Wang, 1998), chap. 1.

57. House Joint Resolution no. 238, 55th Cong., 2nd sess. (May 18, 1898), 30 Stat. 1496; Angelina Grimke, *Appeal to the Women of the Nominally Free States* (Boston: Isaac Knapp, 1838), 19.

58. See Mackenzie v. Hare, 239 U.S. 299 (1915), upholding the denationalization of American women who married aliens. John L. Cable, *Decisive Decisions of United States Citizenship* (Charlottesville, VA: Michie Co., 1967), 41–42; *New York Times*, May 4, 1918.

59. Christina Duffy Burnett, "The Edges of Empire and the Limits of Sovereignty: American Guano Islands," *American Quarterly* 57, no. 3 (September 2005): 798, 795; my italics.

60. Downes v. Bidwell, 182 U.S. 244 (1901); note Justice John Marshall Harlan's eloquent dissent.

61. Torpey, *The Invention of the Passport*, supra note 40, 4.

62. Most of those who entered at Angel Island in San Francisco did have to meet the registration requirements of the Chinese Exclusion Acts.

63. For the Nansen Passport, see Arendt, *The Origins of Totalitarianism*, supra note 29, especially 281 n. 30; and Torpey, *The Invention of the Passport*, supra note 40, 127–29. When the Germans occupied France, they used the Nansen Passport for their own purposes, detaining all the Russians who had one.

64. Despite the severity of U.S. immigration restriction policies in the 1920s and thereafter, Catheryn Seckler-Hudson estimated that some 18.5 million

immigrants entered the United States in the first third of the twentieth century. Seckler-Hudson, *Statelessness*, supra note 28, 1.

65. Richard W. Flournoy Jr., "Nationality Convention Protocols and Recommendations Adopted by the First Conference on the Codification of International Law," *American Journal of International Law* 24 (1930): 467, quoted in Seckler-Hudson, *Statelessness*, supra note 28, 2.

66. I am indebted to Mae Ngai's remarkable essay "The Strange Career of the Illegal Alien: Immigration Restriction and Deportation Policy in the United States, 1921–1965," *Law and History Review* 21 (2003): 69–107, especially nn. 11 and 14. In her analysis, immigration restriction makes the illegal alien; she gives relatively little attention to statelessness, although it is implicit in the situation. On the results of Nazi denationalization, see the moving testimony by a man himself stateless, Marc Vishniac, *The Legal Status of Stateless Persons* (New York: American Jewish Committee, 1945), 34; and David S. Wyman, *Paper Walls: America and the Refugee Crisis, 1938–1941* (Amherst: University of Massachusetts Press, 1968).

67. Roger Daniels, *Guarding the Golden Door: American Immigration Policy and Immigrants since 1882* (New York: Hill and Wang, 2004), 108. For a full history of these developments, see Leonard Dinnerstein, *America and the Survivors of the Holocaust* (New York: Columbia University Press, 1982), especially chap. 8.

68. Candice Lewis Bredbenner, *A Nationality of Her Own: Women, Marriage, and the Law of Citizenship* (Berkeley: University of California Press, 1998), is indispensable on these matters. See chap. 4, especially 134–36.

69. Takao Ozawa v. U.S., 260 U.S. 178 (1922); U.S. v. Thind, 261 U.S. 204 (1923); and Toyota v. U.S., 268 U.S. 402 (1925).

70. *The Nation* 123 (August 4, 1926), cited in Bredbenner, *A Nationality of Her Own*, supra note 68, 135–36.

71. Department of International Protection, UNHCR, "Final Report Concerning the Questionnaire on Statelessness Pursuant to the Agenda for Protection," March 2004, http://www.unhcr.org/protect/ PROTECTION/4047002e4.pdf (accessed January 11, 2007).

72. For an American-born woman of Chinese descent who irretrievably lost her citizenship when she married a Chinese man, see Ex parte (Ng) Fung Sing, 6 F.2d 670 (1925), and the discussion in Bredbenner, *A Nationality of Her Own*, supra note 68, 136. For the exposure to statelessness of foreign women who married U.S. men, see ibid., 157.

73. Seckler-Hudson, *Statelessness*, supra note 28, 23–99.

74. Bredbenner, *A Nationality of Her Own*, supra note 68,174–83.

75. The original agenda of the UN Commission on the Status of Women expressed a grave concern for the risks of statelessness, and a fear for the fragility of married women's nationality. I have written about this aspect of Kenyon's career in "'I Was Appalled': The Invisible Antecedents of Second Wave Feminism," *Journal of Women's History* 14 (2002): 86–97.

76. Convention on the Elimination of All Forms of Discrimination Against Women, Article 9. Full text is found at http://www.un.org/ womenwatch/daw/ cedaw/cedaw.htm (accessed January 11, 2007). For an overview, see Weil, "Access to Citizenship," supra note 7, and on transmission of citizenship only through the father's bloodline, see Anita Fabos, "Transnational Practices of Citizenship and Gender Making for Sudanese Nationals in Egypt," *Northeast African Studies* 8 (2001): 47–68.

77. Convention on the Rights of the Child, 1989, Article 7. Full text is found at http://www.unhchr.ch/html/ menu2/6/crc/treaties/crc.htm (accessed January 11, 2007). This is more elaborate than the provision in the International Covenant on Civil and Political Rights, 1996, Article 24.3: "Every child has a right to a nationality," http://www.ohchr.org/english/law/ccpr.htm (accessed January 11, 2007). For a convenient digest of the rules of transmission of birthright citizenship, see Sarah Adams, supra note 7, 263–64. Algeria will provide birthright citizenship if the father is stateless. In law 1154/2004, Egypt amended its Nationality Law of 1975 to stipulate that anyone born to an Egyptian father or mother is an Egyptian national. See Egyptian state information service, http:// www.sis.gov.eg/EN/Pub/achievements/twentyfiveyears/110301000000000002. htm (accessed August 2, 2008). For a detailed account of an unsuccessful legal challenge to the rule in Bangladesh, see Kif Augustine-Adams, "Gendered States: A Comparative Construction of Citizenship and Nation," *Virginia Journal of International Law* 41 (2000): 93–139. For an international summary (which does not, however, list individual states), see UNHCR, "Final Report Concerning the Questionnaire on Statelessness Pursuant to the Agenda for Protection," supra note 71.

78. Hannah Arendt misunderstood the status of the interned, many of whom were technically enemy aliens, nationals of Japan. But she did articulate a delicious irony that I cannot help but quote here: the test of statelessness is when one would have more rights as a criminal. "A West Coast Japanese-American, who was in jail when the army ordered internment . . . would not have been forced to liquidate his property at too low a price; he would have remained right where he was, armed with a lawyer to look after his interests." *The Origins of Totalitarianism*, supra note 29, 287 n. 42.

79. On Mexican migrant farm workers, and braceros in particular, see Mae M. Ngai, *Impossible Subjects: Illegal Aliens and the Making of Modern America* (Princeton, NJ: Princeton University Press, 2004), chap. 4; and Kitty Calavita, *Inside the State: The Bracero Program, Immigration, and the INS* (New York: Routledge, 1999). Holly Brewer opens the large question of "What 'inalienable rights' do children have?" in *By Birth or Consent: Children, Law, and the Anglo-American Revolution in Authority* (Chapel Hill: University of North Carolina Press, 2005).

80. Trop v. Dulles, 356 U.S. 86 (1958). Mr. Trop, an army private, had escaped from the stockade in Casablanca in 1944. A day later, he was found making his

way back to the base, cold, hungry, and penniless. He served three years at hard labor and received a dishonorable discharge. Some years later, he applied for a passport.

81. The principle was strengthened in 1967, when the U.S. Supreme Court held, in *Afroyim v. Rusk*, that "every citizen in the United States has a constitutional right to remain a citizen . . . unless he voluntarily relinquishes that citizenship." The rules about what counts as voluntary relinquishment are very strict. See nn. 15 and 16 about dual citizenship above.

82. Zadvydas v. Davis, 533 U.S. 678 (2001), argued February 21, 2001. After the German government refused to admit Zadvydas, he filed this writ of habeas corpus. The district court granted the writ, finding that his detention was unconstitutional because Zadvydas was "stateless" and would be detained forever. The Fifth Circuit reversed, finding that despite five years in detention and numerous failed efforts by the INS to establish citizenship for Zadvydas somewhere, there was not yet a definitive showing that deportation would be impossible, so his detention could continue without violating the Constitution. For reflections on *Zadvydas* as an example of the erosion of plenary power, see Hiroshi Motomura, *Americans in Waiting: The Lost Story of Immigration and Citizenship in the United States* (New York: Oxford University Press, 2006), 111–13.

83. Oral Argument, Zadvydas v. Davis, supra note 82; Kneedler, 47; Stansell, 7.

84. This time the Court drew on Justice Robert H. Jackson's legendary dissent in Shaughnessy v. United States ex rel. Mezei, in 1953 at the height of the Cold War, when a legal permanent resident who, after twenty-five years of quiet living in the United States had visited family behind the Iron Curtain, found himself barred from returning, and was imprisoned indefinitely on Ellis Island. Mezei was released only after four years by a presidential "act of grace."

85. Deborah Sontag, "In a Homeland Far from Home," *New York Times Magazine*, November 16, 2003, 48ff.

86. Http://www.nsgtmo.navy.mil/htmpgs/gtmohistory.htm (accessed January 11, 2007).

87. The Patriot Act gave the attorney general expanded power to detain noncitizens who are suspected of terrorist activity; he is not required to notify them of the reason for detention or to share with them the evidence on which detention is based. The draft of Patriot II contemplated stripping even native-born Americans of their citizenship if they provide support for organizations marked as terrorist. For a detailed report on the leaked document, see "ACLU Fact Sheet on Patriot Act II," March 28, 2003, http://www.aclu.org/ safefree/general/ 17383leg20030328.html (accessed January 11, 2007). In December 2004, the Law Lords, Britain's highest court, ruled that the indefinite detention of foreign terrorism suspects is incompatible with the European Convention on Human Rights. See http://hrw.org/english/ docs/2004/12/16/uk9890.htm (accessed January 11, 2007). See also Mark Denbeaux, "Report on Guantanamo Detainees: A

Profile of 517 Detainees through Analysis of Department of Defense Data," Seton Hall Public Law Research Paper no. 46, available at Social Science Research Network, http://ssrn.com/abstact=885659 (accessed January 11, 2007). I am grateful to Elizabeth Hillman for this reference.

88. Judith N. Shklar, *American Citizenship: The Quest for Inclusion* (Cambridge, MA: Harvard University Press, 1991); T. H. Marshall, *Citizenship and Social Class* (Cambridge: Cambridge University Press, 1950); Alice Kessler-Harris, *In Pursuit of Equity: Women, Men, and the Quest for Economic Citizenship in Twentieth-Century America* (New York: Oxford University Press, 2001).

89. See also U.S. Department of State, "Victims of Trafficking and Violence Protection Act of 2000: Trafficking in Persons Report," June 5, 2002, http://www.state.gov/g/tip/rls/tiprpt/2002 (accessed January 11, 2007), and Center for Women Policy Studies, State Laws/Map of the United States, http://www.centerwomenpolicy.org/ programs/trafficking/map/default_flash.asp (accessed August 6, 2008). Also see Judith Resnik, "Law's Migration: American Exceptionalism, Silent Dialogues, and Federalism's Multiple Ports of Entry," *Yale Law Journal* 115 (2006): 1564–1670, especially n. 485.

90. Aihwa Ong, *Buddha Is Hiding: Refugees, Citizenship, the New America* (Berkeley: University of California Press, 2003), 9.

91. See UN Department of Economic and Social Affairs, *The World's Women 2005*, and other resources in Resnik, "Law's Migration," supra note 89, especially 1667 n. 510.

92. *Protocol to Prevent, Suppress, and Punish Trafficking in Persons, Especially Women and Children, Supplementing the United Nations Convention against Transnational Organized Crime*, UN GAOR, 55th Sess., Annex 2, Agenda Item 105, at 31, UN Doc. A/RES/55/25 (2000); "Jobs and Borders: The Trafficking Victims Protection Act," *Harvard Law Review* 118 (2005): 2180–2202, and U.S. Department of Justice, "Report on Activities to Combat Human Trafficking: Fiscal Years 2001–2005" (2006), 75 pp., http://www.usdoj.gov/crt/crim/introduction.pdf (accessed January 11, 2007).

93. Http://www.usdoj.gov/opa/pr/2003/February/03_crt_108.htm (accessed January 11, 2007); and see *New York Times*, April 20, 2002; and Jiang Shunzhe v. Daewoosa Samoa LTD and Kil-Soo Lee, High Court of American Samoa, Trial Division, CA 68–99. Mark Sidel, "Legal Reform in Whose Interests: Illuminations from Vietnamese Labor Export and Its Regulation" (unpublished paper delivered at Institut d'Etudes Politiques de Paris, October 2003).

94. UNHCR, "Statelessness: Prevention and Reduction," supra note 37. EC/57/SC/CRP6, 4.

95. Herman Melville, *Redburn, His First Voyage* (1849; repr. Evanston, IL: Northwestern University Press, 1969), 293; cited in Aristide R. Zolberg, *A Nation by Design: Immigration Policy in the Fashioning of America* (Cambridge, MA: Harvard University Press, 2006), 455.

96. Zolberg, *A Nation by Design*, supra note 95, 454–55.

97. Harlan Grant Cohen, "The American Challenge to International Law: A Framework for Debate," *Yale Journal of International Law* 28 (2003): 552.

98. Ralph W. Mathisen, "Peregrini, *Barbari*, and *Cives Romani*: Concepts of Citizenship and the Legal Identity of Barbarians in the Later Roman Empire," *AHR* 111, no. 4 (October 2006): 1040.

99. New York, 1952.

II

Global Markets, Women's Work

3

IIIIIIIIIIIIIIIIIIIIIIIIIIIIIIIIIIIIIIIIIIIIIIIIIII

Citizenship, Noncitizenship, and the Transnationalization of Domestic Work

Linda Bosniak

In recent political and legal thought, "citizenship" is commonly portrayed as the most desired of conditions: as the highest fulfillment of democratic and egalitarian aspiration. Yet this romanticized portrayal of citizenship tends to obscure deeper challenges that the concept poses. Citizenship talk trades in both universalism and particularism. While the concept is commonly invoked to convey a state of democratic belonging or inclusion, this inclusion is usually premised upon a conception of a community that is bounded and exclusive. And although citizenship as an ideal is understood to embody a commitment against subordination, in fact, citizenship also represents an axis of subordination and exclusion itself.

The divided nature of citizenship as a normative idea presents us with core issues of political and social theory, including feminist theory. It leads us especially to focus on the question of who it is that rightfully constitute the subjects of the citizenship that we may wish to champion and where it is that this citizenship is, and ought to be, located. To the extent that progressive social theorists, including feminist theorists, continue to press to redefine the *substance* of citizenship—to extend our conceptions to include more robust understandings of "social citizenship" or "equal citizenship" or "democratic citizenship," and to incorporate new domains, like the workplace and the home, as sites of citizenship practice—we ought, I think, to be particularly sensitive to the questions of exclusion and subordination implicated in this discussion. Citizenship for whom? Citizenship where? Feminist efforts to reclaim and retheorize citizenship as a core aspirational concept necessarily implicate these questions.

In this chapter, I examine the relationship between the discourses of bounded citizenship as they are implicated in a particular scholarly debate: one concerning the relationship between women's emancipation and work. For many feminists from Western countries, women's struggle to achieve fulfilling, decently remunerated work outside the home lies at the heart of any political effort to achieve their full and equal "citizenship." Yet the idea of citizenship in this context is double-edged. As much feminist scholarship has made clear, it is impossible to think usefully about women and work without addressing a society's organization of its domestic and reproductive labor. As women have entered the formal labor force in Western countries in greater numbers, the domestic labor they traditionally performed in their homes has become increasingly commodified and performed by others—usually women—pursuant to commercial exchange. In many countries, this commodification has taken an increasingly transnational form, with domestic labor being undertaken by migrant women, often from less developed countries. A great many of these women lack the status of citizenship in the countries where they perform that domestic work.

The commodification and transnationalization of domestic labor thus necessarily complicates the conventional feminist story about women's work and citizenship, because it brings another citizenship—citizenship in the exclusive, bounded sense— into the conversation. Thinking about women's work and citizenship, in other words, requires thinking not just about equal citizenship or democratic citizenship or economic citizenship, conceived in universalist terms, but also about citizenship as an exclusive national status. And once we attend to the national-status dimension of citizenship, we see that what many theorists describe as the achievement of "citizenship" for some women through participation in paid work depends increasingly on the labor of citizenshipless others.

The chapter goes on to examine the interplay of citizenships at stake in this situation. What does it mean that, whatever equal citizenship some women in wealthy countries may achieve through market-sphere work, it is often facilitated by the employment of people from poorer countries who themselves lack status citizenship in the country in which they labor? While it is rhetorically tempting to suggest that women in the developed countries acquire their citizenship *at the expense of* the citizenship of their domestic workers, this would be misleading. In fact, I argue, citizenship is not a single quantity transferred from some women to others in zero-sum fashion. Instead, the concept of citizenship designates distinct practices and institutions that are surprisingly autonomous, though certainly not unrelated. The term "citizenship" is conventionally employed to describe both the quality of relationships among members of a political community and the rules associated with the constitution and maintenance of community membership in the first instance. The issue of transnational domestic labor implicates citizenship in both these modalities, and often brings them into tension.

The chapter concludes with some reflections on citizenship's value as a political concept. I argue that citizenship as an idea not only illuminates but also obfuscates, making it less than useful as a tool for studying social phenomena like transnational domestic labor. Yet the discourse of citizenship is itself an important object of study, precisely because it embodies many of the core dilemmas over belonging and exclusion that plague contemporary social and political thought.

I. Citizenship and Domestic Work

In the past several years, social and legal theorists have shown a renewed interest in redistributive concerns. This recent turn to redistribution, though variously formulated, is commonly expressed in the language of citizenship. Many scholars deploy the idea of "economic citizenship," and sometimes "social citizenship," to convey a critique of the material exclusion of the disadvantaged, and to evoke a commitment to redress that exclusion through law and policy. Some argue that the achievement of "equal citizenship" requires close attention to matters of economic justice. Still others maintain that the practice of "democratic citizenship" requires a citizenry that enjoys basic material security. Whatever the specific language or emphasis, however, the idea of citizenship is increasingly linked to the enjoyment of economic rights in the political community.[1]

Among the central concerns of the new economic citizenship literature is the subject of work. Many scholars have urged a shift in conceptual focus from welfare to work in the arena of social citizenship, and many maintain that ensuring "decent work for everyone" is the central condition of equal citizenship today.[2] Some have made the argument in constitutional terms, maintaining that the United States Constitution can and should be understood to require "a right to decent work . . . and an acceptable income for all."[3] Judith Shklar was among the first to write about the indispensable role played by the right to earn as a foundation of American citizenship.[4] Others have made more general political and moral arguments on behalf of policies designed to ensure decent work.

By now, the linkage between economic concerns—work in particular— and citizenship is commonplace. Yet the conjoining of citizenship and economy would not always have seemed either natural or coherent. In its early understandings, citizenship was treated as remote from—even directly opposed to—specifically economic concerns. Aristotelian theory approached citizenship as a mode of distinctly *political* engagement,[5] while in early liberal thought, citizenship came to mean entitlement by some men to legal protection from others' interference in their private lives, including their economic lives. It certainly did not entail any affirmative right to public guarantee of economic goods or benefits.[6] Marxist thought likewise counterposed citizenship to economy by maintaining that the formal equality of citizenship status masks relations of drastic inequality prevailing in "material life,"[7] including—and perhaps especially—the domain of work.

Since the mid-twentieth century, however, application of the concept of citizenship to the economic sphere has been increasingly common. The social theorist T. H. Marshall treated the right to work as an element of "civil citizenship," and further elaborated the concept of "social citizenship," which included the right to basic material well-being through government provision. Many social theorists have since embraced and elaborated this notion.[8] By now, the concept of citizenship is less often confined to the political or civil domains, but is deployed as part of a larger project on behalf of economic justice.[9]

While many scholars have contributed to the process of forging this link between citizenship and work, feminist scholarship has played an especially central role. Feminist scholars have long argued that women need to be fully integrated into the labor market in order to achieve full and equal citizenship.[10] This scholarship stresses meaningful integration as the route to citizenship: women must enjoy equal access, with men, to desirable occupations, and equal pay, respect, and recognition on the job.

Some parts of this integrationist vision, however, have generated controversy among feminists themselves. Among other things, some feminist scholars have posed a powerful, and inescapable, question to its proponents: How, structurally, is women's participation in this work made possible? When women as well as men participate fully in the paid labor market, who is it that will undertake the preconditional work of social reproduction in the domestic arena? How does the work of dependency or care—of child rearing, food preparation, house cleaning, and myriad other physical, emotional, and organizational maintenance tasks—get accomplished?

Work in the traditionally conceived public domain is enabled, according to this critique, by essential but often invisible "care work" at home.[11] And it is traditionally women, both those involved in the paid labor force and those outside of it, who have performed the overwhelming share of this work. For this reason, many scholars have urged that ensuring women the chance to participate in decent, paid work outside the home is an inadequate foundation for equal citizenship. Some sort of public recognition of, and provision for, care work is also necessary.[12]

This idea has been expressed in various ways. Some scholars, like Martha Fineman, have suggested that public responsibility for dependency through social subsidy "marks a right of citizenship no less important and worthy of government protection than civil and political rights."[13] Here, the government support for care is regarded as an entitlement, on grounds that it is necessary for full human functioning and dignity.[14] Others have suggested that care should be treated as a public value for more instrumental reasons. The "republican idea . . . of citizenship . . . could support care as a moral and public value," Linda McClain has written, "and as a precondition to civic and democratic life."[15] Others still have contended that care work must be socially remunerated in some fashion; the idea here is that failure to formally recognize the value of domestic work is itself a denial of citizenship.[16]

Diverse though it is, all of this literature contributes to a critique of the tendency in some feminist scholarship to downplay the domestically based preconditions for the pursuit of citizenship in the "public sphere." Whether urging us to conceive of the activities of the domestic arena as an essential backdrop to public-sphere citizenship or as a locus of recognized citizenship itself, this scholarship insists on highlighting the linkages between women's citizenship and the demands of social reproduction.

Few feminists would disagree with the contention that the domestic sphere needs to become more visible in theory and its activities more valued in practice. Certainly, political and theoretical differences abound here—principal among them, those concerning the normative and economic value feminists should accord to the practices and identities associated with "domesticity," in Joan Williams's term.[17] But all of the critics insist on maintaining a focus on the demands of social reproduction in any discussion of citizenship and work.

These debates about women, work, and citizenship have, of course, un-folded in a specific historical context. This is a moment when, as a matter of fact, increasing numbers of women in developed Western countries, including mothers, do now engage in remunerated work outside their own homes (at least relative to a generation ago). To give just one rel-evant statistic, in the United States, according to U.S. Bureau of Labor Statistics data, 73 percent of mothers in the United States with children ages six to seventeen years old work for pay outside their homes.[18] Ever-growing numbers of families are two-job families; and increasing num-bers of households are headed by single mothers who work in the labor market. These trends reflect the fact that domestic work is not financially compensated, and are a consequence of a broad range of economic and social developments over the past half-century that have brought women in large numbers into the paid labor market.[19]

This development has not meant that women now in the paid labor market are no longer extensively engaged in the practice of social repro-ductive labor at home. Women continue to do a disproportionate share of the domestic work in their own homes in relation to men, even when they work for wages.[20] Their responsibility for the "second shift" affects women's lives not merely at home but also, in blowback fashion, on the job.[21]

One clear concomitant of these various trends, however, is that a good deal of the care work that was conventionally performed by wives and mothers (or female extended-family members) is now performed by non-family members pursuant to commercial exchange or contract. The com-mercialization of domestic work has involved drawing upon, and further developing, a labor market whose great majority of providers are other women. Correspondingly, increasing numbers of women who work out-side their own homes perform aspects of this commercialized care work on a for-pay basis. In this way, women's work in the paid labor market now relies significantly on the commodification of domestic care work, and domestic work has itself become a significant commodified sector of the labor market for women.

A good deal of this newly commodified care work is performed out-side the home in the broader service economy. The surge of employment in—to mention just a few sectors—restaurants and take-out food op-erations, laundries and dry cleaning services, day care facilities, nursing homes, home cleaning services, and tutoring operations reflects the trans-fer to the market of a great deal of care work once performed by women at home. But in addition, and of particular interest here, an important share of the care work traditionally performed by wives and mothers is being performed in the home by other women, pursuant to formal or informal contract, in the form of what the U.S. Census Bureau calls "private household service."[22]

Delegation of care work within the household by some women to others outside the family is certainly not a novel development. There is a long history of both coerced and market-based female domestic labor in the United States and elsewhere. Yet while paid domestic labor was "once the most common female occupation in the United States," in the post-World War II period it declined enormously in economic significance. As noted by the sociologists Ruth Milkman, Ellen Reese, and Benita Roth, "by the early 1970's, some sociologists were writing obituaries for [the occupation.]"[23] Nevertheless, the institution of paid domestic work has been making a substantial comeback in this country and others. Many employed women, especially those of the professional and managerial classes, now "purchase on the market much of the labor of social reproduction traditionally relegated to them as wives and mothers."[24]

In response to these developments, studies of contemporary domestic work have proliferated across the disciplines. There is, by now, an extensive literature in feminist thought about domestic wage labor. Much of the literature makes clear that this broadening of the delegation of care work to third-party women does not bring society closer to eliminating work/family conflict. Indeed, the reliance upon low-wage workers to perform domestic tasks actually reinforces traditional gendered divisions of labor, making it possible to free one class of women from the performance of some of this work while at the same time ensuring that the work remains *women's* work.[25]

Furthermore, this literature shows that commodification of domestic labor is deeply imbricated in relations of class. The scholarship highlights the stratifications that are produced or reinforced among groups of women when domestic tasks "are shifted from unpaid female family members to the shoulders of low wage female . . . workers."[26] This household work is often performed under substandard conditions and is poorly remunerated.[27]

Beyond class segmentation, moreover, the story of care and work is also a story about race. In the United States, especially, the vast share of domestic labor has historically been performed by women of color. Racial stratification has been a critical part of the history of domestic work, as Evelyn Nakano Glenn, Dorothy Roberts, and others have shown, with white women commonly "delegat[ing] the more onerous tasks onto women of color."[28] The trend persists today: the great majority of women doing paid domestic care work in the United States are Hispanic, Asian, and black.[29]

In addition to the class and race features of domestic labor's commodification, however, there is another dimension that is of particular relevance here. Many of the women who perform this commodified household labor, whether in North America or Europe, are (and have for some time been) immigrants who have crossed national borders, often specifically for the purpose of work, and who now reside and labor outside their countries of origin. While many of these immigrants are themselves people of color, the fact of their immigrant identities points to another dynamic in the organization of paid domestic labor. What has developed is a political economy of care that is transnational in scope. The changing place of women in the domestic economy, in other words, draws upon a globalized market in domestic labor,[30] one that is subject to distinct barriers but is nonetheless thriving and expanding.[31]

It is this last, transnational dimension of the political economy of care work that brings us directly to a range of questions about the nature of the relationship between women's work and citizenship.[32] We have seen that many feminists regard access to decent-quality, socially valued work as a necessary precondition for achieving equal citizenship for women. In such claims, the idea of "citizenship" functions as a powerful normative ideal—as the highest political and social aspiration.[33] At the core of this aspiration lies a commitment to an antiexclusionary ethic. "Full stature citizenship" stands, as the United States Supreme Court wrote in 1996, for "equal opportunity to aspire, achieve, participate in and contribute to society based on . . . individual talents and capacities."[34] Those who invoke the idea are responding to long (though differential) histories of exclusion of women from rights and recognition; they are seeking to make real the prevailing "ideal of universal citizenship," in Iris Young's phrase,[35] by reconceiving the character of that citizenship, and by ensuring that the apparent gender-neutrality of the citizenship idea is no longer used to mask structures of gender subordination.

Certainly, the very scope of the "universal" has been one of the principle issues of debate among feminist theorists, including feminist theorists of work. Because the idea of the universal has been deployed to exclude as well as to include,[36] it seems prudent to ask, universal citizenship for precisely whom? Most theorists understand themselves as working on behalf of citizenship for "everyone," including, and especially, "all women."[37] At the broadest normative level, universalism represents a shared and deeply felt commitment among the advocates of women's citizenship.

Yet the fact that the domestic work that lies at the heart of the women and citizenship story possesses an increasingly transnational character complicates the use of the idea of citizenship to express such aspirations. Acknowledgment of the global dimension of this work brings to the table another citizenship discourse—one that is not about universalism at all but about boundaries and exclusivity. Citizenship, in this understanding, is premised on the existence of national borders, and often presupposes an affirmative commitment to them. Most citizenship aspirants in feminist theory, as elsewhere, pay little attention to this "other" citizenship discourse. But given the realities of globalized labor, it cannot be avoided. And once it is addressed, the perennial question "citizenship for whom?" is rendered substantially more complicated.

II. National Borders and Domestic Labor

The transnationalization of labor, including domestic labor, is commonly invoked as a key measure of increasing economic globalization. In recent years, investments, production, and goods have enjoyed increasing (though still partial) freedom from the constraints of borders. But national borders remain relatively rigid when it comes to the movement of persons, including workers. Many people migrate cross-nationally, but most states place restrictions on the numbers of admittees and impose conditions on their stay.

These restrictions are grounded in, and are a function of, a set of institutions we conventionally call "citizenship." This is not the citizenship embraced by feminist theorists, which is concerned with achieving egalitarian and democratic relations among already recognized members of a political community. Here, citizenship is concerned with the community's threshold—with the boundaries of that community in the first instance. This citizenship is a status that assigns persons to membership in specific political communities—ordinarily, nation-states. And the status of citizenship in any given nation is almost always restricted, available only to those who are recognized as its members. While different states have different policies regarding admission to citizenship, citizenship is almost never automatically granted to those who seek it. It is, instead, subject to some rationing by the state. Rationing of this kind is accepted as a matter of international law: states are deemed fully sovereign with respect to decisions about whom to admit to membership.[38]

At the international level, then, citizenship conventionally stands not for normative universalism but for an (at least relative) ethic of closure. It is because of their *lack* of national citizenship status that many prospective immigrants—including many who would seek work in the domestic care sector— are prevented from entering countries of immigration, are required to wait for years to enter, or feel compelled to enter surreptitiously.

But status citizenship does not merely entail closure at the national border. Rather, citizenship's closure operates in the territorial interior as well. This is the case because states of immigration rarely treat an individual's physical entry into state territory as a sufficient condition for full national membership. Rather, foreigners who do enter another state ordinarily enter and reside, at least for some time, in that country in a condition short of full citizenship status. In legal terms, such people reside and work in the state of immigration as aliens—as noncitizens by definition.

Among the immigrant women who engage in domestic labor in the United States and elsewhere, there are considerable numbers who lack formal citizenship status.[39] Some of these noncitizen women are lawful permanent residents, and as such, are theoretically en route to citizenship (though citizenship is not guaranteed by the state, nor will it necessarily be chosen by the immigrants themselves). Yet as noncitizens, or aliens, they are denied certain basic political and social rights, including the right to vote and certain rights of social provision, and they are always potentially subject to the immigration enforcement authority of the state.

A great many other domestic workers are not merely noncitizens but are present on a formally unauthorized basis, as undocumented immigrants or "illegal aliens." Such women are denied many basic rights beyond those denied to lawful permanent residents; in the United States, for example, they are ineligible for virtually all forms of state-sponsored benefits. They are additionally at ongoing risk of apprehension and deportation by virtue of their unauthorized status—and are thus often reluctant to enforce those rights that they do have for fear of coming to the attention of the immigration authorities. Their irregular immigration status renders them vulnerable to subordination in a variety of arenas. The vast majority of these women, moreover, face the prospect of permanent alienage, with no realistic path to status citizenship.

Attention to the increasingly transnationalized character of the domestic labor market thus necessarily introduces the subject of citizenship *status* into the conversation about women and work. And, in fact, a growing number of scholars of domestic labor have recently begun to highlight the issue. Their work vividly describes how a lack of formal citizenship status serves, for these immigrant women, as an additional "axis of inequality" and exploitation on the job.[40] These domestic workers are vulnerable to deportation, they are afraid to invoke the rights they have for fear of being reported to the immigration authorities, and they lack state-sponsored income alternatives to the job.

Here is where the two discourses of citizenship come together. Viewed broadly, this body of scholarship points to an apparent paradox: some women's pursuit of citizenship—whether conceived of as equal citizenship, economic citizenship, or democratic citizenship—by way of work in the developed world is facilitated, in part, by the employment of women from mostly third-world countries who themselves are in a condition of "citizenshiplessness." The citizenship of one group of women seems to be constructed in reliance upon the labor of citizenshipless others. The question thus arises: How are we to understand this picture? How ought we to think about the configuration of citizenships in this situation?

It is rhetorically tempting to suggest that first-world women acquire their citizenship *at the expense of* the citizenship of their domestic workers. Perhaps, on this account, what is at stake is some sort of system of citizenship exploitation, whereby the achievement and enjoyment of citizenship by first-world women is reaped via the expropriation of the citizenship of immigrant others.[41] Some commentators have suggested as much.[42]

Despite its rhetorical attractions, however, this formulation does not quite capture what is going on. It can't be the citizenship itself that is the object of transfer or appropriation. I am very sympathetic with critiques of the transnational organization of reproductive labor developed by various commentators who argue that these arrangements reflect systemic inequality and privilege as between classes of women internationally.[43] There arguably *is* an expropriation—of labor, and care, and maybe even of love (as Arlie Hochschild suggests)[44]—from south to north in the context of a market exchange; and it is one that often redounds to the greater benefit of the employer than of the employee. It is an exchange that is contingent upon economic inequality—international and domestic—and histories of gender and racial subordination, as well as upon the operation of national immigration controls.

But it would be misleading to describe the situation as entailing a transfer *of citizenship* from one group to another—to say that first-world women's citizenship comes at the expense of the *citizenship* of their household workers. It would be misleading because it would represent a conflation of the "citizenships" at stake; it would entail treating them as if they were a single, fungible kind of good, and characterizing the problem as if it were entirely a matter of unequal distribution and control of that good. The trouble with doing so, however, is that there is no single quantity called "citizenship" that is at stake in this situation. The kind of aspirational equal citizenship or economic citizenship that women may hope to achieve through participation in the paid labor market is not the same social good as the status citizenship that many immigrant domestic workers are lacking. The idea of citizenship in each case is constituted by very distinct discourses, associated with an often nonconvergent set of institutions, practices, and normative commitments. Their distinctiveness makes them nontransferable in this way.

III. Divided Citizenships

How, then, are the citizenships at stake in the transnational domestic labor setting related? Here is a place to start to develop an answer: In an article on the history of women's citizenship in the United States, Nancy Cott has argued that citizenship cannot be approached as a unified and internally coherent concept. Among other things, she shows that while white women in nineteenth-century America enjoyed citizenship in "nominal" or "minimal" terms, they were denied many of the rights we now consider fundamental to citizenship in its fullest sense. Specifically, although these women were acknowledged citizens in a formal sense, they lacked most rights of "political citizenship" and certain rights of "civil citizenship," even as understood at the time. Cott observes that "citizenship can be delivered in different degrees of permanence or strength. Citizenship is not a definitive, either/or proposition—you are or you are not—but a compromisable one."[45]

Cott's comments make clear that citizenship is internally more complex and segmented than is usually assumed. Cott is working within a particular tradition of citizenship discourse, one in which citizenship represents the enjoyment of rights.[46] Although she is addressing segmentation *within* the domain of rights-citizenship, her basic insight about citizenship's divisibility or severability can be applied, in relation to the multiplicity of understandings (including, but not limited to, rights-based understandings) that we conventionally maintain about citizenship. Her approach helps us to think about how people can, and do, enjoy partial citizenships—or, stated differently, about how they may be subjects of citizenship in some respects but not in others. To give an example, a person may be afforded many of the basic rights that are commonly characterized as rights of citizenship (whether civil, social, or political), while nevertheless experiencing herself, or perhaps behaving, as a passive political consumer rather than a democratic agent in her political community. In such a case, she might be said to be a rights-citizen in some respect, but not a democratic citizen.

Recognizing the multivalence and divisibility of the citizenship idea brings us back to the conception of citizenship as formal national membership status. This is the citizenship, once again, of borders. It is the citizenship that entitles one to a passport, to diplomatic protection abroad, and, above all, to the right to enter and to remain in a nation's territory without constraint. This is the citizenship that is premised on a commitment to boundaries and closure rather than universalism. It is the citizenship that aliens, by definition, do not enjoy.

As it happens, most political, social, and legal theory that employs the idea of citizenship in normative terms pays little attention to this last form of citizenship. This is certainly true of most feminist theory, including feminist theory on work. Despite all the differences that divide scholars in this area (irrespective of whether these scholars approach the idea of citizenship as a matter of rights or as one of democratic engagement, whether they focus on the domain of market labor or of reproductive labor as the site of women's citizenship) citizenship as formal national status is usually ignored and invisible.[47]

When I say that the national status aspect of citizenship is usually invisible in this literature, I mean not only that these scholars pay little or no attention to the presence and condition of noncitizen immigrants. I mean, more broadly, that their political and social vision tends to be unreflectively insular and nationalist. The feminist scholars of work are concerned with the state of relations that prevails among those who are presupposed members of the national society. These scholars rarely acknowledge that this society is situated in a wider world, and that it is a bounded territorial community that limits access to membership. In most of this work, the national society is treated as the total universe of analytic focus and normative concern.

The invisibility of the world beyond the nation is sometimes palpable (paradoxically) in the text. Legal scholar Vicki Schultz, for instance, has written,

> I believe that it is imperative to create a world in which all women and men can pursue their chosen callings and all working people can live with justice, equality and dignity. . . . [I support] a utopian vision in which women and men from all walks of life can stand alongside each other as equals, pursuing our chosen projects and forging connected lives. In the process we come to view each other as equal citizens and human beings, each entitled to equal respect and a claim on society's resources because of our shared commitments and contributions. . . . We must remake our laws and culture to create a world in which *everyone* has the right to participate in the public world of work. . . . Paid work has the potential to become the universal platform for equal citizenship.[48]

Schultz here treats "world" and "society" as fully substitutable concepts. The society with which she is concerned is a national society, though this is presumed rather than stated. The "everyone" she invokes is a national "everyone," and the universality she champions is clearly a nationally framed universality. In this vision, "we," apparently, *are* the world, and as a consequence, the world beyond the national society is simply effaced.

This is not to say that Schultz would decline to endorse a vision of equality, justice, and dignity through work for people beyond the nation; but the matter of the world beyond the nation is never directly addressed. If it *were* to be addressed, it would raise some sticky policy and normative questions, especially about how universal achievement of decent work in this country can be achieved under conditions of economic globalization. There is, in particular, the subject of international labor competition—the so-called race to the bottom. Is a nationally framed, work-based economic citizenship even achievable in the absence of various protectionist measures such as trade tariffs, investment restrictions, and plant-closing laws? This is the position of many labor unions and other workers' rights organizations that are specifically dedicated to achieving decent work for Americans. Obviously, though, the imposition of protectionist measures would implicate the well-being and interests of people beyond our nation. To what extent, if any, are these interests of relevance here?[49]

These commentators avoid addressing the fact that the national community *within which* universal citizenship is championed is constituted by boundaries that keep nonmembers out. Such disregard means that all the challenging questions that some theorists (usually, the immigration scholars) ask about migration, work, and justice remain unaddressed. Among others: Under what circumstances is it legitimate for a wealthy national society to restrict access to territory and membership? To what extent is the achievement of economic justice—or economic citizenship—within the national society contingent upon such restriction? What obligations do we owe to people whose opportunities for decent work in their own societies have been thwarted, in part, by a system of international political economy that has served to benefit our own nationals? Do such obligations, if any, include the obligation to provide access to our own national labor market? In short, when scholars approach the national community as the world entire, its boundaries are going to be difficult to see, and critical questions will remain unaddressed.

Moreover, it is not merely the boundaries at the community's territorial edges that will be rendered invisible. The status of alienage—noncitizenship in the status sense—represents the legal operation of national boundaries *within* the national territory. Even granting that the "everyone" with whom these analysts are concerned is a nationally framed "everyone," one still needs to specify precisely how far this construct actually extends. Is the goal of economic citizenship (or equal citizenship, or democratic citizenship) meant to extend to all status citizens? To all "Americans"? To all residents? To all territorially present workers? For a group of scholars whose project is guided by a stated commitment to "universalism," disregard of the internal boundaries of citizenship may be a more serious failing than inattention to the territorial threshold.

I have so far suggested that disregard of the exclusionary national aspect of citizenship in the women-and-work literature is partly a product of tacit and habitualized nation-centered thinking.[50] But it also reflects something else: reliance on a particular conception of what the necessary preconditions are for equal or democratic citizenship. This is a conception about the normative structure of citizenship that is common to most of the aspirational scholarship on citizenship, including the women-and-work literature. At its core, this conception is that citizenship, to mean anything, has to be *more than* "mere status."

It is a staple of normative citizenship scholarship to contrast "thin" and "thick" versions of citizenship. Thin citizenship is citizenship-as-status, "mere status," in the disparaging phrase of some commentators.[51] This thin version of citizenship is contrasted with more robust, substantive conceptions—whether based on rights, democratic participation, or identity/recognition. Whichever substantive conception of thick citizenship is invoked, however, a hierarchy between thick and thin is posited: to possess the legal status of citizenship is to enjoy citizenship only in the most formal and nominal sense. True and full enjoyment of citizenship requires much more.[52]

Accompanying this hierarchical ordering of the thin and the thick, one commonly finds an unspoken empirical premise: that achievement of thin, status citizenship is no longer much of a pressing issue in our society. It is generally assumed that universality of status has by now been largely achieved; the formal attributes of citizenship have been extended, as Iris Young has written, to "all groups in liberal capitalist societies."[53] The pressing concern, instead, is to make citizenship more substantive and meaningful to various groups in various ways.[54] The critical focus is thus not on exclusion from citizenship status but on forms of "second-class citizenship."

The idea of second-class citizenship is a powerful trope of social criticism, used to evoke the condition whereby individuals or groups possess formal citizenship status but nevertheless experience de facto exclusion and powerlessness.[55] And it represents an indispensable form of critique. It has been very effective, in rhetorical terms, in conveying the idea that the extension of the formal status of citizenship, alone, can mask real oppression and may thereby represent a largely empty shell.[56] However, the bifurcated approach to citizenship that this critique relies on suffers from important weaknesses. First, the general disparagement of "thin" citizenship, as distinguished from "thick," seems out of touch with the realities of immigration. In a world of vast transnational inequalities and bordered nation-states, the achievement of citizenship status in a wealthy country like the United States is hardly a negligible matter for many people outside its borders. More to the point here, there is a substantial class of people residing and working *within* the borders of many wealthy liberal democratic states who nevertheless lack the formal status of citizenship. As we have seen, the lack of status citizenship that defines alienage sometimes serves as a basis for exclusion and subordination in the broader society. Here, again, we see that status citizenship is neither universally available nor unimportant.

The second difficulty with the thick/thin citizenship duality is conceptual. Citizenship theorists tend to assume the existence of a certain kind of relationship between the thin and the thick. The usual assumption is that the status of citizenship is a necessary precondition for the enjoyment of citizenship in its more substantive and robust versions. Citizenship status, in this view, is an embryonic form of citizenship—a necessary, though insufficient, antecedent to citizenship in its more substantive modes. Citizenship status, we like to assume, is "the right to have rights."[57]

Viewing citizenship status as the ground floor for the larger edifice of equal or democratic citizenship is certainly understandable. It seems intuitively right to say that citizenship is *for citizens*, to assume that substantive citizenship (however defined) will and should be extended to people who are formally designated by law *as citizens*. And things do often work this way. The right to vote, for example, is a right we think of as a core citizenship right—one closely associated with aspirations to both equal citizenship and democratic citizenship. Today, in most political communities, that right is contingent upon possession of status citizenship. There are various other rights, particularly certain rights of social provision, which in many countries depend on possession of citizenship status as well. Indeed, this is one reason why alienage serves as a source of disadvantage: their lack of citizenship status disqualifies aliens from enjoyment of a range of rights in many political communities.

Yet this is not the whole story. Status citizenship is not, and has not always been, a prerequisite for the enjoyment of many important rights. In the United States, aliens—even undocumented aliens—formally enjoy expressive and associational rights, procedural rights in the criminal and civil contexts, contract and property rights, and the right to attend public schools with other children. While always subject to government power to regulate immigration (and certainly that power looms large), aliens continue to enjoy important incidents of community membership. Within the framework of U.S. law and the laws of other democratic states, such rights have often been described as attaching to territorially present *persons* rather than to status citizens. But what is notable is that many of the entitlements that aliens enjoy are commonly described in contemporary social and political thought as forms of "citizenship," or as fundamental elements of equal citizenship or democratic citizenship.

Status citizenship is, therefore, not always a precondition for the enjoyment of essential elements of equal or democratic citizenship as they are conventionally understood. The citizenships at stake are at least relatively autonomous. This relative autonomy, moreover, is not of entirely recent origin. We know, for example, that certain key incidents of democratic citizenship have not always been confined to status citizens. The paradigm example is the right to vote. While today this is a right usually confined to status citizens, it was not always so: aliens possessed the franchise in many states in the United States until the late nineteenth century (this, of course, at a time when women who enjoyed status citizenship were nevertheless denied such right). Even today, aliens vote in a handful of local elections.[58]

All of which belies the idea that thick citizenship necessarily presupposes thin. As an analytical matter, it is possible to enjoy aspects of equal or democratic citizenship without *being* a formal citizen. It is not incoherent, in other words, to speak of the citizenship enjoyed by aliens. The citizenship of aliens (rights without status) is the inverse of second-class citizenship (status without rights). What we see here is that citizenship rights and citizenship status are not always coextensive or mutually entailed.

This brings us back to the question I posed earlier: What sense are we to make of the apparently paradoxical configuration of citizenships that characterizes the subject of women and work? What does it mean that one of the primary preconditions of women's citizenship—understood as the guarantee of decent, socially valued work, however defined—is increasingly contingent upon the labor of women who themselves lack citizenship?

I would submit that there is less of a paradox here than meets the eye. As we have seen, the "citizenships" at issue are neither coextensive nor mutually necessary. In a certain respect, they are incommensurable. Perhaps the best way to see this is to contrast the meaning of *non*citizenship in each context. When we speak of "noncitizenship" in the case of immigrant domestic workers, we are usually talking about their lack of formal standing vis-à-vis the state and their lack of entitlement to remain in the national territory. In various ways outlined above, noncitizenship works as a *mechanism* of subordination. In contrast, in the aspirational work and citizenship literature, the kind of "noncitizenship" suffered by many women is conceived as a lesser form of citizenship, a form of incomplete, or second-class, citizenship. Here, the idea of "non-citizenship" simply *characterizes* an excluded social condition.

Certainly, there is functional overlap between these two forms of noncitizenship, and they are often closely correlated. Exclusion from status citizenship and economic citizenship often go together. Furthermore, it must be emphasized that noncitizen domestic workers have an interest in achieving equal, democratic, and economic citizenship as much as anyone else. This may be facilitated, though not guaranteed, by their acquisition of status citizenship.[59] But not always and not necessarily.

The point, therefore, is that the citizenship that women in this society may seek by way of decent paid work is not dependent upon the expropriation of the *citizenship* of the immigrant domestic workers. Expropriation occurs—exploitation of labor and care in the context of a market exchange, one that often redounds to the greater benefit of the employer than the employee, in part because of the greater vulnerability of the employee across a variety of axes. It is an exchange that is contingent upon international economic inequality and histories of gender and racial subordination as well as the operation of national immigration controls. But it is not the citizenship itself that is the object of expropriation and transfer.

IV. Complementary and Competing Citizenships

Yet even if it is true that status citizenship is analytically severable from both equal and democratic citizenship, we are still left with the question of how to think about the nature of the relationship that does exist between them. It can hardly be an accident, some will argue, that a single word is conventionally used to describe both bounded and universal belonging. Even allowing for citizenship's internal divisions, should we not view the concept as representing a single overarching idea that denotes community membership? On this argument, citizenship may have various dimensions and aspects, but they *all add up* to a single broader phenomenon.

The most compelling way of making this argument would be to say that universal citizenship and bounded citizenship have different domains of action. Universal citizenship is the prevailing ethic (however imperfectly achieved) within the political community, while bounded citizenship operates at the community's threshold. These boundaries are enabling boundaries: exclusivity at the edges allows universality to flourish within. In this approach, universal and bounded citizenship are complementary parts of a larger whole.[60]

This "hard-on-the-outside, soft-on-the-inside" model of citizenship, I believe, represents our commonsense view of how citizenship works. But though it may be intuitive, it doesn't entirely capture important contemporary understandings and practices of citizenship. As I have argued, bounded citizenship operates not only at the threshold but also inside the community's territorial perimeters through the state's laws on alienage. Meanwhile, the ideals and institutions and practices of equal/ democratic citizenship are not always confined to the national inside but operate at the territorial borders; this occurs, for example, by way of sometimes-liberal asylum and refugee policies and norms of due process afforded in some deportation proceedings.

In fact, one might even argue that the ideals and practices of universal citizenship transverse national borders. The international human rights regime, transnational political advocacy networks, and commitments to cosmopolitan ethics have all been described, plausibly, as forms of citizenship that take place across or beyond national borders.[61]

The domains of action of universal citizenship and bounded citizenship are thus not always jurisdictionally separate; rather, these citizenships sometimes occupy the same terrain. And when they do, there are often jurisdictional conflicts over which citizenship norm—one based on universal equality or one based on communal loyalty[62]—should prevail in any given situation.[63]

V. Conclusion: The Language of "Citizenship"

It is possible to take the position that the kinds of conceptual divisions and normative conflicts that characterize citizenship as we conventionally understand it reflect, more than anything, an unfortunate linguistic turn of events. In this view, the idea of citizenship has become a terribly over-worked concept in social, political, and legal thought over the last decade and a half. It is now invoked to represent so many diverse practices and institutions and experiences that it ceases to be analytically meaningful or useful. It is the overly casual, and even promiscuous, use of the term, together with a habit of unconsciousness about its multiple meanings and their implications, that is responsible for all of the confusion.

One might argue, moreover, that the profusion of citizenship talk in our normative political and legal theory is not only confusing but rhetorically dangerous. In particular, the aspirational uses of the idea of citizenship—the ideals of equal citizenship, democratic citizenship, and economic citizenship—may work to undermine the claims and interests of aliens. If ideas about social justice are expressed in the language of citizenship, doesn't this appear, by implication, to exclude from the scope of protection those people defined as noncitizens under the law? Intended or not, this may be the practical result in discursive terms. Additionally, when aspirational and legal definitions of citizenship are conflated, certain social realities disappear from view. In the context of transnational domestic labor, in particular, characterizing the equality aspirations of employer women as matters of citizenship can work to obscure the status citizenship deprivations experienced by many of their female employees.

Perhaps, in this view, we should redress the confusions by confining our use of the idea of citizenship to designate formal membership status. "Citizenship" would then really mean the possession of "nationality," with all the other rights characterized in different terms—terms like justice, democracy, and freedom.[64]

I feel some sympathy with this suggestion and have advanced it myself.[65] But I have also come to think that what is important in scholarly terms is the fact that we *do* use the term in the ways that we do. The conceptual and normative dividedness in conventional ideas about citizenship is precisely what is of interest and what requires accounting. In the end, our ideas about citizenship reflect many of the core political and moral dilemmas that engage us, and they also serve to shape the way we think about these dilemmas. For this reason, the study of the idea of citizenship, and of the multiple practices and institutions and experiences that the term is used to represent, are fundamentally inseparable.

NOTES

1. These scholars employ the language of citizenship in largely liberal terms to describe rights and entitlements that individuals hold against the state. Arguments for "economic citizenship" *qua* rights also sometimes have republican overtones: the claim in some work is that basic economic rights are a necessary condition for achievement of engaged, republican citizenship in the national polity. These uses should be distinguished from claims on behalf of "workplace citizenship" that have also recently proliferated in the legal and sociological literature: here, the idea of citizenship is deployed explicitly in republican terms to refer to active democratic engagement in the life of the community. Unlike classic articulations of republican citizenship, however, the community at issue is not the polity but the firm. For a comprehensive review of the various uses of the concept of citizenship, see Linda Bosniak, *The Citizen and the Alien: Dilemmas of Contemporary Membership* (Princeton, NJ: Princeton University Press, 2006), 17–36.

2. There are other strands of the economic citizenship literature. One group urges public provision of a financial stake in society to all Americans at the age of majority. Bruce Ackerman and Ann Alsott, *The Stakeholder Society* (New Haven, CT: Yale University Press, 2000). A second strand emphasizes more familiar welfare strategies that ensure a right to a decent livelihood. For example, Joel F. Handler, "Questions about Social Europe by an American Observer," *Wisconsin International Law Journal* 18 (2000): 437; Nancy Fraser and Linda Gordon, "Contract vs. Charity: Why Is There No Social Citizenship in the United States?" in *The Citizenship Debates*, ed. Gershon Shafir (Minneapolis: Minnesota University Press, 1998), 113–30.

3. William Forbath, for instance, maintains that addressing the crisis of work requires us to recover American constitutional and political traditions that embrace a firm commitment to an inclusive economic citizenship, and Kenneth Karst likewise posits a central linkage between work and constitutional citizenship. William E. Forbath, "Why Is This Rights Talk Different from All Other Rights Talk? Demoting the Court and Reimagining the Constitution," *Stanford Law Review* 46 (1994): 1790 (reviewing Cass R. Sunstein, *The Partial Constitution* [Cambridge, MA: Harvard University Press, 1993]). Kenneth L. Karst, "The Coming Crisis of Work in Constitutional Perspective," *Cornell Law Review* 82 (1997): 559.

4. Judith N. Shklar, *American Citizenship: The Quest for Inclusion* (Cambridge, MA: Harvard University Press, 1991). A decade later, Vicki Schultz argued that ensuring to "everyone full and equal participation in decently-paid, life-sustaining, participatory forms of work" must serve as the "platform on which equal citizenship [is] built." Vicki Schultz, "Life's Work," *Columbia Law Review* 100 (2000): 1928.

5. J. G. A. Pocock, "The Ideal of Citizenship since Classical Times," in *The Citizenship Debates*, ed. Gershon Shafir (Minneapolis: University of Minnesota Press, 1998), 31–42.

6. Michael Walzer, "Citizenship," in *Political Innovation and Conceptual Change*, eds. Terrence Ball, James Farr, and Russell Hanson (Cambridge, MA: Cambridge University Press, 1989).

7. Karl Marx, "On the Jewish Question," *Deutsch-Französische Jahrbücher* (February 1844).

8. Bryan Turner, *Citizenship and Capitalism: The Debate over Reformism* (London: Allen and Unwin Hyman, 1986); Nancy Fraser and Linda Gordon, "Civil Citizenship against Social Citizenship? On the Ideology of Contract vs. Charity," in *The Condition of Citizenship*, ed. Bart van Steenbergen (Thousand Oaks, CA: Sage, 1994), 90–107; Alice Kessler-Harris, *In Pursuit of Equity: Women, Men, and the Question for Economic Citizenship in 20th-Century America* (Oxford: Oxford University Press, 2002). These efforts represent part of a broader resurgence of interest among scholars in the subject of citizenship in recent years. For an

overview, see generally, Linda Bosniak, "Citizenship," in *Oxford Handbook of Legal Studies,* eds. Peter Cane and Mark Tushnet (New York: Oxford University Press, 2003).

9. The idea of "cultural citizenship" was once similarly regarded as an impossible conjoining of concepts, but the concept is in wide use today.

10. Recent exponents of this view include historian Alice Kessler-Harris, who has maintained that "access to economic equality" through work is "a necessary condition of citizenship" for women. Kessler-Harris, *In Pursuit of Equity,* supra note 8, 283. Kessler-Harris defines "economic citizenship" as meaning

> the achievement of an independent and relatively autonomous status that marks self-respect and provides access to the full play of power and influence that defines participation in a democratic society. . . . Access to economic citizenship begins with self-support, generally through the ability to work at the occupation of one's choice, and it does not end there. Rather, it requires customary and legal acknowledgment of personhood, with all that implies of expectations, training, access to and distribution of resources, and opportunity in the marketplace. (Ibid., 12–13)

See also Schultz, "Life's Work," supra note 4, arguing that paid labor constitutes the necessary foundation of equal citizenship for women.

11. These terms are contested. See Joan Williams for a critique of the idea of "care-work" as "still ha[ving] the little pink bow and the sacralizing heritage, of domesticity." She prefers the term "family work," in part because it serves to "use the legitimate claims of family life as a pivot to redefine the ideal worker." Joan Williams, "From Difference to Dominance to Domesticity: Care as Work, Gender as Tradition," *Chicago-Kent Law Review* 76 (2001): 1446.

12. One commentator has written, "care work must become a recognized component of citizenship, for both women and men." Madonna Harrington Meyer, ed., *Care Work: Gender, Labor, and the Welfare State* (New York: Routledge, 2000), 3.

13. Martha Albertson Fineman, "Contract and Care," *Chicago-Kent Law Review* 76 (2001): 1403, 1437. See also Linda C. McClain, "Care as a Public Value: Linking Responsibility, Resources, and Republicanism," *Chicago-Kent Law Review* 76 (2001): 1681; Deborah Stone, "Why We Need a Care Movement," *The Nation,* March 13, 2000, 13, 15.

14. Such an entitlement would be achieved either through thoroughgoing state-sponsored programs of child care provision, or through more gradualist (though in today's political environment, still utopian) proposals to "eliminate the ideal-worker norm in the benefits related to market work," thus ensuring that receipt of benefits to unemployment insurance, Social Security, and the like are not "contingent on ideal worker schedules that mothers do not work." Williams, "From Difference to Dominance to Domesticity," supra note 11, 1456.

15. McClain, "Care as a Public Value," supra note 13, 1689. In this latter argument, the family is conceived as a "school for citizenship," as well as the site of bodily reproduction. For example, Mary Ann Glendon and David Blankenhorn, eds., *Seedbeds of Virtue: Sources of Competence, Character, and Citizenship in American Society* (Lanham, MD: Madison Books, 1995).

16. E.g., Katharine Silbaugh, "Turning Labor into Love: Housework and the Law," *Northwest University Law Review* 91 (1996): 1; Martha M. Ertman, "Commercializing Marriage: A Proposal for Valuing Women's Work through Premarital Security Agreements," *Texas Law Review* 77 (1998): 17. For an earlier statement of this position, see Ellen Malos, ed., *The Politics of Housework* (Cheltenham, UK: New Clarion Press, 1980).

17. Joan Williams, *Unbending Gender: Why Family and Work Conflict and What to Do about It* (Oxford: Oxford University Press, 2000).

18. See United States Bureau of Labor Statistics, Table 4, Families with own children: Employment status of parents by age of youngest child and family type, 2005–06 annual averages, available at http://www.bls.gov/news.release/famee.t04.htm (last accessed May 20, 2007). In the European Union, the rates overall are somewhat lower (though they vary sharply among EU countries), but the rate of increase in the past thirty years has been steep. See, for example, Jan Dirk Vlasblom and Joop J. Schippers, *Increases in Female Labor Force Participation in Europe: Similarities and Differences,* Discussion Paper Series nr: 04-12, Tjalling C. Koopmans Research Institute, School of Economics, Utrecht University (2004), available at http://www.uu.nl/content/04-12r.pdf (last accessed May 8, 2007).

19. Kessler-Harris, *In Pursuit of Equity,* supra note 8.

20. Feminists have advanced various reasons for this, including internalized gender roles and "gatekeeping." See, for example, Arlie Russell Hochschield, *The Second Shift: Working Parents and the Revolution at Home* (New York: Viking Penguin, 1989); Naomi R. Cahn, "Gendered Identities: Women and the Household," *Villanova Law Review* 44 (1999): 525.

21. For example, Williams, *Unbending Gender,* supra note 17, esp. chap. 3. See also Gillian K. Hadfield, "Households at Work: Beyond Labor Market Policies to Remedy the Gender Gap," *Georgetown Law Journal* 82 (1993): 89.

22. See United States Bureau of Labor Statistics, Table 10, Employed Persons by Major Occupation, Annual Averages, 1987–2000, available at http://www.bls.gov/opub/rtaw/pdf/table10.pdf (last accessed May 20, 2007).

23. Ruth Milkman, Ellen Resse, and Benita Roth, "The Macrosociology of Paid Domestic Labor," *Work and Occupations* 25 (Nov. 1998): 483–510.

24. Ibid. Milkman, Reese, and Roth describe what they call "a partial reversal of the decline" and emphasize that "paid domestic labor is far more widespread in some metropolitan areas than others," including Los Angeles, Miami, Houston, and New York.

25. Judith Rollins, *Between Women: Domestics and Their Employers* (Philadelphia: Temple University Press, 1985), 104, reprinted in *Working in the Service Society,* Cameron Lynn Macdonald and Carmen Sirianni, eds. (Philadelphia: Temple University Press, 1996) ("The middle-class women I interviewed were not demanding that their husbands play a greater role in housekeeping; they accepted the fact that responsibility for domestic maintenance was theirs, and they solved the problem by hiring other women to assist.").

26. Mary Romero, "Unraveling Privilege: Workers' Children and the Hidden Costs of Paid Childcare," *Chicago-Kent Law Review* 76 (2001): 1652–54. According to Romero, the domestic workers' own families are themselves disadvantaged by virtue of enjoying "lower amounts of unpaid reproductive labor."

27. For example, Grace Chang, *Disposable Domestics: Immigrant Women Workers in the Global Factory* (Cambridge: South End Press, 2000), 57 (stating that "[m]embers of *Mujeres Unidas Y Activas* (MUA), a support group for Latina immigrant domestic workers, report that they commonly endure conditions approaching slavery or indentured servitude").

28. Evelyn Nakono Glenn, "Cleaning Up/Kept Down: A Historical Perspective on Racial Inequality in 'Women's Work,'" *Stanford Law Review* 43 (1991): 1341; Dorothy E. Roberts, "Spiritual and Menial Housework," *Yale Journal of Law & Feminism* 9 (1997): 51.

29. Milkman, Reese, and Roth, "The Macrosociology of Paid Domestic Labor," supra note 23, table 4 ("African Americans, Latinas and the foreign born . . . are all overrepresented in this occupation." The trend is similar in many European countries. See generally Bridget Anderson, *Doing the Dirty Work? The Global Politics of Domestic Labor* (London: Zed Books, 2000).

30. Pierrette Hondagneu-Sotelo, *Domestica: Immigrant Workers and Cleaning and Caring in the Shadows of Affluence* (Berkeley: University of California Press, 2001).

31. Many of the immigrants who perform this care work also have families in their countries of origin. The transfer of care work from the family of origin to the family of employment in the developed country has been described by some commentators as a global care chain. See, for example, Arlie Hochschild, "The Nanny Chain," *American Prospect*, January 3, 2000; Pierrette Hondagneu-Sotelo, "International Division of Caring and Cleaning Work," in Meyer, *Care Work: Gender, Labor, and the Welfare State*, supra note 12, 160 (In a new system of "transnational mothering," domestic workers experience "separations of space and time from their communities of origin, homes, children, and sometimes husbands. In doing so, they must cope with stigma, guilt and criticism from others. As they do care work and cleaning work for others, they lose the right to do care work and cleaning for their own families.").

32. In her contribution to this volume, Aihwa Ong describes the comparable but distinct regime of female migrant domestic labor in emerging countries in Southeast Asia. Women from the Philippines, Indonesia, and elsewhere are contracted as an expendable, overworked, and underpaid servant class—not so much to support their female employers' return to the labor market but to enable middle- and upper-middle-class families to sustain their lifestyle. Aihwa Ong, "A Bio-Cartography: Maids, Neoslavery, and NGOs" in this volume.

33. There are, however, differences of opinion among feminists about what citizenship as a normative ideal consists in substantively (with some emphasizing rights, others democratic participation), and differences as well regarding their conceptions of citizenship's domain of action (whether public sphere, workplace, domestic arena, or elsewhere).

34. United States v. Virginia, 518 U.S. 515, 532 (1996). In this volume, Vicki Jackson discusses American courts' inconsistent protection of "full stature citizenship" for women. See Vicki C. Jackson, "Citizenships, Federalisms, and Gender," in this volume.

35. Iris Marion Young, "Polity and Group Difference: A Critique of the Ideal of Universal Citizenship," *Ethics* 99 (January 1989): 250–74.

36. Ibid., 250.

37. For example, Vicki Schultz writes that "[i]n order to make paid work the basis for equal citizenship, we will have to take steps to ensure that what the market produces is both substantively adequate and universally available for everyone." Schultz, "Life's Work," supra note 4, 1885.

38. In this volume, Jacqueline Bhabba's treatment of citizenship emphasizes this status-based dimension. She shows how for many citizen children, the right to residence usually associated with status citizenship, as well as other rights associated with "equal citizenship," are effectively nullified by virtue of the noncitizenship status of their immigrant parents and therefore they often face constructive deportation. See Jacqueline Bhabha, "A Mere Fortuity of Birth? Children, Mothers, Borders, and the Meaning of Citizenship," in this volume.

39. Analysts estimate that close to half of all private household workers in the United States are immigrants, of whom more than two-thirds are noncitizens. Randy Capps, Michael Fix, Jeffrey S. Passel, Jason Ost, Dan Perez-Lopez, "A Profile of the Low-Wage Immigrant Workforce," in *Policy Briefs/Immigrant Families & Workers* (November 2003), available at http://www.iza.org/conference_files/iza_ui_2004/capps.pdf (last accessed May 8, 2007). In major urban areas, the concentration of immigrant low-wage workers, including domestic workers, is far higher than in the country as a whole." Ibid.

40. For example, see Hondegneu-Sotelo, *Domestica*, supra note 30, 13 ("Immigration status has clearly become an important axis of inequality, one interwoven with relations of race, class, and gender, and it facilitates the exploitation of

immigrant domestic workers."); Mary Romero, "Immigration, the Servant Problem, and the Legacy of the Domestic Labor Debate: Where Can You Find Good Help These Days?," *University of Miami Law Review* 53 (1999): 1062–63.

41. For a particularly stark, and in some respects, overly simplified, statement of the position, see Grace Chang, *Disposable Domestics: Immigrant Women Workers in the Global Factory* (Philadelphia: South End Press, 2000), 58:

> The efforts of primarily white, middle-class professional women to "have it all," including careers . . . [and] leisure . . . are secured by exploiting immigrant women and women of color as cheap laborers. . . . The employment of undocumented women in dead-end, low-wage, temporary service jobs makes it possible for middle- and upper-class women to pursue salaried jobs and not have to contend with the "second-shift" when they come home.

For a critique of this kind of framing of the issue, see Romero, "Unraveling Privilege," supra note 26, 1062 (Characterizing the domestic labor question "as an elite-class issue . . . completely ignore[s] the realities of the working poor, working class and lower-middle class. Although child care options for these classes are limited by finances, they too face overtime and long commutes to and from work, making day care options less than adequate.").

42. The case of migrant domestic workers illustrates, one author has written, "how the rights of citizenship in one state can be gained precisely because these are denied" to noncitizen immigrants. Anderson, *Doing the Dirty Work?*, supra note 29, 195.

43. For example, Hondagneu-Sotelo, *Domestica*, supra note 30; Romero, "Immigration, the Servant Problem, and the Legacy of the Domestic Labor Debate," supra note 40; Hochschild, "The Nanny Chain," supra note 31; Rhacel Salazar Parrenas, "The Care Crisis in the Philippines: Children and Transnational Families in the New Global Economy," in *Global Woman: Nannies, Maids, and Sex Workers in the New Economy*, Barbara Ehrenreich and Arlie Russell Hochschild, eds. (New York: Henry Holt, 2004).

44. Arlie Russell Hochschild, "Love and Gold," in *Global Woman: Nannies, Maids, and Sex Workers in the New Economy*, supra note 43, 15–30.

45. Nancy F. Cott, "Marriage and Women's Citizenship in the United States, 1830–1934," *American Historical Review* 103 (1998): 1448–49.

46. In other work, I have discussed in more detail the multiple substantive understandings of citizenship. See Linda Bosniak, "Citizenship," in *The Oxford Handbook of Legal Studies*, supra note 8; Linda Bosniak, "Citizenship Denationalized," *Indiana Journal of Global Legal Studies* 7 (2000): 447.

47. The significant exception here is some of the literature on domestic work and migration, to which I have referred and to which I will return below.

48. Schultz, "Life's Work," supra note 4, 1885 (emphasis added).

49. Schultz gestures briefly toward the subject of economic globalization when she notes that "as corporations seek more flexible forms of production and labor around the globe, more and more people face greater insecurity and less ability to shape their lives through a coherent narrative involving a commitment to work performed in stable settings over the course of a lifetime." Schultz, "Life's Work," supra note 4, 1919. But there is no follow-up. The nation-centered analytic that Schultz and others employ effaces all that is outside the national frame and therefore avoids all issues, practical and normative, that arise about cross-national distribution, trade, and production—questions that are necessarily implicated in any claims about achieving justice through paid work within the national community.

50. On liberalism's implicit nationalism, see generally Samuel Scheffler, *Boundaries and Allegiances: Problems of Justice and Responsibility in Liberal Thought* (Oxford: Oxford University Press, 2001), 79.

51. For example, Chantal Mouffe, ed., *Dimensions of Radical Democracy: Pluralism, Citizenship, Community* (New York: Verso, 1992), 227 (disparaging concern with citizenship as "mere legal status"); Sanford Levinson, "National Loyalty, Communalism, and the Professional Identity of Lawyers," *Yale Journal of Law and the Humanities* 7 (1995): 53–54 (distinguishing between the concept of "good citizens[]" on the one hand, and "mere citizens" on the other). Constitutional theorist Kenneth Karst describes citizenship status as "a simple idea," a "constitutional trifle." Kenneth L. Karst, "The Supreme Court, 1976 Term—Forward: Equal Citizenship under the Fourteenth Amendment," *Harvard Law Review* 91 (1977): 43; Kenneth L. Karst, *Belonging to America: Equal Citizenship and the Constitution* (New Haven, CT: Yale University Press, 1989), 10. He contrasts this with the broader conception of equal citizenship, which entails "the dignity of full membership in the society." Karst, "Forward," 5. For further discussion, see Linda Bosniak, "Constitutional Citizenship through the Prism of Alienage," *Ohio State Law Journal* 63 (2002): 1304.

52. Part of this paragraph is borrowed from Bosniak, "Constitutional Citizenship through the Prism of Alienage," supra note 51, 1304–5.

53. Iris Marion Young, "Polity and Group Difference," supra note 35, 250.

54. For further discussion of this point, see Linda Bosniak, "Universal Citizenship and the Problem of Alienage," *Northwestern University Law Review* 94 (2000): 968–71.

55. In this volume, Valentine Moghadam uses the idea of "second-class citizenship" to critically describe the status of Muslim women. See Valentine Moghadam, "Global Feminism, Citizenship, and the State: Negotiating Women's Rights in the Middle East and North Africa," in this volume.

56. Bosniak, "Constitutional Citizenship," supra note 51, 1305.

57. Hannah Arendt, *The Origins of Totalitarianism* (New York: Harcourt, Brace, Jovanovich, 1951, 1968). See Seyla Benhabib, *Transformations of*

Citizenship: Dilemmas of the Nation-State in the Era of Globalization (Spinoza Lectures) (Koninklijke Uitgeverij: Van Gorcum, 2001), for extended discussion of the idea of "the right to have rights." In Benhabib's reading, the second use of the word "right" in the phrase is premised upon the first. As Benhabib writes, "The second use of the term . . . is built upon th[e] prior claim of membership" as expressed in the first. Ibid., 16.

58. Gerald M. Rosberg, "Aliens and Equal Protection: Why Not the Right to Vote?" *Michigan Law Review* 75 (1977): 1092; Gerald L. Neuman, "We Are the People: Alien Suffrage in German and American Perspective," *Michigan Journal of International Law* 13 (1992): 259; Jamin B. Raskin, "Legal Aliens, Local Citizens: The Historical, Constitutional, and Theoretical Meanings of Alien Suffrage," *University of Pennsylvania Law Review* 141 (1993): 1391.

59. The point is not that noncitizens, including noncitizen domestic workers, don't need ready access to citizenship status. A good argument can be made that anyone who labors here is entitled to acquire citizenship swiftly. See Walzer, "Citizenship," supra note 6. My point for the moment is an analytical one: that the decent work scholars like Vicki Schultz and Alice Kessler-Harris are championing is not the same citizenship as that which alien domestic workers lack. Nor is one a necessary condition of the other. Certainly, they often coincide, but they are "severable." Cott, "Marriage and Women's Citizenship in the United States, 1830–1934," supra note 45, 1448–49.

60. This separate spheres model bears much resemblance to Michael Walzer's understanding of membership. Walzer argues that "while a political community is morally entitled to regulate the constitution of its own membership, the scope of action of its membership-defining policies must be confined to the territorial border. If membership regulation is carried on inside the community in ways that affect the status or experience of persons residing there, this is an exercise of power outside its sphere, as he sees it, and a violation of the principle of complex equality. Setting to one side Walzer's normative argument, his analytical premise is that the domain of membership distribution, or what I am here calling "exclusive citizenship," can, in fact, be separated from the various other distributive domains that constitute life inside the political community." Bosniak, *The Citizen and the Alien*, supra note 1, 40–49.

61. Bosniak, "Citizenship Denationalized," supra note 46, 447.

62. In earlier work, I have characterized the law regarding the treatment of aliens within the United States and at the territorial borders as structured by a dispute about whether the norms of exclusivity or universal personhood should apply in any given case. Such conflict is a version, I think, of the perennial tension between commitments to loyalty and commitments to equality that famously plagues liberal democratic thought more generally. Samuel Scheffler, *Boundaries and Allegiances*, supra note 50, 79. See also Chantal Mouffe, *The*

Democratic Paradox (New York: Verso, 2000); Benhabib, *Transformations of Citizenship,* supra note 57.

63. Linda S. Bosniak, "Membership, Equality, and the Difference That Alienage Makes," *New York University Law Review* 69 (1994): 1047.

64. Of course, what exactly those terms would be raises difficult questions: Would they be conceived as rights of membership? Rights of persons? These are the substantive questions that drive the debates over citizenship to begin with.

65. For example, Linda Bosniak, "The Citizenship of Aliens," *Social Text* 56 (1998): 29–35.

4

|||||||||||||||||||||||||||||||||||||||||||||||||||||||||

A Bio-Cartography:
Maids, Neo-Slavery, and NGOs

Aihwa Ong

The underpaid, starved, and battered foreign maid, while not the statistical norm, has become the image of the new inhumanity in the Asian metropolis. The following cases illustrate the range of assaults against Indonesian maids by well-off households in neighboring countries:

- In 2002, an Indonesian maid in Malaysia was found to have been held as a "sex slave" for nearly two years by a government employee.
- In the same year, an Indonesian maid, who had been starved and repeatedly tortured by her Singaporean employer, died from a final blow. The employer was sentenced to eighteen and a half years and to receive twelve strokes of the cane.
- In early 2003, a Hong Kong housewife, who "filled her afternoons with golf lessons, facials and hair treatments," beat her Indonesian maid until her liver ruptured. The housewife was later charged with assault and is serving a 3.5-year sentence.
- In July 2004, news pictures of a foreign maid with extensive burns on her face, breasts, and back exposed a harrowing tale of sadistic torture. Nirmala Bonat, a nineteen-year-old from East Indonesia, had been repeatedly scalded with hot water and burned with an iron by her employer. The media disseminated shocking images of Nirmala's wounds, arousing a sense of national shame. The prime minister apologized publicly to the victim, and some lawmakers called for imposing a lifelong sentence on the employer *before* her trial.[1]

In addition to the above cases of maid abuse and disfigurement, there are other incidents that remain murky and concealed. For instance, over the past five years, about a hundred foreign maids have fallen from Singapore's high-rises, plummeting to their deaths. The main causes cited were maids slipping off window sills while cleaning the outside glass or hanging laundry to dry on bamboo poles. Others suspect that maids "imprisoned" in apartments were trying to escape or to commit suicide.[2]

The frequency and ferocity of abuses against foreign maids index a brewing human rights crisis over the emergence of neo-slavery in Southeast Asia. Over the past decade, having a foreign maid in the household has become an entrenched entitlement of the middle and upper-middle classes throughout Southeast Asia. Foreign domestic helpers (FDHs) from the Philippines and Indonesia compete to cook, nurse babies, clean bathrooms, and perform other bottom-drawer chores for the middle classes throughout the region, and beyond.[3] There are approximately 140,000 foreign domestic workers in Singapore,[4] 200,000 in Malaysia,[5] and 240,000 in Hong Kong.[6] As an expendable and underpaid servant class, they have become key to the maintenance of the good life in affluent Asian sites. It has been said that these are countries where "the middle classes have no idea how to cope without a maid."[7]

The cases of abuses by employers and recruiters remain small, compared to the total number of female migrant workers. Nevertheless, there is no easy way to assess the actual number of attacks on foreign domestic workers, and the gruesome nature of the violence that has come to light reflects a widespread attitude towards foreign domestic workers as a separate category of subhumans. "Maids as slaves" is "Asia's hidden shame," a novel mix of rising affluence and mounting abuse that exposes the "vulnerable millions" of young women on the move.[8] Low-skilled foreign women circulate in zones of exception that support the citadels of Asia's new rich.

Ethico-Political Spaces of Humanity

Social theorists have argued that the paradox of humanity is its birth in the nation-states, an inscription of the particular in the universal.[9] Giorgio Agamben's concept of bare life points to the seemingly contradictory situation whereby sovereignty is predicated on the exclusion of living beings not recognized as modern humans.[10] Observers note that categories such as migrants, refugees, and illegals have been defined in such a way as to make their rights claims external to citizenship and the law.[11] Agamben maintains that the logic of exception constructs "a zone of indistinction . . . in which the very concepts of subjective right and juridical protection no longer made any sense . . . power confronts nothing but pure life, without any mediation."[12] The juridical-legal division between a zone of citizenship and a zone of bare life, while compelling, is a static and restrictive model, although at the end Agamben seems to be searching for a politics that is not founded upon the biopolitical fracture, or oscillation between the two poles of inclusion and exclusion.[13] In contrast, a temporal conceptualization of the politics of exception would recognize that the state system interacts with other ethical regimes that also operate along a continuum of inclusion and exclusion, though without mapping onto the same division between citizens and bare life. We should not discount shifts in the lines dividing the human and the inhuman, the virtuous and the evil, that are crystallized in the interplay between the sovereign exception and other systems for valuing and disvaluing bodies.

Another binary model that should be challenged is the strict division between human rights and situated ethics. Nevertheless, there is an extravagant claim that a "human rights culture" now prevails. Michael Ignatieff argues that "[t]he existence of a single normative rights standard leaves no room for . . . moral and political evasions" in non-Western countries. The human rights discourse, he maintains, provides "a moral vernacular for the demand for freedom within local cultures."[14] This approach envisions a universal standard of the moral good that will provide the language for articulating human freedom in a range of presumably "bad" cultures in the global south. Ignatieff seems to discount the relevance of the great religions that have long existed as universal systems of civic virtue. Indeed, only by recognizing the relevance of the "moral and political" elements that Ignatieff dismisses as mere evasions can we study the way moral problems are posed, claims articulated, and resolutions arrived at in a particular milieu.

Such dichotomies, between the licit and the illicit, between a universal human rights regime and local cultures, are simple abstractions with little relationship to actual ethico-political negotiations on the ground. Instead of a rigid division between zones of humanity and zones of inhumanity, I propose that the space for problematizing the human is a milieu that is constituted by a nexus of multiple ethical regimes. A situated constellation of citizenship regimes, moral systems, and NGO interventions defines the space within which the translation and transmission of human rights discourse proceeds. Because the site of problematization is shaped by diverse systems of value, it cannot be claimed that only the human rights regime creates a moral vernacular, as if situated ethics have nothing moral to say in the matter of labor and life.

In Southeast Asia, interrelationships among labor markets, nationalisms, and moral economies crystallize conditions of possibility for diverse notions of the human. The neo-slavery of migrant women emerges out of a postcolonial intersection of racialized nationalism, neoliberal strategies, and disjunctive moral economies based on kinship and ethnicity. In postcolonial nations built upon founding or dominant races, questions of who is considered human or subhuman are still inscribed by ethnic biases or hostilities.[15] This racialistic opposition is reinforced by moral schemes that are skeptical about the attachability of mobile alien women detached from their own moral communities. The biopolitical concerns of the more well-off nation to secure middle-class entitlements depends on the availability of foreign others, creating an environment of class privilege and bias that tolerates slavelike conditions for poor female migrants. Thus, in addition to the biopolitical fracture, ruptures between racial and moral economies further complicate notions about who can or cannot be considered morally worthy human beings.

Into this knotted field of situated power and ethics, local NGOs introduce an ethical debate on the plight of female migrants, articulating political claims for their moral dignity beyond a condition of neo-slavery. It is widely assumed that NGOs, as actors in the global public sphere, operate as watchdogs of human rights vis-à-vis the state.[16] But in practice, NGOs both local and transnational have had to engage the nation-state in a variety of practical ways shaped by the nexus of variables. The question is raised whether, in their actual representations of excluded populations, NGOs can operate independently of relationships to the nation-state and to the market. Furthermore, is the discourse of human rights effective for bringing about social improvements, or do NGO interventions require translations of their humanitarian goals into situated ethical notions about the common good? Because NGOs work in a fluid space of contending regimes, their negotiations on behalf of the politically excluded are contingent, and the resolutions are at best ambiguous.

As practitioners of humanity, NGO interventions are technical as well as ethical, since NGO work is fundamentally about managing the risk and security of marginalized populations by giving them value. In order to make claims on their behalf, NGOs define and sort out different categories of excluded humanity, so as to give them resources that *may* be convertible into entitlements and rights. Such ethical work of giving moral value to the politically excepted increasingly has a spatial dimension. NGO interventions entail mapping of spaces of sheer survival that challenge the political spaces of inclusion and exclusion demarcated by individual nation-states. Such techno-ethical strategies are necessary for redrawing the map of moral inclusion.

The argument is in two parts. First, I discuss the way the disjunctures between nations and moral economies create conditions that foster neo-slavery for some foreign maids. As "transient aliens," foreign domestic workers are subjected to a household-based disciplinary regime and to techniques of securitization at the national level. Because they are mobile women, foreign domestic workers are not considered attachable to moral economies despite their role in reproductive labor. As a migrant population, female foreign workers tend to be viewed as aliens and threats to the security of the host society.

Second, interventions into this specific milieu of household-based neo-slavery must first address the moral economies of the new middle classes. In Malaysia and Singapore, NGO interventions stir ethical reflections on the moral obligations of employers by invoking cultural values that can protect the welfare of female foreign workers. NGOs seek to align the bodily integrity of migrant women with their availability as cheap labor, thus projecting their biological claims on a regional scale.

Biopolitical Otherness

The Moral Economy of the Female Migrant

The emerging cross-race, cross-ethnic economy of female migrant workers intersects with multiple moral economies rooted in kinship, religious ethos, and ethnic communities. Conceptually, a "moral economy" is a web of unequal relationships of exchanges based on a morality of reciprocity, mutual obligations, and protection.[17]

In anthropological terms, moral economies involve substantive relationships of exchange that are governed primarily by morality (peasant, religious, "culture") or ethics governing a particular vision of the good life.

Moral economies in villages and urban milieus are the bedrock stimulus for the outflows of young women as migrant workers in Southeast

Asia. Young, mainly unmarried women are central to the capacity of the family, community, and even homeland to sustain a level of development otherwise not available without remittances from abroad.[18] Labor migrations responding to the moral obligations of family and kin have created opportunities for organization by state agencies as well as labor syndicates that seek to channel migrant women to overseas markets.

The Philippines is famous for supplying the world with nannies. Whereas other Southeast Asian nations seek to position themselves in manufacturing chains and knowledge webs, the Philippines' neoliberal strategy has been to transform the country into a labor-brokering nation. There is an overseas employment administration program that makes contractual agreements with foreign countries to hire "the great Filipino worker." The government advertises in global news magazines, claiming that "Filipino workers . . . were born with a natural ability to adapt to many cultures and even delight in discovering new ways to improve their craft."[19] Labor recruiters for overseas markets stress the flexibility and docility of female Filipino workers. At the same time, the state appeals to women to seek overseas jobs as a patriotic duty of "modern-day heroes" whose overseas earnings support the country.[20] There is thus a process of feminization of migrant labor, as well as a masculinization of their national roles as soldiers and "ambassadors" who must not let down the national image of their country as the home of global workers.

Nongovernmental agencies, or NGOs, play a crucial role in training and indoctrinating would-be migrants, focusing in particular on self-managing techniques that instill proper attitude and conduct abroad. Feminist NGOs offer lessons linking overseas employment with Catholic feminine values. Using terms such as "empowerment," NGOs foster a moral connection between free choice in seeking overseas employment and the young women's sense of moral indebtedness and desire to sacrifice for their families. With rape and even murder a real risk faced by workers overseas, NGOs give advice on balancing the vulnerability of their working lives and the vulnerability of their families. They must protect the precariousness of their own families, not forgetting to send money home to their relatives and home towns. At the same time, they should be "friendly but not familiar" with overseas employers—should not be "sexually available" but instead be assertive and confrontational with men who proposition them.[21] Thus, NGOs play a crucial role in reinforcing the moral economic justifications of overseas employment, and in sustaining the moral economy of the family, all the while teaching female migrants to be free economic agents in overseas markets.

The massive, informal outflows of migrants from Indonesia to more developed neighboring countries have been less organized. Village families have been sending their daughters—often by perilous routes operated by criminal syndicates—to Malaysia or Singapore, where they can earn ten times the wages they can make at home. The government is not directly involved in the organization of the maid trade, relying instead on moral economic systems to mobilize young women from towns and villages, and on NGOs to train them for overseas work. Dar Rudnyyckyj reports a *calo* (meaning "patron" or "boss") system of labor recruitment that exploits the notion of moral indebtedness and obligations. *Calo* agents advance cash to would-be female migrants, thus binding them by economic indebtedness and moral obligations to circuits of labor recruitment.[22] Female migrants are collected in camps where NGOs train them in the "techniques of servitude," which include stock English phrases of compliance, keeping to a time schedule, and the use of modern appliances. These two regimes of female out-migration are in competition across the region.

Differences in nationality and educational levels will come to color their moral assessment in the receiving sites. Filipino maids—English-speaking, frequently college-educated, and exuding a sense of Western style—reign as a kind of labor aristocracy in the regional and global domestic service industry. The Philippine state and NGOs also promote the "export value" of their female migrants as responsible workers who are professional and worthy of respect.[23] In contrast, the Indonesian authorities and NGOs have not (yet) undertaken a campaign to sell the virtues of their female migrants. But nevertheless, in both countries, NGOs enhance the capacity of the state in making female migrants available for employment overseas,[24] where they are exposed to conditions of violence and neo-slavery.

Incarceration and Securitization

The interplay of moral economies, state policy, and NGOs has created conditions whereby tens of thousands of female migrants are sent across lines of ethnicity, religion, class, and nationality. The circulation of transient female labor engenders both biopolitical availability and biopolitical othering. Under two-year contracts, these "temporary aliens" become part of a revolving labor pool that sustains thousands of middle-class households in affluent neighboring countries. The contingent legal status of foreign workers reinforces their "biopolitical otherness" [25] as noncitizens and lower-class subjects in tension with upwardly mobile Asian identities. The very biopolitical availability of foreign maids for sustaining a high standard of living becomes the reason for their exception from the good life and the body politic. In the host society, foreign domestic workers are subjected to two technologies of control: a house-bound form of labor incarceration, on the one hand, and a technology of securitization that treats them as potential political threats, on the other.

The influx of foreign domestic workers to the glittering, high-rise cities—Singapore, Hong Kong, Kuala Lumpur—is a vital prop to the new entitlements of the growing middle classes. [26] These cities are in competition to achieve global city status, and satisfying the demand for cheap domestic help is part of the bargain with two-income families. A high standard of living is considered impossible without one or even two foreign maids to take care of household chores as well as of children or the elderly. Having a maid at home is a social right, like access to good schools, housing, shopping malls, and leisure, all entitlements of the middle classes bent on buying their way to the good life. But even as the host country finds itself more intimately entangled with poor neighbors who participate in the reproduction of family life, disciplinary mechanisms and ethical exclusions invest the foreign maid with a biopolitical otherness in the public and in the domestic realms.

Foreign maids are shipped in to be confined in the households that employ them. In Hong Kong, Singapore, and Malaysia, contracted foreign domestic helpers can apply for the renewal of contract but not citizenship. In Singapore, work permits confine foreign domestic workers to "duties of a domestic nature," exclusively within the confines of an employer's home. [27] In Singapore and Malaysia, there are no rules for regulating the work conditions of foreign nannies. The Singapore employment act "prefers to leave the free market to determine the wages and other conditions of service for foreign maids because it is too impractical to impose standards terms." [28] Only in Hong Kong do foreign maids get special work visas that protect the minimum wage and the right to days off. In practice, in all three sites, the majority of foreign maids are not guaranteed good working conditions, minimal earnings, or rest days.

The unregulated nature of domestic employment is based on a logic of incarceration. The employer controls every aspect of the foreign maid's life. It is common practice in Singapore and Malaysia for the employer to hold the maid's passport and work papers, on the excuse of preventing her from running away, but in effect confining her within the household. The employer thus gains a de facto ownership over the foreign domestic, who is thus entrapped and vulnerable to exploitation of her labor and sexuality. Such incarcerating control over an individual who can be subjected to abuse is a form of neo-slavery.[29] Furthermore, even benign employers in these countries do not as a matter of norm observe days off for domestic workers, this in effect imprisoning them within the confines of the house and the endless round of housework. Given such conditions, foreign domestic helpers are often reduced to the status of nonbeings, with no legal claims on their employers or society at large. Also, because foreign women are allowed in specifically for domestic employment, there is widespread public skepticism of their right to a public presence in the affluent cities.

In Hong Kong and Singapore, the incarceral tendencies extend to time-space limits on the maids' days off. The public gatherings of foreign domestic workers are restricted to Sundays and to certain urban spaces. The conditional tolerance of their public presence enhances the hypervisibility of foreign maids as an embarrassing third world presence in upscale metropolitan sites. In Hong Kong, Filipina maids gamely resist such public exclusions by regularly staging street festivals, costume pageants, and parades to establish their claims to a public presence in the host society.[30] Filipina workers enjoy some kind of glamour derived from their English-language skills, a kind of "trophy" maid status that enhances their employers' prestige. Nevertheless, in the Hong Kong environment, any Filipina-looking woman is hailed as "foreign maid" (or *"fan-miu"* in Cantonese), in a process of interpellation that frames an individual as "always-already" a subject of ideological construction.[31] In Singapore, domestic workers are frequently referred as "menials," a term that reinforces their association with lowly, filthy work. Symbolically, then, foreign domestic workers are reminders of a too recent past from which Singaporeans and Hong Kongers have escaped by scaling the heights of urban living. Singaporeans consider foreign maids in public a "social nuisance" and even those who tolerate their presence avoid their weekend enclaves, which are associated with dirt, noise, and chaos.[32] There is a synergy between a racial/dirty personal profiling and a racial/dirty spatial profiling, a sense of the contaminating presence of the transient but ever-present foreign female labor force. So despite the gloss of Westernized cultural skills, Filipina maids operate as a ubiquitous contrastive racial or alien other to the dominant ethnic Chinese populations in the two metropolitan sites.

At a regional scale, the ethno-racial differences between Chinese-dominated middle-class employers and their domestic helpers is projected onto the relationship between the glamorous and glittering cities and their poorer and "darker" neighboring nations. The scramble to become "global cities" has reinforced laws against public expressions of racism in Hong Kong, Singapore, and Kuala Lumpur, but these rules do not apply when it comes to the treatment of foreign migrants who perform a variety of "low-skilled" or "unskilled" jobs avoided by local citizens. But the daily intimate association with these "backward," racial others threatens to subvert the self-image of affluent Asians who themselves have so recently sloughed off menial labor and paddy fields. There is suppressed fear that the increasing presence of poor migrants will blur the ethno-racial distinction of the nation, which in postcolonial Asia is based on ideological constructions of race, kinship, language, religion, and culture.

Filipina domestic workers as a category are actually better treated than Indonesian maids in Southeast Asia. Many Filipina domestic help had worked as teachers or nurses at home, and thus command the highest wages in the region. They are viewed as a kind of status symbol for well-off families and expatriates in Asian cities. While some Filipina maids have been victims of rape, as a group they are less likely than Indonesian workers to be routinely mistreated by their employers and by the police. The Philippine government has bilateral agreements with host societies that give some measure of protection to Filipino workers, so that their chances of recourse to compensation and justice are greater than for other categories of foreign nannies. Filipina workers abroad are thus a kind of female migrant labor aristocracy who enjoy the best low-skilled working conditions for migrants in Asian cities.

Other foreign female workers—from Indonesia, India, Sri Lanka, and Thailand—are frequently treated as a migrant population that has high probabilities of being trafficked and thus entering the host society illegally. There is indeed a huge and not easily controllable system of labor smuggling that ferries low-skilled Indonesian workers to Malaysia. There is a widespread perception of Indonesian workers as the source of crimes and social ills. Poor Indonesians are blamed for petty crimes and an array of other risks such as prostitution and the AIDS disease.[33] They have been accused of practicing a kind of radical Islam not generally welcome in the country. These perceptions of Indonesians as potential enemies also color the treatment of Indonesian women who enter seeking work as domestic help.

While most Indonesian maids in Malaysia are recruited under a two-year contract, they are all tarred by the perception of being "illegal." Their status as less skilled migrant workers, compared to Filipina maids, also reinforces their negative image. They are also under constant surveillance, suspected of being home wreckers and prostitutes, and in public frequently threatened with violence. Indonesian maids are subjected to frequent checks by the police. Public intimidations include police destruction of their documents, demands for bribes, or even gang rape. In addition to the lack of protection from labor exploitation and nonpayment of wages, foreign maids in Malaysia lack a mechanism for the redress of abuse. The Indonesian diplomatic service has not been able to help beyond providing shelter for dismissed migrants who are awaiting deportation. Where foreign maids are concerned, Malaysians tend to be "pro-employer and anti-employee," with the result that abused migrants are criminalized,[34] while crimes against them go unpunished in the vast majority of cases.[35] The situation in Hong Kong is slightly better, but employers charged with maid abuse often avoid punishment.[36] Singapore has set up a procedure for maids to complain about abuses suffered by foreign workers.

Foreign domestic workers are thus situated in a transnational field of labor exchange and traffic that strips them of the most basic political rights. In addition, they are frequently treated as a threat to the social body. Securitization techniques include the manufacture of ruptures, which provokes panic and fears of disruption in the political order.[37] I already mentioned that Indonesian migrants are frequently targeted as a threat; on occasion, they are subjected to mechanisms of international penology. During economic downturn or social panics, a cascade of "emergency" acts reworks the divide between internal and external enemies. For instance, in the aftermath of the Asian financial crisis in 1997–98, close to nine hundred thousand migrant workers, the majority of them female, were expelled from host nations.[38] In Malaysia, campaigns such as "Operation Get Out" pushed migrants to nearby Indonesian islands that act as holding stations. There, migrant women survived by providing sexual services to tourists from Singapore and Malaysia. The combination of routine police harassment and transnational securitization measures gives the host society great flexibility in keeping borders open or shut to migrants, depending on the economic climate or public moral outrage, as the case may be. Indonesian workers are always assessed in terms of a calculation of probabilities that they are illegal, criminal, and a threat to the host country. It is no surprise therefore that Indonesia has come to see itself as a "coolie nation" that makes available its own citizens as cheap workers for richer neighboring countries. The incarceral logic thus imprisons foreign female workers in employers' households, but the logic of securitization keeps them in constant motion as a transient labor pool. An editorial in the leading Singapore newspaper comments on the expulsion of Indonesian workers, observing that "[i]f we must grow calluses on our hearts, so be it."[39] Indeed, foreign maids have a precarious claim on the moral economies of the host society.

Disjunctive Moral Economies

Besides political controls of disciplining and securitization, the moral economies of the host society also erect moral barriers to their presence. Foreign domestic workers are considered a necessary evil who are needed to maintain the household and yet can pose a threat to the host family. This moral ambivalence underlies social demands for strict controls over foreign maids. The employer comes to have unrestricted personal power over the foreign domestic helper, including holding her passport and work permit, and determining her wages, work, and living conditions. But while such privatized power gives the employer wide latitude in dictating the hours of work, there is a difference between a slave driver and a slave owner who feels no compunction in repeatedly abusing the foreign domestic worker.

Incidents of torture and murder of maids escalated in the aftermath of the Asian financial crisis. In Singapore, the authorities do not deal with the problem of maid abuse through legal protection, but on a case-by-case basis. The government recently introduced a half-day orientation for new employers of foreign maids, with the hope that employers can be socialized to treat their foreign maids with respect. Such mechanisms do very little to prevent violence against maids, which continues despite severe punishments for criminal acts of employers. Perhaps recognizing the limits of such legal action, an official made the following plea. "It is vital that employers respect their domestic maids and look after them properly, as invaluable helpers in our households, and not as slaves or chattel."[40] We are thus faced with a situation where the difference between exploitative working conditions and abuse of the foreign worker, between being a slave driver and being a slave owner, suggests a profound moral denigration of the domestic worker as a *female migrant*.

The biopolitical otherness of foreign maids is mapped onto ethno-racial politics surrounding the production of life, and by the disjunctive terrain of ethics through which foreign domestic workers circulate. Among the employing population, there is profound ambivalence about the fact that foreign maids play a crucial role in the material and social reproduction of middle-class families and yet belong to an external ethno-racial servant class. Tensions between a perception of foreign maids as racially and socially contaminating and their involvement in the intimate economies of family care engender complex mechanisms of internal exclusions. There are three contributing factors to an explosive situation whereby an ordinary household employment of foreign female labor can escalate into a situation of neo-slavery.

First, among ethnic Chinese populations, there is a historical practice of servitude that constructs the unattached, mobile woman as an unprotected category.

Many in Southeast Asia are familiar with the old practice of *mui-jai* (in Cantonese), or the bonded maidservant who faithfully served a single family throughout her life. In the early twentieth century, *mui-jai* were young, unattached girls who could be bought and sold as a form of dowry or for concubinage, prostitution, or slavery. The *mui-jai* was therefore as essential outsider, marked by her kinless state, and thus assigned a slave status. A more negative term was "*yong-yan*," an individual who exists for the personal use of the owner. The *mui-jai* could only overcome her social condition by becoming attached through kinship to the employer's family. "A woman was nothing unless she could be validated through kinship relations with a man."[41] The enslavement of poor, unattached young women was a pervasive practice throughout British colonies in Southeast Asia. In 1921, the new professional class in Hong Kong led the fight against the *mui-jai*, in the name of modern progress and support for female liberation.

It is therefore ironic that some of the attitude toward *mui-jai*, or bonded maidservants, seems to have survived among the new middle-classes in Hong Kong, Singapore, and Malaysia. There is the perception that as unattached female migrants, domestic workers are moral outsiders, despite the performance of reproductive work and incorporation into the household. Her externality to kinship is what marks her as having a slavelike status, making her highly vulnerable to physical abuse. Furthermore, unlike earlier generations of *mui-jai*, who were by and large ethnic Chinese, like their employers, contemporary domestics are ethnic others, and therefore impossible to transform into kin. The moral unattachability of foreign domestic helpers makes permanent their exclusion from kinship considerations and obligations that in former days would have been extended to outside women brought in to work as servants. The Filipino or Indonesian maid is an unalterable alien to the moral economy of the Chinese family.

Second, from the perspective of the employer, the short-term employment of the foreign maid creates a sense of being "cheated" by the maid leaving after she has been trained to cook Chinese food and perform other chores that are specific to Chinese domestic life. Thus, in many complaints voiced by mistresses, and in many of the abuse cases, there is mention of the foreign domestic help as a drain on the family resources, requiring the family to incur a loss from employing her. There is an urgency that given the economic investment in her upkeep, the mistress should try to extract the maximum service from the helper during her short employment contract. According to Christine Chin, female employers in Kuala Lumpur frequently refer to their foreign maids as "garbage" or "slave." One employer summed up her distrust of foreign domestic helpers in the phrase, "love to hate them, hate to love them."[42] Despite the foreign maid's contribution to household maintenance, she is also perceived as an outsider who can waste family resources such as food, utilities, and money, and even betray affection from the host family.[43] With the relationship to the foreign maid reduced to one of necessary evil, there is often little room for affection or for developing a sense of moral obligation, so that in extreme cases, such employer resentments can be expressed in kicks, beatings, and burning on the maid's body.

Third, the mistress sometimes views the foreign maid's presence in the household as a double-edge sword. The maid's material and emotional labor are props to the well-being of the host family, but the presence of an exotic young woman in the household stirs worry and jealousy about her sexual allure. The many cases of seduction or rape by male employers contribute to a widespread hostility to the maid's sexuality, a negative view of her as neither kin nor friend but a potential marriage wrecker.[44] In Malaysia, middle-class women share stories about the "sexploits" of their maids, as well as their potential threat to the family as carriers of sexual diseases.[45] Such extreme mistrust disrupts the chances that employers will develop a sense of moral obligation to and protection of the foreign maid. Female employers are more likely than male to view the maid as a potential economic and sexual threat, and they are also more likely to be the oppressors of foreign domestic workers.

In Malaysia, even the moral economies of Malay-Muslims and their Indonesian maids, while they have commonalities in Islam, race (*bangsa*), and similar *kampong* (village)-derived cultures, do not always guarantee good treatment for the latter. Domestic workers from Indonesia are viewed as "social pariahs" undeserving of public sympathy. They are commonly perceived to be perpetrators of moral and sexual crimes who should be locked up in "depots" and deported.[46] The limits of Malay moral economy indicate that national and class divisions break down the extension of ethnic-based moral obligations to poorer coethnics from overseas. There is thus a convergence of language and national bias, with the nationality of the foreign worker recast as a racial otherness, making it less likely that a sense of kinship obligation and mutuality can be extended to foreign domestic workers. In short, the ethical exclusions of foreign maids contribute to the widespread view of their moral inferiority, a kind of suspension of moral obligations that permits their treatment as subhumans, or bare life.

Indeed, the detachment of poor migrant women from moral economy is most concretely inscribed by the technologies of sterility. During the two-year contract, the foreign maid is not permitted to have sex, or to marry a local citizen. To ensure that she will have no biological recourse to citizenship, the foreign domestic helper is tested every six months to check for HIV and pregnancy. Pregnancy results in the termination of the employment contract and expulsion from the country. Meanwhile, there is no regular health coverage for foreign maids, and their health costs are to be borne by their employers, something that is not guaranteed. There is thus a total suspension of the female worker's biological rights during her overseas employment. She cannot express corporeal desires and activities. She is hired to perform reproductive services for the host family, but is excluded from reproductive activities in her own family. This denial of her reproductive role vis-à-vis her own family has led to the transnational relay of family care. Filipino maids working overseas hire poorer women in their home villages to care for their own children.[47] In short, within this realm of biopolitical otherness and disjunctive moral economies, migrant women's legal, moral, and biological statuses are highly contingent, making them vulnerable to the harsh working conditions, rapes, beatings, and disfigurements one associates with neo-slavery.

Remapping the Ethical Terrain

A Milieu of Ethical Reflection

Modern situations of inhumanity become the milieus within which ethical reflection on modern humanity arises. In Asian locations, some critics, following Habermas, have pointed to the "democratic deficit" in public life.[48] For instance, a study of the mistreatment of foreign domestics in Singapore identifies the lack of a lively civil society scene.[49] But while that may well be the case, the model of the public realm is an abstracted space that does not take into account the diverse elements and contending visions, of which democracy is only one element, that shape the political and spiritual visions of the good life. Furthermore, the radical democracy model seems to predetermine only one outcome—full democratic citizenship. But when we investigate the actual unfolding situation for resolving the migrant worker problem, specific milieus of humanitarian crisis shaped by various elements—politics, markets, and ethical systems—also crystallize conditions of possibility for the ethical problematization of and search for ways to give value to the politically excluded.

Communitarian theorists have pointed to the centrality of cultural norms and practices in any conception of the public sphere. But in any one milieu, debates must take into account situated political and ethical reasoning about the public good, especially the kind of thinking about sheer life.[50] Below, I will consider the role of NGOs as they enter into the fray of middle-class entitlements, disjunctive moral economies, bio-welfare, and market calculations that surrounds the plight of foreign domestic workers, and through which the ethical treatment of aliens crystallizes.

The growth of the foreign maid trade coincided with the rise of the discourse of "Asian values." As I have discussed elsewhere, this discourse arose in the context of the "Asian tiger boom," fundamentally as an ideological claim that capitalism in Southeast Asia was a kinder and gentler system in which collective interests were not displaced by unfettered individual interests.[51] Thus tied to nationalist development, the narrative of Asian values became part of the governing process designed to draw moral support for development despite social dislocations. The talk of a "caring society" in Malaysia and Singapore, which claims that wealth accumulation need not be incompatible with kindness, operates as a kind of regulatory discourse that lines citizens up behind development projects. The treatment of migrant workers who are crucial to national development has never been addressed by Asian values discourse, nor has the plight of migrant domestic women who have become indispensable to middle-class life. Nevertheless, the gap between the "caring society" and the treatment of foreign maids cannot be entirely attributed to state developmentalist ideology. Ethnic-based moral economies reinforce the common view of foreign maids as people from coolie nations who are morally unattachable to the host society. In order to intervene in this constellation of values regimes, feminists must articulate an alternative geography of moral accountability.

NGOS: Mapping a Bio-Geography

A common view about migrant workers is that the host country should award them citizenship, in recognition of the contribution of their labor to the national economy.[52] But in Southeast Asia, NGOs that intervene in the crisis of foreign maids do not demand citizenship on their behalf. In fact, the majority of foreign migrant workers do not wish to have citizenship in the host country; they wish to have moral legitimacy and market access. At the same time, competition for foreign jobs among labor-sending countries precludes insistence on the human rights of their own migrant workers. Thus, while NGOs may formally invoke United Nations conventions to claim rights for migrant women and their families,[53] their interventions respond directly to the specific conditions in the space configured by labor markets, biopolitics, and divergent moral economies.

It is useful to think of NGOs as a form of social technology, i.e., like other kinds of governing entities, that defines "objects, rules of action, strategic games of liberties."[54] NGOs give moral value to bare life by defining their clients' biological existence in relation to political space. NGOs thus gain power over the politically excluded, and exercise the power to regulate, frame, and represent their interests to various parties. For instance, in Singapore, some church-based NGOs "govern" foreign maids by helping them submit to their lot through religious disciplining and forbearance. "What we do is help them [the maids] cope using the Bible. . . . We don't encourage complaining, because that's not Biblical. So you either learn to forbear, or seek alternative solutions."[55] State-controlled NGOs thus create a religious space for inducing self-discipline among foreign maids.

But NGOs in Malaysia operate in a different direction, by mapping a different geography of claims for female migrants that cross-cuts the space of the nation-state. This space is scaled at the level of regional migrant flows, and is intended to bridge over disjunctive nations and moral economies that devalue the moral status of female migrants and tolerate conditions of neo-slavery. These NGOs discover that a space of migrant claims to sheer survival can benefit from aligning the claims with neoliberal interest in cheap labor.

Bio-Welfare

The respatialization of migrant claims at a regional level is suggested by the commonality of dangers encountered by migrant women in many national, racial, and moral economic contexts. NGOs throughout Asia have collected data on the array of abuses that female workers suffer in the course of their migration and work in host societies. Migrant women are highly vulnerable to being trafficked, raped, deprived of their earnings, and getting infected with the HIV virus. The labor conditions are defined by the three-D jobs (dirty, demanding, and dangerous) and the three-D stigmas (disease, depravity, and drugs). NGOs remind the public that a majority of migrant workers are females who provide "the cheapest, flexible, and most docile labor . . . for dirty, demanding, and dangerous jobs which locals shun."[56] The extensive documentation of abuses inflicted on female migrant workers at the regional level exposes the hypocrisy of official discourses such as that of "the caring society" (in Malaysia) and the "educated society" (in Singapore). Such self-representations do not come with legal and moral protections for foreign female workers whose circulations make possible the realization of neoliberal standards of living.

Using "the media as their ally," feminists broaden the ethical debates on the treatment of foreign domestic workers, also challenging the Malaysian state to increase the protection of migrant women.[57] Reports on the abuse, maltreatment, torture, and even death of migrant women have provided ammunition in negotiations with local authorities to consider making medical coverage part of the work contract for female migrants. One outcome has been stricter controls over agencies that recruit and transport migrant workers. But there is unanimous support for the government's position that foreign maids should not be given opportunities for citizenship.

Therefore, a major strategy of NGOs is to change public perception about the moral obligation to support and protect the lives of migrant women who have contributed to the realization of their middle-class dreams. Press reports of maid abuse have increased public awareness of the problem, bringing shame and horror to Malaysians who are accustomed to viewing themselves as a warm and hospitable people. The director of a women's shelter in Malaysia said that people need to realize that "poorer people who are working for you also have rights. This is not slavery."[58] The focus is on the mobile female body and its vulnerability to enslavement. What kind of representation can be made that will shift the perception of the migrant female body from a site of a biopolitical otherness to a site of biological claim?

Talking about undocumented workers with AIDS in France, Didier Fassin maintains that "the *suffering body* proposed in the name of common humanity is opposed to the illegitimacy of the *racialized body*, promulgated in the name of insurmountable difference." The discourse of the suffering body, he argues, has created "bio-legitimacy" as a new legal claim whereby health and illness become legitimate grounds for awarding citizenship to the asylum seeker.[59] In Southeast Asia, NGO discourses of the "enslaved or at-risk body" of foreign maids is not proposed in the name of common humanity in order for maids to gain legal status as citizens. Indeed, Southeast Asian countries and their populations are very firm in their political beliefs that it is legitimate for the state to discriminate in favor of its own citizens against aliens. Thus, NGOs are not invoking human rights as a legal status, but are appealing to basic cultural values about the moral worthiness of women's bodies. The focus is on *bio-welfare*, an ethical claim that skirts the issue of political rights by focusing on the sheer survival of foreign female workers. Only by invoking cultural understanding and compassion, not abstract rights discourse, can the moral legitimacy of alien women's bio-security be persuasive to the host society.

The bio-welfare of foreign domestic workers, as women at risk, is an even more fundamental claim on Asian ethics. The bodily integrity of women, the female body confronted with potential violence, is something that can elicit greater moral importance from Asian society, more than the demand for gender or migrant rights. In the course of their work, migrant women suffer from violence and exposure to life-threatening diseases and have little or no access to health services. The foreign maid, who is not a machine, also requires rest, and a limit to overtime labor. Feminists ask, If Singapore is such a civilized society, why are maids treated as "emotionless and slavish working machines," not as human beings?[60] In the absence of enforceable laws for maids to have rest days, feminist NGOs are now insisting on the moral obligations of employers to let their domestic helpers have days off for "rest and relaxation," or to attend to religious practices. The language avoids demanding "worker rights," stressing instead the moral and health benefits of time off, since the foreign worker should not be treated like a slavelike thing. After all, migrant women and foreign maids are frequently also mothers and nurses, life givers and life nurturers who are cherished in Asian traditions.

By focusing on the *at-risk* female body, NGOs compel the Asian middle classes to acknowledge the vulnerable female body and their own responsibility as host society to secure the bio-welfare of their foreign workers. Islam, Hinduism, Buddhism, and Christianity all stress special protection of the weak and vulnerable, especially women and children. These religions also support moral traditions of hospitality to foreign visitors in a region long shaped by international trade and migration flows. Advocates of migrant workers thus stimulate a coherent reflection on ethics into which the public is drawn. In other words, how to reconsider the situation of the domestic worker, whose very biopolitical availability denies her bodily security and human dignity, but instead reduces her to a slavelike status? NGOs raise questions such as whether living the good life (in the material sense) should entail the mistreatment of less fortunate others. Although foreign maids have no citizenship, their enslaved, threatened bodies are a rebuke to the modernity of Southeast Asian societies, suggesting a backward slide to dependency on slaves in the feudal past.

In contrast, the healthy and secure body of the foreign maid can only redound favorably in sustaining the higher standard of living enjoyed by well-heeled Asians. Such ethical reflection will correct the new, ugly face of Asian affluence, and perhaps stimulate a recovery of a sense of Asian hospitality that combines the value of the life of the female migrant with the moral economy of Asian families. The questions posed are tied to wider moral questions of how Asians should live, and how they should treat others who provide their daily comfort and family security. The calls for a restoration of the heart to the Asian treatment of migrant others induce them to rethink the questions of the daily activities that support families and the nation as both a political and ethical problem. In particular, can the middle-class employer break from his or her sense of entitlement and complacency, reenvisioning his or her relationship with the foreign maid as a kind of moral economy, i.e., an ethical relationship, one that minimally secures the biological health of the migrant woman? In the absence of legal rights protecting the foreign helper, can her bio-welfare be guaranteed through the moral economy of the family?

Bio-welfare refers to the rights to life and bodily integrity, which have been called "the first genre of human rights," the fundamental elements of individual rights.[61] But the moral demands for bio-welfare by Asian NGOs are not antecedent to claims for full-fledged legal rights for migrants to become legal citizen subjects. The question remains whether this kind of strictly moral claims for migrant workers can be reinforced through market reasoning.

Market Rights

NGOs are not just content with promoting the bio-welfare of female migrants; they want foreign domestic workers to be truly free economic agents as well. As discussed above, NGOs have subcontracted the role of making available contracted labor migrants for overseas markets. Now, in order to be effective protectors of abused migrant workers, other NGOs ramp up the claims of migrant workers to job freedom in overseas labor markets. Although the foreign domestic helper is not as glamorous as the globe-trotting corporate warrior of neoliberalism, she is also a risk-taking subject, someone who crosses mountains and oceans to reach a labor situation where her chances of biological and economic well-being are highly uncertain. So NGOs are linking the demand for a healthy migrant body to a kind of neoliberal calculation, claiming that as foreign workers, maids should enjoy the freedom of residence, employment, and family life, i.e., the conditions of social reproduction that are enjoyed by foreign professionals in Asia. Foreign domestic workers should have the right to reside in the host city, to bring their families, and to change jobs or find other lines of work. This right of market access and freedom to operate across the region is very different from demands for citizenship.

In surveys conducted by local NGOs, the vast majority of female migrant workers are not interested in becoming citizens in Hong Kong, Singapore, and Kuala Lumpur. Perhaps at the most, 10 percent want to settle down in the host country, and most of these are migrant women who have married local people.[62] What migrant workers want is legal residence, as well as unrestricted movement back and forth to the home country. For Filipino workers, the demand for residency rights and easy mobility also ensures that the Philippines can continue to be a labor-exporting country. Indonesian domestic helpers also feel that migrant rights of residence abroad will enable them to contribute to the development of their country. The Asian Migrant Center, a Hong Kong–based umbrella of

migrant-oriented NGOs, is currently fighting for the right of foreign domestic workers to be temporary residents in the city of employment and
to work and move between Asian cities without the limits imposed by the
contract system.

The ethics of healthy and unharmed migrant bodies becomes the
grounds for their claim to be freely competitive in the regional labor
markets. Furthermore, the health and security of the female migrant is
unavoidably entangled with the well-being of her family left back home.
Claims for the integrity of the migrant body, and freedom of choice in the
regional marketplace, will make migrant workers (and their families) less
vulnerable. At the same time, this alignment of gendered biological security and neoliberal logic also highlights the economic benefits to the host
society. Health security and market flexibility will ensure that the foreign
servant class continues to be available to affluent Asians, but preferably
under better material, moral, and economic terms. The demand for migrant biological welfare is thus embedded in economic interdependency
between the sending and the receiving countries.[63]

Such NGO reasoning thus creates an ethics of exception for foreign
maids, making a good moral economic argument for why, despite their
status as aliens, they deserve biological justice. By inscribing a bio-cartography of migrant workers, NGOs reterritorialize their moral claims on a
regional scale. Unfortunately, given the contingencies of the forces at play,
NGO governance can only safeguard the biological security of migrant
women by foregrounding their capacity to serve the insatiable demands
of the neoliberal sector. For the moment, such moral bargains provision-
ally maintain migrant wages below those of the citizens of the employing
countries.

*   *   *

We need to maintain skepticism toward claims that NGOs are building the
institutional skeleton of a "global public sphere." We have seen that NGO
activities are situated within particular constellations of power and ethics;
their interventions can actually generate new moral hierarchies. In action,
NGOs have not so much converted the globally excluded into humanity
with legal rights as they have redefined and reordered different categories
of the human in connection with various moral systems, markets, and the
state. This is the case because specific NGO problems are crystallized by,
and their interventions take shape through, situated constellations of economic, political, and ethical relationships. NGOs thus are not the actors

of a "postnational constellation," in the Habermasian sense of an emerging global civil society,[64] for three reasons. First, in Southeast Asia, NGOs are demanding moral guarantees of biological welfare, not rights of citizenship for migrant workers as members of a global humanity. Even if they formulate their demands in terms of "migrant rights," there is no juridical institutionalization of migrant rights outside national treaties between sending and receiving countries, and even these are minimal and easily thwarted by the host society. The shocking case of Flor Contemplacion, a Filipino maid executed in Singapore for causing the deaths of the child in her care and of another maid, raised questions of the sending country's capacity to protect the individual rights of its citizens in the host country.[65] Rather, within the Southeast Asian matrix of economic, moral, and political economies, NGOs invoke values shared by various ethical regimes: the female body deserves moral status and physical protection. Such an ethical reasoning can bypass if not displace the ethno-racialized stigma of foreign domestic workers as alien and illegitimate bodies. The bio-welfare claims construct a moral status that may reduce incidents of brutal attacks and disfigurements of foreign maids. But given the current nexus of nationalisms, migrant labor, and moral economies, it is not clear that claims of bio-welfarism will be an antecedent to formal citizenship in the host society.

Second, the NGOs are not postnational in that they play a variety of roles for the nation-state, and become somewhat party or subject to national agendas and capitalist interests. NGOs in labor-exporting countries are part of the institutional infrastructure that supports the state development strategy of making migrant workers available overseas. At the same time, other NGOs protest the dangerous and violent conditions of migrant employment and movement, seeking a kind of basic security and freedom for migrants as mobile workers. NGOs thus directly or indirectly subcontract for states and work with market interests. Such connections to strategic political and market institutions and enmeshment in normative structures actually make NGOs more effective in pursuing grass-roots causes.

My ethnographic discussion shows that NGOs in operation are not autonomous entities entirely devoted to an abstract notion of universal democracy. Rather, the NGO modality in action is one of complex attachments and detachments—embeddedness in cultural affiliations but solidarity with the plight of migrant workers; links to the nation and capitalism but contingent ties to notions of common humanity; use of situated

ethical beliefs but rare mention of human rights; and investment in regional attitudes toward migrant women as a priority over abstract ideals
of global humanity. As actors intervening in particular milieus, NGOs are
vulnerable to regulation and manipulation by the state, the media, and
public opinion, even as they struggle to build an ethical solidarity between foreign domestics and their affluent employers. For the millions of
intrepid young women traveling afar in order to support their own families back home, the geography of labor circulations becomes the unstable
ground of their claim for biological security.

This formulation of situated attachment and detachment is a different
modality than the concept of "detachment" proposed by the "new cos-
mopolitanists" as distance from particularistic ties and disinterested affiliations based on universalism.[66] The point is not that there are no "new
cosmopolitanisms," but rather that NGO missions must be translated and
negotiated within particular alignments of institutional power, and the
ethical outcomes are not solely predetermined by human rights. In order
to be effective at all, NGOs must work with and thus become subjected to
the conjunctural force of overlapping political, moral, and economic systems. Furthermore, most NGOs in the south receive funding from transnational NGOs based in the Netherlands, Denmark, Sweden, the United
Kingdom and Canada, and are thus also subjected to the governance of a
universalizing human rights regime that often pushes human rights agendas without dealing with the practical problems of millions of impoverished peoples living on the edge. NGOs are caught betwixt and between
transnational and situated regimes of living, trying to safeguard lives as
well as living conditions. NGOs try to negotiate in the interstitial space
among diverse ethics regimes.

Third, the concept of constellated ethical systems challenges Agamben's
pessimism that bare life exists in a zone of exception bereft of any possibility of moral intervention.[67] NGOs' interventions on behalf of noncitizens and the politically excluded operate in a realm of diverse traditions
that can be tapped for ethical principles that cherish and protect life. Humanitarian work relies on the interplay of rhetorical claims and counter-
claims, constantly translating values across a range of exceptions, always
making special cases for bringing in one more baby, one more tortured
victim, from the ambiguous edge of humanity. The temporal dimension
of NGO labor is one of continually undoing the binarism institutionalized in citizenship, or the conceptual separation between rights and ethics. When we recognize the fruitful interplay of diverse forms of virtue,

we know that there is no permanent zone of indistinction, only endless ethical challenges to established dichotomies of human and nonhuman, or of good and evil.[68]

NOTES

This chapter is reprinted from A. Ong, *Neoliberalism as Exception* (Durham, NC: Duke University Press, 2006).

1. These are abstracted accounts drawn from reports in *The Straits Times* (Singapore), *The New Straits Times* (Kuala Lumpur), and *The Wall Street Journal* (Washington, DC).

2. Jason Szep, "In Wealthy Singapore, Maids Push for Protection," March 19, 2004, available at http://in.news.yahoo.com/040319/ 137/2c31c.html (last accessed May 1, 2007).

3. At the turn of the century, there were an estimated ten million Asian migrant workers, half of whom were female. Asian Migrant Center, *Baseline Research on Racial and Gender Discrimination towards Filipino, Indonesian, and Thai Domestic Helpers in Hong Kong* (Hong Kong: Asian Migrant Center, 2001), 14.

4. Szep, "In Wealthy Singapore," supra note 2.

5. "Malaysia Maid Abuse Shocks PM," May 21, 2004, available at http://news.bbc.co.uk/2/hi/asia-pacific/3734695.stm (last accessed May 1, 2007).

6. Hazlin Hassan, "Maids as Slaves: Asia's Hidden Shame," *The Manila Times*, June 3, 2004.

7. Jonathan Kent, "Malaysia Angry at Maid Abuse," *BBC News*, May 21, 2004.

8. Hassan, supra note 6; Philip Bowring, "Abuse Shed Light on Vulnerable Millions," *International Herald Tribune*, May 25, 2004.

9. Seyla Benhabib, *The Claims of Culture: Equality and Diversity in the Global Era* (Princeton, NJ: Princeton University Press, 2002).

10. Giorgio Agamben, *Homo Sacer: Sovereign Power and Bare Life*, trans. Daniel Heller-Roazen (Stanford, CA: Stanford University Press, 1998).

11. Etienne Balibar, "Outlines of a Topography of Cruelty: Citizenship and Civility in the Era of Global Violence," *Constellations* 8 (2001); Catherine Dauvergne, "Making People Illegal," in *Critical Beings: Law, Nation, and the Global Subject*, eds. Peter Fitzpatrick and Patricia Tuitt (London: Ashgate Press, 2003), 83.

12. Agamben, *Homo Sacer*, supra note 10, 170–71.

13. Ibid., 179–80.

14. Michael Ignatieff, "Human Rights," in *Human Rights in Political Transitions: Gettysburg to Bosnia*, eds. Carla Hesse and Robert Post (New York: Zone Books, 1999), 318–20.

15. See Stephen Castles and Alastair Davidson, *Citizenship and Migration* (New York: Routledge, 2000), ch. 8.

16. See, e.g., David Held, *Democracy and the Global Order: From the Modern State to Cosmopolitan Governance* (Stanford, CA: Stanford University Press, 1995).

17. For the trail-blazing study of moral economy in Southeast Asia, see James C. Scott, *The Moral Economy of the Peasant: Rebellion and Subsistence in Southeast Asia* (New Haven, CT: Yale University Press, 1976).

18. For specific case studies, see Aihwa Ong, *Spirits of Resistance and Capitalist Discipline: Factory Women in Malaysia* (Albany: State University of New York Press, 1987); and Mary Beth Mills, *Thai Women in the Global Labor Force: Consuming Desires, Contested Selves* (New Brunswick, NJ: Rutgers University Press, 1999).

19. "Invest in the Philippines: Home of the Great Filipino Worker," advertisement in *The Far Eastern Economic Review*, June 13, 2002, 11.

20. Anna Guevarra, "Manufacturing the Ideal Work Force: The Transnational Labor Brokering of Nurses and Domestic Workers from the Philippines" (Ph.D. diss. in Social and Behavioral Sciences, University of California, San Francisco, 2003).

21. Ibid., 164.

22. Daromir Rudnyckyj, "Technologies of Servitude: Governmentality and Indonesian Transnational Labor Migration," *Anthropology Quarterly* 77 (Summer 2004): 407–34.

23. Guevarra, "Manufacturing the Ideal Work Force," supra note 20, 8.

24. Rudnyckyj, "Technologies of Servitude," supra note 22, 407.

25. The term "a biopolitical backwardness" is borrowed from Didier Fassin, "The Biopolitics of Otherness," *Anthropology Today* 17 (February 2001): 4.

26. Christine Chin has argued that in Malaysia, the demand for cheap foreign workers is so high that it is a kind of "social contract" between the state and the middle classes. See Christine B. N. Chin, *In Service and Servitude: Foreign Domestic Workers in Malaysia and the Malaysian "Modernity Project"* (New York: Columbia University Press, 2000).

27. B. S. A. Yeoh and S. Huang, "Spaces at the Margins: Migrant Domestic Workers and the Development of Civil Society in Singapore," *Environment and Planning A* 31 (1999): 1155.

28. Cited in ibid., 1156.

29. This new kind of household slavery shares a startling similarity to the sexual slavery produced by the traffic of women in Asia. See Kathleen Barry, Charlotte Bunch, and Shirley Castley, eds., *International Feminism: Networking against Female Sexual Slavery* (New York: International Women's Tribune Centre, 1984), 22.

30. Nicole Constable, *Maid to Order in Hong Kong* (Ithaca, NY: Cornell University Press, 1997).

31. Louis Althusser, "Ideology and Ideological State Apparatuses," in *Lenin and Philosophy and Other Essays*, trans. Ben Brewster (New York: Monthly Review Press, 1971), 174–75.

32. Yeoh and Huang, "Spaces at the Margins," supra note 27, 1156.

33. See Chin, *In Service and Servitude*, supra note 26, 109–11.

34. Interview with Tenaganita, June 2002.

35. Although the government does allow legal migrants temporary visa extensions to stay in the country in order to testify against an abuser, they are unable to work. In almost all cases, the worker settles for a sum of money and leaves the country. See Sydney Jones, *Making Money off Migrants: The Indonesian Exodus to Malaysia* (Hong Kong: Asia 2000, 2000).

36. Constable, *Maid to Order*, supra note 30.

37. Claudia Aradau, "Beyond Good and Evil: Ethics and Securitization/Desecuritization Techniques," *Rubikon* (December 2001), available at http://venus.ci.uw.edu.pl/~rubikon/forum/claudia2.htm (last accessed May 1, 2007).

38. Asian Migrant Centre, *Asian Migrant Yearbook 2000* (Hong Kong: Asian Migrant Center, 1999), 72.

39. Seth Mydans, "As Boom Fails, Malaysia Sends Migrants Home," *New York Times*, April 9, 1998.

40. Rebecca Buckman and Trish Saywell, "Domestic Disputes: For Asia's Maids, Years of Abuse Spill into the Open," *Wall Street Journal*, February 19, 2004, A6.

41. Maria Jaschok, *Concubines and Bondservants: The Social History of a Chinese Custom* (London: Zed Books, 1998), 76–77.

42. Chin, *In Service and Servitude*, supra note 26, 144–45.

43. Constable, *Maid to Order*, supra note 30, 148–49.

44. Constable, *Maid to Order*, supra note 30, 71, 106–8.

45. Chin, *In Service and Servitude*, supra note 26, 144–45.

46. Chin, *In Service and Servitude*, supra note 26, 111.

47. For an instructive and poignant view of this transnational relay of family care, see the documentary, "The Chain of Love," directed by Marika Meerman (2003). See also Rhacel Salazar Parrenas, *Servants of Globalization: Women, Migration, and Domestic Work* (Stanford, CA: Stanford University Press, 2001).

48. Jürgen Habermas, "Why Europe Needs a Constitution," *New Left Review* 11 (Sept.–Oct. 2001): 14.

49. Yeoh and Huang, "Spaces at the Margins," supra note 27.

50. See Stephen J. Collier and Andrew Lakoff, "On Regimes of Living," in *Global Assemblages, Technology, Politics, and Ethics as Anthropological Problems*, eds. Aihwa Ong and Stephen J. Collier (Malden, MA: Blackwell, 2005).

51. See Aihwa Ong, *Flexible Citizenship: The Cultural Logics of Transnationality* (Durham, NC: Duke University Press, 1999), chap. 7.

52. Saskia Sassen, *Globalization and Its Discontents* (New York: New Press, 1998); and Michael Hardt and Antonio Negri, *Empire* (Cambridge, MA: Harvard University Press, 2000).

53. Since the 1990s, the United Nations has introduced an international convention on the rights of migrant workers and their families, but it remains unratified by the majority of countries.

54. Michel Foucault, *Power: Essential Works of Foucault, 1954–1984*, vol. 3, ed. James D. Faubion, ser. ed. Paul Rainbow (New York: New Press, 2000), 319.

55. Yeoh and Huang, "Spaces at the Margins," supra note 37, 1170.

56. Tenaganita, *Implications of the Economic Crisis on Migrant Workers* (Kuala Lumpur: Tenaganita, 1998), 8.

57. Seth Mydans, "Malaysians Are Stunned by Reports Detailing Abuse of Servants," *New York Times*, February 20, 2000.

58. Cited in ibid.

59. Fassin, "The Biopolitics of Otherness," supra note 25, 4.

60. Lee Ching Wern, "Not Slaves: Maids Speak Out against Unfair System," *Aware*, March 10, 2003, available at http:/www.aware. org.sg/twc2/news2003Mar-10Today.html (site no longer accessible).

61. James C. Hsiung, "Human Rights and International Relations: Morality, Law, and Politics," in *Human Rights of Migrant Workers: Agenda for NGOs*, ed. Graziano Battistella (Quezon City: Scalabrini Migration Center, 1993), 185.

62. Interview with Tenaganita, July 18, 2002.

63. This point is also made in Hsiung, "Human Rights and International Relations," supra note 62, 186.

64. Jurgens Habermas, *Postnational Constellations* (Cambridge, MA: MIT Press, 2001).

65. For a discussion of this case, see Ninotchka Rosca, "Mrs. Contemplacion's Sisters: The Philippines' Shameful Export," *The Nation*, April 17, 1995.

66. Amanda Anderson, "Cosmopolitanism, Universalism, and the Divided Legacies of Modernity," in *Cosmopolitics: Thinking and Feeling beyond the Nation*, eds. Pheng Cheah and Bruce Robbins (Minneapolis: University of Minnesota Press, 1998), 267.

67. Agamben, *Homo Sacer*, supra note 10, 170–71.

68. Aradau, "Beyond Good and Evil," supra note 37.

||||||||||||||||||||||||||||||||||||||||||||||||||||||||||

III

Citizenship of the Family,
Citizenship in the Family
Women, Children, and the Nation-State

II

The "Mere Fortuity of Birth"? Children, Mothers, Borders, and the Meaning of Citizenship

Jacqueline Bhabha

The rights of the child [are] the first rights of citizenship.[1]
—President Hoover's Children's Charter, 1930

There are fundamental rights of the State itself as well as fundamental rights of the individual citizens, and the protection of the former may involve restrictions in circumstances of necessity on the latter.[2]
—*Osheku v. Ireland*, per Gannon J., 1986

The most natural right, one which inheres in citizenship, is the right to reside in the State of that citizenship.[3]
—*D.L., A.O. & Ors v. Minister for Justice, Equality and Law Reform*, per Fennelly J., 2003

Stories of Mothers and Children

On July 27, 2002, two contrasting immigration stories appeared in the U.S. press. Both concerned families of U.S.–citizen children[4] and noncitizen mothers facing an identical dilemma: the choice between family separation and exile from their family home. One story reported on the British widow of a trader killed in the World Trade Center on September 11, 2001, and her two U.S.–citizen children aged seven and four. In a textbook case of "family migration," the woman had left her country and moved because of her husband's job. As a result, her U.S. visa was dependent on that of her British husband. Following his death, the U.S. Immigration and Naturalization Service had taken steps to deport her.

Her role as full-time caretaker of young citizen children did not afford her the immigration benefits that flowed from her former role as spouse of a noncitizen worker. Following intensive lobbying, including support from Tony Blair and Hillary Clinton, however, the authorities granted her a green card under an exceptional provision in the USA Patriot Act allowing foreign-born spouses of 9/11 victims to apply for residency.[5] High-profile leverage, British heritage, and the sympathy surrounding the events of September 11 resulted in these two American children being spared the trauma of being uprooted from their country or being separated from their mother.

The other story concerned a Guatemalan woman, "handcuffed and arrested in front of her stunned husband and sobbing eight-year-old daughter," both of whom were U.S. citizens. Though the news report does not contain details, it seems probable from the sparse facts available that this woman did not follow her husband but set out on her own or with her birth family, probably in search of an unskilled job in the informal economy, jobs for which visas are not available. While the male trader secured a lawful immigration status that was derivatively transmitted to his wife, the female service-sector worker became an undocumented worker. The woman was deported to Guatemala after spending seventeen days in jail. She had missed the date for a hearing to regularize her status in immigration court because the notification sent to her had listed the date incorrectly. At a subsequent interview she was told that the deportation order had already been signed.

Lobbying by the Parent Teachers Association at the child's school and by a Latino organization was to no avail. The woman's lawyers requested a waiver to allow her to return to the United States as a legal resident; such requests can take years to process. Failing that, the woman would have to attempt to have her deportation case reopened, an arduous legal challenge. Meanwhile, the mother had to stay with a friend in Guatemala City since no family resided there any longer. The daughter complained, "I can't sleep, I can't eat, I can't do my work or my arts."[6] In neither case did the citizen child have an enforceable right to preserve family unity at home. Nor did the mother have any recourse based on her critical relational role within the family. From the perspective of international human rights,[7] both the mothers and the children experienced a radical rights deficit. In one case, government discretion was exercised in favor of family unity, in the other case it was not—a bonus for the privileged white family but a casualty for the working-class Hispanic one. In both cases, the parent's legal and social credentials rather than the child's nationality were the deciding factor.

Since July 2002 other such stories have been appearing. The exodus of Pakistani and other long-term but undocumented migrants from the United States to Canada to seek asylum in the face of new registration requirements includes hundreds of citizen children uprooted from their homes with their parents. Of the 82,880 noncitizens from twenty-five listed countries who had registered with the Department of Homeland Security by the end of September 2003, more than thirteen thousand, many of them parents, faced the possibility of deportation.[8] Others face the prospect of indefinite detention without trial or any public scrutiny of the accusations against them.[9] This immigration dragnet has also led to the detention and threatened deportation of forty-three thousand long-term permanent-resident foreign nationals with old criminal convictions. More generally, the overall numbers of noncitizens being detained by the U.S. government have reached unprecedented highs, increasing by a factor of nearly thirty in less than ten years.[10] In addition, the scale of forced removals from the United States is huge and growing. Between 2001 and 2004, over 4.7 million people were compelled to leave the United States for immigration reasons.[11]

This has resulted in the destruction of family life for thousands of citizen children. Included among these were the three Miguel children, aged eleven months, seven, and twelve, all American citizens and each requiring extensive medical attention because of a genetic defect necessitating liver transplants. Their father, a long-time legal resident, had been in detention facing deportation since April 2002 because of an old conviction. His American-born wife had to quit her job as a farm worker to care for the three sick children alone.[12] Also included are the two Andazola-Riva children, aged eleven and six, both of whom are also American citizens. Their single-parent mother, who had lived undocumented but fully employed in the United States for fifteen years with her entire family, was unable to prove that her removal from the United States would result in "exceptional and extremely unusual hardship" to her two children, the required standard under U.S. immigration and nationality law. The children had to leave their home, their school, and their friends for an insecure future with an unemployed parent in Mexico—or stay on in the United States without their sole caregiver.[13] Approximately three million U.S.-citizen children have at least one parent who is in the United States without a regular immigration status; tens of thousands each year live through the deportation of a parent.[14] What does citizenship amount to for these children?

Citizenship: A Social Fact and a Genuine Connection

Little consideration has been given to what it means for a child to be a citizen. This is surprising given that many of the cardinal formal attributes of citizenship—including the rights to vote, to serve on a jury, and to stand for public office—are denied children. No other group of citizens in the developed world today has such legally sanctioned partial access to the benefits of membership. In other societies, and during other historical periods, as suffragettes[15] and Islamist feminists[16] have forcefully demonstrated, the same has been true of women. But the inequities of that discrimination are considered increasingly indefensible. Where they persist, most notoriously in the case of Saudi women, they are the subject of near-universal public condemnation.[17] Other gender-related inequalities in access to the benefits of citizenship, while still pervasive and significant, are not legally sanctioned but rather a matter of de facto discrimination—against homosexuals and transsexuals, or HIV positive/AIDS people. Age-based discrimination, by contrast, is universal and unquestioned. And it has dramatic consequences given the centrality of citizenship to the organization of social life.

Citizenship is a fundamental, constitutive social fact. It governs the relationship between the individual and the collectivity—does one "belong" or is one an "outsider"? It may or may not affect the actual emotional attachment that a person feels to the place in which he or she lives (residence and the presence of family networks are other key factors), but it certainly regulates and stimulates the insertion of the personal into the public—that is, it regulates access to an effective voice in local or national government.

Citizenship also defines the framework in which the balance between self-interest and public concern is negotiated, both by the individual citizen and by the polity, because citizens' interests are central to the assessment of what is a public good. Citizens have a privileged claim to public concern and expenditure where noncitizens do not; citizens exemplify the norm, the standard, the instantiation of national interest where noncitizens do not. In short, through their vote, their agency in public office, their civic participation, their clout as addressees of politicians, citizens have a role in shaping the society they live in that is radically different from that of noncitizens.

A key consequence of this bundle of social facts is that public life is dominated by and organized around the perspectives of citizens. Groups excluded or marginalized from membership find their interests subordinated and their point of view neglected, even ignored. To establish their "genuine connection" to the policy and achieve their political goals, those who are excluded have to garner the support of citizens. This requires an engagement in the public sphere that may present an insurmountable hurdle—for example, for a young child of undocumented parents. The invisibility of children's interests in the framing of much public policy exemplifies this and is a point that will be returned to below.

Citizenship is not only a social fact. It is also the legal correlate of territorial belonging. It signifies official recognition of a particularly close relationship between person and country, typically characterized as a bundle of reciprocal rights and duties, a set of entitlements owed to the citizen by the country and of duties owed to the country by the citizen. The International Court of Justice articulated a classic definition of citizenship in the famous *Nottebohm* case: it is "a legal bond having as its basis a social fact of attachment, a genuine connection of existence, interest and sentiments, together with the existence of reciprocal rights and duties."[18]

Domestic constitutions also enshrine the special status of citizens. The Fourteenth Amendment to the U.S. Constitution, for example, states, "All persons, born or naturalized in the United States, are citizens of the United States and of the State wherein they reside. No State shall make or enforce any law which shall abridge the privileges or immunities of citizens of the United States."[19] Article 2 of the Irish Constitution reads, "It is the entitlement and birthright of every person born in the island of Ireland, which includes its islands and seas, to be part of the Irish nation. That is also the entitlement of all persons otherwise qualified in accordance with law to be citizens of Ireland."[20] As a matter of constitutional law, therefore, citizenship is distinguished as a marker of belonging from other close relationships between person and country also based on "the social fact of attachment," most significantly indefinite or permanent lawful residency. Though generally not an immediately visible or audible marker of belonging in multiethnic societies, it becomes salient as an aspect of someone's identity at key moments—on election day, in the choice of queue at international borders, as a trump to possible deportation proceedings.

Since September 11, the citizenship of terrorism suspects, "unlawful combatants," and nonresidents has become a critical[21] biographical attribute. Citizenship affects the choice of applicable regime relating to national security concerns and the threshold of suspicion. As a marker of identity, citizenship signals "belonging" and "insider status" in a privileged way. The border- and mobility-related entitlements owed by a country to its citizens have become particularly significant: they include the entitlement to a passport, the right to consular protection abroad, the right to move in and out of the country freely and to reenter at any time irrespective of the length of absence abroad, and the entitlement, in some states such as the United States or under European Union (EU) law, to privileged family reunification opportunities.

But arguably the most significant citizen-specific entitlement today is the guarantee of nondeportability, irrespective of criminal offenses. Even treason cannot lead to deportation of a citizen. And yet, for all intents and purposes, some of the American children described above were de facto—or constructively—deported; if a young child's parents are forced to leave a country, so in effect is the child. This is an extremely severe sanction inflicted on an innocent party, a vivid example of the invisibility of the child's perspective. For what could be more devastating for a child than the loss of a parent or a home? From a child's perspective, parenting should be regarded as a critical activity capable of qualifying the impact of a deportation order. But family separation is viewed primarily through the lens of its impact on the adult deportee. Why does a citizen child's nondeportability not impinge more effectively on the family's residency rights?

The Primacy of Nondeportability as an Incident of Citizenship

In contemporary Western society, citizenship is a demographically inclusive status—it is not generally race-,[22] gender-, class-, or age-determined, as it was in antiquity[23] and other earlier periods, as recent as the nineteenth century. It is a status that has no minimum age requirement—children are citizens, as are adults. Indeed, the vast majority of people acquire their citizenship at birth. But, as already mentioned, children cannot vote, stand for public office, serve on juries, or (according to international law)[24] be

The "Mere Fortuity of Birth"? 193

called to bear arms in defense of their country. Thus the bundle of special attributes reduces itself, in the case of children, to the migration/border-crossing rights of protection that I just listed, particularly the entitlement to reside in their country indefinitely without fear of deportation.

These residency rights are no less vital for children than they are for adults, though this point is usually overlooked. The ties and influences that result from belonging to a particular territory are critical, even for very young children. Indeed, they may be as critical as the much more widely acknowledged dependence on and need for consistent parenting. Institutional acceptance of the fact that separation from close relatives can cause permanent psychological damage is pervasive, a bedrock of international law as much as it is a core principle in the immigration systems of developed states.[25] How family unity is to be achieved is more contentious, as I will show below, but the principle itself is universally accepted.

Unlike concerns with family unity, the importance of residency rights for children is not universally accepted. And yet, the place of residence has pervasive impacts and lifelong consequences: it affects children's life expectancy, their physical and psychological development, their material prospects, their general standard of living. The fact of belonging to a particular country determines the type, quality, and extent of education the child receives, as well as the expectations regarding familial obligations, employment opportunities, gender roles, and consumption patterns. It determines linguistic competence, social mores, vulnerability to discrimination, persecution, and war. It affects exposure to disease, to potentially oppressive social and cultural practices, to life-enhancing kinship, social, and occupational networks. In short, the fact of belonging to a country fundamentally affects the manner of exercise of a child's family and private life, during childhood and well beyond. Yet children, particularly young children, are often considered parcels that are easily moveable across borders with their parents and without particular cost to the children.

Family Mobility: A Mismatch between Theory and Practice

What determines who moves with whom? The sovereign prerogative of states to control their own borders and to regulate the admission and residence of aliens on their territory explains the traditional limitations on the right to freedom of movement that underpins all legal migration. It does not, however, explain the striking asymmetry in the family reunification rights of similarly placed adults and minor children, just as it did not explain the gender bias of earlier immigration rules relating to married couples that accorded primacy to the interests and life choices of men over those of women. Parents with claims to asylum can travel across borders with children and subsume them in their applications whether the children have valid claims to asylum or not; immigrant parents can generally bring their minor children to join them once they have established themselves in a new country; parents, if they defeat attempts at deportation or removal directed against themselves, can thereby also prevent the removal of their minor children, whether the latter are independently eligible for settlement or not; parents can even obtain residence and citizenship for biologically unrelated children whom they choose to adopt transnationally. Yet children cannot exercise such choices and have no such enforceable rights with respect to their parents. A citizen child cannot generally use the fact of citizenship to block the removal of parents facing deportation or to secure entry for a parent abroad.

The right to family unity is radically asymmetrical as between parents and children. Like gendered immigration differentials prevalent in an earlier era of contemporary migration,[26] so too this age- and relationship-based asymmetry reflects a discriminatory set of assumptions about the nature of family life in a globalized era. Moreover, it unthinkingly reflects the adult-centered perspective that pervades policy and assumes the absolute primacy of parental over child migration considerations.

Massive global migration has multiple and complex impacts on the conduct of family life. The assumption of a unitary family, all of whose members share the same nationality, live in the same country, travel together or follow the (male) bread winner, have the same short- or long-term interests, and have easy access to each other, is outmoded. It is disrupted by new patterns of mobility: wage earners, visitors, students, entrepreneurs, and creative artists who embark on transnational migration leaving family members behind. New patterns are also evident in family structures with changing gender roles, which more and more frequently result in women becoming primary bread winners, or single heads of household, or initiators of international migration for economic or personal reasons, including escape from oppressive marriages, or the pursuit of new relationships. External forces, including calamities of war, upheaval, and persecution, destroy, separate, or disperse families and result in long-term warehousing of populations, predominantly women and children,[27] in refugee camps in neighboring countries, or in flows of increasingly shunned asylum seekers into developed destination states. In addition, more and more children are born in host countries to parents with different nationalities and immigration statuses; settled immigrant situations are disrupted by visa expiry, criminal conviction, family breakup, and economic vulnerability, while new birth technologies disaggregate formally overlapping ingredients and roles in parenting.

In the majority of these situations, parents provide the anchor to which children are attached. Where parents are divided, as they increasingly are, children, particularly young ones, are predominantly attached to their mothers. But as the scale of global migration increases and with it the number of families encompassing within them different nationalities, so too, in a growing number of cases, it is children who provide or have the potential to provide the migration stability—children who would, but for the asymmetry just mentioned, have the right to establish family unity around them. And yet, precisely because they are children, they do not.

The assumption that children's immigration status must derive from that of their parents rather than vice versa recalls the earlier set of gendered assumptions discussed above—that women traveled with or to follow their husbands, but not vice versa, that "home" was where the man lived. And like those assumptions, it reflects ideological bias rather than factual reality. It also highlights a striking divergence between the foundational assumptions of family and immigration law. Where families are divided by matrimonial or relationship breakdown, courts traditionally allocate the family home to the party with custody of the children—home is where the children are, and the custodial parent's residence derives from the child; but if families face separation because of immigration law, the presumption is that the anchoring role of the children must give way—their primacy evaporates. If children have no right to use their citizenship as a basis for exercising family reunion or shoring up family unity, then—if their parents face deportation—they too risk constructive deportation, despite being citizens. This risk increases as the significance of children's citizenship is minimized.

The Attack on Birthright Citizenship

In recent years and especially in the post–9/11 period, as immigration battles are increasingly fought out on the terrain of citizenship,[28] so the citizenship rights of children in general and birthright citizenship in particular have come under political and legal attack. The citizenship benefits that a child acquires because of birthplace (*jus soli*) or parentage (*jus sanguinis*) are increasingly criticized for being fortuitous or random. The accident of birthplace is singled out as a self-evidently arbitrary basis for the acquisition of an important civic and political status.

This critique is particularly targeted at children born to illegal or undocumented migrants who acquire citizenship by territorial birthright despite their parents' tenuous legal relationship to the state. A U.S. appeal court judgment contains a typical statement:

> A minor child who is fortuitously born here due to his parents' decision to reside in this country, has not exercised a *deliberate decision* to make this country his home, and Congress did not give such a child the ability to confer immigration benefits on his parents. It gave this privilege to those of our citizens who had themselves chosen to make this country their home and did not give the privilege to those minor children whose noncitizen parents make the real choice of family residence.[29]

Which minor children, one wonders, are in a position to make deliberate decisions about the country they reside in or call home? And yet, since the turn of the century, supreme courts in the United States,[30] Canada,[31] and Ireland,[32] to name but three, have all attacked the alleged arbitrariness of birthright citizenship.

The attack on birthright citizenship has several sources. One is exclusionary—a desire to restrict eligibility for community membership. According to Peter Schuck, birthright citizenship is an "infringement of consensualism"[33] because illegal alien parents with very little effort or commitment and no enduring ties to the United States are able to secure citizenship for their children by mere border crossing. The "powerful lure of the expanded entitlements conferred upon citizen children and their families by the modern welfare state" constitutes, it is claimed, an incentive to illegal migration.[34] However, as Bonnie Honig points out, the premise that undocumented migrants are present on the territory without consent is questionable. Significant economic advantages to the nation accrue from their presence;[35] steps to remove illegal migrants have been erratic and inconsistent, even half-hearted, suggesting a lack of serious political will to eject this key element of the U.S. work force.

And yet, the attack on birthright citizenship is not purely academic. Prominent politicians and judicial figures have vociferously criticized the birthright-citizenship rule. For example, the chief justice of the Seventh Circuit Court of Appeals and one of the most influential judicial figures, Judge Richard Posner, delivered the following opinion in a 2003 asylum case: "[O]ne rule that Congress should rethink . . . is awarding citizenship to everyone born in the United States (with a few very minor exceptions . . .) including the children of illegal immigrants whose sole motive in immigration was to confer U.S. citizenship on their as yet unborn children. This rule . . . makes no sense."[36]

Opponents of birthright citizenship, however, have a hard time proving what the "sole motive" of immigration is. Citing the number of births to undocumented mothers[37] without comparable statistics for similarly placed documented or citizen mothers proves nothing. Moreover, the argument seems to ignore the economic roles that migrant women play, casting them essentially as breeders. In fact, migration is a notoriously multifaceted human activity: survival or economic advancement, protection from persecution or enhanced personal security, adventure, career development, family reunification, keeping up with neighbors or relatives may all be part of the purpose of migration, and identifying a single factor across a large and diverse population is inherently problematic.

The British government discovered this in the 1980s when it used equally simplistic and discriminatory assumptions about immigration to curb the rights of some groups. It legislated to restrict the entry of young South Asian men to join their British-born wives or fiancées and settle in the United Kingdom by establishing that only marriages where the "primary purpose" was not the fiancé's or husband's immigration into Britain would be considered valid, and for a period of ten years used the rule to refuse approximately half the applications from these South Asian men.[38]

Indignant judges criticized the sexist and racist assumptions behind the primary-purpose rule. In the words of one judge, "where arranged marriages are the norm, the fact that a marriage is an arranged marriage . . . does not show that its purpose is or was to obtain admission to the United Kingdom."[39] Another judgment highlighted the Eurocentric and gender biases in the refusal decisions of immigration officers by posing a culturally contrasting hypothetical:

> [I]n the context of arranged marriages in Muslim society, the absence of . . . a passionate relationship or indeed of being "in love" [is] not itself indicative of [immigration] being the primary purpose of a marriage. . . . To draw an analogy with English society at the turn of the century, the fact

that an American heiress was so keen to be a duchess that she was prepared to marry an Englishman whom she did not love would not lead one to suppose that the primary purpose of the marriage was for her to obtain admission to the UK. She may have been after his title and he after her money.[40]

Eventually, protracted criticism from civil society, advocates, and the European Court of Justice persuaded the British government to moderate the application of the rule. In doing so it had to concede that immigration decision makers could not unquestioningly apply their stereotypes and biases to assess the motivations of populations they had little understanding of.

By analogy, the argument of critics such as Schuck and Posner against birthright citizenship is grounded in an unapologetically adult-centric view of the world. Schuck defends the proposal to remove birthright citizenship on the basis that this does not interfere with the moral obligations, such as they may be, to illegal aliens: "citizenship status is not necessary to afford illegal aliens and their children at least minimal protection and public benefits."[41] But what of the state's moral obligations towards its own citizens?

Attention to the claims of the citizen child is displaced by a focus on the noncitizen parent. Most citizens acquire their claims on their state through the accident of birth in the territory, not through the moral obligations owed their parents or other relatives. No child consents to his or her citizenship at birth or shortly thereafter. For all citizens, consent to citizenship, in the sense of personal commitment and affirmation of a common historical or cultural project, only develops cumulatively, gradually, and with maturity—citizen children have the incipient right to consent as they reach adulthood. Depriving a subset of children born within the state of that right on the basis of parental immigration status places an extra burden of active consent on one category of children that is not logically related to their link with the state. It also unfairly penalizes the child because of the parent's behavior.

The attack on birthright citizenship also stems from another, quite different set of preoccupations: recent critical work investigating questions of social justice. Here the concern is for equity across groups rather than restriction. Seyla Benhabib, for example, argues that "*territoriality* has become an anachronistic delimitation of material functions and cultural identities; yet, even in the face of the collapse of traditional concepts of sovereignty, monopoly over territory is exercised through immigration and citizenship policies."[42] She calls for much greater acknowledgement of the interdependence of different "peoples" and suggests that "the right to membership [of a society] ought to be considered a human right, in the moral sense of the term and it ought to become a legal right as well."[43]

From this more inclusionary perspective, the legitimacy of birthright citizenship as the basis for allocating valuable resources must be questioned because it is an irrational basis for allocating such resources. According to Ayelet Shachar, citizenship is akin to a property right that must be distributed according to systematic, not arbitrary, criteria: "National affiliations, guaranteed or denied on the basis of considerations such as ancestral pedigree or the brute and random luck of birthplace, should no longer be taken for granted."[44] In theory this sounds like a laudable call to reconsider the equitable basis of access to the privileges associated with the citizenship of developed states. But in practice, and in the absence of an alternative set of viable proposals, it is far from clear that attacking birthright citizenship will result in citizenship proposals that reduce inequality.

The attack on birthright citizenship is, first and foremost, an attack on the existing rights of citizen children. But it has not been discussed in those terms. In fact, in debates on the allocation of entitlements to citizenship, the perspective of the citizen child is remarkably absent. As argued earlier in this chapter, concern about differential or discriminatory access to the benefits of citizenship and about asymmetries in the flow of citizenship rights has typically focused on questions of race and gender, but not age. In the case of gender, in particular, the parallels are dramatic. The obliteration of the woman's perspective or agency was justified by assumptions about her dependence—social, political, economic, and personal—on male relatives, typically her father first and her husband second. Since she was considered an appendage of male agency and dependent on male protection, her legal status, and with it her citizenship and immigration rights, flowed from those of her male relative.

A clear example of this approach is nineteenth-century British nationality law. The 1844 Naturalisation Act granted any foreign woman married to a British subject automatic British nationality; conversely, the 1870 Naturalisation Act deprived British-born women marrying aliens of their British nationality. These laws simply codified long-standing gendered assumptions. As Judge Lord Hale had held as early as 1664, "it is without question that if an English woman go beyond the Seas and marry an Alien, and have Issue born beyond the Seas, the Issue are Aliens, for the wife was *sub potestate viri* [under the power of the man]."[45]

It took decades of concerted pressure from suffragettes, feminist advocates, and their supporters to dislodge these deep-seated prejudices, and to replace them with gender-neutral citizenship laws. Not until 1948 were British women finally allowed to keep their nationality following marriage to a noncitizen. And yet, over thirty years earlier, the problem underlying the gross gender inequality had been clearly identified by a member of Parliament: "We must feel that there is something ironical in a Parliament of men, elected by men, settling once and for all the citizenship and civic rights of women who have no voice in the matter directly at all."[46] The parallels with age discrimination are dramatic. Because the child is absent from the political and legislative process, his or her interests are unvoiced. And so, by a strange twist of logic, the claim that children exercise the normal rights that flow from citizenship, including security of home, family, and residence, is cast as an "abuse."

The so-called abuse of birthright citizenship to secure immigration advantages for undocumented or criminal alien parents is the prime contemporary concern. Even when the focus on citizenship inequalities turns to the deleterious impact of disparate, divided, or dependent nationalities on family relationships, the emphasis is on the inequalities in the rights of similarly placed adults (mothers vs. fathers, women vs. men), rather than on the legitimacy of differences between adults and children.[47] There seems to be an assumption that children's disabilities as citizens are self-evidently justified, a consequence of the fact that they are citizens in the making, "future"[48] rather than actual citizens. The one-way descending flow of familial transmission of citizenship, from parent to child rather than from child to parent, is accepted as a natural rather than a constructed asymmetry, just as its gendered antecedent was. A consequence of this approach is that retrospectivity rather than prospectivity dominates the discussion about justification for access to citizenship: the importance of connection to a community or territory is assessed in terms of the length and depth of past association, rather than the salience or value of future connection. This perspective thus privileges the existing connections sustained by adults or parents over the potentiality for future connections of babies or children.

Child Citizens: A Rights Deficit

It is a strange paradox of modern public policy that children are considered to have a fundamental right to family life[49] and yet no legally enforceable right, unlike their adult counterparts,[50] to initiate family reunion or resist family separation where a family is divided by national borders. Most notable is the disparity in the position of citizens. In the United States, nondeportability and preferential access to family reunification with immediate relatives are considered among the most significant attributes of adult citizens, distinguishing them from legal resident aliens who, in many other respects, share the benefits of modern "postnational" welfare entitlements—access to education and social security, for example,[51]

For U.S. children, however, these cardinal attributes of citizenship are not available. Citizen children are not entitled to any preferred immigration status for their immediate relatives, until they reach majority and can demonstrate links of marriage or dependency by parents. Though not deportable themselves, citizen children are constructively deportable when their alien parents face deportation. As shown earlier in this chapter, their right to permanent residence in their home country does not extend to an entitlement to protect other necessary aspects of that residence, vis-à-vis the continued presence of parent caregivers. The citizen child's interest in protecting family unity is pitted against the state's interest in enforcing immigration control. Deportation of parents, particularly of mothers, usually amounts to a de facto or constructive deportation of dependent minor children—a reality that is obscured by the extreme option of placing citizen children with guardians or others in the home state.

States adopt differing criteria and standards in balancing these two contradictory pressures, reflecting their own domestic legislative frameworks, policy agendas, and approaches to the mandates of international human rights law. These policies span a continuum of approaches. At one end of the spectrum are policies based on the presumption that immigration-control considerations are paramount and that children have no independent claim to full enjoyment of the attributes of citizenship: in these situations, only exceptional and unusually compassionate circumstances can militate against the deportation of a citizen child's parent, and then only if such circumstances relate directly to the citizen child, not the parent or the family as a whole. At the other end of the spectrum are policies that privilege the citizen child's right to enjoy family life in the home country, a right that trumps immigration-control considerations unless there are serious exclusion considerations, implicating national security or comparable threats to the state. In between these two extremes are policies that require a balancing of citizenship and immigration considerations, to determine whether the justifications for deportation override the child's best-interest rights. The contrast between European and North American approaches is illustrative.

Balancing the Individual's Right to Family Life and the State's Interest in Immigration Control: The European Approach

The European approach is governed by the European Convention on Human Rights (ECHR) and the jurisprudence of the Council of Europe institutions that regulate implementation of the convention, the European Commission,[52] and the European Court of Human Rights. Article 8 of the ECHR establishes that the right to respect for one's family or private life can only be interfered with by the state where this is the result of a lawful and legitimate government aim and is "necessary in a democratic society." The implementation of immigration laws is considered a legitimate goal aimed at promoting the economic well-being of the receiving country. So, the critical question in cases involving challenges by deportable alien parents of citizen children has been whether the test of necessity has been met.

In determining whether the correct balance has been reached between the competing interests of the individual asserting the right to family life and the state seeking to enforce immigration control, the European Court of Human Rights has tended to focus on the equities involved in the alien parent's behavior and status. It has articulated a demanding standard for states, insisting on a robust enforcement of the right to respect for the family life of deportable aliens; but for the most part, the perspective of the citizen child has been strikingly absent. In all but one of the reported court decisions, the citizen child is not a coapplicant to the proceedings, nor is the impact on a young child of long-term separation from a parent considered; rather, the emphasis is on rights of parental access to the child. Parents—in nearly all the reported cases, fathers—who have been law abiding, who have been solicitous towards their children, and who have diligently pursued their child-rearing responsibilities have been rewarded for their behavior by being allowed to reside in their child's home country. Parents who have committed serious criminal offenses, or who have been erratic in their exercise of "parental obligations" as understood by the court, have been penalized, even where no threat to state security exists. Family unity and the right to respect for family life has thus generally been viewed as a privilege of parents, earned by good or reasonable behavior, rather than as a right of children, or an incident of citizenship independent of parental conduct.

Several cases are illustrative of a long line of decisions, dating back to the leading 1988 case of *Berrehab v. the Netherlands*,[53] wherein a Moroccan father who lost his right of residence following the breakdown of his marriage to a Dutch citizen was found by the court to have had his right to respect for family life violated by his ensuing expulsion, since this prevented him from regular contact with his Dutch child. In *Berrehab*, the court noted that the father had lived and worked without reproach in the Netherlands for six years prior to his expulsion, had seen his daughter four times a week since her birth, and had contributed to her education and maintenance. The rights of the citizen child to the continuing presence of her father were not addressed, nor was the child a party to the proceedings. Nevertheless, the father's irreproachable behavior was rewarded.

By contrast, in *Yousef v. United Kingdom*,[54] a strong, loving relationship between a Kuwaiti father and British son was restricted to limited-access arrangements because of the impending threat of the father's removal from the United Kingdom following the breakdown of his marriage to a UK citizen. A matrimonial court welfare report described "a strong and affectionate bond between the father and the child" and commented that it would have "been beneficial to the child if that could be maintained in more normal circumstances, i.e. without the threat of the applicant's removal from the United Kingdom which effectively prevented his reasonable access to the child."[55] But the European Commission found no violation of the right to respect for family life: the fact that the father had a minor criminal conviction (for wrongly appropriating one hundred pounds' worth of electricity), was unemployed, and had failed to maintain consistent contact with his son "because of [his] preoccupation with [a] second British woman"[56] meant that his conduct compared unfavorably with the irreproachable behavior of Berrehab. The decision has strong moralistic overtones about the father's less than exemplary conduct; the rights of the citizen child to continue his strong and affectionate bond with his father were not addressed.

Parental equities rather than children's rights were once again the basis for the later decision of the European Court of Human Rights, in *Ciliz v. the Netherlands*.[57] In *Ciliz*, the facts resembled those in *Berrehab*, except for the fact that the Turkish father had had less opportunity to develop and establish an ongoing relationship with his Dutch son because his expulsion had prejudged the outcome of access proceedings. The father was expelled "at the moment when the official investigation into the closeness of the ties between father and son had not yet been concluded, and . . . he was subsequently denied an entry visa allowing him to take part in the proceedings concerning access."[58] Since his removal from the Netherlands was not warranted by any criminal proceedings but rather simply by the breakdown of his marriage and his subsequent unemployment, the court found a violation of his right to respect for family life. In all these cases, blameless parents were rewarded with the right to remain close to their citizen child, but the child's right to family life and the impact of deportation on the citizen child were not part of the decision.

A welcome and novel departure from this line of cases is the approach adopted by the European Court of Justice (ECJ), the court that regulates the implementation of European Community law. Not to be confused with the European Court of Human Rights, which oversees the implementation of the ECHR in the forty-six states of the Council of Europe, the ECJ is an institution of the European Union and is responsible for ensuring that the extensive and growing body of community law (on free movement, on the elimination of trade barriers, on a range of other economic and social matters) is appropriately implemented by the twenty-five EU member states.

Two ECJ cases provide an interesting model for future policy and a challenge to the adult-centered thinking that dominates the ECHR case law just described. The most relevant case for the purposes of this discussion is *Zhu and Chen v. Secretary of State for the Home Department*.[59] It concerned the rights of an EU citizen child to have her noncitizen mother reside with her in an EU member state. Though the case turns on the rights to free movement and residence enjoyed by EU citizens as a result of European community law, its exploration of the relationship between age and the exercise of citizenship rights has much wider resonance.

The facts of the *Zhu and Chen* case can be simply summarized. Man Chen and her husband, prosperous Chinese nationals with a controlling interest in a successful company with a significant presence in the United Kingdom, decided, after the birth of their first child, to avoid the negative repercussions of having a second child in China in violation of the one-child population policy by arranging for a foreign birth and residence rights. Accordingly, Catherine Zhu was born in Belfast, Northern Ireland, and when she was six months old, mother and daughter moved to the United Kingdom. Northern Ireland is part of the United Kingdom, but because neither of her parents had a lawful permanent status in the United Kingdom at the time of her birth, Catherine did not acquire British citizenship by birth. Northern Ireland is also, of course, part of the Irish island, and therefore, as a result of Irish law, Catherine acquired Irish citizenship by virtue of her birth on the island.[60] Catherine was covered by private health insurance and supported by her parents' ample resources; she therefore fulfilled the residency requirements of EC law.

Relying on Catherine's birthright Irish citizenship and the free-movement and residence rights that flowed from it, Mrs. Chen applied for residence permits in the United Kingdom for both Catherine and herself. The British government refused, arguing that the deliberate choice of Belfast as a birthplace, designed to generate Irish nationality and thus immigration entitlements against Britain, was an abuse of EC law. This argument closely matches the Schuck and Posner critiques of U.S. birthright citizenship described earlier.

The Irish government also participated in the proceedings before the ECJ, and advanced the additional argument that, because of her age, Catherine lacked the capacity to exercise EC rights: "While a minor, and unable to exercise a choice of residence, Catherine cannot be a 'national' for the purposes of Article1(1)[of the Council Residency Directive]."[61] It followed from this that Mrs. Chen had no claim to residence rights within the European Union either.

The ECJ disagreed. It held that "a very young minor who is a Community National" and fulfills the legal insurance and resource requirements for residency, enjoyed "a right to reside for an indeterminate period" within the European Union and that it was not for the court to look behind the reasons why the family decided to arrange their affairs in this way. What mattered was whether the legal requirements for citizenship (as determined by the individual member state, Ireland, in this case) and for residency (as determined by community law) had been met. Moreover, in order for Catherine to enjoy the residency right that she was entitled to, the Court determined that she needed the continued presence of her primary caregiver; without this, her right of residence would be rendered ineffective. In the court's words, "refusal to allow the parent . . . would deprive the child's right of residence of any useful effect."[62]

This judgment illustrates the impact of a child-centered approach that explores the substantive meaning of a right from the perspective of the affected applicant, in this case a baby, rather than from the standpoint of a generic adult claimant. In so doing, it follows the reasoning of an earlier ECJ case, *Baumbast and R. v. Secretary of State for the Home Department*,[63] which held that noncitizen children who had moved to a member state with a citizen parent had independent rights to continue pursuing general educational courses they had embarked on, even after the citizen parent had left the member state. Failure to permit this, and *with it the continuing residence of the children's primary caregiver (irrespective of nationality)*, would, the court held, discourage freedom of movement of member-state workers by unduly restricting their families' access to stable and beneficial services (in this case education). As the ECJ correctly appreciated, without consideration of the substantive conditions necessary for the exercise of rights, they become illusory.

The U.S. Approach to Deportation of Parents of Citizen Minors

The U.S. approach to removal of alien parents of citizen children provides a dramatic contrast to this rights-respecting approach. Though the impact of removal on the citizen child is explicitly listed as a relevant factor in the immigration regulations, in practice, the outcomes of appeals against deportation are much less favorable to the stability of family life in the child's home country. The harshness of the overall approach militates against effective or substantive recognition of the rights of the citizen child. There is no forum in which, unlike in the ECJ cases just discussed, the child can be a party to the proceedings. The citizen child's interests are represented, if at all, only indirectly through the alien parent, as a subsidiary consideration. Generally, international human rights norms relating to children's rights are not included in the decision-making process.

The U.S. approach has been governed by a series of legislative acts impinging on the relief available to aliens seeking to resist deportation from the United States. Until 1996, U.S. immigration law provided some opportunities for discretionary relief from deportation for aliens who were lawfully admitted as permanent residents but faced removal because they had criminal convictions. Section 212(c) of the Immigration and Nationality Act (INA) enabled those aliens who had substantial ties to the United States, including spouses and children, to prove to an immigration judge that the negative aspects of their convictions were outweighed by their U.S. connections. Moreover, for aliens who had not been lawfully admitted, there was also the possibility of suspension of deportation, if the alien could establish three points: (a) that he or she had been physically present in the United States continuously for at least seven years before the application for suspension; (b) that he or she was of good moral character; and (c) that the deportation would result in extreme hardship to the deportee or his or her spouse, parent, or child who are U.S. citizens or permanent residents.

Though both of these remedies have similarities to the European approach of balancing the interests of individual and state, in practice neither of these remedies for aliens facing separation from their citizen children was at all easy to obtain. Illegal aliens faced particular difficulties. For them, the critical question revolved around demonstration of "extreme hardship," a term that was not defined by the Immigration and Naturalization Service (INS) or by the Supreme Court, but that was left to the attorney general to construe, "narrowly should [he] deem it wise to do so."[64] By definition, the normal, intense hardship that separation from a parent or enforced deportation from one's home country entails was not sufficient to enable the parent of a citizen child to resist removal.

Thus, the Board of Immigration Appeals (BIA) has established that "the mere fact that an alien's child is born in the United States does not entitle the alien to *any* favored status in seeking discretionary relief from deportation."[65] Economic loss, inadequate medical care, and lower standards of education have been held to be insufficient to establish extreme hardship; the impact of economic difficulties combined with language problems facing two children who had spent their entire lives in the United States, only spoke English, and faced constructive deportation to the Philippines was held not to constitute extreme hardship. Life-threatening medical conditions or unusually pressing individual circumstances are required—it is only the exceptional case that will benefit from the narrowly drawn provisions. Suspension was granted in the extreme case of a Colombian mother of a citizen child who claimed that deportation to Colombia would put both of them in mortal danger because of risks from her husband, who had severely abused her repeatedly and was serving a sentence for shooting two men who had tried to restrain him from attacking his wife and daughter.

Other cases that also exhibit very powerful negative equities affecting citizen children have not, however, yielded outcomes that protect their family unity rights in their home country. A Mexican couple who had lived continuously in the United States for twelve years prior to their deportation proceedings, with three U.S.–citizen children who could not read or write Spanish, substantial assets, and strong credentials as an exemplary family that, according to a majority court opinion (later reversed), "any of us would be happy to see . . . gain citizenship," was denied suspension of deportation. It was held that the children would not suffer extreme hardship, which the court defined as hardship that is "uniquely extreme, at or closely approaching the outer limits of the most severe hardship the alien could suffer."[66]

The contrast with the approach of the ECJ court in the *Zhu and Chen* case just discussed is instructive. In that case, the court's express goal was to facilitate the applicant's effective exercise of her treaty rights. In these cases, by contrast, the court's goal is to limit exceptions to the government's sweeping power to deport. As a result, according to one scholar, "the term 'extreme hardship' as it is presently, albeit vaguely, defined provides practically unattainable relief for the citizen child whose parents are subject to deportation."[67] Yet, as she points out, the fundamental right of a child to parental companionship has been recognized by U.S. courts in other areas concerning children. Reducing the citizen child to a "mere bystander" in his or her parent's deportation suspension proceedings denies the child constitutional rights as an American citizen. "While the procedural due process rights of the illegal immigrant parent may be satisfied by suspension of deportation hearing, the citizen child is not granted the same protection."[68]

Since 1996, both of these already seriously limited forms of relief have been even more severely curtailed. Legislative acts have become progressively harsher, to the point where discretionary relief from deportation is virtually unavailable except in the "most extreme and unusually compassionate circumstances." In this very limited subset of situations, consideration of the impact of removal of an alien parent on a citizen child may in theory prevent the removal from being carried out. The Antiterrorism and Effective Death Penalty Act and the Illegal Immigration Reform and Immigrant Responsibility Act together have stripped aliens convicted of a large number of offences defined as "aggravated felonies" from the relief they were eligible for under Section 212(c). For illegal aliens, the three-pronged test described above has been rendered even more restrictive by several changes, including the following: (a) the continuous-residence period is increased from seven to ten years and (b) the alien must establish that removal would result in "exceptional and extremely unusual hardship" to the alien's citizen or lawful permanent resident spouse, parent, or child. If the earlier relief was considered "practically unattainable," its more recent substitute is virtually illusory.

A 2001 BIA precedent decision, interpreting the new hardship standard, stated that it was "obvious" that the new standard was even higher than the preceding "extreme hardship" threshold![69] Rather than acknowledging and mitigating the trauma of family separation, particularly for young children, the rule requires decision makers to revoke deportation only when the applicant demonstrates that the hardship incurred is "substantially different from, or beyond, that which would normally be expected from the deportation of an alien with close family members here."[70] In these situations, where the parent's alienage trumps the right of the citizen child to parental care and companionship at home, citizenship loses all real meaning for children.[71]

Over the years applicants and their advocates have attempted to argue that these harsh standards are unconstitutional, in that they deprive U.S. citizens of the equal protection of U.S. law to which they are entitled. They have had no success. In one case, the deportable parents of a U.S.–citizen child argued that the de facto deportation faced by their child amounted to discrimination on the basis of her alien parentage;[72] in another, parents challenged the difference in the rights of under– and over–21-year-old U.S. citizens, since the latter but not the former can transmit immediate immigration benefits to their parents.[73] Constitutional challenge has not advanced the position of citizen children on this issue.[74]

U.S. Judicial Disquiet over Neglect of Child Citizens' Rights

Two U.S. court decisions evidence some disquiet about the radical neglect of the interests and voice of the citizen child that results from these harsh measures. In *Beharry v. Reno*, a New York district court judge granted a writ of habeas corpus to a convicted Trinidadian permanent resident seeking relief from deportation on the basis of his strong familial ties to the United States, including a six-year-old citizen daughter. The court held that to do otherwise would be to contravene American obligations under international law. Drawing on international law provisions protecting the right to family life and the child's best interests to challenge U.S. statutory provisions, the court held that "forcible separation of a non-citizen legal resident [of the United States] from his citizen child or spouse implicates this right to familial integrity."[75]

However, this decision was reversed on appeal.[76] Though the court of appeals dismissed Beharry's habeas corpus petition on technical legal grounds, it went out of its way to distance itself from the reliance on international human rights law arguments in the earlier decision: "Nothing in our decision to reverse on other grounds the judgment of the district court should be seen as an endorsement of the district court's holding that interpretation of the INA in this case is influenced or controlled by international law."[77]

In the second case, *Nwaokolo v. INS*, the Seventh Circuit Court of Appeals also granted a stay of removal proceedings to the parent of two citizen children, because the immigration authorities had failed to consider the likely consequences of enforced removal on the citizen children. In this case, the parent had sought to resist removal from the United States by claiming that she and her two daughters would be subjected to female genital circumcision if she were returned to Nigeria. Both the INS and the BIA failed to consider the irreparable injury that the citizen children would suffer.

The Seventh Circuit, in reversing the BIA, commented indignantly— but quite accurately—that "the record before us offers no reason to believe that the BIA even considered the threat to Victoria [the four-year-old citizen child] from the widespread practice of FGM in her mother's home country of Nigeria."[78] Neither child had ever been represented by counsel nor had their interests been directly considered by the authorities. "The government could never do to these girls in this country what the INS seems all too willing to allow to happen to them in Nigeria."[79] The court concluded that the BIA abused its discretion by failing to consider the relevant factor of the hardship to U.S.–citizen children that would result from the deportation of the alien parent.

However, the impact of this decision has also been circumscribed by subsequent judicial pronouncements. They mirror the European Court of Human Rights's reasoning discussed above in the cases challenging deportation of a citizen child's alien parent, because, as in those cases, the U.S. courts base their decisions on the parent's behaviour and on how "deserving" he or she is, rather than on the impact on the citizen child. In *Oforji v Ashcroft*,[80] the Seventh Circuit refused to reverse a decision denying asylum to the Nigerian single-parent mother of two young U.S.–citizen girls. The court distinguished the case from *Nwaokolo* because the mother in that case had, unlike Oforji, initially entered the United States legally and resided here continuously (albeit unlawfully as an overstayer) for over seven years, thus qualifying to make an "exceptional hardship" claim for her children under the terms of the regulations discussed earlier.

The *Oforji* court acknowledged that "as United States citizens, [the two children] have the right to stay here without [the mother], but that would likely require some form of guardianship—not a Hobson's choice but a choice no mother wants to make." The citizen children's perspective is not seriously explored: "Undoubtedly, any separation of a child from *its* mother is a hardship. However, the question before us is whether this *potential hardship* to citizen children arising from the mother's deportation should allow an otherwise unqualified mother to *append to the children's rights to remain* in the United States. The answer is no."[81]

The court also distinguished the interests of the Oforji children from those of a noncitizen boy whose exclusion from his parents' deportation hearing resulted in the reversal of the parents' deportation so that the child would not be deprived of the right to challenge his own removal.[82] Apparently, the Oforji court saw no irony in depriving the citizen children in the case before it of a remedy that would match the one granted to the noncitizen child in the case they distinguished. Sadly, the window of legal opportunity for citizen children to challenge deportation proceedings affecting their parents is no longer open.

Public Controversy over the Rights of Irish-Born Children

Until January 1, 2005, Ireland had a constitution that, like that of the United States, enshrined the right of everyone born in the country to citizenship.[83] This constitutional right to citizenship brought with it the right to reside in the country indefinitely and to be immune from deportation. The unqualified right of residence "is one of the fundamental, absolute and imprescriptible rights of a citizen."[84] But the precise boundaries of this right increasingly have become a matter of controversy.

Ireland has changed, in recent years, from a country of emigration to a country of immigration. One consequence of this rise in immigration has been an increase in the numbers of children born in Ireland to noncitizen parents, including parents who do not have a legal immigration status in Ireland. The arrival of numbers of women in the third trimester of their pregnancy has elicited particularly critical comment. It has been used both as evidence of callous disregard of the mother for her child's well-being and as proof of the calculatingly instrumental "abuse" of Irish citizenship rights for immigration purposes. Where immigration authorities sought to deport these parents, they had to consider whether the citizenship rights of Irish-born children (IBCs) constituted an impediment to the deportation because of the children's right to remain in the state with their parents. Since the late 1990s, this question has recently attracted considerable controversy.

Stories of families refused asylum in the United Kingdom and traveling to Ireland with women in advanced stages of pregnancy gradually became the subject of banner headlines in the tabloids. In the public debate, concerns about the efficacy of the immigration control system were pitted against commitment to the nondiscriminatory enjoyment of the Irish child's full citizenship rights. In a landmark decision in 1990, *Fajujonu v. Minister for Justice*,[85] the Irish Supreme Court upheld the residency and family-unity rights of three IBCs of nonnational parents. The court recognized the constitutional right of the citizen children to "the company, care and parentage of their parents within a family unit." It held that "prima facie and subject to the exigencies of the common good, . . . this is a right which these citizens would be entitled to exercise within the State."[86] Only if there existed "a grave and substantive reason associated with the common good"[87] could parents of Irish-born minors be deported. Upholding the general provisions of Irish immigration control did not constitute such a reason.

In this case, the parents had lived illegally in Ireland for two and a half years before the birth of their first child, and had subsequently had two more children. By the time of the court judgment the couple had lived in Ireland for nine years. The court noted that they had "resided for an appreciable time in the State and ha[d] become member[s] of a family unit within the State containing children who are citizens." This decision, uniquely, reflects the cardinal value of citizenship for a child: the ability to enjoy the company, care, and parentage of their parents within a family unit within the state. As a result of this precedent, IBCs with nonnational parents gained an advantage in securing family unity in the state compared to their noncitizen counterparts—being a citizen child really made a difference to the geographical location of the child's family life.

Twelve years later, in January 2003, the Irish Supreme Court revisited the family-unity rights of IBCs. During the intervening years, the numbers of asylum seekers arriving in Ireland had increased dramatically, from thirty-two in 1992[88] to 10,324 in 2001.[89] In the year 2000, there were some three thousand births to asylum seekers. According to one newspaper article, "up to half of female asylum-seekers are pregnant at the time of making their applications."[90] Hospital authorities confirmed a trend of asylum seekers arriving in Ireland very late in the third trimester of pregnancy, often days before delivery.[91] The number of nonnationals claiming residency on the basis of IBCs increased from approximately fifteen hundred in 1999 to over six thousand in 2001.[92]

This trend was seized on by advocates of immigration restriction to call for an end to the abusive "loophole" opened up by the *Fajujonu* case. While no one advocated the withdrawal of birthright citizenship per se, critics of the prevailing situation argued that the incidents of such citizenship, in particular, the family-unity benefit developed by *Fajujonu*, should be reversed. Immigrants' rights groups countered by decrying moves by anti-immmigrant organizations to discriminate against a small group of IBCs by using the legal status or nationality of IBCs' parents to deny the children the right to family life in their own country.

Against this high-stakes media discussion, the Irish Supreme Court heard the cases of two families of rejected asylum seekers with IBCs. One family consisted of five Czech nationals and an IBC; the family, parents and three young children, had arrived in Ireland when the mother was in the early stages of pregnancy. The other family was Nigerian, parents and a young child and, eventually, an Irish child born five months after the family's arrival in Ireland. In a divided judgment (five to two), the Court reaffirmed the constitutional right of children born in the state to citizenship but distinguished the new cases from *Fajujonu*, where the family had been resident for nine years and had had three IBCs by the time of the court hearing.

A majority of the court held that while children, including Irish children, had a constitutional right to be in the care and company of their families, they had no constitutional or absolute right to do so within Ireland. Any such right, they held, was qualified by the government's inherent sovereign power to control immigration and restrict the entry and stay of noncitizens. Thus, the court found that the Irish state could proceed with the enforced removal of the parents of the IBCs as long as it took into account factors such as the family's length of residency in the state and the IBCs' ability to integrate into their parents' country of origin. It was not necessary to show that the parents represented a security threat to the state or that they were guilty of criminal misconduct—a much broader range of reasons associated with the common good would be admissible to justify removal of the family.

In a key section of the court's decision, Chief Justice Keane emphasized that the quality of rights flowing from citizenship was not the same for adults and for children:

> In the case of adult citizens, it is of course a corollary of the right of citizenship that they are also entitled to . . . reside in Ireland. The position of the minor applicants in the present case is, however, significantly different. . . . Infants . . . are incapable of making, still less articulating, any decisions as to where they will reside. . . . The children have never been capable in law of exercising the right [to choose where to reside] and *in practical terms, as distinct from legal theory, it may reasonably be regarded as a right which does not vest in them until they reach an age at which they are capable of exercising it.*[93]

Given the absence of this right, the majority held that immigration considerations could trump the best interests of IBCs and that Irish citizenship did not entail a presumption in favor of the right to enjoy family life within the home state. The court did not examine whether citizens' constitutional right to reside in their country implied an obligation on the state to render that right effective rather than illusory.

The court was clearly influenced by the xenophobic hysteria raging outside the courtroom doors. By substituting the actual capacity of the child to make a residency decision for the entitlement to have a certain residency decision made on the basis of the child's best interests, the court effectively attacked birthright citizenship and undercut the most significant value of citizenship to an already marginalized group of IBCs. As one of the dissenting justices concluded,

> The fact that the parents have resided in the State for a longer or shorter period may be relevant to the consideration of *their* rights and interests. It seems to me that the State has throughout the conduct of the appeals approached the matter on the assumption that they are concerned with the rights of the parents. It has always been clear that they are not.[94]

By the time the court handed down its judgment in the case, eleven thousand applications for residency by parents of IBCs were pending, many from parents who had withdrawn their asylum applications on the strength of their claim for residency based on the birth of an IBC. Within ten months of the court's decision, the Irish government issued seven hundred letters to parents, proposing deportation unless written representations were made within fifteen days from the date of the letter.[95] Actual deportations followed thereafter. But this did not quell the public outcry.

On June 11, 2004, a public referendum on the constitutional right to citizenship was held; 79.17 percent of valid votes were cast in favor of removing the automatic constitutional right to birthright citizenship.[96] An amendment to the Constitution followed quickly, depriving children born in Ireland, both of whose parents were nonnationals, of the constitutional right to citizenship.[97] Though birthright citizenship had not been eliminated, the nondiscriminatory and inclusive basis for it had. The U.S. route of decoupling children's citizenship rights from their parents' residency rights, briefly adopted after the *D.L. and A.O.* case, was eventually rejected in favor of a radically reconceived notion of national membership and belonging. Parents' status and claims to inclusion within Ireland henceforth determine the citizenship rights of their Ireland-born children.

Canada and the Weakening of Residency Protections for the Families of Citizen Children[98]

As in the United States, Canadian citizenship law is based on *jus soli*. And as in both the United States and Ireland, Canadian courts have wrestled with the tension between citizenship and immigration considerations in deportation cases involving alien parents and citizen children. In *Baker v. Canada (Minister of Citizenship and Immigration)*,[99] a landmark decision in 1999, the Supreme Court of Canada (SCC) reversed the ruling of the lower court and the leading prior case.[100] The SCC held that, though the Convention on the Rights of the Child (CRC) had not been implemented by Parliament and did not therefore have direct application to Canadian law, nevertheless the CRC's values should be recognized and reflected in the interpretation of Canadian law by immigration authorities. The court held that, when immigration officers make humanitarian and compassionate (H&C) decisions about the deportability of a noncitizen parent of citizen children, "attentiveness and sensitivity to the importance of the rights of children, to their best interests, and to the hardship that may be caused to them by a negative decision is essential."[101] Thus, though the

SCC avoided ruling that the child's "best interests" should trump all other considerations, it did state that H&C decisions that minimized the child's interests in a manner inconsistent with Canada's humanitarian and compassionate tradition would be found unreasonable.

As in Ireland following the *Fajujonu* decision, so in Canada following the *Baker* case, immigration authorities and reviewing courts adopted a new perspective on family deportation cases involving Canadian-born children, taking serious account of their best interests. Cases where the immigration officer dealt with the children's interests dismissively were overturned on appeal.[102] However, in subsequent years, in line with the developments in Ireland and the tightening of rules in the United States, Canadian courts have been weakening the protections afforded citizen children and their families by *Baker*.

In a series of rulings, the court has placed less emphasis on the best interests of citizen children in deportation decisions relating to their parents. In some cases it has ruled that the very fact that an immigration officer has, as a procedural matter, considered the impact of parental deportation on the citizen child is sufficient to validate the decision, whether or not the outcome of that enquiry is favorable to the child; in other cases it has investigated the substantive nature of the review, to assess whether the officer's empirical decision was correct in the eyes of the court.

In *Legault v. Canada (Minister of Citizenship and Immigration)*,[103] the court, remanding a deportation decision for reconsideration, agreed with an immigration officer's decision that the noncitizen parent's criminal history should prevail over any humanitarian and compassionate factors, because the emotional loss to the child resulting from the deportation of the father would not result in "disproportionate hardship."[104] The best interests of the child were only one among several factors immigration officers should take into account; the parent's continuing illegal presence in Canada and the government's right to control its borders and enforce immigration laws were others. The court noted that, if the Baker principles were applied, there would be few cases where an immigration officer would be able to conclude that the child's best interests did not demand exemption from deportation of the parent. A later case followed but somewhat tempered the position in *Legault* by holding that consideration of the child's best interests did not require that an immigration officer demonstrate that the child would face disproportionate hardship.[105]

The Immigration and Refugee Protection Act (IRPA), which came into effect in June 2002, incorporates these case law developments but stipulates that H&C decisions must "tak[e] into account the best interests of a child directly affected."[106] Since H&C decisions frequently take several years to come through, during which time the child's parent(s) can be deported, Canadian advocates have attempted to use family court custody orders to prevent family separation and parental deportation by arguing that removal of a parent would violate the family court order. However, in *Alexander v. Canada*, the Federal Court defeated this strategy. The court held that "the grant of custody or sole custody, does not necessitate that the custodial parent maintain physical care of a child at all times."[107] Canada thus imposes a nuanced decision-making exercise on immigration officers and courts. By rejecting a requirement that the child of a deportable adult face "disproportionate hardship," the Canadian approach differs from the harsh U.S. standard[108] and is, rather, reminiscent of the European balancing strategy, though the inclusion of the child's perspective and best-interests considerations is an improvement on the adult-centered European approach.

Citizenship Rights and Nondiscrimination

The position adopted in *Fajujonu* and *Baker* reflects the traditional view that citizenship signals a particularly close connection between person and territory. This view is trivialized when young children are given the "option" of staying in their home country only without their adult caregivers, or when, as with the U.S. rules, child citizens have no impact on the deportability of their parents unless they face extreme medical emergencies or the threat of torture.

Birthright citizenship should bring with it a presumption of nondeportability for children just as it does for adults. In fact, a fortiori, given the significance of developmental experiences, of educational access, and of the powerful resource implications of continued residence within a developed state, the arguments for not deporting citizen children would appear to be even stronger than those for not deporting citizen adults. This is true from the viewpoint of the child's best interests. It is also true from the viewpoint of equity and nondiscrimination; for why should the right to family unity, to enjoyment of family and private life of the child, be less enforceable than the corresponding right for adult citizens? Why should past time spent in a state rather than the prospect of future time enjoyed be the determining criterion of connection? What does citizenship bring to a child, if not the right to grow up in his or her country in the company and with the care of family?

Citizenship for a child very easily and quickly becomes a denuded status. In the absence of the other cardinal civil and political attributes of citizenship, citizenship for the child effectively means the entitlement to enjoy permanently and indefinitely the attributes of social and private life in the home country. Since, increasingly, permanent residents are also entitled to the full range of social provisions, it is the *permanence of access* to these social goods, the fact of nondeportability for the present and the future, that distinguishes the rights of the citizen child from those of the noncitizen child, not the access itself. A just legal framework that incorporates a child's perspective would acknowledge this and increase the burden on the deporting state to demonstrate that the benefits of parental removal outweighed the costs of child separation, institutionalization, or disorientation. In short, a new set of variables would have to enter the reconfigured calculation of what was just, equitable, and proportional in a democratic society.

Residence as Apprenticeship for Future Citizenship

Apart from nondeportability, children share with permanent residents access to all the social goods and provisions available in the state of residence. What then does citizenship mean for a child? At the outset it is an ascriptive status, not chosen, not consented to, which provides the basis for future assumption of the obligations and responsibilities that eventually attach to the status for adults: the civic responsibilities, the legal benefits, the affiliative identifications. As the child develops, so the balance between ascriptive status and consensual identification shifts—the child changes from a repository of protective concerns, a recipient of enabling inputs, to an active participant, an autonomous contributor, a member of the community.

For children, then, citizenship is a status in process. It has to be conceived of principally in terms of rights rather than obligations—rights to family life, to traditional civil and political freedoms as they apply to education, social support, and protection from exploitation. Decisions about accessing and enforcing these rights are vested in the child him- or herself, insofar as the child is a "mature minor" capable of so doing; otherwise parents, or failing that the state in its capacity as *parens patriae*, have the responsibility. But access to these rights paves the way for the assumption of obligations on majority—the child is an adult in process, entitled to a "moral minimum" in order to be apprenticed into future effective participation in the citizenry.[109] Ability to enjoy the attributes of the apprenticeship is a prerequisite for the assumption of the obligations of citizenship on majority. Citizenship, to be meaningful, then, is a civic practice that has to be lived and experienced, which requires participatory presence and engagement, not simply a juridical status that is learned by watching from a distance.[110]

What sort of juror or voter with a contribution to make to his or her peers is one who has been forced to live outside the community during the premajority period? How is such a person to engage with the concerns of the polity in a meaningful and contributory way? The child's enduring presence in the home country is thus not simply an important guarantee for the child of access to the rights and benefits of the community's social goods; it is also a prerequisite for the exercise of the obligations of citizenship as an adult.

A Final French Story

The transformation from ascriptive to consensual participation in citizenship happens gradually; but it underlies the obligation to give some practical meaning to the citizenship of children. Depriving citizen children of the entitlement to continued residence in their home country with the benefit of parental care and companionship undermines that obligation. It leads to discrimination within the class or category of child citizens, between those with alien parents and those with citizen parents, something that is utterly irrelevant from the perspective of the child citizen as a rights bearer and future participant in the citizenry. It introduces uncertainty, stress, and insecurity into the lives of families already living in the shadow of deportation and deprivation.

The poignancy of this situation is well illustrated by the case of the undocumented, so-called *sans papiers* in France.[111] The *sans papiers* are parents of children born in France who are considered "nonexpulsables" because of their French-born children but are also considered "nonregularizables" unless they have spent ten years on French soil, because no amnesty procedure has been afforded them.[112] As a result of their indeterminate status, they have faced constant state harassment.

In response, some of these parents organized politically, becoming involved in a hunger strike in 1995, in order to draw public attention to the impossibility of their situation as long-term, settled "irregulars" with strong moral obligations and claims to remain in France but no legal remedies to enable them to do so.[113] An Aliens Bill, approved on its first reading in July 2003 and signed into law on November 26, 2003,[114] allowed parents of French-born children the right to apply for a residence permit if they had had at least five years of uninterrupted undocumented residence in France, or at least two years of residence since the expiration of a temporary visa, provided they could prove "exercise of parental responsibility" and financial support for the child.[115]

This is a far cry from focusing on the child's interest in having the care and company of his or her parents in the home country irrespective of the official acceptability of the parent's behavior. However, it did provide an avenue for short-circuiting the painful limbo of insecurity and discrimination that citizen children of alien parents were otherwise subjected to. The law was clearly a response to the strength of public feeling about the injustice of penalizing citizen children for the immigration irregularities of their parents. Given the volatile racial politics of contemporary France, however, the prospects of longevity for this progressive legislation were poor. And indeed, only one year after its enactment, the law was amended to deprive parents of citizen children of the access to regularization of their immigration status, the amendment taking effect on March 1, 2005.[116]

For an excluded and marginalized group such as the children of *sans papiers* to have received, albeit for only a year and a quarter, the right to legitimate their parents' stay because of their citizenship, was a dramatic and inspiring achievement. For it to have lasted so briefly is a sobering illustration of the tenuous access to just public policy that this group has. But the vision of a rights-respecting approach to the interests and needs of child citizens is there, in the record. All that remains is for it to be realized again, through the force of persuasion and political mobilization of antiracist and child-rights advocacy. Since children have to rely on the political clout of their more powerful elder peers, perhaps adult self-interest in avoiding deportation, rather than adult dedication to protecting children's rights, will turn out to be the most promising engine of change.

NOTES

1. Children's Charter, distilling recommendations of President Hoover's White House Conference on Child Health and Protection in 1930, cited in Beverly C. Edmonds and William R. Fernekes, *Children's Rights: A Reference Handbook* (Santa Barbara, CA: ABC-CLIO, 1996), 182–85.

2. Osheku v. Ireland, [1986] I.R. 733, 746 (Ire.) (opinion of Gannon, J.), cited in A.O. and D.L. v. Minister for Justice, Equality, and Law Reform [2003] 1 I.R. 1 (Ire.) (opinion of Fennelly, J.)

3. Ibid.

4. I use the term "children" to refer to children under eighteen, following international law and in particular the definition in the 1989 UN Convention on the Rights of the Child, art. 1, G.A. Res. 25, U.N. GAOR, 44th Sess., Supp. No. 49, U.N. Doc. A/44/49 (Nov. 20, 1989).

5. Toby Harnden, "Twin Towers Widow Wins Fight to Stay in US," *The Daily Telegraph* (UK), July 27, 2002.

6. Anastasia Hendrix, "An INS Mistake, a Mother Deported," *San Francisco Chronicle*, July 27, 2002.

7. Article 16(3) of the 1948 Universal Declaration of Human Rights states, "The family is the natural and fundamental group unit of society and is entitled to protection by society and the State." U.N. GAOR, 3d Sess., 1st plen. mtg., U.N. Doc A/810 (Dec. 12, 1948). Similar sentiments are expressed in Article 23(1) of the 1966 International Covenant on Civil and Political Rights, opened for signature Dec. 16, 1966, 99 U.N.T.S. 17, and Article 9 of the 1989 Convention on the Rights of the Child.

8. Sam Stanton and Emily Bazar, "Uprooted Again: Fearful Muslims Find Refuge in Canada," *The Sacramento Bee*, September 23, 2003.

9. For example, Ali Saleh Kahlah al-Marri has been detained in a South Carolina brig since 2001, though no evidence has ever been presented against him. A. C. Thompson, "'Enemy Combatant' Languishes in a South Carolina Brig," *The Progressive*, March 2007, available at http://progressive.org/mag_thompson0307 (accessed March 8, 2007).

10. In 1996, eighty-five hundred noncitizens were detained, compared with 237,667 in 2005. Human Rights Watch, *Locked Away: Immigration Detainees in Jails in the United States* (1998), available at http://www.hrw.org/about/initiatives/insjails. htm (accessed March 8, 2007). *See also* Department of Homeland Security, *Immigration Enforcement Actions: 2005* (2006), http://www.dhs.gov/xlibrary/ assets/ statistics/yearbook/2005/Enforcement_AR_05.pdf (last accessed March 8, 2007).

11. Department of Homeland Security, *2004 Yearbook of Immigration Statistics*, Table 35, cited in Dan Kanstroom, "Post-Deportation Human Rights Project" (seminar presentation, Kennedy School of Government Colloquium on Children, Trauma, and Migration, Cambridge, MA, November 3, 2006).

12. Charles Rabin and Alfonso Chardy, "Immigration Dragnets Target Ex-cons," *Miami Herald*, March 4, 2003.

13. The U.S. rule's disjunction from other established norms regarding the protection of family life prompts quixotic judicial reasoning. In contrast to the Andazola-Rivas case, the Board of Immigration Appeals found "exceptional and extremely unusual hardship" in Matter of Gonzalez Recinas, 23 I. & N. Dec. 467 (BIA 2002). How do the two cases differ? Both cases concerned a single parent with young English-speaking children and no family in Mexico: but instead of two children, the single-parent mother in *Recinas* had six children, and instead of a father who "could" (but did not) provide support in Andazola-Rivas, the Recinas children had had no contact at all with their father. Despite the wording of the rule, an assessment of relative hardships facing the two mothers, not the children, seems to have driven the BIA's contrasting findings.

14. Randy Capp and Michael Fix, *Undocumented Immigrants: Myths and Realities* (New York: Urban Institute, October 25, 2005), http:// www.urban.org/ UploadedPDF/900898_undocumented_immigrants.pdf.

15. Fran Abrams, *Freedom's Cause: The Lives of the Suffragettes* (London: Pro-file Books, 2003).

16. Norani Othman, *Muslim Women and the Challenge of Islamic Extremism* (Malaysia: Sisters in Islam, 2005).

17. See Convention on the Elimination of All Forms of Discrimination Against Women, Dec. 18, 1979, art. 7, 1249 U.N.T.S. 13, 18 (entered into force Sept. 3, 1981).

18. Nottebohm Case (Liechtenstein v. Guatemala), 1955 I.C.J. 4, 23 (Judgment of April 6, 1955).

19. U.S. Const. amend. XIV.

20. Ir. Const., art. 2.

21. At the same time, though, citizenship has become less decisive in protect-ing individual freedom as naturalized citizens find their citizenship of origin in-troduced to qualify and discredit the significance of their U.S. citizenship—as in "a U.S. citizen of Yemeni origin" or Saudi-American. See Joel Brinkley and Eric Lichtblau, "U.S. Releases Saudi-American It Had Captured in Afghanistan," *New York Times*, October 12, 2004.

22. Of course, stringent language and general knowledge tests may in prac-tice operate to exclude certain disadvantaged groups from access to citizenship. Moreover, it is worth noting that, despite the pervasive prohibition against race and ethnic discrimination in today's world, there is a remarkable permissiveness towards them in international (and some domestic) law regarding citizenship. See Joanne Mariner, "Racism, Citizenship, and National Identity," *Development* 46 (2003): 64–70.

23. "Mature civic identity as masculine citizenship is a way of life Aristotle portrays as rich and full," Jean Bethke Elshtain, *Women and War* (Chicago: Uni-versity of Chicago Press, 1995), 55. However, see Cynthia Patterson, "Citizenship

and Gender in the Ancient World," in this volume, for an interesting qualification of the traditional view that women were not citizens in the ancient world. She argues that, though excluded from political citizenship, they were involved in multiple forms of active participation within the community.

24. See 1989 UN Convention on the Rights of the Child, art. 38, as amended by the 2000 Optional Protocol to the Convention on the Rights of the Child, on the involvement of children in armed conflict.

25. In the United States, family reunification accounts for the majority of lawful immigration each year. See Jeanne Batalova, *Spotlight on Legal Immigration to the United States* (August 1, 2006), available at http://www.migrationinformation.org/ Feature/display.cfm?ID=414#6 (last accessed March 8, 2007).

26. For a full discussion of the issues focused on the situation in the United Kingdom, see Jacqueline Bhabha and Sue Shutter, *Women's Movement: Women under Immigration, Nationality, and Refugee Law* (Stoke-on-Trent, UK: Trentham Books, 1994).

27. Jacqueline Bhabha, "Demography and Rights: Women, Children, and Access to Asylum," *International Journal of Refugee Law* 16 (2004): 227–43.

28. "The concept of citizenship has become a central device by which the law distinguishes those subject to it and served by it from strangers. Thus, citizenship has come to play a vital role in the fundamental question of politics." J. Donald Galloway, "The Dilemmas of Canadian Citizenship," *Georgetown Immigration Law Journal* 13 (1999): 206–7.

29. Acosta v. Gaffney, 558 F.2d 1153, 1157 (3d Cir. 1977) (emphasis added), citing Perdido v. INS, 420 F.2d 1179, 1181 (5th Cir. 1969).

30. Nguyen v. INS, 533 U.S. 53 (2001).

31. Janice Tibbetts, "Federal Rulings Make Deportations More Likely: Canadian-born Children Now a Less-important Factor," *Southam News* (UK), February 10, 2003.

32. L. & O. v. Minister for Justice, Equality, and Law Reform [2003] 1 I.R. 1 (Ire.).

33. Peter Schuck, *Citizens, Strangers, and In-betweens: Essays on Immigration and Citizenship* (Boulder, CO: Westview Press, 1998), 213.

34. Ibid., 212.

35. Bonnie Honig, *Democracy and the Foreigner* (Princeton, NJ: Princeton University Press, 2001), 102.

36. Oforji v. Ashcroft, 354 F.3d 609, 620–21 (7th Cir. 2003).

37. Federation for American Immigration Reform estimates that 165,000 babies are born each year in the United States to illegal immigrants and others who come here to give birth. Kelley Bouchard, "An Open Door Refugee Policy Has Its Critics," *Maine Sunday Telegram*, June 30, 2002.

38. Bhabha and Shutter, *Women's Movement*, supra note 26, 76–86.

39. Ibid., 83.

40. Ibid., 84.

41. Schuck, *Citizens, Strangers, and In-betweens*, supra note 33, 214.

42. Seyla Benhabib, *The Rights of Others* (Cambridge: Cambridge University Press, 2004), 5.

43. Ibid., 73.

44. Ayelet Shachar, "Citizens of a Lesser State," in *Children, Family, and State (Nomos XLIV)*, eds. Stephen Macedo and Iris Marion Young (New York: NYU Press, 2003), 347.

45. Bhabha and Shutter, *Women's Movement*, supra note 26, 16–17.

46. Ibid., 18.

47. Linda Kerber, "The Asymmetries of Citizenship" (paper on file with the author); Karen Knop, "Relational Nationality: On Gender and Nationality in International Law," in *Citizenship Today: Global Perspectives and Practices*, eds. T. Alexander Aleinikoff and Douglas Klusmeyer (Washington, DC: Brookings Institution Press, 2001), 89–119.

48. Stephen Macedo and Iris Marion Young, introduction to *Children, Family, and State (Nomos XLIV)* (New York: NYU Press, 2003), 1.

49. According to the preamble to the CRC, states parties are convinced that "the family [is] the fundamental group of society and the natural environment for the growth and well-being of all its members *and particularly children*." 1989 UN Convention on the Rights of the Child, preamble (emphasis added).

50. This right is by no means unqualified or absolute, see chapter by Sarah van Walsum in the volume.

51. Schuck, *Citizens, Strangers, and In-betweens*, supra note 33, 166–67.

52. The commission was the court of first instance within the Council of Europe system until it was abolished. Now all cases brought under the ECHR go straight to the European Court of Human Rights.

53. Berrehab v. the Netherlands, App. No. 10730/84, 11 Eur. H.R. Rep. 322 (1988) (Eur. Ct. H.R.).

54. Yousef v. United Kingdom, App. No. 14830/89, ECHR (adopted on June 30, 1992).

55. Ibid., para. 22.

56. Ibid., para. 43.

57. App. No. 29192/95, Eur. Ct. H.R. (July 11, 2000).

58. Ibid., para. 55.

59. Case C-200/02, Zhu & Chen v. Sec'y of State for the Home Dep't, 3 C.M.L.R. 48 (2004) (ECJ).

60. For more discussion of the Irish situation, see Siobhan Mullally, "Crossing Borders: Gender, Citizenship, and Reproductive Autonomy in Ireland," in *Women and Immigration Law: New Variations on Classical Feminist Themes*, eds. Sarah van Walsum and Thomas Spijkerboer (London: Routledge-Cavendish, 2007), 223–40.

61. Chen and Zhu v. Secretary of State for the Home Department, Written Observations of Ireland, para. 4.4, September 17, 2002 (on file with the author).

62. Case C-200/02, Zhu & Chen v. Secretary of State for the Home Department, 3 C.M.L.R. 48 (2004), para 45. The ECJ delivered its judgment in May 2004; by June 2004, Ireland had passed a constitutional amendment withdrawing the constitutional right to Irish citizenship from children born in Ireland without an Irish parent, see discussion below.

63. Case C-413/99, Baumbast & R. v. Sec'y of State for the Home Dep't, 2002 E.C.R. I-7091 (ECJ).

64. INS v. Jong Ha Wang, 450 U.S. 139, 145 (1981).

65. Villena v. INS, 622 F.2d 1352, 1359 (9th Cir. 1980) (emphasis added).

66. Hernandez-Cordero v. INS, 819 F.2d 558, 563 (5th Cir. 1987) (en banc).

67. Edith Z. Friedler, "From Extreme Hardship to Extreme Deference: United States Deportation of Its Own Children," *Hastings Constitutional Law Quarterly* 22 (1995): 491. The cases cited in the previous three notes are described in detail in this article.

68. Ibid., 526.

69. Matter of Montreal, 23 I. & N. Dec. 56, 59 (BIA 2001).

70. Ibid., 65.

71. Where the board determines that the draconian standard has not been met, there is no possibility of review by a higher court, nor appeal for the exercise of discretion, see Romero-Torres v. Ashcroft, 327 F.3d 887 (9th Cir. 2003); Martinez-Maldonado v. Gonzalez, 437 F.3d 679 (9th Cir. 2006).

72. Acosta v. Gaffney, 558 F.2d 1153, 1155 (3d Cir. 1977).

73. Lopez v. Franklin, 427 F. Supp. 345 (E.D. Mich. 1977).

74. It may however be that the constitutional position is underexplored and that the leading precedent, Perdido v. INS, 420 F.2d 1179 (5th Cir. 1969), widely cited to support the proposition that constructive deportation does not violate U.S. children's constitutional rights is ripe for reconsideration. I am indebted to Christina Coll for these unpublished observations, "U.S. Citizens Deported: The Rejection of American Children Born to Immigrant Parents" (term paper for ISP 229 course at Kennedy School of Government, submitted January 8, 2007, on file with the author).

75. Beharry v. Reno, 183 F. Supp. 2d 584, 588 (E.D.N.Y. 2002), overruled by Beharry v. Ashcroft, 329 F.3d 51 (2d Cir. 2003).

76. Beharry v. Ashcroft, 329 F.3d 51 (2d Cir. 2003).

77. Ibid., 63.

78. Nwaokolo v. INS , 314 F.3d 303, 308 (7th Cir. 2002).

79. Ibid., 310.

80. Oforji v. Ashcroft, 354 F.3d 609 (7th Cir. 2003).

81. Ibid., 617–18 (emphasis added).

82. Salameda v. INS, 70 F.3d 447 (7th Cir. 1995).

83. "It is the entitlement and birthright of every person born in the island of Ireland, which includes its islands and seas, to be part of the Irish nation," Irish Constitution, art.2, prior to the Twenty-seventh Amendment of the Constitution Act 2004, which removed this automatic right from children born to nonnationals. This is reiterated in Article 6 of the Nationality and Citizenship Act 1956, which provides that "[e]very person born in Ireland is an Irish citizen from birth."

84. A.O. and D.L. v. Minister for Justice, Equality, and Law Reform [2003] 1 I.R. 1 (Ire.) (opinion of Fennelly, J.)

85. [1990] 2 I.R. 151.

86. Ibid., 164 (opinion of Finlay, C.J.).

87. Ibid., 163.

88. Nuala Haughey, "State Contesting Right of Non-EU Parents of Irish Children to Stay," The Irish Times, January 9, 2002.

89. Population Data Unit, UNHCR, Population Statistics, Asylum Applications in the EU in 1999–2001 (2002).

90. Haughey, ibid.

91. Roisin Boyd, "The Immigrant Dreams That Are Dying in Irish Maternity Wards," www.metroeireann.com/content.htm.

92. Paul Cullen, "What's to Befall These Irish Children?," The Irish Times, April 9, 2002.

93. See A.O. and D.L. v. Minister for Justice, Equality, and Law Reform, 15 (opinion of Keane, C.J.) (emphasis added). This argument is similar to the one advanced in the Irish government submissions to the Zhu and Chen European Court of Justice case discussed earlier in this chapter.

94. A.O. and D.L. v. Minister for Justice, Equality, and Law Reform, [2003] 1 I.R. 1, 54 (Ire.) (opinion of Fennelly, J.)

95. Human Rights Commission, Position of Non-National Parents and Their Irish-Born Children, October 21, 2003, available at http:// www.statewatch.org/news/2003/nov/IHRC%20non%20national%20parents.pdf.

96. Brian Lavery, "Voters Reject Automatic Citizenship for Babies Born in Ireland," New York Times, June 13, 2004.

97. The Twenty-Seventh Amendment of the Constitution introduced a new clause: Article 9.2(1) now reads, "Notwithstanding any other provisions of this Constitution, a person born in the island of Ireland, which includes its islands and seas, who does not have, at the time of the birth of that person, at least one parent who is an Irish citizen or entitled to be an Irish citizen is not entitled to Irish citizenship or nationality, unless provided for by law." Ir. Const. art. 9.2(1).

98. I am indebted to Geraldine Sadoway, of Parkdale Community Legal Services, Toronto, for enlightening comments and assistance with this section of the chapter.

99. [1999] 2 S.C.R. 817.

100. Langner v. Canada (Minister of Employment and Immigration), [1995] 29 C.R.R. (2d) 184 (F.C.A.).

101. Ibid., 74.

102. See, e.g., G. v. Canada (Minister of Citizenship and Immigration), [1999] 177 F.T.R. 76 (F.C.T.D.); Jack v. Canada (Minister of Citizenship and Immigration), [2000] 7 Imm. L.R. (3d) 35 (F.C.T.D.); Wynter v. Canada (Minister of Citizenship and Immigration) [2000] 24 Admin. L.R. (3d) 99 (F.C.T.D.); Navaratnam v. Canada (Minister of Citizenship and Immigration), [1999] 179 F.T.R. 294 (F.C.T.D.); Naredo v. Canada (Minister of Citizenship and Immigration), [2000] 192 D.L.R. (4th) 373 (F.C.T.D.).

103. Legault v. Canada (Minister of Employment and Immigration), [2001] F.C.T. 315.

104. Ibid., 51.

105. Canada (Minister of Citizenship and Immigration) v. Hawthorne, 2002 F.C.A. 475.

106. Immigration and Refugee Protection Act, S.25(1) (2002) (Can.).

107. Alexander v. Solicitor General of Canada, [2006] 2 F.C.R. 681; 2005 FC 1147.

108. Also, unlike the U.S. position, the *Baker* ruling is not explicitly restricted to Canadian citizen children, and can therefore be prayed in aid for any children facing the deportation of parents.

109. Karl Eric Knutson, "A New Vision of Childhood," in *The Child as Citizen*, ed. Parliamentary Assembly, Council of Europe (Strasbourg: Council of Europe Publishing, 1996), 17–18.

110. Honig, *Democracy and the Foreigner*, supra note 35, 102 (quoting Michael Walzer).

111. For more about the Sans Papiers Movement, see Catherine Raissiguier, "French Immigration Laws: The '*Sans-Papières*' Perspective," in *Women and Immigration Law: New Variations on Classical Feminist Themes*, eds. Sarah van Walsum and Thomas Spijkerboer (London: Taylor & Francis, 2006), 204–22.

112. Migration Policy Group, *Migration News Sheet*, August 2003, 3. Hard copy available from Migration Policy Group, 205 rue Bellard, box 1, B-1040 Brussels (mns@migpogroup.com).

113. Johanna Simeant, *La Cause des Sans-Papiers* (Paris: Presses de Sciences Po., 1998), 137.

114. Law 2003-1119, art. 21 (November 26, 2003).

115. Migration Policy Group, *Migration News Sheet*, 3.

116. Ordonnance No. 2004-1248, art. 4(1), entered into force March 1, 2005.

6

||||||||||||||||||||||||||||||||||||||||||||||||||

Transnational Mothering, National
Immigration Policy, and European Law:
The Experience of the Netherlands

Sarah K. van Walsum

In the summer of 1997, Joyce, a young Colombian mother, traveled to the Netherlands, leaving her six-year-old daughter, Emily, behind with family.[1] Joyce had never married Emily's father, and their paths had separated soon after Emily's birth. Joyce therefore had to support both herself and her daughter. Her purpose in coming to the Netherlands was to visit a sister who was already living there and to explore the possibilities that Europe might have to offer. Once she had established herself there, she hoped to have Emily come over to join her.[2]

Joyce's tourist visa expired after three months, but she decided to stay on in the Netherlands and try her luck a little longer. After a year or so of staying with her sister and friends, earning money with odd jobs, cleaning, and babysitting, she met a Dutchman, fell in love, and decided to stay for good. Getting a residence permit, however, took longer than she had hoped. Her new boyfriend had his own business, and it took some time before he was able to convince the authorities that he would be able to support Joyce.

As soon as she had acquired a residence permit, Joyce booked a flight to Colombia to visit Emily. By then, they had been separated for well over two years. Back in the Netherlands, Joyce applied for a residence permit for her daughter. By early 2000, she had collected all the necessary papers and sent in an application for a permit. When she received a summons from the immigration authorities, she went to her appointment expecting good news. But Emily's request for a residence permit had been rejected.

At the time, Dutch law on family reunification required proof that there was an "effective family bond" between the petitioning parent and the child, that is, that the parent had been effectively involved in the financial support and upbringing of the child, despite the geographic separation. In the eyes of the Dutch immigration authorities, the family bond between Joyce and Emily was no longer strong enough to justify the child's admission on the legal grounds of family reunification.

Joyce lost her appeal. By that time, she had become a Dutch citizen, she had given up her Colombian nationality, and she and her Dutch boyfriend of five years had had a child together. Returning to Colombia to start a new life with Emily was not an acceptable option. Were mother and daughter to remain separated indefinitely?

Joyce and Emily's story is by no means unique in the Netherlands. Until recently, in fact, Dutch case law has been replete with such examples.[3] As I shall explain in more detail below, while families all over the world enlist the help of family, friends, or paid day care for their children, the need to do so is especially strong for individual women (single or divorced) who work outside the home to earn a living. Women who migrate for work in another country, in search of better pay, may need to have children stay in the homes of others in the country of origin. That "good mothering" may take many forms was not initially recognized under Dutch immigration law. The approach in the Netherlands eventually brought it into conflict with European human rights law and with the emerging immigration law of the European Union (EU).

This chapter proceeds as follows. I begin with a discussion of the "effective care" criterion in Dutch immigration law, which provided the basis for the rejection of claims such as those of Joyce and Emily. I then examine the advantages and disadvantages of applying effective care as a criterion for granting rights to parents vis-à-vis their children. Although linking rights to care may seem attractive from a feminist perspective (particularly in the context of family law), the experiences with Dutch immigration law show that such a legal strategy can also work to the detriment of women as mothers.

The Netherlands does not, however, have exclusive jurisdiction over matters of family reunification. European human rights law and, increasingly, immigration law of the European Union is also relevant. Thus, I analyze appeals of domestic Dutch decisions and discuss the interaction between Dutch and European jurisprudence around the ideas of care and family reunification. Given the still-embryonic state of EU harmonization of immigration law, my main focus is on the by now well-developed jurisprudence of the European Court of Human Rights (ECtHR)[4] concerning the application of Article 8 of the European Convention of Human Rights and Fundamental Freedoms (European Convention).[5] I explore the increasingly complex jurisdictional landscape in Europe and the implications for national policies regarding the admission of family members from outside of the European Union. It is this complexity that helps to explain how some single and divorced mothers coming from outside of the European Union have been able to use gains previously made by single and divorced fathers and EU citizens and be reunited with their families.

While the appeal to European human rights law ultimately prevailed, success was neither immediate nor self-evident. A complaint against the application of the effective family bond criterion was declared admissible in 1984,[6] but it took until 2001 before the ECtHR ruled in favor of such a complaint.[7] And the effective family bond criterion continued to be applied in Dutch immigration policies for nearly five years after that ECtHR case was decided.

I conclude with a discussion of the impact of European human rights law upon national immigration policy.[8] While proponents believe that a universalist human rights regime, as expressed through, for example, European human rights law, is gaining ground over the exclusionary effects of domestic immigration policies, skeptics point out that international human rights law, like any other form of law, can only be effective to the extent that it is implemented within a concrete national context. Law alone, they contend, is incapable of ensuring a fair and just society.[9] In their view, whether nationally or internationally based, law's effectiveness remains dependent on the specific context of power relations in which it is being mobilized.

As an example of the way the tensions among national, international, and supranational jurisdictions are played out in present-day Europe, the story of the effective family bond criterion in Dutch immigration law can help us understand how and when international human rights law may in fact serve to mitigate restrictive national immigration policies. At the same time, set in the context of contested family norms, on the one hand, and layered and complex identity politics within Europe, on the other, a discussion of the effective family bond criterion also sheds light on both these sites of contestation and on the complex relationship between them.

Care as a Legal Criterion in the Dutch Context

In the late 1990s, when Joyce applied for a residence permit for Emily, Dutch family reunification policies required that parents provide written proof that they had been effectively involved in the upbringing of their children during the entire period of separation, and that they had also provided full financial support during that period.[10] The burden of proof was considerable, and, after a separation of only several months, many parents were unable to meet these requirements, let alone after several years.[11] What these policies meant in effect was that only those parents who had brought their children with them when migrating to the Netherlands could be sure of getting a residence permit for their children, assuming all other requirements (passport, certified birth certificate, sufficient income, no criminal record) had been met. Parents who, like Joyce, felt they had to leave their children behind temporarily ran a very real risk of being refused permission for family reunification.

Many Dutch immigration lawyers were critical of the effective family bond criterion. In their eyes, certain parents were being denied specific rights in the sphere of family life because of choices that they had made regarding the care and upbringing of their children. Other parents with different opportunities were, on the other hand, entitled to those rights. The Dutch state was in effect rewarding certain parental decisions and punishing others. Normally, Dutch law would not allow for such interference in parental authority, unless vital interests of the child were at stake. On these grounds, it was claimed that the effective family bond criterion formed a violation of basic principles of Dutch law and of international human rights law as well, since both Article 8 of the European Convention and various articles of the UN Convention on the Rights of the Child placed the primary responsibility for the care and upbringing of children with the parents, only allowing for marginal interference, by member states, in parental authority.[12]

Concurrent with this debate, a comparable one was being carried out in the field of family law but in the opposite direction. At the same time that the use of effective care was being criticized in immigration law circles, in family law circles, feminist lawyers were pleading for the application of ongoing daily provision of care as a criterion for determining parental rights. In their view, parental rights should be primarily based on which parent actually provided care, rather than on formal legal or biological ties. This position was taken in reaction to Dutch family law jurisprudence that had followed the ECtHR's 1979 judgment in the *Marckx* case,[13] and that gave single and divorced fathers in the Netherlands visiting rights, the right to formally recognize a child against the express wishes of the mother, and the right to exercise parental authority over a child, while the mother had been the primary caregiver.[14]

While mainstream family rights advocates were very much against application of care as a criterion for attributing parental rights, feminist lawyers supported their case with the following arguments. First, by attaching legal significance to the provision of effective care, adults who had no legal tie with a child (whether by choice or because of a same-sex relationship) could nonetheless acquire legal protection of the affective bond that had been established between them and the child they were nurturing. Second, applying care as a criterion would do more justice to the social position of women, who are generally more involved in providing care than men. While formal equality between men and women became a part of Dutch family law, substantive inequalities continued to persist within Dutch society. Women still had fewer positions of power than men, worked fewer hours, and earned less per hour. Feminist lawyers worried that, unless the substantive implications of women's caring responsibilities were somehow taken into account in family law, the legal protection of family life against state interference would continue to benefit fathers more than mothers.[15]

While this criterion was appealing in some respects as a legal principle in family law, family lawyers needed to take note of how it worked out in Dutch immigration law. For there too the initial expectation was that the introduction of care as a criterion would serve to protect family bonds, not to disrupt them. When this criterion was first introduced in the 1970s, it promised to expand the scope of family reunification policies to include foster children and children born out of previous relationships along with a married couple's own children.[16] In other words, the initial intention was to include children who had substantive family ties with migrant parents, and who would otherwise have been excluded from reunification by the strict application of formal legal criteria.

By the mid-1980s, however, it became apparent that this criterion could also be used to exclude some children. In some of the earlier cases, the effective care criterion served primarily to prevent divorced migrant men from bringing over children they had left behind with their ex-wives. The Dutch state argued that divorced men should be prevented from bringing over their children in the interest of protecting the family life of the mothers they had left behind. Both the Administrative Jurisdiction Division of the Council of State (in the Netherlands, the highest court of appeals in administrative law) and the regional courts supported this application of the care criterion.[17]

This concern for the family life of Third World mothers proved to be of short duration. Once single and divorced mothers started migrating to the Netherlands, the effective family bond criterion came to work to their disadvantage as well.[18] Two examples serve as illustrations. Both concern applications for family reunification made by migrant mothers.

One woman had left her children with her mother after having remarried a man with children of his own, who had refused to take her children into his home. During the day, this woman had stayed at her mother's and looked after her own children, feeding them, taking them to school, and, as the regional court later would put it, "generally doing all that a mother who actually lives with her children would do for them." In the evenings, she had left her children and returned to her new husband's home to look after his needs and those of his children. When this case came before the Dutch regional court, it ruled that she and her children had in fact shared an effective family bond, even though they did not sleep under the same roof, and she won.[19]

The second case involved a single mother who had left her children with her mother and moved to a larger city so that she could earn enough money to look after herself and her family. In that city she lived with a new partner but returned to her home town each weekend to stay with her mother and the children. In her case, the Dutch regional court registered its doubts that there had ever been an effective bond between mother and children. In any event, the court did not consider the bond sufficiently strong to justify reunification.[20] In applying substantive care as a criterion, state authorities and courts gave expression to moral judgments as to what constitutes a "good" or a "bad" parent.[21]

Family Life Seen from the Perspective of Migrant Mothers

Such judgments display little or no awareness of the lived realities of the women concerned. Examples taken from my earlier research shed some light on those realities.[22] Although my research focused on a specific group of immigrants, people originating from the former Dutch colony of Surinam and moving to the Netherlands, their experiences, as parents, are exemplary of those of anyone having to deal with parental responsibilities in a country lacking social benefits and publicly financed child care.

One of the things that I discovered was that, in such a context, child care is structured via a complex interplay of nuclear family and extended family ties and of the responsibilities and obligations that these entail. While parents (and particularly mothers) are primarily responsible for raising, supporting, and caring for children, they may only be able to meet these responsibilities by delegating the day-to-day work to (primarily female) family members.

Thus working mothers or housewives with more children than they can manage may ask their mothers or other female relatives to take one or more children into their homes. Mothers living in the countryside may ask family in the city to take in one or more of their children so that they can attend school there. Mothers living and working in the city, on the other hand, may send their children to family in the countryside to be looked after there. Conversely, couples who are unable to have children of their own may ask if they can take on someone else's child to raise and set to work in the home, on the farm, or in the family business.

Such arrangements may be for shorter or longer periods of time. Some children stay outside the parental home during the week, returning to their parents on the weekends. Others may be removed from the parental home at birth and never know, until they reach maturity, that the woman who has raised them is not their birth mother. In most cases, however, the biological parents, and particularly the mother, continue to see themselves as ultimately responsible for their children's welfare. In fact, their identity as parents and the responsibilities that this entails form a core aspect of their identity as adults. Often they view the alternative caring arrangement as temporary, and will take the children back into their own home once circumstances allow.

Given the wide prevalence of shared child care, it is hardly surprising that parents who migrate internationally leave their children behind in the care of relatives while they explore the possibilities abroad. Children are often taken up in the grandparents' or some other relative's home before the parents actually consider leaving the country. Consequently, mothers and fathers—both married and single—may prefer to leave their children in the care of relatives until they are properly settled in new homes.

Additional Challenges for Single and Divorced Mothers

For single or divorced mothers, who lack the support of a partner or other breadwinner, the need for assistance in raising and caring for their children is particularly acute. Like many male breadwinners, these women too must consider migration as one of the possible options for supporting their families. And like emigrating couples, they too will generally prefer to leave their children behind with family or friends, rather than put them through the hardships and uncertainties of an initial period abroad. After all, many of the jobs that await these women in their countries of destination could be in sweatshops, as prostitutes, or as nannies or live-in maids. These options do not combine easily with child care. Moreover, these are not the sort of professions that generally lead to a residence permit, so that the women involved remain illegally resident and often uninsured as well.

Most single and divorced mothers who migrate to the Netherlands will only be able to acquire a secure position there through marriage to a Dutch national or to a settled immigrant. Even then, many will have to wait before they can apply to have their children legally admitted. During the first three years of married life in the Netherlands, immigrant wives remain dependent on their relationship for maintaining legal status. In the event that the marriage breaks down, they will be thrown back into the uncertainties of a clandestine existence. Since not all men are willing to take in the child of another, some women, fearing a conflict that could end their relationships, wait the three years before applying to have their children legally admitted. But, as Joyce's story shows, as long as the effective family bond criterion is applied, a long period of separation could prove fatal under Dutch law for the child's chances of legally rejoining his or her mother.

Norms about Family:
Intersecting Modes of Exclusion and the "Good Mother"

Given the disconnect between the experienced needs and responsibilities of migrant single and divorced mothers and the way in which the effective family bond criterion was applied in Dutch immigration law, care as a legal principle does not necessarily serve women's interests as mothers.

But does this mean that such a criterion could not be helpful in another field of law, namely, family law? Although immigration and family law clearly serve different interests, it is my conviction that in the sphere of family law, too, one should be very wary of applying substantive care as a criterion for granting parents rights vis-à-vis their children.

A characteristic of family law is that it concerns mutual obligations based not on free contract but on interdependency and mutual moral commitments to provide care and financial support.[23] In this sense, family relationships provide important guarantees for material security and emotional support for children, but also for the dignity of parents whose identities as adults find expression in the responsibilities that they take upon themselves as mature family members. It is precisely because family relations are so significant for all concerned that the right to respect for family life has been included in the arsenal of fundamental human rights.

There is a real risk that applying substantive care as a legal criterion in family law can lead to the devaluation of formal legal ties, meant to define and protect family relations between parents and children, as this has occurred in Dutch immigration law. In the context of family law, too, certain mothers could be disqualified as parents because they do not conform to preconceived notions of what it means to be a "good mother."

Two assumptions currently inform Dutch family law: first, that parents should be given the freedom, as mature adults, to fulfill their responsibilities towards their children as they see fit, and second, that the bond between a child and its biological parents is of essential significance for the child's psychological development. As argued above, these assumptions are not necessarily applied by courts where single and divorced migrant mothers are concerned. When the effective family bond criterion was applied in Dutch immigration law, migrant mothers had to adhere to a specific notion of the "good mother." While this idealized figure no longer reflected the realities of child raising among the white Dutch mainstream, it was used as a standard for reunification with children from developing countries. In such cases, the bond between mother and child was assumed severed when the children were placed in the care of another adult. Where policing the actual involvement of parents in the care of their children had been rejected in Dutch family law as an unacceptable invasion of the privacy rights of those involved,[24] Dutch immigration law actually required immigration authorities to do just that.

These discrepancies between Dutch family law and Dutch immigration law reflected another, related mode of distinction that was, by then, being drawn between *autochthonous* Dutch (the white "native" population) and non-Western *allochtonen* (immigrants and their descendents)[25] residing in the Netherlands. The stigma attached to single motherhood decreased for white, middle-class, single and divorced women throughout the 1970s. These single and divorced mothers became a more or less accepted phenomenon,[26] and those who managed to combine their caring responsibilities with paid employment were even depicted in the Dutch media as living proof of women's emancipation in the Netherlands.[27]

At the same time, however, there was a growing concern about a specific category of unwed mothers, namely, young single mothers among the non-Western *allochtoon* communities. These young women were not lauded as emancipated but were depicted in the same terms that used to apply to all single mothers in the 1960s: unknowing, irresponsible, and incapable of bringing up their children to become responsible citizens. Consequently, these women and their children were depicted as a threat to the moral cohesion of Dutch society.[28] The assumed increase in the number of single mothers coming to the Netherlands from the Dutch Antilles was, for example, quoted as a reason for trying to limit the migration from those islands.[29]

Since women from the Dutch Antilles possessed Dutch nationality, proposals to exclude them could not be explained in terms of nationalist ideology as expressed through immigration law but must also have stemmed from exclusion related to culture and/or phenotype. As Ann Stoler has made clear, processes of racialization in the European context have always been complex and unstable, linking physical traits to assumed cultural attributes and vice versa.[30] Where ethnicized and/or racialized categories are linked to countries of origin, as with the term "non-western *allochtoon*," the line between nationality and ethnicity/race becomes blurred as well.

When family norms are used to distinguish dominant from subdominant groups, distinctions may also be made regarding the measure of responsibility and pedagogical insight that is to be attributed to the different categories of parents. When care is introduced as a substantive criterion for according certain parental rights, the danger that the dominant group of parents will be privileged above the subdominant ones in terms of parental rights becomes very real.

Negotiating the Limits to State Interference in Family Life:
Domestic and European Human Rights Law

Should courts and state authorities never intervene in parent-child relations for reasons related to the substantive quality of care that is, or is not,
being provided? My answer would be no. There are many examples where
interference in family life can be justified on grounds of public interest
such as the enforcement of compulsive education, prevention of conta-
gious diseases, management of public spending, and control over immigration. The individual needs of family members, and the right to respect
for family life, will always, to some degree, have to be measured against
public interests. And while family members should be granted a considerable margin of freedom in meeting their mutual commitments and enjoying the intimacy of family life, states do have a responsibility to ensure
that such freedom is not abused for purposes of fraud, or for the perver-
sion of family relations. The right to respect for family life furthermore
finds its limits in state obligations to protect individuals against incest,
domestic violence, neglect, and other forms of abuse.

My approach is grounded in European human rights law, as the right
to respect for family life, as guaranteed by the European Convention, is
a qualified right and does not offer absolute protection. Article 8 of the
ECHR reads as follows:

> (1) Everyone has the right to respect for his private and
>   family life, his home and his correspondence.
> (2) There shall be no interference by a public authority
>   with the exercise of this right except such as is
>   in accordance with the law and is necessary in
>   a democratic society in the interests of national
>   security, public safety or the economic well-being of
>   the country, for the prevention of disorder or crime,
>   for the protection of health or morals, or for the
>   protection of the rights and freedoms of others.

Interference can be justified, therefore, on the grounds and under the conditions named in the second paragraph. In the process of negotiating the
range of freedom that should be allowed to parents in raising and looking
after their children, the quality of the care provided will inevitably figure

as one of the factors to be taken into account. But in doing so, the states concerned will also have to take into consideration the margins of their own freedom to interfere. In the European context, the margins of state freedom are determined, in part at least, by the European Convention, and enforced by the ECtHR. Determining the limits to the member states' sovereign freedom is, however, a delicate exercise.

The ECtHR has always been conscious of its need to take into account the differences in culture and tradition among its forty-six member states. When the ECtHR deems itself unable to gauge the practical consequences of certain choices that must be made concerning social or economic relations within one or more of the member states, it tends to be quite reticent to impose its mandate. Otherwise, the reasoning goes, it would interfere too much in the sovereign right of those states to make essential choices regarding social and economic issues via democratic processes of decision making.[31]

On the other hand, the European Convention also assumes a minimum standard of human rights and fundamental freedoms to which the member states have committed themselves via Article 53. This minimum standard does limit the range of choices that can be made via the national democratic decision-making process. By deploying its doctrine of the "margin of appreciation" with regard to the level of discretion to be allowed the member states in making their decisions, the ECtHR endeavors to allow the member states enough scope to exercise their sovereign rights, while holding them to the minimum standards guaranteed by the European Convention.[32]

Given the sensitive balance that the European Court must seek to maintain, it is not surprising that it generally grants member states a wide margin of appreciation in immigration law cases. Immigration law, after all, lies close to the heart of national sovereignty, something the ECtHR has been careful to acknowledge since it first passed judgment in an immigration law case.[33] Certainly, among the states parties to the European Convention, immigration continues to be a politically sensitive issue to this day, with the present consensus leaning towards more, rather than less, restrictive measures.[34] Although immigration and integration issues should be distinguished from each other, one can safely say that post–9/11 tensions within current European societies have contributed to the pressure to limit immigration. In this political context, a ruling by the ECtHR that the universal right to respect for family life should prevail over national immigration policies is not likely to fall on willing ears.

On the other hand, the ECtHR has been anything but timid in championing the right to respect for family life in the field of family law. In the case of *Kroon v. the Netherlands*,[35] for example, the ECtHR set aside the Dutch law of succession so that the child of an adulterous relationship could be recognized by the father. Remarkably, the ECtHR didn't even bother to explain why, in this case, it was justified in bypassing the Dutch legislature. Although they may have agreed on the substantive issues in this case, some authors—in my view rightly—have criticized the ECtHR for having shown so little concern for processes of democratic legitimization.[36]

The difference in degrees of freedom that the ECtHR has allowed member states in family law and in immigration law has not gone unnoticed among legal academics and practitioners.[37] Nor did it escape the attention of the judges presiding over the first case in which the ECtHR passed judgment on a complaint against the effective family bond criterion in Dutch immigration law, the case of *Ahmut v. the Netherlands*.[38] In the following section, I shall review this case and those that followed, to trace how the tension between ECtHR's family and immigration law jurisprudence has been resolved.

Challenging Dutch Family Reunification Policies before the ECtHR

The *Ahmut* case concerned the admission of a nine-year-old boy, Soufiane Ahmut, to the Netherlands in order to join his father there. Soufiane's father had left his children behind when, after having divorced his first wife, he left Morocco in 1986. He remarried in the Netherlands and acquired legal residence status as a marriage migrant. In 1987, Soufiane's mother died in a car accident and those children who were still living at home were taken up by their paternal grandmother. Three years later Mr. Ahmut, who by then had acquired Dutch citizenship, requested to have his youngest son, Soufiane, admitted for family reunification, since Soufiane's grandmother had grown too old to look after him any more.

The Dutch immigration authorities refused admission on the grounds that the effective family bond had been severed. The father lost his case before the Dutch courts and proceeded on to Strasbourg, where his case was declared admissible. In the end, the ECtHR took a reticent stance. Considering that the father had made the deliberate choice to leave his children behind, that he could, in theory, return to Morocco to join his son there, and that Soufiane could be looked after in Morocco (his father had, for the time being, placed him in a boarding school), the ECtHR ruled that "in the circumstances the Netherlands Government cannot be said to have failed to strike a fair balance between the applicants' interests on the one hand and its own interest in controlling immigration on the other."[39]

Four of the nine judges presiding over the *Ahmut* case explicitly rejected this reasoning in three separate dissenting opinions, the most extensive of which was written by the Dutch judge, Martens. Martens argued that once a state had allowed an immigrant to settle within its territory, that state was, in principle, bound to respect the choices made by that immigrant concerning family life. Accordingly, one should, as a rule, admit members of the family he or she had left behind and especially, in Martens' view, when the reunification with young children was at stake.

Following the *Ahmut* case, several more complaints concerning the Dutch effective bond criterion were submitted in Strasbourg. Most of these cases were judged inadmissible on the basis of the same arguments that had been put forward in the *Ahmut* decision. On November 7, 2000, however, a case was judged admissible: the case of *Sen v. the Netherlands*.[40]

The Sen Case: An Ambiguous Judgment

The *Sen* case centered around the admission of a nine-year-old Turkish girl, Sinem Sen. Sinem's father had joined his own father in the Netherlands in 1977. In 1982, he went back briefly to Turkey and got married there. Following the wedding, he returned to the Netherlands, leaving his bride in Turkey. She followed him in 1986, but left their three-year-old daughter, Sinem, with family in Turkey. Six years later, Sinem's parents decided to have her join them in the Netherlands. In October 1992, they applied for her admission.

Their application was refused on the grounds that the effective family bond had been broken. By the time the Administrative Jurisdiction Division of the Council of State had turned down Sinem's appeal, her parents had two more children, one born in November 1990 and the second in December 1994, both of whom were born in the Netherlands and continued to live there.

On December 21, 2001, the ECtHR unanimously found that Sinem Sen's case violated Article 8 of the European Convention. Yet despite this unanimity, or perhaps in order to achieve it, the ECtHR took a rather unclear stance regarding its previous case law as expressed in the *Ahmut* case.[41] In paragraph 36, the ECtHR explicitly referred to its earlier judgments and repeated its previously applied criteria. In paragraph 40, the court explained that the facts of the *Sen* case diverged from those in *Ahmut* on one essential point, namely, the presence of two children born and bred in the Netherlands. In the eyes of the ECtHR, this circumstance formed a major obstacle to reunification in Turkey and justified declaring the complaint valid.

Yet in the remaining paragraphs of its judgment, the ECtHR incorporated virtually all of Martens' objections to the judgment in *Ahmut*. The ECtHR emphatically stated that the initial decision made by Sinem's parents to leave her behind ought not be taken to be final. Pointing explicitly to earlier jurisprudence in the field of family law, the ECtHR acknowledged that family life was dynamic and that the state was obliged to allow for and facilitate the normal development of family ties.[42]

With this explicit reference to jurisprudence developed within family law, the ECtHR brought into relief the tensions between its jurisprudence in family and in immigration law. In the eyes of the court, the right to respect for family life applied to all parents and their children in the same way, regardless of nationality. In other words, the exclusionary implications of national immigration rules were overruled by the universalizing principles of human rights. Read this way, the *Sen* case seems to confirm the optimistic expectations of those who expect that universal human rights will, in good time, come to mitigate the exclusionary effects of restrictive national immigration policies.

However, another, more conservative, reading of the *Sen* case is also possible. In reaction to questions posed by Dutch members of Parliament concerning the implications of the *Sen* case for Dutch family reunification policy, the Dutch government replied that this case involved a very particular set of circumstances and hence was of no general significance for Dutch policy.[43] In court cases, too, the Dutch minister for immigration and integration continued to maintain his position that the *Sen* case was specific in two respects. First, it involved a family with two children brought up in the Netherlands. Second, this case did not involve a single or divorced parent who had come to the Netherlands, remarried, and subsequently sought to bring a child over, but rather a married couple that had come to the Netherlands to settle there as a family.[44]

Following the *Sen* case, several more complaints were brought before the ECtHR, but none was declared admissible. Although the Dutch regional courts were consistent in applying *Sen*, the import of that judgment remained subject to debate.[45] Some claimed that *Sen* illustrated the ECtHR's criticism of the Dutch effective family bond criterion. Others argued that *Sen* was the exception that proved the rule, expressed in the earlier jurisprudence, that this point of policy fit comfortably within the Dutch government's margin of appreciation. A second complaint against the effective family bond criterion was declared admissible, however, on October 19, 2004. Judgment was subsequently granted in favor of plaintiff Tuquabo-Tekle on December 1, 2005.[46]

This case concerned a daughter who had been left behind for six years before her mother initiated admission procedures, and again the family involved included two children born and bred in the Netherlands. There were significant differences with *Sen*, however. In this case, the mother, a widow, had traveled to Europe as a single parent and subsequently remarried. The ECtHR, however, made no distinction on this point, and explicitly referred back to the position taken in *Sen*, namely, that "parents who leave children behind while they settle abroad cannot be assumed to have irrevocably decided that those children are to remain in the country of origin permanently and to have abandoned any idea of a future family reunion."[47]

The Intersection between EU and European Human Rights Law

On September 25, 2006, the former Dutch minister for immigration and integration, Rita Verdonk, sent a letter to Parliament regarding the effective family bond criterion in Dutch immigration law.[48] She announced that no distinction would be made any more between the term "effective family bond" as applied in immigration law and the term "family life" as applied in family law on the basis of Article 8 of the European Convention. What this in fact meant was that, for purposes of family reunification, all children legally related to a parent and all children sharing a biological bond with a parent would forthwith be assumed to share an effective family bond with that parent.[49] Only in the event that the child was living on its own and supporting itself or in the event that it had established a family of its own would the authorities still be allowed to conclude that the effective family bond had been broken.

In her letter, the minister explicitly referred to the judgment of the ECtHR in the *Tuquabo-Tekle* case. But this judgment alone cannot explain the policy change. For one thing, more than ten months separated the court's judgment and the minister's letter. In the intervening period, the effective family bond criterion had been the subject of a number of court cases in the Netherlands. The question being put before the Dutch administrative courts was not only whether the effective family bond criterion had been applied in accordance with Article 8 of the European Convention but also whether or not a European Directive on Family Reunification, which had become effective as of October 3, 2005, allowed for the application of such a criterion.[50]

During the negotiations that had preceded the adoption of this European directive, the Dutch government had tried to find support for its position that the effective family bond criterion should be included in it. This proposal was rejected. In fact, it appeared that the Netherlands was the only one among the member states of the European Union to apply such a criterion in its family reunification policies. Nevertheless, the Dutch minister for immigration and integration saw no reason to modify or eliminate the effective family bond criterion when implementing the European Directive on Family Reunification in Dutch immigration law. Her reasoning was that Article 16 of the European Directive on Family Reunification allowed the member states to refuse family reunification in the event that the sponsor and his/her family member(s) did not or no longer lived "in a real marital or family relationship." In her eyes, the effective family bond criterion, as applied in Dutch immigration law, could serve to determine the existence of a real marital or family relationship. This position was challenged before the Dutch regional courts, and, subsequently, before the Administrative Jurisdiction Division of the Council of State.

. The complaints that came before the Administrative Jurisdiction Division were declared ungrounded on formal grounds,[51] leaving the question as to their substantive merits unresolved. It would be only a question of time, however, before the Administrative Jurisdiction Division would have to decide on the substantive issue. Since this would require interpreting EU law, ultimately the Administrative Jurisdiction Division would have to submit prejudicial questions to the European Court of Justice (ECJ) in Luxemburg.

Since the European Directive on Family Reunification had only just been implemented, there was little jurisprudence on which to rely.[52]

Nevertheless, there was good reason to suspect that the ECJ would grant the Dutch state little leeway in deciding on this issue. Although the European Union is not (yet) party to the European Convention, the articles of the convention are accepted as guiding principles of EU law. In particular, Article 8 of the Convention is referred to explicitly in the preamble to the European Directive on Family Reunification. Existing jurisprudence of the ECJ in Luxembourg strongly suggests that the ECJ takes a more activist stance in applying Article 8 than the ECtHR in Strasbourg is inclined to do. I am particularly referring to the position that the ECJ has taken in the past regarding the significance of Article 8 of the European Convention for the freedom of movement of EU citizens with family members originating from outside of the EU.[53]

Many factors can explain the difference in approach between the two courts, and it would go well beyond the scope of this chapter to explore them all. But one at least should be mentioned, namely, the fact that the European Union as a whole has an interest in promoting the free movement of persons within the EU—including those with family members originating from outside of it. Moreover, as the member states strive to achieve integration on a political and normative plane, as well as on the level of economics, the concepts of EU citizenship—with the accompanying right to settle in each of the member states—and of universalistic human rights—promoted as a shared normative heritage—have gained significance. In determining the degree of freedom to be left to the member states, the ECJ has to take such shared concerns into account. If for no other reason, the role that it plays in adjudicating conflicts regarding the right to respect for family life and the freedom to move among and reside within the nations of the European Union will differ from that played by the ECtHR.

Conclusion: Immigrant Mothers, Agency, and European Law

What this story about the effective family bond criterion in Dutch immigration law teaches us is that law, and hence also universalistic principles as expressed through European human rights law, is not monolithic, but fragmented and fraught with contradictions and logical flaws. In serving conflicting interests, it can also facilitate surprising coalitions. It is, after all, nothing more and nothing less than the result of dynamic processes of human interaction. The question that I have addressed in this chapter is to what extent immigrant women have been able to take an active part in these processes in order to mobilize the law so as to increase the scope of their agency in realizing one of the most vital aspects of their identity as mature adults: that of parents responsible for the welfare and future of their children.

As it happens, this story has a happy ending—at least for the Joyces and Emilys involved. But that happy end was not self-evident. There is nothing inevitable or irreversible about the workings of European human rights law. The effectiveness of this, or any other expression of human rights law remains dependent on the concrete power relations in which it is mobilized. In fact, in the context of the gendered conflicts surrounding parent-child relations in the Netherlands and of the specific identity politics being played out there and in the rest of the European Union, single and divorced migrant women of "non-Western" origin have many cards stacked against them. To understand the role that the European Convention has played in helping them resist restrictive Dutch immigration policies, it is important to realize that their success built on gains already made by more mainstream actors: single and divorced Dutch fathers claiming access, parental authority, and the right to acknowledge their children, on the one hand, and, on the other, EU citizens laying claim to their right to freedom of movement and settlement within the European Union and to a "typically European" commitment to human rights protection.

NOTES

1. An earlier version of this chapter was published under the title "Transnational Mothering, National Immigration Policy, and the European Court of Human Rights," in *Migration, Diasporas, and Legal Systems in Europe,* eds. Prakash Shah and Werner Menski (London: Routledge-Cavendish, 2006), 185–203.

2. This story is based on a real case. The names of those involved and other details have been changed in the interest of privacy.

3. Sarah van Walsum, "De feitelijke gezinsband onder de loep genomen (deel II)," *Migrantenrecht* 1 (2000): 10–18.

4. The European Convention was drafted by the Council of Europe following the Second World War, with the intention of implementing the UN Charter of Human Rights. The convention created a catalogue of civil and political rights and freedoms and established the ECtHR (among other instititions) to enforce these rights, in 1959. The ECtHR has an official database, HUDOC (http://www.echr.coe.int/ECHR/), which includes all judgments dating from 1959 and

all admissibility decisions dating from 1986. Unless otherwise noted, the cases quoted in this chapter can be found in that database. The ECtHR should not be confused with the European Court of Justice (ECJ), which is the highest court of the European Union (EU). Unlike the ECtHR, the ECJ deals primarily with cases related to the operation of the common European Union market, and not with human rights claims.

5. Article 8 of the ECHR guarantees the following:

(1) Everyone has the right to respect for his private and family life, his home and his correspondence. (2) There shall be no interference by a public authority with the exercise of this right except such as is in accordance with the law and is necessary in a democratic society in the interests of national security, public safety or the economic well-being of the country, for the prevention of disorder or crime, for the protection of health or morals, or for the protection of the rights and freedoms of others. (European Convention for the Protection of Human Rights and Fundamental Freedoms art. 8, Nov. 4, 1950, 213 U.N.T.S. 222 [hereinafter European Convention on Human Rights])

6. Taspinar v. the Netherlands, App. No. 11026/84, 8 Eur. H.R. Rep. 47 (1984). According to the rules of procedure that apply before the ECtHR, complaints must first be examined for admissibility, before being referred to one of the court's chambers for a procedure on merits. Cases can be declared inadmissible on formal grounds (for example, because national remedies have not been exhausted) or on substantive grounds, one of the most important being that the complaint is considered to be manifestly unfounded.

7. Sen v. the Netherlands, App. No. 31465/96, 36 ECtHR 7, 40 (2003).

8. Yasemin Soysal, for example, argues that a reconfiguration of citizenship has taken place. Whereas it was formerly viewed as a particularized concept, based on nationhood, it is now regarded as a universalistic one based on personhood. As a result, rights that used to belong solely to nationals are now, according to her, being extended to foreign populations. More and more, in her view, claims of individuals are being legitimated by ideologies grounded in a transnational community. She relies on the jurisprudence of the European Court of Human Rights to substantiate this assertion. Yasemin Nuhoglu Soysal, *Limits of Citizenship: Migrants and Postnational Membership in Europe* (Chicago: University of Chicago Press, 1994).

9. Linda Bosniak, for example, has pointed out that national immigration law regimes have recently become more rather than less restrictive, curtailing the human rights of immigrants rather than extending them. Although she does not deny the significance of universalist human rights for debating the legitimacy of such measures in the national context, she is less convinced than Soysal of the inevitable triumph of the universalistic principles of international law over nationalism as a political factor. Linda Bosniak, "Universal

Citizenship and the Problem of Alienage," *Northwestern University Law Review* 94 (2000): 963–84.

10. Later (in 2002), the rules were modified in the sense that, as long as parent and child had not been separated for longer than five years, the effective family bond between them was assumed to be still intact. Once they had been separated for more than five years, family reunification was no longer possible except in two instances, namely, the child had no one to look after it in the country of origin; or the parent had been unable to trace the child due to a situation of (civil) war in the country of origin. "Tussentijds Bericht Vreemdelingencirculaire" (TBV 2002/4) St. Crt. 58:15 (2002).

11. Sarah van Walsum, "De feitelijke gezinsband onder de loep genomen (deel I): Gezinshereniging van twee kanten belicht," *Migrantenrecht* 6 (1999): 147–52.

12. FORUM, Clara Wichmann Instituut, and Defence for Children International, *Gezinsleven met kinderen in het vreemdelingenbeleid. Gezichtspunten en aanbevelingen* (Utrecht: FORUM, 2001).

13. Marckx v. Belgium, App. No. 6833/74, 31 ECtHR 33 (1979). This case, which concerned the rights of children born out of wedlock, was a watershed judgment regarding the significance of Article 8 of the European Convention in the field of family law. Ironically, this case actually addressed the issue of family life between a single mother and her child, and not that of single fathers.

14. For a review of changes that took place in Dutch family law following the ECtHR's judgment in the *Marckx* case, see Caroline Forder, "Legal Establishment of the Parent-Child Relationship: Constitutional Principles" (dissertation law, University of Limburg, 1995).

15. Jenny E. Goldschmidt and Rikki Holtmaat, *Vrouw en recht: trendrapport* (The Hague: Directie Coördinatie Emancipatiebeleid/Stimuleringsgroep Emancipatie Onderzoek, 1993), 122–25; Carla van Wamelen, "De eerbiediging van een zorgrelatie. De rol van zorg bij echtscheiding," *Nemesis* 3 (1996): 76–82.

16. Vreemdelingencirculaire (Dutch Immigration Circular) 1975 (unpublished), chapter G.44: 13–14.

17. Afdeling bestuursrechtspraak van de Raad van State [ABRvS] [Administrative Law Court], 3 februari 1989, Nederlands Juristen Blad 1989, 4, 432–433 (Neth.); Rb. Den Haag Kort Geding 1990: 360 (Sept. 11, 1990).

18. See for example R. v. the Netherlands, App. No. 13654/88 (Dec. 8, 1988).

19. Rb. Den Haag, seated in Haarlem, AWB 99/296 (unpublished) (June 2, 1999).

20. Rb. Den Haag, seated in Zwolle, AWB 96/8085 (unpublished) (Jan. 15, 1997).

21. Cf. Alison Diduck, "In Search of the Feminist Good Mother," *Social & Legal Studies* 7 (1998): 129–36.

22. Sarah van Walsum, *De schaduw van de grens. Het Nederlandse vreemdelingenrecht en de sociale zekerheid van Javaanse Surinamers* (Deventer: Kluwer/ Gouda Quint, 2000). In the course of preparing this thesis, I interviewed roughly

forty people who had migrated from the former Dutch colony of Surinam to the Netherlands. The purpose of my research was to trace the way care and material support, provided via transnational family obligations, were being affected by Dutch immigration policies. Among other things, I was interested in the way child care was being affected.

23. Dorien Pessers, "Liefde, solidariteit en recht" (dissertation, law, University of Amsterdam, 1999).

24. Forder, "Legal Establishment," supra note 14, 406.

25. This term, which includes both foreign immigrants and Dutch nationals of (second-generation) foreign origin, can probably best be translated as "of foreign origin." The category of non-Western *allochtonen* includes all persons with at least one parent born in Africa or Asia (with the notable exceptions of Japan and Indonesia), Latin America, or Turkey. It is used in contrast with the term "autochtoon," which generally denotes the "native" (white) population of the Netherlands.

26. Holtrust, "Geschiedenis van de afstandsmoeder. Dikke bult, eigen schuld," in *Publiek geheim. Deprivatisering van het vrouwenleven*, ed. Carla van Splunteren (Amsterdam: Clara Wichmann Instituut, 1995), 56–57.

27. "Zonder zappende man gaat 't ook; Moderne alleenstaande moeders zijn niet zielig. Zij zijn trots op hun gezin, en op hun zelfstandigheid," Aleid Truijens, *Volkskrant* (a Dutch daily), March 5, 2003.

28. See, e.g., "Amsterdam heeft het" on the editorial page of a leading Dutch daily, the *NRC*, on September 10, 1999.

29. *Nota migratie Antilliaanse jongeren*, Tweede Kamer 1998–1999, 26 283, Nr. 1, p. 5.

30. Ann Laura Stoler, *Racism and the Education of Desire* (Durham, NC: Duke University Press, 1995).

31. L. C. M. Meijers, "Rechtsvormende taak van de rechter bij implementatie van Straatsburgse rechtspraak," *NJCM-Bulletin* 1 (1996): 123.

32. In effect, the jurisprudence of the ECtHR amounts to a practical exercise in negotiating the philosophical tensions explored by Seyla Benhabib in her book *The Rights of Others: Aliens, Residents, and Citizens* (Cambridge: Cambridge University Press, 2004).

33. Abdulaziz, Balkendali, and Cabales v. United Kingdom, App. Nos. 9214/80; 9473/81; 9474/81, 7 Eur. H.R. Rep. 471, para. 67 (1985).

34. An initially liberal proposal regarding family reunification that was put forward by the European Commission has, for example, been heavily amended in favor of more restrictive policies by the national ministers making up the European Council.

35. Kroon v. the Netherlands, App. No. 18535/91, 35 ECtHR (1994).

36. T. Loenen, "Het Europees Hof voor de rechten van de mens als toetser of steller van de wet? Enkele beschouwingen naar aanleiding van de zaak *Kroon*," *NJCM-Bulletin* 1 (1996): 75–82.

37. J. van der Velde, "Positieve verplichtingen," *EVRM R&C*, 33d volume (March 2002): 1–21.

38. Ahmut v. the Netherlands, App. No. 21702/93, 61 ECtHR (1996).

39. Ibid., para. 73.

40. Sen v. the Netherlands, App. No. 31465/96, ECtHR 888 (2001). The admissibility decision was rendered on November 7, 2000, and the judgment given on December 21, 2001.

41. See also, Gül v. Switzerland, App. No. 23219/94, ECtHR 5 (1996).

42. Cf. Marckx v. Belgium, ECtHR, Appl. No. 6833/74 (June 13, 1979), para. 31.

43. Letter of July 8, 2002, from the Dutch Minister of Foreign Affairs to the Chairman of the Permanent Committee on Foreign Affairs of the Dutch Parliament (Second Chamber) concerning the *Sen* case (DJZ/IR-211/02). Available at http://www.minbuza.nl/nl/actueel/ brievenparlement,2002/07/uitspraken_europese_hof_voor_de_rechten_van_de_mens.html (last accessed on May 22, 2007).

44. See the arguments presented by the Dutch State in Rb. Den Haag, seated in Zwolle, AWB 01/67498 (May 22, 2002).

45. I.M. v. the Netherlands, App. No. 41226/98, ECtHR (2003); Ebrahim & Ebrahim v. the Netherlands, App. No. 59186/00, ECtHR (2003); Chandra v. the Netherlands, App. No. 53102/99, ECtHR 13 (2003).

46. Tuquabo-Tekle v. the Netherlands, App. No. 60665/00, ECtHR 1 (2005).

47. Ibid., para. 45. A problematic point of difference in the eyes of the ECtHR was that, in this case, the daughter was already fifteen years old when her mother applied for admission, whereas in *Sen,* the child concerned had been only nine. The ECtHR ruled for the plaintiff. In the event that she would have to remain in Eritrea, Mrs. Tuquabo-Tekle's daughter ran a real risk of being forced to leave school and enter into marriage. Moreover, the fact that Mrs. Tuquabo-Tekle had fled to Europe after the death of her husband and during civil war may have led the ECtHR to take a more critical stance in reviewing the Dutch state's decision in this case than it might have done had there been no asylum-related claims. See also Mayeka & Mitunga v. Belgium, App. No. 13178/03, ECtHR (2006), para. 75.

48. Tweede Kamer, 2006–2007, 19 637, nr. 1089. The policy change announced in this letter was made effective retroactively, valid as of September 8, 2006.

49. Arguably, the term "family life" has been given a broader definition by the minister than by the ECtHR. While the latter will almost always assume there is family life between parent and child when the child has been born out of a marital relationship, in other situations some evidence of a substantive bond will have to be present to justify the claim that the relationship entails family life. See Caroline Forder, "Family Rights and Immigration Law: A European Perspective," *Irish Journal of Family Law* 3 (2003): 2–18.

50. Council Directive 2003/86/EC, 2003 O.J. (L 251) 12–18.

51. The complaints concerned decisions taken before the directive had become effective and/or involved parents with dual citizenship, who fell outside of the scope of the directive. See, e.g., Comment, C. A. Groenendijk, Afdeling Bestuurrecht van de Raad van State [ABRvS] [Administrative Law Court of the Netherlands], 29 maart 2006, 200510214/1, *Jurisprudentie Vreemdelingenrecht* (JV) 2006/172 (Neth.).

52. The only judgment until now is Case C-540-03, European Parliament v. European Council, E.C.R. 2006.

53. Case C-60/00, Carpenter v. Sec'y of State for the Home Dep't, 2002 (E.C.R. I-6279 (UK); Case C-109/01, Akrich v. Sec'y of State for the Home Dep't, 2003 ECR I-9607 (UK).

IV

##

Engendered Citizenship in Practice

Global Feminism, Citizenship, and the State: Negotiating Women's Rights in the Middle East and North Africa

Valentine M. Moghadam

Globalization is a complex economic, political, cultural, and social pro-cess in which the mobility of capital, organizations, ideas, discourses, and peoples has taken on an increasingly global or transnational form. Much has been written about the economic, political, and cultural dimensions of globalization, and many debates revolve around the nature and capac-ity of the state in an era of globalization. The growing literature on the globalization of women's rights movements includes attention to "global feminism" and its participation in, and contribution to, a transnational public sphere. Not all feminist theorists are comfortable with the term "global feminism"; some prefer "transnational feminist practices" while others have insisted that all feminist practice is localized.[1] But are lo-cal communities or national borders impenetrable to globalized norms? What of the migration and mobility of feminist ideas and of their practi-tioners? How do local struggles intersect with global discourses on wom-en's rights? What role is played by feminists in the diaspora, and what is the impact of the state?

The late twentieth century saw the emergence of women's rights move-ments across the globe, including the Middle East and other parts of the Muslim world. This took place in the context of a number of socio-demographic, political, and cultural developments: the rise of a critical mass of educated, employed, politically experienced, and mobile women; their participation in the UN Decade for Women and the UN confer-ences of the 1990s, especially the International Conference on Population and Development (the ICPD, which took place in Cairo in 1994) and the Fourth World Conference on Women (the Beijing Conference, which took place in 1995), where they networked with other women activists; the rise of Islamic fundamentalism and conservative revisions to family laws by neopatriarchal states, which alarmed women in the Muslim-majority countries of the Middle East, North Africa, South and Southeast Asia, and West Africa; and increasing access to the internet.

These developments led to several types of women's mobilization, but here I highlight two: the formation of women's rights or feminist organizations within countries, and the creation of transnational feminist networks such as Women Living under Muslim Laws (WLUML) and the Women's Learning Partnership (WLP).[2] Like the transnational networks, the nationally based women's organizations seek to end women's second-class citizenship and help bring about women's equality, autonomy, and empowerment—the objectives of "global feminism."[3] Among their key strategies is legal reform.

Classic theories of citizenship have focused on national-level dynamics in the explication of rights (e.g., the state, social development, class struggles, political resources). But in an era of globalization, supranational factors are increasingly influential; international pressure from other states or from transnational advocacy networks can affect domestic movements and campaigns.[4] Studies show, too, the emergence of a "global civil society" or "transnational public sphere" consisting of networked social movement organizations and international NGOs that engage with intergovernmental and multilateral organizations in pursuit of the expansion of human rights, environmental protection, women's rights, and other issues.[5] Many theorists of globalization have posited the withering away of the national state with the emergence of powerful institutions of global governance and indeed of a "transnational state apparatus."[6]

But the fact is that women's organizations around the world remain focused on their societies and states. Some lobby for the return of the welfare and developmental state and social rights that prevailed before the onset of neoliberal economics; others for the protection or expansion of reproductive rights; and yet others for equality and empowerment in the family. The state still matters to women, especially in the areas of reproductive rights and family law. As Mary Ann Glendon, Ayelet Shachar, and others have shown, family laws reflect and reinforce the state of gender relations and especially the status of women, but they are also subject to change.[7] In Muslim-majority countries, family law is the battleground upon which women's organizations, Islamists, and neopatriarchal states vie for influence. At stake are social change and women's empowerment versus the status quo and male privilege.

States guided by Islamic law have been reluctant to endorse the UN Convention on the Elimination of All Form of Discrimination Against Women (CEDAW) without qualification. The reservations entered typically pertained to articles in the convention that call for women's equal rights in family matters and as such contravene Sharia-based family laws.[8] But women activists have increasingly set their sights on global civil society, the transnational public sphere, and institutions of global governance to accomplish their goals at home. They look to the UN's women's rights agenda for legitimacy, and they appeal to transnational feminist networks for solidarity and support with campaigns. Both nationally based women's organizations and transnational feminist networks make the reform of Muslim family law and the implementation of CEDAW—without reservations—among their principal objectives.

In this paper, two cases from Muslim-majority countries in the Middle East and North Africa region will elucidate the salience and interplay of the local and the global in the pursuit of women's citizenship rights, and the ways in which the migration and mobility of concepts of women's rights and of feminists themselves reflect a global feminism accessible to activists throughout the world. The Islamic Republic of Iran exemplifies the case of an active movement for women's citizenship in the face of a strong state and—until recently—weak global links. The case of the Kingdom of Morocco shows how coalition building and possibilities for a state-feminist alliance can result in law reform favorable to women. In both cases, local struggles for women's rights have been influenced by global institutions and norms and by the nature of the state.[9]

The Problem of Women's Second-Class Citizenship under Muslim Family Law

Family laws—also known as personal status codes—govern marriage, divorce, maintenance, paternity, custody of children, and inheritance. Based on interpretations of the Sharia, which differentiate between men and women in the allocation of rights and responsibilities, the laws in the Middle East and North Africa typically place women in the position of minor and dependent.[10] Codified restrictions on women's mobility exist and privileges, notably "guardianship" over women, are granted to male kin. Women's interactions with the state and society are thus often deter- mined and mediated through their husbands, fathers, brothers, or other male family members. Guardianship also provides justification for wom- en's second-class citizenship in the public domain, as well as for male au- thority over women in the private sphere of the family.

All societies are stratified by gender—and by class and ethnicity or race—but Muslim societies governed by Islamic legal frameworks exhibit extreme forms of gender stratification and discrimination. In the Middle East and North Africa in particular, this is manifested in differential legal rights of women and men, and in women's underrepresentation in politi- cal structures and their limited access to paid employment. The sources of women's second-class citizenship lie in patriarchal gender relations, politi- cal economy, legal frameworks, and the nature of the state.

Patriarchal gender relations are maintained by precapitalist forms of economic and social arrangements—such as petty commodity production, kinship-ordered agrarian systems, the predominance of the social institu- tions of the family and religion—and by the power of "the father." Here, property, residence, and descent proceed through the male line; women's principal role is marriage and child bearing; the senior man has authority over everyone else in the family, including younger men; and women are subject to distinct forms of control and subordination.

Such patriarchal social and gender arrangements, which were once common in Europe, persist in Asia and North Africa and are evidenced by early marriage, high fertility, and the importance of female virginity and virtue to the family's honor. "Classic patriarchy," as described by Deniz Kandiyoti, is particularly evident in Afghanistan, where precapitalist so- cial forms prevail, but patriarchal gender relations are the norm in other Muslim countries and remain salient in the rural areas of the Middle East and North Africa.[11]

Certain forms of political economy limit women's access to economic resources and employment. The oil economy and high wages of the Middle East and North Africa from the 1960s to the 1980s tended to de- press female employment from both the demand and supply sides; this reinforced women's economic dependence and strengthened what I have called the patriarchal gender contract.[12] In the 1990s, oil prices declined and women entered the labor force in greater number in order to aug- ment the household budget. Although female labor force participation in- creased, so did female unemployment. In addition to economic obstacles to full employment, cultural attitudes prevent female labor incorpora-tion. The male breadwinner/female homemaker ideal remains dominant and finds expression in family laws, marriage contracts, and popular dis-courses, limiting women's choices, opportunities, and participation, in-cluding access to paid employment.

To conservative believers, Muslim family laws are based on correct interpretations of divine Sharia law. From a more critical social science stance, they are the result of historical processes; they mirror patriarchal attitudes and codify women's subordination. The persistence of Muslim family law is in some cases the legacy of state-tribe compromises in the years of postcolonial state building. Where newly created states relied on tribes and clans for legitimacy and support, they left the patrilineal kin-ship systems—with their controls over women's behavior, mobility, and sexuality—intact. Mounira Charrad has described these processes for the Maghrib, showing the different ways in which state-building elites in Al-geria, Morocco, and Tunisia dealt with kin-ordered tribes and how these had divergent outcomes for women's rights in the family. Her analysis can be extended to Jordan, Saudi Arabia, and Yemen, where state-tribe com-promises similarly took place.[13]

Elsewhere in the Middle East, the legacy of the Ottoman *millet* system can be seen; Lebanon, Syria, and Palestine have no uniform civil code to govern matters of marriage and divorce because these matters are legally differentiated by religious community. Iran has a very small population of non-Muslims, but among them, too, religious institutions have always retained control over family matters. For the majority Muslim population in Iran, liberalization of family law took place in the late 1960s and early 1970s, but a very conservative interpretation of women's status in the fam-ily was adopted by the Islamic state after the 1979 revolution.[14]

One factor that complicates and confuses women's citizenship is the discrepancy, in some countries, between constitutions that award equal rights to men and women and the family laws that undermine this equal-ity.[15] Contrary to constitutional guarantees of equality of citizens, and to labor laws that construct women as workers, the family laws delineate dif-ferent rights and obligations for men and for women and render women minors and dependents of fathers, husbands, or other male guardians. In so doing, the family laws reinforce the distinction between the pub-lic sphere of markets and governance—which are cast as the province of men—and the private sphere of the family, with which women are iden-tified. Moreover, family matters have been considered to be outside the purview of human rights because they are based on Sharia law, which is considered by believers to be off-limits to reform or revision.

There are significant variations in women's legal status and social positions across the Muslim world; in the Middle East/North Africa, Tunisia stands out for its progressive family law, women-friendly social policies, and access by women to employment and to political office. In general, however, similar patterns of women's second-class citizenship may be identified. Religious law is elevated to civil status, and religious affiliation is a requirement of citizenship. Children acquire citizenship, nationality, and religious status through their fathers, not their mothers. In marriage, the husband has rights over his wife; he may take another wife (up to four) and he may divorce his wife, whereas a woman must remain monogamous and cannot easily initiate divorce. A Muslim man may take a non-Muslim wife, but Muslim women may not marry non-Muslim men. Marriage gives the husband the right of access to his wife's body, and marital rape is not recognized.[16] In many countries, the criminal code provides for acquittal or a reduction of sentence for men who commit "honor crimes," and premarital sex and adultery are considered serious offenses, especially for women. In the Islamic Republic of Iran, for example, the penal code adopted during the Islamization process of the early 1980s calls for the stoning of an adulterous woman.

Muslim family law has implications for women's economic citizenship and their welfare. Although Islamic law gives women the right to own and dispose of property, they inherit less property than do their male kin. They are entitled to a *mahr* (dower, a financial sum given or promised by the groom), but they could forfeit it if they are deemed to be at fault in the case of divorce. In the absence of a concept of marital assets to be divided in the case of divorce, the wife could lose access to the family home. Inasmuch as laws require that women obtain permission of father, husband, or other male guardian to marry, seek employment, start a business, travel, or open a bank account for their children, this means that women are seen as incapable of entering contracts on their own. The highly formal Islamic marriage contract does require the consent of the wife, and in some countries women may insert stipulations into the contract, such as her right to divorce should her husband take another wife. But here, too, the option of divorce could mean forfeiture of the *mahr* (if it has been deferred, as is often the case). Marriage, moreover, remains largely an agreement between two families rather than two individuals with equal rights and obligations. Elite women or wives with family support systems have protection from willful husbands, but poor women and those without family backing are easily devastated by divorce or widowhood.

Another source of women's second-class citizenship lies in the nature and role of the state, which in the context of the Middle East and North Africa has been defined as "neopatriarchal."[17] Although in more recent decades tension has developed between the state and communal entities such as tribes and extended families, the neopatriarchal state continues to uphold the traditional order in a modernizing context. Over the decades, some Middle Eastern states have encouraged women's social participation in a manner described as "state feminist" (e.g., Egypt under Nasser in the 1960s and the People's Republic of Yemen in the 1970s), but only in Tunisia has family law remained consistently "Westernized" since the 1950s (except in the matter of equal inheritance).[18] Thus it is the state that has reinforced discriminatory family laws and upheld kin and social controls over women. The neopatriarchal state, moreover, is authoritarian; male citizens have few political rights, and women even fewer. Democratization has begun in parts of the region, but the region as a whole is regarded as a "laggard" in the so-called third wave of democratization—and the process may have been further stalled by the highly unpopular American war in Iraq. With a few exceptions (Lebanon and of course post-Saddam Iraq), states are strong and highly centralized in the region—and this despite the ability of globalization processes to weaken state capacity in economic and political matters elsewhere.

Feminist Responses: Transnational and National

Since the 1980s, women's movements in the Middle East and North Africa, and elsewhere in the Muslim world, have had to contend with patriarchal Islamist movements, neopatriachal states, and religious-based family laws—a rather formidable combination of forces. One response was the formation of Women Living under Muslim Laws (WLUML), a network of Muslim and secular feminists who link with other transnational feminist networks to advance the human rights of women. Another transnational feminist network, the Sisterhood Is Global Institute (SIGI), came to be directed by an expatriate Iranian feminist who went on, in 2000, to form the Women's Learning Partnership for Rights, Development, and Peace (WLP). These networks were centrally involved in solidarity work, in raising international awareness about the plight of Muslim women in various parts of the world, in publicizing feminist activism and campaigns, and in providing local women's groups with material or technical support.

WLUML emerged in response to concerns about changes in family laws in the countries from which the founding members came. In July 1984, nine women—from Algeria, Sudan, Morocco, Pakistan, Bangladesh, Iran, Mauritius, and Tanzania—set up an Action Committee in response to state actions that accommodated Islamist demands for the stricter application of Muslim family law. The committee soon evolved into an international network of information, solidarity, and support.

Tasks for the network, set at the first planning meeting in April 1986, were to create international links between women in Muslim countries and communities and to exchange information on their situations, struggles, and strategies, through publications and an Alert for Action system.[19] Since then, WLUML has become a network of women who are active in their local and national movements but who meet periodically to reach consensus on a Plan of Action.

Because WLUML includes women activists who are nonreligious and those, like Malaysia's Sisters in Islam, who are religiously observant women, the network deploys diverse strategies and discourses to champion women's rights, including reinterpretation of religious texts. WLUML is, however, resolutely antifundamentalist and committed to the separation of religion from the realm of politics and the law. Its most prominent strategy is to provide solidarity to women experiencing oppression and to publicize their condition. Over the years, WLUML has been active in raising international awareness about the dangers of fundamentalism for women, issuing many appeals concerning the plight of women during the civil conflict in Algeria, the oppression of women under the Taliban in Afghanistan, and the trend toward legal Islamization in parts of Nigeria and Malaysia.

The Women's Learning Partnership (WLP) involves feminist activists and intellectuals from Africa, Asia, and Latin America who had been part of SIGI's activities in the 1990s, but the focus of its activities remains the Muslim world. Based in Bethesda, Maryland, it carries out activities with institutional or individual partners. During the 1990s, SIGI had been active in publicizing the second-class citizenship of Iranian women and in supporting the work of Iranian feminists, and had developed links with the Moroccan feminist group Association Démocratique des Femmes Morocaines, one of the groups that led the campaign to reform the family law in Morocco. In the new millennium, and as the Moroccan feminist campaign grew in momentum, WLP increased its efforts to publicize the campaign and supports its efforts. One method was to arrange for travel by Moroccan feminist leaders and involve them in seminars and conferences. Another was to include detailed information about the campaign, in English as well as the original French, on the WLP website. A major contribution was the early translation into English of the new Moroccan family law. This is the sense in which the WLP, among other transnational feminist networks, has helped to create an active, and interactive, transnational public sphere, "a real as well as conceptual space in which movement organizations interact, contest each other, and learn from each other."[20]

Nationally based women's organizations have proliferated in the Middle East and North Africa, and their demands may be crystallized as follows: (1) the modernization of family laws, 2) the criminalization of domestic violence and other forms of violence against women, (3) nationality rights for women, and (4) greater political and economic participation.[21] They emphasize, too, that existing family laws are at odds with the universal standards of equality and nondiscrimination embodied in international instruments such as CEDAW. The legal and discursive strategies they deploy to achieve their goals are diverse; some women's groups use a secular discourse and take a confrontational stance while others frame their demands in Islamic discourse and engage in consensus building.[22] These strategies, as well as the objectives delineated above, have been central to feminist demands and claims in Iran and Morocco.

Until recently, feminist organizations in the region exhibited two distinct characteristics. One was their tendency to work with men and to engage with state agencies and authorities in order to further their objectives. The kind of "radical feminist" discourse present in North America and Europe is not found in the feminist movements of the Middle East and North Africa. Instead, in negotiating women's rights, feminist discourses and strategies have been nearer to Western liberal and socialist traditions, with the Islamic feminist discourse being a more recent innovation. The second characteristic has been their relative marginalization from the transnational feminist networks that emerged in the mid-1980s and proliferated in the 1990s. This may be attributed to state repression and in some cases to difficulty in communicating in English (the dominant language of transnational feminist networks on-line). Feminist strategies, therefore, were largely localized in the region and therefore unfamiliar to scholars of women's movements or of social movements.

However, the new millennium saw heightened cooperation between nationally based women's movements and transnational feminist networks such as WLUML and WLP around specific campaigns, notably the reform of the family law in Morocco and the campaign to end stoning in Iran. In both cases, but especially in the Iranian case, expatriate feminists have played a key "bridging" role by linking the local struggle and the relevant global institutions, networks, and norms.

The Islamic Republic of Iran: Local and Transnational Campaigns for Women's Rights

Until the mid-1990s the Islamic Republic of Iran was relatively isolated, a condition ensured by legal measures banning the use of satellite TV dishes, limiting international travel, and restricting access to the internet. Delegates to the UN women's conferences in 1980 and 1985 were Islamists who staunchly defended the *chador* (the fully enveloping black veil) and the Islamic Republic's record, notwithstanding overwhelming evidence of oppression, discrimination, and second-class citizenship for women and religious minorities. Both the legal restrictions and the highly charged ideological climate prevented contact between women activists in Iran and expatriate Iranian feminists.

Post-Khomeini liberalization under President Rafsanjani, however, lessened the restrictions on travel, with the result that expatriate Iranian feminists began to visit Iran and make connections with women's rights activists, both Islamic and non-Islamic. They were able to observe dissidence, resistances, and alternative discourses, including a staunchly antistate and secular feminism and a more consensus-building Islamic feminism.[23] The Islamic Republic failed to deliver on its promise to liberate women; faced with clerical insistence on the perfection of Iran's Sharia-based family law and unhappy with a legal environment that allowed men to divorce their wives at will or take second wives, disillusioned Muslim women turned their attention to the Islamic texts. Their rereading led them to emphasize the egalitarian and emancipatory spirit of the Quran, the Prophet's message, and early Islamic history. In this way, interpretation (*ijtihad*) became a strategy for questioning the legitimacy of patriarchal laws and women's second-class citizenship.

Another strategy was to create a prodigious women's press, including feminist magazines and women's publishing collectives.[24] Reflecting the

development of a collective identity and expressing the grievances and aspirations of contemporary Iranian women, the feminist press revealed the
importance of the international arena for Iranian women activists; editions included translations of feminist essays published in other countries,
and articles were solicited from expatriate Iranian feminists.[25] In the latter
half of the 1990s, under the presidency of Mohammad Khatami and with
the rise of the reform movement, women's rights activists were deeply
immersed in domestic battles for political reform, the relaxation of cultural and social restrictions, and women's rights. On all these issues, they
worked with men, although they also expressed criticism of the male-led
reform movement for its neglect of feminist issues.[26]

Throughout the 1990s and into the new millennium, grievances about
women's legal status and social conditions abounded in the feminist press,
where there was a strong emphasis on women's inequality within the family.[27] The activist lawyer Mehrangiz Kaar had conducted a systematic analysis of Iran's laws pertaining to women's status in the family and society;
her paper was widely distributed within Iran, and in the late 1990s she
was invited by expatriate Iranians to address them in the United States. A
key objective of Iranian women's rights activists, both secular and Islamic,
became the modernization of family law and women's equal rights in matters of marriage, divorce, and child custody. Another concerned domestic violence, with many articles in the feminist press describing domestic
violence as both a social problem and a violation of women's rights.[28] A
third concern was women's underrepresentation in formal politics and the
need for greater participation in Parliament, the local councils, and the
highest political offices. Azzam Taleghani's self-nomination for president
in 1997—and her disqualification on grounds of sex—brought the question of women and political participation to the fore. In 2001, some forty
women sought the nomination, and all were summarily disqualified. Several documentary films were made on the subject of women's pursuit of
the presidency.

Negotiating women's rights took place in the press and in parliamentary debates, especially during President Khatami's second term. Feminists
framed their grievances and demands in Islamic terms and drew from the
"cultural stock" to press for women's rights and equality. But they also
used secular language and pointed to international conventions and standards, thus challenging the dominant political and ideological framework.
They called for the adoption of international conventions and norms such
as CEDAW and the implementation of the Beijing Platform for Action;

they participated in or followed international forums such as the Beijing Plus Five meeting in New York in June 2000; and they forged ties with feminists in the diaspora.

Throughout this period, expatriate feminists strengthened their ties to activists back home, publishing in the feminist press and meeting with activists in Iran (e.g., the activist lawyer Shirin Ebadi, who later would become the Nobel Peace Prize laureate). They facilitated international networking by inviting Iran-based feminists to conferences in Europe and the United States; distributing edited volumes, calendars, and other publications of the Iranian women's press; organizing screenings of films with feminist themes; circulating petitions protesting the mistreatment of feminist leaders in Iran; and writing and lecturing about Iranian women's activism. When lawyer Mehrangiz Kaar was imprisoned on spurious charges in spring 2000, protests could not be organized on her behalf in Iran due to the repressive climate that had followed the suppression of the student movement the previous summer. But a vigorous campaign to secure her release and allow her to travel abroad was launched by expatriate feminists, WLUML, and WLP, in partnership with international human rights organizations.

The incremental steps of the 1990s and early twenty-first century led to the first open protests by Iranian women since March 1979. On March 8, 2005, feminists gathered in front of Tehran University to demand women's rights, and repeated the action the following June, on the eve of presidential elections. In June 2006, they gathered again, but this time they were attacked by the police. Photos of the attack were widely distributed by expatriate feminists and by transnational networks. Indeed, the bridging role played by expatriate feminists has linked domestic feminist groups to a wider array of transnational feminist and human rights networks, and this became evident in the campaign launched in 2006 to end the practice of stoning for adultery and to abrogate the relevant laws from the penal code.[29] In addition, feminists in Iran and the diaspora launched a million-signature petition campaign—a strategy learned from the Moroccan women's movement.

Reforming Family Law in Morocco

Drafted in 1957, the Moroccan *mudawana* was based on the Maliki school of Islamic jurisprudence and was one of the most conservative family laws in the Muslim world. In the face of major resistance to change and arguments that the *mudawana* was fixed and could not be revised, women's organizations initiated a million-signature petition drive for family law reform, leading to amendments to five articles in 1993. The amendments limited the guardian's control and emphasized that the woman should give her consent and sign the marriage contract; allowed women over twenty-one who did not have a father to contract their own marriage without a guardian; and stipulated that before taking a second wife, a husband would have to inform his first wife. The mother was given the right to legally represent her children if their father died, though the mother still could not dispose of the children's property.

The *mudawana* continued to assume that women were subordinate to men: there were double standards in marriage and divorce, for example. Social change in Morocco, including women's rising employment, left the *mudawana* looking increasingly outdated. What is more, violence against and harassment of women seemed to be increasing, and the plight of low-income women who were divorced and left without a home needed to be addressed. During this time, Moroccan civil society became increasingly organized and more women's associations were formed. Women's rights and feminist organizations formed the Collectif 95 Maghreb Egalité, a transnational network that was the major organizer behind the "Muslim Women's Parliament" at the NGO Forum that preceded the Beijing conference. In preparing for the post-Beijing followup, the Collectif formulated an alternative "egalitarian family code" and promoted women's political participation.[30]

The appointment in 1998 of a socialist prime minister and a minister of women and family affairs (a former Communist) who was committed to women's rights led to the formulation of the National Action Plan for the Integration of Women in Development, which contained a chapter suggesting the need to reform the *mudawana*. Huge rallies for and against the Action Plan and family law reform took place in March 2000, and sustained hostility from Islamist groups forced the government to put the plan on the back burner. The women's organizations and their allies in government, however, pressed ahead, and a new mechanism to enhance women's political participation was put in place. In the 2002 elections, thirty-five women entered the Moroccan Parliament, assisted by a new quota system adopted by the political parties.

Meanwhile, King Mohammad VI, who was personally committed to women's rights, had appointed a royal commission to advise him on the family law. Women's rights organizations organized a series of workshops,

roundtables, and discussion groups to analyze the details of the draft legislation and renew their efforts to educate the public and lobby the Parliament for what they argued would be reforms in favor of the well-being
of women, children, and the family. In October 2003, in his capacity as
Commander of the Faithful, the king announced a new family code—
which he asserted was consistent with the spirit of the Sharia—and then
sent it to the Parliament. This code, which Parliament passed in January
2004, was heralded as a giant leap in women's rights as well as a huge advance in children's rights.[31] The main features of the new Moroccan family
law are as follows:

- Husband and wife share joint responsibility for the family.
- The wife is no longer legally obliged to obey her husband.
- The adult woman is entitled to self-guardianship and may exercise it
  freely and independently.
- The right to divorce is a prerogative of both men and women, exercised under judicial supervision.
- The principle of divorce by mutual consent is established.
- The woman has the right to impose a condition in the marriage contract requiring that her husband refrain from taking other wives.
- If there is no preestablished condition in their marriage contract, the
  first wife must be informed of her husband's intention to remarry,
  the second wife must be informed that her husband-to-be is already
  married, and the first wife can ask for divorce due to harm suffered.
- Polygamy is subject to the judge's authorization and to stringent legal conditions (no objection by the first wife) that make the practice
  nearly impossible.
- In the case of divorce, the woman is given the possibility of retain-
  ing custody of her child even upon remarrying or moving out of the
  area where her ex-husband lives.
- The child's right to acknowledgment of paternity is protected in
  cases where the marriage has not been officially registered.
- For both men and women, the minimum legal age of marriage is
  eighteen years.

New family courts were established in support of the reformed family code. Training for the judiciary was improved, and women could be
appointed as family judges. Morocco now joins Tunisia and Turkey as
the only countries in the Middle East and North Africa region where the

husband and wife have shared responsibility for the family.[32] Aspects of the new family law represent a challenge to the patriarchal gender contract. Because of this, and because of continued resistance from Islamist critics, the challenge to both state agencies and women's organizations is to raise popular awareness about the new law and women's new rights through education, media campaigns, and other activities.

The Moroccan case is a striking example of how women's rights advocates can build coalitions to generate social dialogues, have an impact on key policy debates, and help effect legal reform and public policy changes. What is remarkable is that the feminist campaign succeeded in breaking the long taboo against touching the *mudawana*—and this in a very conservative culture. Feminists' success derived partly from their strategic use of Islamic sources in defense of their case for an emancipatory interpretation of *Sharia* to frame the new family law, along with arguments about the need to fully involve women in all aspects of public life in order to further socioeconomic development.[33] It is important to note, too, that the long campaign to improve the status of women was an entirely domestic matter, although local-global linkages were evident in the latter part of the campaign. Moroccan women's rights groups clearly benefited from a global environment conducive to women's rights; they took part in the Beijing process; they teamed up with feminist groups in Tunisia and Algeria to write an alternative, egalitarian family code; and their struggles were supported and publicized by transnational feminist networks such as WLUML and WLP. Yet their decade-long struggle was carried out and won by dint of their own efforts. The success of the Moroccan campaign for family law reform can be replicated in other countries in the region, though not in exactly the same way, for Moroccan women had the advantage of a sympathetic and supportive political leadership—a factor not present in all the countries in the region.

Conclusions

The mobility of feminists and feminist ideas, participation in the transnational public sphere, and new international institutions and norms conducive to women's rights are among the opportunities afforded by the era of globalization that have positive implications for women's citizenship within and across borders. National-level dynamics—including changes in the characteristics and aspirations of the female population, and feminist

A Model of the Extension of Citizenship Rights

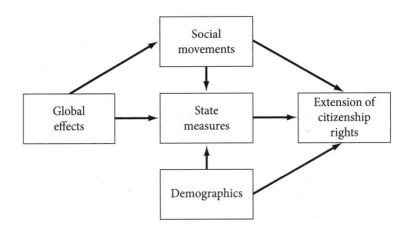

conflicts with states and Islamist movements—are clearly behind the drive for women's rights, lending credence to classic theories of citizenship. And yet, in an era of globalization, supranational institutions, norms, and movements intersect with national-level factors, although not in exactly the same way in every case. Thus, as seen in the figure above, the combination of global effects, sociodemographics, social movements, and state measures leads to the extension of citizenship rights.

A major impetus for the movement for women's citizenship rights in Muslim countries has been political Islam. The rise of Islamic fundamentalism—and the stark clarity of its patriarchal agenda—has been a key factor in galvanizing women in the Muslim world and setting in motion movements for the definition and expansion of women's rights. This has coincided with the growth of the population of middle-class and educated women with aspirations of equality, mobility, and empowerment.

The cases of Iran and Morocco (and other cases not examined here, such as Algeria, Bahrain, Jordan, Tunisia, and Turkey) show that many women in the Middle East and North Africa are unwilling to accept notions of "difference" that translate into subordination within the family and second-class citizenship—hence the emphasis on reform of Muslim family law and the insistence on greater political rights and participation. Moreover, the struggle for citizenship is rooted in domestic issues of political/cultural contention and social conflict; certainly it should not be seen as a manifestation of Western feminism's reach.

And yet, the late twentieth century saw the expansion of global institutions, movements, and norms pertaining to trade, governance, and rights. Among these processes has been the migration and mobility of feminist ideas across borders once seen as intractable or as the embodiment of some absolute cultural difference. The integration of north and south in the global circuits of capital and the construction of a transnational public sphere in opposition to the dark side of globalization has meant that feminism is not "Western" but global. The struggle for women's citizenship is a global phenomenon—indeed, one of the defining features of the era of globalization—and domestic struggles often find support, legitimacy, or inspiration in transnational ideas, movements, and organizations. This is why, in Iran and Morocco, the struggle around family law and women's rights more broadly has entailed both state-centered and transnational strategies. [34] These cases also show how feminist networks participate across borders in the transnational public sphere. They show that the transnational public sphere, while "an opportunity structure that is recognized most clearly in the core countries of the industrialized West, is appreciated even in relatively marginalized sites in the non-Western world as well."[35] For women in the Middle East, North Africa, and elsewhere who seek the expansion of citizenship rights, the most critical sites and resources are the state, civil society, the transnational public sphere, and transnational feminist networks.

NOTES

1. For some, global feminism is a kind of colonial or imperial feminist discourse, of the kind that Laura Bush may espouse for Afghan or Iraqi women under U.S. hegemony. For others, it is inscribed in the Beijing Platform for Action and the UN Convention on the Elimination of All Forms of Discrimination against Women. For diverse perspectives see, e.g., Mahnaz Afkhami, "Introduction," in *Faith and Freedom: Women's Human Rights in the Muslim World*, ed. Mahnaz Afkhami (Syracuse, NY: Syracuse University Press, 1995), 1–6; Amrita Basu, ed., *The Challenge of Local Feminisms: Women's Movements in Global Perspective* (Boulder, CO: Westview Press, 1995); Inderpal Grewal and Caren Kaplan, "Introduction," in *Scattered Hegemonies: Postmodernity and Transnational Feminist Practices*, eds. Inderpal Grewal and Caren Kaplan (Minneapolis: University of Minnesota Press, 1994), 1–34; Valentine M. Moghadam, *Globalizing Women:*

Transnational Feminist Networks (Baltimore, MD: Johns Hopkins University Press, 2005); Nancy Naples and Manisha Desai, eds., *Women's Activism and Globalization* (London: Routledge, 2002).

2. Islamist women's organizations and various kinds of women-run NGOs also were formed, but they will not be considered here.

3. A "transnational feminist network" (TFN) brings together women from three or more countries around a common agenda, such as women's human rights, feminist economics, reproductive health and rights, or antimilitarism. Some of the better-known TFNs include Development Alternatives with Women for a New Era (DAWN), Women Living under Muslim Laws (WLUML), Women in Development Europe (WIDE), and the Women's International Coalition for Economic Justice (WICEJ). Although TFNs of the present wave appeared in 1984–1985, one of the earliest is the Women's International League for Peace and Freedom (WILPF), formed in the early part of the twentieth century. For an elaboration, see Moghadam, *Globalizing Women*, supra note 1.

4. Margaret Keck and Katherine Sikkink, *Activists beyond Borders: Advocacy Networks in International Politics* (Ithaca, NY: Cornell University Press, 1998).

5. Jackie Smith, Charles Chatfield, and Ron Pagnucco, eds., *Transnational Social Movements and Global Politics* (Syracuse, NY: Syracuse University Press, 1997); John A. Guidry, Michael D. Kennedy, and Mayer N. Zald, "Introduction," in *Globalizations and Social Movements: Culture, Power, and the Transnational Public Sphere* (Ann Arbor: University of Michigan Press, 1999), 1–29; Robert O'Brien, Anne Marie Goetz, Jan Aart Scholte, and Marc Williams, *Contesting Global Governance: Multilateral Economic Institutions and Global Social Movements* (Cambridge: Cambridge University Press, 2000).

6. See, for example, William I. Robinson, "Social Theory and Globalization: The Rise of a Transnational State," *Theory and Society* 30 (April 2001): 157–200; and Leslie Sklair, *Globalization: Capitalism and Its Alternatives*, 3rd ed. (Oxford: Oxford University Press, 2002).

7. Mary Ann Glendon, *State, Law, and Family: Family Law in Transition in the United States and Western Europe* (Amsterdam: North-Holland Publishing, 1977); Ayelet Shachar, "Should Church and State Be Joined at the Altar? Women's Rights and the Multicultural Dilemma," in *Citizenship in Diverse Societies*, eds. Will Kymlicka and Wayne Norman (Oxford: Oxford University Press, 2000), 199–224.

8. This is not fundamentally different from objections raised in the United States to CEDAW's ratification and implementation, based on arguments that prevent federal judges from employing or relying on foreign law. See Judith Resnik, "Law's Migration: American Exceptionalism, Silent Dialogues, and Federalism's Multiple Ports of Entry," *Yale Law Journal* 115 (2006), where she argues that such reservations are in fact unworkable, given "law's migration."

9. This paper is part of a larger project on women's movements in the Middle East, in which I examine the role of states, strategies, and global linkages. The project has been partially funded by a grant from the American Sociological Association's Fund for the Advancement of the Discipline (2003–2004). In addition to reliance on the relevant secondary sources, research methods have included participant observation in conferences and campaigns, a close reading of publications by women's organizations, and interviews with movement activists.

10. See Abdullahi An-Naim, *Islamic Family Law in a Changing World* (London: Zed Books, 2002). In Israel they are based on the Jewish *Halacha*, and in Lebanon there are fifteen personal status codes for the eighteen recognized ethnic-religious communities, including Christian ones. In Muslim-dominant countries, non-Muslim communities are exempt from Islamic family law, and family matters are governed by religious codes supervised by churches (thus, Catholics cannot divorce because their churches do not allow it).

11. See Deniz Kandiyoti, "Islam and Patriarchy: A Comparative Perspective," in *Shifting Boundaries: Women and Gender in Middle Eastern History*, eds. Nikki R. Keddie and Beth Baron (New Haven, CT: Yale University Press, 1992), 23–44; Valentine M. Moghadam, *Modernizing Women: Gender and Social Change in the Middle East*, 2nd ed. (Boulder, CO: Lynne Rienner Publishers, 2003), esp. chapter 4.

12. Valentine M. Moghadam, *Women, Work, and Economic Reform in the Middle East and North Africa* (Boulder, CO: Lynne Rienner Publishers, 1998). In the oil-rich countries, the use of contract labor, including Asian women workers, substituted for native women's labor. In more recent years, and with the growth of unemployment, governments have barred certain occupations from foreign labor, though the use of Asian women in the service sector and domestic work persists throughout the Gulf countries, as well as in Jordan and Lebanon.

13. See Mounira Charrad, *States and Women's Rights: The Making of Postcolonial Tunisia, Algeria, and Morocco* (Berkeley: University of California Press, 2001). Honor killings in Jordan are an extreme form of such male kin control over females.

14. It should be noted that legal pluralism, wherein two different legal systems (here, Sharia and secular) may govern a particular body of law, is not only confined to family matters and is not accepted in all Muslim countries. Saudi Arabia uses Sharia law almost exclusively; in Iran, criminal matters may be adjudicated in both Sharia and civil courts; finally, Sharia courts are not present at all in Turkey.

15. This is the case in Egypt and Algeria but not in the Islamic Republic of Iran, whose constitution specifically subjects equality of citizens to "Islamic criteria."

16. See Lamia Shehadeh, "The Legal Status of Married Women in Lebanon," *International Journal of Middle East Studies* 30 (1998): 501–19; and Lynn Welchman, "Capacity, Consent, and Under-Age Marriage in Muslim Family Law," in *The International Survey of Family Law, 2001 Edition*, ed. Andrew Bainhaus (Bristol, UK: Family Law, 2001).

17. Hisham Sharabi, *Neopatriarchy* (Oxford: Oxford University Press, 1988); Hillel Frisch, "Modern Absolutism or Neopatriarchal State Building? Customary Law, Extended Families, and the Palestinian Authority," *International Journal of Middle East Studies* 29 (1997): 341–58.

18. Turkey's legal code was made secular in the 1930s, but its family law remained conservative until the women's movement emerged in the 1980s and began to force amendments. Yesim Arat, "Gender and Citizenship in Turkey," in *Gender and Citizenship in the Middle East*, ed. Suad Joseph (Syracuse, NY: Syracuse University Press, 2000), 275–86.

19. Marieme Helie-Lucas, "Women Living under Muslim Laws," in *Ours by Right: Women's Rights as Human Rights*, ed. Joanna Kerr (London: Zed Books, 1993), 225; and Seema Kazi, "Muslim Laws and Women Living under Muslim Laws," in *Muslim Women and the Politics of Participation*, eds. Mahnaz Afkhami and Erika Friedl (Syracuse, NY: Syracuse University Press, 1997), 142.

20. Guidry, Kennedy, and Zald, "Introduction," supra note 5, 3.

21. Moghadam, *Women, Work, and Economic Reform*, supra note 12, ch. 7; and Moghadam, *Modernizing Women*, supra note 11, ch. 8.

22. Suad Joseph, ed., *Gender and Citizenship in the Middle East* (Suracuse, NY: Syracuse University Press, 2001); Valentine M. Moghadam, "Engendering Citizenship, Feminizing Civil Society: Reflections on the Middle East and North Africa," *Women & Politics* 25 (2003): 63–88; Moghadam, "Organizing Women: The New Women's Movement in Algeria," *Cultural Dynamics* 13 (July 2001): 131–54. For more details on women's movements and collective action, see contributions in *Journal of Middle East Women's Studies* 2 (Spring 2006), special issue on "Women and the Public Sphere in the Middle East and North Africa."

23. The Islamic feminist discourse in Iran was represented by the women's magazine *Zanan*, which began to publish in 1992. For details on this phenomenon, and on the debates that took place in the diaspora on secular versus Islamic feminism, see Valentine M. Moghadam, "Islamic Feminism and Its Discontents: Towards a Resolution of the Debate," *Signs: Journal of Women in Culture and Society* 27 (Summer 2002): 1135–71.

24. These include *Jens-e Dovvom?*, *Farzaneh*, *Hoghough-e Zanan*, *Roshangaran Press*, *Fasl-e Zanan*, and the output of the Women's Cultural Center, directed by secular feminists Noushine Ahmadi-Khorassani and Parvin Ardalan.

25. For example, a 2000 issue of *Jens-e Dovvom?* [The Second Sex?] carried a translated article on Madonna by a U.S. sociologist and an article on

preparations for the Beijing+5 conference in New York as well as interviews with expatriate feminists and articles on domestic topics.

26. See, for example, Mahboubeh Abbas-Gholizadeh, in *Farzaneh* 5 (Winter 2000).

27. Parvin Abyaneh's survey of seventy-two articles in the magazine *Zanan* that dealt with problems of women's legal status showed that fully 61 percent of them dealt with family issues. See Parvin Abyaneh, "Islamic Feminism: Shortcomings and Challenges," paper presented at the annual meetings of the Center for Iranian Research and Analysis, Bethesda, MD, April 2000.

28. See *Fasle Zanan* [The Season of Women: A Collection of Feminist Articles] 1 (2001): 1380 and 2 (2002): 1381. See also the article by Shahla Ezazi in *Farzaneh* [Journal of Women's Studies and Research] 5 (Winter 2000).

29. For details on the campaign, see http://www.meydaan.com/ English/ aboutcamp.aspx?cid=46 and www.change4equality.com/english.

30. This project was assisted by German foundations, which also financed the publication of the egalitarian code—along with other reports—in Arabic, French, and English.

31. Women's Learning Partnership, *Morocco Adopts Landmark Family Law Supporting Women's Equality*, available at http://www.learningpartnership.org/ events/newsalerts/morocco0204.phtml#adfmdoc (last accessed on July 13, 2004).

32. Ibid. See also Fatima Sadiqi and Moha Ennaji, "The Feminization of Public space: Women's Activism, the Family Law, and Social Change in Morocco," *Journal of Middle East Women's Studies* 2 (Spring 2006): 86–114.

33. One women's rights leader explained, "I wouldn't say that we are Islamic feminists, but we live in a religious society and so we had to teach ourselves more about Islam in order to reach the people." Author interview with Latifa Jbabdi of l'Union d'Action Feminine, in Helsinki, Finland, September 9, 2004.

34. It is interesting, if ironic, that at a time when Middle Eastern and North African feminists argued for a uniform and egalitarian civil code governing family matters, "multiculturalists" in Ontario sought to institute sectarian arbitration. (For an elaboration, see Audrey Macklin, "Particularized Citizenship," in this volume). It is no accident that an exiled Iranian feminist led the campaign against the introduction of Muslim family courts in Ontario—and that WLUML was a key player in raising international awareness of this matter. These are further examples of the migration and mobility of feminists and feminist ideas.

35. Guidry, Kennedy, and Zald, "Introduction," supra note 5, 9.

|||||||||||||||||||||||||||||||||||||||||||||||||||||

8

Particularized Citizenship:
Encultured Women and the Public Sphere

Audrey Macklin

Borders are gendered: most women and girls admitted as permanent immigrants to the global north still enter on the basis of their relationship to a man (typically a husband or father) and would not otherwise qualify as independent immigrants.[1] Gender is bordered: enforcement of the boundaries of gender identity is sufficiently strict that crossing these borders is not called migration, but transgression. In multicultural societies of the global north, it is not uncommon to seize upon immigrant women who belong to diasporic communities as victims of illegitimate gender discipline by minority cultures or faiths. The bordering of gender in the broader society tacitly emerges as appropriate, benign, or even natural.

This chapter attempts to depart from this pattern by examining two case studies in which encultured women publicly challenged communal practices as oppressive and unjust. They did so through the vehicle of law reform advocacy, or what Vicki Jackson might call acts of "public citizenship."[2] Claiming their entitlement as legal citizens of Canada to participate in governance, they demanded equal citizenship as Canadian women. At the same time, they pointedly refused to renounce their cultural citizenship or to confine their gender critique to a specific cultural context. In other words, they rejected the ultimatum described by Ayelet Shachar as "your culture or your rights."[3]

How did the encultured women manifest their citizenship in the public sphere (represented here by law reform), and how was that citizenship regarded in the wider polity? My hypothesis is that the encultured woman's disruptive presence in the public domain of law reform was managed by casting her as a "particularized citizen." By this I mean that she was admitted (even welcomed) into the political realm of citizenship, but only heard insofar as she spoke of "her own" community.

Law simultaneously configures and reflects the social meaning and political implications of cultural difference and of equality. This fact undermines any attempt to assign an unreflexively prescriptive role to law as solvent for the normative tension between individual equality and group autonomy in the multicultural context, insofar as law itself is implicated in the production of these norms. This interactive relationship between law and public discourse also reveals the dynamic processes whereby citizens participate in shaping the laws that shape them as citizens. It is at these moments that encultured women become agents in the production of substantive rules that mediate between and structure their citizenship in the state and in their cultural/religious community.

The first case study concerns the explicit prohibition of female genital cutting or mutilation (FGM) in the Canadian Criminal Code. The second addresses the recent debate about the legal recognition of Islamic faith-based family law arbitration in Ontario, Canada. The challenge and the paradox for the women engaged in law reform lies in asserting political citizenship (as encultured Canadians) to redress the denial of civil citizenship (as women), while defending their cultural citizenship (as Africans or Muslims) against external denigration. Members of diasporic communities quickly learn that legal citizenship does not necessarily secure the respect, access to resources, and recognition associated with substantive citizenship. These groups utilize the incidents of political enfranchisement to advance the substantive recognition that formal citizenship itself fails to provide. In other words, they bootstrap their citizenship into a campaign for redressing the unfulfilled promise of citizenship.

Vulnerable groups may feel alienated from law but also seek law's protection. For instance, some racialized and immigrant women subject to domestic violence fear that contacting police will expose their partners to a racist criminal justice system, reinforce negative stereotypes about the violent/sexist/primitive character of their male cohort, and leave them even more susceptible within their communities than before. Their reluctance to access the legal system becomes symptomatic of their exclusion from citizenship and the protection that citizenship is meant to entail.

Minority communities' relationship with the civil justice system remains underexamined and probably varies across the spectrum of legal disputes (property, commercial, family, employment, personal injury, etc.).

It would be unwise to generalize about when, why, and how individuals from within diasporic communities litigate internal disputes. Apart from the usual financial barriers, other variables might include the perceived correspondence of mainstream legal norms with those to which individuals subscribe; the confidence members have in the mainstream system; the availability of normative and institutional alternatives within the community; and intragroup pressure to resolve disputes internally. A crucial difference between criminal and civil law is that the former imposes state coercion on everyone, whereas the latter depends on private individuals voluntarily accessing the state's judicial system.

The Prohibition of Female Genital Cutting in the Canadian Criminal Code

The advocacy campaign by a group of African-Canadian women (mainly Somali and Sudanese immigrants) to eradicate female genital cutting or mutilation (FGM) fit squarely within the criminal law model. A conventional framing of this issue in multiculturalism debates queries whether respect for cultural difference requires toleration of a practice that appears irredeemably violent, debilitating, and misogynistic.[4] The answer is almost invariably "no": FGM is the poster child for the limits of liberal tolerance.

Many commentators note that the practice is contested within the affected diasporic communities, but implicitly treat this as a contingent fact of little theoretical interest. The case study that I present takes as its starting point the recognition that FGM is opposed by many, if not most, men and women in the affected communities.

At one level, the narrative I describe may be dismissed as an easy case for liberals concerned about multiculturalism to the extent that everyone involved was publicly committed to eradicating FGM. Yet, it bears noting that multiculturalist analyses of FGM rarely cite actual defenses of the practice asserted by members of the affected communities.[5] In general, it appears that scholarly inquiry has been preoccupied with the question of whether FGM should be tolerated, without much attention to what is being said and done within the relevant diasporic communities. One may contend that this academic fixation is politically benign. I am not so sure. I worry that it is a marginalizing narrative[6] that reifies and perpetuates a story of Africans as lawless, disordered, and primitive. Actual discussions in the north among virtually all participants—African and non-

African—has not turned on whether the practice should end, but on how best to hasten its demise.

Anecdotal reports suggest that FGM is performed in Canada, probably by health care professionals,[7] but numbers are unknown. Anti-FGM activists from within the various communities attempt to discourage it through education about the adverse health and psychological effects of FGM. They also engage in consciousness raising to dispel the alleged cultural or religious justifications for the practice. These activists are also keenly aware that publicity about FGM elicits revulsion from mainstream culture.

The Canadian Department of Justice first considered the desirability of amending the Criminal Code to make FGM a criminal offense in 1991. It initially decided to do nothing, on the grounds that FGM already constitutes a criminal offense under existing laws prohibiting aggravated assault, assault causing bodily harm, and failure to provide necessaries of life to a child.[8] No one seriously believed that a perpetrator could avoid conviction by raising a so-called cultural defense of FGM.[9]

A few years later, in 1997, the government reversed its earlier position. First, it amended the Criminal Code to explicitly define FGM as a subcategory of aggravated assault. The phrase "wound or maim" now includes to "excise, infibulate or mutilate, in whole or in part, the labia majora, labia minora or clitoris of a person."[10] The amended law declares that FGM constitutes an assault to which no person can consent, except under stipulated circumstances. The exceptions are cases of medical necessity, or where the woman "[is] at least eighteen years of age and there is no resulting bodily harm."[11] In effect, the law contains a therapeutic defense and a delimited defense of consent.

Why did this happen, and what message did the government intend to convey through the explicit criminalization of FGM? The practice was already illegal under the general law prohibiting various forms of assault. From a purely doctrinal perspective, it would have made more sense to create an exemption from the law of assault for male circumcision, a common cultural and religious practice in North America (to which a small but feisty network of men has recently raised loud objections). Technically, male circumcision also constitutes an aggravated assault, even though its physical and psychological impact on males pales in comparison to the potential damage wrought by FGM on females. Nevertheless, the fact that no one fears criminal prosecution for circumcising their male child speaks to the power of dominant cultural norms to supersede the letter of the law and determine what the law is "really" about.

Singling out FGM for special mention in the Criminal Code seems to implant a marginalizing narrative into legal text. It risks reinforcing negative stereotypical associations among immigrants, culture, and criminality, while affirming mainstream Canadians' self-perception as enlightened, liberated, and law-abiding. Thus, explicit criminalization of FGM may add nothing to the existing state of the law except more stigma.[12]

Surprisingly, the political pressure to criminalize FGM in Canada emanated from encultured women who inserted and asserted themselves directly in the legislative process. This contrasts notably with the sequence of events in other jurisdictions where, according to critics, the leaders of the campaign tended to be white activists, while women from affected communities were selectively recruited to perform the role of exoticized victim.

In speaking with the Canadian activists, I learned that criminalization was supported by many, but not all, among those who opposed the practice of FGM.[13] During the 1990s, advocates of explicit criminalization embarked on a sophisticated campaign that built coalitions with mainstream feminist organizations and drew on popular organizing. In fact, a major impetus for the 1997 amendment appeared to be a 5,000-person petition launched by a woman from one of the affected communities that she presented to the federal minister of justice. It contained signatures gathered from a wide cross-section of Canadians.

In late 1996, the House of Commons Standing Committee on Justice and Legal Affairs invited submissions on a draft amendment to the Criminal Code regarding child prostitution, child sex tourism, criminal harassment, and FGM (Bill C-27). Community-based organizations such as Women's Health in Women's Hands, the Female Genital Mutilation Legal Community Committee, the African Canadian Legal Clinic, as well as the National Action Committee on the Status of Women (among others), weighed in favoring explicit criminalization.

The FGM Legal Community Committee explicitly framed their interest in participating in law reform as a democratic right flowing from citizenship:

> The FGM Legal Community Committee, as part of our movement to eradicate female genital mutilation and in fulfilling our duty and responsibility as citizens, demand our right as citizens of this country, to be part of the decision making process, using our expertise and experience in the determination of female genital mutilation legislation that so vitally affects our lives.[14]

Supporters of the amendment claimed that naming FGM as a criminal offense would unequivocally convey the message of its illegality to affected communities, thereby delivering a more potent deterrent than the status quo.[15] At the same time, these supporters invariably prioritized education and consciousness raising within the community as the primary route to eradicating the practice. The form and substance of the criminal sanction was assessed in accordance with its didactic value.[16] When I asked one advocate if she was concerned about the stigmatizing effect of specifically naming FGM in the Criminal Code, she surmised that the affected communities were already so alienated from mainstream Canadian society that criminalizing a particular cultural practice associated with these communities would make little difference. In her estimation, the women had little to lose in terms of group reputation, and something to gain in terms of protecting vulnerable members.

To a large extent, the anti-FGM campaign was a debate over means, not ends. All participants in the public process avowed their opposition to the practice of FGM, and the main task of advocacy groups was to persuade the state to adopt a more explicit criminal law instrument than hitherto existed. The campaign took the form of a dialogue between the federal government and a group of interlocutors expressing a common position. No discussion about the representativeness of the advocates was necessary, since no one claiming to speak on behalf of community members from the "other side" came forward publicly. The recent and ongoing controversy over family law arbitration by practitioners operating according to Islamic law presents a more complex array of issues and actors.

Legal Recognition of Islamic Faith-Based Family Law Arbitration

A cursory outline of the family law regime is necessary to situate this debate. The family law rules governing relationship breakdown in Ontario are a complicated admixture of federal and provincial laws. The relevant statutes set out default rules for distribution of property, child custody, and support (spousal and child). Reformist projects over the last thirty years have made considerable progress in addressing the gendered consequences of relationship breakdown. Property-division rules recognize the role that the unpaid labor of wives plays in enabling husbands to maximize their career development and wealth accumulation. Spousal support guidelines acknowledge that many women forfeit their own careers in the paid labor force to stay home with children, and some may simply never be in a position to attain full financial self-sufficiency. The default rules have moved far beyond regarding the traditional role of stay-at-home wife as a choice for which husbands bear no financial responsibility.

Despite (or perhaps because of) these relatively progressive rules, the state permits parties to opt out of the process and most of the substance of the statutory family law regime. Rather than litigating property division, custody, child support, and spousal support in the ordinary courts, parties may resolve these issues by negotiating an agreement on their own or with the assistance of lawyers and/or a mediator. The resultant agreements are labeled "domestic contracts." Parties may also engage an independent arbitrator of their choosing to adjudicate the dispute, albeit in a less formal manner than would a judge. Arbitrations are governed by the Arbitration Act,[17] which enables judicial enforcement of arbitral awards across a range of private disputes. Arbitration of family law matters under the Arbitration Act is seldom used in comparison to mediation and negotiation under family law legislation.

Having embarked on any of these private mechanisms of alternative dispute resolution (ADR), parties may adopt the default legislative rules as the framework for resolving their dispute. Alternatively, they may bargain according to their own preferences, values, and priorities. These can range from maximizing economic self-interest to abiding by religious norms. If they employ the services of a mediator, they may stipulate that the person guide them according to whatever norms they choose. Prior to the arbitration controversy, they could also instruct the arbitrator to apply the legal regime of their choosing, including religious law.[18] Apart from child support, a court will probably never examine the content of the ensuing domestic contract or arbitral award as a prerequisite to enforcement.

In late 2003, Syed Mumtaz Ali, retired lawyer and self-styled "patron-in-chief" of the newly established Islamic Institute for Civil Justice (IICJ), announced that the IICJ would begin arbitrating in family and inheritance matters in accordance with Muslim law, the arbitral awards would then be enforceable under the terms of the Arbitration Act. These proposed tribunals were quickly dubbed "Shari'a courts" in the media, and the prospect of their establishment generated considerable apprehension about the importation of oppressive, patriarchal practices associated with Islamic law in other countries. Ali himself did little to dispel the anxiety when, among his various inflammatory comments, he declared that any "good" Muslim would be obliged to use such tribunals to the exclusion of the ordinary courts.

In response to public outcry, the Ontario government appointed a former attorney-general, Marion Boyd, to conduct a review of the use of arbitration in family and inheritance law. Her mandate, explained in her report "Dispute Resolution in Family Law: Protecting Choice, Promoting Inclusion" (hereafter "Boyd Report"), was to "explore the use of private arbitration . . . and the impact that using arbitrations may have on vulnerable people."[19] Over the course of six months, Boyd received submissions in person, by phone, and in writing from over fifty groups as well as many private individuals. She met with women's organizations, religious bodies, immigrant settlement organizations, family lawyers, arbitrators, mediators, and concerned citizens.

In her final report, Boyd endorsed the continued use of binding, enforceable arbitration of family law issues under the Arbitration Act. In so doing, she rejected the Quebec example, where family law arbitrations have no legal force, although informally they may be taken into account by a court as "advisory opinions." While sympathetic to the possibility that women might be coerced into agreeing to faith-based arbitration, Boyd rejected the notion that explicit or implicit threats of social, religious, financial, or immigration reprisal—essentially, anything short of physical violence—would or should vitiate consent to arbitrate.[20] She believed that informed consent would be facilitated by supporting community organizations who could "explain rights under Ontario and Canadian law in a way that is likely to be comprehensible to people of diverse backgrounds and culture."[21] As a safeguard, Boyd recommended that if and when an arbitral award was challenged in court, a judge could set aside the award on the same grounds as mediated or negotiated domestic contracts, including on the basis of a legally specific type of extreme unfairness called "unconscionability."[22]

Unsurprisingly, the Boyd Report's conclusions did not quell the controversy, and opponents of faith-based arbitration intensified their campaign. Finally, in September 2005, the Ontario government announced that it would not adopt the recommendations of the Boyd Report. Instead, it would amend the law to preclude faith-based family law arbitration under the Arbitration Act. Eventually, the Ontario government passed legislation restricting enforceable family arbitrations to Canadian law.[23] The law does not prohibit parties from engaging religious authorities to arbitrate their disputes; it simply states that such arbitrations awards have no legal effect.[24] Although some grumbled that the amended law would violate the guaranteed freedom of religion under Section 2 of the Canadian Charter of Rights and Freedoms, it seems unlikely that any Canadian court would construe freedom of religion as imposing a positive obligation on Canadian courts to enforce the judgments of religious authorities. Because the legislation denies recognition to all legal orders external to Canadian law, it is probably secure from the complaint that it discriminates against religious law.

Performing Citizenship: Encultured Women's Articulation of Claims in the Public Sphere

My present goal is not to measure the policy outcomes on FGM and faith-based arbitration against a substantive vision of multicultural accommodation. To take possession of the normative project would divert attention from the less explored terrain of how encultured women exercise citizenship through the formulation and promotion of their own normative stance. I am interested, first, in how encultured women articulate their claims in the public sphere (here represented by the domain of law reform) and, second, in the alignment between substantive outcomes and that discursive performance.

To illuminate the first issue, I examine the formation of alliances across overlapping identity categories, the discursive negotiation of liberal norms of equality and liberty, and the instrumental deployment of law and law reform as a means of reconfiguring gendered power relations within the encultured community.

Building coalitions is smart strategy. Not only does it boost numbers; it also facilitates translation and transmission of a message to diverse audiences. The Somali and Sudanese women who led the anti-FGM advocacy effort succeeded in recruiting the formal support and participation of the African-Canadian Legal Clinic, the National Action Committee on the Status of Women, and several thousand unaffiliated petition signers. However powerful the defenders of FGM within their communities, they had no reasonable prospect of attracting external allies. I found literally no trace of their presence in the public discourse around the criminalization issue.

The arbitration debate featured a much wider array of interlocutors. The dominant institutional voice opposing Muslim arbitration was the

Canadian Council of Muslim Women (CCMW). While linked by common self-identification as Muslims, members include immigrants and native-born Canadians and women of Middle Eastern, African, and Asian background. The CCMW mobilized to gather the support of organizations variously comprised of non-Muslim women, mixed-sex Canadian Muslims, immigrant women, Canadian nongovernmental human rights organizations, and international progressive, feminist, and Muslim activists. Prominent individuals, including male Muslim scholars outside Canada, and high-profile Canadian white feminists, also endorsed the CCMW position against faith-based arbitration.

One of the most important allies was Women Living under Muslim Laws (WLUML). WLUML is a transnational network of women from Muslim countries who are dedicated to contesting local and patriarchal interpretations of Islam. By pooling and sharing the plurality of interpretations of Muslim law in the multiple jurisdictions where it is deployed, WLUML offers an internal critique of the allegedly fixed and invariant content of Islamic laws. By measuring state practice against international human rights norms, they also condemn the failure of states to honor their international obligations with respect to women's equality.[25] With the benefit of personal experience living in Islamic states and through the global clearinghouse of data gathered by WLUML, local opponents of Muslim arbitration tacitly encouraged the public to situate the Ontario proposal against a transnational landscape of Muslim governance. This tactic was politically astute and effective, though arguably somewhat inattentive to national context. By this I mean that it appealed to the fears of an uninformed public that enforcement of faith-based dispute resolution would somehow push Canada onto a slippery slope toward theocracy.

Rather than remaining a local provincial matter, the prospect of so-called Shar'ia courts drew attention from media, NGOs, and activists around the world. The Ontario government was keenly aware of the sudden and intense scrutiny focused on their handling of the issue. Much of this was accomplished through the assiduous efforts of the CCMW and the International Campaign against Shari'a Courts in Canada.[26] They utilized networks based on their multiple affiliations—as Canadians, as women, as immigrants, and as Muslims—to build solidarity with overlapping constituencies both domestically and transnationally. They convened conferences and workshops to publicize the issue, orchestrated demonstrations in front of Canadian embassies and consulates in major European cities,[27] organized international letter-writing campaigns to provincial politicians, and invited activists from around the world to Canada to publicize the negative impact of Islamic law on women's rights in various countries. While engagement by feminists from the north in women's struggles in the south is well documented,[28] the "Shari'a court" controversy is probably one of the few episodes where women from the global south were recruited to lend their support and expertise to a campaign by women situated in the global north.

A few individual women did figure prominently among the supporters of faith-based arbitration, but the list of participants compiled in the Boyd Report indicates that all but one ad hoc group of Muslim women opposed arbitration of family law matters and/or faith-based arbitration of family law matters. Religious bodies whose members already engaged in some form of faith-based dispute resolution, such as the Christian Legal Fellowship, the Salvation Army, B'nai Brith, the Sunni Masjid El Noor, and the Ismaili Muslims all supported faith-based arbitration. The Christian Legal Fellowship rather tellingly (if ironically) qualified their support by cautioning that "[i]t is much more difficult to balance competing rights of religious freedom and equal treatment under the law when a religious community does not believe that all members of the community are to be treated equally (for example if women are considered less worthy)."[29]

Some theorists of deliberative models of democracy query the exclusionary impact of the formal structures of public deliberation on marginalized groups. Whatever the general cogency of this point, it appears that the proponents of criminalizing FGM and the opponents of Muslim family law arbitration were demonstrably able to articulate their objectives and their reasons by reference to public norms that commonly recur in the arena of Western democratic political debate. I cannot say if this required distortion of their preferred mode of argumentation in order to accommodate the formal requirements of participation, but my point is simply that the mode of discourse did not impose an insurmountable barrier.

On the discursive level, appeals to the liberal principle of equality fit easily within both campaigns. This is unsurprising, given that both groups resisted a multiculturalist argument that recognition of cultural diversity requires respect for practices or processes that, in their view, systematically disadvantage encultured women. Both groups demanded equal benefit and protection of the general law, whether in the criminal or family law sphere. (Recall that explicit criminalization of FGM did not alter the content of the criminal law so much as provide greater precision.)

Opponents of enforceable, faith-based arbitration contended that whatever theoretical space existed for progressive interpretations of Islamic law, historical and contemporary precedent reliably predicted that it would be construed and applied in a manner that was relatively more patriarchal and detrimental to women than secular, public law. They also maintained that a commitment to Islam was not inimical to obedience to the secular laws of the state. Just as the CCMW promoted Canadian Muslim women's overlapping membership in national, religious, and transnational communities, so too did the organization insist that statist, spiritual, and cosmopolitan normative frameworks converged in their commitment to equality:

> CCMW holds that human rights as declared in the United Nations Universal Declaration are consistent with the ideals of Islam, and as believing Muslim women we can adhere to the Quran and to the U.N. Declaration. We see no contradiction between the rights and responsibilities as expressed in the divine message and those articulated by the nations of the world. As Canadian Muslim women we uphold the Charter of Rights and Freedoms and expect it to apply to us as fully as to any other Canadian.
>
> There is no incongruity between the Quran and the U.N. declaration which recognizes [that] the "inherent dignity and . . . the equal and inalienable rights of all members of the human family is the foundation of freedom, justice and peace in the world." Further, it states that "a common understanding of these rights and freedoms is of the greatest importance for the full realization of this pledge." We believe that all peoples must come to a recognition of the commonality and universality of these rights as they do not contradict nor are they limited to a specific culture or country.
>
> An important right in the Universal Declaration of Human Rights, Article 7 states "all are equal before the law and are entitled without any discrimination to equal protection of the law."[30]

Equality discourse thus served the aspirations of both groups. The more daunting task confronting the advocacy groups was to reconcile their stance with another (potentially competing) core principle of liberalism, namely, respect for liberty and individual autonomy. In both instances, the vehicle for its articulation was the legal doctrine of consent.

First, it was unproblematic for the anti-FGM advocates to assert on behalf of an even more vulnerable group (girls) that minors could never consent to FGM; indeed, it appears that the procedure is usually inflicted on girls. Nevertheless, the anti-FGM campaigners also opposed an exemption from liability "where the person is over 18 and no bodily harm resulted." Their position left little room for the (hypothetical) adult woman who freely consented to any form of the procedure.

Second, the prospect of adult Muslim women consenting to enforceable Islamic arbitration was not hypothetical. Nor could the CCMW easily escape a charge of parentalism toward other Muslim women. The CCMW took the position that the low legal threshold for valid consent to enter arbitration was simply inadequate to protect many women from coercion by spouses, kin, and community to accede to a process and to rules that would predictably leave them worse off than the ordinary civil justice system. They argued that the social, legal, and cultural vulnerability of many Muslim women in Canada sharply constricted the possibilities for genuine consent.

In adopting their respective positions, both groups risked appearing dismissive of autonomy and individual choice. These values stand at the core of most versions of the liberal tradition. Indeed, promotion of choice is touted as a specific virtue of the various forms of alternative dispute resolution. Additionally, their critique of consent also bore the undesirable risk of depriving encultured women of agency. Therefore, the manner in which these actors broached the issue of consent warrants closer attention.

Since FGM is usually performed on minors, the real issue regarding consent was whether the offense would encompass cosmetic genital surgery. In principle, cosmetic surgery among mainstream women was not a preoccupation of the advocates for FGM criminalization. However, a notable feature of the FGM intervention was a conscious refusal to segregate FGM from other disfiguring and misogynistic bodily practices. When responding to draft legislation, the group argued that describing alteration of women's genitalia as "therapeutic" or as not inflicting "bodily harm" is a Western conceit that can be traced back to the Victorian era, where clitoridectomies and removal of ovaries were performed to "cure" nymphomania, promiscuity, lesbianism, and masturbation:

Female genital surgeries continue to be practised today in the West that have questionable or no medical benefits for the woman herself—for example, "father's stitches" (extra stitches during episiotomy repair) to make the vaginal opening tighter after vaginal delivery, vaginoplasty for cosmetic purposes to "snug" the vagina to enhance male sexual pleasure, or so-called "labia reductions" and "female circumcisions."[31]

The submissions provocatively invert the lens back on the ideology and practices of the dominant culture to critique the defenses contained in the draft legislation, thereby disrupting the conventional dichotomy of the "liberated First World woman" and "oppressed Third World woman." One might argue that the alleged parallels between FGM and cosmetic genital surgery trivialize the physiologically and anatomically damaging effects of FGM. It is, however, worth noting that the range of practices encompassed by FGM does include forms that are not debilitating. Meanwhile, recent media accounts suggest the growing popularity of gratuitous cosmetic genital surgery in mainstream society, including among minors.[32]

In other words, it is not wholly fanciful to imagine an overlap between certain forms of FGM and elective genital surgery. To assert that they transpire in radically different cultural fields only begs the question. The salient point is that the proponents of explicit criminalization drew the comparison between FGM and cosmetic surgery not in the service of crude cultural relativism, but rather as a means of unsettling the legal meaning of bodily harm through attention to historical and contemporary mainstream practices. This, in turn, placed consent to cosmetic genital surgery in a social context of gender relations that made it more difficult to sustain consent to cosmetic genital surgery as a qualitatively different and unproblematic exercise of individual autonomy.

The discourse of liberty broadcast over two frequencies in the arbitration debate. One involved the individualist claim that offering devout Muslims, Christians, or Jews the choice of resolving their family law matters according to religious norms would respect and enhance the autonomy of group members. Another was the multiculturalist assertion that religious liberty entails the entitlement of religious groups to engage in family law dispute resolution mechanisms of their own design.

As noted above, the CCMW emphasized that many Muslim women are recent immigrants to Canada, financially and otherwise dependent on their husbands, isolated from the wider community by linguistic and cultural barriers, inculcated with a narrow, authoritarian, and inflexible version of Islam, and uninformed of their legal rights. Beyond acknowledging that real or apprehended domestic violence would vitiate consent to arbitration, legal criteria for ensuring free, informed consent to arbitration did not extend to an analysis of disparities in bargaining power or structural forms of coercion. Adapting a standard feminist critique of alternative dispute resolution, the CCMW disputed the presupposition that genuine consent could and would result if only participants were free from physical violence and received enough accurate information about the likely consequences of their participation in the process.

One evident difficulty with this advocacy strategy was that its focus on the most vulnerable Muslim women played directly into stereotypes of Muslim women as veiled and subordinated victims, Muslim men as sexist, violent abusers, and Islam as an inherently and essentially misogynist, retrograde, and oppressive faith. The CCMW deplored becoming instruments for the demonization of Islam, and reiterated that fidelity to Islam did not require adherence to traditional renditions of Muslim law:

> CCMW is cognizant that our stand, regarding Muslim law, places us in a difficult position. We are a pro-faith organization of Muslim women, we do not want to provide further ammunition to those who are keen to malign Islam and yet we must be honest about the issues which affect us within the Muslim and non-Muslim communities. Silence is not an option.[33]

Indeed, the CCMW's own leadership by example furnished the most compelling refutation of the stereotype of the meek and mute Muslim woman. Ironically, the Boyd Report used the CCMW's success against it. The fact that the CCMW "has worked hard since its inception within the various Islamic communities to enhance the role of women within the faith and to foster an understanding of the principle of equality so central to Islamic teachings" earned it the assignment of educating Muslim women "about rights, obligations and options with respect to family law."[34] The CCMW would, could, and should according to Boyd, empower Muslim women to choose or reject religious arbitration. While the CCMW did and does engage in grassroots education, it did not share Boyd's optimism that information alone would empower women to withhold consent.

With respect to the liberty claim on behalf of the religious community, it is important to recognize that the debate about arbitration transpired on a discursive terrain already circumscribed by the logic of privatization. The Arbitration Act already permitted private arbitration of family law disputes, already permitted parties to choose alternative rules (tacitly including religious law) and already permitted parties to shield outcomes from effective judicial oversight. To put it another way, faith-based arbitration and its normative driver, multiculturalism, were already nested within the domain of privatization and constrained by attendant neoliberal invocations of choice, liberty, and autonomy. Indeed, had proponents of faith-based arbitration asserted jurisdiction to erect a parallel system of justice *ab initio*, I suspect that the claims of equal application of law would have prevailed handily over competing claims of religious autonomy. For all of Canada's celebrated commitment to multiculturalism, demands for exceptional jurisdiction remain contentious even when asserted within the domain of federalism by Quebec or indigeneity by aboriginal people.

This local historical context of arbitration opened certain discursive doors for proponents and closed others for opponents of faith-based arbitration. Proponents, in effect, could correctly assert that they asked for nothing more than the benefit of the existing legal regime. Opponents could not easily target religious law from among the options permitted within the arbitration regime without allegedly breaching the constitutionally protected freedom of religion and/or commitment to multiculturalism.[35] Freedom of religion and multiculturalism could each be deployed—in good faith—in favor of state-enforced faith-based family law arbitration.

Opponents of Islamic arbitration were thus placed in the unenviable position of demanding retraction of some aspect of the status quo. The CCMW, along with the National Association of Women and Law (NAWL) and the National Organization of Immigrant and Visible Minority Women (NOIVMW), took a principled position that corresponded to the common denominator binding them as a coalition. In effect, they reargued the case against binding, enforceable arbitration of family law disputes: the privatization of family law via arbitration subverted the equality gains achieved in the legislation's default allocation of property, custody, spousal support, and child support.[36] To the extent that certain renditions of Islamic law were particularly inequitable toward women, devout Muslim women (especially recent immigrants) were especially vulnerable to forms of coercion that law does not recognize. Islamic family law arbitration was an exemplar of what is wrong with family law arbitration as currently practiced.

In presenting their arguments in this fashion, the CCMW performed a delicate balancing act similar to that of the women who advocated for explicit criminalization of FGM. On the one hand, they criticized certain practices, attitudes, and belief systems within their community; on the other hand, they refused to accede to an image of their faith as uniquely or intrinsically misogynistic. Nor would they identify Islamic law as the sole or primary menace to gender equality, but instead drew attention to the institutional configuration of family law into a regime that permits parties to "opt out" of public norms and public scrutiny, leaving vulnerable women of all faiths and ethnicities with inadequate legal protection.

This critique threatens the implicit assumption that the secular operation of the status quo provides the normative standard of fairness, gender equality, and justice against which faith-based alternatives should be measured. Just as the anti-FGM campaigners drew connections between FGM and distorted Western attitudes and practices toward the female body, the CCMW linked their opposition to Muslim arbitration to wider feminist concerns about the privatization of justice.[37] As I discuss below, neither gambit won wider support.

Securing Women's Citizenship through Law

How do participants in law reform perceive law's role in the advancement of citizenship? A common feature of both the FGM and Islamic tribunal campaigns was a pronounced ambivalence toward the mainstream justice system, expressed in an endorsement of it as a lesser evil rather than an unqualified good.

Advocacy groups who called for a Criminal Code amendment prohibiting FGM viewed law as a potent pedagogical instrument that would speak directly to their communities. Yet they could not discount the risks attendant in engaging with a criminal justice system known to be insensitive, or even hostile, to racialized and ethnic minorities. For example, the anti-FGM advocates proposed a two-tiered sentencing regime that would expose those who actually perform the operation to more serious penalties than the parents of the girl. In particular, they were concerned that lengthy imprisonment of parents would not be in the best interests of the child, and that racial bias would infect the sentencing process.[38]

As noted above, the groups also rejected a therapeutic defense, or a defense of consent, regardless of age or physical impact. Despite their success in obtaining explicit criminalization of FGM, the defense of consent remains where the person is over eighteen years of age and "there is no resulting bodily harm."[39] The combination of the therapeutic and consent defense effectively exempts mainstream practices of cosmetic genital surgery (labia reduction, vaginoplasty, etc.) from the ambit of deviant behavior. The law prohibiting FGM in Canada carries a maximum fourteen-year sentence for parents and perpetrators alike. Thus, measures proposed by the advocacy groups that did not distinguish FGM from mainstream forms of genital disfigurement, and sentencing provisions that attempted to balance protection of vulnerable girls and women against subjecting parents to racist elements of the criminal justice system, both failed to win acceptance. As it happens, only one incident of FGM has ever resulted in criminal charges being laid, and no one has ever been convicted in Canada with an offense related to FGM,[40] before or since the 1997 amendment.

Opponents of faith-based arbitration of family law matters could not credibly dispute the evidence that the mainstream justice system fails many participants in its management of family law cases. The evidence of overburdened court dockets, chronic backlogs, paltry legal aid funding, burgeoning numbers of unrepresented litigants, and generalist judges lacking experience and expertise is simply overwhelming. The process in general, and the adversarial trial in particular, are frequently criticized by feminists (among others) as alienating and intimidating experiences for all concerned. Indeed, avoiding the expense and ordeal of litigation is a major incentive driving parties into alternative dispute resolution, be it negotiation, mediation, or arbitration.

The best rejoinder that the CCMW and other opponents could muster in the face of irrefutable deficiencies in the justice system's management of family law matters was that, as between family law arbitration under the Arbitration Act and the default regime under the mainstream justice system, the latter was less bad in terms of exploiting and exacerbating women's inequality. In making this argument, the CCMW and its allies confronted strong resistance from the government (who sought to reduce pressures on the court system through ADR), individual participants in the system (who viewed arbitration as preferable to litigation), and an array of lawyers, mediators, and arbitrators (who supported ADR for both professional and principled reasons).

It emerges from reading submissions that proponents of the FGM law and opponents of faith-based arbitration imagined law's power in contradictory ways. In my view, the anti-FGM campaigners systematically underestimated the coercive power of the criminal justice system, while the anti–Islamic tribunal activists overestimated the equilibrating power of the civil justice system.

In January 2002, almost five years after the introduction of the FGM amendment of the Criminal Code, a Sudanese-Canadian couple in a small Ontario city became the first people charged under it. The charges were based on their elder daughter's allegation that she was subjected to FGM at the age of eleven, while in Canada, by an unidentified "practitioner."

The accused parents replied that the girl was infibulated in Sudan more than ten years earlier, at a time and place where the practice was inflicted on about 90 percent of females. The family left the country before the youngest daughter reached the age where the procedure is customarily performed, and the parents disavowed any intention or desire to inflict it on her in Canada. The alleged practitioner was never identified, apprehended, or charged. According to my conversations with the prosecutor and a defense counsel, as well as a female community leader, it seems that neither police, child welfare authorities, nor the lawyers consulted with anyone from the affected community for guidance on the cultural dynamics potentially in play. The family was wrenched apart through various state interventions, which included temporary detention of the parents in custody, apprehension of two daughters by child welfare authorities, and placement of the complainant daughter in foster care.

As is so often the case, real life did not follow the theoretical script. The parents did not attempt to justify the commission of FGM on their daughter by claiming ignorance of Canadian law or the primacy of cultural traditions over Canadian law. The sole issue was one of credibility in relation to when and where the FGM occurred. Media accounts of the case tended to ignore or gloss over this question, and instead used the prosecution as a segue to the stereotypical and entirely hypothetical scenario of parents who wilfully subject their daughters to FGM in Canada and attempt to defend the practice through invocation of cultural norms. Notably, in none of the media coverage did anyone step forward to justify the practice. Some tried to provide a contextual explanation of why it happens, but all opposed its perpetuation.

Some ten months after this case first came to the attention of state authorities, the Crown withdrew all charges against the parents. The prosecution's case depended entirely on the credibility of the complainant about when and where the FGM occurred, and the Crown eventually concluded that it could not obtain a conviction based on the complainant's testimony.[41] The complainant remained a ward of the court from December 2001 until late 2002, before returning to live with her family at the age of fifteen.

The experience of this family may well serve as an object lesson and a deterrent to any other parents in Canada who might contemplate subjecting their daughters to FGM. But this is not the scenario envisaged by those who advocated the new law. They appeared not to anticipate the trajectory of the criminal justice system once unleashed. When a criminal investigation is launched, the matter henceforth "belongs" to the state. Individual citizens exercise little or no influence on the exercise of state power. This dissociation is especially evident where the members of the group are largely absent from the ranks of state actors charged with investigating, prosecuting, and applying the law.

Apart from anything else, the fact that the daughter made a complaint of this nature to public authorities surely signals serious problems within the family, the sources of which are probably inseparable from the intense intergenerational stress that migration detonates in many immigrant families. But this is a different story about immigration, citizenship, and gender than the dominant narrative recited about FGM.

A central issue for feminists in both the FGM and the Islamic arbitration debates concerned the way secular law could protect encultured women from the risk of oppressive intracommunal practices. The answer regarding criminal law is straightforward, insofar as the criminal law prohibits conduct and punishes violations. But prohibiting Muslim couples from relying on religious authorities to arbitrate the consequences of marital dissolution was never on the horizon. The state has neither the will nor the resources to police informal dispute resolution; instead, the narrower question was whether the ordinary courts would enforce these religious judgments.

The power of law in this civil context is rather more limited than the media and the interlocutors attribute to it. Denying judicial enforcement to religious arbitration does not preclude parties from resorting to and abiding by the edicts of religious authorities. It will simply keep the practice in the shadows and out of the glare of public scrutiny. Moreover, parties have in the past and may continue in the future to rely on these authorities to mediate and to facilitate negotiations. Preserving enforceability of these domestic contracts means that the same concerns about religious arbitration will persist in the mediation and negotiation context.

Ultimately, law reform operated in both cases as a mechanism for reconfiguring intragroup power relations. Those who opposed FGM evidently felt that they had not been able to prevail on the strength of existing legal, medical, cultural, feminist, and religious arguments against the practice. Whether this was due to their status within the communities as women and/or as feminists, or the rejection of their arguments, or some combination of factors is not clear. In any event, passage of a specific law prohibiting FGM accorded them a tactical advantage over those who had disregarded them until that point, thereby improving their access to norm-generating discourse within their community. In effect, they used their public citizenship to leverage their position within their cultural community. Put another way, they boosted the heft of their citizenship qua encultured women.[42]

Outside of their communities, the form of visibility gained through the criminal law warrants a cautionary response. Recognition as perpetrators and victims of a culturally distinct crime is hardly the type of recognition ethnic communities usually seek. The mixed record of advocacy on this matter underscores the way cultural and racialized minorities take a gamble when they decide to engage with law, even for limited and strategic purposes. Activists within the community can control the form and content of internal grassroots education, and may believe that the role of law should be confined to that of preemptive deterrent. They may carefully craft a balanced approach to legislative reform, only to see one side of the balance discarded by legislators. They cannot control the way the power of the criminal law, once triggered, will be exercised by mainstream police, prosecutors, and judges against the members of their community who allegedly transgress the law. Nor can they determine how the law will be read by mainstream culture and the impact this will have on the affected communities.

I suspect—along with activists in other jurisdictions who opposed criminalization—that the law will in fact be read as mainstream (white, Judeo-Christian) Canadians inscribing their moral superiority on (African Muslim) bodies through the text of the criminal law. The fact that the proponents of the law came from the communities who are the law's object will probably remain unknown to the vast majority of Canadians. This is the case because the de facto marginalized status of Canadians of African origin means that they are unlikely to be recognized as law makers. Instead, they are more frequently characterized as law breakers, a perception that can only be exacerbated by the anti-FGM law itself.

I would add here that once a new criminal offense is added to the Criminal Code, it is rarely removed. For example, the Criminal Code still prohibits dueling. Even if FGM ceases to be practiced, and even if no one is ever convicted of the crime, I suspect that an offense named "FGM" will communicate a message to and about certain Canadians for a very long time.

The denial of judicial enforcement to faith-based arbitral awards was celebrated as a triumph for the CCMW and its allies, even though most acknowledged that it could simply drive (or maintain) the practice underground. The complex and crucial question of the institutional interface between public justice and private ordering was largely deflected throughout the debate and remains unaddressed.[43] Cast against broader normative debates about the state, multiculturalism, and gender, the issue of public judicial supervision of private dispute resolution may appear parochial and technical. Yet, it bears reiterating that this is precisely the locus where the relationship among the state, the community, and the individual will be managed.

These concerns are not intended to suggest that the outcome in either case was wrong. However, they lead me to question Melissa Williams's proposal that a "difference principle as applied to reasons" might justify collective decisions based on reasons supplied by marginalized groups "even when those reasons are not immediately available from one's own social or cultural experience." I am skeptical that deferral to the reasons of marginalized groups can substitute for persuasion on the substantive norms at issue. Deference clearly encounters an obstacle when confronted with diverse opinions, as illustrated by disparate views among Muslim women about religious arbitration. This does not preclude struggling to achieve an "enlarged perspective" that might make one more receptive to persuasion by hitherto unfamiliar arguments, but such a stance is not reducible to deference.

Once one takes intragroup diversity seriously, the availability of deference as a method of resolving intergroup perspectival differences is constrained by the absence of a formal mechanism for ranking different voices within a specified community. This is especially the case if the community in question is too large, diverse, or diffuse to permit identification of leaders, or if the process by which leaders emerge raises doubts about whether they can be considered truly representative. One might adopt a Rawlsian position requiring that accomodationist policies by the state ought to prioritize improving—or at least not worsening—the welfare of the worst off in a cultural community. However, this is not tantamount to deference on the means of accomplishing that objective. Ultimately, one cannot escape the need for argument and persuasion, whether expressed through logocentric analysis, narrative, deliberation, or other means.

If one assumes that there were no voices from the affected communities willing to speak against explicit criminalization as a necessary means of deterring FGM in Canada, I concede that it would be highly problematic for nonmembers of the community to resist the campaign, especially on the grounds that legislative action would not be in the best interests of their own community. Such a stance would appear patronizing at best. Both the desired benefits and the apprehended costs of explicitly criminalizing FGM will redound to the advocates' respective communities. If there is a compelling reason for deference, it arises mainly from the empirical uncertainty regarding the effects of the legislation, and the fact that those who will feel its impact are perhaps in the better position to select which risks to assume.

In the case of Islamic arbitration, two factors rendered deference on policy choices impracticable. The first was the lack of unanimity among Muslim women, the group posited as most vulnerable to the greatest harm from enforceable, faith-based arbitration. The second was that the choice of policy instrument had a direct bearing on who constitutes the pool of affected persons. Excluding Muslim or faith-based or family law arbitration altogether from the purview of the Arbitration Act affects progressively broader constituencies in different ways. The first affects Muslims, the second affects all faith-based groups, and the third affects all parties to family law disputes.

Encultured Women's Citizenship

What lessons do these two episodes offer about the meaning of citizenship and gender among encultured women? First, it is evident that some encultured women can and do express political citizenship in the public sphere of law reform, deploying the form and content of discourse that hold currency in that domain.[44] Second, it should not escape notice that in both episodes, encultured women deliberately framed their respective issues with analyses of gender and race that transcended the cultural specificity of their situation.

Yet, both the anti-FGM advocates and the CCMW conspicuously failed to persuade their audience at precisely those moments where they enlarged the scope of analysis beyond their own cultural community. It is certainly true that advocates for law reform rarely get everything they want. Nevertheless, as I have argued elsewhere, when cultural practices are scrutinized through the prism of equality, mainstream liberal social and legal practices almost invariably operate as the normative referent against which other cultures will be judged and solutions devised.

Reminding the mainstream of the gendered impact of the privatization of family law, or the misogyny embedded in "cosmetic" genital surgery, or the racism of the criminal justice system, disrupts this conceit, especially when the critique comes from an "other" who demands equal protection of the law but stubbornly refuses to be rescued by it. In this sense, the rejection of policy options that internalize broader race and gender critiques warrants scrutiny beyond an assessment of the merits of a given proposal. It also hints at a tendency to confine the exercise of encultured women's citizenship to the precise space where their various identities intersect.

This "particularized citizenship" manifests in at least two ways. First, to paraphrase Gayatri Spivak, while white women may now join white men in the "civilizing mission" of rescuing brown women from brown men, brown women cannot be seen to be saving white women from white men.[45] Second, it is not so much that the encultured woman is put to the invidious choice of "either your culture or your rights"; it is rather that she is not yet fully heard when she replies "neither, as presently constituted, and both, as I envision them."

By offering an account of the "particularized citizenship" of encultured women, I do not purport to describe a necessary, permanent, or universal condition. The exercise of citizenship is an iterative process, not a static end state. Over time and at its best, it does not merely enable traversal of the polity's internal borders; it challenges, reimagines, and transforms the borders themselves.

NOTES

1. The author thanks Anver Emon, Robert Leckey, Judith Resnik, and an anonymous reviewer for insightful comments and suggestions.

2. Vicki Jackson defines public citizenship as "an act involving visible participation in public processes with the capacity to influence or direct governmental decisions affecting the lives of other members of the polity." See Vicki Jackson, "Citizenships, Federalisms, and Gender," in this volume. The multiple meanings ascribed to citizenship and the complex interrelationship among these various conceptions is elegantly surveyed in Linda Bosniak, "Citizenship," in *The Oxford Handbook of Legal Studies*, eds. Peter Cane and Mark Tushnet (Oxford: Oxford University Press, 2003), 183.

3. Ayelet Shachar, *Multicultural Jurisdictions* (Cambridge: Cambridge University Press, 2001), 5.

4. See, e.g., Susan Moller Okin, *Is Multiculturalism Bad for Women?*, eds. Joshua Cohen, Matthew Howard, and Martha C. Nussbaum (Princeton, NJ: Princeton University Press, 1999).

5. The nearest to a public endorsement I have seen is in Doriane Lambelet Coleman's description of the "Seattle Compromise" in which a Seattle hospital agreed to perform a symbolic circumcision by nicking the labia of female infants and drawing blood. Her article described Somalis who warned that they would subject their daughters to traditional (debilitating) circumcision in the absence of the proposed alternative. Doriane Lambelet Colemen, "The Seattle Compromise: Multicultural Sensitivity and Americanization," *Duke Law Journal* 47 (1998): 723

6. I thank Ruth Rubio-Marin for this helpful phrase.

7. This hypothesis is based on the fact that in Canada, unlike in Britain and France, girls have not been showing up in hospital emergency wards suffering the consequences of botched procedures.

8. Canada Criminal Code, R.S.C., ch. C-46, §§ 215, 267, 268 (1985).

9. In 1993, the Criminal Code was amended to add the offense of removing a child under the age of eighteen with the intention of committing, outside Canada, an act that would constitute an aggravated assault or an assault causing bodily harm if committed in Canada. The objective was to deter parents from evading Canadian law by taking their daughters to be circumcised overseas. The effect of the revision was to criminalize taking a girl out of Canada with the intent of subjecting her to FGM elsewhere. Canada thereby extended its criminal law jurisdiction extraterritorially to take precedence over competing normative frameworks in other jurisdictions. Canada Criminal Code, R.S.C., ch. C-46, § 4.1 (1985) (as am.).

10. Canada Criminal Code, R.S.C., ch. C-46, § 268(3) (1985) (as am.).

11. Id. § 268(3)(b).

12. See David Fraser, "The First Cut Is *Not* the Deepest: Deconstructing Female Genital Mutilation and the Criminalization of the Other," *Dalhousie Law Journal* 18 (1995): 310. It is important to recall that the criminalization of migrants did not begin with September 11. One strand of anti-immigrant backlash from the 1990s appropriated migrant women's activism around domestic violence, FGM, and the *hijab* to argue for immigration restrictions from so-called nontraditional source countries because male nationals did not respect women's human rights.

13. My thanks to Sadia Gassim, who organized the petition I refer to here, Lucya Spencer of the National Organization of Immigrant and Visible Minority Women (NOIVM), and Khamisa Baya of Women's Health in Women's Hands, each of whom generously gave their time to discuss their involvement in the legislative process with me. I am also grateful to Ms. Baya for sharing with me an extensive package of submissions and briefs from various participants.

14. FGM Legal Community Committee, "Brief to the Parliamentary Standing Committee on Justice and Legal Affairs Re: Bill C-27," Nov. 26, 1996, 7 (on file with author).

15. Women's Health in Women's Hands, "Brief on Bill C-27," Nov. 26, 1996, 23 (on file with author).

16. See, e.g., FGM Legal Community Committee, "Brief to Parliamentary Standing Committee," supra note 14, 29; African Canadian Legal Clinic, "Bill C-27," 13 (on file with author). The National Organization of Visible and Minority Women of Canada also created a Workshop Manual on FGM as a resource for organizations and groups interested in educating their communities about FGM.

17. Canada Arbitration Act, S.O., ch. 17 (1991).

18. Canada Arbitration Act, S.O., ch. 17, § 35 (1991).

19. Marion Boyd, *Dispute Resolution in Family Law: Protecting Choice, Promoting Inclusion*, December 20, 2004, at 5, *available at* http://www.attorneygeneral.jus.gov.on.ca/english/about/pubs/boyd/fullreport.pdf.

20. Boyd's main proposals for change fell into three categories. First, she suggested building more procedural safeguards into the existing arbitration regime in order to ensure that individual consent to arbitrate is voluntary and informed. Second, Boyd made a number of recommendations directed at professionalizing the practice of arbitration and mediation. Third, Boyd proposed maintaining an archive of redacted arbitral decisions that would be publicly available and form the basis for a periodic governmental review of the practice of faith-based arbitration. Boyd, *Dispute Resolution*, supra note 19, 134–44.

21. Ibid., 141.

22. Ibid., 134.

23. Family Statute Law Amendment Act, S.O., ch. 1 (2006).

24. Id. ch. 1, § 2.2(1)(b).

25. For a fuller description of the activities of Women Living under Muslim Laws, see Valentine Moghadam, "Global Feminism, Citizenship, and the State: Negotiating Women's Rights in the Middle East and North Africa," in this volume; Madhavi Sunder, "Piercing the Veil," *Yale Law Journal* 112 (2003): 1399.

26. The International Campaign against Sharia Court in Canada appears to be the brainchild of its coordinator, Homa Arjomand, whose extraordinary personal commitment to the issue is evident from the organization's website: www.nosharia.com (last accessed April 6, 2007).

27. Demonstrations were held in autumn 2005 in London, Paris, Stockholm, Dusseldorf, and The Hague. See www.nosharia.com (last accessed April 7, 2006).

28. See Valentine Moghadam, "Global Feminism, Citizenship, and the State: Negotiating Women's Rights in the Middle East and North Africa" in this volume.

29. Boyd, *Dispute Resolution*, supra note 19, 68.

30. Canadian Council of Muslim Women, *Position Statement on the Proposed Implementation of Sections of Muslim Law [Sharia] in Canada,*, May 25, 2004, available at http://www.ccmw.com/ Position%20Papers/Position_Sharia_Law.htm.

31. Women's Health in Women's Hands, "Brief on Bill C-27," supra note 15, 7.

32. Jill Mahoney, "Designer Vaginas: The Latest in Sex and Plastic Surgery," *Globe and Mail* (Toronto), August 13, 2005, A1.

33. Canadian Council of Muslim Women, *Position Statement on the Proposed Implementation of Sections of Muslim Law [Sharia] in Canada*, supra note 30.

34. Boyd, *Dispute Resolution*, supra note 19, 131.

35. Similarly, one could not single out Islamic law for exclusion from the arbitration regime without meeting the accusation of discrimination as between religions.

36. The overarching concern about the privatization of justice applies to mediation as well as arbitration. A rich body of feminist and critical legal scholarship in the 1980s and 1990s addressed these issues, primarily focusing on mediation. See, e.g., Trina Grillo, "The Mediation Alternative: Process Dangers for Women," *Yale Law Journal* 100 (1991): 1545; Isabelle R. Gunning, "Diversity Issues in Mediation: Controlling Negative Cultural Myths," *Journal of Dispute Resolution* (1995): 55; Martha Shaffer, "Divorce Mediation: A Feminist Perspective," *University of Toronto Faculty Law Review* 46 (1988): 162. For a more recent reflection on mediation within religious communities, see Clark Freshman, "The Promise and Perils of 'Our' Justice: Psychological, Critical, and Economic Perspectives on Communities and Prejudices in Mediation," *Cardozo Journal of Conflict Resolution* 6 (2004): 1. For a recent iteration of the argument against arbitration of family law issues, see Andre R. Imbrogno, "Arbitration as an Alternative to Divorce Litigation: Redefining the Judicial Role," *Capital University Law Review* 31 (2003): 413.

37. Judith Resnik offers a creative historical glimpse into the architecture of justice (literally and metaphorically) to critique post-9/11 practices of privatizing justice through the "devolution of the power of judgement to private processes" that impose state power "without seeming to need to show it to legitimate it." Guantanamo Bay is the iconic example. Judith Resnik, "Places of Power: From Renaissance Town Halls to Guantanamo Bay" (paper presented at University of Cincinnati College of Law, Cincinnati, OH, March 29, 2006), 38.

38. According to the brief submitted by Women's Health in Women's Hands,

> These concerns regarding overly lengthy incarceration of parents and/or guardians are neither unfounded nor exaggerated, and are strengthened by documented reports of endemic systemic ethno-racial discrimination in the criminal justice system and similar biases in the sentencing process of the judicial system. The result of such institutionalized discrimination is not only higher than average conviction rates but also relatively lengthier incarceration periods for Canadians from ethno-racial communities. (Women's Health in Women's Hands, "Brief on Bill C-27," supra note 15, 14)

39. Canada Criminal Code, R.S.C., ch. C-46, § 268(3)(b) (1985) (as am.).

40. The significance of this fact is unclear. Maybe FGM is not happening in Canada, maybe it is not happening anymore, or maybe it goes unreported by members of the affected communities and undetected by teachers, doctors, social workers, etc.

41. James Ramsay (Crown Prosecutor, St. Catherine's Ontario), in telephone interview with the author, June 18, 2002.

42. For an elaboration of the idea of the "heft of citizenship," see Audrey Macklin, "Who Is the Citizen's Other? Considering the Heft of Citizenship," *Theoretical Inquiries in Law* 8 (2007): 333–66.

43. A detailed account of a desirable institutional arrangement lies beyond the scope of this chapter. However, a compelling argument could be made that vulnerable women will be better protected where private processes *are* enforceable by the ordinary courts, but only on condition that the outcomes are automatically and mandatorily reviewed by ordinary courts for substantive alignment with basic norms of fairness, gender equality, and responsiveness to material need. The onus would not be on the vulnerable party to seek judicial protection. Religious authorities would have an incentive to adopt legal interpretations that conform to these basic norms in order to secure the benefits of respect and recognition that come with public enforcement.

44. The Canadian Council of Muslim Women's own research indicates that it is exceptional. A report commissioned by the CCMW in 2006 concluded that "Muslim women tend to be disengaged from the civic and political life" in Canada, as evidenced by low levels of civil and political participation by Muslim women. CCMW, "Muslim Women Embrace Canada as Home but Remain on the Margins of Civic And Socio-Economic Life of the Country" (press release), November 17, 2006, available at http://www.ccmw.com/Press%20Release/News%20 Release%20_Engaging%20Muslim%20Women.doc.

45. Gayatri Chakravorty Spivak, "Can the Subaltern Speak?," in *Marxism and the Interpretation of Culture*, ed. Cary Nelson and Lawrence Grossberg (Chicago: University of Illinois Press, 1988), 297. Thanks to an anonymous reviewer for reminding me of Spivak's trenchant phrase.

9

‖‖

Multiculturalism, Gender, and Rights

David Jacobson

The status of women has loomed large in recent times in immigration matters in the courts and in public opinion. Honor killings, forced arranged marriages, female genital mutilation, "ritualized" rape, and other such matters now mark contemporary discussion on immigration and immigrant communities, especially in Europe. Much as ethnic and ideological criteria framed debates about immigration in the past, so questions about gendered practices do today; and much as issues of ethnicity and ideology reflected then-present global fissures, so gendered practices today tell a story of deeper global, cultural, and religious fault lines.

This intersection of immigration and women's rights has produced a mixed response from feminist scholars. If judicially it appears that the rights of women and other gendered groups such as gays have—as I will argue—on the whole trumped the claims of unfettered multiculturalism, the responses of others, from political figures to academics, has been less certain. Notably, for a not insignificant group of feminists, postcolonial sensibilities have, in effect, trumped women's rights—at least when it comes to women in immigrant communities.

I have two objectives here. The primary goal is to describe and suggest explanations for the response of the courts to the sometimes competing demands of immigrant communities, multicultural aspirations, and women's rights (and on occasion those of other gendered groups). The secondary goal is to suggest that the argument criticizing concerns about women's rights in some immigrant communities as obscuring repression of women in Western countries is empirically and normatively on weak footing. Such a critique is (unwittingly) making for a distressing retreat in the global movement for women's rights, on issues as fundamental as bodily integrity.

Let me begin with the core argument: I suggest that the evolution of international norms of justice, along with erosion in the sovereign ambit of the nation-state, has created a tendency in the courts to privilege individual "bodily self-possession" and free choice, including that of women, and that this is leading the courts to uphold women's human rights to bodily integrity and freedom from patriarchal and communal fiat. This development is, in practice at least, geographically bounded and, in Western countries, socially and politically fraught vis-à-vis some immigrant communities.

The Stories behind the Violence

Statistics on violence tell two stories. One regards the events between perpetrators and victims. Curiously, however, the deeper, socially more fundamental story is hidden. For example, although the number of suicides is proportionally small, the patterns of this particular form of violence reflect significant, underlying social phenomena. The social fabric of whole communities or demographic categories is revealed in findings such as the historical tendency for Protestants to commit suicide at greater rates than Catholics, or the fact that single people commit suicide more often than married people, or that suicide rates have tended to go down in wartime. And so the story of violence against women is the story of the status of women more broadly.

The problem of violence and discrimination against women is, however, further compounded in communal and social contexts where the violence is actually viewed as justifiable. Rather than being labeled as a deviant act to be extirpated, just as suicide is viewed largely as beyond the pale, the degradation of women is normatively acceptable within certain subsets of immigrant and other communities. This is the case even if such practices are at variance with the accepted norms of the larger society. We see this clash of scripts play out with painful regularity in Europe and, to a lesser extent, in the United States.

Violence and discrimination against women is not, of course, limited to any one group, and no one community or religion can be characterized on these grounds. However, if we are to try to address this fundamental problem, we need to study the varying patterns in the status of women across different sociological groupings or subgroupings and draw out the underlying bases for such differences. The statistics on violence against women are very difficult to ascertain; even when a sophisticated institutional structure is in place (as in Britain, where special units have been set up by the police on domestic violence and on violence in immigrant communities, as well as an honor killings unit), there is a strong likelihood of marked underreporting. Suicide statistics, if analytically intriguing, are open to different forms of interpretation. That said, we do know to a good degree of suggestive detail from United Nations cross-national data and rankings on gender-related development (an index that considers life expectancy, adult literacy, enrollment in education, and income), gender empowerment measures (women with seats in Parliament, female legislators, senior officers and managers, female professional and technical workers, and the ratio of income vis-à-vis males), and gender inequality in education and women's political participation that the cross-national differences are stark and Western countries consistently occupy almost all the top twenty-five places.[1]

As immigrants migrate they take with them, or shed, different cultural practices. The patterns here are complex, and sociologists and demographers have for decades been seeking to track the variegated patterns of structural, cultural, and spatial integration, and the way these patterns shift from first- to second- to third-generation immigrants. There have been related discussions about assimilation and multiculturalism. I am not aware of work that has systemically distilled research on the impact of the host societies on different immigrant groups as regards women's empowerment and freedom from violence, or other discriminatory practices within subsets of immigrant communities. But much suggestive information, from the patterns in sending countries to newspaper reports to available statistics to court cases, indicates a situation of significant concern for many immigrant women.

The cases reported in the media display a grim, repetitive quality, such as the following examples from the United Kingdom. Abdalla Yones, a Kurd living in London, cut his daughter Heshu's throat, leaving her to bleed to death. This followed months of beatings before he killed her in what was described as a frenzied knife attack. He had disapproved of his sixteen-year-old daughter's "Western way of life" and her Christian boyfriend. In this recent case, the judge, sentencing Yones to life in prison, stated that the killing was "a tragic story arising out of irreconcilable differences between traditional Kurdish values and those of Western society."[2]

Samaira Nazir sought to elope with her Afghan boyfriend after rejecting Pakistani suitors chosen by her family. She never got the chance: she was killed with eighteen stab wounds inflicted by her brother and cousin at her home in Southall, England. Violence, of course, does not always involve murder: girls are reportedly beaten up, for example, for carrying cell phones, seen as signs of the modern world. The British government set up an agency in 2006 to help British citizens whose parents are trying to force them to marry partners from overseas. The unit deals with upwards of three hundred cases a year.[3]

More than a dozen women are victims of honor killings each year in the United Kingdom, and, when the whole range of "honor offenses" are counted, they are estimated to be in the thousands. Such purported offenses include abduction, forced abortion, rape or victimization because of relationships with outsiders, or sexual orientation.[4]

Outrage has been expressed across a number of Western countries regarding the cultural practice in which parts or all of a young girl's external genitalia are excised, also known as female genital mutilation or cutting. When the Harborview Medical Center in Seattle agreed to perform a symbolic "female circumcision" to serve the local Somali community, whereby a small cut would be made to the prepuce (the hood above the clitoris) and no tissue would be excised, and with children old enough to understand and consent to the procedure, the hospital was besieged by an angry response from the public and politicians. Harborview consequently retreated from its effort, even though it was an attempt to prevent local Somalis from taking their daughters to their homeland, where their daughters were at risk of complete removal of the clitoris and labia.[5]

The Limits of Multiculturalism

Cases like this cast light on debates on multiculturalism and postnationalism and, more broadly, on changing patterns of political and social engagement. The rights and status of women prove to be remarkable prisms in part because the multicultural project, and the largely unproblematic depiction of transnationalism and postnationalism, splinters on women's issues.

Postnationalists have argued that, in essence, through international human rights norms, we have an emerging category of "personhood," that is to say, a social and legal identity or claim that, in principle, transcends states. States, in turn, have become much more accountable to persons within their jurisdiction under international human rights law. The dramatic rise in dual citizenship, both in its increasing legal sanction and in carriers of dual nationalities, has often been seen as an expression of this new postnationalism. Different threads followed from, or were implied in, these arguments: postnationality led to the suggestion of "transnational citizens" and, more broadly, an assertion of a growing phenomenon of transnational communities. And insofar as postnationality eroded the legitimacy of homogenously defining nation-states through assimilation or exclusion, it was related to the practice of multiculturalism.

The problem with the debates on multiculturalism, postnationalism, and transnationalism is that the way these social patterns are incorporated *institutionally* (in the institutions of government and society) has not been sufficiently elucidated. Individuals within themselves may represent both transnational and national elements at different times or even simultaneously, for example, expressing Dominican pride by voting in "homeland" elections and patriotically supporting, or even fighting for, the United States in something like consecutive moments. As the ambiguity of the concepts of postnational and transnational attest, trying to tease out what these concepts mean, and who exactly are these "postnationals" and "transnationals," has proven notoriously difficult to ascertain when we are trying to delineate discrete groups and individuals. Rather, I argue that we need to locate the institutional "matrix" through which such activities are expressed.

In this chapter, I consider forms of political participation, less from the perspective of individuals or groups mobilizing politically than with regard for the legal and institutional channels that enable political or social engagement. I concentrate primarily on the United States and Europe. By taking this institutional approach, we can attain a more nuanced understanding of social and political practices than blanket terms like "national," "postnational," or "multicultural" suggest. Indeed, it may be a way of getting at the evolving form of the nation-state itself, such as the growing role of judicial bodies and integration in international legal and normative frameworks.[6] The institutional configuration of the state allows us to essentially "map" the patterns of political and social engagement facilitated by these institutions. This also addresses the problem of delineating what groups, which individuals, and at what moments transnationalism or multiculturalism is being expressed. When one speaks of multiculturalism and transnational communities, the place of women can be ambiguous. When we take this institutional approach, I argue that women's status (and that of "gender minorities" more broadly) actually becomes much less ambiguous, and the renderings of multiculturalism more nuanced.

Put another way, viewing immigration and immigrant communities through the lens of gender reveals the institutional limits of multiculturalism and transnationalism.

In so doing, I argue that the state, which in these debates tends to take on a static and somewhat opaque quality, is in fact fluid, dynamic, and often contradictory. It is constantly evolving in ways that play a critical role in determining the patterns whereby individuals engage "the state" or one another. Part of the fluid character of the state in this regard is that it is made up of multiple institutions that are sometimes at cross-purposes, and policy on, say, immigration matters can be formed in competitive or symbiotic ways within the state itself.

Judicial Politics

I suggest here that the institutional configuration of the state has changed significantly in recent decades, with a growing role of judicial and judicial-like bodies. This is a development that has been concomitant with, and partly related to, the growing role of international human rights norms. A couple of points need to be stressed here. In contrast to democratic citizenship with its emphasis on active involvement of the citizenry in self-government, this "judicialization," which involves not just courts, but today infuses almost any social organization, enables what I refer to as the "proprietary self." "Proprietary self" may have a negative tone to it, but I am using it descriptively, and I will momentarily expand upon it. By "judicialization" I am referring to judicial or quasi judicial bodies replacing formerly nonjudicial proceedings of administration, legislation, the executive branch, or in dispute settlement with judicial arbitration. The term "judicialization" can also describe a usually partial shift of authority from the legislature and the executive branch to the judiciary.[7]

An example of the use of judicial agency, and this form of political engagement that has grown in recent decades (changing the nature of the state in the process), was a ruling by the European Court of Human Rights that "closed off" the sex of a spouse as a criterion in determining immigration status. An individual's sex in this context ceased to be a category that member states could turn to in determining who could enter or not enter their country. The 1985 judgment was triggered by (women) applicants, resident in the United Kingdom, whose foreign husbands had been refused permission to remain with or join them under the U.K. immigration rules of the time. (These rules did not preclude men settled in the United Kingdom from bringing in their foreign wives.) This and many other judicial rulings have had an especially striking impact on Britain, where the political system has traditionally been one in which the sovereign Parliament was paramount, and the courts were second-ary, possessing very limited powers of judicial review. British judges have been much emboldened by turning to European legal rulings and instru-ments.[8] Judicialization is equally striking on the international level. Citing the World Trade Organization's arbitration mechanisms, two law scholars note how "legal briefs are replacing diplomatic notes, and judicial decrees are displacing political compromises."[9]

Through a panoply of rights, such judicial agency enables individuals to pursue "private" cultural, economic, social, and political goals. This de-velopment, of the proprietary individual empowered through judicially sanctioned rights, has not supplanted the democratic forms of political engagement—expressed through the legislative and executive branches, and through other forms of popular action—but has created a distinct form of political participation.

The cultural dimension of multiculturalism is derivative of the propri-etary individualism described here. Cultural groups are derivative in the sense that cultural, religious, and ethnic expression is legitimate, insofar as it is grounded in the determination of individuals of their own, volun-tary self-expression to celebrate a cultural identity of one kind or another. In so doing, however, traditional cultures that have relied on communal or patriarchal custom or fiat are fundamentally changed. We can see this effect when women's rights clash with patriarchal culture; in the great pre-ponderance of cases the rights of women trump the claims of such cul-tures, legally and in public opinion.[10]

Self-Possession

Nationally based courts are now more likely to reach across borders of the nation-state, whereby judges invoke international law, and, more strik-ingly, courts like the European Court of Justice and the European Court of Human Rights now make judgments enforceable across almost a whole continent. One could even argue that the European Union itself is pri-marily a judicial, administrative, and regulative mechanism, and in this respect Europe has led the charge of "judicialization."[11]

This process has expressed itself not only across borders but "vertically" as well. International and transnational norms (usually but not always in an explicit legal sense) are cascading downward, especially in the democratic world, leading to and reinforcing a surge of domestic rule making and regulations. This cascade impacts not only government agencies but also private and corporate institutions. Thus this process goes beyond high-profile court cases: it is explicit in public and private organizations' rules on "diversity," "hostile work environments" (regarding both ethnic and gender matters), and sexual harassment. It is in this larger sense that we must understand judicialization, the seemingly exponential growth in administrative rules, and the overarching role of human rights, rather than narrowly focusing on actual litigation and the actual litigants (though these are centrally important), or even the courts themselves. Although less noticeable, legal hearings within private and public organizations have surged as well, alongside and in response to growing judicial review in Europe and in the United States.[12] This phenomenon cuts across, if unevenly, the democratic world and is particularly marked in Europe.

The expansion of judicial rights, domestically and internationally, is associated with the growing salience of the *proprietary individual*. What is meant by that concept? I have noted elsewhere a revealing historical development in the English language. The use of the term "self" as a prefix—such as "self-realization" or "self-defense"—first appears in the English language, according to the Oxford English Dictionary, in the sixteenth century and multiplies rapidly in use in the seventeenth century. The significance is, if I may put it this way, self-evident: it indicates the emerging importance of the individual qua individual, rather than as an extension of social categories like class, guild, or nation.

This semantic change mirrors the Protestant Reformation, which put the individual and his (and sometimes her) conscience front and center, pushing central religious authority to the background. It marks the beginning of a very gradual move towards the presumption that the individual is the proprietor of her own self, be it in terms of the body or the mind. The individual *owns* herself, and thus *chooses* what to do with herself. The proprietary self is about ownership and choice, and is tightly related to self-reflexiveness. It could also be termed an "autobiographical self." Implicit in the concept is also the individual as consumer, which develops only in the nineteenth and twentieth centuries, but I will leave this for discussion in another work.[13]

The proprietary self evolves slowly and unevenly, in both geographic and sociological respects, and is mirrored by the centuries-long expansion of rights and institutions that underwrite the individual. The expansion of rights that accelerated through revolutionary changes in government and at the impetus of social movements was mostly about the access of individuals, at first filtered by race, class, and sex, to the civic and political arena. In the last forty years, in contrast, we see the growing stress on postnational rights—rights that inhere in the individual per se, independent of nationality or communal affiliation.

A trajectory can be seen through this process, at least among democracies, of the erosion of "communal sovereignties." That is to say, the assumption that individuals—who they are and how they are defined—are predicated on communal constructs has gradually given way to an assumption that communal constructs are instead, normatively speaking, predicated on individuals. In the "ideal-typical" sense, communities are a function of individual choice, not ascription. Religion, race, nationhood, and their construction, reflect this. Signposts along the way include the following: the Catholic Church loses its monopoly in Western Europe; slavery based on race is revoked in places across the world; dual citizenship, once thought akin to bigamy, expands dramatically and globally from the 1990s in law and in practice.

In the struggle for woman's "self-possession," we observe many markers. It is a process that is geographically and sociologically very uneven. One can safely say, I think, that the constraints on women—legal, political, and social—are the most prominent barriers in the world today to the expansion of the proprietary self. The global cultural divides on issues of sex and gender mirror past struggles over race, nationhood, and class. Struggles on these issues still continue, but sex and gender have been given priority. This is the salient finding in a recent, highly publicized study regarding Western countries and the Islamic world: if there is a cultural divide, issues related to gender and sexuality are central.[14] In this light, the struggle of women's movements in Muslim countries takes on a particularly difficult set of negotiations, aptly brought out in Valentine Moghadam's chapter in this volume.

This trajectory also points to a broader evolution of the forms of political engagement. Indeed, issues of proprietary individualism have supplemented, and even in part supplanted, more republican and democratic modes of politics.[15] The proprietary self suggests the ability of the individual to act as an "initiatory" and "self-reliant" actor, and to be an active participant in determining his or her life, including the determination of social, political, cultural, ethnic, religious, and economic ends.[16] The foundational mechanism of self-possession is the dense web of legal rights and restraints, which are mediated or adjudicated by judicial, quasi judicial, and administrative bodies of different kinds. In contrast to the past, little in life today is beyond the potential reach of the law. Its tentacles, for better or for worse, reach into every sphere of life, from families to corporations to nation-states. Individual access to the dense web of judicially mediated legal rights and restraints has become perhaps the primary mechanism of individual "self-determination," rather than the traditional democratic route of voting, civic participation, and political mobilization.

Integrating Gender

What this analysis suggests is that we have largely missed the mark in the debate over postnationalism, transnationalism, and multiculturalism. We have done so not in terms of favoring one side or another's argument, but in terms of how we have *framed* the discussion.

What if we approach these issues "institutionally"? Rather than focusing on the emergence of transnational communities, postnationalism, or even multiculturalism as the most significant, if not fully articulated, development, we should recognize the growing salience of proprietary individualism. From this perspective, we see the significance of women's rights, particularly in the area of culture in its immigrant or national variants.

Self-possession concerns the individual, not families or even ethnic and religious groups. This is an important point when it comes to immigration, ethnicity, and nationality. For in many of the cases of ethnicity, religion, and nation, women have been subsumed to ethnicity or nation, for both the immigrant groups and the host nations. That is to say, the image and role of women has often been celebrated in ethnic, religious, and national traditions but celebrated in familial and maternal roles and in terms of their critical place in cultural reproduction. That maternal status had a figurative as well as literal bearing on the community's future.[17]

The irony is that the proprietary self is most evident today, at least in official institutional terms, through the liberating of women rather than via the "cultural liberation" that is so celebrated in multicultural and transnational motifs. Indeed, judicial agency in the sense I have described here has transformed many a cultural form in its traditional sense—precisely because it has upturned the traditional role of the woman in many cases. And this, indeed, is why questions relating to the status of women have fractured the linkages of host societies and some immigrant groups (or subsets of those groups) where women have a particularly subordinate or culturally specific role.[18]

The cultural dimension that is so exclaimed by governments, various nongovernmental groups, and academics, is a function of the proprietary self. It is something of a paradox that we use the term "postnational" or "transnational" in the discussion on immigration and identity when what has achieved "postnational" status in the sense of a truly transnational category are, in legal terms, the rights of women. This cross-national legal convergence on women's rights happened relatively early in immigration law, though this has not captured as much attention as the place of ethnic groups.[19] One could argue that to describe an ethnic or religious group as postnational may be a contradiction in terms (insofar as an ethnic group claims some form of nationhood or national home, as in the cases of Mexico and Turkey).

Cultural groups—be they ethnic or religious—are derivative in the sense that cultural, religious, and ethnic expression is considered legitimate (in the framing of government and societal institutions, notably the courts) insofar as affiliation is determined by individuals according to their own, voluntary decision to celebrate a cultural identity of one kind or another. In this process, however, many traditional cultures are fundamentally changed. This is a story that is being played out across much of the democratic world, in cases from child brides to female genital cutting, from forced arranged marriages to honor killings (though this narrative is less marked in some cases, most notably India).[20] It is also remarkable in cases such as these that the court crafts a cultural "space" to accord with broadly multicultural ideals, but almost always it is predicated on fundamental women's rights.

A number of cases that have caught the public eye, and academic attention, tend to suggest the reverse, namely, that "my culture made me do it" has been a successful defense, even at the expense of women's rights and integrity. Among the cases: the drowning by a Japanese-American mother of her two young children and her failed suicide attempt was defended on the basis that parent-child suicide was a customary and honorable response to the shame caused by her husband's unfaithfulness; the abduction and rape of a Laotian American woman was justified by the perpetrators, Hmong men, as a customary way to choose a bride, known as "marriage by capture"; and a New York Chinese man explained that he bludgeoned his wife to death because of her unfaithfulness, which he stated would be acceptable under Chinese custom.[21] These defenses, where a cultural practice or belief was invoked to mitigate the defendant's crimes, were called "cultural defenses," though there is no legally codified concept as such.

However, these cases—or rather the *popular interpretation* of these cases—have veiled the more pertinent trajectory regarding women's rights. They hide a more general pattern of judicial and statutory responses to countercultural practices that implicate women's agency (and obscure the generally very unfavorable light in which judges regard cultural defenses). Furthermore, even in these *cause célèbre* cases, and where cultural practices involving the subordination of women are legally invoked, a cultural defense is not an absolute legal defense; rather, it comes into play to reduce charges or at the point when the defendant is up for sentencing.

The crime is still a crime; a cultural practice is at best a mitigating factor. Such invoked cultural practices, involving the subordination of women, are almost never considered in and of themselves "justified" or exculpatory. The number of cases where the cultural defense has been used successfully, even in this qualified sense, is still rather limited. This is remarkable given the number of immigrants in the United States with customs that conflict with American law. According to several criminal lawyers with experience working with immigrants, if the cultural defense were effective, we would be seeing it raised in many more cases.[22]

We can see a similar dynamic in European cases. In Norway, a woman of Moroccan ancestry named Nadia was kidnapped by her parents, who feared she was rejecting Islam for a Western way of life. They took her, apparently drugged, to Morocco and married her against her will. After their return to Norway, the state prosecuted the parents for holding a person against his/her will, but did not have sufficient evidence for a forced marriage charge. The court found the parents guilty, but granted reduced sentences, due to Nadia's request for leniency for her parents. The court noted, however, that "traditions cannot supersede Norwegian law." The Norwegian case, which took place in 1998, drew widespread attention.[23]

Also widely noted was a British case, where an English mother, described as a nonpracticing Christian, opposed the application of her former husband, a nonpracticing Muslim of Turkish origin, to have their male child, "J," circumcised. The official solicitor supported her. The father appealed, suggesting that the judge had confused the child's religion with the child's upbringing because, under Muslim law, the father's religion determines the child's religion. The Court of Appeal dismissed the appeal in a 1999 judgment, noting *inter alia* that J had a mixed heritage and secular lifestyle, though the court accepted the father's "passionate" concern for J to be given a Muslim identity. Furthermore, the court endorsed the view that, under United Kingdom law, one parent could not arrange circumcision without consent of the other parent (itself an assertion of individual agency of each parent over patriarchal custom).

Two further comments in the court's judgment are of interest in the context of proprietary individualism. First, the court noted that "[t]he fact that the child is recognized as a Muslim under religious law was not and is not an issue [for the court]," a statement that speaks for itself in indicating which law and custom is privileged. Second, the judgment notes, "It is clear that adherents of Islam would regard him as a fellow Muslim and that his father so regards him. There is no reason to suppose the child himself at present perceives himself as a Muslim or as belonging to any faith grouping." This suggests that the question of J's religious identity is to be determined by him, through his own (voluntary) agency, and not through religious and communal fiat.[24]

A methodological note: It is exceptionally difficult to get the full universe of cases, in the United States or in Europe, where a cultural defense of some kind may be proffered. They can't all be identified in indexes, as the terms used for such cases are not standardized. "Culture" can invoke all manner of issues, or the term "culture" may not be used in a relevant case. Cultural and gender dimensions may enter at a variety of points in the legal process but remain unpublished. These cases also involve myriad jurisdictions. It is in practical terms impossible to get a fully scientific sampling of the cases. That said, the evidence from any extensive and reasonable search does indeed point to the conclusion above, that the efficacy of the cultural defense has been limited. The countervailing examples are few. This conclusion is borne out in other studies as well.[25]

Inventing Culture

What is striking is how judges and other actors in the judicial system can be conscious of multicultural sensitivities, but at the same time try to predicate multiculturalism on individual agency or "self-proprietorship."

Since women's agency is in question across a range of cultural practices, it becomes an issue of trying to elicit, or invent, a thread imputably endogenous to the culture in question that recognizes women's agency.

Notable in this regard is a much publicized Nebraska case. This case involved an Iraqi refugee from the first Persian Gulf War who arrived in the United States in 1995. He was ultimately convicted of first-degree assault on a child. On November 9, 1996, the refugee, Latif Al-Hussaini, thirty-four years old, "married" a thirteen-year-old girl who had been "given away" by her father. After the ceremony, Al-Hussaini took his "bride" to a new home where he engaged in sexual intercourse with her, despite her objections. Al-Hussaini was later arrested. He claimed he did nothing wrong, as arranged marriages with young girls were customary in Iraq and legal under Islamic law. The court nonetheless sentenced him, in September 1997, to four to six years' imprisonment.

The Nebraska example is telling and not only in that the rights of the girl negated any cultural claim that subordinated women. The case also illustrates how the legal system edits or reinvents culture through redefining what that culture (or, in this regard, religion) is in its purportedly true, authentic form.[26] In Al-Hussaini's appeal in 1998 against the state of Nebraska, the prosecutor for Nebraska argued that, to quote from the judge's decision, "while Al-Hussaini attempts to lessen his culpability by claiming that the acts were sanctioned by religion, there is evidence in the pre-sentence investigation report that such a marriage would not be universally accepted in Iraq and, in fact, was highly unusual and would be considered wrong in the majority of Iraqi communities."[27] The Court of Appeals affirmed the sentence of the lower court, noting, "there is really only one victim of this crime and that is the 13-year-old child with whom Al-Hussaini had sexual intercourse without her consent."[28] The court here takes a global perspective, placing itself in the role of an imaginary anthropologist expounding on different world cultures.[29]

The court's role in inventing culture is telling. Defining boundaries— gender boundaries and boundaries on the freedom of association—is more than simply stating a rule. As Robert Cover writes, the judge "becomes constitutive of a world." Such "jurisgenesis" takes place through a cultural form (broadly Western in the cases described here) while transforming another (for example, of one immigrant community). The judge, as in the Al-Hussaini case, adjudicates law as the "social organization of power" but, in a real sense, has to tell a story in order to legitimize the court's judgment. In this latter regard, it is the "organization of law as meaning." Law here is about the destiny of individuals and nations. "Law must be meaningful," writes Cover, "in the sense that it permits those who live together to express themselves with it and with respect to it."[30] In that regard, when a "foreign" cultural claim fails, the plaintiffs (and by extension, their community) are still invited to express themselves within the cultural framework represented by the state.

The debate around female genital mutilation is perhaps most symbolic and illustrative of the normative and institutional trajectory, in the West at least, of the "women's rights versus culture" clash. I use the term "symbolic" with a specific purpose here. Female genital mutilation has not generated that many court cases outside of France. But the cases that have taken place have elicited substantial public attention, and produced the following effects. First, both judicial and legislative actions to proscribe female genital cutting have privileged a particular cultural form, and in this regard such mutilation becomes a focal point for a larger "clash of cultures."

Second, genital mutilation goes to the core issues of women's rights, autonomy, and sexuality (and suppression of women's sexuality, literally), and in this regard epitomizes the social configuration of gender. Finally, nearly all the religious and cultural rituals associated with female genital mutilation metaphorically and, in a sexual sense, bodily, take away women's agency. Indeed, the excision of a women's sexuality through such mutilation has been justified for the sake of essentially domesticating women, so they will think of "keep[ing] house" rather than their "own sexual pleasure" (with the interesting presumption that keeping house and a woman's sexual pleasure are mutually exclusive).[31]

This "symbolic" process regarding female genital mutilation, and the role of judicial or quasi judicial bodies in promoting women's agency, is evidenced in the way the issue arose in the United States, and in France. In the United States, it was a judicial asylum case that prompted legislation to ban female genital mutilation. The case was heard before the Board of Immigration Appeals in 1996, and coerced female genital mutilation was found to be grounds for granting asylum. The court noted in its decision the coercive character of the applicant Fauziya Kasinga's marriage (into a polygamous union) and how she was pressured to undergo female genital mutilation.[32] Here the judicial body did not hide its abhorrence of female genital mutilation, in this regard associated with the Tchamba-Kunsuntu tribe in Togo. Mutilation of this kind, the Board of Immigration Appeals determined, was persecution under the law, the board noting that, in its extreme forms, the "female genitalia are cut away" and the "vagina is sutured partially closed," which can cause serious, sometimes life-threatening complications.

The Immigration and Naturalization Service, fearful of being inundated by asylum claims of this nature, asked to limit such claims when tribal members believed "they were simply performing an important cultural rite that bonds the individual to the society" and to exclude past victims of female genital mutilation if they "at least acquiesced" to the rite. The voluntary quality of the act (implicating the question of individual agency) became the yardstick, even for the INS.[33]

The federal law criminalizing the act of circumcising, excising, or infibulating anyone under the age of eighteen years, except for surgery essential for the health of the patient performed by a licensed physician, was passed following Kasinga's asylum request (granted in June 1996) and went into effect in March 1997. One section of the law specifically rejected any justification of the law on religious or cultural grounds, such that "no account shall be taken of the effect on the person on whom the operation is performed of any belief . . . [nor] that the operation is to be performed as a matter of custom or ritual." Any cultural defense on the matter is simply negated as a legal option.[34] Federal legislative history on the issue of female genital mutilation pointed to the similar position of UNICEF, the World Health Organization, international human rights groups, and laws in other countries (particularly the United Kingdom).[35] It is significant (in the context of judicialization) that an administrative and judicial action, itself reflecting changing international norms, generated the public concern that, in turn, spurred legislative action.

France was the first Western country to prosecute acts of female genital mutilation within its borders. France has no specific law against female genital mutilation, but the judicial system took action in a series of cases by linking female genital mutilation to the French Penal Code, in particular to Article 312, which concerns violence committed against a child under fifteen years, including "mutilation, amputation . . . or other permanent disability."[36]

Among the French cases that generated public interest are the following. In 1990, an African father who arranged to have his daughter "circumcised" against his French wife's wishes, was given a five-year suspended sentence by the end of the appeal process. The first trial against an "excisor" took place in 1991 and, in contrast to the suspended sentences that characterized prior female genital mutilation cases, the court meted out a three-year prison sentence. The first parent to serve time in jail was a Gambian woman who was sentenced to five years in jail, four of them suspended, for "causing the wounding and mutilation" of her two daughters. The French government also ran public campaigns in immigrant communities to warn that female "circumcision" is illegal.

Though France was at the forefront of prosecuting cases of female genital mutilation, it has been criminalized in a number of Western countries, including Sweden, the United Kingdom, Switzerland, Belgium, Canada, Australia, and, with the exception of the mostly symbolic Sunna form of female genital cutting, in the Netherlands.[37] (The *Sunna* form of cutting is considered the "mildest"; it involves the removal of the tip of the clitoris and, or alternatively, of the prepuce.)

Postcolonial Retreats from Women's Rights

Ayaan Hirsi Ali was compelled as a 22-year-old to marry a Canadian Somali. On her way from Somalia to Canada, however, she requested refugee status in the Netherlands. Her arrival in the West was, she says, her "real birthday." Her husband showed up at the refugee camp in Holland and she was able to say "no," reassured by the presence of a Dutch policeman. As one Dutch reviewer of her autobiography noted, Hirsi Ali "experienced an imperative that to most of us is a mere abstraction: individual freedom needs the rule of law." Although she was elected to the Dutch Parliament in 2003 and the scriptwriter of a film protesting violence against Muslim women (the director of which, Theo van Gogh, was subsequently murdered by an Islamist), even the rule of law could not fully protect her—a cautionary warning in the fight for human rights generally—and she fled to the United States, haunted by constant death threats. The death threats were preceded by a television documentary, apparently intent on undermining her because of her criticism of aspects of multiculturalism.[38]

Hirsi Ali's story is an example of what, in my mind, are unfortunate directions taken in prominent arguments regarding the human rights of women in some immigrant communities. Many have argued that to suggest that multiculturalism and woman's rights may be oppositional—in certain, delimited respects—obscures repression of women within Western countries and masks the way women's agency may be realized in patriarchal cultures.

A nuanced version of this argument is that of the political theorist Bonnie Honig. She suggests that "feminists ought to be careful lest they participate in the recent rise of nationalist xenophobia by projecting a rightly feared backlash—whose proponents are mostly native-born Americans—onto foreigners who come from somewhere else and bring their foreign, (supposedly) 'backward' cultures with them." She criticizes Susan Okin—who first raised the rhetorical question, "is multiculturalism bad for women?"—for "denuding veiling, polygamy, [and] clitoridectomy of all their context, signification, and meaning." In a common complaint, Honig notes that cultures are not univocal: "There are brutal men (and women) everywhere. Is it their Jewish, Christian, or Moslem identity that makes them brutal . . . or is it their brutality?" She notes further that "extinguishing cultures is not the answer" and that we "must resist the all-too-familiar and dangerous temptation to make foreignness itself fundamentally threatening to women."[39] Audrey Macklin makes a similar point in this volume.[40]

Another frequent criticism is that, in the words of law professor Catherine Powell, "the West/Rest dichotomy shields the cultural roots of gender inequality in Western States, such as the United States, from scrutiny by either advocates or foreign governments." Powell notes critically that the "West is assumed to provide a culturally neutral baseline or measuring rod against which to evaluate the progress of the rest of the world."[41]

In addressing these critiques, let us note what all those at the core of this argument agree upon. No culture is "univocal." No culture is immune from misogynist violence and other forms of discrimination against women. All cultures, in their myriad diversity, contain elements that are attractive and elements that, from a liberal perspective at least, are less than attractive. And I think most writers in this debate can agree that criticisms of certain gender-related practices do not constitute ipso facto hostility to immigrants or immigration as such, let alone participation in nationalist xenophobia.

However, from the perspective of human rights and democratic norms, what differences in patterns in the status of women can we discern? What do those patterns reveal about underlying social structures? What are the institutional differences? Rather than comparing "ideals," which academics are wont to do, or comparing the ideals of one society against the practices of another, we need to compare actual practices—this, I suggest, is a normative as well as an empirical measure. Where patriarchal practices systemically discriminate against women, and where cultural practices like forced marriage, female genital mutilation, child brides, and even honor killings take place, arguments about avoiding "essentialist" descriptions of the "other" are correct, but are on a level of such abstraction that they miss the point. These arguments severely underplay, in effect, the qualitative jump of institutionalized discrimination against women in such patriarchal circumstances compared to, say, the United States or Britain more generally—and do the women in such circumstances no favors.

A test of our thinking is to take ourselves out of the overwrought arena of postcolonial politics. Here South Africa in the era of apartheid is a striking example. Its apologists argued that racism was characteristic of the United States as well and that, therefore, Americans had no right to criticize South Africa. One could take that further: white South Africans were a diverse group and did not speak "univocally." Apologists could add that we should be careful when addressing apartheid as, like most authoritarian regimes, it was a cultural as well as political practice, and we should not want to "extinguish" the culture itself. But of course the apologists were wrong, and any extension of such arguments would be wrong: both the extent and, most importantly, the institutionalization, of racism in South Africa were on an order of magnitude that was much more severe than racism in the United States of the same period—say, in the 1960s or 1970s. And if the West had turned exclusively inward, addressing its own flaws, I am not sure the apartheid regime would have been undone when it was undone.

The basic argument here is empirical, with normative implications: how do practices differ across sociological, demographic, and geographical settings? (Those settings differ also across immigrant groups but also, it must be stressed, are variegated within the respective immigrant communities.) In turn we must ask a pragmatic question: what, in such circumstances, is the best way to combat discrimination against women? (Extending the comparison with South Africa, I note that the American case illustrates that dealing with, in that case, domestic racial discrimination was not mutually exclusive from seeking to undermine apartheid; the same is true for combating other forms of discrimination.) We need to, I suggest, shift from abstract arguments over principles to arguments over practices and how to change practices, especially where those practices display the most severe and institutionalized forms of discrimination.

Host societies benefit enormously from immigration, and the more tolerant the host the better it does—the United States is of course the classic example of that oft-stated observation (other countries reap the pain of exclusionary practices, as we have witnessed recently in France). Normatively, we should not object to the fact that immigration into the United States, or any other country for that matter, can also involve the transformation of status for some immigrant women, or their daughters or their daughters' daughters. As in the ending of racial apartheid, "extinguishing" gender apartheid, albeit a cultural practice, should not be a source of concern.

Conclusion

What the gradual (though in recent decades accelerated) emergence of the proprietary individual does is to make it more difficult to demand exclusive loyalties, including compelling the full assimilation of "outsiders." But—and this point needs to be stressed—this development applies to immigrant ethnic and religious groups as much as to "the nation" itself. We can no longer enforce singular loyalties nationally, but nor can a father force his daughter to remain an orthodox coreligionist or to marry the man of his choosing. Proprietary individualism is a fundamentally distinct social form, and we are mistaken in thinking that the state has "declined" and that immigrant ethnicities or religious communities have conversely, as a result, been "empowered." It is not that one player has won out and the other has lost—it is a new game with altered rules. To the extent that we have postnational, transnational, and multicultural social and political forms, they must be understood in the context of the proprietary self.

Two central reasons contribute to the significance of sex and gender in contemporary conflicts, domestically and internationally. One reason, already noted, is that gender-related issues reveal the normative institutionalization of proprietary individualism, mirrored in and expanding through judicial agency. The expansion of the proprietary self concerns not only women. However, the subordinate status of women cuts across so many "organizations," from nation-states to corporations, from tribal customs to religions, from ethnic groups to the family, that such gender issues have "floated" to the top. The nested judicial institutions have been a critical mechanism in generating women's rights in that it appears to be breaking down, from the nation-state on down (in most, if not all, democratic states), the patriarchy that has characterized so many social organizations. The second related reason is that lines of contention within democracies and globally cultural divisions are drawn by, or revealed through, issues related to the status of women. Race and even nationhood are secondary, at least in the way these conflicts are represented or made manifest.

The role of the judicial and judicial-like organizations is also notable not only in and of itself but specifically as it relates to the status of women and certain other gendered groups. Democracy as a political form emerged well before women's rights began their expansive reach of recent decades. Without a doubt, it is judiciaries that have played a critical role in that expansion. But that institutional dynamic also points to the fragility of women's rights, particularly for women in certain geographic, social, and cultural settings. This relates to the evolving relationship between, and vulnerabilities of, different bodies—legislative, judicial, executive, and administrative—within the state.

The interaction of judicial and other branches of government around the rights of women is striking. The judicial bodies, at different levels, are in this regard animated by liberal values that are informed by international human rights norms (if not necessarily by formal international instruments), but the locus of their "effect" is still within the bounds of the state. The judicial bodies can have an effect through *informing* the state normatively. The state, in its executive and legislative sense, has to address concerns of national and democratic accountability—which includes concerns about immigration flows, populations, and the like. The state uses—or coopts—international norms in defining inclusion and exclusion.

Thus issues of gender serve as a means of excluding certain "undesirable" cultural practices. Curiously, where once we saw, to take the American case, ethnic criteria as a basis for determining immigration concerns, or ideological criteria (such as in the anticommunism McCarran-Walter Act), we now witness gender as a way of delineating the "inside" and the "outside."[42] As in the anticommunist case, the gender dimension represents a wider, global divide, especially vis-à-vis much of the Muslim and Arab world. For all the progress in women's rights, however, there is a certain vulnerability: political and popular pressures on legislators or the executive branch, internally or externally, could equally swing against the interests of women's rights and "self-possession."

The expansion of proprietary individualism is profoundly unsettling to certain cultures, or more accurately certain subsets of cultures, and nowhere is this fissure more apparent than with regard to the status of women. Resistance to such expansion, sometimes seen at its core as (overstated in my opinion) Americanization or Westernization, takes a variety of forms. In its darkest form, that resistance is expressed through terrorism, which violates the most fundamental precept of civil society. "The new unit of totalitarianism is the terrorist cell," notes Seyla

Benhabib, adding, "the goal of this new form of war is not just the destruction of the enemy but the extinction of a way of life." Terrorism strains democracy and the rule of law; "violence lurks at the edges of everyday normalcy" and is the most extreme threat to civility, by definition targeting civilians.[43] When suicide bombers are promised seventy-two virgins, we are introduced to the ugliest and most perverse caricature of relations between men and women and of the image of women themselves—men go to war to die in "glory" with the "pure" female awaiting to serve them. Globally, we are once more at the abyss, once more staring into the heart of darkness, and the rights of women are a key leitmotif of that struggle.

NOTES

1. United Nations, *Human Development Report,* 2005, available at http://hdr.undp.org/en/media/hdr05_complete.pdf. See also the discussion in Judith Resnik, "Categorical Federalism: Jurisdiction, Gender, and the Globe," *Yale Law Journal* 111 (December 2001): 658.

2. Sue Clough and Sean O'Neill, "Muslim Cut[s] His Daughter's Throat for Taking a Christian Boyfriend," *The Daily Telegraph,* September 30, 2003. See also Sandra Laville, "Tide of 'Culture Clash' Violence Worries Police," *The Daily Telegraph,* September 30, 2003. The United Kingdom has seen increased pressure for tougher action against honor killings, not just from the public at large but also from activists within immigrant communities who complain that the police do not act assertively due to "political correctness." In parts of the Asian community, there are growing reports that women are being subjected to violence, and sometimes murdered, for refusing to obey the traditions of "their culture." In a number of documented cases, women have been subjected to violence by family members for choosing to follow an "independent path. Their perceived crimes can include wanting to go to university, refusing an arranged marriage or having a boyfriend." Sandra Laville, "Police to Target Wave of Murders in the Name of Family Honor," *The Daily Telegraph,* March 10, 2003.

3. Caroline Alexander and Charles Goldsmith, "U.K. 'Honor Killings,' Cloaked in Family Silence, Stymie Police," *Bloomberg.Com,* January 16, 2007, available at http://www.bloomberg.com/apps/ news?pid=newsarchive&sid=aQe8VVyUR.qk (accessed February 21, 2007).

4. Ibid. Dr. Veena Raleigh, University of Surrey, is cited for the suicide statistics.

5. Doriane Lambelet Coleman, "The Seattle Compromise: Multicultural Sensitivity and Americanization," *Duke Law Journal* 47 (1998): 717–84.

6. The rationale for this approach is that any set of "ideas," norms, and social practices, to exist in a quotidian sense, needs to be institutionally embedded (and institutions themselves represent certain normative conceptions). Consequently we need to "locate" the institutions first, before launching into the kinds of categories used in the debate. Note that such an approach does not necessarily address whether, for example, immigrants are changing the institutions or vice-versa.

7. See, for example, Alec Stone Sweet's article on judicialization, "Judicialization and the Construction of Governance," *Comparative Political Studies* 32 (1999): 147–84, available at http://cps.sagepub.com/cgi/content/abstract/32/2/147?ck=nck.

8. See David Jacobson and Galya Benarieh Ruffer, "Courts across Borders: The Implications of Judicial Agency for Human Rights and Democracy," *Human Rights Quarterly* 25 (February 2003): 87–89. On gender and immigration law see Abdulaziz, Cabales & Balkandali v. United Kingdom, 94 Eur. Ct. H.R. (Ser. A) (1985).

9. See Susan Esserman and Robert Howse, "The WTO on Trial," *Foreign Affairs,* January/February 2003.

10. I am using the term "gender" here as shorthand for the rights of women and other gendered groups, and "culture" as shorthand for groups that portray themselves as expressing a specific cultural or religious identity. Clearly, "gender" is culturally constructed in important ways, and cultures generally involve the stipulation of gendered identities.

11. This section draws partly on David Jacobson, "Europe's Post-Democracy?" *Society* 40 (January–February 2003): 70–76.

12. This is not a unidirectional "top-down" process, whereby a global normative order scripts the activities of state and nonstate actors. International norms evolve as states react to structural challenges, such as responding to waves of migration, changing themselves in the process (notably in the growing role of the judiciary). These responses enmesh the state on an ad hoc basis in a set of institutional relationships and obligations that, given prior knowledge, would not have been necessarily viewed as desirable. I discuss this at greater length in David Jacobson, "New Border Customs: Migration and the Changing Role of the State," *UCLA Journal of International Law and Foreign Policy* 3 (1998–99): 443–62; and in David Jacobson, *Rights across Borders: Immigration and the Decline of Citizenship* (Baltimore, MD: Johns Hopkins University Press, 1996).

13. There is some intersection between the concept of the proprietary self, as I present it here, and C. B. Macpherson's "possessive individualism," but it is also significantly different. The "proprietary self" in the sense I refer to connotes self-possession in the existential and sociological sense, and does not necessarily imply "selfishness" or indifference to society. There is a certain affinity with the marketplace, but the "proprietary self" is not solely, or fundamentally, defined

through the marketplace or capitalism. Nor do I view it as a necessarily negative phenomenon. On the contrary, there is much to welcome in its emergence. See C. B. Macpherson, *The Political Theory of Possessive Individualism: From Hobbes to Locke* (Oxford: Clarendon Press, 1962). On the history of consumerism, see Charles F. McGovern, *Sold American: Consumption and Citizenship, 1890–1945* (Chapel Hill: University of North Carolina Press, 2006).

14. Ronald Inglehart and Pippa Norris, "The True Clash of Civilizations," *Foreign Policy* 135 (March/April 2003): 1–3.

15. This development is discussed at greater length in David Jacobson and Galya Benarieh Ruffer, "Courts across Borders," supra note 8, 74–92.

16. The quoted terms, used in a different context, are taken from James E. Block, *A Nation of Agents: The American Path to a Modern Self and Society* (Cambridge, MA: Harvard University Press, 2001).

17. Gila Stopler argues that the fact that women are a "group," not a "community," has handicapped women's rights. Women's affiliations, Stopler suggests, are primarily with various religious, ethnic, racial, and national communities, which precludes women being a community in and of themselves. For a contrast to Stopler's argument, see Valentine Moghadam's analysis of women's associations in this volume. In a sense, one could say then that, traditionally, nation or religion has trumped gender. But Stopler's argument can also be viewed as a test of the sociological presence of the proprietary individual. It is because the proprietary self is predicated on the individual, and not on "communities," from nations down to families, that women in particular benefit from institutionalized (and judicialized) agency, such that in that context, gender may trump culture. See Gila Stopler, "Countenancing the Oppression of Women: How Liberals Tolerate Religious and Cultural Practices That Discriminate against Women," *Columbia Journal of Gender and Law* 12 (2003): 189–98.

18. The very act of immigration to countries like the United States can bestow agency on women: Saskia Sassen notes in her chapter, "Culture beyond Gender," in *Is Multiculturalism Bad for Women?*, eds. Joshua Cohen, Matt Howard, and Martha C. Nussbaum (Princeton, NJ: Princeton University Press, 1999), 76–78, how immigrant women are empowered through their presence in the United States—pointing in this regard to the advantages of American (national) culture: such women gain personal autonomy and independence vis-à-vis men; immigrant women have greater control of budgeting and over domestic decisions; and they even gain leverage in requesting help from men for household chores. Similarly, such women are more likely to integrate into mainstream society. "Group rights," writes Sassen, "did not help these immigrant women achieve a greater sense of self and confidence."

19. Nationality law, once determined almost exclusively down the patrilineal line, is now, in most democratic countries at least, gender neutral. See Randall Hansen and Patrick Weil, "Citizenship, Immigration, and Nationality: Toward

a Convergence in Europe?" in *Toward a European Nationality: Citizenship, Immigration, and Nationality Law in the EU*, eds. Randall Hansen and Patrick Weil (London: Palgrave Publishers, 2001), 9–10.

20. One example of an exception to the claim that gender trumps culture is at the nexus of federal and American Indian tribal law. In the 1978 Santa Clara Pueblo case, the United States Supreme Court held that tribal sovereignty was preeminent vis-à-vis concerns about membership rules that disadvantaged women. See discussion in Judith Resnik, "Dependent Sovereigns: Indian Tribes, States, and the Federal Courts," *University of Chicago Law Review* 56 (Spring 1989): 671–759.

21. See Doriane Lambelet Coleman, "Individualizing Justice through Multiculturalism: The Liberals' Dilemma," *Columbia Law Review* 96 (June 1996): 1093–1113.

22. This observation was made by Doriane Lambelet Coleman, personal communication, September 13, 2003. I also benefited in this regard from discussion with Yxta Maya Murray, personal communication, October 8, 2003. It is striking the extent to which the culture defense continues to appear—and fail. See, for example, In re Israel Wendemagengehu (Santa Clara County Super. Ct. No. C9884181), *habeas corpus petition denied*, 2005 Cal. App. Unpub. LEXIS 9747, at *1 (Oct. 25, 2005). This case deals with an Amhara Christian who claimed a cultural defense, namely, that he was culturally humiliated when his wife left him and spat on him. He was convicted of second degree murder in 2005. Another case that took place in Alabama involved a man who killed his three children after his wife left him, and claimed this was a normal reaction of a Vietnamese to save face; he was sentenced to death. For a discussion of the facts of this case, see Bui v. State, 551 So. 2d 1094 (Ala. Crim. App. 1988).

23. Alison Dundes Renteln, "Cross-Cultural Dispute Resolution: The Consequences of Conflicting Interpretations of Norms," *Willamette Journal of International Dispute Resolution* 10 (2002): 108–11. The court statement cited here is quoted in Renteln.

24. Quotations cited, and case reported, in Jane Maynard, "Re J (Child's Religious Upbringing and Circumcision)," *Family Court Reports* 1 (2000): 307–14. A separate European case that I have not discussed here is the *l'affaire foulard*, or scarf affair, in France. I have not done so as the issue of women's agency here is ambiguous, and the affair may more reflect the idiosyncrasies of French republicanism than anything else. As Seyla Benhabib writes, "in the *foulard* affair we encounter public officials and institutions who supposedly champion women's emancipation from [their] communities by suppressing the practice of veiling. . . . [Yet] some women resisted the state not to affirm their religious and sexual subordination as much as to assert a quasi-personal identity independent of the dominant French culture." See Seyla Benhabib, *The Claims of Culture: Equality and Diversity in the Global Era* (Princeton, NJ: Princeton University Press, 2002), 94.

25. Alison Dundes Renteln scoured available cultural defense cases, not only limited to gender-related issues, through legal indices, briefs, transcripts, newspapers, and other documents. She reached the conclusion that courts are indeed reluctant to accept the culture defense. See Alison Dundes Renteln, *The Cultural Defense* (New York: Oxford University Press, 2004). She discusses methodological issues on pp. 6–8.

26. On "invented" or "edited" culture, see Eric Hobsbawm, *Nations and Nationalism since 1780: Programme, Myth, Reality* (New York: Cambridge University Press, 1990); John W. Meyer, John Boli, George M. Thomas, and Francisco O. Ramirez, "World Society and the Nation-state," *American Journal of Sociology* 103 (July 1997): 144–81.

27. State v. Latif Al-Hussaini, 579 N.W.2d 561, 563 (Neb. Ct. App. 1998).

28. Ibid.

29. That is an innovation from the traditional judicial position of not crossing national borders; earlier cases would ascertain, for example, the "whiteness" (often understood in cultural, not racial, terms) of Muslims, Hindus, and others in order to measure successful assimilation into American society. Congress had, in its first formal pronouncement on citizenship, restricted naturalization in 1790 to "white persons." This requirement for citizenship remained in force until 1952. Applicants from China, Japan, Burma, the Philippines, as well as those of mixed-race background, failed in their efforts to become citizens. Mexicans and Armenians were classified as white. Then there were borderline cases as far as the courts were concerned, and in such cases the courts wavered. See, for example, Ex Parte Mohriez, 54 F. Supp. 941 (D. Mass. 1944) (granting an Arabian immigrant's petition because he was found to be a member of the white race). For a general discussion, see Ian F. Haney López, *White by Law: The Legal Constructions of Race* (New York: New York University Press, 1996).

30. Robert M. Cover, "*Nomos* and Narrative," *Harvard Law Review* 97 (November 1983): 11, 18, 23, 29.

31. Celia W. Dugger, "Rites of Anguish: A Special Report: Gender Ritual Is Unyielding in Africa," *New York Times*, October 5, 1996, A4, quoted in Susan Moller Okin, "Is Multiculturalism Bad for Women?" in *Is Multiculturalism Bad for Women?*, eds. Joshua Cohen, Matt Howard, and Martha C. Nussbaum (Princeton, NJ: Princeton University Press, 1999), 14. See also Elizabeth Heger Boyle, *Female Genital Cutting: Cultural Conflict in the Global Community* (Baltimore, MD: Johns Hopkins University Press, 2002), chap. 5.

32. Although her name appears as Kasinga in the legal case materials, in her autobiography she spells her name "Kassindja." For the sake of simplicity, I retain the "legal" spelling. See Fauziya Kassindja and Layli Miller Bashir, *Do They Hear You When You Cry?* (New York: Delacorte Press, 1998).

33. In re Kasinga, 21 I. & N. Dec. 357 (BIA 1996).

34. Pub. L. No. 104-208, 110 Stat. 3009 (1997), cited and quoted in Carol M. Messito, "Regulating Rites: Legal Responses to Female Genital Mutilation in the West," *Buffalo Journal of Public Interest Law* 16 (1997–98): 33–77.

35. Boyle, *Female Genital Cutting*, supra note 32, 90.

36. Bronwyn Winter, "Women, the Law, and Cultural Relativism in France: The Case of Excision," *Signs: Journal of Women in Culture and Society* 19 (1994): 943.

37. Boyle, *Female Genital Cutting*, supra note 32, 83–110, and Messito, "Regulating Rites," supra note 34, 49–54. The term "female *circumcision*" is something of a misnomer, implying equivalence to male circumcision, and understates the profound impact for women's sexuality of most female genital mutilations. The male equivalent (sexually, not reproductively) would be, as a number of observers have noted, "penidectomy," or the removal of all or most of the penis.

38. See Ayaan Hirsi Ali, *Infidel* (New York: Free Press, 2007), and the review of the book by Luuk van Middelaar, "Out of Europe," *Wall Street Journal*, February 3, 2007, P12.

39. Bonnie Honig, "My Culture Made Me Do It," in *Is Multiculturalism Bad for Women?*, eds. Joshua Cohen, Matt Howard, and Martha C. Nussbaum (Princeton, NJ: Princeton University Press, 1999), 35–40.

40. Audrey Macklin, "Particularized Citizenship," in this volume.

41. Catherine Powell, "Lifting Our Veil of Ignorance: Culture, Constitutionalism, and Women's Rights in Post–September 11 America," *Hastings Law Journal* 57 (December 2005): 331–35. See also Leti Volpp, "Feminism versus Multiculturalism," *Columbia Law Review* 101 (2001): 1181–1218.

42. This is revealed in certain respects in Sarah K. van Walsum's chapter on transnational mothering in this volume. See Sarah K. van Walsum, "Transnational Mothering, National Immigration Policy, and European Law," in this volume.

43. Seyla Benhabib, "Political Geographies in a Global World: Arendtian Reflections," *Social Research* 69 (Summer 2002): 539–66.

V

||||||||||||||||||||||||||||||||||||||||||||||||||||||

Reconfiguring the Nation-State
Women's Citizenship in the Transnational Context

10

||||||||||||||||||||||||||||||||||||||||||||||||||

Globalizing Fragmentation: New Pressures on Women Caught in the Immigration Law–Citizenship Law Dichotomy

Catherine Dauvergne

The advancing forces of globalization have pushed citizenship discourses in new directions. Within the discourse of formal legal citizenship, challenges to the traditional coupling of citizen and nation have come from the marked increases in provisions of dual citizenship, as well as from the innovation of an aggregated citizenship status in the European Union. On the plane of substantive citizenship, globalization has ushered in a debate about whether the emerging structures of global civil society are a boon for participatory governance or whether the increased importance of the international realm for significant policy making has generated a growing democratic deficit. Psychological or identity-linked discourses of citizenship are also at stake as an important branch of globalization theory defines the phenomenon in terms of a reframing of our understanding of our place in the world. Given that citizenship is an essentially contested concept,[1] it is no surprise that globalization is now a key feature of that contestation.

This chapter takes up the question of globalization's effects on citizenship and examines it in light of two propositions. The first of these is that in response to the pressures of globalization, control over membership is being transformed into the last, and best defended, bastion of national sovereignty. The second proposition is that for Western liberal states with well-developed immigration programs, immigration law and citizenship law have long had a dichotomous relationship in which the liberal discourses of equality and inclusion are left to citizenship law while immigration law performs the dirty work of inequity and exclusion. The intersection of these two propositions means that under contemporary conditions of globalization, immigration law is more effective than ever at excluding women from access to formal citizenship. This analysis also illustrates one of globalization's central paradoxes: its fragmented and contradictory forces magnify both inclusion and exclusion. The line between inclusion and exclusion is gendered in the case of citizenship.

My focus in this chapter is on formal legal citizenship. This traditional version of citizenship has received comparatively less attention in recent scholarship, which focuses primarily on the meanings given to citizenship that have accreted to it that go beyond the bare legal assertion of a relationship between the individual and the state. Formal legal citizenship remains vital, as it underlies work considering interpretations of the relationship it asserts, or perspectives that can be added to it. When Alexander Aleinikoff argues, for example, for a new legal status of "denizen" to acknowledge the membership of those who are neither citizens nor "others," the argument is grounded in the persistence of formal legal citizenship.[2] Inquiries into how citizenship is "denationalized" or how it is disaggregated also set some markers against the formal categorization.[3] Citizenship has also retained a role as a bare legal status, the importance of which is being reasserted in the face of the contemporary politics of a global war on terror. From Guantanamo Bay to Syrian jails, the thin line of formal citizenship is asserting itself with crucial consequence.[4]

Citizenship in this legal sense is a creature of the law, a formalized categorical designation; but it also attracts the protection of the law and triggers the now somewhat old-fashioned right of the state to act on behalf of its citizens. The original version of the international legal principle of state diplomatic protection is what has been asserted in the Guantanamo Bay and Mahar Arar cases.[5] In both instances, the importance of citizenship formulated as *a right of the state* has prevailed where human rights arguments have failed.

Legal citizenship remains, as Audrey Macklin has described it, "a thin but unbreakable guard rail."[6] It is true that the formal rights associated with legal citizenship make for a brief list, far short of the aspects of participation and identity that are the basis of a robust participatory engagement in social and political life. Nonetheless, the pressures of globalization are affecting even the permanence of permanent residency status.[7] Narrow, formal, legal citizenship has never been irrelevant. As I will discuss below, it is undergoing a resurgence of importance in globalizing times. Persistent inequalities in access to this bare legal status are, therefore, worthy of attention in this volume alongside analyses of other exclusionary aspects of citizenship.

I will first describe the immigration law–citizenship law dichotomy and consider the variety of implications this has for women as migrants embarking on the path to formal citizenship. I will then consider how globalization is transforming immigration laws, both through a far-reaching "crack-down" on extralegal migration and by an intensified global competition for the best and the brightest migrants. These new trends have important consequences for women. The chapter concludes by considering how control over membership in the national community has become the last bastion of sovereignty, how this affects citizenship as the marker of that membership, and how this shift makes the fragmented exclusions from formal citizenship more important than ever.

Immigration Law and Citizenship Law

In prosperous Western nations with developed immigration programs, immigration law rather than citizenship law is the effective hurdle to formal membership.[8] This is especially true in settler societies, such as Australia, Canada, the United States, and New Zealand, that have built part of their national mythology around being "nations of immigration." In part this is the case because the distinctions between those with permanent legal residency status and those with citizenship are small.[9] More important, however, is the fact that once newcomers are accepted as migrants, the hurdle for full membership in the form of citizenship is a low one. Typically, a certain number of years of legal permanent residency must be accumulated,[10] one must have a minimal knowledge of the "national" language,[11] and then pledge to defend the nation and respect its laws. Applicants must also be of good character, a hurdle that may become more significant in these ominous times. Australia, Canada, and the United States also require that new citizens have some knowledge of the nation they are joining, but this testing requirement is not onerous for those who have lived in the country for the required number of years.[12] In general, applying for citizenship is cheaper, easier, and quicker, with a far greater likelihood of success, than applying for permanent immigration status.

Applications for permanent residency are more onerous, as well as more expensive. Applicants are subject to medical examinations and to more rigorous character assessments. In the United States, Canada, and Australia, the three broad categories of permanent immigration are family, economic, and humanitarian.[13] The state scrutiny of an immigration application varies with the category. For family class applicants the focus of eligibility, and therefore scrutiny, is personal relationships. For economic applicants, scrutiny focuses on financial affairs and on qualifications. In humanitarian categories (the most formalized of which is refugee status),[14] the scrutiny will depend on the particular nature of the claim being made. The basic element of a refugee claim is an individualized risk of persecution for a legally defined reason. Refugees must have a story to tell, and must be able to tell it.[15] They are confronted with legal regimes where, generally speaking, the state agents have more powers than the police and individuals have fewer rights protections than criminal suspects.

The group of permanent residents that is eligible to become new citizens is a group recruited and constituted by immigration law. What this means for women is both important and complicated. Immigration laws aim to discriminate—to determine who will be admitted and who will be excluded. Significant scholarly work has focused on the overt racism of Western countries' immigration provisions over the course of the twentieth century, and on how racist preferences continue to be communicated through facially neutral law. Much less attention has been drawn to the way immigration provisions are gendered. In each of the major admission categories—family, economic, and humanitarian—gender is played out in the law. But the role that gender plays is fragmented. It is different in each category, taking varying forms depending on the underlying logic of the particular need the category aims to address.

It is at this juncture that a focus on formal citizenship is directly linked to the concerns of substantive inquiries into citizenship. The underlying assumption of the immigration preferences of prosperous Western nations is that liberal nations are morally justified in closing their borders, subject to exceptions of their choosing.[16] That is, the discrimination inherent in this law is justified by the need of the liberal community for closure and its right to identity.[17] Racist provisions eventually came to be seen as abhorrent to liberal principle, but the basic logic of an immigration law that discriminates among applicants on the basis of choosing those who best meet the needs and values of the nation has not been impugned overall. The criteria that immigration laws enshrine read as a code of national values, determining who some "we" group will accept as potential future members. These messages of acceptance overlap the preoccupations of substantive citizenship: Whom do we value and why? Who can contribute to vital social sectors: the economy and the family? Who is deserving of our protection and our humanity? The immigration law filter gives legal form to

Australia: Principal Applicants, Family Class: 1994 to 2005[18]

	Female	Male	Percentage Female
1994–95	17,987	11,153	61.3
1995–96	23,948	14,407	62.4
1996–97	16,929	11,297	60.0
1997–98	12,732	8,410	60.2
1998–99	13,266	8,235	61.7
2000–01	10,633	6,587	61.8
2001–02	12,528	7,184	63.6
2002–03	15,055	8,744	63.3
2003–04	15,266	9,481	61.7
2004–05	16,759	10,377	61.8

Canada: Principal Applicants, Family Class: 1995 to 2004[19]

	Female	Male	Percentage Female
1995	29,084	22,275	56.6
1996	28,625	21,153	57.5
1997	26,360	18,831	58.3
1998	24,022	15,618	60.6
1999	26,479	16,971	60.9
2000	28,727	18,516	60.8
2001	30,574	20,337	60.1
2002	27,627	18,618	59.7
2003	30,677	18,769	62.0
2004	31,349	18,718	62.6

United States: All Admissions, Family Categories: selected available years[20]

	Female	Male	Percentage Female
1994	262,210	201,389	56.6
1995	261,846	198,519	58.9
1996	340,227	256,025	57
2002	388,810	284,180	57.8
2003	286,038	205,503	58.2
2004	359, 425	261,003	57.9

Note: Publicly available American statistics do not separate principal applicants. This is probably the reason why the "percentage female" is smaller in this table than in the table above.

the answers to these questions. The bodies for whom these answers are a fit can pass through this filter and become formal legal citizens. This is not the only kind of membership, and is arguably not the most valuable kind of membership, but it is a privileged form of membership nonetheless.

Family reunification is by far the largest admission category in the United States and was the largest category in Canada and Australia until the mid-1990s, when those two nations led the worldwide move to tailor immigration requirements to fit immediate market needs. Women pre-dominate in the family category.

The story told by these numbers is broadly similar in each of the three nations: family reunification immigration includes a significant propor-tion of what might sardonically be called "wife import." A tiny portion of these women fit the stereotypical descriptor "mail-order bride." The vast majority do not. Nonetheless, it remains the case that under the heading of family reunification immigration, women arrive as migrants on the ba-sis of their legally defined relationship of dependence. While children and some other family members are in the category, approximately 80 percent of admissions are under various "partnership" headings.[21] In the United States, Australia, and Canada, this dependence is reinforced through the mechanism of sponsorship agreements, whereby the sponsoring part-ner must undertake to ensure that the sponsoree will not accept various welfare state payments from the government for a set number of years. The sponsor must demonstrate that he or she is financially independent from the state.[22] The statistics do not follow the same categorization in the United States, but some preference for women in this category still per-sists. In addition, the publicly available American statistics are not broken down in the same way (i.e., by gender *and* principal applicant status) and therefore mask these trends.

The economic immigration categories are tailored in an attempt to en-sure that those granted admission will find good jobs immediately and begin contributing to the economy upon arrival. Whether the indicator used is guaranteed job placement, particular skills, experience, education, or personal wealth, the category is tailored to indicate a preference for men. Gendered disparities on these indicators persist in the wealthy na-tions that are sought-after immigration destinations. In migrant-sending nations, such disparities are often more pronounced. The immigration provisions therefore serve to import gendered disparity. The economic in-dicators that are preferred for their "neutrality," of course, reflect gendered and racialized dimensions of privilege. Some nations even label these skilled migrants as "independents," signifying overtly the parallel with the citizenship discourse emphasis on individuality and autonomy.

Humanitarian immigration is also gendered. Women and men are ap-proximately equally represented in the international population of refu-gees and other persons of concern to the United Nations High Commis-sioner for Refugees. Despite this, however, admission figures for refugees and asylum seekers[23] in the United States, Canada, and Australia show

Australia: Primary Applicants in Economic Categories, 1999-2000 to 2004-05

	Female	Male	Percentage Female
1999–00	4,213	8,647	32.76
2000–01	5,166	10,342	33.31
2001–02	5,005	10,194	32.92
2002–03	5,596	10,395	35.00
2003–04	7,324	13,672	34.88
2004–05	7,638	14,099	35.14

Canada: Primary Applicants in Economic Categories, 1995-2004

	Female	Male	Percentage Female
1995	15,663	28,075	35.81
1996	16,742	34,656	32.57
1997	15,908	36,500	30.35
1998	12,444	29,308	29.80
1999	13,090	34,207	27.68
2000	14,891	43,206	25.63
2001	17,016	48,269	26.06
2002	15,397	42,821	26.45
2003	14,667	36,557	28.63
2004	16,773	38,406	30.40

United States: All Admissions in Economic Categories, recent available years[24]

	Female	Male	Percentage Female
1994	60,413	62,864	49.01
1995	42,265	43,066	49.53
1996	58,634	58,862	49.90
2002	84,678	90,219	48.42
2003	40,362	41,761	49.15
2004	75,025	80,289	48.31

that more men than women are admitted. There are overlapping explanations for this: men are more able or willing to make the often dangerous journey to a prosperous nation; a family that can only afford one smuggler's fee may elect to send a father or a son; men may be more successful at attaining refugee status because the focus of the definition fits men's experiences more easily than women's.[25] Whatever the explanation for a particular case or series of cases, the result is that proportionately more men than women benefit from the particular type of "solution" to refugee status that is represented by resettlement in a prosperous nation.

As migrants in each of these categories, women's and men's experiences are distinct. The distinctions reflect fault lines of privilege and dependence that are familiar to citizenship theorists. Many women arrive as

Australia, Humanitarian Admissions, all subclasses, all categories of applicant

	Female	Male	Percentage Female
1994–95	4,518	7,110	38.85
1995–96	4,742	6,927	40.64
1996–97	3,310	5,087	39.42
1997–98	3,157	4,400	41.78
1998–99	4,364	4,426	49. 65
2000–01	904	1,603	36.06
2001–02	766	1,312	36.86
2002–03	1,072	1,870	36.44
2003–04	1,212	1,868	39.35
2004–05	1,572	2,386	39.72

Canada, Refugee Admissions, Principal Applicants[26]

	Female	Male	Percentage Female
1995	5,468	10,186	34.93
1996	5,435	10,216	34.73
1997	4,257	8,893	32.37
1998	4,270	7,856	35.21
1999	4,662	8,441	35.58
2000	5,786	10,195	36.21
2001	5,475	9,367	36.89
2002	5,250	8,129	39.24
2003	5,729	8,951	39.03
2004	7,498	10,561	41.52

Refugee and Asylee Adjustments, United States[27]

	Female	Male	Percentage Female
1994	59,633	61,790	49.1
1995	55,630	59,020	48.5
1996	61,178	67,386	47.58
2002	61,616	64,331	48.9
2003	21,950	22,932	48.9
2004	34,315	36,794	48.3

new migrants because of their relationships of dependence: either as new marriage partners or as defined dependents of skilled migrants. While the legal categories that condition their admittance cannot of course determine their personal outcomes, they do convey to these women and others important messages about how and why they are valued by the nation. These migrants are the pool of new citizens. The universal values of membership as citizenship are made available to women on the basis of their gendered experiences as the objects of immigration law. Access to the citizenship debate about participation, representation, and equality is conditioned for these people on their prior acceptance through the much more rigorous and personal screening of immigration law.

At the outset of the twenty-first century, some new trends responding to globalizing forces are discernable in the immigration laws and policies of the most sought after immigration destinations. I will now turn to considering how the shifting agenda of global immigration laws affects the immigration law–citizenship law dichotomy, and what the implications of these shifts are likely to be for women.

Global "Crack-Down"

We are in the midst of a worldwide crack-down on illegal immigration. The United States has been a leader in this area, with the Illegal Immigration Reform and Immigrant Responsibility Act,[28] the increased spending on enforcement along the Mexican border,[29] and, most recently, a rhetorical commitment to entry and exit controls. The 1999 British Immigration and Asylum Act targeted unfounded asylum applications by fast tracking "out" of the asylum system but not into it, reducing rights for asylum seekers, and introducing new identity controls. More recently, the British have stringently curtailed the provision of welfare state benefits for asylum seekers.[30] Germany changed the form of its constitutional right to seek asylum in 1993 and in 1998 introduced a new law reducing benefits for asylum seekers. France has reduced asylum seeker benefits within the past decade.[31]

The European Union introduced a harmonized approach to asylum seekers in April 2004[32] and is working on developing a common policy on illegal immigration to give effect to the Treaty of Amsterdam commitments in this direction. Since 1999, Australia has removed the possibility of permanent status from some refugees, declared some of its own territory to be "beyond its borders" for the purpose of asylum claims, and introduced a comprehensive privative clause into its legislation, aimed at curtailing the role of the courts in immigration decision making.[33] Canada has introduced a mandatory requirement that its refugee decision makers take into account whether a claimant has adequate documentation and has ratcheted up front-end screening on various inadmissibility criteria.[34] Very few of these changes are attributable to the post–September 11 immigration panic. Those events, however, have added impetus and political appeal to trends that were well established by the close of the twentieth century.

This global crack-down on illegal immigration affects women in several ways. As crossing borders without legal authorization becomes harder, the market for smuggling and trafficking becomes more lucrative, as well as more dangerous.[35] Expense creates a greater barrier for women than for men. Even if migrating illegally is not a social good, it nonetheless has some markings of privilege. Some who migrate illegally do improve their life circumstances. Some who migrate illegally are eventually able to attain membership rights and even full citizenship in prosperous nations.

The increased danger of smuggling in a crack-down atmosphere also affects women independently of cost. In Australia, for example, where one of the crack-down measures has been to remove family reunification rights for some categories of refugees, an immediate result has been more women and children making the boat journey across the East Timor Sea.[36] In this scenario, where women had previously been protected by a paternalistic stereotype, a change of government policy has generated a brutal formal equality of circumstance.

Trafficking, or at least our tracking of and concern with it, is also on the increase. The victims or subjects of trafficking are overwhelmingly women and children, especially girls.[37] Immigration law crack-downs raise the stakes in this business. As in any market system, the costs are passed on, perhaps to the ultimate "consumers" but certainly to subjects, in the form of higher risks and higher prices of freedom. The line between smuggling and trafficking is often not clear. For women with fewer options of moving, trafficking or the risk of being trafficked may be made more attractive by global crack-down measures. While legal sanctions against trafficking are increasing globally, there is little evidence yet to suggest that trafficking itself is being reduced. Many forms of legal crack-down also serve to increase incentives for women to cooperate with traffickers, if the ultimate result of the law is being returned to a place they endured this horror to leave. This form of illegal immigration remains available and highly gendered.

Beyond the effects of smuggling and trafficking, the current international moral panic about illegal immigration has subtly gendered effects because of the way the category of "illegal" is constructed legally and the way it is conjured in our collective imaginations. While technically anyone present in a nation-state without citizenship or authorization has transgressed immigration laws, the label "illegal" draws from, but does not conform to, the law. The "illegals" of our imagination, against whom the current wave of law reform is directed, are not backpacking students who overstay their visas or business people who fall just outside the NAFTA categories. They are instead racialized and destitute. They fill the most dismal sweatshops and sexshops. They come seeking the benefits of our great wealth and generosity, our right to bestow but not their right to claim. The discourse of illegal immigration is filled with images of those who have and those who have not, of desperate transgressors, of the deserving and the undeserving, of "good" or "bad" illegals. Gender insinuates itself into this discourse—not in a way that disadvantages women directly, but by creating a space in which being victimized and powerless can purify one's status as transgressor. The recognition that some illegal migrants are victims with few choices forms an excuse, but it also robs individuals of agency, and is a confining identity from which to advocate for oneself or others.

One potential resolution to "illegality" is political amnesty. Amnesty, in the form of regularized legal status, has been periodically used in a number of countries. Both President Bush and Canada's immigration minister floated tentative amnesty plans in late 2003 and early 2004, although at time of writing neither of these plans had advanced beyond recurrent rhetoric. What both proposals have in common, however, is a direct linkage between regularization of immigration status and paid employment. In the United States, the proposal was aimed at those working in jobs that were deemed unattractive to American citizens.[38] In Canada, the principal target of the plan was construction workers.[39] In other words, the amnesty proposal was in each case tied directly to a need identified in economic discourse. The Canadian day-labor construction industry is predominantly male. Even if recipients of a regularized status were also allowed to extend legal residency to their families, women and children whose status in Canada was secured in this way would, here as in the elite economic categories, have their passage to citizenship marked by dependency. The tentative American proposal is not tied to a specific industry and thus would reach more women than the Canadian plan, but the gender bias of paid employment is still central to the plan, as is evidenced by the argument that these proposals are not truly amnesties but, instead, limited programs for those who are making an economic contribution.

Cracking down on illegal immigration also necessarily affects refugees. International refugee law recognizes that many who flee persecution will not have regular travel documents: Article 31 of the Refugee Convention requires that parties to the convention not penalize refugees for illegal entry into the country. However, there is no provision in international law that prohibits countries from working to ensure that refugees or refugee claimants do not enter in the first place. Crack-down measures have the effect of making entry harder for anyone attempting to cross the border without authorization; they do not distinguish between those seeking to claim refugee status and those who are entering for any other reason.

In addition to this generalized effect, some crack-down measures target refugee claimants directly. One of the most prominent of these is a range of "safe third country" agreements that are being used to limit travel by those seeking refugee status. A safe third country provision is key to the European Union's 2004 harmonization agreement.[40] A similar agreement came into effect between the United States and Canada at the end of 2004. Safe third country agreements aim to ensure that refugee claimants seek protection in the first nation they reach that offers such protection. Advocates of these provisions argue that they discourage asylum "shopping" and that they will not harm anyone facing a genuine risk of persecution. They rest on the principle that someone needing refugee protection ought to be grateful for any type of protection anywhere—that refugees begging protection ought not to be choosers. This sentiment is not supported by refugee law, but is a popular one in refugee politics.

In the case of women fleeing gender-related persecution, safe third country provisions may prove to be particularly dangerous. An important concern of advocates in Canada and the United States has been that women fearing gender-related persecution are being denied access to refugee determination in Canada, where there is a stronger tradition of protection against gender-specific persecution. Political responses to illegal immigration affect refugees directly and indirectly. As refugee status is "determined" in a bureaucratic or judicial process by a receiving nation, there is nothing to separate "genuine" refugees from "illegal" migrants at the border or just outside it.

While prosperous nations have used a variety of legal tools to effect the crack-down on illegal immigration, the difference appears to be related to varying assessments of what is likely to be effective in a given circumstance. The goal of these measures is broadly similar. In this sense, these measures represent a global convergence in policy. This leads to increased vulnerability for those who are already the most vulnerable. Crack-down measures have the effect of protecting the smuggling and trafficking markets, making refugee travel more precarious, privileging those in paid employment, and fostering images of victimization. All of these factors refract gender. While these measures are being developed, the same nations are also altering policies at the elite end of the immigration spectrum, with its own gendered patterns.

Immigrants We Choose

Countries like Canada and Australia have been at the forefront of defining a worldwide competition for the best and the brightest of migrants. Those with particular skills, experience, education, and money are being recruited and welcomed. Some of this immigration is defined as permanent and some as temporary, but those categories are less and less relevant, particularly given the lowered thresholds for citizenship in the nations that have developed these programs. Best and brightest immigration also has serious equity implications for the global brain drain, particularly as it is being closely linked to international university education.

As Canada and Australia have moved since the mid-1990s to reserving a greater number of places to economically skilled immigration over family immigration, they have moved to having a greater number of men than women selected as primary applicants. The United States is contemplating similar moves, but it would take massive changes for economically based immigration to overtake the size of the United States's family reunification program. The size of the American economy alone creates a draw that other nations are adjusting their law and policy to imitate. It is also critical to note that immigration statistics concern those who are admitted to remain permanently. In the United States, millions of people are admitted each year on a temporary basis for work, outstripping the numbers admitted to Canada or Australia. Temporary admission is often a step on the way to later permanent status.

Aggregate statistics about economic immigration often show approximate gender parity. This is partly the case because economic migrants bring their families.[41] (Many women do, of course, qualify as economic migrants.) When a woman arrives as a partner of a primary economic applicant, her right to enter (and sometimes her right to remain) is conditioned by her relationship (usually with a man). While this relationship may not personally be experienced as a dependency, it is legally framed that way. A shift in emphasis towards economic immigration does not, therefore, remove women from the pool of potential new citizens in a straightforward way, but it does ensure that women enter this pool because of their relationships of legal dependence. One element of both Australia's and Canada's new inducements for immigration has been to ensure that the partners of economic migrants do not face labor market restrictions. This is a recognition of some of the gendered barriers that have existed in this category of most privileged migrants, but it does not alter the basic contours of the program.

The United States's diversity visa program is a notable *quasi* exception in the economic category. The program is imaginatively compelling and adds an interesting twist to the standard story of immigration policy fulfilling national aspirations and fueling mythology. It is aimed at providing potentially permanent immigration places for residents of countries with low rates of immigration to the United States. The program is conducted by lottery, and 6.2 million qualified entries were received for the fifty thousand visas available for 2003.[42] Spouses and children are allowed to accompany successful entrants and are not counted against the fifty thousand quota. The animating idea of the program is to foster immigration from nations currently underrepresented in the United States's immigration statistics. It embraces a commitment to diversity in the composition of the American immigration picture that is unparalleled in formal immigration programs. It is also a direct counter to the queuing and bureaucratic wrangling that are a standard part of immigration programs. It is a program embracing the "land of opportunity" slogan, if not quite reaching the appeal of "give us your huddled masses."

In thinking about the diversity program, there are several observations about gender. First, the program confirms that what counts as diversity, or, conversely, discrimination, in immigration is not about gender. It is about racialization, which has been read since the mid-1970s as country of origin. Second, despite the lottery logic and consequent "equal playing field" appeal of the program, there are baseline criteria for entry. These are high school or equivalent education or two years of work experience in a job that requires two years of training (including on-the-job training). While these requirements are framed as minimum, they do eliminate some aspirants, and more women than men. In particular, childcare and domestic work would be unlikely to qualify. Third, in a program structured as a lottery, significantly more visas go to men than to women (approximately 32,000 to 26,000 in 1996; 23,000 to 20,000 in 2002; and 25,000 to 21,500 in 2003). This could be the result of the minimum requirements. It could also be the result of a probabilistic calculation, given that the applicant pool is in the order of magnitude of six million. In other words, it could mean nothing at all (knowing about how the pool is gendered would be more revealing).

Finally, it could also mean that women are less likely than men to want to migrate. There is some evidence to suggest that this may be generally true, and we do know that most people do not prefer, as a first life choice, to permanently leave the country they think of as home. How would this preference affect the immigration law–citizenship law dichotomy? In a world where women and men were equally appealing to migrant recruiting nations, it might mean that more men than women became eligible for the new citizen pool. For the equalizing, homogenizing, starting-over logic of citizenship, this would be, then, one further way in which citizenship is a masculinized concept. The diversity program stands as an example of how immigration is gendered even against a backdrop of "pure chance." Feminists have long been familiar with the masculinity of neutrality. In immigration, neutrality is the exception. Most nations are not content to seek just any migrants; they want instead to select those most likely to meet certain perceived needs.

New Citizenships

A final aspect of understanding the impact of globalizing trends on the immigration law–citizenship law dichotomy is to consider changes to formal citizenship itself. Changing citizenship is becoming easier. An increasing number of nations are tolerant of dual citizenship. An increasing number of individuals hold multiple passports, or in the case of the European Union, achieve the results of so doing.[43] The increasing availability of citizenship is one of globalization's paradoxes. When we seek out this type of measure of inclusion, we find inclusion is on the increase. When we seek out the exclusions seen in the crack-down on illegal immigration and the ratcheting up of border controls, we see exclusion is also on the increase.

For those who are in positions of privilege, globalizing trends enhance and increase that privilege; for those who are excluded, globalization is increasing their exclusion. Current citizenship law reform proposals in Canada illustrate this paradox nicely. Proposals for a new Citizenship Act aim to create a stronger statement of Canadian values and to make it easier to terminate or revoke the citizenship of those who are considered undesirable.[44] In short, the aim is to enrich the meaning of inclusion and to facilitate the speed and certainty of exclusions.

The advent of European Union "citizenship" also reflects paradoxical globalization effects. Those who are citizens of any member nation may now cross European borders freely, and may move to other member nations to work, or to seek work. One effect of this agreement is to enhance the importance of formal legal citizenship in European nations. Formal citizenship of France or Britain or Portugal now carries with it a significant benefit over a mere permanent residency right. In this way, European freedom of movement is a counter to Saskia Sassen's argument that the most meaningful distinction in globalizing times is that between those with legal residency status and those without it. While permanent residency in a European Union nation is still an important right, the distinction between permanent residency and citizenship is underlined by the opening of borders to citizens only. For those who are "included" in the citizenship bundle, inclusion has become more meaningful. Another key feature of the *quasi* citizenship standard emerging in Europe is its ties to participation in the labor market. The right to cross European borders is hinged to a right to work or seek work. Formally, this provision is tied to the logic of an economic union and a single market. While nationals are not uniformly prohibited from seeking welfare state support in states where they do not hold citizenship, there are limits to the right to do this. The rhetoric of this substantive citizenship is economic. It is not a right to move anywhere in Europe to raise one's children or to seek out a gentler climate. In this way, the denationalization of citizenship in Europe reifies market values, and market choices, both of which have been comprehensively demonstrated to be masculinized.[45]

Opening borders to citizens of European nations serves in part to compress the immigration law–citizenship law dichotomy. Reinforcing the significance of formal citizenship entitlements reduces the role of immigration law as the most effective barrier to membership. This effect is partial, as permanent residency in Europe remains an important status. But some of the roles of immigration law are taken over by citizenship law in this reconfiguration. Situating Europe in any consideration of globalization's paradoxes is vital, as Europe is often held up as the exemplar of globalization's most promising future. For citizenship law, the example is a sobering one. The European story thus far shows a reinscription of formal citizenship's exclusionary powers, little immigration by those with free rights to do so, and a harmonization of exclusions at the ever-expanding

European borders. In combination with a trend toward increased dual citizenship (and increasingly meaningful dual citizenship),[46] the importance
of formal citizenship, and the capacity for economic rhetoric to capture
the field of substantive citizenship, are both on the increase.

Sovereignty, Globalization, and Formal Citizenship

I am using the term "globalization" to refer to "an on-going and accelerat-
ing process that is restructuring and increasing the connections among
economies, institutions, and civil societies. This dynamic and multidimensional process is integrating trade, production, and finance as well as
strengthening global norms and global social forces."[47] However the globalization story is told, one theme is that the constellation of forces com-
prising globalization poses, or may pose, a threat to nation-states. Theoretical discussions of globalization also reflect a debate about the nature
of sovereignty. Within this debate is an emerging tendency to define sovereignty in terms of control over people rather than control over territory
or policy generally.[48] In my view, this shift in emphasis in defining sovereignty is a direct result of globalizing forces and of the power of states to
assert themselves in the areas of immigration and citizenship. Sovereignty
is being shifted to the area where the importance of the nation is least
threatened.

While the capacity of states to exert policy control in economic and
financial matters is challenged by increased global interconnectedness,
control over formal admission to the polity is not. Even in these globalizing times, states retain clear powers to admit outsiders, as well as significant rights to work towards curtailing informal admissions. The current
global crack-down on extralegal immigration can be read as a response
to globalized threats to national sovereignty. In the face of these threats,
nations assert themselves as nations by seeking to strongly control their
borders. A strong policy stance against "illegals" is effective in bolstering
this sovereign assertion even when physical borders are not: the label "illegal" ensures exclusion from within. Drawing a line between those with
lawful immigration status and those without it ensures that the value of
membership is protected, even if territorial integrity is not. In this way, a
crack-down on illegal immigration asserts sovereignty on two planes simultaneously. While it is also true that globalization is marked by a great
number of people traveling, this travel is a new marker of privilege. For

those with access to travel, it is more common and more affordable. It has become another reading of globalization's widening of the gulf between privilege and privation.

As globalization enhances the importance of control over formal membership, it reinforces exclusions along the immigration law–citizenship law dichotomy. The impulse to tighten exclusions affects women differently in varying immigration categories. But as it is generally true that women are more vulnerable, each exclusionary provision magnifies this vulnerability. The gendered dimensions of this dichotomy are subtle. Gender is not the only dimension of vulnerability at issue. Similarly, formal citizenship is only one form of membership, frequently not the most meaningful. However, as globalization shifts sovereignty to an emphasis on control over people, the importance of formal membership is strengthened. Together these trends show increased exclusion, somewhat gendered, from a subtly more important formality. Both of these shifts are important, and damaging to women. The dominant logic of globalization is an economic one. In areas where the recent shifts in immigration and citizenship standards have been liberalizing, the underlying rationale has been economic. This is true of European free movement provisions, as it is of India's extension of dual citizenship rights to expatriates, and of tentative amnesty proposals for illegal workers. Economic logic has never fully recognized women's productivity.

Citizenship laws in many sought-after immigration destinations now appear more liberal, but the immigration laws that are citizenship's gatekeepers are not. The formal logic of the immigration law–citizenship law dichotomy corresponds to globalization's paradox: immigration law is about exclusion and citizenship law is about inclusion. The role that each type of law plays in constituting the border of the nation and its membership allows both of these dynamics to operate simultaneously. It also provides for a rhetorical shift from one logic to the other as the politics of the day requires. It remains true in these globalizing times that immigration law does the dirty work of exclusion, freeing citizenship law to uphold the lofty ideals of liberal legalism. For women, access to citizenship is, now as ever, conditioned by an intricately gendered immigration net.

NOTES

This chapter was previously published in one section of chapter 7 in Catherine Dauverone, *Making People Illegal: What Globalization Means for Migration and Law,* Cambridge University Press, 2008.

1. Linda Bosniak draws on the work of William Connelly in defining citizenship in this way in "Citizenship Denationalized," *Indiana Journal of Global Law Studies* 7 (2000): 447.

2. This is one of the key contributions of Alexander Aleinikoff's *Semblances of Sovereignty: The Constitution, the State, and American Citizenship* (Cambridge, MA: Harvard University Press, 2002).

3. Linda Bosniak, in "Citizenship Denationalized," supra note 1, inquires into how citizenship is denationalized across a range of discourses and asks when and why this *should* take place. She notes that denationalization is least likely in legally bounded renditions of citizenship. Seyla Benhabib argues that the elements of citizenship are being disaggregated in a way that separates social membership from political membership and thus creates a space for membership without citizenship; see Seyla Benhabib, *The Claims of Culture: Equality and Diversity in the Global Era* (Princeton, NJ: Princeton University Press, 2002).

4. Citizens of some prosperous Western states have received assistance from their governments after being detained at Guantanamo Bay and have been released earlier than some non-Western prisoners. American citizens have also been treated differently from other Guantanamo detainees. On September 26, 2002, Mahar Arar, a dual citizen of Canada and Syria, was removed to Syria by the United States and reportedly was detained and tortured for more than a year. The Canadian government negotiated his release and return to Canada on October 6, 2003.

5. Ian Brownlie, *Principles of Public International Law* (Oxford and New York: Oxford University Press, 2003), 391–92.

6. Audrey Macklin, "Exile on Main Street: Popular Discourse and Legal Manoeuvres around Citizenship," in *Law and Citizenship,* ed. Law Commission of Canada (Vancouver: UBC Press, 2006), 22.

7. In the United States the scrutiny of permanent residents from the Islamic Middle East was heightened dramatically following the events of September 11, 2001. In Canada, recent legislative changes have reduced rights for permanent residents being stripped of their status for residency violations or criminal activity. In Australia, permanent residency rights for some refugee claimants have been sharply curtailed since 2001.

8. I have made this argument in more detail in "Citizenship, Migration Laws, and Women: Gendering Permanent Residency Statistics," *Melbourne University Law Review* 24 (2000): 280.

9. These distinctions typically include the right to vote, the right to carry a passport, and access to some public service positions, as well as an obligation

to military service and jury service when they arise. Saskia Sassen has argued that the most important distinction is between those with some legal residency status, including citizenship, and those with no legal status. See Saskia Sassen, *Losing Control? Sovereignty in an Age of Globalization* (New York: Columbia University Press, 1996). My argument here is, of course, a partial challenge to this assertion.

10. In the United States the requirement is five years' residency with permitted absence of up to a year. In Australia the requirement is two years, and in Canada it is three years.

11. There is a language component in the United States, Australia, and Canada. In each case the standard is one of basic communication skills.

12. The knowledge requirement is focused on history, politics, and citizenship rights. The United States and Canada both administer a formal written test at approximately a primary school level of difficulty. Some applicants in each country are exempted from this testing. In Australia, testing focuses on rights and responsibilities of citizenship and is administered orally, testing English language skills at the same time.

13. Some nations include a fourth category, those who are admitted because of cultural membership ties. This group includes Germany and Israel.

14. In the United States, status can be granted to both "refugees" and "asylees." Both categories follow the refugee definition set out in the United Nations Convention Relating to the Status of Refugees, July 28, 1951, 19 U.S.T. 6259, 189 U.N.T.S. 150 (entered into force April 22, 1954).

15. This point is well made by Audrey Kobayashi, "Challenging the National Dream: Gender Persecution and Canadian immigration Law," *Nationalism, Racism, and the Rule of Law*, ed. Peter Fitzpatrick (Aldershot, UK: Dartmouth Press, 1995). Kobayashi argues that refugee women are confined by the victimization they must portray to attain their status.

16. Michael Walzer's assertion of this view has been the most influential. See Michael Walzer, "Chapter Two: Membership," in *Spheres of Justice: A Defense of Pluralism and Equality* (New York: Basic Books, 1983), 31–63. See also my discussion in "Amorality and Humanitarianism in Immigration Law," *Osgoode Hall Law Journal* 37 (1999): 597.

17. Some liberal thinkers have taken an "open borders" position (see e.g., several articles by Joseph Carens, "Aliens and Citizens: The Case for Open Borders," *Review of Politics* 49 (1987): 251; "Open Borders and Liberal Limits," *International Migration Review* 34 (2000): 636; "Refugees and the Limits of Obligation," *Public Affairs Quarterly* 6 (1992): 31), but it is less prevalent than a closed borders argument. I have argued that the dispute between open borders liberals and closed borders liberals is not resolvable and is one reason for the intransigence of political debate about immigration provisions. See Dauvergne, "Amorality and Humanitarianism," supra note 16.

18. Australian statistics are reported per fiscal year, which runs July 1 to June 30. These statistics were obtained directly from the Department of Immigration, Multicultural, and Indigenous Affairs in response to an email query. They are not published.

19. Canadian statistics are drawn from Citizenship and Immigration Canada, *Facts and Figures: Immigration Overview: Permanent and Temporary Residents 2004* (Ottawa: Minister of Public Works and Government Services Canada, 2005).

20. U.S. statistics are drawn from three publications: *Immigration to the U.S. in Fiscal Year 19XX* (with "XX" indicating the year in question), *Statistical Yearbook of the Immigration and Naturalization Service*, and since 2002 the *Yearbook of Immigration Statistics*. These reports are available at the Office of Immigration Statistics, online: <uscis.gov/graphics/shared/statistics>. From 1997 to 2001 statistics are given for immigrants admitted by age and sex but are not cross-referenced with category. The number of principal applicants in family categories has been calculated by adding together numbers of principal applicants in the family-sponsored preferences class and those in the immediate relatives of U.S. citizens' class.

21. In Canadian law these are spouse, common law partner, and conjugal partner. On inquiry to the Office of Immigration Statistics, a further breakdown was not available.

22. There is generally a minimum income requirement for sponsorship in the United States (8 U.S.C. § 1183a (2002), Canada, and Australia. In Canada, this requirement is waived when one is sponsoring a partner or dependent child (*Immigration and Refugee Protection Regulations* SOR 2002-227 r 133(4)). However, the prospective sponsor still must not be in receipt of state welfare-type payments (r 133(1)(k)).

23. These categories contain only some of those admitted permanently on the basis of humanitarian considerations. Others include those who do not fit within the internationally agreed upon refugee definition but who are in refugee-like situations as well as people admitted under various categories of humanitarian exception to the immigration rules that exist in each of these countries.

24. The American data are not directly comparable to the Australian and Canadian because primary applicant numbers and dependent numbers are not separated, masking any tendency for men to be the more likely primary applicants. Between 1997 and 2001 publicly available American immigration statistics do not report entry category cross-referenced by gender.

25. There is a considerable body of scholarship on the gender biases of refugee law. Some examples include Susan Kneebone, "Women within the Refugee Construct: 'Exclusionary Inclusion' in Policy and Practice—the Australian Experience," *International Journal of Refugee Law* 17 (2005): 7–42; Melanie Randall, "Refugee Law and State Accountability for Violence against Women: A Comparative Analysis of Legal Approaches to Recognizing Asylum Claims Based on Gender Persecution," *Harvard Women's Law Journal* 25 (2002): 281.

26. It is not possible to identify "all humanitarian" admissions in Canadian statistics, so these data are not identical to the Australian data. The Canadian and American data are more comparable in this regard, but see note 27.

27. It is probably the case that the U.S. statistics are closer to gender parity because these numbers do not disaggregate principal and secondary (dependent) admissions. Without access to this breakdown, I can only guess that the United States follows patterns similar to those of the other states.

28. Pub. L. No. 104-208, 110 Stat. 3009 (1996).

29. Joseph Nevins, *Operation Gatekeeper: The Rise of the "Illegal Alien" and the Remaking of the U.S–Mexico Boundary* (New York: Routledge, 2002).

30. Under Section 55 of the Nationality, Immigration, and Asylum Act 2002, which came into effect on January 8, 2003, and is accessible at http://www.opsi.gov.uk/ACTS/acts2002/20020041.htm. New housing restrictions for asylum seekers are slated to come into effect in the United Kingdom in early 2005.

31. For more information on the French cases, see "Introduction: Implications of the Conseil Constitutionnel's Immigration and Asylum Decision of August 1993," *Boston College International and Comparative Law Review* 18 (1995): 256. For more information on the German cases, see Samuel K. N. Blay and Andreas Zimmerman, "Recent Change in German Refugee Law: A Critical Assessment," *American Journal of International Law* 88 (1994): 361.

32. European Union Council Directive on Minimum Standards on Procedures in Member States for Granting and Withdrawing Refugee Status Interinstitutional File 2000/0238 (CNS), 2004 8771/04.

33. *Migration Legislation Amendment Regulations* 2001 (No. 12). The effect of this clause was curtailed by the High Court of Australia in *S157 v. Minister for Immigration, Multicultural, and Indigenous Affairs*, (2003) 195 ALR 24.

34. *Immigration and Refugee Protection Act*, R.S.C., ch. 27, § 106 (2001)(Can.).

35. Report of the Special Rapporteur on violence against women, its causes and consequences, Ms. Radhika Coomaraswamy, on trafficking in women, women's migration, and violence against women, submitted in accordance with Commission on Human Rights resolution, 1997/44. E/CN.4/2000/68,on February 29, 2000.

36. Mary Crock and Ben Saul, *Future Seekers: Refugees and the Law in Australia* (Sydney: Federation Press, 2002), 107.

37. Office of the Under Secretary for Global Affairs. *Trafficking in Persons Report*, U.S. Department of State Publication 11150 (June 2004).

38. "A Vital Immigration Debate," editorial, *New York Times*, January 8, 2004; Deb Riechmann, "Bush Wins Support from Mexico's President for His New Immigration Proposal," *Canadian Press*, January 12, 2004; Amy Fagan, "Democrats Offer Plan on Aliens," *Washington Times*, January 29, 2004.

39. Maureen Murray, "Hopes, Dreams, but No Status: 'You're Like a Prisoner in a Free Country,'" *The Toronto Star*, November 15, 2003; "Amnesty Encourages Illegal Immigration," editorial, *The Gazette*, November 15, 2003.

40. See European Union Council Directive on Minimum Standards on Procedures in Member States for Granting and Withdrawing Refugee Status, supra note 32.

41. This is shown starkly in the tables presented above. For Australia and Canada, where the numbers are disaggregated in "principal" and "secondary" (for dependent entries), men predominate. In the United States, where everyone is registered together, a veneer of gender parity emerges.

42. On file with author.

43. Kim Rubenstein, "Citizenship in a Borderless World," in *Legal Visions of the 21st Century: Essays in Honour of Judge Christopher Weeramantry*, eds. Anthony Anghie and Garry Sturgess (The Hague: Kluwer Law International Publishers, 1998), 183–206; Kim Rubenstein and Daniel Adler, "International Citizenship: The Future of Nationality in a Globalized World," *Indiana Journal of Global Legal Studies* 7 (2000): 519.

44. Reform of Canadian citizenship law has been called for at least since 1994. *Into the 21st Century: A Strategy for Immigration and Citizenship* (Hull, Quebec: Minister of Supply and Services, 1994). Since that time, two bills have died before being passed by the Canadian parliament. In late 2004, the government announced that it was again pursuing citizenship law reform.

45. See also Patricia Nanz, "Mobility, Migrants, and Solidarity: Towards an Emerging European Citizenship Regime" (on the development of EU citizenship and its impact on the position of women migrants); and Sarah van Walsum, "Transnational Mothering, National Immigration Policy, and European Law: The Experience of the Netherlands" (on women's immigration in search of [better] paid employment and its implications for family reunification), in this volume.

46. One example of how dual citizenship can become more meaningful is the case of Ms. Zahra Kazemi, a dual Iranian and Canadian citizen who was killed in a prison in 2003 in Iran. After initial reluctance to take action, the Canadian government advocated for an inquiry into her death and took moderate diplomatic sanctions against Iran. This was despite the traditional rule that when a national is in the country of her nationality, her dual citizenship does not avail him or her.

47. Peter Dauvergne, "Globalization and the Environment," in *Global Political Economy*, ed. J. Ravenhill (Oxford: Oxford University Press, 2005), 367.

48. See for example, David Jacobson, *Rights across Borders: Immigration and the Decline of Citizenship* (Baltimore, MD: John Hopkins University Press, 1996), 5; Christian Joppke, "Why Liberal States Accept Unwanted Immigration," *World Politics* 50 (1998): 267. Kim Rubenstein, "Citizenship in a Borderless World," supra note 43, also takes this view.

11

||||||||||||||||||||||||||||||||||||||||||||||||||||||||||||

Status Quo or Sixth Ground?
Adjudicating Gender Asylum Claims

Talia Inlender

Sofia Campos-Guardado was forced to watch as her uncle and cousin were hacked to death with machetes in retaliation for their opposition to a controversial agrarian reform proposal in El Salvador. She was then raped, while political slogans were chanted in the background.[1] Olimpia Lazo-Majano was forced to work as a domestic, washing the clothes of a military commander in El Salvador. During the course of her work, she was beaten and raped. The commander threatened that if she defied him he would denounce her as a subversive and would "have her tongue cut off, her nails removed one by one, her eyes pulled out. . . ."[2] These women fled their homes, crossing borders in search of the asylum protections set forth in the 1951 Convention on the Status of Refugees.[3] How their claims—and the claims of others like them—should be understood and adjudicated has been the subject of a long-standing debate among feminist advocates and scholars.

The Convention on the Status of Refugees (hereafter Refugee Convention) requires those seeking asylum to demonstrate both that they have suffered legally cognizable persecution and that their persecutory treatment was on account of one of five enumerated categories: race, nationality, religion, political opinion, or membership of a particular social group (MPSG).[4] Gender is conspicuously missing from among these categories. On one side of the debate lie those who believe that gender claims can and should be understood within the existing enumerated grounds, in particular, as political opinion and social group claims.[5] On the other side of the debate, proponents argue that the addition of gender as a sixth enumerated ground is both practically and theoretically necessary in order to ensure protection for female (and male) asylum seekers[6] persecuted on the basis of their actual (or perceived) gender.[7]

This chapter explores the merits of each side of the debate. First, I briefly recount the history of the Refugee Convention to highlight the way historical tensions play out in the debate over where gender claims should be situated in contemporary applications of the Refugee Convention. Second, I lay out the nature of gender persecution, drawing a distinction between gender-specific and gender-based persecution. "Gender-specific" refers to *forms* of persecution that can be suffered only by women, for example, forced pregnancy and female genital cutting. "Gender-based" refers to persecution *motivated* by particular beliefs about gender, for example, laws that mandate severe punishments for violations of governing mores related to women's proper dress and social status.

Third, I outline several critiques of asylum law's treatment of both of these forms of gender persecution, demonstrating how these weaknesses are visible in the adjudication of cases brought by those crossing borders to seek asylum in the United States, Canada, and England. Fourth, I examine justifications set forth for the two proposed solutions to this shortcoming: incorporating gender claims into the existing grounds and expanding the refugee definition to include gender as a sixth category. I conclude that these justifications support the use of the currently enumerated categories for *gender-specific* claims but that a sixth category is warranted for those seeking asylum from *gender-based* persecution.

I. A Brief History of the Refugee Convention

The first half of the twentieth century was marked by massive civil unrest in Europe. Refugees fled revolution in Russia, the collapse of the Ottoman Empire in Turkey, the rise of fascism in Italy, civil war in Spain, and, perhaps most dramatically, the Second World War. As World War II unfolded, millions of people were forcibly displaced, deported, or resettled. In 1943, the Intergovernmental Committee of Refugees, the body charged with overseeing resettlement of refugees, expanded its mandate to include "all persons wherever they may be who, as a result of events in Europe, have had to leave their countries of residence because of the danger to their lives or liberties on account of their race, religion or political beliefs."[8] This definition of refugee both included those who had lost de jure national protection and extended to those who had lost de facto protection as a result of changing political climates. Although gender was absent from this initial (and from subsequent) lists, the origins of enumerated grounds upon which refugee status might be claimed were born.

The Intergovernmental Committee on Refugees was later replaced by the International Refugee Organization and, ultimately, by the United Nations High Commissioner for Refugees (UNHCR). In July and November 1951, the UNHCR convened delegates from twenty-six countries to address the refugee crisis. The question of the scope of the refugee definition was debated. Records from these proceedings reflect the tension between proposals for a broad definition to ensure the protection of a range of persecuted individuals and proposals to develop group categories based on political, geographic, and time limitations.

Some delegates expressed a desire for an expansive definition of the term "refugee." The Italian representative argued that "protection should be extended to as many refugees of all categories as possible; refugees should all be regarded purely and simply as unfortunate, destitute and homeless persons."[9] Representatives from both Canada and the United Kingdom also expressed a desire for "the widest possible definition" to be adopted.[10]

On the other hand, French and American delegates insisted on time and geographic limitations that would ensure a limited number of those qualifying for protection.[11] Indeed, the majority of the debate surrounding the definition of the term "refugee" was concerned with the proposal that time and geographic limitations be included in the definition such that only those fleeing political events occurring in Europe before 1951 would be eligible for refugee status. In addition to the political, time, and geographic discussions, the Swedish delegate announced his country's proposal that membership in a particular social group be added to race, nationality, religion, and political opinion as a ground upon which refugee status might be granted.[12] This proposal was adopted without debate.[13] A gender ground, however, was neither proposed nor adopted.

Ultimately, the definition of "refugee" included the time and geographic restrictions requested by the United States and France, as well as five enumerated grounds (or groups) that individuals would have to demonstrate belonging to in order to receive protection: race, nationality, religion, political opinion, and a particular social group.[14] It was not until 1967 that the time and geographic limitations were removed.[15]

The history of the Refugee Convention, then, reflects a tension between a desire to provide protection for persecuted individuals and the perceived need on the part of participating member countries to ensure that such protection be limited by a demonstration of group belonging. This tension—between individual suffering and group membership—is played out in a variety of contexts, including the one at issue here: the debate over where gender claims should be situated in contemporary applications of the Refugee Convention. Are women persecuted as individual political dissidents? As members of social groups? Or for their gender itself? The answers to these questions depend on the situation and, as I will argue below, are critical in weighing the arguments for and against adding gender as a sixth enumerated ground.

II. The Nature of Gender Persecution: Gender-Specific vs. Gender-Based Claims

Women are often persecuted for the same reasons as men. They are targeted because of their political beliefs, harmed as a result of their religious affiliations, and punished for their ethnic identifications. However, two distinctions may differentiate the persecution of women: its form and its motivation.

With respect to form, women are targeted in particular, *gender-specific* ways, including rape, sexual violence, forced abortion, compulsory sterilization, and forced pregnancy.[16] In these cases, the gender of the victim may dictate the manner of persecution but is not necessarily the reason for the persecutory act itself. As Andrea Binder notes, "gender-specific harm is not necessarily persecution perpetrated *because of* the victim's gender."[17] For example, rape or sexual abuse may be used to punish a woman because of her controversial political beliefs or identification as a religious or ethnic minority. In this example, gender determines what Heaven Crawley refers to as the "form" rather than the "fact" of persecution.[18]

By contrast, the motivation of the persecutor may differ when a woman, rather than a man, is the subject of persecution. In these cases, which I refer to as "*gender-based* persecution," there is a "causal relationship between gender and persecution."[19] Here, the *reason* for the persecution itself is the victim's gender. The form of the persecution in these cases may be gender-specific (for example, in the event of female genital mutilation) or it may not be (for example, a woman may be arrested and subject to lengthy imprisonment, a more traditional form of persecution, for violation of gendered social mores). What distinguishes gender-based persecution is not the form of persecution but its animating purpose.[20]

III. Weaknesses in Asylum Law's
Treatment of Gender Persecution

Women (and men) bringing gender-specific and gender-based claims face significant obstacles across jurisdictions under current asylum law. First, gender-specific persecution is often not treated as cognizable.[21] As a result, those whose claims rely on "harms that are unique to women"—or, as is demonstrated below, gender—may find their applications rejected for failure to demonstrate that they have suffered persecution.[22] The 1995 Canadian case of *Chan v. Canada*, brought by a man who fled China claiming a fear of forced sterilization, presents an example of how a male's claim of gender-specific persecution was rendered invisible in the eyes of the law.[23] The court dismissed Mr. Chan's appeal from his denial of asylum and—despite the dissent's argument to the contrary—refused to rule on whether forced sterilization of a man constitutes a cognizable form of persecution.[24]

Gender-based claims similarly risk being denied because the form of persecution (for example, regulation of dress and conduct) does not rise to the level of cognizable persecution, even if the reason for maltreatment is seen as unacceptable. This weakness is demonstrated by the denial of claims like the one asserted by Saideh Fisher, an Iranian citizen. Fisher was traumatized by encounters with Iranian police who stopped her initially because of her attendance at a male friend's party, where she witnessed the host in a bathing suit, and then again when she "had a few pieces of hair hanging out [of her chador or veil] by mistake."[25] In *Fisher*, the United States Court of Appeals for the Ninth Circuit found that although "Iran's dress code and conduct rules may seem harsh by Western standards," they did not amount to persecution.[26] Ms. Fisher's gender-specific treatment was not recognized as rising to the level of persecution under the law, leaving unacknowledged the gender-based motivation that lay underneath her discriminatory treatment. As a result, her claim—like that of Mr. Chan—was denied.

The critique that gender-specific and gender-based persecution may be rendered legally invisible is linked to the second concern with asylum law's treatment of gender claims, namely, that asylum law "privileges male-dominated public activities over the activities of women which take place largely in the private sphere."[27] Under the law, an applicant must show that he or she has been or will be persecuted by a government actor or by an actor whom the government is unable or unwilling to control.[28]

As a result, women—who often suffer at the hands of "private" actors, including family and local community members whose behavior in fact is condoned by the "public" sector—are saddled with the extra evidentiary burden of "proving that the government would be unable or unwilling to aid them."[29] This means that *gender-specific* claims may be denied because the perpetrator of a rape or sexual assault may have been a "private" individual rather than a government official. Similarly, *gender-based* claims risk being denied because "privately" held beliefs that lead to gendered or nongendered forms of harm must be shown to be government-sanctioned in order to be cognizable.

The adjudication of claims brought by women who have suffered domestic violence in their home countries demonstrates this weakness.[30] In an early case in the United States, *In Matter of Pierre*, the Board of Immigration Appeals (BIA) denied relief to a Haitian woman whose husband, a government official, threatened to kill her and, indeed, attempted to do so by burning down her home.[31] Despite this demonstration of persecution, the woman's claim was denied because "[t]he motivation behind [the husband's] alleged actions appears to be strictly personal."[32] Similar reasoning was used by the BIA to reject the claim of Rodi Pena-Alvarado, a Guatemalan woman who suffered ten years of abuse at the hands of her husband, a former soldier. After several fruitless attempts to obtain government protection, she fled to the United States in search of asylum.[33] Although the immigration judge initially granted her claim, the BIA reversed, finding that the husband's abuse was an "action[] by a private part[y]" and that the Guatemalan government did not "encourage[] its male citizens to abuse its female citizens, nor [did] the Government . . . suddenly and unreasonably withdraw[] protection from a segment of the population."[34] These domestic violence cases demonstrate that the visibility of gender claims is complicated not only by a hesitancy to identify gender-specific forms of treatment as persecutory but also by the difficulty of proving that acts traditionally conceived of as private matters (often because they occur within the family sphere) are explicitly or tacitly government sanctioned.

Third, even when women are able to overcome the gender-related hurdles of proving the persecution and the government-actor requirements necessary to make their stories "visible" for asylum purposes, their claims must still be located within one of the five enumerated grounds in order to be cognizable. Although case law in the United States and the United Kingdom, among others, demonstrates that successful gender-specific and gender-based claims have been argued on the grounds of political opinion and social group,[35] whether gender claims should continue to be rendered visible only along the traditional axes of political opinion and social group (as opposed to in an explicit gender category)—and what is at stake in this debate—is taken up in part 4 below.

Finally, critics deride the process to which female asylum applicants are subjected during the adjudication of their claims. There are significant emotional and cultural difficulties posed by requiring women to repeat their stories of gender-specific persecution, often before male adjudicators. Nancy Kelly explains that "[o]ften a woman is expected to repeat her story before a male interviewer or immigration judge with the assistance of a male interpreter . . . . This difficulty is exacerbated for women who, for cultural or religious reasons, will be ostracized by their families or communities if the assault becomes known."[36] As a result, "[e]ven where a woman has been persecuted . . . she thus finds it more difficult to establish her claim than a man."[37]

Administrative guidelines released by the UNHCR as well as by the Canadian, American, and Australian governments attempt to address some of these concerns. The UNHCR's "Guidelines on the Protection of Refugee Women"[38] (1991 UNHCR Guidelines) "discuss[] . . . protection from physical, sexual and other forms of violence in refugee camps, legal aspects of status determination, access to food, shelter and other services, as well as repatriation."[39] The guidelines recommend that women "fearing persecution or severe discrimination on the basis of their gender should be considered a member of a social group for the purposes of determining refugee status. Others may be seen as having made a religious or political statement in transgressing the social norms of their society."[40]

Similarly, the Canadian, American, and Australian administrative guidelines provide information, advice, and strategies for adjudicators dealing with gender-related claims.[41] The guidelines all "deal with the process by which women's claims are heard, as well as the substance of the refugee definition as it applies to women making gender-related claims. . . . [T]he content of the advice given is also very similar."[42] For example, all of the guidelines recognize and enumerate gender-specific forms of persecution, including sexual abuse, forced abortion, female genital mutilation, and forced marriage.[43] Likewise, the guidelines all encourage increased sensitivity on the part of adjudicators dealing with gender-related claims.[44] Nevertheless, none of the guidelines suggests the inclusion of gender as an enumerated ground. Rather, "they encourage decisionmakers to let gender inform their assessment under race, religion, nationality, or political opinion if possible."[45]

The UNHCR and country-specific guidelines, however, are advisory. They offer suggestions and strategies but do not have the force of binding law. Their impact is therefore difficult to assess.[46] Whether or not new law—in the form of the addition of a sixth enumerated ground—is preferable, or necessary, in order to better protect those with gender-related claims in the asylum process is the subject of part 4.

IV. Status Quo or Sixth Ground? Engaging the Debate

Advocates offer two potential responses to the treatment of gender-specific and gender-based claims in the asylum process: incorporating gender claims into the existing grounds and expanding the refugee definition to include gender as a sixth category. Below, I examine the justifications offered for both sides of the debate. I conclude that the justifications for maintaining the status quo suffice for the treatment of *gender-specific* claims but that those with *gender-based* claims might better be served by the addition of a sixth ground.

IV.A. Justifications for the Status Quo

Proponents of incorporating gender claims into the existing race, religion, nationality, political opinion, and social group grounds rely on both practical and theoretical justifications for this position. From the perspective of practical implementation, it is difficult to imagine a consensus among nations (or even advocates) forming around the addition of gender as a sixth ground to the well-established refugee definition. As Andrea Binder explains,

> While a reformulation of the refugee definition would be desirable, political realities and trends in immigration policies inevitably lead to the conclusion that this approach is not very promising for the near future. Rather, efforts may be focused on improving the administrative and judicial practices with regard to the existing conventional and statutory framework.[47]

Kristine Fox argues that this practical concern about the ability to reach consensus over a new ground weighs heavily in favor of maintaining the status quo in order to prevent short-term harm to women. She notes that "[a]dding gender to the Convention as an independent basis of persecution would unnecessarily delay assistance to women since member-nations will find it necessary to argue and debate a change of that magnitude."[48]

The question of whether a new ground is practically feasible, however, is distinct from whether such a ground is theoretically desirable. Proponents of the status quo offer several theoretical justifications in support of the incorporation of gender claims into the existing asylum grounds. First, proponents of this view argue that the problem with the adjudication of gender asylum claims does not lie primarily in the law itself but in "the social and political context in which the claims of women are adjudicated."[49] As a result, the appropriate solution to the problem does not lie in the addition of a new legal definition, but in increasing the sensitization of those who adjudicate asylum claims to women's persecution, in particular, by means of sexual violence. Heaven Crawley explains this perspective.

> The problem here does not lie with the refugee definition itself, which does not require decision-makers to view sexual violence as inherently private . . . what is at issue is a particular conceptualization of sexual violence that legitimates and normalizes it. In this context, what we need to address is the way in which a nonlegal conception of violence is used to distort sexual abuse.[50]

This argument addresses the concern that *gender-specific* claims are not recognized as persecution within the current asylum framework and persuasively proposes increased sensitization rather than further legal specification as a means to address this problem. However, it leaves the question of how to deal with *gender-based* claims unresolved.

Second, proponents of adjudicating women's claims within the current legal framework argue that "the addition of 'gender' as a new category . . . would bear the risk of reducing diverse female experience to a specific category of gender related persecution which might lead to an even stronger exclusion of women from the traditional refugee definition."[51] This argument assumes that setting gender claims *apart* by creating a new category will serve to further isolate women from mainstream asylum law.[52] A preferable approach would be to structure "the dominant paradigm of refugee law . . . around a partial, gender perspective . . . compel[ling] representatives to challenge former interpretations and decision-makers to respond constructively and imaginatively to these arguments."[53] This approach has the advantage of raising sensitivity to the ways in which gender may be a motivating factor of persecutors while ensuring that violations against women are seen as part and parcel of violations of broader human rights.[54] Again, however, this justification seems best suited to gender-specific claims in that it draws attention to the ways in which gendered *forms* of harm, for example, rape or forced abortion, are akin to other traditional means of persecution while arguing that at their root, these forms of persecution are inflicted because of divergent political or religious views, rather than because of gender.

Third, proponents of adjudicating gender claims within the existing Refugee Convention framework argue that separating women's claims out from the traditional grounds risks "depolitic[izing] women's lives."[55] As Thomas Spijkerboer notes, "[t]here is . . . a clear tendency to see what women do and what is done to them as related to culture. . . . And, somehow, that which is cultural is considered as non-political."[56] Heaven Crawley clarifies the political nature of the "cultural," explaining "that there is a tendency to misinterpret the causal relationship between gender and persecution. . . . Often women are not persecuted because they are women but . . . because they refuse to be 'proper' women. This is a political issue. . . ."[57] If claims of gender persecution are adjudicated within the traditional grounds of political asylum law, women's stories may be told as stories of political harm rather than as tales of cultural misfortune.

This third justification begins to touch on the way gender-based harms might appropriately be adjudicated within the existing framework. If gender-based persecution is theorized as a form of political persecution, the existing political opinion category is rendered well suited for the adjudication of gender-based claims.[58] Similarly, proponents of incorporating gender claims into the traditional Refugee Convention grounds have argued that gender-based claims might comfortably fit within the race, nationality,[59] and religion grounds. The majority of these theorists, however, believe that membership in a particular social group (MPSG) is the most logical home for gender-based claims. Lesley Hunt, of Australia's Immigration Tribunal, states succinctly the justification for using MPSG to adjudicate gender-based claims:

"[W]omen," . . . whilst being a broad category, nonetheless have both immutable characteristics and shared common social characteristics which make them cognisable as a group which may attract persecution. . . . Another element binding all women, regardless of culture or class, is that of fear of being subjected to male violence. . . . Whilst there does exist separation in lifestyles, values, political leanings, etc., women share a defined social status and as such are differentially dealt with by society as a group.[60]

Opponents of adjudicating gender claims within the MPSG ground raise two arguments. First, the size of the group risks opening the refugee floodgates to half the world's population. Although this concern "has no basis in fact or reason," in that a showing of individualized persecution would still be required of each applicant, it is nevertheless consistently raised in debates over whether women can constitute a particular social group under asylum law.[61] Second, opponents point to the risk that using MPSG "essentializes" women by creating a "false sense of cohesiveness, which women as a group do not in fact possess."[62] As Heaven Crawley explains, "'Women' are not a cohesive group. . . . Whilst there are undoubtedly cases where gender alone is the basis for persecutory treatment, more often the persecution is not applied equally to all women."[63] The tension among theorists over which category is most appropriate for the adjudication of gender-based claims suggests that none of the existing categories comfortably accommodates the claims of women fleeing gender-based persecution. This debate over which ground, political opinion or MPSG, in particular, should serve as the basis for gender-based claims points to room for theorizing about a sixth ground to accommodate claims where gender is responsible for the "fact" and not just the "form" of persecution.

IV.B. Justifications for a Sixth Ground

Proponents of adding gender as a sixth ground within the asylum definition also rely on both practical and theoretical justifications to support their position. These theorists argue that practicality should be measured not in terms of the political feasibility of adding a sixth ground but in terms of what actually makes sense for ensuring the protection of women seeking relief from persecution. They urge that, judged in these terms, it is more effective to create a separate ground that is geared towards and responsive to gender claims than to try to manipulate these claims so that they fit into the existing categories. As Emily Love explains, "By adding a sixth category of persecution, Congress can ensure that immigration judges grant the protection of asylum to those women who face persecution . . . without having to struggle to fit that harm into an existing category."[64]

Several theoretical justifications also support the addition of gender as a sixth ground. First, the methodology by which gender claims are incorporated into asylum law, i.e., through manipulation of the existing grounds or addition of a separate ground, is not neutral.[65] "Methodology[,]" it is argued, "can either empower or shuffle the status quo."[66] In these theorists' view, a methodological approach that reframes asylum law's orientation towards gender claims by allowing women's stories to be told as they experience them is preferable to one that constructs women's claims within the parameters of male-dominated categories. Mattie Stevens explains,

> The proposed approaches to recognizing women's refugee claims [by incorporating them into existing categories] rely on methods that place a great deal of discretion in the hands of judges who are largely white, male, conservative, and unelected. These approaches do not openly challenge the biases against women inherent in the process of petitioning for refugee status. . . .[67]

In order to overcome these biases, Stevens urges the necessity of a major methodological overhaul that "would ensure that claims to refugee status accurately reflect women's reality by allowing them to tell their story as opposed to attempting to tailor it to the current categories."[68]

This theoretical justification for adding a sixth ground is more closely aligned with the concerns raised by *gender-based* rather than *gender-specific* claims. Empowering women to "tell their stor[ies]" as they experience them, rather than adapting them to the existing categories, makes sense for claims where a woman is persecuted *because of* her gender. For example, a woman fleeing female genital mutilation (FGM) might have difficulty telling her story in a way that conforms to the existing categories.[69] Such a woman's asylum claim may arguably be constructed as one of political opinion, in that she believes that she has an affirmative right not to be mutilated by the political leaders of her tribe. Such a claim might also be (and has more typically been) constructed as an MPSG claim, whereby it is argued that the woman is a member of a particular social group of women who are members of tribes that engage in genital mutilation but oppose the practice.[70] However, each of these constructions requires women to tell their stories in a way that sidesteps the root reason for their persecution: the fact that they belong to the female gender. Creating a sixth ground would do away with the need to manipulate stories that are about gender, like those of FGM claimants, into stories that are about abstract "political opinions" and "social groups." If being able to tell one's story accurately is the measure of an empowering methodology, then, in *gender-based cases*, the addition of a sixth ground would empower women to identify the real reason for their persecutory treatment.

The methodological justification, however, is less convincing with respect to *gender-specific* claims. In these cases, the underlying reason for the harm is in line with an already existing category. For example, a political activist who is raped in retribution for her participation in a street protest will be able accurately to recount that she was persecuted on account of her political opinion. Again, if being able to tell one's story accurately is the measure of an empowering methodology, then in *gender-specific* cases, maintaining the status quo by allowing women to tell (and recognizing) their stories as ones of political, religious, or ethnic persecution would be the methodologically preferable approach.

Second, arguments for adding gender as a sixth ground, like those that support using MPSG as a home for gender claims, conceive of women as a coherent group for the purposes of asylum recognition. In particular, advocates identify subordinate social status and vulnerability to persecution as elements that bind all women.[71] Catharine MacKinnon's work, though it does not directly address asylum law, is helpful in clarifying the theoretical basis for this claim. She explains that "[w]omen are a global group in the sense that the distinctive social definition, treatment, and status of women as a sex relative to men is recognizable in diverse forms all over the world. Both women's subordination and their resistance to it have been global all along."[72] Indeed, she argues that the upsurge of transnational feminist movements[73] has solidified women as a global, social group. She notes that "[i]n challenging men's rule . . . women as such have emerged not only as a group in itself—a transnational group created through treatment that is not limited by national boundaries—but also as a group for itself, self-consciously realized through organizing."[74]

Recognizing women as a coherent group, with gender as its identifying marker is, in MacKinnon's view, a critical step in acknowledging and rectifying harms perpetrated against women. Although "[i]ndividuals may suffer discrimination one at a time, . . . the basis for the injury is group membership."[75] In order to pursue real remedies to the persecutory treatment of women throughout the world, it is necessary to recognize and address the group-based nature of the harms they suffer. If the notion that women are (or have become) a global, social group has merit, then the addition of a sixth ground that identifies the group—and recognizes persecution on the basis of it—makes sense. Although this same argument might be used to justify using the existing MPSG ground, for the methodological reasons highlighted above, sixth-ground theorists would probably not find such a response sufficient.

This theoretical justification for the addition of a sixth ground may be met with the same primary critique as that leveled against the inclusion of gender-based claims in the MPSG category—that it improperly "essentialize[s]" women in a way that is neither accurate nor politically desirable.[76] Again, MacKinnon's work is useful in constructing a response to this argument. MacKinnon argues that because feminism emphasizes the social construction of actual women, it does not fall prey to the anti-essentialist critique.[77] She points out that acknowledging that women share commonalities that bind them in relevant ways "improve[s] one's ability to analyze hierarchy as socially constructed."[78] One does not need to view women as "homogenous" in order to acknowledge that women "are marked and defined and controlled by" their sex and gender in ways that have resulted in their subordinate and vulnerable status throughout the world.[79] Anti-essentialist arguments, MacKinnon claims, result in multicultural defenses for gendered violence instead of acknowledging the fact that such violence is a universal phenomenon.[80] This type of argumentation risks reducing all people to "individuals" and hence never being able to give a meaningful account of the group-based nature of persecution, precisely the type of harm that asylum law concerns itself with.[81]

MacKinnon's response to anti-essentialist concerns maps well onto arguments for adding gender as a sixth ground in asylum law. If gender is added as a sixth ground, the asylum definition will recognize the universal nature of gendered harms. At the same time, however, it may avoid the essentialist critique by allowing actual women's experiences (rather than assumptions about what types of harms are or are not gender-based) to drive its application. Analogizing the posited gender category to the current political opinion ground is helpful in illustrating this point. The political opinion ground creates no essential prototype of an opinion that is cognizable for purposes of asylum law. It does not presume that all political activists throughout the world have similar beliefs or are animated by the same factors. As a result, minions of former dictators who fear persecution when their regimes collapse may be eligible for asylum (so long as they have not been perpetrators of persecution themselves), just as those who fight on the front lines for democratic reform are eligible for relief.

Similarly, the creation of a gender ground in asylum law need not presume that all women the world over suffer equally from state-sanctioned rules and violence that target women. Rather, it would make eligible for relief those women who are able to demonstrate that they fear persecution for any number of gender-based reasons, including their opposition to oppressive laws like those that mandate severe punishments for immodest dress or their fear of genital cutting. The creation of a gender category in asylum law need not be "essentializing" in this view. It would be broad enough to incorporate the claims of all who could establish any gender-based reason that resulted in cognizable persecution. Whether or not one agrees with the propriety of the gendered reason (i.e., whether or not one thinks women should dress modestly or should be circumcised) would be irrelevant to the analysis, just as whether or not one agrees with the political views of an asylum seeker is irrelevant to the adjudication of his/her political opinion claim; a gender-based reason that results in persecutory treatment would be enough to establish a claim.

This theoretical justification for a sixth ground is persuasive in addressing the adjudication of claims where the actual or feared persecution is *because of* gender, namely, *gender-based* claims. Because this justification is grounded in the notion that what is cognizable about women as a group is their "distinctive social definition, treatment, and status[,]" only those claims which demonstrate a nexus between this status and the persecution would be served by a gender ground. It would be more difficult to establish such a nexus in a *gender-specific* claim, if, as has been posited, the manner in which persecution is perpetrated is conceived of as distinct from the reason animating the persecution.[82] If this is the case, then a woman who is raped for her political activities might have a harder time showing that it is her gender "status[,]" rather than her political beliefs, that animated the persecution. She would thus not be eligible for relief under the new, gender category, though she would have a cognizable political opinion claim.

A final theoretical justification for adding a gender ground, rather than incorporating women's claims into existing categories, is the healing power of recognizing the collective identity of women who have been destroyed by sexual violence.

> Identification with the identity sought to be appropriated and defiled can reclaim and restore part of what the rape destroyed; the particularity of one's humanity and the particular meaning of collective identity. This partly

explains why understanding that one was raped as a woman, not as an individual—identification with women in that sense—can be experienced as affirming and healing. It can go some distance toward restoring the specific part of one's humanity that sexual violation took away.[83]

The addition of a separate, gender ground may affirm women's collective identity and be healing in a way that subsuming their stories into male-dominated categories may not.

This justification for a sixth ground blurs the line between *gender-based* and *gender-specific* violence that has been drawn throughout the literature and this chapter. It assumes that sexual violence, without regard to the reason for its perpetration, harms women as women in a way that requires acknowledgment and collective healing. Such a justification would support the incorporation of both gender-specific and gender-based harms in a sixth ground. Practically speaking, this justification may ring true. However, as a legal matter, asylum law clearly prohibits defining a social group—or, in this case, an entire ground—by reference to persecutory conduct.[84] It is likely that an asylum adjudicator faced with a *gender-specific* claim would find that the manner of persecution was not sufficient to establish that the reason for the persecution was *gender-based*. Such a finding would be fatal to the claim even if a sixth ground were to be added.

V. Conclusion

Women like Sofia Campos-Guardado and Olimpia Lazo-Majano continue to flee persecution in search of the protections of a Refugee Convention that does not explicitly acknowledge gender asylum claims. I have argued that the convention's currently enumerated categories are sufficient (and, in some ways, preferable) for the adjudication of *gender-specific* claims, but that a sixth category is warranted for those seeking asylum from *gender-based* persecution.

Whether or not one's weighing of the costs and benefits of each approach aligns with my own, it should be clear that the stakes are high in the debate over whether to incorporate gender claims within the existing Refugee Convention grounds or to add a sixth ground. These stakes include whether women (and men) will be able to accurately recount their persecution as stories of gender subordination, political activism, or religious conviction; whether the universality of gender violence is forthrightly acknowledged or the perceived harm of essentializing women is protected against; and ultimately, whether the approach that is chosen will meaningfully assist refugees crossing borders in search of freedom from persecution.

NOTES

1. *See* Campos-Guardado v. INS, 809 F.2d 285, 287 (5th Cir. 1987), cert. denied, 484 U.S. 826 (1987).

2. *See* Lazo-Majano v. INS, 813 F.2d 1432, 1433 (9th Cir. 1987), overruled in part on other grounds by Fisher v. INS, 79 F.3d 955 (9th Cir. 1996).

3. Convention Relating to Status of Refugees, July 28, 1951, art. I(A)(2), 19 U.S.T. 6260, 189 U.N.T.S. 137.

4. The 1951 Refugee Convention definition reads in relevant part,

> The term "refugee" shall apply to any person who . . . owing to well-founded fear of being persecuted for reasons of race, religion, nationality, membership of a particular social group or political opinion, is outside the country of his nationality and is unable, or owing to such fear, is unwilling to avail himself of the protection of that country; or who, not having a nationality and being outside the country of his former habitual residence as a result of such events, is unable or, owing to such fear, is unwilling to return to it. (Convention Relating to Status of Refugees, July 28, 1951, art. I(A)(2), 19 U.S.T. 6260, 189 U.N.T.S. 137)

5. *See, e.g.,* Heaven Crawley, *Refugees and Gender: Law and Process* (Bristol, UK: Jordan Publishing, 2001); Audrey Macklin, "Cross-Border Shopping for Ideas: A Critical Review of United States, Canadian, and Australian Approaches to Gender-Related Asylum Claims," *Georgetown Immigration Law Journal* 13 (Fall 1998): 25.

6. A significant feminist literature examines the distinction between sex and gender as well as analyzes how the relationship between sex and gender intersects with the rights of individuals. I use the term "gender" to refer to a political and social, rather than a biological, ascription. Therefore, many of the arguments here may apply to those of both the female and the male sex, with the notable exception of the arguments with respect to what I define as gender-specific persecution. For further discussion of this distinction, see Judith Butler, *Gender Trouble* (New York: Routledge, 1990); Gayle Rubin, "The Traffic in Women: Notes on the 'Political Economy' of Sex," in *Toward an Anthropology of Women*, ed. Rayna R. Reiter (New York: Monthly Review Press, 1975), 157.

7. *See, e.g.,* Mattie L. Stevens, "Recognizing Gender-Specific Persecution: A Proposal to Add Gender as a Sixth Refugee Category," *Cornell Journal of Law and Public Policy* 3 (1993): 179; Emily Love, Recent Developments, "Equality in

Political Asylum Law: For a Legislative Recognition of Gender-Based Persecution," *Harvard Women's Law Journal* 17 (1994): 152–53; Lindsay M. Gray, Note, "Changing Asylum Law for Afghan Women under the Taliban: Desperate Times, Moderate Measures," *Brandeis Law Journal* 40 (Winter 2001): 557, 572.

8. Karen Musalo, Jennifer Moore, and Richard A. Boswell, *Refugee Law and Policy: A Comparative and International Approach*, 2nd ed. (Durham, NC: Carolina Academic Press, 2002), 21 (*quoting* United Nations High Commissioner for Refugees, *An Introduction to the International Protection of Refugees*, 1992), 4–5, *available at* http:// www.reliefweb.int/rw/rwt.nsf/db900SID/NVEA-5ULK8F/$File/unhcr-RLD1.pdf?OpenElement).

9. Statement of Mr. del Drago, Representative from Italy, U.N. Doc. A/CONF.2/SR.2, at 10, July 20, 1951.

10. Statement of Mr. Hoare, Representative from the United Kingdom, U.N. Doc. A/CONF.2/SR.19 at 17, Nov. 26, 1951. The Canadian delegate explained that "[h]e was personally in favor of the widest possible definition, and only regretted that it has been impossible to reach agreement upon it." Statement of Mr. Chance, Representative from Canada, ibid., 6.

11. *See generally* Statement of Mr. Rochefort, Representative from France, and Statement of Mr. Warren, Representative from the United States, U.N. Doc. A/CONF.2/SR.3, at 10–13, 15–16, Nov. 19, 1951.

12. Statement of Mr. Petren, Representative from Sweden, U.N. Doc. A/CONF.2/SR.3, at 14, Nov. 19, 1951.

13. The social group ground—despite the fact that it was not heavily debated at its adoption—has in some ways come to embody the central tension between generosity and limitation that pervaded the 1951 Convention. On the one hand, its ambiguity leaves room for expansion of protection to those asylum seekers whose stories don't fit comfortably within the other enumerated grounds, including women, homosexuals, and children. *See, e.g., infra* note 35. On the other hand, the social group ground, like the other categories enumerated at the 1951 Convention, reflects a commitment to the use of group belonging as a means of limiting claims to refugee relief.

14. The 1951 Refugee Convention definition reads,

The term "refugee" shall apply to any person who. . . . [a]s a result of events occurring before 1 January 1951 and owing to well-founded fear of being persecuted for reasons of race, religion, nationality, membership of a particular social group or political opinion, is outside the country of his nationality and is unable, or owing to such fear, is unwilling to avail himself of the protection of that country; or who, not having a nationality and being outside the country of his former habitual residence as a result of such events, is unable or, owing to such fear, is unwilling to return to it. (Convention Relating to Status of Refugees, July 28, 1951, art. I(A)(2), 19 U.S.T. 6260, 189 U.N.T.S. 137)

15. Protocol Relating to the Status of Refugees, opened for signature, Jan. 31, 1967, art. I, 19 U.S.T. 6223, 606 U.N.T.S. 267 (entered into force Oct. 4, 1967).

16. *See*, e.g., Andrea Binder, "Gender and the 'Membership in a Particular Social Group' Category of the 1951 Refugee Convention," *Columbia Journal of Gender and Law* 10 (2001): 167, 172–73 (noting that this distinction "relates to the types and forms of persecution that are *gender-specific*").

17. Ibid., 168.

18. Heaven Crawley, "Women and Refugee Status: Beyond the Public/Private Dichotomy in UK Asylum Policy," in *Engendering Forced Migration: Theory and Practice*, Doreen Indra, ed. (New York and Oxford: Berghahn Books, 1998), 324.

19. Binder, "Gender and the 'Membership in a Particular Social Group' Category," supra note 16, 168.

20. Ibid., 175 ("In these cases, gender may act as either the persecutor's single motivation or it can be one factor among others. . . ."). Anjana Bahl has characterized the distinction between gender-specific and gender-based claims by noting that the former

> includes and focuses on persecution that, for the most part, is particular to women—namely sexual abuse, rape, genital mutilation, domestic violence and bride burning" while the latter includes "claims which constitute persecution because of the applicant's gender—persecution for disobeying repressive laws or for not conforming with social mores that are offensive to women. This category also includes situations that discriminate against women and strictly prohibits them from engaging in certain activities." (Anjana Bahl, "Home Is Where the Brute Lives: Asylum Law and Gender-Based Claims of Persecution," *Cardozo Women's Law Journal* 4 (1997): 35–36)

21. *See*, e.g., Lindsay A. Franke, Note, "Not Meeting the Standard: U.S. Asylum Law and Gender-Related Claims," *Arizona Journal of International and Comparative Law* 17 (Fall 2000): 605 (noting that asylum law is not well suited to women's claims, in part, because women suffer unique forms of harm); Mattie L. Stevens, "Recognizing Gender-Specific Persecution," supra note 7, 179, 203 (noting that the current asylum definition does not take into account gender-specific persecution).

22. Franke, "Not Meeting the Standard," supra note 21, 611. *See also* Linda K. Kerber, "Toward a History of Statelessness in America," *American Quarterly* 57 (2005): 729 (noting that "[o]nly recently have gender-specific asylum claims such as rape, dowry-related violence, or coerced female circumcision been recognized, and that recognition has been sporadic").

23. Chan v. Canada (Minister of Employment and Immigration) [1995] 3 S.C.R. 593.

24. Ibid. The Federal Court of Appeal in Canada has ruled that forced sterilization may constitute persecution for the purposes of asylum law, but it did so

in a case brought by a woman claimant. *See* Cheung v. Canada (Minister of Employment and Immigration) [1993] 2 F.C. 314.

25. Fisher v. INS, 79 F.3d 955, 959 (9th Cir. 1996).

26. Ibid., 961.

27. Nancy Kelly, "Gender-Related Persecution: Assessing the Asylum Claims of Women," *Cornell International Law Journal* 26 (1993): 628.

28. 8 U.S.C. § 1101(a)(42)(a)(2006) (defining a refugee as any person outside of his or her country of nationality who is "unable or unwilling to avail himself or herself of the protection [his or her country]." *See, e.g.*, Navas v. INS, 217 F.3d 646, 655–56 (9th Cir. 2000); Llano-Castellon v. INS, 16 F.3d 1093, 1097–98 (10th Cir. 1994).

29. Franke, "Not Meeting the Standard," supra note 21, 613.

30. *See, e.g.*, Laura S. Adams, "Fleeing the Family: A Domestic Violence Victim's Particular Social Group," *Loyola Law Review* 49 (2003): 288 (arguing "that countries that systematically fail to protect victims of domestic violence do so because of a policy choice to defer to private ordering in the context of the family"). Domestic violence is only one example of a type of gender claim that is often denied because of the private actor problem; honor killings represent another. *See also, In re F.O.*, CGRS Case No. 263 (United States) (unpublished decision from Immigration Judge) (denying asylum to a Jordanian woman whose father ordered male family members to kill her on sight for engaging in sexual transgressions).

31. 15 I. & N. Dec. 461, 461–62 (BIA 1975).

32. Ibid., 463.

33. *In re R.A.*, 22 I. & N. Dec. 906 (BIA 1999) (overturned by a 2001 interim decision of the attorney general).

34. Ibid., 922. The denial of Ms. Pena-Alvarado's claim raised serious protest. In January 2005, Attorney General John Ashcroft remanded the case back to the BIA and both advocates and the government submitted briefs in support of granting asylum. The Center for Gender and Refugee Studies, the group representing Ms. Pena-Alvarado, maintains updates of the progress of the case at http://cgrs.uchastings.edu/campaigns/alvarado.php (last accessed on February 16, 2007).

35. *See, e.g.*, Lazo-Majano v. INS, 813 F.2d 1432, 1435 (9th Cir. 1987) (holding that the abuse and rape of Ms. Lazo-Majano was on account of her abuser's political opinion "that a man has a right to dominate" and because of "one specific opinion [her abuser] attributed to her. She is, she has been told by [her abuser], a subversive."); *In re* Kasinga, 21 I. & N. Dec. 357 (BIA 1996) (granting asylum to a woman at risk of female genital mutilation as part of a social group of women who are members of tribes that engage in genital mutilation but oppose the practice). *See also* Islam v. Sec'y of State for the Home Dep't [1999] 2 A.C. 629, 629-30 (H.L.) (U.K.) (granting asylum based on social group membership to two Pakistani women who were abused and then abandoned by their husbands after having been accused of adultery).

36. Kelly, "Gender-Related Persecution," supra note 27, 630.

37. Ibid.

38. Guidelines on the Protection of Refugee Women, Office of the United Nations High Commissioner for Refugees, U.N. Doc. ES/SCP/67 (July 22, 1991) [hereinafter 1991 UNHCR Guidelines].

39. Macklin, "Cross-Border Shopping for Ideas," supra note 5, 29.

40. 1991 UNHCR Guidelines, supra note 38, 40.

41. *See* Immigration and Refugee Board of Canada, Guidelines Issued by the Chairperson Pursuant to Section 65(3) of the Immigration Act, Guideline 4, Women Refugee Claimants Fearing Gender-Related Persecution, *available at* http://www.irb-cisr.gc.ca/en/ about/guidelines/women_e.htm (last accessed December 22, 2006) [hereinafter Canada Guidelines]; Memorandum from Phyllis Coven, Office of International Affairs, Considerations for Asylum Officers Adjudicating Asylum Claims from Women (May 26, 1995), *available at* http://cgrs.uchastings.edu/documents/legal/guidelines_us.pdf (last visited Dec. 22, 2006) [hereinafter U.S. Considerations]; Dep't of Immigration and Multicultural Affairs (Austl.), Refugee and Humanitarian Visa Applicants: Guidelines on Gender Issues for Decision Makers, July 1996, *available at* http://cgrs.uchastings.edu/ documents/legal/guidelines_aust.pdf (last accessed December 22, 2006) [hereinafter Australia Guidelines]. For a useful comparison of the Canadian, Australian, and United States gender guidelines, see Macklin, "Cross-Border Shopping for Ideas," supra note 5, 27–71.

42. Macklin, "Cross-Border Shopping for Ideas," supra note 5, 30.

43. Canada Guidelines, 7; U.S. Considerations, 703–4; Australia Guidelines, 4.4., 4.6, all supra note 41.

44. Macklin, "Cross-Border Shopping for Ideas," supra note 5, 35 ("All three sets of directives counsel decisionmakers to be sensitive to the variety of religious, cultural, and personal reasons why women might experience pain, trauma, humiliation, or shame in recounting certain incidents, especially those of a sexual nature.").

45. Ibid., 52.

46. Macklin believes that "[w]hether directives are formally binding or otherwise, institutional incentives to abide by them do have an effect." Ibid., 33. She does, however, acknowledge that "[i]t is not feasible . . . to measure the impact of the Guidelines and Consideration on number or proportion of successful gender-related refugee claims" for various reasons, including fluctuation in conditions and immigration rates from countries of origin. Ibid., 34.

47. Binder, "Gender and the 'Membership in a Particular Social Group' Category," supra note 16, 193.

48. Kristine M. Fox, Note and Comment, "Gender Persecution: Canadian Guidelines Offer a Model for Refugee Determination in the United States," *Arizona Journal of International and Comparative Law* 11 (Spring 1994): 131.

49. Heaven Crawley, "Women and Refugee Status," supra note 18, 311.

50. Ibid., 316.

51. Birthe Ankenbrand, "Refugee Women under German Asylum Law," *International Journal of Refugee Law* 14 (2002): 45.

52. Thomas Spijkerboer argues that separating gender claims out "invites the idea that the claims do not belong to the core of refugee law and should therefore be dealt with by granting something less than refugee status." Thomas Spijkerboer, *Gender and Refugee Status* (Burlington, VT: Ashgate, 2000), 130. Although this observation was made in the context of acknowledging women as a particular social group, it would apply with equal—if not greater—force to the complete separation of gender claims into a sixth category.

53. C. J. Harvey, Review Essay, "Gender, Refugee Law, and the Politics of Interpretation," *International Journal of Refugee Law* 12 (2000): 685; *Women as Asylum-Seekers: A Legal Handbook* (London: Immigration Practitioners' Assoc., Refugee Action & Refugee Women's Legal Group, 1997), *4.

54. Heaven Crawley explains the challenge as "whether it is possible to design and enforce laws, policies and practices which take into account the specific experiences of women without losing sight of the universalist claims made in this area of legal discourse." Ibid., *1.

55. Ankenbrand, "Refugee Women under German Asylum Law," supra note 51, 56.

56. Spijkerboer, *Gender and Refugee Status*, supra note 52, 131–32.

57. Crawley, *Refugees and Gender*, supra note 5, 62–63.

58. Audrey Macklin offers a strong critique of the use of the political opinion ground to adjudicate gender-based claims, particularly those where domestic violence is at issue.

> Consider that it would be odd to argue that South African whites oppressed blacks because blacks held the political opinion that they were entitled to be treated as human beings (although they presumably did hold that belief). Indeed, apartheid existed because of the racist beliefs of whites—in other words, blacks were persecuted because of their racialized identity, not because of what they believed. By the same token, domestic violence is not about what a woman believes, but about her gender identity—and the sexist beliefs of the man who abuses her. This cannot be captured under the rubric of political opinion because . . . political opinion refers to the victim's beliefs and not those of the persecutor. (Macklin, "Cross-Border Shopping for Ideas," supra note 5, 59)

See also Catharine MacKinnon, *Are Women Human?: And Other International Dialogues* (Cambridge, MA: Harvard University Press, 2006), 60 (explaining that the reality of women's choices and the way women's lives are structured is not explicitly political because women don't have the power to control the social or political contexts in which they live). MacKinnon's insight, though not made specifically with respect to asylum law, is useful for understanding why women's claims might not fit comfortably into the political opinion ground.

59. Heaven Crawley, among others, develops a link between nationality and gender claims, discussing the harm that results from loss of citizenship when women marry foreign men.

[A] gender-related claim of fear of persecution may also be linked to reasons of nationality in situations where a law causes a woman to lose her nationality (i.e. citizenship) because of marriage to a foreign national. Whilst some nationality laws are therefore discriminatory, fear of persecution must not arise from the fact of losing nationality itself but rather the consequences which may be suffered as a result. (Crawley, *Refugees and Gender*, supra note 5, 65)

60. RRT Reference: N93/00656 at 13–17 (Aug. 3, 1994) (Hunt), *quoted in* Macklin, "Cross-Border Shopping for Ideas," supra note 5, 64–66.

61. Crawley, "Women and Refugee Status," supra note 18, 73.

62. Review Essay, "Gender, Refugee Law, and the Politics of Interpretation," supra note 53, 693. I take up the anti-essentialist argument in section IV.B below.

63. Crawley, "Women and Refugee Status," supra note 18, 73.

64. Emily Love, "Equality in Political Asylum Law," supra note 7, 152–53. See *also* Lindsay M. Gray, "Changing Asylum Law for Afghan Women," supra note 7, 572 ("Although the social group and political opinion categories, in theory, provide a basis for a successful asylum claim, in reality, they fall short of consistent protection for women.").

65. *See* Mattie L. Stevens, "Recognizing Gender-Specific Persecution," supra note 7, 213. *See also* Katharine T. Bartlett, "Feminist Legal Methods," *Harvard Law Review* 103 (1990): 830–31 ("Feminists cannot ignore method, because if they seek to challenge existing structures of power with the same methods that have defined what counts within those structures, they may instead, 'recreate the illegitimate power structures [that they are] trying to identify and undermine.'").

66. Stevens, "Recognizing Gender-Specific Persecution," supra note 7, 213.

67. Ibid., 214.

68. Ibid., 215.

69. *See, e.g.,* Gregory A. Kelson, "Female Circumcision in the Modern Age: Should Female Circumcision Now Be Considered Grounds for Asylum in the United States?," *Buffalo Human Rights Law Review* 4 (1998): 207–8 (proposing the "inclu[sion] of gender as a category of persecution" as a solution to the problems he lays out with respect to the adjudication of FGM claims in the United States).

70. *See, e.g., In re* Kasinga, 21 I. & N. Dec. 357 (BIA 1996).

71. *See, e.g.,* Macklin, "Cross-Border Shopping for Ideas," supra note 5, 67 (endorsing Lesley Hunt's argument for conceiving of women as a social group in that it "elaborates on why the subordinated social status of women constitutes them as a particular social group, and links both domestic violence and inadequate state protection in response to that status").

72. MacKinnon, *Are Women Human?*, supra note 58, 13.

73. *See, e.g.,* Valentine M. Moghadam, "Global Feminism, Citizenship, and the State: Negotiating Women's Rights in the Middle East and North Africa," in this volume.

74. MacKinnon, *Are Women Human?,* supra note 58, 12.

75. Ibid., 5.

76. *See* notes 62 and 63 accompanying text.

77. MacKinnon, *Are Women Human?,* supra note 58, 51. Iris Marion Young's work on the nature of social groups also offers a counterargument to the anti-essentialist critique. She explains, "Although social processes of affinity and differentiation produce groups, they do not give groups a substantive essence. There is no common nature that members of a group share." Iris Marion Young, *Justice and the Politics of Difference* (Princeton, NJ: Princeton University Press, 1990), 47.

78. MacKinnon, *Are Women Human?,* supra note 58, 52.

79. Ibid., 51.

80. "Why," MacKinnon asks, "are we coming up with a multicultural defense for *each* culture in which men specifically and particularly are permitted to believe that rape is sex, instead of looking at the assumption that rape happens in a man's mind rather than in a woman's body in all of them?" Ibid., 54.

81. Whether or not—and how—people of the same gender may constitute a "group" is the subject of an ongoing debate in feminist theory. Although this chapter only skims the surface of this debate in its treatment of the anti-essentialist critique, for further insight into this problem, see Iris Marion Young, *Justice and the Politics of Difference,* supra note 77, 42–48.

82. MacKinnon's work indirectly challenges the gender-specific vs. gender-based distinction. She argues that sexual violence, no matter the reason for its perpetration, harms women as women (not only, as has been argued, as political activists). MacKinnon explains that "sexual assault destroys women as women, including their capacity to cohere as such, just as genocidal rape destroys or seeks to destroy Muslims and Croats and Tutsis and Jews, defining, and in so doing in part constituting, the groups as a subordinate people." *Are Women Human?,* supra note 77, 226.

83. Ibid., 229.

84. "There is more than a hint of circularity in the view that a number of persons may be held to fear persecution by reason of membership in a particular social group where what is said to unite those persons into a particular social group is their common fear of persecution." Applicant A v. MIEA [1997] 190 C.L.R. 225, 242 (Austl.) (opinion of Dawson, J.) (concluding that "[t]he 'particular social group' that the appellants rely upon [parents with one child who desire a second child and who are subject to particular persecutory official sanctions or subject to particular persecutory conduct, that is, compulsory sterilization] is impermissibly defined by reference to persecutory conduct"). *Applicant A,* 190 C.L.R.

||||||||||||||||||||||||||||||||||||||||||||||||||||||||

12

Intercultural Political Identity:
Are We There Yet?

Angelia K. Means

Anamnesis and story-telling can also provide reasons. . .
—Juergen Habermas, Religion and Rationality[1]

The Next Step

Before Nicholas Sarkozy was elected president of France, he was the "famous" minister of the interior, who suppressed riots in which immigrants from North Africa set cars ablaze in the suburbs of Paris. He called the protestors "scum" and insisted that France needed a "Ministry of Immigration and Identity" to facilitate assimilation. According to Sarkozy, both Europeanization and immigration have put pressure on French national identity: Europe has expanded so much that it is threatening its own identity (if Turkey joins the European Union "Asia" will be a part of "Europe"), while immigration (by non-Europeans) is threatening to destroy whatever is left over when "Europe" finally exhausts its outward expansion. Is he right?

Is Sarkozy right to imagine that "homeland security" starts with protecting national identity? Will Europe just fall apart if the European Union becomes the Eurasian Union? Will hospitality to the "other shore"—the other discourse of anamnesis—finally divide "European" consciousness and memory *in a way that obviates rather than regenerates?*[2] "Will French political traditions be less strong if they are now carried forth and reappropriated by Algerian(s) [and others]?"[3] Do all mature democracies need a "Ministry of Immigration and Identity" to protect the cultures that have been historically associated with democracy? Do "enlarging" republics have a special need to protect identity from immigrants?

While I disagree with Sarkozy, he understands what is at stake. He understands that anxiety about what Old Europe is about to lose (and the sinking feeling that resistance is futile) "frames" the debate about immigration and democracy. He understands that we are legitimately concerned about the enlargement of democracy, the inclusion of others, the weakening of borders, etc.

This anxious defense of cultural identity in enlarging, inclusive, "strong" democracies is, as Seyla Benhabib argues, nothing more than "a swan song to a vanishing ideology of nationhood."[4] Nonetheless, there are different ways of interpreting the song. In Benjamin Barber's famous formulation, "strong" democracies rely on participatory politics, instead of individual rights, to shape and change democratic processes.[5] In my reformulation, strong democracy is self-confident and self-reflexive, and has the mature consciousness of a society that no longer needs to firmly differentiate positive and negative rights nor to protect the "cultural preconditions" of participatory politics. It is prepared to rely upon the "political" energy of new members who claim the right to reinterpret individual rights. Strong democracy is capable of being deeply self-reflective about its own identity: it is capable of asking itself who has the *right to have rights*—that is, the right to possess them not only in the elemental sense but also in the sense of giving them meaning. Fortuitously, strong democracies are evolving into a new form of political society, a type of society that can leave behind the ideology of national identity; yet, the birth of a form of collective identity that transcends (sublates) national identity is a difficult process that, not surprisingly, is engendering its own countercultural "reaction."

What are the characteristics of this new democracy? Strong democracy (also called "core democracy" by Habermas) has undergone the requisite socioeconomic modernization, is thoroughly adapted to cultural modernity (with its characteristic differentiation between law and ethical/cultural/religious worldviews), and has well-developed (and integrated) formal and informal public spheres. Democracies that meet this definition possess *unprecedented* self-confidence and stability; as a consequence, they are secure enough to recognize human diversity—they are prepared to "refashion the meaning of their own peoplehood" and integrate (not assimilate) cultural diversity.[6] In the context of this democracy, Sarkozy embodies the reaction formation built into the loss of national culture and the ongoing transition to a thoroughly political form of integration.

Only a strong democracy can imagine that the right to democratic citizenship is a human right, the content of which is determined by democratic will formation, and not by traditional forms of cultural identification; yet, and this is the dilemma, the strength of democracy in its most mature form evokes anxiety about an "end of history" in which immigrants actually assert their human right to participate in democracy and *potentially* threaten the only kind of "nation" that is capable of recognizing a new generation of human rights—the *rights* of others. Instead of assimilating others, strong democracies can recognize the right to be different in ways that are fundamental and constitutive of identity, provided immigrants are willing to "fit" difference into the discourse of individual rights.[7]

As long as immigrants accept this proviso, we have no right to protect "our" identity from "them." We cannot protect "our" culture, since "our" culture is "constitutively" intercultural; it is a byproduct of an iterative phenomenon that relies upon a strong democracy that is (finally) prepared to recognize the rights of others. Yet, we must still acknowledge that there will be reasonable disagreement about how much difference democracy can accept and survive.

In what follows, I call for the constitutional courts of strong democracies to take an active role (as meta-public spheres) in determining the boundaries of our *Kulturkampf.* Civil society debate and disagreement about the culture wars will, undoubtedly, continue to frame claim making; however, courts must decide the scope of the other's rights and protect them. Courts need to develop cultural rights—to "frame" an antidiscrimination norm that includes the individual's right to be free from cultural discrimination.

The argument has three parts. First, I argue that strong democracies have neither the right nor the need to protect their historical cultures by discriminating against the cultures of new members. These democracies have a duty to recognize that all the individual members of a democratic society have a right to equal protection that encompasses not only racial and gender discrimination but also cultural discrimination.

Second, I use a European Court of Human Rights (ECtHR) decision to demonstrate the nexus between gender and racial discrimination, on the one hand, and cultural discrimination, on the other. In *Abdulaziz, Cabales, and Balkandali v. United Kingdom*,[8] the ECtHR upheld the United Kingdom's right to use ancestry as a basis for citizenship, and thus, to discriminate on the basis of race/ethnic background. However, the court struck down the application of the law, which treated non–ancestrally British women differently than it did non—ancestrally British men. While the British law at issue in *Abdulaziz* was subsequently amended by the 2003 European Council Directive on Family Reunification,[9] this case illustrates both the complex tie among race, gender, and cultural discrimination and the need to extend the equal protection norm to include cultural identity. Not only is the right to be free of cultural discrimination the next step for democracy (in terms of its normative evolution), but, in some contexts, it is imperative in order to protect all persons from racial and gender discrimination.

Finally, I argue that the individual's equal right to cultural expression is akin to the right to religious expression. While cultural expression, like religious expression, may come into conflict with gender discrimination, in the context of strong democracy, cultures (like religions) can be expected to evolve, to become complex, contrarian, and differentiated, and, ultimately, to make their peace with the idea of equal rights for all, including women's rights. Like religion, culture can be oppressive. But can we even imagine excising the right to free exercise of religion? As equal protection norms developed to protect weak members, we balanced the (oftentimes) countervailing norms of equality and religious freedom, rather than eliminating the latter. We also hoped (not without justification) that the intervention of religiously "inflected" arguments in the public sphere would not only support equality in certain cases but also, *to some extent*, support the transcendence of "inequality norms."

Also, just as religious freedom can be a model for cultural freedom, immigrants can learn from the democratization project of feminism: much of feminism has focused not just on formal rights, but on the interpretative context in which rights are given meaning by those who bring to bear a different "cultural" perspective.[10] Obviously, in addition to sharing an emancipatory project, feminism and multiculturalism can be adversaries. However, while women are often depicted as collateral damage in the cultural wars,[11] I think that culture (like religion) holds the potential to rationalize and integrate as democracy becomes stronger—even to authorize new interpreters as these interpreters take their place as equal coauthors of democratic law and (*intercultural*) peoplehood.

What's Wrong with the "People"?

More than twenty years ago, Michael Walzer argued that most advanced democracies were monocultural "closed societies" and that cultural monism was both compatible with democracy and legitimate. In Europe's democracies, immigrants seemed to reinvigorate the economy and revitalize cultural identity without threatening the core identity of the "people." In Europe, immigration was "manageable." Political integration was only persuasive to Americans because America was an exception to the rule: a strong democracy that was, in the deepest sense, a nation of immigrants. Most strong democracies acted as if "the promotion of moral and intellectual culture and the efficient working of political institutions might be 'defeated' by the *continual creation of heterogeneous populations*."[12] And, while he admitted that "there [is no] firm evidence that culture cannot thrive in cosmopolitan environments,"[13] he nonetheless concluded that anxiety about cultural integration was a "good enough reason" for democratic citizens to choose to protect their ancestry by excluding others.

In the context in which Walzer made these claims, the ineluctability of immigration (that continually regenerates heterogeneity), and its constitutive relation to "democratic iterability" (or revisability) was not yet apparent. It was not yet clear that the strong defense of cultural integration was nothing more than "a swan song."[14] For Walzer, democratic reiteration referred only to sovereign difference—the repetition of "constitutionally" closed societies, each of which was guaranteed the right to self-determination and self-identification.

For Walzer, democratic iterability did not refer, as it does for Benhabib, to the ongoing interior resignification of democratic identity itself. This is not just a normative disagreement, but a socioempirical one as well. For Benhabib, once democracy matures to the point at which national *self*-identification is self-consciously recursive, the "people" are capable of accepting the truth: their own identity is tension-riven and aspirational.[15] In Benhabib's rational reconstruction, democratic peoples have always been "riven by class, gender, ethnicity, and religion" and, as a consequence of the emergence of immigrant nations, their identity is now thoroughly imbricated with cultural heterogeneity as well.[16] What seems to be different now is that we have—in certain types of societies—gained the capacity to recognize, and reconcile ourselves to, the *truth* about political identity.

But, is this rational reconstruction an ideal type, a description of the evolution of the self-understanding of actually existing democracies, or the intellectual's understanding of what is possible? Does this "model" identity reflect who "we" are or, rather, the template for an aspiration to outgrow false consciousness? In actuality, we live in a historical moment in which recognition of who we are (and have been) hangs in the balance, in which democratic peoples are deciding whether they will reconcile themselves to the interiorization of democratic iterability[17] or alienate themselves from it and reaffirm (for as long as possible) the traditional model of democratic reiteration.[18] We are confronted with a *political* choice.

While Walzer has always had critics,[19] twenty years ago he was able to argue that democracies that chose strong cultural integration—as opposed to the type of political integration that protected dialogic norms or the "ongoing process of liberal conversation"[20]—were simply reflecting a reasonable disagreement, an "alternative modernity." Like other left-leaning critics, he thought that the normative project of cultural integration was no excuse for labor exploitation. He also thought that the duty to provide for the naturalization of second- and third-generation "guest" workers was the core content of the *human right to political membership*. If we conceive of the "right" to membership as a bundle of rights (as he does), only the core, Walzer argues, is universal—the remainder must be specified by citizenship legislation or by the will of the people.[21]

For Walzer, the exclusion of cultural alterity (provided it was not a subterfuge to reproduce a castelike structure of labor hierarchy) not only was permissible but was a legitimate *political* choice. The collective right to exclude cultural difference was tied to the general principle of reasonable difference. Hence, the European and Atlantic-American paradigms were simply different "reasonable" interpretations of democratic citizenship, each of which was plausibly arrived at in the context of strong democratic institutions.

Even Walzer's critics had to acknowledge that this claim was plausible: since, a generation ago, most actually existing democratic publics did not identify themselves as "immigrant nations," the immigrant-nations model seemed like a (path-dependent) "choice." Today, these democratic publics must realize that they were mistaken.

In the next section, I turn to the role that courts play in helping us reconcile democratic citizenship and the new paradigm of nationality.

My question is whether courts can help us develop a new normative self-understanding, one which assists us in comprehending the nature of our "mistake."

The Juridification of Culture in Strong Democracies

Should courts presume to usurp political judgment when it comes to political identity? Do constitutional courts actually have a duty to defer to the people's judgment when it comes to immigration and naturalization laws and the extension of private rights to immigrants? Do these courts have a duty to defer to the judgment of citizens who want to protect their historical identity from the reality of cultural heterogeneity? Or do these courts have a duty to recognize the normative potential of cultural heterogeneity, and steer us in the direction of intercultural political culture and recognition of the rights of others?

In my view, courts have a duty to recognize the normative potential inchoate in our structural transformation. In fact, the purpose of a constitutional court—its basic pedagogic role—rests on whether it manages to teach us that the obsessive defense of our ancestry is not an "alternative modernity" but a refusal to reconcile ourselves to the normative potential of our historical moment. The challenge is for courts to do so in ways that will neither alienate democratic citizens nor energize the reaction formation that sustains this alienation.

Ideally, juridical responses to Sarkosyiste-type cultural phenomena will take shape, not as the legitimation of cultural discrimination (to protect "our" identity) but as a universal right not to be discriminated against on the basis of one's culture. However, if juridification of a new category of discrimination is just an abstract right or the latest in a series of rights that constrain the will of the people, then it will not really produce political integration that includes immigrants and respects the "rights of others." To protect rights, we must engrain them in structures of recognition and patterns of political identification.

We must adopt a special form of juridification: *jurisgenerative politics.*[22] Instead of "positing" the law, jurisgenerative politics refers to the dialectic between constitutional norms and democratic will formation. "*[J]urisgenerative politics* refers to iterative acts through which a democratic people that considers itself bound by certain guiding norms and principles reappropriates and reinterprets these, thus showing itself to be not only the subject but also the author of the laws."[23] Concretely, *jurisgenerative* politics takes place in a constitutional court (albeit one that is continuously infiltrated by the resonant voices of democratic civil society).

Constitutional courts are a part of the structural transformation of the public sphere: they act as meta-public spheres when they determine human rights of special standing, i.e., speech norms of public discourse[24] and discursive scope—the question of who constitutes the people, who has the right to be a part of "us" and coauthor the laws.[25] When constitutional courts embrace their role as meta-public spheres, they guarantee the right to membership by rejecting discrimination, by protecting fair procedures and freedom of speech,[26] and by reinterpreting core private rights in light of the new perspectives of new members.[27]

According to Frank Michelman's formulation of *jurisgenerative* politics, "the pursuit of political freedom through law depends on 'our' constant reach for inclusion of the other, of the hitherto excluded—which in practice means bringing to legal-doctrinal presence the hitherto absent voices of emergently self-conscious social groups."[28] Bringing others to legal-doctrinal presence is an essential part of the democratization process; it is the way "new slant(s) on the world penetrate the dominant consciousness" and reframe the people's self-interpretative horizon. Who are "we"? What is wrong with "us"? How can "we" be better? The other's rights bring to consciousness "new slants" on these questions.

Historically, the pursuit of political freedom through law has involved legal recognition of political rights (e.g., voting rights, discursive rights, and nondiscrimination or civil rights legislation), as well as recognition of certain private rights (like the equal right to marriage), which cannot be denied without imperiling the pursuit of political freedom. When African Americans, women, and gays sought equal political freedom, they were part of democracy's iterative process. Their fight for inclusion was a fight to reinterpret political freedom, to make "us" understand that "we" *needed* an entirely new category of law (civil rights legislation). Theirs was also a fight to reinterpret "private" rights, the denial of which constituted a form of public denigration that was incompatible with equal political freedom. To this end, they made "us" understand that "we" *needed* to rethink family law, inter alia, patriarchal rules governing family property and custody, interracial sex and marriage laws, and gay sex and marriage. Today, immigrants are the emergently self-conscious social (cultural) group that demands the transformative authority of legal-doctrinal presence. Today, they are the ones who provoke us to ask, What is wrong with us?

In the next section, I will examine a case from the European Court of Human Rights (ECtHR), *Abdulaziz, Cabales, and Balkandali v. United Kingdom (1985)*, in which the ECtHR affirmed the right of member states to protect cultural identity by "constitutionalizing" Walzer's conception of a human right to membership. The court upheld Britain's "patrial" or ancestry law, which was then in force but has subsequently been changed.[29] Under that law, persons of British ancestry were given preference over nonpatrials. In addition to protecting British culture by favoring immigrants with cultural affinity, the law protected cultural integration by disfavoring (female) immigrants who chose to practice arranged marriage. This decision provides an opportunity to analyze whether democratic peoples violate human rights when they protect their ancestry by preferring new members with the same ancestry. Do they violate human rights when, as in that case, they protect cultural identification by reproducing their own traditional marriage norms?

I am convinced that the court that heard the *Abdulaziz* case was, as Benhabib would say, writing its "swan song." Thus, while I disagree with the decision, I think I understand the court's reasons for allowing strong cultural identification to survive. The growing abstraction of political identity (given the dual pressures of European citizenship and the emergence of immigrant nations in Europe) might motivate citizens to hold onto a "transitional object" that they have already outgrown—and it might lead constitutional courts to let them. As a result, the *Abdulaziz* case is important because it captures both the danger—and the potential—of the juridification of cultural rights.

The European Court of Human Rights and the Rights of Others

In the case of *Abdulaziz, Cabales, and Balkandali v. United Kingdom*, the European Court of Human Rights (ECtHR) adjudicated the claim of three lawful permanent residents of the United Kingdom whose husbands were refused permission to remain or join them under the 1971 British immigration laws, which were amended in 1980 to require British citizenship for women who wished to have a male fiancé or husband remain or join them in the country.[30] No such equivalent rule existed for men seeking to bring female fiancées or wives.[31] As a result of these laws, Ms. Abdulaziz, born in Malawi and a resident of the United Kingdom, Ms. Cabales, born in the Philippines and a resident of the United Kingdom, and Ms.

Balkandali, born in Egypt and a resident of the United Kingdom, were each denied permission to be joined by their husbands in their country of residence.[32]

In adjudicating this case, the ECtHR interpreted several core provisions of the European Convention on Human Rights, and upheld Britain's "patrial" or ancestry law, established in the British Immigration Act of 1971.[33] The court further decided that, while ancestry-based citizenship is legitimate, the application of the law was unfair, since the United Kingdom had discriminated against nonpatrial women by interpreting the right to family life in a way that disadvantaged them more than nonpatrial men.[34]

After the 1980 amendment of its immigration rules, the United Kingdom gave a preference to the wives of male immigrants over the husbands of female immigrants. This preferential treatment was based on the view that wives were less likely to work and hence less likely to compete with citizens for jobs. The female immigrants argued, and the court accepted, that the law discriminated against them on the basis of sex.[35]

While it rejected the government's claim that the right to family life is reserved for European citizens,[36] the court was cautious in defining the "rights of others." It concluded that immigrant rights were limited, and must be interpreted in light of immigrant status.[37] Immigrants, they argued, did not have the right to live with their spouses in the country of permanent residence even if the immigrant had lived and worked in the country for years (and even if she had become a naturalized citizen). Married immigrants had a right to live together somewhere in Europe, but this right could only be enforced against the country of residence if there were nowhere else to go, if there were "no other choice."[38] However, while human rights were partial and incomplete for some people, they had to be applied in a gender-neutral manner. And, since the British law relied upon presumptions regarding "typical" gender behavior in the labor market, it discriminated against women and violated gender-equity norms protected by Europe's Convention on Human Rights.[39]

In short, the court legitimated ancestry-based cultural discrimination while affirming Europe's commitment to an antidiscrimination norm in the gender context. But did the court contradict itself? Is it possible to separate the practice of cultural discrimination from the experience of gender (and racial) discrimination in immigrant communities? Moreover, at the level of moral-juridical justification, can we really disaggregate "social" discrimination and "cultural" discrimination? Can we separate the interior others (women) who have long fought to participate in democratic iterations from exterior others (immigrants)? Can we transform partial rights and status (for all immigrants) into equal rights and standing (in some contexts) so that a new category of "excluded consciousness" can seek full legal doctrinal presence?

When the court invalidated the gender-discrimination feature of the legislation, the ECtHR arguably forced Britain to discontinue a backdoor form of discrimination—in which men from the former colonies who lacked close ethnic ties to Britain were targeted for exclusion. Gender discrimination allowed the state to promote cultural integration without fully discriminating against the entire class of nonpatrials. The state seemed to understand the intersection of gender and cultural discrimination: discriminating against married (or engaged) women from the former colonies, some of whom had arranged marriages, was not just a way of excluding competitors from the labor market but also a way of singling out for exclusion different ideas about marriage and family life. By targeting the intersection of gender and culture, the state enacted a form of parsimonious discrimination; it deployed the law in a way that comprehended the role of women in reproducing culture.

In fact, the government's interpretation of the right to family relied on cultural discrimination. The government had argued that, unlike the right to be free of torture or other "basic" freedoms protected in the Convention on Human Rights, the right to family life was a privilege of European citizenship. Since ideas about family life were intimately related to cultural integration, the government contended that member nations could not protect their own cultural identity if this right applied to immigrants. If the right to family was a human right, guaranteed to everyone in Europe (and not just to "Europeans"), then it was a medium for reinterpreting European cultural identity. As the government understood it, family life was intimately related to human life, and uniting families was a matter of compassion and dignity; yet, it was also a sphere in which "culture matters."

In order to exclude those who practiced the wrong kind of marriage, the government defended the normative "purpose" of marriage. The "primary purpose" of marriage was not "resettlement" or "reunification" or any other instrumental reason.[40] Primarily, there should be noninstrumental reasons for marriage, reasons having to do with intimacy and mutual concern. Arranged marriages did not meet this primary purpose since, putatively, there was no "relationship" prior to marriage. The question is, How does one rebut this presumption? How does one prove a relationship worthy of reunification, but not primarily motivated by reunification?

In the United Kingdom, applicants for family unification had to prove that they had "met" and that they "intended to live together as man and wife."[41] While none of the applicants in the *Abdulaziz* case had practiced arranged marriage, the applicants argued that having to give evidence that marriage partners had met beforehand amounted to a requirement to prove a consensual or voluntarist relationship, which discriminated against those who practiced forms of customary marriage. Accordingly, the applicants argued, the law was *prima facie* invalid.[42]

The court, however, concluded that, since the applicants were not practitioners of customary marriage and thus were not harmed by the government's interpretation of family life, they had no standing to make this claim. Moreover, the court asserted that a concept of family life that excluded arranged marriages and that, therefore, disadvantaged those from the Indian subcontinent (and parts of Africa) is not *necessarily* discrimination, as long as the limitation on arranged marriages was implemented in order to reduce the incidence of bogus marriages for immigration purposes.[43]

However, in cases subsequent to *Abdulaziz*, British immigration judges applied the primary-purpose rules in ways that made the discriminatory intent apparent. As Susan Sterett argues on the basis of her close reading of these cases, immigration judges used gender discrimination as the filter for cultural discrimination.[44] When women attempted to reinterpret the meaning of arranged marriage and actively invert the power hierarchies associated with customary families, the very fact that they were "agreeing to marry a partner chosen through family but [still] insisting on some autonomy"[45] was taken as evidence that their marriages could not be real arranged marriages (which, in any case, were not real, i.e., consensual marriages).

Judges were inclined to exclude spouses (fiancés) in cases of arranged marriage.[46] On the one hand, these spouses were excluded because they could not offer convincing evidence that an arranged marriage was a "real" marriage.[47] On the other hand, they were excluded if their "customary" marriages deviated from traditional practice. In short, the judges concluded, their marriages were not real (in the normative sense) and, assuming *arguendo* the validity of customary "marriage," they held that they were within their rights to suspect fraud if an applicant defended an "idiosyncratic" interpretation of custom.

Women were special targets of discrimination. Their attempt to resignify and hybridize customs was actually taken as evidence of insincerity. In cases where the woman had the "whip hand,"[48] where she was the one who was settled with a job and a home, and who sought to bring in a man who would probably be unemployed and dependent, immigration officials assumed the marriage was not real.⁴⁹

Under the auspices of saving women from their culture, British courts and the ECtHR enacted a perfect storm of gender and culture bias. This bias has been difficult to overcome. Critics contend that cultural rights are opposed to women's rights and reinforce the power of "authoritative" interpretations of culture as opposed to the countervailing interpretations of weaker cultural "authors" like women.⁵⁰ However, as *Abudulaziz* and its progeny demonstrate, guaranteeing the individual's right to be free of cultural discrimination may support both women's "authorship" of countercultural interpretations of traditional cultures, and their equal right to participate in the reinterpretation of rights in ways that are relevant to us all. Guaranteeing the right to cultural expression protects the right to say "yes" or "no." It gives the individual the right of refusal, but also the right of acceptance—*on different terms*.

In response to the *Abdulaziz* case, the United Kingdom ended the gender discrimination feature of its immigration legislation by making it equally difficult for the spouses of all noncitizens to enter. In addition, a 2003 European Council Directive on Family Reunification (implemented in 2005) granted all third-country nationals legally residing in the European Union a right to family reunification. In the latter case, the scope of this "new" right remains unclear. The *Abdulaziz* court had recognized that legal residents, and not just European Union citizens, had standing to claim the convention's right to family, but, in terms of the content of the right, it still allowed for status differences—legal residents, naturalized immigrants, and (native) citizens had different rights, ranging from partial to full rights.

The council's directive⁵¹ reiterates the court's decision that legal residents have a right to family unification, but it remains silent on the most important part of the court's holding: whether legal residents have the *same* right to family life. At the end of this story, women gained the right to equal protection (once the British immigration law was amended to disadvantage equally men and women of nonpatrial descent) and all legal residents gained the right to equal protection (once the European bureaucracy amended the rules to give legal residents a right to family unification, that was initially—albeit ambivalently—articulated by the ECtHR).

Yet, it is important to keep in mind that the post-*Abdulaziz* reforms do not affect two of the most important features of discrimination affirmed by the *Abdulaziz* court: (1) the people's right to protect citizenship based on "close ties" or ancestry-based identity and thus enact cultural discrimination; (2) the government's right to curtail the authority of immigrant women who continue to suffer the substantive effects of gender discrimination in nexus with cultural discrimination—*despite the formal extension of equal protection*. In effect, the European Court of Human Rights "constitutionalized" something like Walzer's understanding of a human right to membership.

Just as in Walzer's formulation, the court envisioned a right with a minimum (albeit evolving) core content. In the last two decades, most of Europe has accepted that after the second (or third) generation, "guest" workers and their descendents have a right to membership. In strong democracies, there is a human right to membership that invalidates the "permanent" political exclusion of immigrant workers. Moreover, strong democracies tend to acknowledge a right to membership that specifically rules out racial, religious, sexual orientation, and gender discrimination in the application of immigration and naturalization laws, as well as discrimination against immigrants in the application of fundamental rights (like the right to family life). *But (pace Walzer and the ECtHR), there is no human right to membership that obligates democratic peoples to be neutral with respect to culture.* And, since cultural discrimination may intersect with and preclude the regulation of other forms of discrimination, the failure to protect persons from cultural discrimination effectively fails to protect them from racial and other forms of discrimination.

The *Abdulaziz* court did attempt to enforce a variant of the antidiscrimination norm, and that was progress. However, to the extent that the court strictly delimited the minimum core content of the human right to membership (and left the remainder of the content to be determined by the "will of the people"), it abdicated its role in *jurisgenerative* politics. Of course, even an ambivalent defense of the antidiscrimination norm is progressive: a *de minimus* egalitarian claim is a "wedge," a point of departure in a legitimation process that can always evolve from partial inclusion to full parity. But, as we shall see, the court has to extend the antidiscrimination principle to include cultural discrimination or it will actually fail in its faltering efforts to secure equality in other ("already protected") domains, i.e., gender and racial equality.

Ordinarily, human rights are codified in civil rights legislation—and, in fact, the iterative process of strong democracy has generated an unprecedented codification of civil rights. However, while courts should not "ordinarily" determine the content of basic rights, they have a duty to function as a meta-public sphere that guarantees the equality of the "authors of the law." This duty includes an obligation to (1) reject (formal) discrimination and protect freedom of speech for all members; (2) protect the iterative process (in all its domains and dimensions) so that human rights can be reinterpreted in light of the new perspectives of new members (who are thereby recognized as equals); (3) articulate a human right to membership that brings to *full* legal-doctrinal presence emergent sociocultural groups that were previously excluded for unjustifiable reasons, inter alia, gender, racial, religious, sexual orientation, or because of their membership in, and choice to identify closely with, a particular cultural group (cultural identity).

In *Abdulaziz*, the ECtHR made two mistakes. First, the court failed to acknowledge that democracy has *in fact* outgrown its original tie to the monocultural "nation" and, hence, *should* forsake its reliance on cultural discrimination as a means of reproducing an identity it has already lost. Instead of identifying national identity as a "transitional object," the court gave its imprimatur to ancestry-based immigration and naturalization rules *as if* such rules represent a reasonable "alternative" to non–ancestry-based rules. (I suspect that the court just decided to allow Europeans to keep their "transitional object" for the time being; however, because it did not openly signal this, the decision is "legitimating" instead of "accommodating.")[52] Second, the court failed to acknowledge the intersection of racial and cultural discrimination, on the one hand, and gender and cultural discrimination, on the other, and thus failed to defend the principle of antidiscrimination in the core areas of race and gender.

Most citizens of strong democracies would reject racial discrimination in immigration and naturalization law (just as they would reject racial discrimination among citizens); yet, in order to justify cultural discrimination, democracies are often forced to justify racism. In *Abdulaziz*, the British law favored those with "close links" to the Old Commonwealth and disfavored those whose "ancestry" was in the "New Commonwealth."[53] The applicants argued that given the history of colonialism, the "ancestry rule" was racist: the rule's *purpose* was to exclude people of color whose ancestors were not white people from the British Isles.[54]

The court acknowledged that some legislators intended to exclude "coloured immigrants" whose presence—in increasing numbers—was experienced as threatening and as an impediment to "good relations between the different communities living in the United Kingdom." Nonetheless, the court held that the applicants were not the victims of racial discrimination.[55] When laws prohibiting racial discrimination are applied to rules of immigration and naturalization, the immigrant's *status* matters—immigrants do not have the *same* rights as citizens. Like most of the rights in the Convention on Human Rights, the right to freedom from discrimination (Art. 14) is limited by formal principles of legality (i.e., any rights-restrictive law must be promulgated and clear) and by substantive norms of democratic legitimacy (i.e., any rights-restrictive law must be shown to be necessary in a democratic society).

In this case, while trying to avoid the absurdity of excluding people of color in order to maintain "good relations between different communities," the court insisted that the preferential treatment given those who have "close ties" with the "indigenous" British population (even though they have never lived and worked in the United Kingdom) is justified if the discriminatory rule is "necessary in a democratic society."[56] The question for the court was, *Are close ties based on ancestry, rather than civil society interaction, "necessary in a democracy"?*[57] Without endorsing the ancestry rule, the court argued, in effect, that ancestry-based citizenship is a reasonable interpretation of substantive norms of democratic legitimacy, and, thus, justifies rights-restrictive discrimination. The court decided that it was legitimate for a democracy to choose to discriminate against those from different cultures, *even if this had the additional effect of (intentionally) discriminating on the basis of race.*

In addition to legitimating cultural discrimination in nexus with racial discrimination, the court justified cultural discrimination in nexus with gender discrimination—despite the fact that the court rejected formal gender discrimination. In fact, the judges failed to recognize that the more indirect form of cultural discrimination—encoded in culturally specific ideas about marriage—is discrimination at all. The refusal to even countenance the idea of cultural discrimination allows this form of discrimination (and the various forms of discrimination that intersect with it) to remain unthematized—to obscure and defer the emergent legal-doctrinal consciousness of those who experience this unarticulated discrimination, and to stall the iterative work of the countercultural perspectives of new members.

The applicants in the *Abdulaziz* case were not even allowed to *argue* an essential part of their case, namely, that the refusal to interpret the "right to family" to include "customary" ideas about family and marriage is a form of cultural discrimination *that also discriminates against women.*

Why is it so obvious that human rights codified in the European Convention must be interpreted in light of "European"[58] traditions? European nations have become diverse polities that, as part of their own democratization process, have extended rights to *others* who, in turn, have a *right* to participate in rights interpretation.

If we citizens of strong democracies continue to take our own democratization process seriously, we will, as an inchoate feature of our own recursive identity, recognize the rights of new members. In order to recognize the rights of these new members, we must be able to imagine how they could persuade us of new interpretations, how they could show us that their rights claim is valid. To this end, we need legal and cultural institutions that allow the full range of reasonable interpretations to emerge in the discursive public sphere and (potentially) reorient democratic decisions.

We need institutions that would allow the women in the *Abdulaziz* case to get a fair hearing. As this case shows, some women have a countercultural *and* contrapunctal[59] view of marriage—these women imagine a hybrid marital institution that is free of coercion yet not fully a matter of autonomous decision, that is predicated on the right of women to work and support their families yet assumes that the marital "relationship" is not based on a history of sexual-romantic attraction. Their understanding of the type of mutual relatedness that sustains reciprocity, intimacy, and partnership with a significant other challenges the "traditional" Western idea of marriage in the same way that gay marriage challenges this tradition. Gay marriage reiterates private and public life—by refuting the idea that the primary purpose of marriage is biological reproduction, same-sex partners lay claim to the authority to reinterpret the marital institution and the plethora of private rights that support it.

Advocates of the new "customary" marriage question our uncritical consumption of the iconic love story, while modeling family life that is egalitarian and intercultural, and then fighting for their families in a public sphere that demands that they justify themselves. When new members remind us that marriage is really about responsibility that limits our freedom, they may help us discover why family life is deteriorating as freedom deepens in democratic societies. They may help us figure out what is wrong with our families and how we might imagine a better interpretation of democracy's private life. At the same time, they may help us find a better interpretation of democracy—one in which the other's right to membership gives us privileged access to a multidimensional critical horizon. We spend a lot of time debating the added value of immigrants, but mainly focus on elemental civil society—the labor market—to the exclusion of the political. We have been so distracted by the need to use immigrants (and then "assimilate" them into "our" culture) that we have failed to take seriously their real productive work.

Intercultural Political Identity: Are We There Yet?

As a consequence of the "real" productive work of immigrants and the developmental trajectory of strong democracy, democracy is prepared for its next structural transformation: the emergence of intercultural political identity.[60] In the alternative modernities literature, there is a great deal of emphasis on the diversity of developmental trajectories. However, I have argued that cultural monism is not an "alternative"; it is, at best, a transitional object—that "condenses" an evolving identity into a form that allows us to feel safe enough to grow up.[61] Moreover, I have argued that constitutional courts "strengthen" democracy: they transform juridification of modern society into *jurisgenerative* politics. And, *jurisgenerative* politics is not just the boundary or wall that contains democratic iteration but a necessary part of its dialectic. Strong democracies have strong constitutional courts.[62]

In my formulation, constitutional courts act as meta-public spheres when they determine human rights of special standing, i.e., speech norms of public discourse[63] and discursive scope or the question of who we are.[64] When constitutional courts embrace their role as meta-public spheres, they guarantee the right to equal freedom by (1) protecting freedom of speech and publicity; (2) rejecting discrimination; (3) reiterating private rights in light of the (countercultural and perhaps contrapunctal) perspectives of new members. Their role, in other words, is not to provide a comprehensive conception of moral freedom that fills in the substantive content of personal liberty and moral autonomy,[65] but rather to pursue "political freedom through law" (Michelman).

By constantly "reach[ing] for inclusion of the other," by "bringing to legal-doctrinal presence" emergent social groups, and, eventually, emergent cultural groups,[66] the meta-public sphere functions as the mediating context that connects the actual public sphere to the ideal community envisioned in constitutional discourse. Bringing others to legal presence is an essential part of the democratization process: the juridification of the others' rights sets free their (juris) generative authority. Yet, it also orients this authority. As the repository of moral learning acquired in the course of an unprecedented effort to communicate with others, the constitutional courts of mature democracies are best situated to orient the regenerative authority of new members.

In the absence of a strong constitutional court, democratic iterations may be stalled by democratic peoples who resist the authorial claims of new members who promise to threaten their identity.[67] Since new members force us to risk self-alienation, it takes a lot of maturity to recognize their rights, whether "they" are racial or religious minorities, women, gays and lesbians, or, finally, immigrants from cultures that are very different from our own.

Moreover, without a strong constitutional court, democratic iterations may deteriorate into postmodern iterability (Derrida). When the democratization process is "radicalized" and set free of the normative idea of political freedom through law, "democratic" politics may be imperiled (instead of emancipated) by "the continuous creation of heterogeneous populations." In *Democracy and the Foreigner,* Bonnie Honig defends this model of heterogeneity by elaborating the idea of radical democracy and postmodern iterability in relation to immigrant populations.[68] She argues that no matter how much we reform immigration and naturalization rules, we will merely "harness" and disempower the legitimating authority of immigrants as long as our constitutional norms exclude the "bad" immigrant who claims the right of radical democracy, i.e., the right of political amendment associated with the (re)founding activity of coleg-islators (as opposed to the activity of constitutional interpretation).[69] To her mind, the immigrant who assimilates to jurisgenerative thinking is reproducing the closed society as much as the iconic good immigrant who assimilates to the dominant culture and renounces the "bad" immigrants (i.e., the "scum") who dare to hold onto countercultural/contrapunctal values.

I think Honig is mistaken for two reasons. First, strong democracies can recognize the immigrant's *right* to countercultural/contrapunctal difference, not despite the rule of law but because of it. Countercultural publics flourish in democratic civil societies *to the extent that* they are supported by a legal tradition that recognizes the rights of others. And, contrapunctal publics are just one form that countercultural identity takes. The former joins a contra-modern worldview (in which value sphere differentiation has been resisted) and a modern worldview (in which cultural-expressive values have been separated from the law). Like counterculturalism, in general, it relies on the receptivity and "foregrounding" of a legal-discursive context that makes freedom possible. In short, contrapunctal publics rely on the achievements of the modern world view.

In strong democracies, civil society is not unregulated so much as it is emancipated; in such societies, juridification may start off disciplining others, but as juridification evolves into *jurisgenesis*, the interpenetration of constitutional normativity and democratic culture reinforces legal *and* cultural freedom. The democratic constitution is not a barrier to iterability *rightly understood*; it is rather itself a communicative or discursive space in which inclusion of the hitherto suppressed or not yet present voice of other people expands the meaning of freedom, the scope of reason giving and reasonable difference, and the discursive scope of "our" identity.

Democratic iterations rely on the political activity of the public sphere, as well as the *political* activity of constitutional courts. Without the interpretative praxis of the court, the only way immigrants could fundamentally alter the "text" of political society would be by galvanizing the people to amend the constitution. Of course, protest movements led by immigrants will, at times, remind us of our founding moment and harness people power, like other civil rights movements. Democratic embers can always be rekindled. But, the political "agency" of heterogeneous identity has its limits—it has to be channeled and made sense of. Democratic iteration is not ontological but historical: it has grown up as part of a democratization process that is continually receptive to heterogeneity because it has a special resource for refining and relating to heterogeneity without being overrun by it.

Constitutional courts can refine and relate, steer and interpolate jurisgenerative politics, and thus avoid the twin evils of either clinging to the type of magical thinking that allows us to still believe in original meaning and ancestral identity or merely reconciling ourselves to alienation and misrecognition, and the ensuing reactionary politics of identity. The *self-conscious* reproduction of heterogeneity without the hindrance of the learning curve embodied in the Constitution would position the advocates of reactionary people power to reassert their right to protect themselves and resist the rights of others for as long as possible.

Today, immigrants are the "emergently self-conscious social [cultural] group"[70] that demands the transformative authority of legal-doctrinal presence. Today, they are the ones that provoke us to ask, What is wrong with us and how can we make ourselves better? Unlike the other groups, however, immigrants have challenged us to be reflexive about the elemental cultural prerequisites of democratic integration. Do democracies need to be culturally integrated? If we don't need it, do we have a right to choose it?

I have been arguing that cultural integration is not an alternative for the citizens of strong democracy: our horizon of moral learning has shifted permanently. Even if we lament the loss of identity, we have to accept that democratic self-determination is not the same as self-identification. In retrospect, we can recognize "our" culture for what it is: a "transitional object" that needed to be decoupled from democracy. While some democratic peoples will continue to resist and defend their cultures from immigration, the presence of immigrants—in an open society with a long history of democratic iteration—evokes self-reflexivity about the core features of the human right to membership. The transition from monocultural nationality to immigrant nations is inevitable, but our reconciliation with that which we can no longer really deny is still a matter of political decision.

Even if we decide to accept the normative consequences of immigration, there will be reasonable differences in the way strong democracies interpret discursive scope. However, the human right to membership has certain core features that narrow the people's power to decide who they are by deciding who will be a member. The core features of this right include (1) admission criteria that repudiate arbitrary discrimination, i.e., discrimination on the basis of gender, race, sexual orientation, religion, and culture; (2) naturalization criteria that deemphasize cultural integration; and (3) a conception of rights that guarantees each the right to bring relevant differences (like culture and religion) to bear when interpreting rights, provided the claimants recognize that participating in the articulation of rights will probably change their cultures (religions).

Following civil, political, and social rights, cultural rights (understood as an individual right to be protected from discrimination) complete a pattern of critical and reflexive rights evolution.[71] Cultural rights are the next step—perhaps the *sine qua non* of rights that finally liberates us from the "last discrimination."[72] "Cultural rights can, indeed must, be understood as the widening of democratic citizenship," and "conversely, democratic citizenship can be expanded only by opening it up culturally."[73]

In a strong democracy, identity politics cannot be the basis of the law—whether it is the identity of the dominant culture or the (balkanized) identity of subcultures. However, identity that is countercultural and contrapunctal, hybridic, and intercultural is open to regeneration in the course of legal mediation. Concrete identity is relevant to articulating individual rights, but only if that identity has already reconciled itself to the abstracting and mediating features of the democratization process.

We have already seen this model of reconciliation at work. Religious freedom plays a pivotal role in constitutional history, and, potentially, offers a model for integrating the "other" into the discourse of rights. Recently, Habermas revised his position on religion, reconstructing both its constitutional and its philosophical content to elevate religion from a "therapeutic" (private) discourse to one worthy of "translation" and intermediation in the public sphere.[74] Religion is worthy of translation, in part, because it has something to teach us about equal freedom. "Religious traditions have a special power to articulate moral intuitions, especially with regard to vulnerable forms of communal life . . . this potential makes religious speech a serious candidate for transporting possible truth contents, which can only be translated from the vocabulary of a particular religious community into a generally accessible language."[75] I think we need to recognize that cultural traditions hold the same potential as religious traditions: the capacity to help vulnerable forms of life attain equality and express moral claims that are relevant to reframing democratic norms.

Just as our historical respect for religious expression is paying off with opportunities for moral learning, similarly we can work to recuperate and elevate the moral content of culture, to make it less a matter of private identity yet conducive to the language of *private* rights *and* accessible to the publicity norms of democracy.[76] We hoped that guaranteeing freedom to religious sects would lead religions to (1) "grow attached to liberal democracy and obey its norms" and (2) "liberalize doctrinally [so that] they would become less credulous and dogmatic, more sober and rational."[77] Even though some cultural institutions—like arranged marriage—are not religious institutions, the type of discrimination at stake is analogous, and so is the promise that guaranteeing freedom will deepen attachment to democracy and integrate (not assimilate) others into practices of reason giving.

If this attachment is to be durable and the "integration" into the public sphere not merely a pretext for assimilation, we must take vulnerable voices seriously, in terms of both content and form. Weak and disenfranchised (deauthorized) participants in "traditional" cultures often experience themselves as similarly disenfranchised by the wider democratic society. The guarantee of cultural freedom authorizes them to speak up and

402 RECONFIGURING THE NATION-STATE

reiterate a particular culture and, at the same, to invoke the iterative logic of democracy in favor of "the rights of others." Integration requires intermediation and translation; it also requires taking seriously the normative potential of other people's contrapunctal and countercultural values.

Anamnesis—speech that recollects, memorializes, and, in some sense, cathartically releases "sectarian" values—can provide reasons if the appropriate institutional framework exists to translate ancestry, tradition, and narrative particularity into arguments that are, more or less, accessible to all of us. Instead of exiling otherness from the public sphere (by "secularizing" religious and cultural difference), we need to construct "translation institutions" that facilitate the participation of religious/cultural citizens by relieving them of the asymmetrical burden of making themselves understood to "secular" citizens, or, worse still, to citizens who attempt to "establish" religious monopoly/cultural monism.[78]

According to Habermas's formulation, translation institutions belong in the "political public sphere" (where citizens can speak freely) but not in the domain of legislative decision making (where only secular reasons count). Citizens, he argues, but not legislators, may speak freely and make claims grounded in their particular traditions *as long as they honestly believe that their reasons could be translated into general claims by translation institutions.* Once narrative claims are translated into arguments, they can enter the public debate of legislatures and (potentially) become legally cognizable. The informal public sphere thus provides the space in which different social-cultural-religious groups give their reasons, and then, hopefully, translate those plural "reasons" into generalizable terms.

If intercultural political integration is to succeed, we need translation institutions that attempt to equalize the duty of translation, while still securing the right to be heard. We need to accommodate culture, as we have long accommodated religion (and now envision the widening of this accommodation). Accomodation will require *jurisgenerative* framing—the extension of political freedom through law (especially for weak, partially authorized speakers who seek to become equal coauthors). Guaranteeing the right to cultural expression, situating it within a framework that protects the rights of a long list of disenfranchised others (African Americans, women, gays, etc.), and relating intersecting (and, at times, conflicting) rights are conditions of the type of translation institutions that makes intercultural political integration possible.

Ultimately, while I have a close affinity with the Habermasian interpretation of strong democracy and its relation to intercultural validity, I think translation institutions should sit on the brink of the political public sphere and constitutional courts. Instead of working exclusively in the former and then attempting to integrate the "wild life" of the informal public sphere to make it usable by legislators, we should also acknowledge the role of courts in articulating cultural freedom and defining the boundaries of cultural conflict and reconciliation through translation. Strong democracies will only develop translation institutions *in a timely manner* if constitutional courts motivate legislatures by recognizing that cultural discrimination violates the rights of residents and citizens of democracies. Not only is cultural discrimination a distinct category of rights that should be "constitutionalized," but it can also intersect with other forms of discrimination; yet, cultural discrimination has been obscured from view because we lack the institutional framework for translating cultural narratives into arguments.

Hopefully, democratic citizens are beginning to recognize that particular cultural communities can articulate "moral intuitions especially with regard to vulnerable forms of life" like immigrants, women, and racial minorities (or people like the *Abdulaziz* claimants, who are all of the above). But, to actually perceive *others* we have to have translation institutions that interpenetrate the spheres of democratic iteration (formal and informal) and the sphere of *jurisgenerative politics*. We need to provide the institutional contexts for immigrants to argue with us so they can redeem their rights and pursue "political freedom through law."[79]

NOTES

1. Jürgen Habermas, *Religion and Rationality: Essays on God, Reason, and Modernity* (Cambridge, MA: MIT Press, 2002).

2. Jacques Derrida, *The Other Heading* (Bloomington: Indiana University Press, 1992), 28–75, trans. Pascale-Anne Brault and Michael B. Naas.

3. Seyla Benhabib, *The Rights of Others: Aliens, Residents, and Citizens* (Cambridge: Cambridge University Press, 2004), 212.

4. Ibid., 207.

5. Benjamin R. Barber, *Strong Democracy: Participatory Politics for a New Age* (Berkeley: University of California Press, 1984).

6. Benhabib, *The Rights of Others*, supra note 3, 212.

7. Elsewhere, I have argued that the same principle applies to Native Americans. See Angelia Means, "Arguing with Natives," *Constellations* 9, no.2 (June 2002): 221.

8. Abdulaziz, Cabales & Balkandali v. United Kingdom, 94 Eur. Ct. H.R. (Ser. A) (1985).

9. European Council Directive on Family Reunification (2003/86/EC).

10. See Maria Pia Lara, *Moral Textures: Feminist Narratives in the Public Sphere* (Berkeley: University of California Press, 1998). See also Means, "Arguing with Natives," supra note 7, 225–30.

11. Susan Okin, *Is Multiculturalism Bad for Women?* (Princeton, NJ: Princeton University Press, 1999).

12. Michael Walzer, *Spheres of Justice* (New York: Basic Books, 1983), 37 (my emphasis). Here, Walzer is paraphrasing Sidgwick. See Henry Sidgwick, *The Elements of Politics* (London: Macmillan, 1891), 295–96.

13. Ibid., 38.

14. Benhabib, *The Rights of Others*, supra note 3, 207.

15. Walzer, *Spheres of Justice*, supra note 12, 82.

16. Ibid., 80.

17. See generally, Benhabib, *The Rights of Others*, supra note 3.

18. See generally, Walzer, *Spheres of Justice*, supra note 12.

19. For central critiques of Walzer's work, see Bruce Ackerman, "Rooted Cosmopolitanism," *Ethics* 104 (April 1994): 516–35; Joseph Carens, *Culture, Citizenship, and Community* (Oxford: Oxford University Press, 2000), esp. chap. 2; Habermas, *Religion and Rationality*, supra note 1.

20. Walzer, *Spheres of Justice*, supra note 12, 50.

21. Ibid. While immigration "norms" were limited to the rights of guest workers, Walzer also argued that there was a duty owed to certain classes of refugees, e.g., war refugees, when advanced democracies "intervene" in other countries.

22. Juridification gradually extends negative rights to include all, and this extension of rights, in turn, produces a demand for the actualization of rights that cannot be met without turning all subjects into equal citizens who decide on the meaning and relevance of rights. Rights are only real when given meaning by rights holders, who eventually transmit this meaning through jurisgenerative politics or a form of politics that enables the subject to gain the status of citizen in the act of claiming rights. Robert Cover first used the phrase "jurisgenerative" to describe the process through which legal meaning is created. See Robert Cover, "The Supreme Court, 1982 Term—Foreword: Nomos and Narrative," *Harvard Law Review* 97 (1982).

23. Benhabib, *The Rights of Others*, supra note 3, 181. Here Benhabib is drawing on the jurisgenerative concept first identified by Robert Cover and then developed by Frank Michelman (who acknowledged that his own ideas on this matter were indebted to Benhabib's explication of the "normative self-understanding of democracies"). See Cover, "Nomos and Narrative," supra note 22, at 19; Frank Michelman, "Law's Republic," *Yale Law Journal* 97 (July 1988): 1502 (citing Seyla Benhabib, *Critique, Norm, and Utopia: A Study of the Foundations of Critical Theory* [New York: Columbia University Press, 1986], 272).

24. Habermas, *Religion and Rationality*, supra note 1.

25. See Benhabib, *The Rights of Others*, supra note 3.

26. See John Hart Ely, *Democracy and Distrust* (Cambridge, MA: Harvard University Press, 1980).

27. See Michelman, "Law's Republic," supra note 23.

28. Ibid., 1529.

29. Subsequently, a 2003 European Council Directive on family reunification established the right of legal residents in the European Union to apply for reunification with their spouse, underage children, and the children of their spouse. This directive made the rule that forced women (but not men) to be British citizens in order to bring in dependents invalid not on equal protection grounds, but on the grounds that it provided for reunification for citizens and not for legal residents. Importantly, the directive extended rights to "naturalized" British citizens, as opposed to the native born. Council Directive 2003/86/EC of 22 September 2003 on the right to family reunification. *Official Journal L 251, 03/10/2003 p. 0012–0018.* (entered into force on October 3, 2003; Member States had to comply by October 3, 2005).

30. Abdulaziz, supra note 8, paras. 10, 28(a).

31. Ibid., para. 24(b).

32. Ibid., paras. 39, 44, 50.

33. The distinction between "patrials" and "nonpatrials" was first made in the Immigration Act of 1971. "Patrials" were defined as those with the right of abode in the United Kingdom, "nonpatrials" as those who did not enjoy this right. For an analysis of the development of British immigration laws, see ibid., paras. 13–15.

34. Ibid., paras. 70–72.

35. Ibid., para. 83 (holding the state's economic interests in protecting its labor market from influx of immigrant workers insufficient to justify differential treatment between men and women under Article 14 of the European Convention on Human Rights).

36. A 2003 European Council Directive subsequently established the right of third-country nationals to family reunification. See note 29.

37. Abdulaziz, supra note 8, paras. 60–62, 85.

38. Ibid., para. 61. It is important that the applicants were not the husbands, but the wives. In other words, this is "clearly" about the rights of lawful residents and naturalized citizens (as compared with unlawful residents, applicant nonresidents, or citizens who were born in the country). Significantly, in this case, one of the applicants was a naturalized citizen, and as such, was still subject to the "no right to choose" rule, just like resident aliens. The United Kingdom changed the law vis-à-vis naturalized citizens after the introduction of the 2003 Directive on Family Reunification, which extended the right to family reunification to third-country nationals and erased the distinction between "ancestrally" British and naturalized British citizens in terms of their rights to be reunited with their families.

39. Ibid, paras. 78–83.

40. Ibid., para. 22.

41. Ibid.

42. Ibid., para. 48. I should note that one applicant from the Philippines did submit that she was married in a customary ceremony that "was solemnised without a license." Under Philippine law, after five years' cohabitation, common law marriage converts to legally recognized marriage. In the absence of five years' cohabitation, there is some controversy as to the law. The applicants argued that, in the Philippines, customary marriage is presumed valid until specifically declared invalid by a court (that makes an inquiry into the time of cohabitation, etc.). The government, by contrast, argued that Philippine law declares customary marriage void ab initio until such time as the cohabitation requirement is filled. Since the couple had not been married five years, the government argued that their customary marriage was void under Philippine law and that the European Court should defer to this law.

43. Ibid., para. 85b.

44. Susan Sterrett, "Intercultural Citizenship: Statutory Interpretation and Belonging in Britain," *Constitutional Dialogues in Comparative Perspective*, eds. Sally J. Kenney and William M. Reisinger (London: Macmillan, 1991), 119–42.

45. Ibid., 121.

46. Ibid.

47. Ibid., 124–25.

48. Ibid., 131.

49. Ibid., 130–31.

50. See Okin, *Is Multiculturalism Bad for Women?*, supra note 11.

51. European Council Directive on Family Reunification (2003/86/EC).

52. Although the Court did not explicitly accept or reject discrimination on the basis of national origin in the Abdulaziz decision, holding only that this discrimination passed the test of proportionality. However, in European Parliament v. Council (Case C-540/03), the European Parliament challenged the directive as a violation of the fundamental freedoms of the Union. The EP's challenge was brought specifically to the sections of the directive that allowed member states the latitude to impose additional requirements in terms of length of residence and on the reunification of children. The ECtHR held that the directive did not violate the fundamental freedoms and recognized the margin of appreciation awarded states when they examine applications for family reunification. Abdulaziz, supra note 8, paras. 22, 54.

53. The Old Commonwealth includes Australia, Canada, and New Zealand; the New Commonwealth is comprised of former colonies in Africa, the Caribbean, and Asia. Ibid., paras. 11–15, 81–85.

54. Ibid., para. 38

55. Ibid., paras. 76, 84.

56. Ibid., para. 58 (2)

57. Ibid.

58. Although the Court does not specifically label such practice as "European," it remains tied to a view that marriage is a voluntary association, chosen by two partners because they are in love with each other—and not because such a marriage would fill another instrumental "normative" purpose.

59. The idea of "contrapunctal difference" refers to those immigrants who embody multiple temporal or historical perspectives, because they are simultaneously oriented by a contra-modern worldview (in which value sphere differentiation has been, to some extent, successfully resisted) and by a modern worldview (in which ethical-expressive values have been, to a large degree, extirpated from the legal sphere). See Homi Bhaba, *The Location of Culture* (London: Routledge, 1994), esp. ch.8, "Dissemination: Time, Narrative, and the Margins of the Modern Nation."

60. As I will argue in this section of the essay, my view of intercultural political identity is not the same as a "fusion of horizons" approach. In fact, I strongly disagree with Bhikhu Parekh and other advocates of this tradition. See Bhikhu Parekh, *Rethinking Multiculturalism: Cultural Diversity and Political Theory* (Cambridge, MA: Harvard University Press, 2000). Like Walzer, Parekh argues that human rights are reiterated in the context of cultural specificity. According to Parekh, democracies should be concerned with pluralizing the interpretative communities that give meaning to "universal" rights instead of imposing a particular culturally inscribed interpretation. Not only will others resist human rights discourse less if they can "legitimately" make it their own—if they can make human rights the rights of others—but we, in the West, can learn from these "alternative modernities." On this view, we have the opportunity to participate in the preconditions of our own moral learning. For the time being, liberal democracies can learn from immigrants. Parekh argues that, if immigrants fail to convince the majority to make an exception in their case or reinterpret the liberal majority's conception of the good life, then immigrants must accept their duty to assimilate to the "operative public values" of liberal democracies. However, liberal democracies, in recognition of their own pluralism norm, should make every effort to learn from immigrants: "rather than use the public values as a crude and non-negotiable standard for evaluating minority practices, society should engage in a dialogue with the minority." Ibid., 270. Dialogue between different cultures will force both minorities and the majority to defend (or abandon) their cultures. In some cases, these cultures will only coexist—with the liberal society giving a patchwork of exceptions and "deferring" deeper integration until a "fusion of horizons" occurs. This fusion of horizons or context of intercultural evaluation is brought about by the "passage of time" and ongoing "formal and informal public discussions." Unfortunately, Parekh fails to admit that his theory implicitly assumes the background context of a liberal democracy. Only

liberal democracies—strong democracies—can serve as the "context of intercultural dialogue" and even among these democracies the ones who take their commitment to the "good life" too seriously tend to exclude those with countercultural values. The "alternative modernities" thesis is a hoax: there is only one type of society that can recognize the rights of others—a democracy that is already "strong" enough to treat its own culture (its own attachment to the specificity of the "good") as a transitional object. Ibid., 272–73.

61. Julia Kristeva, trans. Leon S. Roudiez, *Nations without Nationalism* (New York: Columbia University Press, 1993), 41.

62. The United Kingdom is a notable exception to the rule. Until recently, the United Kingdom did not have a written constitution or a constitutional court; nonetheless, its unwritten constitution protected many of the same rights as the written constitutions of other advanced democracies.

63. See Jürgen Habermas, "Equal Treatment of Cultures and the Limits of Postmodern Liberalism," *Journal of Political Philosophy* 13 (2005).

64. See Benhabib, *The Rights of Others,* supra note 3.

65. Unfortunately, the United States Supreme Court has followed a Dworkin approach to substantive due process for much of recent history. Even its defense of gay rights in Lawrence v. Texas, 539 U.S. 558 (2003), was grounded in a comprehensive conception of privacy and its relation to decisional autonomy. While I applaud the outcome in Lawrence, I think the comprehensive justification of the autonomy norm is at odds with the antidiscrimination norm of cultural discrimination. Like the Abdulaziz applicants, many immigrants identify with both tradition and autonomy—they claim the freedom to "resignify" their traditions and make them compatible with their own relative autonomy and hence the basic normativity of democratic constitutions. See Ronald Dworkin, *Freedom's Law: The Moral Reading of the Constitution* (Cambridge, MA: Harvard University Press, 1996).

66. Michelman, "Law's Republic," supra note 24, 1529.

67. See Walzer, *Spheres of Justice,* supra note 12.

68. Bonnie Honig, *Democracy and the Foreigner* (Princeton, NJ: Princeton University Press, 2001).

69. Ibid., 79.

70. Michelman, "Law's Republic," supra note 24, 1529.

71. See Maria Pia Lara, "Democracy and Cultural Rights: Is There a New Stage of Citizenship?," *Constellations* 9, no. 2 (2002): 218.

72. In an essay on animal liberation, Peter Singer cautions against speaking of the "last discrimination"; nonetheless, I think recognizing cultural discrimination is, in a sense, the end of history. Animal liberation movements will confront us with "species-ism" as will contact with intelligent life on other planets (if there is such life). But, I suspect that the forms of discrimination that now seem so "far-fetched" to the human imagination will one day prove less illusory, if only

we manage to overcome the form of discrimination that vexed us for so long. See Peter Singer, "Animal Liberation," *The New York Review of Books*, April 5, 1973. Also see Peter Singer, "Animal Liberation at 30," *The New York Review of Books*, May 15, 2003.

73. Pia Lara, "Democracy and Cultural Rights," supra note 71, 218.

74. Initially, Habermas viewed "ethical-expressive" discourse as therapeutic, and shoved many forms of concrete identification into this residual category—aesthetics, religion, all forms of social and cultural identity. ("Narrative therapy" allowed individuals and cultures to investigate self-pathology and understand needs and identity in a different light.) Over time, however, he came to acknowledge that, in addition to promoting self-clarification, narratives can serve a moral purpose: aesthetic discourse (Wellmer) and the language of subcultures, e.g., welfare mothers (Frasier), can illuminate the moral domain and change the world. Recently, Habermas applied thinking he adopted in relation to aesthetics and social groups to religion (and cultural groups). See Means, "Arguing with Natives," supra note 7, 227.

75. Jürgen Habermas, "Religion in the Public Sphere," *European Journal of Philosophy* 14 (2006): 10.

76. When Habermas writes directly about the "equal treatment of cultures" and the corresponding justification for cultural rights, he focuses on the psychological and moral development of individuals. Every person needs a culturally "thick context" in which to grow up. The "cultural constitution of the human mind" is one of the core forms of reciprocal recognition on which we rely; it is part of "the (expanded) development of personal identity" on which "the concept of the legal person as the bearer of subjective rights" relies. While I think all this is true, I think cultural rights is primarily justified as an extension of the logic of "political freedom through law"—in this case, via our confrontation with the next (unthematized) form of discrimination. Jürgen Habermas, "Equal Treatment of Cultures and the Limits of Postmodern Liberalism," *Journal of Political Philosophy* 13 (2005): 17.

77. Mark Lilla, "Church Meets State," *New York Times Book Review* (May 15, 2005), p. 39. Cf. Jürgen Habermas, "The Conflict of Beliefs: Karl Jaspers on the Clash of Cultures," *The Liberating Power of Symbols*, trans. Peter Dews (Cambridge: MIT, 2001).

78. Ibid.

79. Michelman, "Law's Republic," supra note 24, 1529.

13

||||||||||||||||||||||||||||||||||||||||||||||||||||||

Mobility, Migrants, and Solidarity: Towards an Emerging European Citizenship Regime

Patrizia Nanz

Union citizenship is destined to be the fundamental status of nationals of the Member States, enabling those
who find themselves in the same situation to enjoy the
same treatment in law irrespective of their nationality.

—European Court of Justice, Case C-184/99,
Grzelczyk [2001], ECR I-6193, para. 31

"Italy is in the EU . . . [so] I have no problems. I don't
know why I should want German citizenship when I
have . . . just as many rights as Germans. . . . I have no
disadvantages as EU-citizen, . . . as a fellow citizen."

—Armando Guerri, nineteen-year-old
migrant in Frankfurt/Main

Citizenship has traditionally been regarded as exclusive—as defining who
belongs to the people of a particular state—with territory and national
authority as its hallmarks.[1] However, contemporary states have become
increasingly porous and open to transborder population movements. Migration across states and, in particular, across states within Europe, poses
unique challenges to traditional notions of citizenship. Cooperation among
European countries around economic practices began in the 1950s. Over
the last half of the twentieth century, cooperation expanded, culminating

in the formation of the European Union (EU) in 1992, with member countries working to harmonize laws around trade, social welfare, and migration. This chapter explores the emergence of a European citizenship regime and the impact of such a regime on women's citizenship.

In Europe, mass labor migration and refugee flows remained relatively constant after 1945 but have accelerated and, as a result, have become more complex since the late 1980s. The bulk of intra-European migrants left rural areas of southern Italy, western Spain, northern Portugal, and northern Greece in the 1950s and 1960s. Generally speaking, in the 1950s and 1960s, Italy was the most common country of origin and West Germany the most common destination of all these flows.[2] At that time, migrants moving from one European country to another were subject to the same national immigration laws as third-country nationals from outside of Europe. The general intra-Europe migration trend in the middle of the twentieth century was for European men to migrate first and have their spouses follow them a decade later through family reunification programs, although this means of entering has never precluded active economic, social, and political roles for these women.[3] Some women were also admitted as economic migrants in the 1950s and 1960s. In Germany, for example, 20 percent of the so-called guest workers recruited were women.[4] Following the oil crisis and economic slowdown in 1973, many countries imposed harsh restrictions on labor migration across states within Europe.

The introduction of European citizenship in 1992 profoundly changed the nature of intra-European migration. Migrants from European Union member states became citizens without being required to acculturate or assimilate to the host country. In the absence of border controls, visas, and sanctions for nonregistration, European citizens are now entitled to move across national borders at their will. The increased mobility of Europeans over the last decade (e.g., transborder professional lives, student exchange programs, cross-national marriages, retirement and resort moves, etc.) has led to the emergence of a "transnationalized space" where growing numbers of individuals are going through experiences in their everyday lives that undermine their sense of national belonging.

This individual experience of transnationalization is reflected in the Reform Treaty (2007),[5] which imagines a distinct political space encompassing Europe's twenty-seven nation-states.[6] The treaty envisions that citizens can and will derive constitutional rights that are directly applicable vis-à-vis the member states; for example, rights that protect fundamental freedoms and those intended to facilitate the free movement of persons within the Union.

But would the enactment of the Reform Treaty, and the transnational aspiration that informs it, actually fuse the peoples of the member states into one European people, a "constitutional *demos*"? Is the European "we" a body of associates based on their likeness or may they remain alien to each other? Does European citizenship establish bonds of trust and solidarity beyond national membership? And, what can women expect from the European unification process? Does mobility across borders help or hinder women in achieving equality of status?

In this chapter, I analyze mobility and its implications for the emerging citizenship regime of the European Union from a normative-legal as well as empirical-sociological perspective. I first show that Union citizenship implies the dissociation of nationality (belonging) and citizenship (legal status). It envisions a more abstract sphere of cooperation among aliens, which depends on their capacity to engage in intercultural and transnational citizenship practices. I demonstrate how the jurisprudence of the European Court of Justice has promoted this transnational vision of EU citizenship. Second, against this normative-legal background, I explore European citizenship from the perspective of migrants who embrace dual national identities and multiple alliances. My empirical findings suggest that mobility creates an emerging "situated postnational citizenship" with new forms of transnational solidarity among individuals based upon the recognition of mutual difference. Finally, I look at the promise that the European citizenship regime may hold for women's citizenship and for the rights of non-EU national residents in the Union.

I. The Construction of European Citizenship

Union citizenship was a conceptual innovation of the 1992 Maastricht Treaty.[7] The creation of this legal status goes beyond the functional integration of member state economies via the fundamental (economic) freedoms: the free movement of goods, services, capital, and labor force. Until 1992, the citizens of EU member states were "market citizens"; they were considered foreigners when traveling and living elsewhere in the Union.[8] Union citizenship established the legal status of European citizenship for every person who is a national of a member state. Legal status confers four main rights: (1) the right to move freely among, and reside in, other member states; (2) the right to vote and run in municipal and European Parliament elections in the member states where they reside; (3) protection in a non-EU country by the diplomatic or consular representatives of other member states if one's own member state is not represented; and (4) the right to petition the European Parliament, and to petition the European Ombudsman.

The governments agreed to these rights because they hoped to engender popular support and alliances to Union institutions and policies.[9] What is striking about these rights is that they only apply to migrants, i.e., to European persons outside their state of nationality or on their return from migration from another European state. Mobility of EU nationals within the European Union is both an important right in itself and a source of other rights.

The Amsterdam Treaty clarified the relationship between national and Union citizenship, insisting on the supplementary role of Union citizenship and making it explicitly a second citizenship.[10] This independent right, however, rests on national membership. The citizenship issue clearly touches on fundamental questions concerning the institutional character of the European Union. So far, the Union is neither a suprastate nor an ensemble of contract partners. Rather, it is a trans- or postnational normative order, in which questions of statehood and the boundaries of political community remain contested.

Since its foundation, fifty years ago, the European Union has evolved into a community of law that increasingly determines the everyday life of the citizens of member states. This change has had an impact on Europe's women: the European Union advanced from a principle of "equal pay for equal work" (Article 119 of the founding Treaty of the European Economic Community in 1957) to its current far-reaching equality provisions (Article 21 on nondiscrimination[11] and Article 23 on gender equality[12]) of the Charter of Fundamental Rights of the European Union (2000) that imposes a duty not just to respect equality but also to take positive measures, e.g., through mainstreaming, to promote it.[13]

Moreover, Union citizenship presents a series of challenges to traditional thinking about the control of borders and their significance.[14] The right of a member state to include certain people and exclude others using border and identity documents as the tools of differentiation has been deeply transformed by EU law on free movement. The effect of the right of equal treatment (in working conditions, as regards family,[15] and in relation to extensive protection against exclusion and expulsion), which nationals of the member states enjoy, has reduced the difference in position between intra-EU migrant workers who are nationals of other member states and nationals of the host state itself.

In nation-states, citizenship is national citizenship: only nationals qualify for belonging to the political community (the *demos*). There are two basic criteria according to which modern states normally define nationality,[16] namely, the *ius sanguinis* (cultural/ethnic criterion) and *ius solis* (territorial criterion).[17] These criteria are supposed to embody those social facts of close attachment to a particular state. They serve as patterns of justification for excluding nonnationals from citizenship. Many states have traditionally prohibited multiple citizenships, concerned that individuals will suffer from conflicting loyalties and split identities.

Union citizenship, although it is contingent upon national citizenship in one of the member states, is a status that is not grounded in a prior belonging to a particular state. It is attached to the idea of a single *polity*[18] but does not presuppose a prior underlying attachment of the citizen to the Union, i.e., it does not convey any kind of cultural or national "European identity." Union citizenship abolishes the hierarchy between different loyalties (national, European) and allows individuals a multiplicity of associative relations without binding them to a specific nationality. People who are alien with respect to their nationalities, i.e., who are separated by their different national identities, are at the same time fellows with respect to their shared European citizenship.[19]

As detailed in the following section, there has been a continual legal expansion of the status of Union citizenship so that it comprises benefits, which in turn may create bonds between individuals and the Union. In this way, nationality (belonging) and citizenship (legal status) are gradually becoming dissociated in the Union. But a feminist criticism has rightly noted that this dissociation has not been gender neutral. For example, benefits for intra-Europe migrants remain focused on traditionally male forms of paid work.[20]

The Making of Europeans and the Jurisprudence of the European Court of Justice

The jurisprudence of the European Court of Justice (ECJ) played a key role in gradually including the citizens of the European Union in the matrix of rights and duties of the treaties a long time before the creation of Union citizenship.[21] Since the *van Gend & Loos* judgment in 1963, the citizens of the member states have been subject to the rules of the European Community (EC).[22] In that case, the ECJ created the doctrine of "direct effect," according to which some unconditional norms of EU law confer rights on individuals that national courts must protect. The most important consequence of this doctrine is that it makes fundamental (economic) freedoms directly enforceable against member states, thereby eroding national sovereignty. Until the creation of Union citizenship, the personal scope of the direct-effects doctrine was limited in application to specific groups to whom European rights were granted: workers, service providers, or persons wishing to form an establishment in other member states.

The logic of market integration, namely, that there should be no obstacles for an EU citizen seeking employment in another state, has opened up space for a parallel logic of universal human rights to take root in ECJ jurisprudence. This parallel logic, which the ECJ has embraced, envisions that there should not be obstacles to the guarantee of fundamental rights for citizens and people moving between member states.

While the European legislature, made up of both the European Council and the European Parliament, has been reluctant to attach substantial rights to the concept of Union citizenship, the ECJ has been much more receptive to an expansive understanding of the concept. In 1969, the court declared that fundamental rights, in spite of lacking textual reference in the treaty, are enshrined in the "general principles of community law."[23]

The jurisprudence of the court challenges the age-old constitutive tension between human rights and national self-determination. In particular, for the protection and integration of citizens, the principle of equality, and especially the prohibition of discrimination on grounds of nationality or of gender, cannot be underestimated. For example, the ECJ adopted a rather progressive position on the relationship between pregnancy and discrimination, particularly when compared with U.S. or Canadian courts.[24] Its jurisprudence holds that pregnancy discrimination is direct and noncomparative discrimination (i.e., a pregnant woman cannot be compared to a sick man).[25] The court also took a strong stand with respect to gender discrimination against part-time workers. Similarly, Union citizenship is grounded by the principle of nondiscrimination, although so far it concerns mainly social and cultural rights.

By extending this nondiscrimination principle to prohibiting any discrimination on grounds of nationality, the European Court of Justice has reconstructed Union citizenship in a way that potentially turns aliens into associates. One of the first cases in which Union citizenship became prominent was *Bickel and Franz*.[26] In that case, due to traffic code violations, a German and an Austrian citizen were involved in criminal proceedings in Bolzano, Italy. German-speaking Italian nationals benefited from a rule allowing the German language in court proceedings in Bolzano. The ECJ held that by prohibiting "any discrimination on grounds of nationality," Article 12 of the EC Treaty requires that persons in a situation governed by community law be placed entirely on an equal footing with nationals of the member states.

In another 2002 ECJ case, *Baumbast*,[27] the court adjudicated the claim of a German national who lived in Britain and worked either there or as a German employee in China. Baumbast's residence permit was not renewed by the British secretary of state, who claimed that he was no longer a worker in the country. Here the ECJ held, against the opposition of two intervening governments, that as a citizen of the European Union, Mr. Baumbast and his family had the right to rely on Article 18 (1) of the EC Treaty, i.e., the right to move and reside freely within the territory of the member states. This case was the first in which the court placed the fundamental right of free movement above purely economic considerations.[28] Until then, the right to work or establish oneself in another member state was not wholly effective unless job seekers and potential entrepreneurs were given the opportunity in law to seek work or attempt to otherwise establish themselves in the new country.[29]

The language of the ECJ on Union citizenship is that of equality before the law, the principle that T. H. Marshall found central to the acquisition of other rights.[30] The 1998 case of *Martinez Sala* introduced another facet of equal treatment into the understanding of Union citizenship, thereby putting a legal end to unequal treatment based on economic status.[31] The question at the heart of the case was whether an unemployed Spanish national, single mother, and long-term resident in the land of Bavaria (although on what precise basis her lawful residence could be deduced was not entirely clear), could claim a child-raising benefit available solely to German nationals or those who had a residence permit. The national court ruled that Ms. Martinez Sala was neither a worker nor an "employed person" under European Community social security regulations. The ECJ, in contrast, held that she could rely upon the nondiscrimination principle enshrined in Article 12 of the EC Treaty. Ms. Martinez Sala could not be obliged to produce a residence permit in order to obtain the benefit, when German nationals only have to prove to be permanently settled in

Germany. The court thereby widened the conferral of social advantages and family benefits beyond the bounds of economic activity and, as a result, undermined a facet of member state sovereignty on welfare matters.

The court's approach in the *Martinez Sala* case, while interpreted as a milestone for the development of Union citizenship, has also been criticized as an example of exclusion of women. This critique is based on the ECJ's refusal to recognize "care work" as a "proper" form of work in the case.[32] While EC law explicitly acknowledges the importance of family and care needs among ascendant relatives in particular, as a potential barrier to the mobility of workers, it does not recognize care as a legitimate form of rights-bearing social contribution.

The leading case on Union citizenship is the ECJ's 2001 decision in *Grzelczyk*.[33] In that case, a French national who was studying in Belgium and who had previously worked there applied for "minimex," a minimum subsistence allowance. The fact that he did not hold Belgian citizenship was the only bar to his receipt of the benefit. Although he was initially refused by the local authorities, the ECJ held that he had to be given the allowance on the basis of his Union citizenship. The court explained, "Union citizenship is destined to be the fundamental status of nationals of the member states, enabling those who find themselves in the same situation to enjoy the same treatment in law irrespective of their nationality. . . ."[34]

It is undisputed that the *Grzelczyk* case is an example of discrimination based solely on nationality. The importance of this case resides in its systematic approach to defining citizenship as including persons who would have traditionally fallen outside the scope of a European Community law. In short, any link with the exercise of the right of free movement appears to be sufficient to bring the case within the scope of the treaty. The court relied on both the right to move freely and the right against discrimination. And, as Elspeth Guild observed, "Marshall's argument that social citizenship is closely linked with the development of universal education which is a prerequisite for the extension of the franchise finds an echo here."[35]

The 2001 *Grzelczyk* judgment is an all-embracing interpretation of what may come within the European Community's ambit. As a result, it has far-reaching consequences for the catalogue of Union citizens' rights. For social rights, the principle of residence gradually overshadows nationality. The court confirmed this ruling in a 2004 case, *Collins*. In *Collins*, an Irish-American national moved to the United Kingdom in order to find work in the social service sector. A month later he applied for the job seeker's allowance, which he was refused on the grounds that he was not habitually resident in the United Kingdom.[36] With express reference to the previous citizenship case law, the ECJ held that any discriminatory national provision—even in terms of financial benefit—was unlawful. Union citizenship has become a "trigger norm" of the ECJ, in particular, for its antidiscrimination jurisprudence.[37]

II. European Citizenship from the Perspective of Intra-EU Migrants

Is the juridico-political conception of a "denationalized" citizenship[38] of EU citizens supported by empirical evidence of people's sense of belonging? In order to explore this question, we should listen to those who live and work between nations, cultures, and languages. Under today's condition of societal denationalization, such "intercultural identities" are far more common than we might assume and are certainly not limited to underprivileged migrants or an elite made up of "global players." By studying autobiographical narratives, this section aims to shed light on new identities that emerge as a result of denationalization and the disintegration of the *demos*. The assumption is that new identities may enrich democratic politics with innovative interpretations of the social world or, for that matter, of an emerging European transnational citizenship regime. Their accounts of citizenship make ideologies[39] of belonging and political loyalties explicit, as well as reveal people's normative ideals with respect to collective identification (boundaries of trust and solidarity, of inclusion and exclusion).

The case of Germany, considered a destination for both high- and low-skilled migrants, invites questions about societal and political membership as framed in specifically cultural terms. German identity is traditionally built on the idea of *Kulturnation*, and until 1999, citizenship, an essential element for the constitution of collective identities, was mainly based on *ius sanguinis*.[40] After the SPD/Greens won the Bundestag elections in September 1998, a heated and wide-ranging debate focused on the desirability of granting German (or dual) citizenship to long-standing resident "guest-workers" and their descendents. In the Hessen Landtag (Parliament of the Province of Hessen) elections of February 1999, the CDU/CSU based their whole election campaign on their opposition to the "dual passport"—and won. The campaign even extended to gathering signatures on the streets of Frankfurt for a petition against the citizenship law reform project. In the context of this public debate, during which my interviews with migrants took place, the question of being a European citizen or a non-European foreigner became increasingly relevant. And, in fact, all my interviewees spontaneously brought up the subject of their European identity and European citizenship, although I had myself been careful never to mention "Europe" or "European citizenship."

Transnational Surveys of Intra-EU Migrants' Perspectives

Before we examine the content from the interviews, it is useful to first briefly consider some rich data from a series of attitude surveys. Eurobarometer data, gathered by the Public Opinion Analysis sector of the European Commission,[41] has shown that negative attitudes towards intra-EU migrants are a key variable that is highly correlated with hostility toward European integration.[42] However, what is perhaps more interesting is that data has revealed that even during the period in which support of the member states for the European Union dwindled (after about 1990), the majority of those surveyed by Eurobarometer identified with Europe—an attachment that grew throughout the beginning of this century.[43] Interestingly, maintaining a European identity does not seem to erode one's feelings towards one's own nation. Contrary to traditional Euro-sceptic discourse in the political science literature, respondents with high levels of national identity are more likely to identify with Europe than respondents who display weaker levels of political identification.[44] Thus, because individuals describe themselves as holding multiple identities, we can reject zero-sum conceptions of national versus European identity. A critical factor involved in mitigating prejudice towards "outsiders" seems to be adopting a sense of collective identity that is not exclusively national.[45] Moreover, the more Europe is identified in "civic-political" rather than in "cultural-ethnic" terms, and the more cultural diversity is welcomed, the less exclusion and categorization of "others" (EU migrants or non-EU third-country nationals) takes place.[46]

The well-respected *Shellstudie*, a national study of the attitudes, values, and behaviors of German youth, showed that foreigners see the future of that country more positively than Germans, and among the foreigners, Italians are more optimistic than Turks, and women more optimistic than men.[47] Young migrants feel that they enjoy roughly the same opportunities as the indigenous population. Recent quantitative and qualitative studies on the life situation of young female migrants show that a considerable number of them want to go their own way without breaking away from their parents' culture or their values.[48] These women are keen on education and see no contradiction between the "modern life" of individualism, on the one hand, and their intense family orientation, the inevitability of marriage, and their belief in religion, on the other hand. They feel free to navigate between their different identities. All these findings support the impression given by my own interviews.

The material providing the principal evidence arises from a set of interviews with Italian denizens[49] from different occupational backgrounds (computer engineer, secretary, construction worker, greengrocer, school student, etc.) in Frankfurt am Main.[50] Although the small sample size of my single case study[51] does not enable me to explore possible gender differences, it may provide the groundwork for more comprehensive research, which could take into account these differences.

My interviews were driven by an interest in the interviewees' views on the issues of citizenship, identity, and sense of belonging. My underlying questions were as follows: (1) Do the interviewees understand their identity to be constructed or as something prediscursively defined by categories such as nation, region, etc.? (2) To what extent do the interviewees mix with those from other cultures, and how willing are they to engage with and learn from them? 3) To what degree are the interviewees self-reflexive, i.e., do they see their own perspectives as partial and are they willing to see the world through the eyes of others?

Four Stories of Belonging under Conditions of Denationalization

Annalisa Corradi, a small, delicate, neat woman in her thirties, greets me in her immaculate apartment. She came to Frankfurt at the age of six and worked for many years as a hairdresser before marrying an Italian waiter who has recently taken over his own pizzeria. She is now a housewife and the mother of two children. Her story is one of success, of moving up the ladder step by hard-earned step. One of the signs of her ambition lies in the fact that she has sent her children to a private school to learn "good German," which in state schools is "impossible because of the huge number of foreign kids." Annalisa's German and Italian *personae* come to the fore at different times.[52]

> I can be an Italian here; I can be a German. . . . What am I? Everything, everything, I am surely an Italian, obviously, . . . but ah, when I have to play the German role, then I play the German role, no problem.[53]

Annalisa displays a self-conscious ability to play different "identity" roles and to switch between them "autonomously." Accordingly, she has no essentializing conception of cultural and national self-understandings and seems aware of their "constructedness."

Riccardo Dente gives a rather different impression. Big, well-dressed, and jovial, he breaks into a fleeting smile when he finds something funny about the stories he tells me. At forty, he runs a law firm with twenty employees on one of the most elegant streets in Frankfurt, but he evidently prefers to be "one of the boys" rather than play the role of the "big boss." He moved to Germany with his father, a physician from Friuli, when he was five years old, after the death of his mother, a Neapolitan musician. Riccardo is now married to a German woman and has four children. He clearly enjoys being at the center of attention, underlining his self-consciously Italian *savoir vivre* with somewhat theatrical gestures, even though he speaks German with a strong Hessian accent. In the middle of recounting his life story he says,

> If I had either the fortune or the misfortune of . . . making a clear choice: . . .
> I am clearly an Italian and a German, then I would also say, yes, I am politically European, and culturally German.[54]

What is most salient about this statement is Riccardo's caution when using his identity categories, his unproblematic (even slightly positive) view on apparently confusing, ambivalent belongings: he "is" Italian, politically European, and culturally German.

I interview Armando Guerri in the back room of the tiny food shop run by his parents. Short of stature and solidly built, the nineteen-year-old apprentice hotelier calls himself a "typical third-generation immigrant brat." He seems at ease with a "hyphenated" or "pastiche" Italian-German identity, an identity that extends even to his gestures and ways of talking. Armando was born in Frankfurt but spent two years at elementary school in Sicily, where he stayed with his grandmother. He is keen to emphasize that his friends are "international." When he goes back to his village in Sicily during the summer, he feels just as at home as he does in Frankfurt, but then, as he points out with a smile, more than half of the other guys are also migrants and normally live in Germany or Holland. He believes that non-EU immigrants can benefit from German citizenship, but he himself, being Italian (i.e., an EU citizen), does not need it, even if this means that he cannot vote in the national elections. He is happy with his right to vote in the local *Kommunal* elections.

> In my case . . . Italy is in the EU . . . so I have no problems. I don't know why I should want German citizenship when I have . . . just as many rights as a German. That is, aside from voting, but otherwise, I find, I have no disadvantages as EU-citizen, a fellow citizen.[55]

His discourse on European citizenship is based on rights and "legal advantages," not on some idea of a shared essentialistic identity or common European culture that non-Europeans do not share. In his narrative there are no such boundaries between "us" and "them," between "friends" and "enemies." For Armando, "European" seems to mean "international" or "intercultural." For him, what counts is the way someone is as a person, regardless of his national or cultural identity. This is a theme that repeatedly recurs in all the interviews.

Armando can see himself living in other European countries—but also beyond, for example, in America. He can also see himself having an African or Moroccan girlfriend. Indeed, rather than excluding non-EU migrants from his European discourse, he tends to place a high value on encountering different cultures. He is also able to put himself in the shoes of non-EU migrants. For example, he tells me that if he were Turkish, he would want German citizenship because non-EU migrants have fewer rights.

> Well, if I were from Turkey . . . I would want to have German citizenship . . . because I know, as a Turk, . . . one doesn't have as many advantages as an Italian in Germany. I feel European, a hundred percent.[56]

Armando feels quite happy with the plurality of coexisting national identities and seems aware of their dynamic constructedness. Depending on the context, he can navigate now as the "third-generation immigrant in Frankfurt" (focusing on common intercultural experience); now stressing

his Germanness (for example, when he is with someone from his Sicilian village who hasn't gone abroad); now his Italian origins (for example,
when he watches football with his friends—they all "play" with their own
and each others' different origins). In his everyday life, Armando draws
on his knowledge of different cultures and languages, mixing them and
picking out the good elements from both.

Teresa Pedrini is a pretty, stylish nineteen-year-old, full of energy but
seemingly uneasy about her life. She left high school (*Gymnasium*) a year
before taking the final examinations, the *Abitur*, a decision she now re-
grets. She works part-time in a clothes shop and plans to go back to the
Gymnasium and then to Italy to carry on her studies. Teresa's life story is
one of transnational coming and going, a pattern more typical of Italian
than, say, Turkish or Spanish migrants. She was born in Frankfurt, but
just after her eighth birthday the whole family returned to Lecce. It was
there that Teresa spent what she calls her "important years" in terms of
socialization. After seven years, however, her father lost his job and the
family decided to go back to Frankfurt. Despite extreme difficulties at the
Gymnasium, she felt immediately socially accepted by the members of her
class, the majority of whom were foreigners.

> No, no, no, there was no real difference between students. . . . You can say
> that they were all Germans, no matter whether one was [also] a foreigner,
> Italian, Spanish, Portuguese. . . .[57]

Teresa, like many of the other interviewees, tells me that her friends are
"Germans, Spaniards, Moroccans, Turks, French, and English." She emphasizes that there were no differences between them and that they were
all fundamentally "Germans" regardless of their background. At the same
time, however, Teresa's narrative underlines cultural diversity, stressing in
particular her own Italian identity, as well as the fact that encountering
all these different cultures was an enriching experience. At school she and
her classmates would often discuss what was happening in their different
countries of origin and that by taking from the ways of life, the cultures,
the religions of others, they broadened their own cultures, and their horizons. She describes this as important for her "personal learning processes."
Although she otherwise speaks highly of her friends in Lecce, she criticizes
them for being somewhat "racist" towards the Albanians and Turks who
arrive on the Italian coast. Although her words belie a degree of nostalgia

for Lecce, she underscores the fact that she has no problem with living as a foreigner in Germany or with the many cultures of her peers.

> It is enriching [in Germany] . . . because you have contact with Germans, with Moroccans, Turks, and many other nationalities and from each nationality you derive a life style, a culture, a religion that enrich your own. . . .[58]

For Teresa and for all of those from her age group who were interviewed by me, "European" describes the mixing and encountering of different cultures that she experiences in her Frankfurt life. For her, the unification of Europe was present all along in her classroom.

> Sincerely speaking, [European unification] is very significant . . . because before I ever distinguish between countries, for me Europe was already united. [When] you live in Germany, you have many friends of different races . . . therefore European unification for me was already happening on a small scale [in class]. . . . I hope that it continues in this way.[59]

Towards a Situated Postnational European Citizenship

As to their self-understanding (my first question), the interviewees indicated that they do not feel "uprooted" but rather feel rooted in two cultures. This is perhaps the most striking feature of the interviews and of the literature: the ambivalence of the interviewees' sense of belonging and their awareness that their identities are multiple and constructed, not ready-made or pregiven by any national or cultural bond. All interviewees reject the either/or classifications of collective identity, which are typical of ready-made conceptions (e.g., the underlying idea of a pregiven identity, which was an important feature of the German debate about dual citizenship). Having developed a certain predisposition to perceive themselves from an intercultural and transnational perspective, migrants are "betwixt and between."[60] They emphasize the fact that they are both foreign (e.g., Italian) and German, and most express an ambivalent but strongly situated idea of citizenship and identity. My interviewees, especially those who attended school in Germany, enact ambivalent self-understandings (simultaneously Italian, German, and "international") but—and in this they differ from their Turkish peers—often spontaneously deem themselves "European" when asked about citizenship issues. Unlike Turkish migrants, they are citizens of an EU member state and say that because of the "legal advantages" of being an EU citizen they "do not need" German citizenship.

As to the degree of openness (my second question), all of my interviewees see this kind of plural belonging and intercultural interaction as enriching. They emphasize that people with different origins can go beyond encounters with others and mix with each other interculturally by actively learning from each other. While they recognize that such encounters can involve conflict or other difficulties, all seem to agree that attempts at mutual understanding and learning are important experiences, which contribute to one's development as a person. They emphasize that we should learn to treat all people "equally." Some of them explicitly refuse to draw boundaries between (other) foreigners, Italians, and Germans, but make clear that this equality should not obliterate cultural differences. Such an open and "constructed" self is a crucial presupposition for transnational citizenship practices.

As to the degree of reflexivity (my third question), my interviews show that exposure to a plural situatedness somehow relativizes the attachment to one's roots. Multiple belongings do not seem to lead to a sort of abstract or detached postnational identity but to a more reflexive, although situated, sense of belonging. The collective identity of migrants is ambivalent and relativized, while their personal identity is strong but flexible—and not at all uncommitted. Their capacity to move among multiple identities according to the context of social interaction is accompanied by a striking willingness (spontaneously expressed in the narratives) to change perspective in order to try to see the world through others' eyes. Some, for example, say that if they were Turkish (i.e., if they were not to have EU citizenship), they too would ask for German citizenship in order to have the same rights as Germans or migrants from EU member states. Two older interviewees, for example, emphasized that today the Turks or the asylum seekers in Germany or the Albanians and Kurds who arrive on the coast of Puglia are like the Italian migrants of the 1960s. Almost all interviewees, especially the younger ones, emphasize EU citizenship in civic-political terms; thus boundaries become arbitrary or "constructed."[61] Their accounts display a "pastiche" self-understanding and a multilayered conception of citizenship, which is surprisingly conscious of the legal status of Union citizenship.

I end this section with an extract from the interview with Chiara Gambaro, a small, lively greengrocer at the *Kleinmarkthalle,* a huge multicultural food and vegetable market. At thirty-eight, she seems uninterested in her appearance, but emanates warmth and a quick intelligence. When she was twelve years old, she came to Frankfurt with her parents, both workers from Agrigento (Sicily). At twenty, she married a Sicilian and now has two sons. During the interview she expresses a strong interest in both Italian and German politics. Certain of the fact that she has the "same rights" as a German citizen (apart from national voting rights), she, like all other interviewees, is uninterested in German citizenship.

Chiara's idea of citizens' rights is detached from questions of identity. Several times she emphasizes the fact that she likes working in the multicultural context of the *Kleinmarkthalle* and is especially fond of her Kurdish friends, for whose political troubles in Turkey she expresses much sympathy. Chiara likes going back to Sicily, but also dislikes the fact that people of different social status are treated differently there when they go to an office, to a bank, or to the doctor. Like two other middle-aged female interviewees from southern Italy, she also emphasizes the fact that women in their home country are "less free." As important features of European identity, Chiara stresses "equality between men and women," as well as among all people regardless of where they come from, as a distinctive quality of European citizenship. To her, Europe reaches out and can include "threatened" Kurds, "oppressed" Indian women, and non-Europeans ("*extracomunitari*"), thereby blurring boundaries drawn by EU citizenship between individuals from member states and individuals from "third" states:

> We are all European, no? I think so. . . . In my opinion, feeling like a European is feeling free, independent, not like some nations of the world like India where [people] have no rights, as women, for example. . . . We Europeans have rights, we are democratic. . . . We are international, we are truly European, and even the non-Europeans living here have adapted a bit as well.[62]

As we have seen from these interviews, under conditions of multiple belongings, cultural and national identity can become more "relativized" and reflexive. Reflexivity, the insight that one's own perspective is partial and that the perspective of others is potentially equally valid, is crucial for the idea of trust and solidarity across national or cultural boundaries. My data provides some evidence that the sociocultural presuppositions for a transnational solidarity based upon the recognition of difference can be obtained in many contexts, and can be fostered in others, for example, by institutionalized citizenship practices promoting cultural self-reflexivity, openness to diversity, and cross-national political dialogue.

III. Considering the Future of Women's Citizenship and the Rights of non-EU National Residents in the European Union

As we have seen, Union citizenship, both in law and in practice, implies the dissociation of nationality (belonging) and citizenship (legal status)— a dissociation that has the potential to foster trust and solidarity independent of national affiliations. The recognition of the alien as a fellow citizen is a basic challenge of Union citizenship. Union citizenship creates an explicitly political status and it does so without relying on a constitutional European *demos*. It offers to the citizens of the member states a new and additional "we," which creates a bond among individuals who accept that they are and remain alien to each other. Situated in one or more nation-state contexts and cultures, they are conscious of a more abstract sphere of communication about common goals among strangers. The European Union is a political space without *demos*, based on the solidarity of citizens who are able to reflect their otherness.

But can Union citizenship be considered truly postnational?[63] And is it gender sensitive? Union citizenship, as defined by the treaty, is on the one hand inclusive for EU nationals, potentially fostering multiple loyalties among them; on the other hand, however, it by definition excludes non-EU nationals residing in the European Union from political participation. Union citizenship has created a "two-tiered status of foreignness":[64] the discrepancy between those who are foreign nationals but EU citizens and those who are third-country nationals has deepened. Although the integration of the latter into the European Union's rights regime is rather advanced,[65] citizenship of the Union is still unavailable to them. As yet, it is unclear whether Union citizenship will ultimately replace the rights and duties specific in the national context, whether it will simply complement national law, or whether the concept of citizenship will "evolve" as such, namely, in a liberal-democratic rather than (supra)national way.

These two tiers of foreignness give rise to a division between a political community and a transnational economic and social community: as yet, non-EU citizens benefit only from certain citizenship rights, namely, those that are not intrinsically linked to nationality of a member state.

Although they are *de jure* not EU citizens, they are entitled to some civil, economic, and social rights.[66] The clear distinction between insiders and outsiders is particularly challenged by a curious position regarding rights to social security within the European Union.[67] Moreover, the Charter of Fundamental Rights of the European Union, signed in Nice in 2000, is reacting to injustices of social exclusion by establishing rights of solidarity.[68] Although the "citizen" behind the charter is clearly a gendered person and European (not global), it allows for an understanding of "citizenship as critical positioning," which does not focus on belonging to nations, "avoids explicit sexing of subjects and opens up spaces for the inclusion of sexual minorities."[69]

Remarkably, the ECJ has been making fewer and fewer distinctions between EU citizens and non-EU third-country nationals. For example, in the *Zhu and Chen* case, a Chinese woman decided to travel to Belfast in order to give birth to her daughter, having deliberately chosen Belfast because anyone born in Northern Ireland acquires Irish nationality and is thus a Union citizen, with the right to move freely to Cardiff in Wales.[70] Ms. Chen invoked the right of residence deriving from that of her daughter. In order not to reduce the monopoly powers of the member states with regard to the determination of nationality, the court notably held that Zhu satisfied the sufficient-resources condition for the right of free movement only via her Chinese mother who, as her primary caregiver, also gained an indefinite right of residence. Ultimately, both mother's and daughter's rights to remain in the United Kingdom were vindicated.

The *Zhu and Chen* case plants an important seed for the realization of the rights not only of third-country nationals residing in the European Union, generally, but also the subgroup of those nationals who are women, in particular. The case demonstrates how women may be able to use transnational forms of citizenship and entitlements to increase their mobility and gain rights. Notwithstanding this far-reaching judgment, however, we have to acknowledge that for non-EU nationals there are, as of yet, no political rights: they are still unable to vote or to run in local, national, and European elections. Welfare and employment rights do not make them "partial European citizens" from a legal point of view.

Parallel to the process of "integration through law," i.e., through rules, court decisions, and agreements, formal and informal citizenship practices are taking place at the European level through social movements and transnational policy networks (e.g., the European Women's Lobby, the women members for trade unions, the European Network against Racism, the European Coordination for Foreigners' Right to Family Life). Scholars have emphasized these "soft" forms of participation in EU institutions as well as transnational associations and networks, which challenge national citizenship as the main access, as well as sign of membership and alliances, to a political community.

The potential for third-country voices to be heard in EU policymaking as a result of the participation of transnational networks suggests that we may indeed be moving toward "a potentially progressive source of post-national rights."[71] As Valentine Moghadam's chapter in this volume discusses, women have successfully used transnational feminist networks (TFNs) to vindicate their rights in the Middle East, North Africa, and around the world.[72] TFNs may similarly play a role in ensuring that any postnational citizenship that emerges in the European Union includes equal political and civil rights for women migrants both from within and from outside of the Union.

At the beginning of the 1990s, the European Parliament gave subsidies to a transnational structure called "Migrants' Forum" to induce non-EU nationals to coordinate their actions beyond the national level and to integrate them into the European Union. By claiming equality of rights and treatment, third-country nationals were striving to promote their status as "European citizens" in the newly shaped political arena.[73] But, although it is remarkable that the European Union does not use EU citizenship to exclude non-EU citizens from "soft" forms of participation, further-reaching expectations that the EU's migration regime might be a source for a postnational polity can empirically not be supported.[74]

The debate on the European Constitution was relaunched by the German president of the European Council in early 2007. Renewed negotiation brought with it an opportunity to intervene on multiple levels in European civil society and the transnational public space.[75] Title II of the as yet unratified Reform Treaty (or "Lisbon Treaty") includes an article on "provisions on democratic principles," which establishes a clear connection between a "regular dialogue" with civil society and democratic governance in the European Union.[76] This article would oblige *all* European institutions to be transparent and open to consultation. If this article enters into force, reflections about the inclusion of civil society organizations in EU policymaking processes will inevitably gain momentum.

The transformative changes in the meaning of Union citizenship are better understood as processes, not as immediate effects of the formal enactment of a legal status. These changes will depend on judicial and political interpretations of citizenship at the national and European level, as well as on people's sense of European citizenship. As Ute Gerhard has recently argued, "with regard to the integration already achieved through law and citizenship practice, women," and we may add migrants, "in Europe have more to win than to lose."[77] As yet, however, both the goal of European integration and the nature of European citizenship is an open-ended project, the outcome of which is unknown.

NOTES

1. I would like to thank Talia Inlender and Chavi Kenney Nana for their excellent editing, as well as Talia Inlender, Judith Resnik, and the editor at NYU Press, Deborah Gershenowitz, for their helpful suggestions. Thanks also to Hannah Müller for library assistance.

2. Ettore Recchi, "Migrants and Europeans: An Outline of the Free Movement of Persons in the EU," 38 *AMID Working Paper Series* (Aalborg, Denmark: Academy for Migration Studies in Denmark, 2005), *available at* http://www.amid.dk/pub/papers/AMID_38-2005_Recchi.pdf.

3. See generally Jane Freedman, ed., *Gender and Insecurity: Migrant Women in Europe* (Aldershot, UK: Ashgate Publishing, 2003).

4. See Monika Mattes, "*Gastarbeiterinnen,*" in *der Bundesrepublik Anwerbepolitik, Migration und Geschlecht in den 50er bis 70er Jahren* (Frankfurt/Main, Germany: Campus Verlag 2005).

5. The as-yet-unratified Reform Treaty (or Treaty of Lisbon) replaces the "European Constitution" that was drafted by a Constitutional Convention under the auspices of the European Council. Remarkably, the Constitutional Convention was open for comments by civil society organizations and citizens. Deliberations were public and a website for comments was established. However, the actual composition of the convention was clearly male dominated: only seventeen out of a total of 107 members were women. Following the failed referenda on the draft EU Constitutional Treaty in France and the Netherlands in 2005, a Reform Treaty was signed by EU leaders at a special summit in Lisbon on 13 December 2007. The Reform Treaty deliberately dropped all constitutional symbolism once included in the draft Constitutional Treaty. Treaty of Lisbon Amending the Treaty on European Union and the Treaty Establishing the European Community, *available at* http://www.consilium.europa.eu/uedocs/cmsUpload/cg00014.en07.pdf.

6. In the spring of 2004, ten new member states joined the European Union: Cyprus, the Czech Republic, Estonia, Hungary, Latvia, Lithuania, Malta, Poland, Slovakia, and Slovenia. On January 1, 2007, Romania and Bulgaria joined the European Union.

7. Treaty on European Union and Final Act art. 8-8^E, Feb. 7, 1992, O.J. (C 224) (1992), *reprinted in* 31 I.L.M. 247 (1992) [hereinafter Maastricht Treaty]. These ideas are included in Articles 17–22 in the Amsterdam revisions to the Maastricht Treaty.

8. Ulrich K. Preuss, "Two Challenges to European Citizenship," in *Constitutionalism in Transformation: European and Theoretical Perspectives*, eds. Richard Bellamy and Dario Castiglione, 139 (Oxford: Blackwell, 1996).

9. Andreas Føllesdal, "Citizenship: Global and European," in *Global Citizenship: A Critical Reader*, eds. Nigel Dower and John Williams, 73 (Edinburgh: Edinburgh University Press, 2002).

10. In October 1997, the Amsterdam Treaty introduced amendments to the principle of European citizenship in Articles 17 and 21 (formerly Articles 8 and 8[d]). The Amsterdam Treaty states that "citizenship of the Union shall complement and not replace national citizenship." Treaty of Amsterdam Amending the Treaty on European Union, the Treaties Establishing the European Communities and Certain Related Acts arts. 17, 21, Oct. 2, 1997, 1997 O.J. (C 340).

11. Article 21 of the Charter of Fundamental Rights of the European Union (hereinafter EU Charter) states that "any discrimination based on any ground such as sex, race, colour, ethnic or social origin, genetic features, language, religion or belief, political or any other opinion, membership of a national minority, property, birth, disability, age or sexual orientation shall be prohibited." Charter of Fundamental Rights of the European Union art. 21, Dec. 1, 2000, 2000 O.J. (C 364) 1, *available at* http://www.europarl.europa.eu/ charter/pdf/text_en.pdf.

12. Article 23 of the EU Charter states that "equality between men and women must be ensured in all areas, including employment, work and pay." Ibid., art. 23.

13. Sandra Fredman, "Transformation or Dilution: Fundamental Rights in the EU Social Space," *European Law Journal* 12(1) (2006): 41–60.

14. See, for example, Elspeth Guild, *The Legal Elements of European Identity: EU Citizenship and Migration Law* (The Hague: Kluwer Law International, 2005).

15. Migrants from EU member states are entitled to family reunification. In fact, the ECJ has been so protective of those seeking family reunification (and, in particular, protecting these individuals against member states' restrictive policies towards their own nationals) that it has created an incentive for European citizens to use their free movement rights in order to establish a right to family reunification with third-country national family members. However, no such solution appears in sight for Europe's migrants who are third-country nationals. Ibid., ch. 6.

16. In the *Nottebohm* case, the International Court of Justice ruled that

nationality is a legal bond having at its basis a social fact of attachment, a genuine connection of existence, interests and sentiments, together with the existence of reciprocal rights and duties. It may be said to constitute the juridical

expression of the fact that the individual upon whom it is conferred . . . is in
fact more closely connected with the population of the State conferring nationality than with any other State. (Nottebohm Case [Liechtenstein v. Guatemala],
1955 I.C.J. 4, 23 [Judgment of April 6, 1955])

17. The EU member states use different combinations of the cultural/ethnic
and territorial criteria for determining national citizenship.
    18. Ulrich K. Preuss and Ferran Requejo, eds., *European Citizenship, Multicul-
turalism, and the State,* 8 (Baden-Baden, Germany: Nomos Verlag, 1998).
    19. Clause Offe and Ulrich K. Preuss, "The Problem of Legitimacy in the Eu-
ropean Polity: Is Democratization the Answer?" in *The Diversity of Democracy:
Corporatism, Social Order, and Political Conflict,* eds. Colin Crouch and Wolfgang
Streeck, 175–204 (Cheltenham, UK: Edward Elgar, 2006).
    20. See Catherine Dauvergne's chapter in this volume, "Globalizing Fragmen-
tation: New Pressures on Women Caught in the Immigration Law–Citizenship
Law Dichotomy." For other examples, see Chiara Saraceno, "Constructing Europe, Constructing European Citizenship: Contradictory Trends," in *Will Europe
Work? Integration, Employment, and the Social Order,* eds. Martin Kohli and
Mojca Nowak, 127–41 (London: Routledge, 2001); Ute Gerhard, "European Citizenship: A Political Opportunity for Women?," in *Women's Citizenship and Political Rights,* eds. Sirkku Hellsten, Anne Maria Holli, and Krassimira Daskalova,
37–52 (New York: Palgrave Macmillan, 2006).
    21. It is important to emphasize that the ECJ does not actually decide cases.
It simply answers a set of questions posed by the national courts, which the latter deem to be necessary for the purpose of resolving an issue of European law,
which arises before it. The preliminary reference procedure does not guarantee
the "right" interpretation and enforcement of EC law at the national level.
    22. Case 26/2, van Gend & Loos v. Netherlands Inland Revenue Administra-
tion, [1963] E.C.R. 1.
    23. Case 29/69, Stauder v. Stadt Ulm Sozialamt, [1969] E.C.R. 419, para. 7.
    24. See, for example, Geduldig v. Aiello, 417 U.S. 484 (1974) (holding that
exclusion from disability benefits due to pregnancy does not constitute an equal
protection violation under the U.S. Constitution). See also Claire Kilpatrick,
"Emancipation through Law or Emasculation of Law? The Nation-State, the EU,
and Gender Equality at Work," in *Labour Law in an Era of Globalization: Transformative Practices and Possibilities,* eds. Joanne Conaghan, Richard Michael Fis-
chl, and Karl Klare, 489–509 (New York: Oxford University Press, 2004).
    25. Case C-177/88, Dekker v. Stichting Vormingscentrum voor Jong Volwassen
(VJV Centrum), [1990] E.C.R. I-3941.
    26. Case C-274/96, Criminal Proceedings against Horst Otto Bickel & Ulrich
Franz, [1998] E.C.R. I-7637.

27. Case C-413/99, Baumbast & R. v. Sec'y of State for the Home Dep't, 2002 E.C.R. I-7091, para. 81.

28. James D. Mather, "The Court of Justice and the Union Citizen," *European Law Journal* 11(6) (2005): 730.

29. However, the ECJ always held that the right in Article 18 of the EC Treaty is not unconditional and is dependent upon the terms of various limitations and conditions laid down elsewhere in the treaty, its secondary legislation, and even national and international provisions.

30. Thomas H. Marshall, *Citizenship and Social Class: And Other Essays* (Cambridge: Cambridge University Press, 1950).

31. Case C-85/96, Martinez Sala v. Freistaat Bayern, [1998] E.C.R. I-2691.

32. See Jo Shaw, "Gender and the European Court of Justice," in *The European Court of Justice*, eds. Grainne de Burca and J. H. H. Weiler, 141 (New York: Oxford University Press, 2001); Louise Ackers, "Citizenship, Migration, and the Valuation of Care in the European Union," *Journal of Ethnic and Migration Studies* 30(2) (2004): 373–96.

33. Case C-184/99, Grzelczyk v. Centre public d'aide sociale d'Ottignies-Louvain-la-Neuve, [2001] E.C.R. I-6193, para. 31.

34. Ibid.

35. Guild, *The Legal Elements of European Identity: EU Citizenship and Migration Law*, supra note 14, 240.

36. Case C-138/02, Collins v. Sec'y of State for Work and Pensions, [2004] E.C.R. I-2703.

37. Stephan Wernicke, "'Au nom de qui?' The European Court of Justice between Member States, Civil Society, and Union Citizens," *European Law Journal* 13(3) (2007): 380–407.

38. For a discussion, see Linda Bosniak, "Denationalizing Citizenship," in *Citizenship: Comparisons and Perspectives*, eds. T. Alexander Aleinikoff and Douglas B. Klusmeyer (Washington, DC: Carnegie Endowment for International Peace, 2001).

39. "Ideology" is intended here to point to social structures, which are reflected in people's narratives about themselves and society. Ideologies are the result of historical processes and social events and thus exist independent of any single individual. For discussions of ideology, see Theodor W. Adorno, Else Frenkel-Brunswik, Daniel J. Levinson, and R. Nevitt Sanford, *The Authoritarian Personality* (New York: Harper & Bros., 1950); Karl Mannheim, *Ideology and Utopia: An Introduction to the Sociology of Knowledge* (New York: Harcourt Brace, 1949).

40. In 1999, the Social Democratic government passed a new citizenship law, which allowed for the first time for *ius soli* citizenship. It paved the way for "guest workers" to seek citizenship. The new act gives automatic citizenship to

children born in Germany to foreign residents. Because of this shift in Germany from the *ius sanguinis* principle toward a residence-based one, Germany provides a useful case study. See Gesetz zur Reform des Staatsangehörigkeitsrechts [Act to Amend the Nationality Law], July 15, 1999, BGBl. I at 1618, art. 1, no. 3 (F.R.G.).

41. For additional information on Eurobarometer surveys, see their website at http://ec.europa.eu/public_opinion/index_en.htm (last accessed April 26, 2007).

42. Lauren M. McLaren, "Immigration and the New Politics of Inclusion and Exclusion in the European Union: The Effects of Elites and the EU on Individual-Level Opinions regarding European and Non-European Immigrants," *European Journal of Political Research* 39(1) (2001): 81–108.

43. Jack Citrin and John M. Sides, "More Than Nationals: How Identity Choice Matters in the New Europe," in *Transnational Identities: Becoming European in the EU*, eds. Richard K. Herrmann, Thomas Risse, and Marilynn B. Brewer, 166–67 (Lanham, MD: Rowman & Littlefield, 2004).

44. Michael Bruter, "Civic and Cultural Components of a European Identity: A Pilot Model of Measurement of Citizens' Levels of European Identity," in *Transnational Identities: Becoming European in the EU*, supra note 43, 204.

45. Ibid., 182.

46. Ibid.

47. Among respondents, Germans were the most pessimistic about the future: 36 percent of male and 37 percent of female Germans surveyed agreed that the "future was rather gloomy." Of the foreign respondents, 35 percent of male Turks and 26 percent of female Turks agreed with the statement, while 26 percent of male Italians and 23 percent of female Italians agreed. See Deutsche Shell, ed., *Jugend 2000*, vol. 1 (Opladen, Germany: Leske & Budrich, 2000), 27.

48. Ursula Boos-Nünning and Yasemin Karakasoglu, *Viele Welten. Zur Lebenssituation von Mädchen und jungen Frauen mit Migrationshintergrund* (Münster, Germany: Waxmann Verlag, 2005); Cordula Weissköppel, *Ausländer und Kartoffeldeutsche. Identitätsperformanz im Alltag einer ethnisch gemischten Realschulklasse* (Weinheim, Germany: Juventa-Verlag, 2001). In terms of qualitative studies, there is quite a lot of literature on Turkish migrants and very little on other migrant groups (Italian, Spanish, Portuguese, etc.).

49. By "Italian denizens," I mean Italian (non-German) citizens who are legally resident in Germany. My focus is on the emergence of a specifically European dimension in collective identity, and as such, it made sense to center my inquiry on migrants from an EU member state.

50. Frankfurt is a multicultural city in the Land of Hessen with a population of over six hundred thousand. A center of international finance and labor mobility, it ranks fifth among the world's "global cities." See Saskia Sassen, *Cities of a World Economy (Sociology for a New Century)* (Thousand Oaks, CA: Pine Forge Press, 1994). At 30 percent, the proportion of non-German inhabitants in Frankfurt is higher than in any other German city. After Turks and nationals of the

former Yugoslavia, Italians—with 13,500 residents—are the third largest group of foreigners and the largest group of nationals from an EU member state.

51. Thirty potential interview candidates were randomly selected from a list provided by the Italian consulate. Using the technique of minimal and maximal contrasting (Grounded Theory), I drew a "theoretical sample" of fifteen from the short list, ensuring that the selection was balanced in terms of sex, age, occupation, education, and time spent in Germany. I established a minimum of five years. Of these fifteen people, seven were men and eight women; four were under twenty years old, eight were between thirty and forty-five years old, and three were over sixty years old. When I contacted these fifteen people, twelve agreed to be interviewed about "how migrants live and think today." For more details on the methodology and setting, see Patrizia Nanz, *Europolis: Constitutional Patriotism beyond the Nation-State* (Manchester, UK: Manchester University Press, 2006), ch. 7.

52. To make the interviewees comfortable, I let them choose the language in which to speak. Perhaps it helped that I am myself half Italian and was raised bilingually in Germany.

53. Original transcript follows: "Ich bin hier, äh, ja, ich kann hier Italienerin sein, ich kann hier Deutsche sein. Was ich bin? Alles, alles, ich bin schon Italienerin, klar logisch, aber äh, wenn ich heute die deutsche Rolle spielen soll, dann spiel' ich die deutsche Rolle, kein Problem."

54. Original transcript follows: "Aber, wenn ich das Glück oder das Pech hätte, wie man's nimmt, ja, 'ne klare Zuweisung zu sagen, ich bin deutlich Italiener, ich bin Deutscher, dann würde ich 'ja' dazu sagen, politisch Europäer, kulturell Deutscher. "

55. Original transcript follows: "Bei mir, bei mir ist es halt, Italien ist halt in der EU, und ich hab' halt keine Probleme, ich wüsste auch nicht, warum ich, äh, die deutsche Staatsbürgerschaft annehmen sollte, ich hab' genauso viele Rechte so gesehen als wie die Deutschen. Also, außer das mit den Wahlen, aber ansonsten, find ich, hab' ich keine Benachteiligung als, äh, EU-Staats, also Mitbürger."

56. Original transcript follows: "Also, wär' ich, was weiß ich, aus der Türkei oder so würd' ich dann schon die, äh, die deutsche Staatsbürgerschaft annehmen wollen. Weil, äh, ich weiß nicht, als Türke hat man, ich weiß nicht, nicht so viele Vorteile wie wenn man Italiener ist in Deutschland. Ich fühl' mich als Europäer, also hundertprozentig."

57. Original transcript follows: "Con tutti, cioè io non, non faccio differenze ormai. No, no, no, non c'era nessuna distinzione cioè proprio tra ragazzi questo non esisteva, cioè non esiste proprio, tutti sono si può dire tutti tedeschi, è uguale se adesso sei straniero, italiano, spagnolo, portoghese."

58. Original transcript follows: "E' un arricchimento sì, assolutamente, perché stai a contatto con tedeschi, con marocchini, con turchi, con tante altre nazionalità e da ogni nazionalità prendi un vivere, un modo di vivere, una cultura, una religione cioè ampli anche il tuo, la tua cultura, la propria cultura personale."

59. Original transcript follows: "Io sinceramente, [l'unificazione dell'Europa] ha un grande significato, si, assolutamente, però che adesso abbiano unificato l'Europa per me già prima, cioè per me personalmente, no adesso per me come paese, ma per me personalmente, perchè prima non avevo mai fatto queste distinzioni tra tutti questi paesi per me era già unita l'Europa. Eh si, perchè, perché tu vivi in Germania, vivi in Germania, hai tanti amici di tante razze, quindi l'unificazione dell'Europa per me c'era già, nel piccolo naturalmente, sperando che continui in questo modo."

60. We can, for example, also observe more subversive ways of coping with double belonging: by enacting a mix of cultural (and often linguistic) tokens in daily interaction, young immigrants blur the boundaries of sociocultural and national identities within the space of a nation-state. By emphasizing their "Turkishness," for example, "ethnic" hip-hop groups of the 1990s subvert their "otherization" as "Turks." Similar to the use of "nigger" in Black American hip-hop lyrics they, for instance, transform the contemptuous term "*Kanake*," which Germans use to insult Turks, into a discursive weapon against discrimination and marginalization. They combine elements of global youth rebellion, like rap music, "cool" modes of dressing, and aggressive (macho) behavior with expressions of "Turkishness" as a device against demands for assimilation: "I'm not the black man / I'm not the white man / I'm just the type between them / I'm a Turkish man in a foreign land." Lyrics from a rap song in English by the Turkish Power Boys in Frankfurt, see Hermann Tertilt, *Turkish Power Boys: Ethnographie einer Jugendbande* (Frankfurt/Main, Germany: Suhrkamp Verlag, 1996).

61. The only interviewee whose boundary drawing is firmly based on cultural and ethnic criteria (and who, as a consequence, displays a sort of federalist Euronationalism) is Marco Cimino, a 39-year-old. He came to Germany at the age of eighteen because he wanted to earn money to buy a house in Foggia. In fact, Marco remained in Germany, marrying a Portuguese woman and eventually becoming an electrician at the Historical Museum of Frankfurt. As an EU citizen, he tells me he could even become a "*Beamter*" (civil servant). When talking about his first job, Marco describes his Turkish colleagues in negative terms. He was happier once he had changed jobs and found himself working with Spaniards, Portuguese, and Greeks (also Germans). It is they, with whom he has lived and worked since, that he views as "European foreigners." This positive identification (e.g., between Italian and Spanish migrants in Germany), which refers to processes of inclusion among Europeans and the creation of a European citizenship, goes hand in hand with negative identification (e.g., of Turkish migrants), which involves the drawing of (more or less rigid) boundaries and processes of exclusion of "non-European" foreigners.

62. Original transcript follows: "Siamo tutti europei no? Io penso di sì, siamo europei. . . . europei, secondo me, sentirsi europei è sentirsi liberi, indipendenti, non come certe nazioni del mondo come l'India che non c'hai nessun diritto, da

donna ad esempio, e che cavolo, sembriamo nel 1600, nel 1500, noi europei ab-biamo i diritti, abbiamo gli stess-cioè siamo democratici ecco, per me è quello. Siamo internazionali, siamo europei veramente, e anche extracomunitari di-ciamo, vivendo qua si sono un po' adeguati anche loro."

63. Yasemin Nuhoglu Soysal, *Limits of Citizenship: Migrants and Postnational Membership in Europe* (Chicago: University of Chicago Press, 1994); Theodora Kostakopoulou, "Towards a Theory of Constructive Citizenship in Europe," *Journal of Political Philosophy* 4 (1996): 337–56; Riva Kastoryano, "Transnational Networks and Political Participation: The Place of Immigrants in the European Union," in *Europe without Borders: Remapping Territory, Citizenship, and Identity in a Transnational Age*, eds. Mabel Berezin and Martin Schain, 64–88 (Baltimore, MD: John Hopkins University Press, 2003).

64. Seyla Benhabib, *The Rights of Others: Aliens, Residents, and Citizens* (Cambridge: Cambridge University Press, 2004), 153.

65. If a third-country national has acquired recognition of status in one member state, she or he is entitled to exercise a right of economic activity and residence in any other member state. She or he can also pursue studies, vocational training, or economically inactive residence (e.g., retirement).

66. In *Recep Tetik v. Land Berlin*, the ECJ referred to the Association Agreements that exist between the European Union and states that are not members of the Union in ruling that Turkish workers and their families have the right to equal treatment in social security usually afforded to EU citizens. Case C-171/95, Joint Party: The *Oberbundesanwalt beim Bundesverwaltungsgericht*, [1997] E.C.R. I-329.

67. To be sure, different member states interpret the rights to social and employment benefits in anything but a uniform way.

68. The Reform Treaty, in Article 6, does refer to it as a document with full legal force.

69. Susanne Baer, "Citizenship in Europe and the Construction of Gender by Law in the European Charter of Fundamental Rights," in *Gender and Human Rights*, ed. Karen Knop, 112 (Oxford: Oxford University Press, 2004).

70. Case C-200/02, Zhu & Chen v. Sec'y of State for the Home Dep't, 3 C.M.L.R. 48 (2004) (ECJ). For further discussion of this case from the perspective of children's rights, see Jacqueline Bhabha, "The 'Mere Fortuity of Birth?': Children, Borders, Mothers, and the Meaning of Citizenship," in this volume.

71. Andrew Geddes, *The Politics of Migration and Immigration in Europe* (London: Sage, 2003), 26.

72. Valentine Moghadam, "Global Feminism, Citizenship, and the State: Negotiating Women's Rights in the Middle East and North Africa," in this volume.

73. Due to internal problems as well as managerial and financial irregularities, this forum lost support by the European Commission and eventually ceased to exist. Currently, there is only loose talk in Brussels about a renewed initiative.

See Andrew Geddes, "Lobbying for Migrant Inclusion in the EU: New Opportunities for Transnational Advocacy?," *Journal of European Public Policy* 7(4) (2000): 632–49.

74. Dawid Friedrich and Patrizia Nanz, "The EU's Civil Society from a Normative-Democratic Point of View: The Case of the EU's Migration Policy," in *Governance and Civil Society: Theoretical and Empirical Perspectives*, eds. Carlo Ruzza and Vincent della Sala, 113–33 (Manchester, UK: Manchester University Press, 2007).

75. For a discussion of the European public sphere, see Patrizia Nanz, "Multiple Voices: An Interdiscursive Concept of the European Public Sphere," in *Public Sphere and Civil Society? Transformations of the European Union*, eds. John Erik Fossum, Philip Schlesinger, and Geir Ove Kvaerk (Oslo: ARENA Report, 2007), ch. 1.

76. Reform Treaty, Art. 8 B.

77. Ute Gerhard, "European Citizenship: A Political Opportunity for Women?," supra note 20, 49.

II

Citizenships, Federalisms, and Gender

Vicki C. Jackson

Though often thought of in terms of rights (political, civil, social) or of membership (affiliation, belonging, exclusion), citizenship also entails relationships among citizens, between citizens and governments, and between levels of governments. Citizenship and governance have both grown considerably more complex in recent decades. Migrations across nation-states, along with modern transportation and communications technologies, now yield multigenerational communities that retain close ties to the original country of emigration.[1] Members of these communities may experience themselves as citizens of both states, seeking to retain their original-country-of-origin citizenship while also obtaining recognition as citizens of the state to which they or their forebears migrated. In part through liberalization of citizenship laws to permit dual nationality, citizenship becomes pluralized. Moreover, as governance grows more complex, citizenship's relational qualities do so as well. The idea of "nested" citizenships in federal polities has been extended, for example, to members of European Union states, and multiple citizenships, reflecting overlapping relationships to multiple governments, are thus becoming more of a norm. At the same time, federal forms of government organization are appearing in creative ways as national territorial states devolve governmental powers both down and up. This chapter examines the implications of these more complex forms of government organization and citizenship for gender equality.

Do these structures and relationships of governance—sometimes expressed through the idea of citizenship, sometimes through the idea of federalism—matter in any systematic way to the pursuit of gender equality at the global, national, and local levels? One answer could be that the institutional structures of governance are not of particular salience to the concerns of gender equality so long as courts are available to enforce gender equality rights. Still another kind of answer might be that national affiliations and institutions are of diminished importance in a postnational regime in which all are human rights holders who have resort to international or transnational mechanisms of norm enforcement. This chapter takes a third perspective, exploring the possible benefits of national territorial states and national citizenship to gender equality and considering how federal structures within those states might matter to gender equality.

In referring to "states," I avoid the terminology "nation-state," which sometimes has connotations of an ethnic or historical unity of the people who make up the population of the state. Rather, I will use the terms "territorial state" or "national state" to refer to those states that are recognized in the world community as states, and to emphasize the territorial basis of their governance.[2]

In the first part of this chapter, I argue that, while transnational and "postnational" forms of governance pose important challenges to territorial states, states will survive for the foreseeable future and, moreover, have something to offer women's equality movements. Although national territorial states can be oppressive, militaristic, and chauvinist, so, too, can some of the communities of identity that may emerge as their alternatives.[3] Territorial states offer prospects for advancing gender equality, first, by providing a space for public participation at some remove from familial and ascriptive group identities;[4] second, by rooting this space in a shared geography of everyday life, in which some degree of territorial government is inevitable for the foreseeable future; and third, by linking legally enforceable equality commitments and the mechanisms to implement them to the particularized communities of identity that human beings seem to need. Because of the likely continued importance of states, there is much worth considering from those who argue for recognition of a right to become a full member, a citizen, of a new state of residence within some reasonable time and on some reasonable terms.[5]

Does this citizenship need to be exclusive? Does assuming the identity of a citizen in a country of migration require abandoning identity as a citizen of one's country of origin? Although in some countries at some times acquiring citizenship has required abandoning a prior citizenship,[6] in contemporary circumstances it should be and frequently is possible to retain multiple national citizenships. As I discuss in the second section below, federal systems provide one model for multiple citizenships at the national level, and the spread of dual nationality regimes suggests the feasibility of similar models transnationally. Federal systems provide legal mechanisms for managing legal relationships among multiple governments and legal regimes with overlapping purposes, such as the principle of "supremacy" or "paramountcy" of national over state or provincial law. As multiple national citizenships grow, law will need to develop other rules, e.g., for defining which citizenship is primary for which purposes.

In the last part of the chapter, I explore federalism more generally, looking at how its institutional features may affect gender equality and associated social movements. Federal systems offer both challenges and benefits to movements for full gender equality—challenges arising in part from the greater difficulty federal systems pose to formal legal change and opportunities arising in part from the proliferation of opportunities for women to serve and participate in governments.[7] In the end, though, the relationships between federal structures of government and women's advancement are too complex and diverse to permit any generalized conclusion about whether federalism as such is harmful or beneficial to establishing and implementing gender equality.

I. From Sovereignty to Legitimacy: Globalization and Territorial Government

The globalization of law has seen the growth of overlapping government structures that arguably have jurisdiction or authority to regulate. With a dramatic increase in the post–World War II era of international agreements regulating relationships between member nations and their own citizens or residents, an increase in regional transnational legal institutions (especially but not exclusively in Europe), and important changes in the structure (and enforcement mechanisms) of the world trading system, the complexity of institutional and legal relationships has increased. Accompanying this proliferation of supranational laws and governance structures has been renewed interest in decentralization of governance under principles of subsidiarity,[8] or democratic experimentalism,[9] as well as a rise in regional or other boundary-crossing movements of ethnic, linguistic, or religious self-determination claims.

Increased pressures for decentralization may well be related to the concurrent development of supranational forms of lawmaking and

governance. In Europe, the success of supranational governance in fulfilling roles formerly performed by national governments (e.g., assuring the
conditions of a common market) has been associated with increases in
regional nationalisms, within or across traditional state lines. The presence of a common European market and the floor of protection for human rights set by the European Convention on Human Rights may make
it less costly (and thus more attractive) to diminish allegiance to existing
multicultural or multiethnic territorial states and to pursue forms of governance corresponding more closely to forms of cultural, ethnic, or linguistic group identities. Renewed interest in decentralization and federal
arrangements may also be a response to the profusion of nongovernmental entities vying with governments and with each other for regulatory or
contractual authority over persons.[10] These contribute to pressures for the
disaggregation of what we might think of as "packages" of governmental powers and responsibilities.[11] Privatization of government functions to
nongovernmental business or nonprofit entities, decentralization of government authority in the sense of devolving power to more local governing bodies, and transfers of national power to supranational or regional
entities are all mechanisms by which the functions of national governments are being disaggregated.[12]

Yet territorially based government remains a human necessity. We
live corporeally in the world and the vast majority of the world's people
have only a single home. Although territorially based governments exist
in a more complex environment, sharing power with other governments,
with markets, and with "civil society" organizations, the existence of these
competitors should not obscure the distinctive capacities of territorial
governments to act with political legitimacy based on democratic internal
arrangements. Among the many governments that exist in the world, it is
national territorial states that have been the principal actors and subjects
of international law, and with which modern conceptions of citizenship
are associated.[13]

Legitimate government authority need not mean exclusive or "sovereign" authority. Although territorial states have been widely associated
with the idea of "sovereignty" at the international level, the idea of sovereignty as exclusive power and dominion over one's territory and citizens
is—in the postwar era of "human rights," international war crimes tribunals, and the World Trade Organization—no longer an accurate description of territorial state power, if ever it was.[14] Concurrent and overlapping legal authority, an accepted feature of federal states, is increasingly a

feature of the relationships between international and national law,[15] suggesting that it is useful to separate the idea of a national territorial state
as a place of *legitimate* governmental authority exercised on behalf of a
territorially based population from the idea of a state as having *exclusive*
authority, or sovereignty, over its citizens or territory.[16]

If we abandon the idea of exclusive sovereignty and come to understand territorial states as having primary, but not exclusive, legitimate
authority over their citizens, then we can consider more flexible conceptions of citizenship that may preserve for gender-equality advocates
the powerful claims for equality within particular states associated
with the idea of citizenship, while at the same time allowing additional
forms of legal status to protect those who live or work or otherwise
find themselves away from their states of original nationality. For this
reason, proponents of gender equality should give attention to moving from concepts of sovereignty to the idea of legitimacy in theorizing
the state, and from exclusivity to concurrency in theorizing governance
jurisdiction.[17]

II. Citizenship, Territorial States, and Globalization

These shifts in government powers and functions in a globalizing environment affect understandings of citizenship. Citizenship is, at the international level, strongly associated with national territorial states. To
the extent that the role of territorial states in the world legal order is in
decline, or contested, these contests will be reflected in efforts to reun-
derstand, abandon, or transform citizenship.[18] Does the idea of territorial
state citizenship—as distinct from personhood—remain important? Are
human rights replacing citizenship as the most important rights-bearing
ideas and legal norms? Should legal systems see their members primarily
as citizens or as bearers of human rights? How do affiliations as citizens
compare with self-understandings as consumers, customers, and preference holders in regional or globalized markets, or as ethno-linguistic-ra-
cial-tribal ascriptive group identity members? Are communities of identity today sufficiently distinct from the territorial states to which citizenship conventionally attached that citizenship loses its meaning as a form
of membership or affiliation? As these questions suggest, pressures on
the concept of citizenship in significant respects parallel those discussed
above in the context of territorial states.

The duties under international law that a state owes uniquely to its national citizens[19]—duties to permit citizens to reenter their home country, or the right to assert claims on their behalf against other countries—remain important. In some circumstances, territorial states can be more effective in asserting claims on behalf of their nationals against other states than are alternative mechanisms of protecting human rights.[20] Although the duty of a state to assert claims against other states on behalf of its own nationals may be of somewhat diminished importance in light of the possibility of individual petitions to human rights bodies to directly assert human rights claims against other nations, the mechanisms for resolving such claims are still quite weak. Human rights regimes with direct petitioning do not extend as fully as the claims international law allows states to assert against one another.[21]

At the same time that "postnational" forms of safeguards are being recognized and legitimated—as well they should be—for migrants, refugees, asylum seekers, and others who are not citizens but have claims in law against a territorial state, citizenship remains valuable as something of an "automatic pass" into one's home country. A world "without borders" in which refugees, asylum seekers, and other migrants could cross what were formerly national borders routinely, as a matter of right, is quite distant (and even in such a world, questions of political participation and democratic legitimacy would be posed).[22] Whether the "right to have rights" will always be associated with belonging to a particular national community,[23] at present to be a "national citizen" of a viable country matters significantly insofar as there is a home country that one can return to, a place in the world where one is presumptively entitled to live.

Citizenship, moreover, does not mean simply the possession of particular rights,[24] nor does it simply mean membership in a sense that is indistinguishable from what social club one belongs to, what religious congregation one affiliates with, or what university one attended.[25] The continued importance of citizenship, both in the international law sense of nationality and as a marker of full membership, is underscored by the report of the International Law Association's Committee on Feminism and International Law in 2000. This report begins by noting the conventional wisdom that the "rise of international human rights, many of which flow from residence or simply presence within the jurisdiction of a state, has diminished the importance of nationality as a basis for rights." The drafters of the report disagree:

[T]he political disintegration of states and widespread economically motivated migration of individuals symptomatic of globalization have shown
the importance of nationality as a means for individuals to become full
members of the societies in which they find themselves or to obtain assistance in returning to the societies they voluntarily or involuntarily left.[26]

The report elsewhere states that, at least in the short term, "the traditional protective function of nationality has assumed even greater importance as the large-scale movement of workers, refugees and others seen in
the late twentieth century means that significant numbers of people live
outside their state of nationality."[27] As the position of this committee suggests, not only does the idea of citizenship in the sense of nationality remain important in international law, but citizenship in a sense internal to
territorial states is important insofar as it embraces concepts of equality of
rights, equality of status, and equal membership within national territorial states.[28] I discuss three senses of this internal concept of citizenship
below.[29]

First, the relational qualities of being a citizen may differ significantly
from the relational qualities associated with or desirable for membership
in other forms of organization.[30] An assumption of equality of citizens
is central to understanding the relational position of citizens in a democratic national state. Private associations may or may not assume the internal equality of members. Membership within polities whose legitimacy
is in some sense founded on self-government differs from membership in
private associations whose legitimacy is founded on, for example, adherence to hierarchical determinations of faith or custom. Thus, even if one
were to view citizenship as primarily about membership and affiliation,[31]
citizenship implies a relationship of equality to others who are citizens of
the same polity and can serve as a powerful basis for the imposition of
duties on the government—as representative of the citizens—to give effect
to that fundamental equality. Citizenship, for example, continues to be deployed in the constitutional rhetoric of the United States Supreme Court
as implying full equality for women, or, in the Court's words, *"full citizenship stature*—equal opportunity to aspire, achieve, participate in and contribute to society based on their individual talents and capacities."[32]

A second meaning of citizenship within a territorial state is tied to
concepts of participation in self-governance and the exercise of regulatory authority over persons by virtue of their physical connection to
the territorial jurisdiction. Human beings have developed capacities to

communicate, associate, and affiliate in noncorporeal ways (through wired and wireless communications), as well as to maintain physical corporeal connections with more than one governmental territorial jurisdiction at a time. Yet we are not likely in the foreseeable future to escape from the needs for territorially based governance to assure the performance of police functions (i.e., stopping violence against persons where it occurs) or public health functions (i.e. assuring a supply of clean water and disposal of sewage)—all of which are tied to corporeal territorial governance. This is not to say that the functions we think of as "governmental" are fixed; indeed they are not, as devolution to the private sphere across the world reflects, as does government involvement in new forms of activity. But the "republican" concepts of deliberative democracy on which participatory meanings of citizenship rest will remain important in territorial states, even though they may be important at other levels and places as well; and the legal apparatus of national states helps secure the democratic functioning of smaller units of government in which more participatory self-governance can occur.[33]

A third meaning of citizenship is that of rights holder (with respect to civil, political, and/or social rights). It is in this sense that international human rights law has arguably diminished (in a relative sense) the importance of citizenship.[34] One now can claim to be a legal rights holder in the world regardless of whether one is or is not a citizen of a territorial national state: for those in need of protection, as migrants, refugees, asylum seekers, or other victims of human rights abuses, international human rights law offers a possibility of relief.[35] But this possibility does not provide a sufficient basis for abandoning national citizenship as a category of importance. Indeed, efforts to decouple citizenship from territorial states may have perverse effects on the ability of those states to enforce legal rights of citizens and noncitizens alike.[36] Citizenship as a basis for claim making and as a strategy for advancing towards greater equality for members of groups, including women, that have traditionally been excluded and disadvantaged through systems of legal and social norms, remains an important strategy and source of rights.

I do not suggest that "citizenship" carries with it an uncontested package of rights—indeed, for vast periods in U.S. history, women's citizenship was not understood to entail even the right to vote.[37] Nor do I suggest that citizenship should be the only basis for rights holding—to the contrary, protections of "persons" from abusive state action is central to any human rights observing state.[38] But citizenship as a concept and a rhetorical trope has been effectively invoked in connection with claims of political rights—including voting and office holding; of civil rights—including the right to enter into contracts, to own property, to marry, to pass on membership to one's progeny; and to social and economic rights—to education, to minimum subsistence, or to health care.[39] Citizenship—in the sense of being a rights-holding and duty-bearing member of a state—has been an important engine for equality in the United States and in some other countries. Thus, the U.S. Supreme Court, in overruling prior case law upholding exclusions of women from jury service, wrote that a system that "operates to exclude from jury service *an identifiable class of citizens*" is unconstitutional.[40] This language resonates with Judith Shklar's conception of citizenship as a form of "standing," of recognition and acknowledgment, that is not fully captured by other descriptions, insofar as it links one's self-concept as a full member of society with the external regard that one's dignity and self-respect entail.[41]

Citizenship rights under national constitutions may have particular resonance in attacking exclusionary practices. Although ultimately unsuccessful, litigation by the Native Women's Association in Canada, objecting to the government's failure to fund it or invite it to join in negotiations over the new charter even though other representatives of aboriginal peoples were, is an example of the possibilities of a robust conception of citizenship as a proactive tool for equality.[42] When this women's group sought to assure that Charter principles of gender equality would apply to aboriginal self-government, it emphasized national equality norms rather than accepting the inegalitarian self-governing autonomy of smaller communities. A postnationalist might query whether their interests might have been as well, or better, served by claiming a "human right" of equal participation.[43] Yet given who the decision makers were—members of the national government, located in Canada—the value of citizenship and its connection with a self-governing, defined polity may have added to the felt urgency and legitimacy of the claims.

Citizenship's capacity to serve as a strategy for equality within a polity may depend in part on its exclusionary edges, thus raising important risks.[44] Those who are not citizens may be treated differently or even excluded. Invocation by wealthier nations of hard-edged citizenship and immigration policies can have unjust effects on those seeking to migrate from less advantaged nations. To the extent that citizenship has power in arguments towards equality, it depends in part on the ability to assert a status *within* the decision-making polity, a polity that is not the international community. To the extent that citizenship is a concept distinct from personhood, it has meaning because it is particular: one is a citizen of this country, or even of these two countries, but not of every country in the world. Citizenship is a kind of enclosure that also excludes. What citizenship should mean—as "standing," as rights holding, as duty bearing, or as membership, affiliation, or identity—is in some sense defined in opposition to those who are not citizens. Advances in gender equality in citizenship may not help, and might even harm, those women who are in immigrant communities, legal or not.

But the harm from the exclusionary content of citizenship may be mitigated if citizenship becomes a status that most people within a polity can expect to acquire as a matter of course and through passage of a reasonable amount of time.[45] The exclusionary edge of citizenship should also be mitigated and constrained by human rights norms.[46] Perhaps international human rights law needs to move in the direction of recognizing "rights" to become citizens of countries in which one lives after some extended but reasonable period of time and subject to reasonable conditions.[47] And there are also risks from abandoning the concept of national citizenship or treating it as an unimportant marker. Undermining the civic affiliations embraced by national citizenship may have costs to maintaining the significance and viability of democratic governmental spaces.[48] It is still primarily national territorial states that provide the legal frameworks for enforcement of individual rights in the world, to the extent that they are enforced.[49] It is those states, again, that provide the frameworks for participation in self-governance based on civic membership in the territory.

Citizenship can thus serve as an important measure of civic identity and civic-mindedness.[50] Treating citizenship as involving only individual choices—like what credit cards to have or what clubs to join—overlooks the relational aspects of citizenship,[51] in linking cocitizens to respect for one another's status, rights, and well-being within a particular community. Devaluing citizenship, the national communities it is associated with, and its possibilities for pluralist democratic creeds or forms of "constitutional patriotism"[52] may make more attractive other ideological commitments that are less tolerant and more likely to lead to violence towards other groups. Preserving the possibility of civic identity may thus be related to prospects for successful democratic polities, in a world in which the possibilities of excessive valuation of unmoored autonomous choice (by "consumers" expressing various "preferences"), on the one hand, and the increasing powers of deeply ascriptive and closed group identities, on the other, threaten to swamp the systemic capacities for public-regarding behavior (or even for taking a long-term view of self-interest) on which pluralist democracies in the long run are likely to depend.

Some of the normative impetus for "denationalizing" citizenship,[53] or for "postnational" citizenship,[54] involves the need for legal rights and concepts to protect migrants, refugees, displaced persons, and transnational workers. These legitimate needs, though, should not cause us to overlook the continued importance of national territorial states and the continued benefits of a concept of citizenship in those states.[55] Nor should they persuade women to abandon a concept—of equality of citizenship and the legal status and rights that it implies[56]—that in so many places and in so many ways could be deployed to enhance women's access to public life, education, and economic advancement.[57] The mechanisms of enforcing gender equality exist at the global, national, and local levels—the claims of equal citizenship in territorial national states need not be the only rhetorical or legal strategy deployed. But its power in dealing with national organs of government and decision making seems undeniable and well worth preserving, even as citizenships become more multiple, and flexible, in character.

It is important to emphasize that one can hold meaningful citizenship in more than one entity.[58] In federal polities the idea of nested citizenships is familiar: one is a citizen of both a subnational unit, like the state of New York, and a national state, like the United States. Federal systems are often built around the idea of "dual citizenship" in this "nested" sense.[59] Dual citizenship in two territorial states is probably increasing, as both wealthier elites and poor migrants develop connections to multiple locations;[60] a number of countries have liberalized citizenship regimes to allow dual citizenship on more generous terms.[61] As I have suggested elsewhere, accommodating dual national citizenships may call for the development of legal concepts of primary citizenship to accommodate the competing rights and demands associated with each, and such accommodations need not necessarily devalue citizenship as a positive institution.[62] Thus, "denationalizing" citizenship is not the only strategy available to prevent or mitigate the harms that citizenship's exclusionary edges may cause, especially to poorer migrants to wealthier countries.[63]

National territorial states and associated citizenship(s), then, should not be abandoned as potential tools by those concerned with women's equality. I have identified three reasons for this view: first, the inevitability of territorially based government with its potential for shared public space;

second, the attractiveness of enhancing connections to and with a territorial form of organization that is not based solely on ascriptive identity or individual preference but on a rooted geography of living; and third, the role of territorial states, and the citizenship associated with them, as mechanisms of improving women's equality. Women and men, it is fair to assume, will continue to live in and participate as citizens in national territorial states, and the next section explores the federalist forms in which some of those states are organized.

III. Government Structures, Federalism, and Gender Equality

State citizenship need not be, and frequently is not, unitary. A national citizen may be a citizen of subnational states or units, as well as of supranational entities (viz., European citizenship) and/or of other countries.[64] Moreover, quasi federal forms of legal organization are likely to become more widespread in responding to the disaggregation of governmental powers both upwards (to supranational levels) and downwards (to local or regional levels); if so, multiple citizenships may likewise become of greater importance. The consequences of this form of institutional organization of government, then, may be important for gender equality advocates to consider. And it can best be studied in the context in which it has longest existed, within national states.

Federalism exists in many forms. Basically, a federal system is one that has a constitutional division of power among different governments exercising jurisdiction over the same territory, in which each level of government has some direct relationship with people as constituents. Concurrency of legislative, regulatory, and/or judicial jurisdiction is a basic feature of federal states. Whether the specific subjects of jurisdiction are understood as concurrent, or as existing in separate spheres of exclusive jurisdiction, or as some combination of these two, the central institutional fact is that citizens of federal nations are subject to the jurisdiction of multiple legitimate governments; they help elect members of multiple legitimate governments; and they frequently, though not invariably, hold at least two forms of citizenship. In these respects, federal systems provide some insight into the possibilities of multiple, shifting citizenships, and multiple disaggregated governmental powers.

It is difficult to make any general statement about the relationship between the structure of government in relation to women, a historically disadvantaged group that is neither geographically concentrated nor a numerical minority.[65] In some polities, federalism has at times provided apparent advantages to gender equality movements, and at other times or places it has been perceived as a significant obstacle.[66] There are many different forms of federalisms, and there has been little systematic research on how federalism affects gender equality, though there have been some excellent case studies of the interaction between particular federal systems and issues of gender.[67] One important factor may be the degree to which the federal divisions correspond to the presence of culturally distinct, geographically concentrated minorities.[68] To facilitate future research, I identify some possible advantages and disadvantages of federalism for gender equality.

A. Advantages of Federal Systems for Gender Equality?

1. LOCATION AND POLITICAL PARTICIPATION

Some feminist scholars, including Kim Rubenstein, who first made the point to me, suggest that governments that function "closer to home" might be thought to offer to all constituents more opportunity for participation and influence.[69] Travel to a more distant location might impose greater costs on women than men, proportionately, either because of current distributions of family responsibilities, or because of increased risks to personal security for women traveling alone. To the extent that travel poses greater obstacles for women than men, governmental arrangements with more power exercised in geographically more proximate units may be better for women as they are presently socially situated.[70] Women's participation can change institutions so as to facilitate more participation by women, as is reflected in the standing orders of the new Scottish parliament after devolution in 1999, which require for all executive bills "a statement of their potential impact on equal opportunities (including gender equality)" and which bring parliamentary meeting times into compatibility with school holidays.[71] Yet much will depend on the size and specific location of different levels and forms of government, and what their governmental powers are, rather on than their federal or unitary character as such.

2. FACILITATING ACTS OF PUBLIC CITIZENSHIP AND PUBLIC OFFICE HOLDING

One might explore a broad array of acts of public citizenship. In addition to public office holding—on city councils, school boards,[72] other special

governmental units, state and county legislative bodies, in national legislatures, in executive positions, and in elected and appointed judgeships[73]—
these would include voting (in elections for local, state, and federal office
or in state or local referenda) or serving on a jury. They might also include less visible forms of participation as a public citizen, including, for
example, attendance at public meetings of boards of education or zoning
boards, writing and having published letters to the editor, participating in
online discussions of governance issues, or even reporting crime to the
police.

Do local and/or state politics and public space offer more opportunities for these acts of public citizenship than the federal? The answer may
vary from polity to polity and may depend on many other factors—including the numbers of other women who hold leadership roles.[74] One
might also consider the effects of differently structured and selected bodies at the national level—such as upper houses of legislatures apportioned
by subnational unit rather than strictly by population—on women's participation.[75] To the extent that there are gender differences in participation at the different levels of governance, other factors may be analyzed,
including voting methods,[76] voting cycles, political party alignments and
internal practices, districting, qualifications for office and for the ballot,
campaign finance and advertising regulations, and other legal constraints.
That there are such gender differences appears clear, at least in the United
States, where women seem to participate more in public office holding at
state levels in both legislative and judicial positions.[77]

Whether differences in office holding at the national and subnational
level (where they exist) can fairly be attributed to or seen as a benefit of
federalism is a complicated question. In Australia, women won election
to state-level legislatures long before they won seats in the national parliament,[78] but more recent studies cast some doubt on the proposition
that women necessarily participate in elective office more heavily in local
and state elections, or suggest that different levels of participation may
be conditioned on other factors (for example, what powers governments
exercise and which political parties are in control at the different levels).[79]
And even if a number of other federal nations have similar phenomena,
this may not be due to federalism so much as to localism and the density
of different levels of government, whether or not they are constitutionally entrenched.[80] If women are better represented in state and local governments, moreover, it may not be because women prefer work closer to
home but because such positions are less competitive; local opportunities

may be so calibrated in terms of subject matter and amount of time required that they are more accessible to those without prior experience or connections. One might then ask whether in federal systems there tend to be more opportunities for nonnational public representation—at the state and local level–than in unitary systems and, if so, whether this is because of a tendency either to proliferate governments, in federal systems, or to preserve more power to more locally elected bodies.[81]

3. DECENTRALIZATION, PREFERENCE SATISFACTION, REDUNDANCY, AND IDENTITY

A standard argument in law and economics is that decentralized government can offer a wider mix of government services and laws, and thus provide more choices to those of the citizenry who are mobile.[82] Given the wide array of views on the relationship of work to family life and other issues of concern to caregivers (who are currently predominantly female), having a range of diverse settings for different governments to experiment with different approaches might offer some benefit. In theory, it allows people to make choices to move to states or localities offering a better mix of benefits and programs—for example, part-time/flex time vs. on-site child care vs. support for parents staying home.[83]

In theory, the preferences of larger numbers can be better realized where different jurisdictions can make different decisions, with "exit" and choice serving to maximize preference satisfaction.[84] To the extent that women are mobile, they may benefit from disaggregating government functions into smaller units at different levels that may provide a broader range of attractive opportunities.[85] Yet as the critical literature suggests, the assumption of citizen mobility—of the capacity for exit—is fraught with error,[86] and job availability may exert a swamping effect on other choices for mobile citizens. In many societies, moreover, women with children will have significantly less mobility than do men.

However, a federal system may offer other kinds of choices relevant to gender equality. First, in a federal system there are at least two levels of government that citizens can try to mobilize to provide services, laws, enforcement of laws, or dispute settlement—the national and the subnational.[87] Federal systems provide multiple (seemingly redundant) avenues for the pursuit of change through government—laws, policies, and in some cases even judicial decisions.[88] These multiple avenues provide choices of where to look for the policy result one favors; even if it cannot be won at the national level it may be obtainable at a smaller level of government with authority to make policy different from that of the national government. In working at the local level, moreover, change can be made that may gradually win acceptance at other levels.[89] Second, federalisms are often designed to accommodate geographically concentrated groups, with distinctive languages, ethnic, racial, and/or religious identities. Identity is a complex amalgam of multiple individual characteristics and group affiliations; women whose identities are positively constructed around affiliative group membership may find benefit in the choices for group autonomy that federalism can provide.

4. EXPERIMENTATION

Justice Brandeis famously referred to the U.S. states as laboratories of experimentation.[90] Although some disagree that federalism serves this value,[91] to the extent that federalism secures the continuous existence of multiple levels of government, and to the extent that having different governments increases the possibility of different policies, federalism may well offer greater prospects for experiments that can be adopted by other jurisdictions where they prove effective. Because women have not held political power to the same extent as men, issues of concern to gender equality may particularly benefit from government experimentation.

For example, in Canada a government agency devoted to the status of women funded a study of different approaches to "state feminism"—or the designation or creation of offices within the government devoted to women's equality—and found that the organization of such offices in Quebec was quite different from that in the rest of Canada and proved to be more effective.[92] Or consider the importance of experiments in the policing and prosecution of gender-motivated assaults, given differences between early and more recent scholarly evaluations of once-experimental policies like mandatory arrests for domestic violence.[93] Although the benefits of having "experiments" from which data can be drawn can also occur in a nonfederal, "unitary" but decentralized government, constitutional federalism guarantees subnational units rights of self-governance and thus may foster greater degrees of localism and whatever experimentation localism facilitates or permits.

5. FEDERAL SYSTEMS AND JUDICIAL REVIEW

Federal polities typically empower a national-level court to enforce some aspects of the basic federal bargain, perhaps, it has been suggested, because the terms of a federal bargain will only work if a relatively neutral umpire is authorized to enforce them.[94] To the extent that the court also has jurisdiction over other kinds of claims, some political scientists suggest, it builds up institutional legitimacy and, hence, capacity to grant relief against governments with respect to individual rights claims.[95] Although it is plainly not necessary to have a federal system to have strong courts, federalism does seem to be positively associated with a form of legalism that often includes a powerful constitutional court.

The existence of independent judicial review does not necessarily mean that litigation will be a productive strategy for gender—a whole subject in and of itself.[96] And there are important differences among federal systems. For example, a recent comparative study argued that the opportunity for judicial protection of equality rights created by the Charter of Rights encouraged Canadian feminists to rely on litigation as a strategy, whereas in Australia (which has no comparable bill of rights), "a tolerance for, and culture of, advocacy in the bureaucracy has encouraged Australian feminists to focus on a 'femocrat' strategy."[97] But to the extent that federalism is associated with strong constitutional courts that also have capacity to enforce individual rights claims against the states, it may tend to make available a judicial system that offers opportunities to feminists to advance gender equality through adjudication.

6. FEDERALISM AS A TOOL FOR INCREASING TOLERANCE, EQUALITY, AND LIBERTY?

To the extent that some regions of a country are more conservative and illiberal, federalism, it has been argued, provides a mechanism to allow those illiberal societies to live in peace with more liberal components and, over time, to develop more of a liberal overlapping consensus conducive to greater tolerance.[98] This phenomenon may, in turn, translate into more receptivity to implementing gender equality norms in formerly quite traditional areas. The premise is that without the brakes of a federal decision-making mechanism, the clash between liberal and illiberal components would yield more violence, or less progress. This proposition is difficult to test empirically, as it depends not merely on the existence of a federal structure but on whether federalism limits are sufficiently enforced to achieve the incremental character of change. Measurement and sample size limitations may well preclude empirical testing. And even if it were correct, it would be a difficult case to make that women in some subnational units must endure present injustice to allow their societies to get used to the idea of their equality.

In many countries, federalism is understood as a way to accommodate group differences within a single polity. In the United States there is an argument in the literature that federal systems protect liberty by preventing any one level of government from becoming too powerful, in part by the limitation on jurisdictional competencies reflected in the Constitution and enforced by a court. Is federalism a "double security" to the rights of the people?[99] This surely can be contested. But it is true that a bad policy at the national level has the capacity to do more harm to more people than bad policy at the local level; federal divisions of authority may provide a check point to slow the worst harms from regressive national policies. Although women have important interests in promoting their own equality, and the positive freedoms required to do so may require strong governments, women also have interests in liberty and thus in checking abusive government.

B. Disadvantages of Federal Systems for Gender Equality?

Although there are some grounds to think that federal systems, in some instances, may help advance gender equality, there are other grounds for skepticism that the proliferation of governmental authorities and the constitutional reservations of powers to more local rather than more centralized government authority, typical in federal systems, will be beneficial.

1. UNITARY GOVERNMENTS AND ORGANIZATIONAL ADVANTAGES

As a traditionally subordinated, historically discriminated against group, women need change to overcome inequality and they may need government to shift levers of power. As one scholar has written, federalism may "divide[] women's interests among levels of government in such a way that determining long-term strategies for women's movements is difficult and the levels of energy and resources required to achieve change are excessive."[100] To the extent that women need government to act to help promote change, it may be easier to galvanize political forces at a national level than to have to do so at multiple subnational levels. In some ways it seems obvious that if an equality movement needs to persuade only a single legislature of the need to change laws, legal change will come more easily than if multiple bodies must be persuaded of the change. Federal systems typically increase the number of veto points through which constitutional change must pass before it can become binding,[101] and the national legislature's capacity to effect change through ordinary statutes may be limited by constitutional allocations of jurisdiction, especially on issues of interest to women.[102] Many other factors, of course, beyond the number of filters or veto points in a constitutionally specified structure of government—such as the nature of civil society, political party behavior, organization and ideology, and voting rules—influence how the opportunities and challenges of a federal system will intersect with women's equality interests.[103] In some polities, federalism may have worked to the advantage of gender equality movements, as in Australia, where it has been reported that "when governments opposed to women's advocacy have been in power at the federal or Commonwealth level, women's groups have been able to shift their lobbying" to the more sympathetic state level.[104] But perhaps this simply indicates that federal systems tend to offer greater opportunities to slow the pace of change, in whatever direction it is moving.

2. UNITARY GOVERNMENTS MAY BE EASIER TO MONITOR

It is easier to monitor action at one central national level than at multiple subnational levels. News media, watchdog groups, or lobbyists can focus energy on a single set of national institutions more easily than on fifty-plus state jurisdictional levels. Although local developments can be monitored at the local level, attracting the attention of national monitoring groups, whether in government, civil society, or the press, has distinct advantages, and once monitoring groups identify an item for action, taking action in a single national legislature is easier than in multiple subnational legislatures.

3. OLDER CONSTITUTIONS AND WOMEN'S DISADVANTAGE IN FEDERAL ARRANGEMENTS

To the extent that federal constitutions are crafted without full participation of women—as was the case in the United States and Australia—allocations of powers to the national government may be more likely to reflect issues of concern to men of the time than to women.[105] In Australia, feminist scholars have argued that the Constitution enacted in 1900 would have been quite different had women been allowed full participation in its drafting and adopting (as some had sought). At the time of its drafting and adoption, women had won the right to vote in South Australia and Western Australia, but not in the four other Australian states. Efforts to guarantee the franchise regardless of gender in the Constitution itself failed (though soon after its enactment women were given the vote nationally), as did the effort by one woman candidate to gain election to the constitutional convention.[106] Scholars have suggested that a broad range of social welfare powers—including power to address hygiene and sanitation, control of prostitution, and authority to enact uniform approaches to child custody and support—might have appeared in the 1900 Constitution based on women's groups' concerns at the time, had women fully participated.[107] While some amendments to the Australian Constitution in 1946 broadened the national government's powers over social welfare, issues remain, for example, with respect to child custody.[108]

National governments operating under older constitutions may face questions as to the extent of their powers to enact legislation to address issues of gender equality, that is, whether the subject matter is *ultra vires* national power. This possibility may create disincentives to focus on the national legislature, and in any event poses added costs and uncertainties to the process of change. An example from the United States involves national legislation to prevent domestic violence. The Violence Against Women Act of 1994[109] not only provided financial support for violence prevention but also created a civil rights remedy for the victims of gender-motivated assaults. Six years later, however, the Supreme Court held that the civil rights remedy was beyond the scope of national power. Neither the 1789 Constitution's provisions authorizing federal regulation of interstate commerce nor the provisions of the Fourteenth Amendment's guarantee of the "equal protection of the laws" were found sufficient to uphold the national civil rights remedy.[110]

The absence of women from full participation in the drafting of precisely those constitutions that are the oldest surviving,[111] whose jurisprudence has exercised influence on others, raises deeper questions about whether constitutional law and constitutionalism are not greater obstacles to, than tools for, achieving women's equality.

Yet original exclusions can be redressed both by amendment and by reunderstanding the constitution's meaning. With respect to Canada, for example, the Privy Council decided that the 1867 Constitution Act was to be treated as a "living tree" and interpreted in an evolving way, such that a woman could be appointed to federal public office.[112] The 1982 Canadian Charter of Rights and Freedoms, moreover, was adopted in a process in which women's groups actively participated to include provisions designed to secure gender equality as a constitutional principle and the authority of governments to undertake affirmative action programs to promote equality.[113] In the United States, the Constitution was amended to permit women to vote, and judicial interpretations of the Equal Protection Clause of the Fourteenth Amendment provided the basis for an edifice of constitutional law protecting women from many, though not all, forms of intentional government discrimination.[114] National powers, however, continue to be affected, and at times to the detriment of women, by judicial interpretations of older constitutional texts.[115]

4. FEDERALISM AND STRUCTURES OF REPRESENTATION?

Federal systems typically have structures of representation at the national level designed to protect the position or interest of subnational governments or territories, often in a bicameral legislature with one "house" devoted to representation of the subnational parts. These structures of representation are often not distributed on a strictly per capita basis— that is, they provide representation on the basis of territory, not population, granting disproportionate voting power to some persons. An upper house may represent an additional filter through which national legislation needs to pass, making change more difficult. Moreover, upper houses that provide disproportionate voting strength to smaller population areas whose views on gender equality are more conservative than those of the national majority may pose a particular barrier if their assent to legislation is required.

Mary Becker has argued for modification of the structure of and voting rules for the U.S. Senate through constitutional amendment in order to require or encourage more women in the Senate and to broaden its perspectives on social issues.[116] Professor Becker has also argued for a shift away from winner-take-all single-seat election contests to greater reliance on proportional representation, for allocating votes for children to be voted by their parents, and for changes to increase the percentage of poor persons who vote.[117] Professor Becker's work was directed at the situation in the United States. In other federal settings, as in Australia, the Senate has had more women than the lower house, in part because of the use of proportional voting for groups of senators.[118] As these examples illustrate, the range of federal structures and voting schemes is large, and would need to be considered in analyzing whether representation of subnational governments in national government structures works to advantage or disadvantage women.

5. FEDERALISM AND PROTECTION AGAINST BIAS
IN DECISION MAKING?

If we focus on the nature of decision making at the subnational level, there is an argument that federal systems—at least those with subnational units dominated by or including highly traditional and gender-biased social and political structures—would be more likely to harm women's equality interests than a unitary system in the same territory.[119] To the extent that traditional societies are more likely to insist on rigid gender roles, and to the extent that rural societies are more traditional than urban settings, federal systems—many of which give extra voting power to rural areas— might be thought systematically to disadvantage gender equality movements.[120] It is sometimes suggested that the national government provides more support for cities than do the state governments, and cities have been fertile grounds for developing innovations in gender equality (for example, rape crisis centers, women's shelters).[121] On these assumptions, and to the extent that one could choose whether to create a unitary or federal nation in the same territory and the same population, then, at least in countries with both large urban populations and some geographically contained highly traditional societies that severely subordinate women, a unitary state might be preferred. But such a choice is often not in fact available.[122]

Moreover, some feminist scholars debate whether subnational or national states are better situated to address issues of concern to women with respect to family matters.[123] As Judith Resnik suggests, it may prove impossible to develop acontextual propositions about the superiority of any particular level of government for advancing gender equality[124]—and for that reason, one might seek to sustain the capacities of all levels of government to address gender equality issues without insisting on hard and fast lines of divisions of authority.

Within particular polities, the relationships between forms of governance and gender equality will also depend on where the most important substantive norms are enacted, implemented, and enforced. For example, one might ask, are national courts more willing to enforce equality norms against the substantive laws enacted at subnational rather than national government levels? Consider two recent U.S. Supreme Court decisions. In *United States v. Virginia* (1996) (*VMI*),[125] the Court held unconstitutional the state's maintenance of a public, men-only college designed to produce "citizen-soldiers." Justice Ruth Ginsburg, writing for the Court, declared, "[n]either the goal of producing citizen-soldiers nor VMI's implementing methodology is inherently unsuitable to women," thereby apparently laying claim to women warriors as part of the national ideology for what may be the first time in the Court's history. The claim was linked to the Court's central analytic:

> that neither federal nor state government acts compatibly with the equal protection principle when a law or official policy denies to women, simply because they are women, full citizenship stature—equal opportunity to aspire, achieve, participate in and contribute to society based on their individual talents and capacities.[126]

Here was the highest national Court, declaring that regardless of whether it was acting for a state or for the nation, no government could deny to women "full citizenship stature." *VMI's* language suggests that a denial by either the federal government or a state government of "full citizenship stature" violates the constitutional requirement of "equal protection," absent an "exceedingly persuasive justification," which, according to *VMI*, "must be genuine, not hypothesized or invented *post hoc* in response to litigation," and "must not rely on overbroad generalizations about the different talents, capacities, or preferences of males and females."[127]

However, five years later in *Nguyen v. INS* (2001),[128] the Court upheld overt gender discrimination in a federal citizenship statute. The statute provided that a child born abroad to an unmarried U.S. citizen mother would be deemed a citizen (provided the mother had met a U.S. residency requirement for the period prior to the birth), but a child born abroad to a similarly situated unmarried U.S. citizen father would be entitled to citizenship only if (in addition to the other requirements) the father's paternity was legally established prior to the child's eighteenth birthday. The Court held that two government objectives justified the differential treatment: first, the greater difficulty in establishing biological parenthood for men than for women (which in an era of DNA testing does not account for the age cutoff); and second, the government interest in assuring that there was an opportunity to develop a parent-child relationship. The latter rationale was particularly surprising on the facts because Nguyen's father had been the custodial and primary care-giving parent since the child was age six and had raised the child in the United States. Given the Court's earlier condemnation of reliance on "overbroad generalizations" about the capacities or preferences of males or females, the application of this statute to these facts would seem to embody why the generalization represented in the statute was overbroad, as the dissent argued.

Why the apparent retreat from the more intense scrutiny of *VMI* to the *Nguyen* decision? The U.S. Court is not generally reluctant to take on coordinate branches of its government, as evidenced by the Court's invalidation of congressional legislation to provide a remedy for gender-motivated assault in 2000.[129] Perhaps the difference may be explained by judicial deference to national political authority in an area of particular national concern, as in the Court's decision upholding the male-only draft.[130] Further research could consider these and other possible explanations.

The complexity of analysis in a single national state is daunting; developing comparative data to explore systematic connections between federalism and gender equality may prove impossible; and extending that research to the more complex, quasi federal, or overlapping systems of government on the horizon, even more speculative. Even rigorous empirical investigation may not permit systematic conclusions about the relationship between federalism(s) and opportunities for women's public life or for women-friendly policies.[131] Yet perhaps identifying particular risks and benefits of the federal form for gender equality will lead to a better understanding of the possibilities for equality-improving legal strategies at global, national, and/or other levels.

Conclusion

Federalism and citizenship are both concepts rooted in ideas of differentiated governments with distinctive members—and thus might seem in tension with some of the universalizing aspects of women's human rights. Yet federal systems illustrate the possibilities for sustaining both universal (i.e., nationally uniform) rights and differentiated subnational policies. Just as federalism in the United States has not obliterated the states but has allowed the balance of federal and state power to shift over time, globalization and transboundary movements of people need not lead to the demise of national territorial states, but instead may shift their status among different levels and forms of governance. These changes may require complex adjustments of the relationships between national states and international legal entities, within and among national states, and among different parts of these various levels of government. Globalization may also mean that many more of us live in "nested" (or overlapping) forms of civic affiliations and must think "federally" about layers of government and layers of rights. And as has arguably been the case with federalism within states, there may be some benefit to unresolved tensions in these relationships and in concurrency rather than exclusivity of jurisdiction, at least over human rights issues of equality. Given wide divergences in particular normative aspirations, social practices, and effective enforcement of legal norms, the interests of women in overcoming subordination may be best served by an overlapping multiplicity of sources of law, affiliations of identity, and legal fora for rights enforcement, which layered forms of governmental jurisdiction can provide.

NOTES

1. See generally Kim Barry, "Home and Away: The Construction of Citizenship in an Emigration Context," *New York University Law Review* 81 (2006): 11. Research for this chapter, originally prepared for a 2003 Conference on Citizenship, Borders, and Gender: Mobility and Immobility, at Yale University, was essentially completed in 2006 and generally does not reflect later developments.

2. To be recognized as a state, a territorial entity must fulfill the following requirements: it must have a permanent population and territory, a government in effective control of the territory, and a capacity to deal and make agreements with other states. See Montevideo Convention on the Rights and Duties of States art. 1, December 26, 1933; Restatement (Third), Foreign Relations Law of the United States, §201 (1987).

3. See, e.g., Thomas M. Franck, "Clan and Superclan: Loyalty, Identity, and Community in Law and Practice," *American Journal International Law* 90 (1996): 359, 367–69.

4. For example, although not all territorial states are secular, the great majority of states in the world provide some formal legal protection of religious freedom and many provide in fact considerable levels of religious freedom for their populations. See U.S. Dept of State, 2006 *Annual Report on International Religious Freedom*, available at http://www.state.gov/g/drl/ rls/irf/2006 (last accessed on July 17, 2007) (more than a majority of the countries evaluated [at least 115 of 191] were found to have legal protections for religious freedom that were "generally respected" in practice). For a less sanguine view, see Robert F. Drinan, *Can God and Caesar Coexist?* (New Haven, CT: Yale University Press, 2001).

5. See Seyla Benhabib, *The Rights of Others: Aliens, Residents, and Citizens* (Cambridge: Cambridge University Press, 2004), 50–69; see also, Michael Walzer, "The Distribution of Membership," in *Boundaries: National Autonomy and Its*

Limits, eds. Peter G. Brown and Henry Shue (Totowa, NJ: Rowman and Little-field, 1981), 1, 31–32 (stating as a principle of "political justice" that "[t]he processes of self-determination through which a territorial state shapes its internal life must be open, and equally open, to all . . . who live in the territory, work in the local economy, and are subject to local law. . . . Every new immigrant, every refugee taken in, every resident and worker must be offered the opportunities of citizenship.")

6. See Linda Kerber, "The Stateless as the Citizen's Other: A View from the United States," in this volume, at 97.

7. For helpful discussion of the possible benefits of increasing the numbers of women in public office, including bringing diverse perspectives of women into legal and political decision making on issues that may not have been foreseen at the time of election or appointment, and building trust among groups working on issues of special concern to women and government offices, see Jane Mansbridge, "The Descriptive Political Representation of Gender: An Anti-Essentialist Argument," in *Has Liberalism Failed Women? Assuring Equal Representation in Europe and the United States,* eds. Jytte Klausen and Charles S. Maier (New York: Palgrave, 2001), 19–38.

8. For a discussion of subsidiarity in Germany and the European Union, see, e.g., George A. Bermann, "Taking Subsidiarity Seriously: Federalism in the European Community and the United States," *Columbia Law Review* 94 (1994): 332, 338–403; Gráinne de Búrca, "Reappraising Subsidiarity's Significance after Amsterdam" (Jean Monnet working paper, New York University School of Law, New York, 1999); Greg Taylor, "Germany: The Subsidiarity Principle," *International Journal of Constitutional Law* 4 (2006): 115–30.

9. See, e.g., Michael C. Dorf and Charles F. Sabol, "A Constitution of Democratic Experimentalism," *Columbia Law Review* 98 (1998): 267.

10. On the importance of the growth of global markets and of privatization in challenging the national state, see Philip C. Bobbitt, *The Shield of Achilles: War, Peace, and the Course of History* (New York: Knopf, 2002). Cf. Jean-Marie Guéhenno, *The End of the Nation-State,* trans. Victoria Elliott (Minneapolis: University of Minnesota Press, 1995) (describing move from era of "politics" to era of "networks"). On the importance of migration and of elite and working-class transnational communities, see Yasemin Nuhoğlu Soysal, *Limits of Citizenship: Migrants and Postnational Membership in Europe* (Chicago, IL: University of Chicago Press, 1994); Paul Johnston, "The Emergence of Transnational Citizenship among Mexican Immigrants in California," in *Citizenship Today: Global Perspectives and Practices,* eds. T. Alexander Aleinikoff and Douglas Klusmeyer (Washington, DC: Carnegie Endowment for International Peace, 2001), 253–77.

11. See Vicki C. Jackson and Mark Tushnet, *Comparative Constitutional Law,* 2d ed. (New York: Foundation Press, 2006), 1005.

12. Whether on balance these processes are creating more government or less is unclear. While there may well be a proliferation of bodies that in some formal sense exercise governmental powers, the disaggregation of authority may reflect a shift or transfer of authority to private entities. See, e.g., Saskia Sassen, *Losing Control? Sovereignty in an Age of Globalization* (New York: Columbia University Press, 1996) (discussing the impact of financial markets' transnational growth and increased power of businesses on government power); Bobbitt, supra note 10. The degovernmentalization of responsibility, whether to private business corporations, NGOs, or other nonstate holders of power (e.g., tribes, religious groups, family clans), raises important questions of application of human rights beyond governments.

13. Cf. Anna Yeatman, "The Idea of the Constitutional State and Global Society," *Law/Text/Culture* 8 (2004): 83 (arguing that globalization of society makes states, as political organizations, more important).

14. See generally David Kennedy, "International Law and the Nineteenth Century: History of an Illusion," *Quinnipiac Law Review* 17 (1997): 99, 116–17, 122–28 (arguing that association of territorial state with exclusive "sovereignty" is a phenomenon, largely of late nineteenth and twentieth centuries; earlier in the nineteenth century states were assumed to be constrained by international customary law and thus not wholly "sovereign" in the formal sense of having exclusive authority).

15. As noted, it is unnecessary that territorial states also be regarded as "nations"—to the extent that the word "nation" implies a homogenous ethnicity or background. Rather, Canada, the United States, India, and South Africa, among many others, exist as multiethnic, complex national territorial states. The "self-determination" of "peoples," a right recognized in international law, can occur *within* legal and political frameworks provided by territorial states. See Thomas M. Franck, "The Emerging Right to Democratic Governance," *American Journal of International Law* 86 (1992): 46.

16. See John Jackson, *Sovereignty, the WTO, and Changing Fundamentals of International Law* (Cambridge: Cambridge University Press, 2006) (arguing for a focus on appropriate power allocations rather than assumptions of exclusive sovereignty); cf. Thomas Franck, *The Power of Legitimacy among Nations* (New York: Oxford University Press, 1990) (arguing for shift from focus on bindingness of rules of international law to their legitimacy and arguing that legitimate rules exercise a compliance pull).

17. For a recent example of theorizing concurrency with respect to constitutional power to remedy gender and other forms of disadvantage, see Beverley Baines, "Federalism and Pregnancy Benefits: Dividing Women," *Queen's Law Journal* 32 (2006): 190 (arguing for "equity federalism").

18. See, e.g., David Jacobson, *Rights across Borders: Immigration and the Decline of Citizenship* (Baltimore, MD: John Hopkins University Press, 1996), 7

(citizenship as linchpin of the nation-state); Linda Bosniak, "Multiple Nationality and the Postnational Transformation of Citizenship," *Virginia Journal of International Law* 42 (2002): 979 (noting relationship between possible decline in the importance of territorial state sovereignty and perceived increases in "postnational" or "transnational" subjects or citizens).

19. See Universal Declaration of Human rights, arts. 13(2), 21, G.A. Res. 217A (III) (Dec. 10, 1948); see also International Covenant on Civil and Political Rights, art. 12(4), 99 U.N.T.S. 171 (entered into force March 23, 1976); Restatement 3d of the Foreign Relations Law of the United States, §711, comment c (1987). Although there is a distinction between nationality and citizenship, for purposes of this chapter, I treat them together as a single concept of national citizenship. "Nationality" refers to the relationship between a person and a state under international law that, for example, permits the state to assert claims on behalf of its nationals. "Citizenship" is a concept under national law, implying full inclusion as a member of a polity, internally. In theory, one can be a "national" of a country without being a "citizen" for purposes of equal status within that country. See generally Lori F. Damrosch et al., *International Law: Cases and Materials* (4th ed. 2001), 427; Restatement 3d, Foreign Relations Law, supra, §§ 211, 212. In this chapter, I refer to citizenship as embracing the idea of nationality under international law.

20. Note the relative success of the United Kingdom in asserting claims against the United States on behalf of its nationals held at Guantanamo. See John Daniszewski, "British Inmates at Guantanamo to Be Released," *Los Angeles Times,* January 12, 2005, A3 (reporting that the last four British inmates at Guantanamo were being released following negotiations between the two governments). See also Patrizia Nanz, "Mobility, Migrants, and Solidarity: Towards an Emerging European Citizenship Regime," in this volume, at 413 (noting that EU citizenship confers right to "protection in a non-EU country by the . . . representatives of other member states if one's own member state is not represented"). Disparities in the powers of states of nationality may, however, influence their efficacy in asserting claims on behalf of their nationals.

21. Thus, for example, the CEDAW Convention only recently added an Optional Protocol allowing individual petitions to be filed, and many signatories to CEDAW have not adopted that Optional Protocol.

22. See Seyla Benhabib, *Transformations of Citizenship: Dilemmas of the Nation State in the Era of Globalization* (Spinoza Lectures) (Assen, The Netherlands: Van Gorcum Uitgeverij, 2001), 36–41.

23. Hannah Arendt, *The Origins of Totalitarianism* (New York: Harcourt Brace, 1973), 296–97.

24. In both the United States and Australia, women were long considered "citizens" even though they lacked such basic rights as the right to vote. See, e.g., Minor v. Happersett, 88 U.S. 162 (1875); Kim Rubenstein, "Citizenship and the

Constitutional Convention Debates: A Mere Legal Inference," *Federal Law Review* 25 (1997): 301–3.

25. In this respect I disagree with Peter Spiro, "Dual Nationality and the Meaning of Citizenship," *Emory Law Journal* 46 (1997): 1411, 1417 (suggesting that citizenship is like a "club" membership).

26. International Law Association, Committee on Feminism and International Law, "Final Report on Women's Equality and Nationality in International Law" (69th I.L.A. Conference, London, 2000) (Christine Chinkin, Chair; Karen C. Knop, Rapporteur), *International Law Association Report of Conferences* 69 (2000): 248, 251. (This report is also available on the ILA website, http://www.ila-hq.org. Click on "committees," click on "Feminism and International Law," and scroll down to "committee documents.")

27. Ibid., 258.

28. Many scholars discuss two or three central meanings of citizenship: first, the idea of citizenship as rights-bearing; second, the idea of citizenship as participation in self-governance; and third, the idea of citizenship as membership, or affiliation, with a specific political community. Citizenship is also discussed in terms of duties—of jury service, of military service—duties sometimes seen as correlative of rights and sometimes of status. Citizenship can also be understood as part of a project of maintaining spaces for civic commitments—commitments that transcend more ascriptive features of social identity and demand (or facilitate) the development of the virtues of citizenship, including toleration; citizenship thus might be understood as a status not only vis-à-vis governments but relationally, vis-à-vis other citizens. See generally William A. Galston, *Liberal Purposes: Goods, Virtues, and Diversity in the Liberal State* (New York: Cambridge University Press, 1991).

29. My categories do not entirely correspond with T. H. Marshall's famous classifications of the three stages of citizenship—from civil rights, to political rights, to social rights. See T. H. Marshall, *Class, Citizenship, and Social Development* (New York: Doubleday, 1964), 71–72. All of these rights may be necessary for full citizenship today, but the order in which they arrived in the English system he studied will not necessarily hold true in other times and places: immigrants, for example, may benefit from some social welfare rights, and civil rights, long before they are eligible to vote.

30. Compare Galston's list of the virtues/aptitudes of citizens in democracy—see Galston, *Liberal Purposes*, supra note 28, 220–27—with what we might describe as virtues of members of a university community, or a congregation, or a social club. See also Karen Knop, "Relational Nationality: On Gender and Nationality in International Law," in *Citizenship Today: Global Perspectives and Practice*, ed. T. Alexander Aleinikoff and Douglas Klusmeyer (Washington, DC: Carnegie Endowment for International Peace, 2001), 89–124. On the relationship between citizenship and equality, see Marshall, *Class, Citizenship, and Social Development*, supra note 29, at

84 ("Citizenship is a status bestowed on those who are full members of a community. All who possess the status are equal with respect to the rights and duties with which the status is endowed."); see also ibid., 87, 92.

31. See T. Alexander Aleinikoff, *Semblances of Sovereignty: The Constitution, the State, and American Citizenship* (Cambridge, MA: Harvard University Press, 2002), 178–79 (discussing citizenship as a sense of identification and belonging).

32. United States v. Virginia, 518 U.S. 515, 532 (1996) (emphasis added). For discussion, see Jill Elaine Hasday, "The Principle and Practice of Women's 'Full Citizenship': A Case Study of Sex-Segregated Public Education," *Michigan Law Review* 101 (2002): 755 (urging focus on history and effects of educational settings on gendered role differentiation).

33. On the importance of "civic republicanism," see Linda McClain, *The Place of Families: Fostering Capacity, Equality, and Responsibility* (Cambridge, MA: Harvard University Press, 2006), 16–17. On whether federalism is related to the availability of participatory self-governance at even more local levels, see also, Andrzej Rapaczynski, "From Sovereignty to Process: The Jurisprudence of Federalism after Garcia," *The Supreme Court Review* 34 (1985): 341; Vicki C. Jackson, "Federalism and the Uses and Limits of Law: Printz and Principle?," *Harvard Law Review* 111 (1998): 2180, 2218 n. 176. For a more pessimistic view that participatory self-governance in the liberal tradition is no longer possible, see, e.g., Guéhenno, *End of the Nation-State*, supra note 10.

34. For a classic discussion of citizenship as entailing equality of rights holding, see Marshall, *Class, Citizenship, and Social Development*, supra note 29, 71–88.

35. Asserting "legal rights" in this context implies a jurisprudential theory that does not require strong notions of enforceability to claim a legal right, for enforcement at the international level depends on relatively weak mechanisms. Thus, for example, the United Nations Human Rights Committee monitors reports from signatory countries, and may express "views" on individual complaints filed against those countries that are signatory to the first Optional Protocol of the International Covenant on Civil and Political Rights.

36. Vindication of rights under international human rights law typically depends on enforcement apparatuses associated with territorial states, many of whose national courts are increasingly willing to look to international human rights to interpret domestic statutory and constitutional law. See generally Vicki C. Jackson, "Transnational Discourse, Relational Authority, and the U.S. Court: Gender Equality," *Loyola of Los Angeles Law Review* 37 (2003): 271.

37. On marriage and citizenship in the United States, see Nancy Cott, *Public Vows: A History of Marriage and the Nation* (Cambridge, MA: Harvard University Press, 2000).

38. See, e.g., U.S. Const., Amend XIV ("No state shall . . . deny to any person within its jurisdiction the equal protection of the laws.").

39. Cf. Nancy Fraser and Linda Gordon, "Contract versus Charity: Why Is There No Social Citizenship in the United States?," in *The Citizenship Debates*, ed. Gershon Shafir (Minneapolis: University of Minnesota Press, 1998), 113–27 (noting tension between "civil" rights of contract and property, and more "social" rights and arguing for greater attention in the United States to conceptions of "social citizenship").

40. Taylor v. Louisiana, 419 U.S. 522, 525 (1975); but see Rostker v. Goldberg, 453 U.S. 57 (1981) (upholding statute that required only men to register for military draft, in light of purportedly unchallenged exclusion of women from combat).

41. Judith N. Shklar, *American Citizenship: The Quest for Inclusion* (Cambridge, MA: Harvard University Press, 1991), 2, 15–18. Shklar focuses on the meaning of citizenship through the perspective of those—slaves, women, nonproperty-owning whites—who were excluded from its full realization. Shklar writes, "To be a second-class citizen is to suffer derogation and the loss of re-spectable standing." Ibid., 17. Shklar argues that the essence of citizenship in the United States is not participation, which people do more in private organizations, clubs, or churches, but rather is *standing*. Ibid., 30–31. Disfranchised Americans have not asked for Athenian-style participatory politics but "that citizenship be equally distributed, so that their standing might also be recognized and their interests be defended and promoted." Ibid., 29–31.

42. See Native Women's Association of Canada v. Canada (1994) 3 S.C.R. 627. Although plaintiffs' claims were based on the freedom of association and gender equality provisions of the Charter, linkages between citizenship and claims of equality in rights to participate in public processes were apparent (albeit invoked against the plaintiffs' claims) in the court's reasons. Ibid., 654–55 (quoting Justice L'Heureux-Dubé's judgment in Haig v. Canada, 1993 2 SCR 995, 1041–41, disagreeing that a government has an "'obligation to consult its citizens through'" a referendum). For discussion of the varying views of aboriginal women in Canada about the entrenchment of equality rights, see Marian Sawer and Jill Vickers, "Women's Constitutional Activism in Australia and Canada," *Canadian Journal of Women and the Law* 13 (2001): 1, 19–20.

43. International law recognizes both gender equality and rights of "peoples" to self-determination; potential conflicts could be imagined between gender equality and claims rooted in asserted "traditions" supported by a majority of a "people" even if discriminatory against one part of that people. Insofar as a number of national constitutions provide stronger support for gender equality claims than for the protection of autonomous self-governance by minority groups, they may be more potent tools for gender equality.

44. Cf. Walzer, "The Distribution of Membership," supra note 5, 9–10 (arguing that restraints on entry into a country "serv[e] to defend the liberty and welfare, the politics and culture of a group of people committed to one another and to their common life").

45. See Benhabib, *Transformations of Citizenship*, supra note 22, 60–61; Jacobson, *Rights across Borders*, supra note 18, 10–11 (suggesting that nationality is being recast from a principle that reinforces state sovereignty to "a concept of nationality as a human right").

46. Given the complex historical relationships between some strands of the women's suffrage movement and racism or nativism, this is an important concern. See, e.g., Ellen Dubois, *Feminism and Suffrage: The Emergence of an Independent Women's Movement in America, 1848–1869* (Ithaca, NY: Cornell University Press, 1978), 92–103, 174–79; see also Kathleen M. Blee, *Women of the Klan: Racism and Gender in the 1920s* (Berkeley: University of California Press, 1991), 116, 117.

47. See generally Benhabib, *The Rights of Others*, supra note 5. If international law is coming to recognize what Thomas Franck has called a right to democracy—see Franck, "The Emerging Right to Democratic Governance," supra note 15—it might well follow that international law must also come to recognize a right to acquire nationality—or the related ability to participate in self-governance—in the country in which one has resided for a significant period of time. For a controversial proposal to treat "immigration as [a] transition" to citizenship, with a "presumed equality" of rights for immigrants (except for those who fail to seek citizenship as soon as they are eligible), see Hiroshi Motomura, *Immigrants in Waiting: The Lost Story of Immigration and Citizenship in the United States* (New York: Oxford University Press, 2006), 9, 13, 189–99.

48. But cf. Linda Bosniak, "Denationalizing Citizenship," in *Citizenship Today: Global Perspectives and Practices*, eds. T. Alexander Aleinikoff and Douglas Klusmeyer (Washington, DC: Carnegie Endowment for International Peace, 2001), 237 (providing sympathetic evaluation of postnational concepts of citizenship).

49. See Thomas Buergenthal, "The Evolving International Human Rights System," *American Journal of International Law* 100 (2006): 783.

50. Cf. Aleinikoff, *Semblances of Sovereignty*, supra note 31, 178–81 (arguing that citizenship should be decentered from rights bearing and be associated more with membership and belonging than with individual rights).

51. See also ibid. (developing the idea of citizenship as relationships of those in a community with each other). For a different kind of emphasis on relational citizenship, see Knop, "Relational Nationality," supra note 30.

52. I am referring here more to a historically or empirically grounded concept of constitutional patriotism, see, e.g., Mark Tushnet, "Thinking about the Constitution at the Cusp," *Akron Law Review* 34 (2000): 21, 29, 35 n. 35, than to a concept of constitutional patriotism grounded in universalist commitments, see Jürgen Habermas, *Between Facts and Norms: Contributions to a Discourse Theory of Law and Democracy*, trans. William Rehg (Cambridge, MA: MIT Press, 1996), 465–66; but see Frank I. Michelman, "Morality, Identity, and Constitutional Patriotism," *Denver University Law Review* 76 (1999): 1009, 1010, 1025–26.

53. See Bosniak, "Denationalizing Citizenship," supra note 48.

54. See Soysal, *Limits of Citizenship,* supra note 10.

55. Soysal's argument is a subtle one, which at times recognizes the continued centrality of the territorial state as the location of citizenship and the enforcement mechanism. See also Rainer Bauböck, "Introduction [to Part III]," in *From Migrants to Citizens: Membership in a Changing World,* eds. T. Alexander Aleinikoff and Douglas Klusmeyer (Washington, DC: Carnegie Endowment for International Peace, 2000), 305 (arguing that Mexico and the European Union "illustrate how the traditional conception of citizenship as a singular membership in a sovereign national polity is gradually eroding under the impact of geographical mobility and regional integration"); but cf. Marco Martiniello, "Citizenship in the European Union," in *From Migrants to Citizens,* supra this note, 342, 354 (expressing caution about significance of EU citizenship as still largely derivative of national citizenship, a "complementary supracitizenship"). For an argument that dual nationality arising out of "emigrant citizenship" does not "eliminate[e] geographic borders in some postmodern sense" because "[t]he society in which the emigrant participates is still territorially bound," see Barry, "Home and Away," supra note 1, 58.

56. Cf. Stephanie Palmer, "Feminism and the Promise of Human Rights: Possibilities and Paradoxes," in *Visible Women: Essays on Feminist Legal Theory and Political Philosophy,* eds. Susan James and Stephanie Palmer (Champaign: University of Illinois Press, 2002), 90, 97–98 (urging feminists to embrace law and rights and thus support human rights as strategy for women).

57. See, e.g., United States v. Virginia, 518 U.S. 515, 532 (1996) ("[N]either federal nor state government acts compatibly with the equal protection principle when a law or official policy denies to women, simply because they are women, full citizenship stature—equal opportunity to aspire, achieve, participate in and contribute to society based on their individual talents and capacities."); see also Noëlle Lenoir, "The Representation of Women in Politics: From Quotas to Parity in Elections," *International and Comparative Law Quarterly* 50 (2001): 217, 243–47 (describing how parity for women on electoral lists is reconciled with universalist basis of citizenship).

58. See Nanz, at 419 (reporting data indicating that "maintaining a European identity does not seem to erode one's feelings towards one's own nation" and that "respondents with high levels of national identity are more likely to identify with Europe" than those with weaker levels of national identification).

59. On nested federal citizenship, see Vicki C. Jackson, "Citizenship and Federalism," in *Citizenship Today: Global Perspectives and Practices,* eds. Alexander Aleinikoff and Douglas Klusmeyer (Washington, DC: Carnegie Endowment for International Peace, 2001), 127–82; see also Peter Schuck, "Citizenship in Federal Systems," *American Journal of Comparative Law* 48 (2000): 195; Rubenstein, "Citizenship and the Constitutional Convention Debates," supra note 24, 303, 299.

("'[T]he whole purpose of this Constitution is to secure a dual citizenship. That is the very essence of a federal system.'" [quoting Josiah Symon, delegate from South Australia, debating proposed Australian constitution]). As Rubenstein also notes, the Australian Constitution, after some debate acknowledging that Australia would also continue as part of the British empire, used the words "subject of the Queen" to refer to Australians—thus arguably embracing and eliding two forms of dual citizenship—the double citizenship in a particular state within Australia and the dual character of being a citizen of Australia and a subject of the queen. Ibid., 304–5. (Only in 1984 did Australian citizens cease to regard themselves as British subjects. Ibid., 308). At the same time Rubenstein also notes the important debate over the capacity to exclude Asians from Australian citizenship, thus emphasizing the exclusionary, discriminatory edge of citizenship. Ibid., 306.

60. See, e.g., Ayelet Shachar, "The Race for Talent: Highly Skilled Migrants and Competitive Immigration Regimes," *New York University Law Review* 81 (2001): 148.

61. See David A. Martin and T. Alexander Aleinikoff, "Double Ties: Why Nations Should Learn to Love Dual Nationality," *Foreign Policy*, no. 133 (Nov.–Dec. 2002): 80–81; see also Franck, "Clan and Superclan," supra note 3, 378–80.

62. Jackson, "Citizenship and Federalism," supra note 59, 151, 159–61, 177–78.

63. On the denationalization concept, see Bosniak, *Denationalizing Citizenship*, supra note 48. In addition to the idea of a right to acquire citizenship within a reasonable time, on alternatives consider denizenship for permanent resident aliens, see Tomas Hammar, "State, Nation, and Dual Citizenship," in *Immigration and the Politics of Citizenship in Europe and North America*, ed. William Rogers Brubaker (Lanham, MD: University Press of America, 1989), 81–95; multinational citizenships for persons with strong affiliative connections between two or more states; and adherence to international human rights norms to protect basic human rights and dignity of all persons.

64. Federal nations often, though not always, recognize a form of nested dual citizenship. See Jackson, "Citizenship and Federalism," supra note 59, 134–37. For a tripartite nested citizenship, consider a citizen of Germany, who would have membership in a subnational entity or land, in the German state, and in the European Union. Dual citizenship—that is, non-nested memberships in two different states—is on the increase as international presumptions in favor of single identities yield to liberalization of conditions of dual citizenship. See also, Patrizia Nanz, "Mobility, Migrants, and Solidarity: Towards an Emerging European Citizenship Regime," in this volume, for a discussion of the interaction between EU and national citizenship, and the impact that perceptions of supranational belonging have on the importance of national citizenship.

65. For a classic study of ethnic conflict, territorial government, and law, see Donald L. Horowitz, *Ethnic Groups in Conflict* (Berkeley: University of California Press, 1985).

66. Thus, for example, in Switzerland delays in providing full women's suffrage have been attributed in part to its federal structure and culture. See, e.g., Lee Ann Banaszak, *Why Movements Succeed or Fail: Opportunity, Culture, and the Struggle for Women Suffrage* (Princeton, NJ: Princeton University Press, 1996); see also Regula Stämpfli, "Direct Democracy and Women's Suffrage: Antagonism in Switzerland," in *Women and Politics Worldwide*, eds. Barbara J. Nelson and Najma Chowdhury (New Haven, CT: Yale University Press, 1994), 690–704 (attributing delay in full women's suffrage from 1959—when both houses of the national legislature recommended allowing women to vote—to 1990, when women were allowed to vote in the last canton, to the effects of federalism and rules for direct democracy among an initially male electorate). A Canadian study of state feminism noted the need to "bea[t] the 'federalism foxtrot'" because responsibility for government policy, e.g., with respect to violence against women, was unclear; Canadian feminists suffered from "limited co-ordination among governments, and minimal coordination among femocrats working at various levels on anti-violence strategies." L. Pauline Rankin and Jill Vickers, "Women's Movements and State Feminism: Integrating Diversity into Public Policy" (Ottawa: Status of Women Canada, 2001), at http://www.swc-cfc.gc.ca/pubs/pubspr/0662657756/ 200105_0662657756_e.pdf (last accessed on May 13, 2007). The report also found that women activists were often told they had gone to the wrong office, and were "expected to figure out a division of power so complex that even political scientists find determining lines of responsibility difficult." By contrast, in Australia the "femocrats" in the state and national governments coordinated their own work and cooperated. See Marian Sawer, "Femocrats and Ecocrats: Women's Policy Machinery in Australia, Canada, and New Zealand," *UNRISD/UNDP Occasional Paper #6* (March 1996), 4–10, available at http://www. unrisd.org/ unrisd/website/document.nsf/ 0/D1A254C22F3E5CC580256B67005B6 B56?OpenDocument (last accessed on July 25, 2007).

67. See, e.g., Theda Skocpol, *Protecting Soldiers and Mothers* (Cambridge, MA: Harvard University Press, 1992); Suzanne Mettler, *Dividing Citizens: Gender and Federalism in New Deal Public Policy* (Ithaca, NY: Cornell University Press, 1998); Louise Chappell, *Gendering Government: Feminist Engagement with the State in Australia and Canada* (Vancouver, Canada: University of British Columbia Press, 2002); Banaszak, *Why Movements Succeed or Fail,* supra note 66; Sawer and Vickers, "Women's Constitutional Activism," supra note 42, 1. See also, Jane Mansbridge, *Why We Lost the ERA* (Chicago, IL: University Of Chicago Press, 1986).

68. See, e.g., Sawer and Vickers, "Women's Constitutional Activism," supra note 42, 34 (concluding based on their study of Canada and Australia that "[a]symmetrical federations . . . foster the emergence of different political orientations within feminism, whereas a cohesive 'women's position,' for example, on centralization/decentralization will be more common in congruent federations").

69. For a helpful discussion of the relationship between gender and federalism in Australia, and in particular of the opposition of prominent Australian suffragists to federation because of the potential loss in the colonial governments' powers with ensuing diminution of women's powers to influence important public policies, see Kim Rubenstein, "Feminism and Federalism: Pushing Federalism beyond Territory," text at nn. 28–31 (unpublished manuscript, August 2006, on file with author) (a shorter version of this paper is available at http://www.gt-centre.unsw.edu.au/ publications/papers/docs/2006/7_KimRubenstein.pdf); see also Joni Lovenduski, "The Rules of the Political Game: Feminism and Politics in Great Britain," in *Women and Politics Worldwide*, eds. Barbara J. Nelson and Najma Chowdhury (New Haven, CT: Yale University Press, 1994), 298, 302 (speculating that it might be easier for women who live close to London to combine "domestic life" with participation in Parliament).

70. See Rubenstein, "Federalism and Feminism," supra note 69, text at note 31.

71. Fiona MacKay, Fiona Myers, and Alice Brown, "Towards a New Politics? Women and the Constitutional Change in Scotland," in *Women Making Constitutions: New Politics and Comparative Perspectives*, eds. Alexandra Dobrowolsky and Vivien Hart (Houndmills, UK: Palgrave Macmillan, 2003), 84, 87–88; see also Fiona MacKay, "Descriptive and Substantive Representation in New Parliamentary Spaces: The Case of Scotland," in *Representing Women in Parliament: A Comparative Study*, eds. Marian Sawer, Manon Tremblay, and Linda Trimble (London: Routledge, 2006), 171–87.

72. A 1995 federal census study reported that in 1992, 31 percent of elected school board members in the United States were women—a higher percentage than in any other set of elected positions in the United States, including city councils, state legislatures, or the national Congress. See "Number of Elected Officials Exceeds Half Million, January 30, 1995," describing *Popularly Elected Officials, Preliminary Report No 2* GC92-2(P) (reporting that 24 percent of local government officials in 1992 were female and that, at the local level, school districts had the highest percentage of female elected officials, at 31.2 percent), available at http://www.census.gov/Press-Release/cb95-18.txt. Another study, in 2002, found that 38.9 percent of school boards were female. See Frederick M. Hess, "School Boards at the Dawn of the Twenty-First Century" (National School Boards Association, 2002): 5, available at http://www.nsba.org/ site/docs/1200/1143.pdf (last accessed on May 13, 2007). For comparable data on women in Congress, and state legislatures, reflecting lower representation, see note 77 below.

73. On women in elected legislatures, see, for example, Beth Reingold, *Representing Women: Sex, Gender, and Legislative Behavior in Arizona and California* (Chapel Hill: University of North Carolina Press, 2000); Michele L. Swers, *The Difference Women Make: The Policy Impact of Women in Congress* (Chicago, IL: University of Chicago Press, 2002); the set of essays in *Representing Women in Parliament,* supra note 71.

74. See Raghabendra Chattopadhyay and Esther Duflo, "Women as Policy Makers: Evidence from a Randomized Policy Experiment in India," *Econometrica* 72 (February 2004): 1409, 1427–28 (reporting data from an experiment in 265 villages in one state in India). The study also found policy differences: women were more concerned than men about drinking water, for example, and in village councils where reserved seats for female heads resulted in a female head, more resources were devoted to improving water supply than other councils.

75. Thus, for example, in Australia, a higher percentage of women serve in the Senate than in the House. For one explanation, see Ann Millar, "Feminising the Senate," in *A Woman's Constitution? Gender and History in the Australian Commonwealth*, ed. Helen Irving (Sydney: Hale & Iremonger, 1996), 127, 128–29, 135 (suggesting that the Senate holds less power than the House; has longer terms and smaller numbers and is thus a less confrontational body; and relies on proportional voting for groups of senators, allowing smaller and newer parties to win election, as factors explaining women's greater representation in the Australian Senate than in the House). See also Sarah Maddison and Emma Partridge, "How Well Does Australian Democracy Serve Australian Women?" *Audit Report No. 8* (Canberra: Democratic Audit of Australia, Australian National University, 2007), 61–63, available at http://democratic.audit.anu.edu.au/papers/focussed_audits/ 200703_madpartozdocwom.pdf (last accessed May 13, 2007) (attributing differences both to different voting systems and the role of minority parties, noting that women's representation in legislatures varies substantially among political parties). But cf. text at notes 115, 116 below (noting Mary Becker's critique of U.S. Senate as impairing progress towards women's substantive equality).

76. A number of studies suggest that proportional representation tends to increase women representatives over first-past-the-post or plurality winner systems characteristic of single-member districts. For a helpful overview, see Drude Dahlerup, "Introduction," in *Women, Quotas and Politics*, ed. Drude Dahlerop (London: Routledge, 2006), 3–31; see also, e.g., Pippa Norris, "The Impact of Electoral Reform on Women's Representation," *Acta Politica* 41 (July 2006): 197–213. Indeed, the first woman to run for elective office in Australia, Helen Spence, was an advocate of proportional representation, adopted some decades later and considered of importance in women's gaining seats in the Australian Senate. See Millar, "Feminising the Senate," supra note 75.

77. A "snapshot" of women in legal positions in the year 2000, prepared by the American Bar Association, reported that women were 16 percent of the U.S. court of appeals judges and almost 15 percent of the U.S. district court judges. See http://www.abanet.org/women/ snapshots.pdf (last accessed on May 13, 2007). At that time, two of the nine Supreme Court justices were women (now, in 2007, there is only one female Supreme Court justice). In contrast to these numbers, over 26 percent of justices on state courts of last resort were female (aggregating data from elected and appointive positions). And in 2003, twenty

of the fifty-two current state court (or equivalent) chief justices were women. See www.feminist.com (women's e-news) (February 9, 2003). This number fell slightly (seventeen out of fifty-three state courts of last resort) in 2007. See "Judicial Selection and Retention, Membership on State Courts of Last Resort by Sex, National Center for State Courts," available at http://www.ncsconline.org/WC/Publications/KIS_JudSelCOLRsex.pdf (last accessed on May 13, 2007). A similar percentage gap seems to exist between female members of the U.S. Congress (about 14 percent in the 108th Congress, up to 16.1 percent in the 110th Congress) and state legislatures (in 2002, about 22.4 percent and in 2007, 23.5 percent). See Center for American Women in Politics, Rutgers University, http://www.cawp.rutgers.edu/ Facts.html (last accessed on May 13, 2007).

78. Deborah Cass and Kim Rubenstein, "From Federation Forward," in *A Woman's Constitution*, ed. Helen Irving (Sydney: Hale & Iremonger, 1996), 108–26 (first woman elected to a state assembly in 1921 in West Australia, with women elected to state assemblies in at least three other Australian states before the first women were elected to the national legislature in 1943); see ibid., 119–20 and note 49.

79. See Maddison and Partridge, "How Well Does Australian Democracy Serve Australian Women?," supra note 75, 60, 65 (showing that women in Australia are only slightly better represented in state and territorial parliaments than in the national parliament in Australia and attributing the difference in part to the dominance of Labor parties at the subnational level). Interestingly, and "[c]ontrary to popular belief," this report found that the lowest percentage of women's participation occurred at the local government level in Australia, ibid., 60. It reported that Canada, Sweden, and New Zealand have a similar pattern of lower percentages of women in local elected governments than in state or national government, while in the United Kingdom the opposite is true, ibid. at 70, as in the United States. See notes 73, 77 above. The Maddison-Partridge report suggests that the higher participation of women in local government in the United Kingdom "may be a result of the different spread of responsibilities—local government in the UK has a stronger role in education, health and housing compared to Australia." Maddison and Partridge, "How Well Does Australian Democracy Serve Australian Women?," supra note 75, n. 92. (I am grateful for the assistance of Professors Kim Rubenstein and Marian Sawer in identifying this source for me.) See also Rubenstein, "Federalism and Feminism," supra note 69, text at note 112.

80. See Alain Brewer-Carías, "Venezuela," in *Handbook of Federal Countries (2005)*, eds. Ann Griffiths and Karl Nerenberg (Montreal: McGill-Queens University Press, 2005), 393, 402–3 (comparing number of persons per democratically elected governments, ranging from [greater to lesser densities of governments] 1,614 in France to 2,333 in Switzerland to 3,872 in the United States to 5,086 in Germany to 71,006 in Venezuela). This data suggests that federal constitutions do not have a linear relationship with democratic decentralization of government,

France being a unitary state and the others—including Venezuela—being, as a formal matter, federal states.

81. Institutional isomorphism is the tendency of institutions to replicate the forms and structures of other apparently similar organizations even if the mimicry is not as functional. See Ryan Goodman and Derek Jinks, "Toward an Institutional Theory of Sovereignty," *Stanford Law Review* 55 (2003): 1749; Paul J. DiMaggio and Walter W. Powell, "The Iron Cage Revisited: Institutional Isomorphism and Collective Rationality," in *The New Institutionalism in Organizational Analysis*, eds. Paul J. DiMaggio and Walter W. Powell (Chicago, IL: University of Chicago Press, 1991), 63–64. Isomorphism might imply that federal governments will tend to have more complex systems of governance at the subnational level as well, as the federal pattern of divided authority is replicated at other levels—that is, the apparent decentralization of legislative authority from central to subnational governments might be replicated in the allocations of authority among subnational units and more local levels of government. Some federal systems also provide constitutional status to a third level of government involving constitutional protections for some self-governance by cities or other local government units.

82. See Charles Tiebout, "A Pure Theory of Local Expenditures," *Journal of Political Economy* 64 (1956): 416–24. For comparative analysis of the option of "exit" as compared with "voice" in markets and government, see Albert O. Hirschman, *Exit, Voice, and Loyalty: Responses to Decline in Firms, Organizations, and States* (Cambridge, MA: Harvard University Press, 1970).

83. One study, for example, found differences in the preferences expressed by female courthouse employees, based on their race, with respect to interest in part-time work and on-site child care. See "Report of the Special Committee on Gender to the D.C. Circuit Task Force on Gender, Race, and Ethnic Bias," *Georgetown Law Journal* 84 (1996): 1657, 1842. But whether these kinds of differences in preferences would correspond to different geographic areas of residence and voting is a separate question.

84. Of course, this argument depends on people, here women, having actual mobility and ability to exit, which—for reasons not unconnected to traditions of care giving—may be more hypothetical than real. Second, the argument ignores the complexity of decision making about residence, the large number of factors relevant, and the often high transaction costs of relocation.

85. Again, these opportunities need not be limited to those in a federal system, but federalism's emphasis on multiple levels of self-governing polities may help assure that such opportunities are present. For a fascinating argument that it is polities that are in some sense on the periphery of established powers that are more likely to innovate by, for example, embracing women's suffrage and office holding, see John Markoff, "Margins, Centers, and Democracy: The Paradigmatic History of Women's Suffrage," *Signs: Journal of Women in Culture and Society* 29 (2003): 85–116.

86. See, e.g., Jonathan Rodden and Susan Rose-Ackerman, "Does Federalism Preserve Markets?," *Virginia Law Review* 83 (1997): 1521, 1541 (noting barriers to labor mobility); Susan Rose-Ackerman, "Risk-Taking and Reelection: Does Federalism Promote Innovation?," *Journal of Legal Studies* 9 (1980): 593–616.

87. On the potential benefits of redundancy of government protection, see, e.g., Judith Resnik, "Tiers," *Southern California Law Review* 57 (1984): 840.

88. Cf. Ann Althouse, "Vanguard States, Laggard States: Federalism and Constitutional Rights," *University of Pennsylvania Law Review* 152 (2004): 1745 (arguing that in a federal system there will typically be both "vanguard" states and "laggard" states with respect to contentious issues).

89. See Rubenstein, "Federalism and Feminism," supra note 69 (describing how women's suffrage was adopted in some Australian states in the late nineteenth century; local option was preserved in the Constitution of 1900; yet by 1902, women [white] had suffrage); see also Markoff, "Margins, Centers, and Democracy," supra note 85. It is also, of course, true that in a federal system progressive change won at a local level can be defeated by action at the national level—for example, in the United States, the federal Defense of Marriage Act, 1 U.S.C. §7, deprives civil unions authorized by some states of their effects in establishing a legal marital relationship for purposes of national legislation.

90. New State Ice Co. v. Liebmann, 285 U.S. 262, 311 (1932) (Brandeis, J., dissenting).

91. See Rose-Ackerman, "Risk-Taking and Reelection: Does Federalism Promote Innovation?," supra note 86 (arguing that states lack incentives for experimentation because of external benefits to free-rides); Edward L. Rubin and Malcolm Feeley, "Federalism: Some Notes on a National Neurosis," *UCLA Law Review* 41 (1994): 903, 914–20 (arguing that federal constitutional division of authority is unrelated to the possibilities for experimentation in any form of decentralized government).

92. See Rankin and Vickers, "Women's Movements and State Feminism: Integrating Diversity into Public Policy," supra note 66, chapter 1. Among the specific aspects noted were the decentralization of the office, with regional offices through the province, and the nominating process for membership on the Conseil du Statut de la Femme, with "[f]our members recommended by feminist organizations, two by universities, two by socio-economic groups and two by unions." This departure from "the norm for advisory council appointments," the report observed, reflected "a substantial commitment on the part of the Quebec government to representing its women citizens appropriately through state feminist institutions."

93. Mandatory arrest began on the local level as an innovative effort to respond to domestic violence. See Lawrence W. Sherman and Ellen G. Cohn, "The Impact of Research on Legal Policy: The Minneapolis Domestic Violence Experiment," *Law & Society Review* 23 (1989): 117. The importance of continued

study in different communities is emphasized by more recent critical discussion. See, e.g., Elizabeth M. Schneider, *Battered Women and Feminist Lawmaking* (New Haven, CT: Yale University Press, 2000): 182; Donna Coker, "Crime Control and Feminist Law Reform in Domestic Violence Law: A Critical Review," *Buffalo Criminal Law Review* 4 (2001): 801, 852–53; Holly Maguigan, "Wading into Professor Schneider's 'Murky Middle Ground' between Acceptance and Rejection of Criminal Justice Responses to Domestic Violence," *American University Journal of Gender Social Policy and Law* 11 (2003): 427, 435–36 (describing study finding that "mandatory arrest policies are associated with fewer killings of white women and of Black unmarried men . . . [and] increased legal advocacy resources are associated with fewer white women being killed by their husbands and more Black women being killed by their boyfriends"); Linda G. Mills, "Killing Her Softly: Intimate Abuse and the Violence of State Intervention," *Harvard Law Review* 113 (1999): 550, 585 (referring to data that "mandatory arrest may endanger the lives of some survivors of intimate abuse, particularly African-American women").

94. See Jenna Bednar, William N. Eskridge, Jr., and John Ferejohn, "A Political Theory of Federalism," in *Constitutional Culture and Democratic Rule*, eds. John Ferejohn, Jack N. Rakove, and Jonathan Riley (Cambridge: Cambridge University Press, 2001), 223–70; Donald P. Kommers, *The Constitutional Jurisprudence of the Federal Republic of Germany*, 2d ed. (Durham, NC: Duke University Press, 1997) (discussing divisions of competencies in German constitutional history). Longstanding federal countries—the United States, Canada, Australia, Germany, Argentina, Switzerland—all provide that a national court has competence to review at least subnational unit compliance with the constitutional division of powers.

95. See, e.g., Martin Shapiro, "The Success of Judicial Review and Democracy," in Martin Shapiro and Alec Stone-Sweet, *On Law, Politics, and Judicialization* (Oxford: Oxford University Press, 2002), 149–83.

96. On the possible benefits of rights-based litigation for gender equality claims, see Catherine A. MacKinnon, "The Logic of Experience: Reflections on the Development of Sexual Harassment Law," *Georgetown Law Journal* 90 (2002): 813. There is an extensive feminist literature that is critical of rights as strategies. For discussion, see Palmer, "Feminism and the Promise of Human Rights: Possibilities and Paradoxes," supra note 56, 95–97; Deborah L. Rhode, "Feminist Critical Theories," *Stanford Law Review* 42 (1990): 617, 635 (describing feminist critique of rights as coexisting with recognition that rights have rhetorical power and can be used contextually to advance gender equality; "Since rights-oriented campaigns can both enlarge and restrict political struggle, evaluation of their strategic possibilities requires historically situated contextual analysis."). See also David Jacobson, "Multiculturalism, Gender, and Rights," in this volume at 324 (concerning the role of judicial organizations in advancing women's rights by "informing the state normatively").

97. Chappell, *Gendering Government*, supra note 67, 6. For a recent discussion of the "femocrat" strategy in Australia, noting its initial efficacy, its positive influence on international standards, its complications, and its declining efficacy under recent governments in Australia, see Maddison and Partridge, "How Well Does Australian Democracy Serve Australian Women?," supra note 75, 33–76.

98. See Mark Tushnet, "Federalism and Liberalism," *Cardozo Journal of International and Comparative Law* 4 (1996): 329 (arguing that constitutional federalism, if formalistically enforced, may delay centralization of law enough to allow time for cross-cutting differences to develop between groups formerly characterized by reinforcing cleavages); cf. Graham Walker, "The Idea of Nonliberal Constitutionalism," in *Nomos: Ethnicity and Group Rights*, eds. Ian Shapiro and Will Kymlicka (New York: New York University Press, 1997), 172 (suggesting that federalism may function as a way to graft liberal and illiberal constitutional orders).

99. James Madison, "The Federalist No. 51," in Alexander Hamilton, James Madison, and John Jay (writing as Publius), *The Federalist*, ed. Terence Ball (Cambridge: Cambridge University Press, 2003), 251, 254; for further discussion, see Jackson, "Federalism and the Uses and Limits of Law," supra note 33, 2217–20.

100. Jill Vickers, "Why Should Women Care about Federalism?," in *Canada: The State of the Federation 1994*, eds. Douglas M. Brown and Janet Hiebert (Kingston: Queen's University Press, 1994), 135, 136; see also Chappell, *Gendering Government*, supra note 67, 169.

101. It is instructive to look at the jurisdictions in which women were first allowed to vote: women began to be allowed to vote in the second half of the nineteenth century in some unitary nations, such as Britain (1869, unmarried women who were householders were allowed to vote in local elections), Sweden (1862–1863, selected women were allowed to vote in local elections), and New Zealand (1893). See "Woman Suffrage Timeline: Winning the Vote," at http://womenshistory.about.com/ library/weekly/aa091600a.htm (last accessed on May 14, 2007). Moreover, women were allowed to vote in particular subnational units of federal nations, such as Wyoming (1869 as a territory, 1890 as a state) and the Australian states of South Australia (1895) and Western Australia (1899). See International IDEA Women in Politics, "Table 8, Women's Access to the Rights to Vote and to Stand for Elections: World Chronology," available at http://www.idea.int/gender/ (last accessed on May 14, 2007); "Women of the West Museum Website," http:// www.museumoftheamericanwest.org/explore/exhibits/suffrage (last accessed on May 14, 2007).

102. See supra note 110, 115 for a comparative study of women's suffrage movements in the United States and Switzerland, see Banaszak, *Why Movements Succeed or Fail*, supra note 66, 3–4, 217–20 (arguing that use of federal form for national suffrage organizations in the United States allowed the women's suffrage movement to succeed more than sixty years before all women could vote in Switzerland, where the women's organizations operated more independently,

reflecting an internalization of autonomous traditions of cantonal decision making that prevented effective coordination). See ibid., 217 ("[T]he U.S. movement took full advantage of its own federal structure to spread the knowledge and information about tactics to local areas."); ibid., 218 (arguing that even effective local organization tactics were not spread to other parts of Switzerland, "mainly because Swiss suffrage activists were themselves divided by language, religion, politics, and region," which "inhibited the flow of information between activists and reinforced the belief that the tactics of one segment of the movement were not applicable elsewhere"); cf. Lenoir, "The Representation of Women in Politics, from Quotas to Parity in Elections," supra note 57, 224–25 (noting important role of associations in the United States in promoting feminism by facilitating women's capacity to organize themselves). These findings are consistent with the work of Theda Skocpol and others on the role of federalism in the organization of voluntary associations. See Theda Skocpol, Marshall Ganz, and Ziad Munsion, "A Nation of Organizers: The Institutional Origins of Civic Voluntarism in the US," *American Political Science Review* 94 (2000): 527, 528 (emphasizing the importance of federal organization for national associations through the development of "translocal linkages," with a key finding that fully three-fourths of the U.S. membership associations that grew larger over time used a federal-state model of organization and the most successful organizations took advantage of the leverage of government at different levels).

103. See, e.g., Najma Chowdhury and Barbara J. Nelson, "Redefining Politics: Patterns of Women's Political Engagement from a Global Perspective," in *Women and Politics Worldwide*, eds. Barbara J. Nelson and Najma Chowdhury (New Haven, CT: Yale University Press, 1994), 3, 14–18.

104. Rankin and Vickers, "Women's Movements and State Feminism: Integrating Diversity into Public Policy," supra note 66, 16 (summarizing findings of Marian Sawer and Jill Vickers, "Women and Constitutional Activism in Australia and Canada," unpublished manuscript, 1998). See also Maddison and Partridge, "How Well Does Australian Democracy Serve Australian Women?," supra note 75, 39 ("Feminists . . . have long used Australia's federal system to their advantage. In periods where the federal government has been unsympathetic to feminist demands, progress has been pursued at other levels."); Sawer and Vickers, "Women's Constitutional Activism," supra note 42, 35 (noting that in Australia, the "multiple points of initiation within a federal system have meant that some momentum in terms of feminist policy may be maintained even when unsympathetic governments are elected at one level or another").

105. See, e.g., Helen Irving, "A Gendered Constitution? Women, Federation, and the Heads of Power," in *A Woman's Constitution? Gender and History in the Australian Commonwealth*, ed. Helen Irving (Sydney: Hale and Iremonger, 1996), 98, 101 (noting failure of the constitution to guarantee women's suffrage and arguing that "women might well have written, if not an entirely different

Constitution, at least one significantly different in parts"). Cf. Helen Irving, "Fair Federalists and Founding Mothers," supra this note, 1–20 (arguing that despite being denied the vote on the constitution women's organizations were success-ful in bringing some, though not all, of their concerns into the drafting pro-cess of the Australian constitution). On whether women's interests and claims differ systematically from those of men, compare, e.g., Hilary Charlesworth, "Transforming the United Men's Club: Feminist Futures for the United Nations," *Transnational Law and Contemporary Problems* 4 (1994): 421, with Deborah L. Rhode, "Changing Images of the State: Feminism and the State," *Harvard Law Review* 107 (1994): 1181, 1206–7 (noting that while women legislators' priorities differ from men's, women legislators vote differently from male legislators on a small range of issues and the "similarities have been far stronger than the dif-ferences"). A number of studies of legislative voting in the United States suggest that in many areas a legislator's gender does not affect voting, but in some areas, including some issues directly relating to gender equality, the gender of the leg-islator does matter.

106. For discussion, see, e.g., Irving, "Fair Federalist and Founding Mothers," supra note 105; Millar, "Feminising the Senate," supra note 75; Cass and Ruben-stein, "From Federation Forward," supra note 78, 110 (describing early Court de-cision interpreting provision of 1900 Constitution guaranteeing existing suffrage as intended to leave it to each state to define who could vote). No women voted for delegates to the 1891 constitutional convention; women in South Australia were allowed to vote for delegates to the 1894 convention, though not from any other Australian state; no women were present at the 1897 convention either. In the ratifying referenda on the proposed constitution, women were excluded from voting in four of the then six states. Ibid., 118. (The Constitution, enacted into law in 1900, came into force January 1, 1901.)

107. Irving, "A Gendered Constitution? Women, Federation, and the Heads of Power," supra note 105, 102.

108. See ibid., 102–3; Rubenstein, "Feminism and Federalism: Pushing Feder-alism beyond Territory," supra note 69, text at notes 51–73 (discussing division of jurisdictional competence over children depending on whether they are nuptial or not as adversely affecting handling of child abuse cases).

109. See Violence Against Women Act of 1994, Public Law 103-322, tit. IV, 108 Stat. 1902 (codified as amended in scattered sections of 8, 18, and 42 U.S. Code).

110. See United States v. Morrison, 529 U.S. 598 (2000).

111. Cf. Jan Lewis, "Representation of Women in the Constitution," in *Women and the United States Constitution: History, Interpretation, and Practice*, eds. Sibyl A. Schwarzenbach and Patricia Smith (New York: Columbia University Press, 2003), 23–33 (observing that, although not at the drafting table of the U.S. Con-stitution, women were intended to count among "the people" for purposes of de-termining the number of representatives to which each state was entitled).

112. Edwards v. Attorney-General for Canada, 1930 A.C. 124, 136 (P.C. 1929) (appeal taken from Can.). For discussion see Vicki C. Jackson, "Constitutions as Living Trees? Comparative Constitutional Law and Interpretive Metaphors," *Fordham Law Review* 75 (2006): 921.

113. See Canada Charter of Rights And Freedoms §§ 15, 28; Sawer and Vickers, "Women's Constitutional Activism," supra note 42, 18–27 (describing multiple positions of different communities of feminists on the Charter and women's active participation in the framing of Section 15); Lorraine Eisenstat Weinrib, "Of Diligence and Dice: Reconstituting Canada's Constitution," *University of Toronto Law Journal* 42 (1992): 207, 222 n. 69 (describing impact of women's group protests in excluding sex equality [Section 28] from rights subject to notwithstanding clause [Section 33] in drafting of 1982 Charter).

114. See Reva Siegel, "She the People: The Nineteenth Amendment, Sex, Equality, Federalism, and the Family," *Harvard Law Review* 115 (2002): 947; Vicki C. Jackson, "Holistic Interpretation, Comparative Constitutionalism, and Fiss-ian Freedoms," *University of Miami Law Review* 58 (2003): 265; Vicki C. Jackson, "Holistic Interpretation: *Fitzpatrick v. Bitzer* and Our Bifurcated Constitution," *Stanford Law Review* 53 (2001): 1259; Jackson, "Transnational Discourse, Relational Authority, and the U.S. Court," supra note 36, 271.

115. See, e.g., United States v. Morrison, 529 U.S. 598 (2000).

116. Mary Becker, "Patriarchy and Inequality: Towards a Substantive Feminism," *University of Chicago Legal Forum* (1999): 21, 78–79.

117. See ibid., 68–78.

118. See note 75 above.

119. James Madison, "The Federalist No. 10," in *The Federalist*, supra note 99, 40, 44–46, suggested that representative bodies encompassing a wider range of interests and perspectives might be less prone than smaller and more homogenous bodies to control by powerful factions motivated by self-interest rather than the general good. By definition, national governments are larger than the subnational (in any given setting). Would women's interests be "better" represented in the larger national legislature than in the profusion of smaller representative bodies entailed in a federal system? Any such claim would rest on a number of contestable assumptions. To begin with, the choices may not be between unitary or federal nations of the same size but between a federal nation or several smaller unitary ones. There is no recognized ideal size for a territorial national state: there are vast differences in the population size of those governmental units called states; California is a subnational unit whose population is larger than that of most countries in the United Nations. Even if there is something to the idea that a body encompassing more interests will be harder to take over than a smaller body, at some point a representative body may represent so many interests that it permits capture by those that are best organized or have existing power; determining the maximally beneficial size

for decision making by a legislative body is a daunting task. Thus, Madison's basic claim, that the plurality of interests at the national level will prevent factions, or imprudent passions, from dominating the national legislature, may be contested. Finally, the majoritarian status of women as voters may also confound application of his thesis. See also text at note 98 (noting Tushnet's argument that formally enforced federalisms may promote greater tolerance over time).

120. But note that the states that first allowed women to vote in the United States were not states with large cities, but rather were Wyoming, Utah, Idaho, and Colorado. June Johnson Lewis, "Winning the Vote: American Woman Suffrage Timeline," at http://womenshistory. about.com/library/weekly/aa031600a. html (last accessed on May 14, 2007).

121. See, e.g., Marian Sawer, Manon Tremblay, and Linda Trimble, "Introduction: Patterns and Practice in the Parliamentary Representation of Women," in *Representing Women in Parliament*, supra note 71, 1, 6 (noting that federal systems "may enshrine the power of state or provincial government at the expense of local government"). On cities and their constitutional relationships to national and state governments in the United States, see, e.g., David J. Barron, "Why (and When) Cities Have a Stake in Enforcing the Constitution," *Yale Law Journal* 115 (2006): 2218; Richard Schragger, "The Role of the Local in the Doctrine and Discourse of Religious Liberty," *Harvard Law Review* 117 (2004): 1810; Gerald E. Frug, "The City as a Legal Concept," *Harvard Law Review* 93 (1980): 1059; Richard Briffault, "Our Localism: Part I—The Structure of Local Government Law," *Columbia Law Review* 90 (1990): 1. On the transnational importance of cities, see Saskia Sassen, *The Global City* (Princeton, NJ: Princeton University Press, 1991). Note the possibilities for direct constitutional protection for the powers of cities found in some constitutions. See, e.g., Constitution of Brazil (1988), arts. 18(4), 23, 29–31; Constitution of the Russian Federation (1993), arts. 130–33.

122. Instead, the choice may be between a federal nation or many smaller nations, in which case a federal state that exercises some mitigating influences on the most illiberal subnational societies might have advantages.

123. See, e.g., Naomi R. Cahn, "Federalism, Family Law, and the Federal Courts," *Iowa Law Review* 79 (1994): 1073 (objecting to "domestic relations" exception to federal jurisdiction in diversity cases and arguing that federal courts should decide diversity cases raising state law issues of domestic relations); but cf. Anne C. Dailey, "Federalism and Families," *University of Pennsylvania Law Review* 143 (1995): 1787 (arguing that, in the United States, states are better situated to develop family law than the national government because developing a moral view of families benefits from localism, and that the normative character of family law arises from communitarian visions more possible at state than federal level).

124. See Judith Resnik, "Categorical Federalism: Jurisdiction, Gender, and the Globe," *Yale Law Journal* 111 (2001): 619, 629 (challenging the "naturalness" within the United States of allocating issues of particular concern to women's equality (including family relations, gender-motivated violence, and marital status) to the states as a matter of legislative and judicial jurisdiction and also challenging presumption of superiority of federal courts over state decision makers).

125. 518 U.S. 515 (1996).

126. Ibid., 532.

127. Ibid., 531, 533.

128. 533 U.S. 53 (2001).

129. United States v. Morrison, 529 U.S. 598 (2000).

130. See Rostker v. Goldberg, 453 U.S. 57 (1981). Another possibility might be that there is less reason to be skeptical of purportedly benign motivations for statutory gender differences at the federal, compared to state, levels. Although such a stance would be consistent with the power given to Congress under Section 5 of the Fourteenth Amendment and with the early case law distinguishing between the constitutional standards to review state and national affirmative action laws, it is inconsistent with more recent case law on affirmative action for racial minorities, which has insisted on applying the same standard to federal and state laws. Compare Richmond v. J.A. Croson, 488 U.S. 469 (1989), with Adarand Constructors Inc. v. Pena, 515 U.S. 200 (1995).

131. Theoretical obstacles include, first, the difficulty in distinguishing between localism and federalism, which raises cautions about attributing benefits from local government for women's participation to constitutional federalism; second, federalism as a system in place now, especially under older constitutions that do not (or did not) protect women's rights to equality, may prove an uncertain guide to whether future decisions to federalize in other systems would be good or bad for women; third, disagreement over the meaning(s) of greater gender equality might influence evaluation of the possibilities of federal as compared to unitary forms of organization.

About the Contributors

SEYLA BENHABIB is Professor of Political Science and Philosophy at Yale University and was Director of its Program in Ethics, Politics, and Economics, and she was the president of the Eastern Division of the American Philosophical Association in 2006–2007. She is the author or coauthor of many books, most recently *The Rights of Others: Aliens, Citizens, and Residents* and *Another Cosmopolitanism: Hospitality, Sovereignty, and Democratic Iterations.*

JACQUELINE BHABHA is the Jeremiah Smith Jr. Lecturer in Law at Harvard Law School, the Director of the Harvard University Committee on Human Rights Studies, and a lecturer on public policy at the Kennedy School of Government. She is the coauthor of *Women's Movement: Women under Immigration, Nationality, and Refugee Law.*

LINDA BOSNIAK is Professor of Law at Rutgers University and author of *The Citizen and the Alien: Dilemmas of Contemporary Membership.*

CATHERINE DAUVERGNE is Professor and Canada Research Chair in Migration Law for the University of British Columbia Faculty of Law. She is author of *Making People Illegal: What Globalization Means for Migration and Law* and *Humanitarianism, Identity, and Nation: Migration Laws of Australia and Canada.*

TALIA INLENDER is an Equal Justice Works Fellow at Public Counsel in Los Angeles. She is a former judicial clerk to the Honorable Stephen Reinhardt on the United States Court of Appeals for the Ninth Circuit.

VICKI C. JACKSON is currently Carmack Waterhouse Professor of Constitutional Law at Georgetown University Law Center and practiced law for several years before joining the Georgetown faculty. She is coauthor (with Mark Tushnet) of *Comparative Constitutional Law* and coeditor (with Tushnet) of *Defining the Field of Comparative Constitutional Law*.

DAVID JACOBSON is Professor of Global Studies at Arizona State University and codirector of the Global Resolve Initiative, a program for assisting women in developing countries through biofuel microbusinesses. He is the author of, among other works, *Rights across Borders: Immigration and the Decline of Citizenship* and *Place and Belonging in America*.

LINDA K. KERBER is May Brodbeck Professor in the Liberal Arts and Professor of History, Lecturer in Law at the University of Iowa. Her books include *No Constitutional Right to Be Ladies: Women and the Obligations of Citizenship* and *Women of the Republic: Intellect and Ideology in the American Revolution*.

AUDREY MACKLIN is Associate Professor at the Faculty of Law, University of Toronto. She researches, teaches, and writes about migration, citizenship, law and gender, multiculturalism, and human rights. A list of her publications is available at www.law/utoronto.ca/faculty/macklin.

ANGELIA K. MEANS will be a Visiting Professor of Politics at Sarah Lawrence for the 2008–2009 academic year.

VALENTINE M. MOGHADAM joined Purdue University in January 2007 as Professor of Sociology and Women's Studies and Director of the Women's Studies Program. She is the author of *Modernizing Women: Gender and Social Change in the Middle East* and *Globalizing Women: Transnational Feminist Networks*, among other publications.

PATRIZIA NANZ is Professor of Political Theory at the Institute for Intercultural and International Studies (InIIS), University of Bremen. She is the author of *Europolis: Constitutional Patriotism beyond the Nation State* and coeditor of *Civil Society Participation in European and Global Governance: A Cure for the Democratic Deficit?*

AIHWA ONG is Professor of Sociocultural Anthropology and Southeast Asian Studies at the University of California, Berkeley. She is the author of many books, including *Flexible Citizenship: The Cultural Logic of Trans-nationality* and *Neoliberalism as Exception: Mutations in Citizenship and Sovereignty.*

CYNTHIA PATTERSON is Professor of History at Emory University. She is the author of *Pericles' Citizenship Law of 451/0 B.C.* a *The Family in Greek History,* and editor of *Antigone's Answer: Essays on Death and Burial, Family and State in Classical Athens.*

JUDITH RESNIK is the Arthur Liman Professor of Law at Yale Law School. Her books include *Adjudication and Its Alternatives* (with Owen Fiss), and her recent articles include "Law as Affiliation: 'Foreign Law,' Democratic Federalism, and the Sovereigntism of the Nation-State"; "Gendered Borders and United States Sovereignty"; and "Law's Migration: American Exceptionalism, Silent Dialogues, and Federalism's Multiple Ports of Entry."

SARAH K. VAN WALSUM is Senior Researcher in Migration Law at the Free University of Amsterdam (VU University), Faculty of Law, Department of Constitutional and Administrative Law. She is the coeditor (with Thomas Spijkerboer) of *Women and Immigration Law: New Variations on Classical Feminist Themes.*

Index